# CASES IN
# MARKETING
# MANAGEMENT

# CASES IN MARKETING MANAGEMENT

EDITED BY

## KENNETH E. CLOW
*University of Louisiana at Monroe*

## DONALD BAACK
*Pittsburg State University*

Los Angeles | London | New Delhi
Singapore | Washington DC

Los Angeles | London | New Delhi
Singapore | Washington DC

FOR INFORMATION:

SAGE Publications, Inc.
2455 Teller Road
Thousand Oaks, California 91320
E-mail: order@sagepub.com

SAGE Publications Ltd.
1 Oliver's Yard
55 City Road
London EC1Y 1SP
United Kingdom

SAGE Publications India Pvt. Ltd.
B 1/I 1 Mohan Cooperative Industrial Area
Mathura Road, New Delhi 110 044
India

SAGE Publications Asia-Pacific Pte. Ltd.
33 Pekin Street #02-01
Far East Square
Singapore 048763

Senior Executive Editor:  Lisa Cuevas Shaw
Editorial Assistant:  Megan Krattli
Production Editor:  Libby Larson
Copy Editor:  Megan Speer
Typesetter:  C&M Digitals (P) Ltd.
Proofreader:  Wendy Jo Dymond
Cover Designer:  Janet Kiesel
Marketing Manager:  Helen Salmon
Permissions Editor:  Adele Hutchinson

The Ivey cases have been prepared solely to provide material for class discussion. The authors do not intend to illustrate either effective or ineffective handling of managerial situations. The authors do not intend to provide legal, tax, accounting, or other professional advice. Such advice should be obtained from a qualified professional. The authors may have disguised certain names and other identifying information to protect confidentiality.

Printed in the United States of America

*Library of Congress Cataloging-in-Publication Data*

Cases in marketing management / editors, Kenneth E. Clow, Donald Baack.

p. cm.
Includes bibliographical references and index.

ISBN 978-1-4129-9603-7 (pbk.)

1. Marketing—Management—Case studies.
I. Clow, Kenneth E. II. Baack, Donald.

HF5415.13.C33 2012 658.8—dc22 2010051833

This book is printed on acid-free paper.

11 12 13 14 15 10 9 8 7 6 5 4 3 2 1

# Contents

# Preface

In the majority of colleges and universities, the marketing management capstone course helps students review and integrate the materials they have studied in the business major, with the primary focus on marketing concepts. The techniques used to assist in the conceptualization and application process include case studies, visits and lectures from marketing professionals, simulations, tests, term papers, and other methods. The degree to which managerial principles appear in the class largely depends on the background and preferences of the professor.

Oftentimes, the management perspective in a marketing management course concentrates on the strategic level. Students are asked to review lines of products and brands, or the marketing process, from the vantage point of the chief marketing officer or chief executive officer. This approach may be useful in many ways, especially in terms of conceptual and integrative reasoning; however, it also tends to require students to think about managerial positions they will not hold for a number of years, if ever.

In early 2010, SAGE released *Marketing Management: A Customer-Oriented Approach*. The design of the text is slightly different from the traditional marketing management course. Instead of a chief executive/strategic viewpoint, the emphasis shifts to a first-line supervisory and lower-level management perspective, as these will be the positions most students will hold in the first few years after graduation. The text provides strategic concepts to add context and understanding of how lower-level positions fit with the larger company direction. And, as the book title suggests, the primary focus is on customer service rather than brand management or other key marketing ideas. To help students prepare for the jobs they are likely to occupy in the early years of their careers, the text seeks to more fully integrate the fields of marketing and management into one presentation and also provides numerous quantitative analysis problems, such as break-even analyses, calculations of consumer lifetime values, and others.

*Marketing Management: A Customer-Oriented Approach* contains eight full-length cases for students to analyze. Initially, several professors indicated that they would prefer a larger number of cases. Consequently, this book—*Cases in Marketing Management*—was written to help professors teach the marketing management course in several ways. For some professors, this book offers a supplementary set of cases to accompany the main textbook.

Other professors prefer using a case-only approach. They will be able to require *Cases in Marketing Management* as a stand-alone text. To assist in this method, this book provides a brief review of the materials presented in each chapter prior to the set of cases chosen for that topic area. Finally, the cases may also be used as a supplement to an MBA course in marketing management.

The cases in this book were selected from a high-quality Ivey list. They should serve several purposes. First, students and professors can enjoy the advantage of using a casebook structured in the same manner as the textbook, with cases corresponding to each chapter and section. Second, a variety of cases were chosen to correspond with the goals of the textbook, which means students will be able to apply conceptual, strategic thinking as well as tactical and operational ideas and methods. Third, both small companies and larger corporations are included, thereby presenting a greater range of potential jobs that students might take in the coming years.

For each chapter, we briefly summarize marketing management concepts and theories and describe the relevance of the issues/problems in the case. Each case is also accompanied by questions that help the students think critically about the material in the case. This organization provides students with opportunities to analyze the cases and apply the lessons learned to situations they will encounter in the future.

We have also included a password-protected instructor website that includes teaching notes for all the cases, along with suggested answers to the end-of-case questions. Instructors can access the site at http://www.sagepub.com/clowcmm.

The field of marketing evolves and changes at a rapid pace. Marketers must adjust to changing lifestyles, shifting product preferences, evolving media usage habits, new technologies, and increasing global competition; however, the basic tenets of marketing remain the same. A well-designed marketing management course allows students to integrate key marketing concepts and adapt them to the new circumstances that may arise in the coming years.

# Acknowledgments

We want to acknowledge and thank all those involved in the writing of this book. We would like to thank the staff at Ivey Publishing, without whom this casebook would not have been possible. Kenneth E. Clow would like to thank Ron Berry, the dean of the College of Business at University of Louisiana at Monroe, for his support and confidence for projects such as this. He would also like to thank his wife, Susan, and his children, Dallas, Wes, Tim, and Roy, for their support, encouragement, and understanding.

Donald Baack would like to thank Eric Harris, the department chair for management and marketing at Pittsburg State University, for his encouragement and support in pursuing projects such as these. He also wishes to acknowledge Paula Palmer, departmental administrative assistant, for all her work. Finally, his wife, Pam; his children, Daniel, David, and Jessica; plus his grandchildren add a great deal of richness and meaning to his life.

We would also like to thank the following individuals who assisted in the preparation of the manuscript through their careful and thoughtful reviews:

Yun Chu, *Robert Morris University*

Dr. Timothy Donahue, *Chadron State College*

Michelle B. Kunz, *Morehead State University*

Dr. Steven Lysonski, *Marquette University*

Michael K. Rich, *Southwest Minnesota State University*

Al Rosenbloom, *Dominican University*

*From Kenneth E. Clow:*

*To my sons, Dallas, Wes, Tim, and Roy, who provided encouragement, and especially to my wife, Susan, whose sacrifice and love made this book possible.*


*From Donald Baack:*

*I would like to dedicate my efforts on this book to John Mulvaney, in appreciation of his continuing friendship and support over many, many years.*

# CHAPTER 1

# The Nature of
# Marketing Management

The term *marketing management* describes two separate but related topics. First, it is a common name for the capstone course taken by marketing majors as they prepare to graduate. In that context, integrating management and marketing concepts to help prepare individuals for careers constitutes the primary goal.

Second, marketing management is a business process. It includes managing marketing activities in profit-seeking and nonprofit organizations at the supervisory, middle-management, and executive levels. Success in these endeavors will be based on a strong knowledge of a variety of marketing functions combined with a clear understanding and application of supervisory and managerial techniques.

Both of these topics may be examined and discussed using case analyses. Students and professors can learn from the case content and from each other when examining the concepts and actions taken by companies in a range of industries. This first case was chosen to accompany a review of the basic marketing management field. As the name implies, marketing management combines the fields of marketing and management.

## Marketing

Marketing experts agree that an effective marketing program should be driven by customers, whether it is a for-profit, a nonprofit, or a governmental organization. The traditional definition of marketing has been

1. discovering consumer needs and wants;

2. creating the goods and services that meet those needs and wants; and

3. pricing, promoting, and delivering those goods and services.

The definition suggests that the primary elements of marketing include understanding and meeting the needs of consumers. Doing so requires attention to six major areas:

- Markets
- Products
- Prices
- Places (distribution systems)
- Promotion
- People

Markets consist of customers with wants and needs, financial resources, and the willingness to spend resources to satisfy those wants and needs. Market segments are made up of groups of buyers in consumer markets and business-to-business markets.

Products are the physical goods sold to customers and services rendered to them. Physical goods include both durable goods that last longer than 1 year and nondurable goods with shorter uses. Nondurable goods include convenience items, shopping goods, and specialty products. Services consist of the intangible items sold to others, including banking, financial, insurance, transportation, credit, and personal services.

Prices are based on costs, demand/supply, competition, and profit goals. Pricing activities include setting base prices, offering discounts, and amending or changing them when needed.

Place or distribution involves deciding where, how, and when products are made available to potential customers. The first decision is often the choice between exclusive, selective, or intensive distribution. Then physical distribution methods are chosen, including methods of storage and inventory, modes of transportation, forms of inventory control, and billing and payment processes.

Promotional activities include creating the advertising programs, consumer and trade promotions efforts, personal selling tactics, and supporting public relations activities. The term *integrated marketing communications* has often been applied to promotions. Promotional programs are strongly influenced by changing preferences for media.

The people involved in marketing are those who produce and sell products and the individuals who render services. In recent years, customer satisfaction and customer retention have received a great deal of attention. High product quality and outstanding customer service can be key elements in a successful marketing program.

Company leaders also recognize that strong brands offer major advantages to marketing programs. Effective marketing accounts for the growing influence of the Internet and the trend toward internationalization and global competition.

## ⊠ Management

Management is the process of getting things done through other people. A distinction should be made between *doing* and *managing*. Managing consists of the ability to get others to complete work while helping improve their skills and knowledge of the business. Managers engage in five key activities:

- Planning
- Organizing
- Staffing
- Directing
- Control

Planning outlines a course of action for the future in the operational short term (1 year), tactical/ medium range (1–3 years), and long-range or strategic time horizons (3 years or more). Plans are created by first assessing the company's environment, where managers seek to identify the opportunities and threats that exist. Then managers assess company strengths and weaknesses. Forecasts are developed to help in the planning process, typically in the areas of economic conditions, future sales, and changes in technologies. Decisions can then be made with regard to the options to pursue and those to leave behind. Plans are drawn, and then goals and standards are set for the purposes of assessment and control.

Organizing combines people and resources to create goods and services through the processes of job design, departmentalization, and drawing lines of authority and responsibility. Staffing consists of attaining and preparing quality employees.

Directing, or actuating, involves seeking to achieve the highest levels of performance. Achieving success is made possible by teaching, motivating, leading, communication, and working with teams and groups. Actuating represents the people side of business.

The control process consists of comparing performance with standards, making corrections when needed, and rewarding success. Control occurs at three levels: individual (or the performance appraisal process), departmental, and companywide. Control includes correcting problems and making sure those who succeed are recognized with tangible rewards.

Marketing management implies the integration of these concepts. The tools to be used include marketing strategies, which are the sweeping marketing efforts based on the company's mission; marketing tactics that support strategies in the medium term; and operational plans for day-to-day marketing efforts. Most students will at first be involved in developing and carrying out operational plans but should also be aware of the tactical and strategic directions the plans are designed to support. Each will be devoted to creating solid customer acquisition, customer interaction, and customer retention programs.

## ⊠ The Case

### Chantale and Clinton Call for Service

Chantale and Clinton are the names of two consumers who purchased a new refrigerator from The Canadian, a large department store chain. It subsequently began to malfunction. They received poor service from the vendor's repair division over an extended period of time and, at the end, wondered what to do next. The primary issues are service failure and poor service recovery. The story demonstrates how regular customers become disenchanted when entry-level employees and supervisors take them for granted and inconvenience them without concern. In the end, the couple passes along negative word of mouth about the department store chain to several friends and acquaintances. The experience also could affect their future intentions to purchase from the retailer and the refrigerator's manufacturer.

# Chantale and Clinton Call for Service

*By Christopher A. Ross*[1]

On the evening of July 5, 2007, the Rileys were sitting around their dinner table reminiscing about the events of the past few weeks. Early in February, the Rileys had bought a new compact refrigerator that had started to malfunction. They had subsequently called the vendor's repair service and had received extremely poor service. They were now wondering what they should do. Should they do nothing and treat the poor service as an isolated incident? Should they walk away vowing never to deal with this particular retailer and the brand? Should they write to the retailer, complain about the service, and demand some form of apology or compensation? Or was there something else that they could do? Underlying all of these questions was the issue: Was it worth the trouble?

## The Rileys

Chantale and Clinton Riley were two professional consultants: Chantale worked as an accountant and Clinton was a financial advisor. Clinton was 60 years old and Chantale was 56 years old. They had met each other while at university in the 1970s and had been living in Montreal since 1980. They resided in Côte-des-Neiges-Notre-Dame-de-Grâce, one of the boroughs of Montreal. They had two children: a boy, 23 years old, who had just completed a bachelor's degree at McGill University, and a girl, 18 years old, who had just completed her first year of CEGEP.[2] All members of the family were completely bilingual in English and French. In fact, McGill University was the first educational institution where the boy had been schooled in English; the girl had always attended French schools.

The Rileys had always been loyal to the Bryand brand of appliances, the private brand of The Canadian, one of the largest department store chains in Canada. The Canadian had more than 40,000 employees and annual sales of more than $5.5 billion. During their 27 years of marriage, all of the Rileys' appliances had been purchased at this chain. Yard equipment such as lawn mowers and snow blowers had also been bought at this chain. One could describe this couple as loyal The Canadian customers. Prior to meeting Clinton, Chantale had been employed as a department manager at The Canadian for three years and she had always described the policies of The Canadian as being very customer-oriented.

The Rileys' refrigerator for the past 25 years had been a Bryand and it was still in good working order, even though it was a bit noisy. In February 2007, however, after reading an article about the electrical inefficiency of refrigerators that were more than 20 years old, both Chantale and Clinton were persuaded to purchase a new refrigerator as a way to save energy and to do their part for the environment. The family also needed more refrigerator space in order to accommodate the special dietary needs of the youngest child. Because the Rileys already owned a separate freezer, they felt that a full-size compact refrigerator, one that did not include a freezer, best suited their needs. It would provide enough space for special foods as well as for regular perishables.

After doing some shopping around, they discovered that only the brands Frigidaire, Kenmore, and Bryand had the features they were looking for. The Rileys subsequently evaluated all three brands and found them to be identical except that the Bryand was on sale at about $100 cheaper than the others. After some discussion, they decided to purchase The Canadian brand, Bryand, since they had always had good experiences with The Canadian regarding service. For example, Chantale recalled that they had bought a front-loading washing machine the year before, but the machine had a persistent and constant vibration when used. After trying

Version: (A) 2009–03–25

unsuccessfully to correct the problem, The Canadian agreed to accept the return of the washing machine and the Rileys had received a full reimbursement. The couple subsequently bought a traditional top-loading washing machine from The Canadian.

## The New Refrigerator

The Canadian delivered the new refrigerator on February 8, 2007. It did not have a freezer as expected; the panelling of the door was made of stainless steel and it had a capacity of 16.7 cubic feet. The delivered price was $1,401.56. This price included the cost of delivery, federal and provincial sales taxes, and an extended five-year warranty. This warranty included a general warranty of one year parts and labor, and five years parts and one year labor for the compressor and sealed system.

On the day of delivery, Clinton noticed that the appliance was much noisier than the one that it had replaced. He thought that the noise was coming from the compressor, which seemed to be tripping on and off quite frequently. One morning he decided to time the compressor and noted that it functioned for about four minutes, tripped off for about three minutes, and then the pattern repeated itself. Not having any technical knowledge about refrigerators, he called The Canadian's customer service department and spoke to a representative. The employee informed him that the recommended setting for the dial that controlled the internal temperature of the refrigerator was four degrees Celsius but that that was a U.S. recommendation. The representative told Clinton that since Canada was colder he should lower the setting to three and this lower setting should have a positive effect on the operation of the compressor. Clinton was somewhat skeptical about this information but he did what the representative suggested. He did not notice a difference in the functioning of the compressor but thought that maybe that was the way modern refrigerators functioned. Apart from the noisiness of the refrigerator, the family of four was quite happy with the new appliance.

The representative had also told Clinton that buying a new refrigerator in order to save energy did not make sense because the annual savings were miniscule and in any case modern refrigerators were not as durable as the one that the Rileys had replaced. He said that if he had been in the same position he would not have purchased a new refrigerator. Clinton took that information with a "grain of salt" but wondered about the wisdom of what the technician had said.

Sometime in April, the Rileys' Bryand dishwasher developed a problem: the dishes were not being washed properly. They called for service and a technician visited them the following day. It turned out to be a simple problem that was repaired in about half an hour. But while doing the repairs, the technician said that he was leaving the employ of The Canadian because its service had deteriorated. He felt that repairs that should be covered by the warranty or extended service were no longer being covered by The Canadian. He gave the example of the hose that connected a clothes-washing machine to the water tap. According to the repairman, if that hose sprung a leak it was not covered by the warranty because The Canadian claimed that it was not part of the machine.

## June 11

On the evening of June 11, Clinton noticed that the internal temperature of the new refrigerator, bought only four months ago, seemed to be less cold than it should be. In order to confirm this, he placed a thermometer inside the refrigerator and left it there overnight. The following morning the thermometer showed that the internal temperature of the refrigerator was 16 degrees Celsius instead of the generally recommended four degrees Celsius. A telephone call to The Canadian's repair department produced good results. That same day, June 12, a technician arrived at the Rileys' home. He was accompanied by an apprentice and, together, they diagnosed the problem as being leaking refrigerant. The two technicians changed some parts of the line that held the refrigerant and added a valve to make future repairs easier. They also added new refrigerant. The refrigerator was soon working well and the technicians left.

As a result of the failure of the refrigerator, the Rileys had to throw away several food items but they were grateful that the problem had been solved relatively quickly. When they had inquired from the technician if the cost of the lost food would be reimbursed, as stated in the five-year extended warranty that they had purchased at the cost of $79.99, they were told that because the problem occurred during the first year, no reimbursement would be forthcoming since the extended warranty reimbursed the cost of lost food only after the expiration of the manufacturer's warranty. This explanation sounded odd to Clinton and Chantale since they had purchased a Bryand, The Canadian brand. They decided, however, not to pursue the matter since they had lost only about $50 worth of food. The amount was relatively small because they had saved several items by storing them in the family freezer and in a camping cooler. Clinton had bought ice for the cooler at a service station at a cost of $5.89 for two bags.

## June 27

Clinton opened the refrigerator at about 6:00 P.M. on Wednesday, June 27, and suspected that something was wrong once again. The appliance appeared to be not as cold as usual. Once more, he installed a thermometer in the refrigerator, mentioning to Chantale that he suspected something was wrong with the refrigerator. Subsequently, the family went to bed.

## June 28

When Clinton checked the refrigerator on the morning of Thursday, June 28, the temperature was once more at 16 degrees Celsius, a good 12 degrees above the recommended temperature. He called The Canadian's service department at 6:30 A.M. and was told that a technician would be there the same day since this was an emergency. The representative also indicated that someone would call the Rileys at their home. At about 8:00 A.M., Clinton left to buy ice for the cooler so that some of

the foodstuffs from the refrigerator could be saved. Fortunately, the refrigerator was less than half full since it was a Thursday and the family normally did their grocery shopping on Saturdays.

A little while later, Clinton had to leave home for an appointment in downtown Montreal and Chantale offered him a lift. They both left the house and asked the cleaning lady, who normally came each Thursday, to take any messages because they were expecting a call from The Canadian. Upon Chantale's return, the cleaning lady said that no one had called. Chantale, who had some errands to run, decided to remain at home to wait for the call. At about 3:00 P.M., a representative from The Canadian called to say that because the repair department was extremely busy, no one would visit that day and that a repair person would only come the following day, on Friday, June 29. The Canadian could not say whether it would be in the morning or in the afternoon. That same evening, Clinton bought some more ice for the cooler.

## June 29

On the morning of June 29, a Friday, Clinton, after apologizing profusely, cancelled an appointment with a client so that he would be available when the technician arrived. Chantale called The Canadian to find out whether it could be more precise regarding the arrival time of the technician. The representative from The Canadian indicated that someone would visit between 10:00 A.M. and 2:00 P.M. The technician, Miguel, arrived at about 1:00 P.M. After spending about one hour going through various diagnostics, Miguel announced that the refrigerant was not flowing and that there was a blockage in the gas line. His tests indicated, however, that the compressor was sound. He needed a special gas, nitrogen,[3] to be able to clear the blockage, but he did not have a supply in his truck. Another repair person would have to revisit the Rileys at another time, he said.

A long weekend was coming up and the Rileys had planned to be away for a family reunion. They were scheduled to return to Montreal on Monday evening, July 2. The technician therefore suggested that someone could be available first thing on Tuesday, July 3. After some discussion, the technician called his office, spoke to someone and scheduled the next appointment for early on Tuesday morning. He mentioned to the Rileys that he might be the one to return but that he was not certain. Just in case, on the invoice, he wrote a note to the technician who would be coming on Tuesday that he or she would need nitrogen in order to complete the repair job. Chantale mentioned to the technician the amount of food that had been lost and Miguel indicated that The Canadian would reimburse her. He subsequently provided her with a form that she could use to indicate the cost of what was lost.

Both Clinton and Chantale were disappointed that the refrigerator had not been repaired that day because Chantale was expecting her brother who lived in France to arrive that evening at Pierre Elliott Trudeau airport and she had wanted to prepare a special meal for him. With the refrigerator not working, they had to make do with leftovers from the previous day that had been stored in the cooler. Her brother could not have his favorite drink, a cold beer, because there was no room in the cooler for beer.

On Monday evening, when they returned to Montreal, the Rileys stopped once more to buy ice for the cooler and milk for their Tuesday morning coffee and breakfast. That Monday evening, all members of the family had cereal with milk and some fruits for dinner. After making an inventory, Chantale threw away all the food that was left in the refrigerator.

## July 3

On the morning of Tuesday, July 3, Clinton had to take the family car to the tire dealer. During the weekend trip he had found that there was an excessive vibration on the steering wheel. He had had the wheels balanced the previous week and was therefore returning the car to have the wheel balancing rechecked. While at the tire dealer, he phoned Chantale to suggest that she call The Canadian to verify what time the technician was coming to repair the refrigerator. Meanwhile at the dealership, it turned out that the wheel balancing of the car had to be adjusted but the dealer also suggested that it was possible the car would continue to vibrate because the tires seemed to be a problem. Clinton said he would check them on the road and if there was a problem, he would like to have new tires and a credit for the unused portion of the old tires. The dealer agreed and suggested a price of $175.00 for four new tires instead of the $600.00 that they would normally cost.

When Clinton arrived home from the tire dealer at about 9:00 A.M., he decided to remain at home because Chantale had called The Canadian's customer service and was told that The Canadian would investigate and call her back. At 10:00 A.M., no one had called so Chantale called again and she was told that someone would visit the Rileys before noon. At 2:30 P.M., no one had arrived and no one had called.

Chantale, therefore, called The Canadian to inquire about the delay. She once more repeated the whole story to the customer service representative since, at each call, she spoke to a different person. She was told to be patient; that the file clearly indicated that a technician would visit her home that day. Clinton was under the impression that the repair department remained open for business until 8:00 P.M. and was therefore not overly concerned. He felt fairly certain that a technician would turn up, as had happened in the past.

By this time, Clinton and Chantale had been without a refrigerator for about five days. They had to buy more ice to preserve a small quantity of food. At about 3:30 P.M. Clinton called the customer service and inquired about the delay after repeating the sequence of events. The representative promised to investigate and have someone call the Rileys.

At about 6:30 P.M., Chantale again called the repair department. She was now quite incensed because no one had called back, as promised. A man answered. He said that no one would visit the Rileys that day, since the repair department closed at 4:30 P.M. He also said that he would write a note to the person in charge of scheduling the repair jobs, telling him to call the Rileys and to schedule the repair for Wednesday. Additionally, he said that if the couple did not receive a phone call by 8:30 A.M., they should call the department. The whole family was quite unhappy with the situation and tried to make do with a meal prepared with canned goods and bread. Partly because of the allergies of the youngest child, they were used to preparing their meals each day, using basic ingredients, and found it difficult to continue eating canned food.

# July 4

On Wednesday, Clinton visited the tire dealer and had the tires on the family car changed. The steering wheel vibrations disappeared and he returned home at about 9:30 A.M. Meanwhile, having heard nothing from The Canadian, Chantale had called the service department at 8:25 A.M. Someone named Christiane answered the phone. She said that there was a note in the couple's file and that she would communicate with the repair department, asking the person in charge to call the Rileys. This was to be done by sending the employee an e-mail message. Apparently, the service department and the repair department did not communicate with each other by phone but only in writing. She said that she would phone Chantale as soon as she had heard from the repair department.

At 9:30 A.M., having heard nothing from The Canadian, Chantale phoned again. After waiting a few minutes for a service employee to take the call, and after recounting the whole story once again to another representative, she was told that Christiane had not yet heard from the repair department and that she would send another note to it. At that point, Chantale lost her cool and asked the person on the phone where else could she call if nobody called her back saying what time the repair would be done. She was given the 800 number of the service department of the corporate office. Chantale told the woman on the line that if no one had called her back after one hour, she would call the 800 number, which she did, at 10:45 A.M.

Again, she told the complete story to Diane, the person who answered the phone. After apologizing on behalf of the company, Diane told Chantale that she would check things out herself, since the file clearly stated that the repair was supposed to

have been done the previous day. She said that someone would call the Rileys as soon as possible. Clinton and Chantale subsequently had a small lunch, since there was no fresh food in the house anymore. They waited for the phone call in vain. Finally, Clinton decided to call again but this time to the store where the refrigerator had been bought.

Clinton called the store at about 2:15 P.M. He was hoping that after listening to the story, the store manager would be sufficiently concerned so that he or she would put pressure on the repair department to respond. When Clinton called the store, he was told that the manager was busy with a client and was therefore not available. Clinton insisted on talking to someone in a supervisory capacity. Finally, the store representative said that maybe she could help. Her name was Johanne. Clinton recounted the events of the past month. When he had finished the story, Johanne responded that she worked in a store and therefore had nothing to do with service and that she could not help. She suggested that Clinton should call customer service. Clinton, somewhat angrily, pointed out that sales in the store depended on The Canadian providing good service and that as a salesperson she had better be concerned about service. Johanne laughed sheepishly and agreed. Clinton, by this time, was so exasperated that he said that he felt like putting the refrigerator in his minivan, taking it to the store, and dumping it at the entrance. Joanne then said that the store did have a service where a small refrigerator could be loaned to clients. Clinton asked if he would have to visit the store to collect it. Joanne said yes. Clinton said that that was unacceptable and that The Canadian should deliver it. Finally, Johanne said that the only thing she could do was to give Clinton the number of the president's office, which she did.

Clinton called the number at about 2:30 P.M. on July 4. The person who answered the phone, Nicole, listened to the story and offered to send an e-mail to the manager in charge of repairs. Clinton indicated that it was about the third or fourth time someone had told his wife or him that an e-mail would be sent, and nothing had happened the previous times. Nicole then asked Clinton to hold. When she returned, she said that the manager was taking another call and that she could not speak to him. She was willing to leave a voice message as well as send an e-mail. Clinton was adamant that he wanted some action now and that he was completely frustrated. He indicated that he owned about three other appliances from The Canadian and that he was always a loyal The Canadian customer. He also said that his wife had worked at The Canadian as a department manager and that she was also loyal, but at this point he had no faith or confidence in the way the matter was being handled. Nicole again asked him to hold. When she returned, she said that she had spoken to the repair manager and that as soon as he had heard the phone number of the client, he said that he was aware of the problem and that he was working on it. Nicole told Clinton that he would receive a phone call within the hour. Clinton responded that this was about the fourth time he was given this promise but that no one had called in the past. Nicole was always polite. Clinton subsequently hung up, not very hopeful that the situation would be corrected soon.

A customer service representative from The Canadian finally called at about 3:00 P.M. on July 4. The employee said that a technician would visit the Rileys on July 5. She asked if that was OK. Clinton replied that that was terrible because he had been expecting a technician that same day, July 4. The representative explained that no appointment had been made for July 4, since the previous appointment had been scheduled for July 3. Finding this answer completely unacceptable, since in the past someone had called when a service visit had to be postponed to the next day, Clinton again pointed out how terrible the service from The Canadian was. He added that it made no sense to say that since no one had turned up on July 3, he should not have expected someone on July 4, and that clearly she must realize that the problem of the refrigerator still existed and the family had been without a refrigerator for approximately seven days. He continued that he knew that it was not the caller's fault but that she was the only person he could talk to. She listened and continued to ask politely if July 5 was a good day. Clinton explained that someone would have to stay home another day and asked whether under the circumstances, she could give a precise time when the technician would arrive. The representative responded that

the best she could do was indicate that the technician would come in the morning. At that point, Clinton terminated the call in exasperation.

That same day, a neighbor of the Rileys knowing about the situation invited the family over for dinner. The family went over and had dinner with their friends. While there, Dorothy, the neighbor, said that she too was a customer of The Canadian but that after hearing about the experience of the Rileys, she was beginning to think that she should search for a new supplier. She worked in an office that was in the process of buying new appliances and it had more or less decided to purchase the Bryand brand. But after hearing about the problems with the refrigerator of Chantale and Clinton, the office was going to re-evaluate its decision and more than likely buy an alternative brand. Dorothy also recounted that she had heard in her office a story about a The Canadian technician who, while repairing a refrigerator, had to be advised by a plumber who was at the same site. She believed that the service of The Canadian was deteriorating very badly.

Chantale and Dorothy, continuing their conversation, discovered that they were both facing the same situation, as home owners. Indeed, one couple had been married for 27 years and the other, for 18 years. Their home appliances, purchased new at the time their homes were bought, had reached or were approaching the end of their useful life and needed to be replaced. During the past 18 months, the Rileys had purchased a new dishwashing machine, a new clothes washer, and a new refrigerator. They knew that they would soon have to change the dryer, the stove, and the microwave oven. Dorothy faced the same situation. She thought that all her electrical appliances would need changing within the next five years. Both of them mentioned that since their disposable income was higher than before, they were able to buy more expensive appliances compared to the first time.

## July 5

On Thursday morning, the cleaning lady arrived at 9:00 A.M. and was surprised that the refrigerator had still not been repaired. She inquired about the brand and said that she would make a mental note not to buy that brand.

At about 9:45 A.M., a technician called to say that he would be there in 30 minutes. At 10:30 A.M., he arrived and Clinton and Chantale were happy to see that the technician was Miguel. When he heard the story he was quite surprised that no one had visited the Rileys on Tuesday morning. He began the repairs immediately by using nitrogen to clear the blocked lines. The job took about two hours and Miguel left at 12:30 P.M. The refrigerator appeared to be functioning properly when he left. Miguel also took the food claim with him after suggesting that Chantale add the cost of the ice bought to the list of expenses. Including the ice, Chantale calculated the total loss at around $108. Miguel promised to call in about five days to check if all was well with the refrigerator.

Chantale and Clinton, after doing a big grocery run and cooking their first complete meal since the trouble started seven days before, discussed their ordeal. Chantale mentioned that it could have been worse. One of them had to stay at home to deal with the problem for five days altogether but, given that they were consultants who had the luxury of working at home occasionally, they had postponed a few appointments but they did not lose five days of pay. But the couple was still very angry with the treatment they felt they had received during the past week. They understood that the problem with the refrigerator could necessitate two service calls but they did not understand that promises were broken and appointments were not respected. They were also puzzled that the employees of the company seemed to communicate only by e-mail. They agreed that the company had been a major disappointment and they wondered if they could ever trust it again regarding the purchase of future appliances. Chantale ended the conversation by adding that, unfortunately, due to their habit of buying extended service warranties, they would probably have to deal with The Canadian's repair service department again in the next five years. At the dinner that evening, the family raised questions regarding whether they should do anything further.

The next day, to the surprise of Chantale, Miguel called to inquire about the refrigerator. Upon learning that it seemed to work well, he promised that he would call the following week to see if all was well with the refrigerator. True to his promise, Miguel called again on Tuesday. Chantale felt that at least one person from The Canadian cared.

## CASE QUESTIONS

1. Have you ever experienced a similar situation with telephone services, cable or satellite television systems, financial institutions, airlines, or service providers such as hair-care professionals? If so, what did the company do wrong? What was the most important thing the company could have done to make you feel better about the poor service?

2. From the perspective of marketing, what element of the marketing mix (e.g., markets, products, prices, place, promotion, people) is most at risk for the department store chain?

3. From the perspective of management, what should the repair department's supervisors do to deliver better-quality service in the future?

4. If you were going to serve as a consultant to The Canadian, what recommendations would you make at the strategic, tactical, and operational levels? How would your recommendations connect with one another?

5. This case is largely presented from the perspective of "what not to do." In other words, it focuses on the mistakes made by the company. If you were to rewrite the case, could you show how to manage this department from a "what to do" perspective, tying your answer with the essential link between the service department and future marketing efforts?

# Market Analysis

A market analysis entails the study of a company's customers and competitors along with the overall industry and environment. From these analyses, the marketing team identifies whom to target, the products to market, and the best promotional approach to influence potential customers. A market analysis program consists of

1. an environmental analysis,

2. a competitive/industry analysis,

3. analysis of product positioning,

4. a market segment analysis, and

5. a customer analysis.

## Environmental Analysis

An environmental analysis begins with careful monitoring of all external variables that have an impact on an industry. Assessments of all political, social, economic, technological, and semicontrollable forces should be made. Political forces include laws, courts, governmental taxes and subsidies, and times when the government competes with business. Shifting demographics, cultural trends and changes, and rising educational levels constitute some of the primary social forces affecting business and marketing activities. Economic forces include economic conditions and the price and availability of raw materials. Companies are influenced by new products, product improvements, improvements in production methods, and other technological forces.

Semicontrollable forces act on companies, but methods exist to influence them in return. Those forces include local community, financial institutions, labor unions, suppliers, stockholders, retailers, and other channel members. These strategic variables impact individual products, companies, and consumers.

## Competitive/Industry Analysis

A competitive/industry analysis first identifies the levels of competition, from the closest and most intensive competitors to those that are the most distant but still viable organizations that are able to take away customers. Each is investigated using as many resources as needed to understand methods of competition as well as the individuals and companies other firms target with marketing efforts. In this context, competitive rivalries offer not only potential benefits in terms of increased focus by employees but also present challenges to a firm's well-being through lost sales and lost customers.

## Analysis of Product Positioning

Product positioning involves the place a good or service occupies in the minds of consumers and relative to the competition. Four components to be considered include

1. the target audience,

2. the good or service being offered,

3. the frame of reference or category, and

4. points of differentiation or uniqueness.

Once completed, positioning strategies may be put in place.

Positioning strategies are formulated based on attributes, use or application, competitors, product users, product class, price/quality relationships, or cultural symbol status. Attributes are those features that make a product unique, distinct, or superior. Use or application positioning is similar to attribute positioning; however, the ways to use the product are stressed more than the product's characteristics. Positioning against competitors involves a comparison that places a company's product in a better light than what another company offers. Product-user positioning focuses on the ways in which a product is superior as it is being used. Product-class positioning suggests the item is superior when compared with others within a set of products. Price/quality-relationship positioning is designed to convince consumers they are getting a better value for the money they pay. Cultural symbol positioning associates the product with a cultural icon or some other facet of culture.

A perceptual map may assist in identifying the optimal product positioning strategy. It typically employs two axes representing the key variables that affect perceptions of a product—most often, price and quality. Marketers seek to avoid brand parity, where all products are perceived to be basically the same, by building brand equity—the perception that a given brand is different and better.

## Market Segment Analysis

A market segment analysis categorizes customers into groups and identifies the characteristics of members of the groups. This is achieved by analyzing demographic characteristics, psychographic variables, behavioral actions, and geographic location. Then, segments are identified in terms of the potential for profit based on the match of the product to the market, the size of the segment, sales potential, growth potential, reachability, consumer responsiveness, retention potential, and levels of competition.

## Customer Analysis

A customer analysis is designed to provide marketers with an in-depth understanding of the company's customers, which consists of consumers, other businesses, and nonprofit organizations. The "Ws" of a customer analysis include understanding the "who, what, when, and where" of consumer purchases. The "H" suggests how purchases are made.

An effective marketing program necessitates careful study of the consumer buying decision-making process. Each step offers the potential to reach and attract customers. The steps include problem recognition, an internal information search, the evaluation of alternatives, the purchase decision, and a customer's postpurchase evaluation of the process. The concepts "share of mind" (awareness, recall) and "share of heart" (loyalty, affection) provide helpful ideas about how customers view a company and its products.

## Market Potential and Market Demand

The marketing team can also benefit from methods that help with understanding market potential and market demand. Market potential consists of the total number of individuals or businesses that might purchase a product. Market demand is the total current existing demand for a product. Company or brand demand expresses the demand for a particular company's brand and is often referred to as market share.

Demand may be estimated using consumer surveys, sales force estimates, executive opinions, or one of several quantitative methods, including trend projections, moving averages, exponential smoothing, and regression analyses. Producing quality demand estimates keeps a company from over- or under-producing items.

Two additional market analysis tools are contribution margins and break-even-point analyses. Contribution margin is calculated by subtracting marginal costs from additional revenues. The contribution made is to fixed costs and profit. Break-even analysis identifies the number of units that need to be sold in order to cover fixed costs and variable costs.

The purpose of a market analysis should be to increase understanding of the key targets of a marketing effort. It identifies the context in which products are sold, the competitors involved, the company's standing relative to those competitors, and the consumers that might be acquired and retained through various marketing efforts.

## The Cases

### GENICON: A Surgical Strike Into Emerging Markets

GENICON is a U.S.-based firm that manufactures and sells medical devices for laparoscopic surgery. The company's owner and founder, Gary Haberland, concluded that expanding in the more well-developed U.S. market was difficult. He was presented with the opportunity to expand into Europe, and GENICON subsequently entered a total of nearly 30 countries. At that point, 85% of company sales were made in foreign markets. To continue to grow the company, additional expansion was necessary. The case suggests that Haberland believed that the BRIC countries—Brazil, Russia, India, and China—offered the most promising new markets. Each had quantifiable and nonquantifiable advantages and disadvantages. A market analysis of each country would help him make the best decision for the company.

## HyundaiCard's Marketing Strategy

The HyundaiCard credit card company entered the competitive South Korean market in 1999. An innovative program tying credit card usage to automobile purchases gave the company a quick start; however, sales soon slowed. Strong competition with well-known brands had halted the firm's growth. HyundaiCard's marketing response was based on its electronic customer relations management program, which helped the firm customize interactions with customers and with target market segments. The program was a success and demonstrates the value of a well-designed market analysis program. Questions remain as to the direction the company should take in the future.

## TerraCycle, Inc.

TerraCycle's main product, an all-natural fertilizer that helps plants grow, was part of owner Betsy Cotton's desire to create goods that have a low impact on or even replenish natural resources. This approach was in contrast to two major competitors, Scott's and Spectrum. Relying on relationships with retail giants Walmart and Home Depot, the eco-company looked for ways to continue to grow. Individual gardeners constituted the company's primary market. The marketing management team considered the development of two specific plant foods, one for orchids and another for African violets. With limited resources, the marketing team assessed whether to develop one of the two products or both.

# GENICON: A Surgical Strike Into Emerging Markets

### By Allen H. Kupetz, Adam Tindall, and Gary Haberland

In January 2010, Gary Haberland, president and founder of GENICON, a U.S.-based firm that manufactured and distributed medical devices used in laparoscopic surgery, sat at his desk poring through rather encouraging fourth quarter financial statements. Impressed with GENICON's recent performance, he reflected on how he had arrived at this point and what the future might hold for the young company. It was not long ago that GENICON was near bankruptcy, as had been the case with many small companies in this industry. GENICON, unlike most of the startup companies that had succumbed to the pressures of the medical device industry, was not only able to remain open but actually thrived: it did this by focusing on its international distribution strategy since the early stages of its launch. This strategy not only saved GENICON from the vast and often fickle barriers of the U.S. market, but also came to define the company.

Haberland knew that in order for GENICON to grow and diversify, new markets would have to be identified, evaluated, and developed. Although the minimally invasive surgery (MIS) device market in the United States had long been the largest in the world, international markets were expected to grow at a much faster rate than the five percent growth forecasted for the U.S. market for the foreseeable future. According to the 2009 GENICON business plan, growth for the Pacific Rim was estimated to be 14 percent, with 11 percent for the Middle East, nine percent for Europe and six percent for Latin America; additionally, it was extremely difficult to gain market share in the United States. Since the early 1990s, distribution of MIS devices had been controlled by companies

Version: (A) 2010–06–30

receiving contracts through group purchasing organizations (GPOs). The GPOs' financial structure had long favored purchasing products from only the largest companies, some of which included Ethicon and Covidien, subsidiaries of Johnson & Johnson and Tyco respectively: this factor presented nearly insurmountable barriers to many start-up MIS device companies. Survival for GENICON depended on its ability to sell products abroad.

Early international success did not change the fact that GENICON needed to constantly identify what market it should enter next. The capital investment and risk associated with entering a new market was high for a firm the size of GENICON. Although the cost varied depending on the market and the local regulatory process, it would cost approximately $50,000[1] per market up front, with another $20,000 in costs for distributor assessment, market sampling and channel contracting. There was also an opportunity cost, as Haberland did virtually all the new business development and thus he was often out of the office attending tradeshows and meeting potential new distributors; furthermore, the time between initial investment and the point at which the first revenues were realized had been as much as three years. As was the case with many start-up companies, capital resources were difficult to come by and entering various markets simultaneously was simply not feasible.

## A Look Inside the Laparoscopic Industry

Laparoscopic surgery, a subset of MIS, allows physicians to examine, diagnose and treat problems within the abdomen. These surgical interventions can be performed through either traditional open or minimally invasive techniques. During laparoscopic surgery, the abdomen remains closed while specialized surgical instruments are inserted through a number of small incisions. Compared to open surgery, laparoscopy reduces trauma to the skin and muscles and reduces post-operative pain: this leads to shorter hospital stays and recovery times, providing clear advantages for both patients and hospitals.

The global market for MIS devices and instruments was worth an estimated $12 billion in 2005 and was expected to reach $18.5 billion by 2011, an average annual growth rate (AAGR) of 7.5 percent between 2006 and 2011. The United States accounted for approximately 60 percent of the world market, or $7.2 billion in 2005, and was growing at an AAGR of 7.2 percent. The U.S. market for all MIS procedures was approximately $7.7 billion in 2006 and was expected to reach $11 billion by 2011;[2] thus, there was a market outside the United States of more than $7 billion for GENICON to pursue.

While strong future sales growth was expected, this growth rate was forecasted to decline year-over-year (YOY). This declining growth rate was indicative of several market forces. The laparoscopic device market was limited by hospitals aiming to contain laparoscopic surgery costs by purchasing less expensive reusable and/or reprocessed devices instead of premium-priced disposables. With the market becoming very competitive and reaching a period of slower growth, coupled with the recent downturn in the worldwide financial condition, hospitals did not want to invest large sums of money in instrumentation. Many hospitals argued over the value of owning the assets they used and whether disposable or reusable instruments were appropriate in their business models; additionally, in some developing international markets, issues involving the re-use of disposable instruments put downward pressure on sales in those markets. GENICON was certain, however, that the ease-of-use and innovation of the disposable device markets would continue to guarantee their use and market share. When taking all factors into account, the outlook for the entire laparoscopic device industry was deemed very promising by Haberland and many industry observers.

## The Genesis of GENICON

In 1996, while working for a large medical device company, Haberland and a small development team were tasked to perform an analysis as to whether the company should mature its soft goods line to include laparoscopic medical devices. The firm was hesitant, considering it was primarily involved in orthopaedics and this would represent a significant deviation from their current operations; additionally, maturing their line to include laparoscopic devices would require a large investment of capital resources. After several months of research and negotiations with the development team, upper management decided to forgo entry into this field, citing high barriers to entry and compatibility with the company's current operational structure as factors in their decision. Haberland, baffled by management's assessment, resigned and created GENICON.

Being part of a large corporation lent Haberland little knowledge or experience concerning how to create a company of his own. Although it was clear to Haberland that there was an enormous unmet need in the endoscopic industry, he was unaware of how to go about meeting this need; for example, he knew nothing of the process to gain approval from the Food and Drug Administration (FDA) to manufacture and market medical products. Haberland learned that in order to file with the FDA he needed a company, and in order to have a company he needed his first product. After vetting the various devices used in laparoscopic surgery, he decided to start with a trocar, a device used in every laparoscopic procedure to provide the initial means of access into the abdominal cavity (see Exhibit 1).

Considering his limited resources for development, the trocar was the most logical option. Being a one-man company meant that Haberland had to outsource any research and development requiring specific technical skills. The knowledge base for these instruments was well established and readily available, reducing the capital investment needed to produce a prototype; more importantly, several of the patents on these devices had expired since many had been on the market for more than a decade. Taking this approach was much less costly than developing a completely new product, which was extremely important considering Haberland's limited financial resources.

In 1998, GENICON achieved its first sale to an Atlanta-based distributor for $20,000. This was a monumental achievement for the company at the

| Exhibit 1 | Sample of GENICON'S Products |

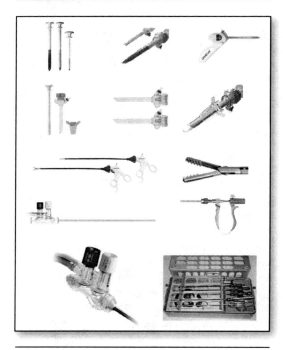

*Source:* Company records.

time, but further sales had to be obtained quickly as expenses rapidly began to pile up. Haberland initially targeted U.S. customers. Considering that approximately half of the world's laparoscopic procedures were performed in the United States, and given GENICON's location, this market seemed to be the logical choice. Expecting brisk sales within the first year, GENICON would then use that capital to sustain operations and grow the company.

Though there was a large and increasing demand for laparoscopic surgical devices, unforeseen barriers to obtaining these sales loomed large. The U.S. health care market heavily favored purchasing through GPOs, which then sold to hospitals and other primary care facilities. While larger medical device firms had few problems selling their products under this arrangement, smaller companies faced a daunting challenge to obtain contracts from GPOs. This industry structure led to GENICON's inability to sell any significant amount of product during its initial year of operation. To further compound the young company's problems, it was quickly running out of capital. If these issues persisted, the company would almost certainly fail within a year.

## GENICON Goes International

In 1998, Haberland learned that the American College of Surgeons would be holding their annual meeting at the Orlando Convention Center, just minutes from his home. Although it was not a trade show, Haberland figured it would be a good place to network and gain input from surgeons.

It was not inside the convention, however, where Haberland received advice that would drastically change GENICON's market focus. While walking to the convention center, he ran into an employee of British Standards Institution (BSI), an organization involved in licensing products for the European market. The pair briefly discussed their respective businesses and their motives for being at the conference. Upon learning of GENICON's troubles doing business in the United States, the gentleman asked if Haberland had ever thought of taking his business to the European market. Haberland had envisioned one day being an international company, but to this point had never given it any serious consideration. As the two spoke and Haberland dwelled on his recent experiences trying to penetrate the U.S. market, he expressed interest in the proposal. Following the discussion and some additional research, Haberland found that a potential opportunity existed in Europe, and that it was in his company's best interest to exploit this opportunity. With BSI's assistance, GENICON became the smallest company ever to receive the regulatory authority allowing its products to be sold throughout the European Union (EU).

While gaining this approval, GENICON's domestic business continued to remain sluggish. Realizing that it was going to be impossible to conduct business in the United States until GPO

contracts were obtained, Haberland decided to focus his efforts on the newly opened European market. Though this strategy posed its own set of risks, there was no other option. Learning of GENICON's recent European approval, a shareholder recommended that Haberland attend MEDICA in Germany, one of the largest tradeshows for medical devices in the world: this would provide an opportunity to meet distributors from every country in the EU and negotiate contracts with medical device suppliers.

There were several crucial factors taking place around the time of the MEDICA exhibition in 2000. The European market for medical devices, once composed of many suppliers—none of which had significant market share—was in transition. Prior to the late 1990s, relatively small to medium-sized manufacturers would use an array of distributors throughout the EU to get their products into hospitals. By using the distributor network, these companies were able to reach beyond their national borders into nearby foreign markets. This changed, however, when Tyco Healthcare (now Covidien) entered Europe in the 1990s: a series of strategic acquisitions by Tyco Healthcare consolidated the once-fragmented market. Being a much larger company, Tyco Healthcare used its size to negotiate favorable contracts with only a few regional distributors. Shortening the distribution channel provided significant cost savings for Tyco, but devastated many distribution companies that now had no products to sell.

It was in this environment that Haberland entered the market, having no ties in Europe at the time. The local distributors, desperate for products to sell, were more than willing to take GENICON's products into the European market. The MEDICA tradeshow was a huge success and marked a turning point for the small company. The local distributors would provide a steady stream of sales for GENICON, allowing it to remain a viable company without having significant revenues in the United States.

After obtaining several contracts in Europe, the future for GENICON seemed bright: however, Haberland found that this new market presented its own challenges, and that the company was again facing internal issues of its own. The EU was primarily composed of socialized health care systems, which provided medical care much differently than in the United States. Sales of medical devices would be directly correlated with the number of tenders won. A tender allowed a company to sell its products to a given health care system for a certain length of time. Winning tenders did not guarantee immediate sales, as these were contracts to sell to selected hospitals and health care facilities at some point in the future, usually one to three years. Though distributors typically bought some stock to build their inventories, this was not a substantial amount. Outside the EU, many developed countries provided health care to their citizens in a similar manner. Under these conditions, Haberland was able to establish business in almost 30 countries around the globe (see Exhibit 2 and Exhibit 3).

| Exhibit 2 | Genicon's International Markets (February 2010) |
|---|---|

| | | |
|---|---|---|
| Argentina | Greece | Singapore |
| Australia | Hong Kong | South Africa |
| Belgium | Ireland | South Korea |
| Canada | Italy | Spain |
| Chile | Japan | Sweden |
| Colombia | Malaysia | Switzerland |
| Denmark | Mexico | Thailand |
| Ecuador | New Zealand | Turkey |
| Egypt | Peru | U.A.E. |
| Finland | Portugal | U.K. |
| France | Saudi Arabia | |

*Source*: Company records.

| Exhibit 3 | Top 10 Markets for GENICON (2008) |
|---|---|

| Top 10 Markets ($) | 2008 | | |
|---|---|---|---|
| | Sales | Cost | Gross Margin |
| United Kingdom | 654,733 | 405,443 | 249,290 |
| United States | 588,488 | 403,958 | 184,530 |
| Italy | 540,556 | 449,140 | 91,416 |
| Turkey | 331,936 | 212,398 | 119,538 |
| Saudi Arabia | 311,221 | 187,828 | 123,393 |
| Spain | 304,263 | 151,056 | 153,207 |
| Greece | 298,763 | 92,399 | 206,364 |
| United Arab Emirates | 92,958 | 58,467 | 34,491 |
| Puerto Rico | 79,378 | 40,292 | 39,086 |
| Ireland | 57,714 | 33,401 | 24,313 |
| Total | 3,260,010 | 2,034,382 | 1,225,628 |

*Source*: Company records.

## International Market Selection

Considering that approximately 80 percent of GENICON's business was derived outside the United States, a critical factor in its success had been choosing the right international markets. There were usually moderate fees associated with obtaining the proper regulatory approval, averaging around $20,000 per market, but there were also recurring fees in the United States: GENICON spent approximately $55,000 per year for U.S. federal and state regulatory issues associated with exporting, certifications, and inspections. Furthermore, other elements such as taxes and tariffs, government regulations, exchange rates, and even corruption affected the ability and profitability of doing business in a given country. Due to GENCION's limited human and capital resources, it was critical that only countries with great market potential were chosen.

Deciding to invest in a country that was unsuited for GENICON's products would lead to minimal sales, wasted manpower and lost revenues. On the other hand, not choosing to enter suitable markets would have equally negative effects in terms of lost opportunity. Haberland narrowed down the list to four of the most promising countries for GENICON to enter: India, China, Brazil, and Russia. Each had its own set of benefits and shortcomings, and Haberland—not having the human or capital resources to go into all markets at once—was conflicted as to which market presented the best opportunity for GENICON (see Exhibit 4).

### India

According to some reports, India would overtake China in terms of population by 2050. Despite rapid economic growth, India remained a very poor country. According to the International Monetary Fund (IMF) estimates, India's gross domestic product (GDP) per capita was $1,016 in 2008, compared with $2,969 in China.[3] India's emerging middle class would continue to drive demand for new goods and services. A wealthier society, combined with tax reforms, would serve to boost revenue receipts and relieve some of India's fiscal pressures.

---

**Exhibit 4**  Selected Medical Device Market Forecasts (2003–2013)

**India**

|  | 2003 | 2004 | 2005 | 2006 | 2007 | 2008 | 2009f | 2010f | 2011f | 2012f | 2013f |
|---|---|---|---|---|---|---|---|---|---|---|---|
| Medical device market (US$bn) | 1.38 | 1.54 | 1.72 | 1.91 | 2.12 | 2.35 | 2.61 | 2.91 | 3.24 | 3.60 | 4.01 |
| Medical device market (INRbn) | 66.82 | 70.76 | 77.14 | 84.50 | 92.83 | 101.17 | 120.24 | 141.06 | 153.76 | 167.58 | 182.61 |
| Medical device market as % of total healthcare market | 6.11 | 5.72 | 5.37 | 5.28 | 5.12 | 4.43 | 4.50 | 4.32 | 4.22 | 4.40 | 3.64 |

*Source:* Association of Medical Devices and Suppiers of India (AMDSI). The Associated Chambers of Commerce and Industry of India (Assocham). Central Drugs Standard Control Organization (CDSCO). BMI.

*Note:* f = forecast.

*(Continued)*

| Exhibit 4 | (Continued) |

### China

|  | 2003 | 2004 | 2005 | 2006 | 2007 | 2008 | 2009f | 2010f | 2011f | 2012f | 2013f |
|---|---|---|---|---|---|---|---|---|---|---|---|
| Medical device market (US$bn) | 6.90 | 7.79 | 3.79 | 9.92 | 11.20 | 12.64 | 14.28 | 16.12 | 18.21 | 20.58 | 23.25 |
| Medical device market (CNYbn) | 57.15 | 64.50 | 72.01 | 79.09 | 85.12 | 87.87 | 97.65 | 108.35 | 117.48 | 127.60 | 139.51 |
| Medical device market as % of total healthcare market | 8.68 | 8.50 | 8.32 | 8.04 | 7.54 | 6.80 | 6.61 | 6.40 | 6.06 | 5.75 | 5.48 |

*Source:* China Association of Medical Devices Industry (CAMDI), State Food and Drug Association (SFDA), China Customs, BMI.

*Note:* f = forecast.

### Brazil

|  | 2006 | 2007 | 2008 | 2009f | 2010f | 2011f | 2012f | 2013f |
|---|---|---|---|---|---|---|---|---|
| Medical device market (US$bn) | 2.1 | 2.5 | 3.0 | 2.5 | 2.8 | 3.7 | 4.8 | 5.7 |
| Medical device market (BRLbn) | 4.6 | 4.9 | 5.5 | 6.1 | 6.9 | 7.7 | 8.6 | 9.7 |
| Medical device market as % of total healthcare market | 2.6 | 2.2 | 2.1 | 2.2 | 2.2 | 2.3 | 2.3 | 2.4 |

*Source:* BMI, ABIMED, WHO, US Commercial Service.

*Note:* f = forecast.

### Russia

|  | 2006 | 2007 | 2008 | 2009f | 2010f | 2011f | 2012f | 2013f |
|---|---|---|---|---|---|---|---|---|
| Medical device market | 1.67 | 1.82 | 1.98 | 2.04 | 2.18 | 2.38 | 2.59 | 2.88 |
| Medical device market (RUBbn) | 45.37 | 46.50 | 49.23 | 61.57 | 67.05 | 69.51 | 69.94 | 74.76 |
| Medical device market as proportion of total healthcare market (%) | 4.23 | 3.61 | 3.08 | 3.97 | 4.05 | 3.66 | 3.42 | 3.32 |
| Diagnostic equipment | 0.34 | 0.37 | 0.41 | 0.43 | 0.47 | 0.52 | 0.58 | 0.64 |
| Therapy and rehabilitation equipment | 0.29 | 0.32 | 0.34 | 0.35 | 0.38 | 0.41 | 0.44 | 0.49 |
| Disposables | 0.26 | 0.27 | 0.29 | 0.30 | 0.31 | 0.33 | 0.35 | 0.38 |
| Monitoring equipment | 0.23 | 0.26 | 0.29 | 0.30 | 0.32 | 0.36 | 0.40 | 0.44 |
| Medical aids | 0.16 | 0.17 | 0.18 | 0.18 | 0.20 | 0.21 | 0.23 | 0.25 |
| Surgical | 0.10 | 0.11 | 0.12 | 0.12 | 0.13 | 0.14 | 0.15 | 0.17 |
| Other | 0.29 | 0.32 | 0.34 | 0.35 | 0.38 | 0.41 | 0.45 | 0.50 |

*Source:* BMI, RMBC, WHO, US International Trade Administration, Coalition for US-Russia Trade.

*Note:* f = forecast.

India would continue to struggle to provide adequate health care services to its rapidly growing population. Publicly funded health care would be the main provider for the bulk of the poor population, although people were increasingly turning to private providers offering better facilities and shorter waiting lists. Public facilities would continue to suffer personnel shortages, which the government had been unprepared to address in recent times. Private health care boasted superior quality and facilities: it accounted for more than 65 percent of primary care and more than 40 percent of hospitals, resulting in some personnel shortages in the public sector. India's vast population generally paid for health care out of pocket. According to the World Health Organization (WHO), the private sector accounted for nearly three-quarters of total health care spending in 2007.[4]

Regulations improved significantly after 2000, and India was on the brink of forming the Medical Device Regulatory Authority (MDRA). The agency would ensure the quality, safety, efficacy, and availability of health care equipment used in the country. India's intellectual property (IP) laws left a lot to be desired, but were improving; likewise, approval times were shortening, with some innovative products being introduced in a relatively short period after mature market launch. Despite these improvements, India was held back by an entrenched bureaucracy. On a positive note, the country scored high for policy continuity, which was backed up by the longest and most exhaustive constitution in the world.

Through 2013, Business Monitor International (BMI) forecasted 11.3 percent YOY growth for India's $2.35 billion medical device market, which was higher than both the pharmaceutical and overall health care industries: this demonstrated the buoyancy of the sector.[5] Imported, high-end goods would continue to account for the majority of sales, but domestic production would increase its share through 2013. Other key trends included more transparent regulations, a reduction in levies and an influx of foreign firms. In 2005–2006, imports of medical devices rose by 23 percent to top $365 million, and similar growth was expected for the following years.[6]

## China

As early 2010, China had the fastest-growing major economy in the world, lifting hundreds of millions of people out of poverty over the past generation. A massive trade surplus and almost $2 trillion of foreign reserves served as a cushion against external economic volatility. China's policy makers appeared to be committed to continuing gradual economic reform. Caveats to its success included a heavy reliance on imports of energy and food, and a large segment of the population still living in poverty. China's dependency on exports to sustain growth made it vulnerable to the global recession. Private consumption was weak, at less than 40 percent of GDP. The first quarter of 2009 saw the Chinese economy grow at its slowest pace since quarterly records began in 1992, as collapsing exports and retreating consumers resulted in real GDP growth slowing to 6.1 percent YOY. The deceleration was felt across all sectors of the economy, including health care. Despite the economic slowdown in the face of a global recession, China fared extremely well and was poised for continued economic expansion into the future.

China's health care system was highly centralized. It came under close scrutiny following the 2003 outbreak of severe acute respiratory syndrome (SARS). The event highlighted the inadequacies of China's central planning in terms of efficient health care delivery across such a large country. As a result, the private sector made further inroads in the following years, especially as China opened up to outside suggestions and continued with its health care system reform, encouraging hospitals and clinics to turn a profit. Health care facilities in China suffered regional disparities. Approximately 40 percent of the Chinese population lived in cities that boasted considerably superior health care services, although the accelerating rate of urbanization threatened to worsen access to services as cities struggled to meet rising demand and villages lost qualified medical personnel. Further improvements to the sector were required, although the rising reliance on market forces would stimulate faster changes.

The regulatory framework was also improving, but it still hindered the path toward more efficient operations, particularly those used to dealing with defined and transparent roadmaps to commercialization because it was so difficult for companies to predict when, if ever, regulatory approval would be granted. Companies could not prepare reliable sales funnels or forecasts. The State Food and Drug Administration (SFDA)—China's premier food, drug, and medical device watchdog—completed a draft version of the revised regulations for the Supervision and Administration of Medical Devices in September 2009, giving a clear signal that quality was becoming increasingly important: this was good news for non-Chinese firms. The approval system for medical devices was decentralized. Input from the local governments was needed for registration of new devices, leaving firms facing significant bureaucratic pressures to roll out products swiftly. Typically, it took 12 months to approve a new piece of equipment, but this time period was expected to shorten. Unfortunately, as of February 2010, the reuse of data and analyses previously given to other regulatory agencies was not permitted: this lengthened the process. The SFDA sent some encouraging signals: in January 2009, a senior official at the agency said that the improvement of the medical device registration system would be the agency's top priority in 2009.

China's $12.6 billion medical device sector was expected to post double-digit growth between 2008 and 2013, driven by a booming economy and an ageing population. Domestic firms were expected to move up the value chain, while foreign players would continue to increase their presence. Challenges included inconsistent IP enforcement and relentless downward pricing pressures. Cutting-edge medical equipment was expected to experience the greatest demand. By 2012, the value of the medical device industry was expected to reach $20.6 billion, an impressive 8.2 percent share of the overall health care market. A key driver of the medical equipment market was the increase of private insurance and the privatization of state-owned health care facilities. The growing commoditization of health care in China would likely result in increased demand.

## Brazil

The Brazilian economy was one of the largest in the world: it benefited from a rich abundance of agricultural and mineral resources. Onshore and offshore oil discoveries catapulted Brazil toward the status of global oil giant almost overnight. This would help the country attract a wide range of investors and businesses over the long term. The Brazilian economy was highly reliant on strong consumer spending levels, which were driven by a credit boom. Tighter credit and liquidity conditions amid the global financial crisis of 2009 instigated signs of consumer retrenchment, casting growing uncertainty over Brazil's potential for a prompt economic recovery down the road. Long-term growth prospects were generally positive, with nominal GDP growth rate expected to average 6.6 percent annually through 2013.[7]

Brazil's rapidly growing population and the government's commitment to expanding access to essential health care were key drivers of future growth in the market. Despite many changes between the 1980s and the 2000s, the country made significant inroads on public health. In May 2008, the government passed a law obligating the country to increase health care spending to a minimum of 10 percent of GDP, compared to the seven percent spent on health care in previous years.[8] Total health expenditures were forecasted to rise steadily well into the future, assuming stable economic conditions prevailed and that population growth continued at a steady rate.

Medical device registration was controlled by The National Health Surveillance Agency (ANVISA), which required companies to establish a local office or manufacturing unit, or appoint a local distributor in order to access the market. Although ANVISA has its own regulatory standards, international certification was generally accepted. Approval of medical devices in Brazil could become subject to greater risk-based differentials, following two proposals from ANVISA. The adoption of a four-tier system was being considered, similar to the system used in the EU in which low-risk health products were allowed easier access to the market, while higher-risk products required suitable Good Manufacturing Practice (GMP) certification. Industry observers welcomed this move, noting cost benefits for certain manufacturers, safety benefits for patients and greater efficiencies for health regulation. The registration process was relatively swift, taking an average of 10 months, and product registrations were valid for five years. The cost of device registration varied according to the annual revenue of the company and was generally in the range $1,200 to $11,900.[9]

Brazil's medical device market, valued at $3.0 billion in 2008, was the largest in Latin America. The strong growth experienced since economic liberalization in the 1990s was expected to continue well into the future. A compound annual growth rate (CAGR) of 13.8 percent was anticipated through 2013, fuelled by increases in health care expenditures: a large part of this spending would be channelled towards the modernization of health care services. Brazil remained overwhelmingly dependent on imports of medical equipment and supplies, with official statistics showing a $1.9 billion deficit in these products in 2007. The public sector, which accounted for 44 percent of domestic demand for medical devices, offered strong potential for firms able to win government tenders. The Ministry of Health's budget increased by 21 percent in 2006, and strong public sector funding was expected to continue, offering strong growth potential for domestic manufacturers.[10]

The medical device distribution sector was highly fragmented, creating the biggest challenge for foreign firms looking to bring their products to the Brazilian market. There were approximately 3,000 importers and distributors, of which most were small companies that operated regionally or in niche markets; for this reason, many multinationals chose to tie up with local device makers to gain access to the market. As the market continued to grow, it was anticipated that there would be consolidation in the inefficient distribution sector, which would boost market access.

With few large-scale domestic manufacturers and a large rapidly growing market, Brazil's medical device sector offered strong potential for foreign device makers to exploit imports. Indeed, the medical device market suffered from a major trade deficit that grew by an estimated 20 percent between 2006 and 2007 to reach $1.8 billion. The United States accounted for approximately 50 percent of the import market. The widening trade gap was not helped by low import tariffs: there were no import duties or value-added taxes on 42 medical devices. This was in contrast to many other emerging markets, where only high-tech products that could not be manufactured locally were import duty exempt.

## Russia

The post-1998 rebound from the economic crisis, combined with significant reductions in personal and corporate income tax rates, made Russia a much more attractive place to do business than in the decade following the Soviet Union's collapse. Stability increased dramatically as the economy rebounded on the back of high commodity prices and the currency's 1998–1999 devaluation. Despite these improvements, the Russian economy was still in a state of transition, with large account and fiscal surpluses being eroded significantly and challenging the country's macroeconomic stability. Russia's dependence on the oil sector made it particularly vulnerable to a sustained decline in energy prices; additionally, many foreign investors were put off by poor legal safeguards, high levels of bureaucracy, and corruption.

The ongoing modernization of the health care system was the key driver of the medical device market's growth, though this was often pursued in an inconsistent and piecemeal manner. Positive factors fueling a growth in healthcare expenditures included vastly improved government finances, a commitment to health care improvement, and the rise of private health insurance, as many large companies routinely provided supplementary insurance for employees. Significant structural challenges remained, including antiquated and poorly funded hospitals, a lack of primary care networks and physicians, a poor logistics infrastructure, and a wide variability in terms of the quality and availability of health care across regions. The state of medical facilities was expected to improve substantially over the long–term, but conditions were problematic. Encouraging to many in the medical manufacturing industry was the general trend toward greater healthcare expenditure levels, and forecasts were that total private and public health care spending would reach $97.4 billion by 2013, equivalent to 3.8 percent of GDP.

The potential of the Russian market was balanced by significant political risk. Roszdravnadzor, the main government health regulator, lacked enforcement teeth and had seen significant disruption from changes in leadership since late 2006. Registration of foreign-made medical devices was handled by this department. All imports had to go through either a Russia-based subsidiary or an authorized local distributor; in addition, there was the risk that future changes to legislation could actually make the situation worse for foreign producers, as the government sought methods (short of punitive tariffs) to increase the share of local producers in the overall marketplace. This scenario was expected to benefit from the reduction in tariffs for medical devices to an average of five percent for these products, as a result of Russia's likely future accession to the World Trade Organization (WTO).

Russia's $1.98 billion medical device sector displayed robust long-term growth potential, driven predominantly by an expanding economy and improving health investment by both the state and private sector. Though the economic crisis of 1998 served as a stimulus for the domestic medical devices market—as the price of imported equipment rose sharply—local players failed to consolidate their position and imports still made up approximately 75 percent of the market.[11] The medical device sector was expected to suffer some short-term setbacks due to the economic slowdown in 2009, but demand from increased state investment should mitigate a substantial amount of this negative impact. By 2013, the total market valuation should reach $2.88 billion after growing at a CAGR of 7.74 percent.[12]

The sheer size of the Russian healthcare network, comprising almost 10,000 hospitals, meant that there was great opportunity for this sector, even if the majority of financing came from the government. Healthcare expenditures were growing at a reasonable pace as well: it was estimated that healthcare expenditures stood at a total of $39.4 billion in 2007.[13] Spending was forecasted to fall slightly to 3.8 percent of GDP by 2012, which was low by European standards. Nevertheless, as Russia's middle class grew, the number of private clinics and hospitals was expected to increase accordingly, which would help fuel sector growth.

## Where to Go Next?

Haberland's review of GENICON's 2009 performance made him feel confident about the future. The company had 21 employees: six in operations, six in sales, five in administration, three in research and development, and him. Annual revenues were above $5 million, which had been achieved with a marketing/business development budget of under $225,000.

With more than 10 years of experience and some real international success, Haberland was ready to enter one or more of these emerging markets: but where should GENICON go next? Was it possible that none of these four emerging markets were right for GENICON? Should it skip these four for now and focus on growing its business in its existing international markets, or large, wealthy countries, such as Germany, that were adjacent to one of its existing markets? Taking GENICON's current situation into account, Haberland took the data and used it, along with his instincts, to decide where to go to next.

## CASE QUESTIONS

1. The market for minimally invasive surgical instruments in the United States was growing but at a slower rate than in other countries. Did Gary Haberland make the best decision to simply shift all the company's efforts to international markets, or should he have first tried harder to expand sales in the United States?

2. A market analysis of each of the potential countries designated for expansion would include a quantitative and a qualitative evaluation. Based on the information in the case, which quantitative figures would be most important for the market analysis? How would the concepts of market potential and market demand apply to the analysis? Make a case for the country Gary Haberland should choose based solely on a quantitatively based market analysis.

3. The market analysis of each of the potential countries designated for expansion could also be conducted using "gut-reaction" or qualitative-decision variables, such as cultural similarity, ease of conducting business, and perceptions of corruption. Based on the information in the case, which qualitative variables would be the most important for the market analysis? Make a case for the country Gary Haberland should choose based solely on a qualitatively based market analysis.

4. Using both quantitative and qualitative variables, which country should Gary Haberland choose?

5. What complications emerge from conducting a market analysis in a foreign country as compared with the United States?

# HyundaiCard's Marketing Strategy

### By Chan Soo Park and Ronald D. Camp II

In January 2009, the vice-president of HyundaiCard's marketing division (see Exhibit 1), Jae-Woo Park, and several marketing managers discussed the marketing strategies of HyundaiCard in Korea. Following a review of HyundaiCard's marketing plans, the marketing managers put forward many ideas for marketing strategies and anticipated possible difficulties for HyundaiCard as a market follower in the competitive Korean credit card market. Jae-Woo reported the marketing strategies to Ted Chung, president of HyundaiCard.

HyundaiCard entered the competitive Korean credit card industry in 1999 and branded itself as "Hyundai M Card" (see Exhibit 2). Its creative

business model forecasted HyundaiCard holders would be pre-discounted as much as 2,000,000 won (US$1,800) for buying Hyundai automobiles when paying with the HyundaiCard. They could then pay the discount back with credit card point mileage within five years. Although this creative business model achieved tremendous success within the Korean market, the company's performance had not progressed since 2002. HyundaiCard suffered from minimal customer count (i.e., number of cards distributed) and had difficulty relating its creative business model to the strong personas of leading players in the credit card industry. As a result of the innovative marketing strategy, however,

Version: (A) 2009–12–09

| **Exhibit 1** HyundaiCard's Organization | | |
|---|---|---|
| President & CEO | Strategic Planning Division | Strategic Planning Dept. <br> Process Innovation Dept. |
| Risk Management Committee | Finance Division | Corporate Planning Dept. <br> Finance Dept. |
| Customer Protection Committee | Corporate Service Division | Public Relations Dept. <br> Corporate Service Dept. <br> IT Dept. <br> Customer Satisfaction Dept. <br> Business Legal Dept. |
| Audit Committee | Risk Management Division | Collection Management Dept. <br> Early Collection Dept. <br> Risk Management Dept. <br> Underwriting Dept. |
| | Sales Division | Personal Sales Dept. <br> Corporate Sales Dept. |
| | Marketing Division | CRM Dept. <br> Marketing Dept. <br> Brand Marketing Dept. <br> PRIVIA Dept. <br> Financial Business Dept. |
| | Integrated Marketing Division | Alliance Sales Dept. <br> SME Business Dept. |
| | Finance Business | Cross-Sell Business Dept. |
| | Finance Business Division | Cross-Sell Business Dept. |

**Exhibit 2** HyundaiCard M, as a HyundaiCard Representative Product

Source: Company files.

HyundaiCard successfully positioned itself as a market leader.

Yet challenges remained for senior management. How could HyundaiCard, a market follower, successfully position itself as a market leader? Could HyundaiCard's marketing strategy keep enhancing its competitive edge in the market? What future strategy would be best for HyundaiCard?

# HyundaiCard Co., Ltd.

HyundaiCard was the country's fourth largest credit card company. HyundaiCard, sponsored by Hyundai Kia Automotive Group, was established in 1999 when the Hyundai Motor Group acquired Diners Card as a subsidiary and changed the card's name in 2001 to "HyundaiCard" (see Exhibit 3), thereby challenging the highly competitive credit card industry. Hyundai Motor Group prepared a long-term strategy in order to transform itself from an automobile manufacturer into the world's leading provider of additional services related to automobile businesses. The company's goal was to strengthen its financial services, retail businesses and Internet fields, etc.

| **Exhibit 3** | Corporate Milestones | |
|---|---|---|
| 1967 | | Diners Club Card, the world's first credit card, launched in Korea by its agent, Korea National Tourism Organization |
| 1984 | June | Citi Corp. opened the Korean branch of Diners Card |
| 1993 | Feb. | Daewoo Group took over the management of Diners Club Korea |
| 1994 | Sept. | Launched prepaid cards |
| 1996 | June | Launched overseas travel supporting services |
| 1997 | Dec. | Began overseas ATM cash withdrawal service |
| 1998 | July | Increased capital to W100 billion |
| 2001 | Oct. | Changed company name to HyundaiCard Co., Ltd. |
| | Nov. | Became an affiliated company of Hyundai Motor Group |
| 2002 | Jan. | Released Hyundai "M" Card |
| | Oct. | Opened wireless Internet site |
| 2003 | March | Increased capital to W180 billion |
| | April | Remodeled and opened Internet shopping mall site (http://shop.hyundaicard.com) |
| | June | Increased capital to W310 billion |
| 2004 | Jan. | Disclosed HyundaiCard's corporate identity |
| | June | Selected as Korea's most respected enterprise |
| | Sept. | Won first place in Service Quality Index for the Credit Card |
| | Oct. | Opened customized travel site |
| 2005 | May | Opened HyundaiCard VIP Lounge at Incheon International Airport |
| | Aug. | Established a strategic alliance with GE Consumer Finance |
| 2006 | April | Renewed Alphabet Card marketing |
| | Dec. | Selected top in the Credit Card category of National Consumer Satisfaction Index (NCSI) |
| 2007 | Jan. | Released HyundaiCard M Lady |
| | Apr. | Released HyundaiCard V Completed first successful overseas US$400 million bond by an Asian card company |
| | July | Attainment of an impressive 5,000,000 cardholders under HyundaiCard M |
| 2008 | Feb. | Released Family Discount Card, HyundaiCard H |

In 2005, HyundaiCard strengthened its funding base through the formation of a strategic alliance with GE Consumer Finance (GECF), a unit of General Electric (GE). GECF invested 678.3 billion won in the firm, thus becoming the largest shareholder. HyundaiCard's largest shareholders became Hyundai Motor and GE Consumer Finance (see Exhibit 4). After years of gaining cumulative expertise and know-how, through its association with GE Consumer Finance, HyundaiCard made efforts to become a market leader in the credit card industry by initiating a unique, customized service via alphabet card marketing activities. HyundaiCard secured a more stable financial base with this alliance; the BIS capital adequacy ratio increased to 43 percent from 11.3 percent, addressing a significant improvement in the company's risk profile. HyundaiCard upgraded creditability and reinforced financial stability through the formation of the strategic alliance. A sustainable growth base was firmly laid by introducing GE's advanced financial product planning and risk management systems. The partnership formed a solid foundation upon which HyundaiCard could become a market leader in South Korea.

"HyundaiCard M," a HyundaiCard representative product, had enjoyed yearly high performance.

### Exhibit 4   Ownership Structure (%)

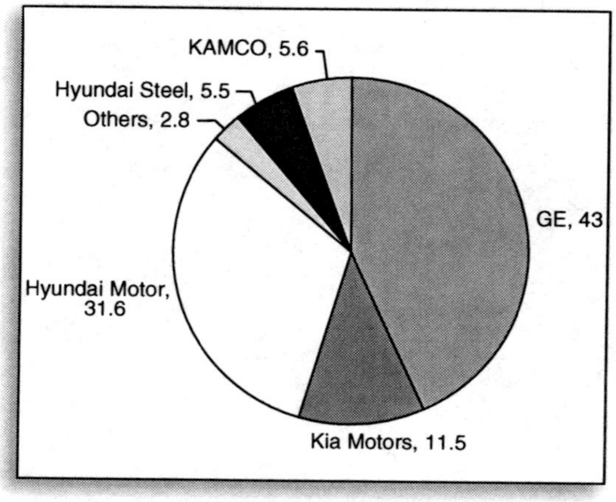

KAMCO, 5.6
Hyundai Steel, 5.5
Others, 2.8
GE, 43
Hyundai Motor, 31.6
Kia Motors, 11.5

*Source:* HyundaiCard, 2009.

It secured more than one million subscribers within the first year of its launch. As a single credit card brand, it had the largest subscriber base of any credit card in Korea. In addition to "HyundaiCard M," which created a huge sensation among male customers, HyundaiCard released the "M Lady" card, designed to offer additional beneficial services to female customers. The "M Lady" credit card brand also gained a favorable response from the Korean market (see Exhibit 5).

## The Credit Card Market in South Korea

### South Korea Credit Card History

The concept of paying merchants by using a credit card was invented in 1950 by Frank X. McNamara, an American businessman who left cash in his hotel room and, as a result, was unable to pay his bill at a restaurant. The Diners Club produced the first general purpose credit card; shortly thereafter, it was followed by American Express and Carte Blanche. The Bank of America created the BankAmericard in 1958, which evolved into the VISA card. MasterCard appeared in 1966.

In Korea, the concept of the credit card was introduced in 1969 by a Korean department store, Shinsaegae. In 1978, Korean Exchange Bank launched its first credit card under a joint venture with VISA International, issuing the credit card to its clients who travelled frequently (see Exhibit 6). In the 1980s, bank and non-bank credit card companies began to do business in Korea. It was not until the year 2000 that the market saw an annual growth rate of 80 percent and more than 100 million cards issued.

### Credit Card Consumption Patterns and Trends

Between the 1990s and 2002, the number of credit cards issued in South Korea increased tenfold, from 10 million to 100 million. Bank of Korea records show the credit card usage amount at that time was 40 percent or higher of private final

| Exhibit 5 | HyundaiCard's Products |
|---|---|

| Products | Target Customers | Main Services |
|---|---|---|
| HyundaiCard M | The all-around, all-purpose multi-point card for driving, dining out, flying or even shopping. | Clients earn up to three percent of their purchase in points each time they use their card and in turn save points to redeem a discount voucher worth up to US$2,000 on a Hyundai/Kia car, or redeem points at a growing list of locations including GS Caltex gas station, CJ Home Shopping, Lotte Cinema and more. |
| HyundaiCard M Lady | The multi-point card and service exclusively for women. | Clients benefit from multi-rewards points when buying a car, filling up their gas tank, dining out, flying or shopping. They acquire additional movie discounts and interest-free payments on purchases made at alliance stores. |
| HyundaiCard S | A serious shopping card for serious shoppers. | Clients receive a five percent discount on all purchases at Hyundai Department Stores and 80 points per liter of gas purchased during weekends at four major fuel gas stations. Clients can earn points to save five percent on cell phone charges and get additional discounts for movies and dining out. |
| HyundaiCard W | The weekend travel card that earns free travel benefits while you travel. | Clients spend US$12,000 and receive one Travel Ticket redeemable for airline tickets at all airlines. They also enjoy a variety of complimentary travel services. |
| HyundaiCard U | The value card made for university students. | Clients earn up to one percent in U points on all purchases. They also trade points for points at cooperative partner businesses. |
| HyundaiCard K | A premium mileage card doubling as a Korean Air SKYPASS Membership card. | Clients earn and save up to three miles on every purchase. Discount vouchers worth up to 10 percent off airfare are also offered and clients may receive up to 15 percent off purchases at major duty-free shops. |
| HyundaiCard K VIP | An ultra-premium card doubling as a Korean Air SKYPASS Membership card. | Clients receive all the benefits of HyundaiCard K, plus free round trip ticket vouchers for a travel companion around South Korea. |
| The Black | The first VIP card made exclusively for the top 0.019 percent of South Korea. High-class benefits for high-class customers. | Clients may receive free upgrades to first class on Korean Air and Asiana Airlines. They may also receive 10 percent off coupons for air travel and US$300 gift vouchers for use at top hotels, beauty shops and more. Full access to Club Services. |
| The Purple | A VIP card made for the top five percent of South Korea, including medical doctors, pharmacists, successfully self-employed individuals and CEOs. | Double Rewards are offered on M points and airline mileage. A free airfare voucher may be redeemed for a companion on trips to Hong Kong, China, Japan, and most countries in Asia. |

*Source*: HyundaiCard IR, 2007.

| Exhibit 6 | Timeline of the Korean Credit Card Market |
|---|---|

| Year | Development | Credit Card Service Companies |
|---|---|---|
| 1960s | In 1969, the first card was issued by the Shinsaegae Department Store to Samsung Corporation employees. | Shinsaegae Department Store |
| 1970s | The first VISA card was introduced by the Korean Exchange Bank Credit Service Co., LTD (KEBCS), in a joint venture with VISA International. | KEBCS and VISA International |
| 1980s | In 1987, the credit laws were amended and the credit card market began to develop more aggressively. Four mono-line credit companies were established. | Four mono-line credit companies: LG in 1987, Kookmin in 1987, the Korean Exchange Bank Credit Service (KEBCS) in 1988 and Samsung in 1988. |
| 1990s | Tax laws were modified at the end of 1999. A tax deductible system was introduced—a portion of credit card purchases could be deducted from income before tax. | I: Department stores<br>II: Bank: BC, Suhyup, Kwangju<br>III: Mono-line credit<br>companies: LG, Samsung<br>IV: Automobile and oil companies |
| 2000s | Private consumption with credit cards was approximately $210 billion annually. The average South Korean had at least four credit cards. | 64 types of credit card service products by 2002.<br>Distribution industry: 38<br>Mono-line issuers: 10<br>Banks: 16 |

*Source:* Financial Supervisory Committee and Credit Finance Association.

consumption. Koreans paid for many purchases with credit cards, even small purchases of a few dollars at convenience stores. Private consumption with credit cards amounted to approximately $210 billion in 2006. According to the Bank of Korea (BOK), Korea ranked 34th in per capita income in the world, but the credit card penetration in South Korea was quite high, with the world's second highest per capita card issuance. The average South Korean cardholder held 3.78 credit cards in 2008, trailing only the United States with 5.3 cards. Trailing behind were Singapore with per capita card issuance of 2.98 cards, followed by the United Kingdom (2.36), the Netherlands (1.92), and Belgium (1.57).

A unique characteristic of the Korean credit card was its multi-functionality. South Korea's credit card companies offered competitive incentives in order to entice credit card customers to use their products frequently (see Exhibit 7). A great deal of credit card use was tied to retail chains or conglomerates. For example, consumers who had a HyundaiCard bought products at the Hyundai Internet shopping mall (www.Hmall.com) and at Hyundai department stores run by the Hyundai conglomerate. Similarly, consumers who had a Samsung credit

| Exhibit 7 | Various Incentives Provided by Dynamic Korean Credit Card Companies |
|---|---|

| Credit Card Services | Incentives |
|---|---|
| Cash discounts | Five to 10 percent discount to consumers who purchase products with their credit cards |
| Interest-free installments | Several online shopping websites provide credit card consumers with the option of interest-free installments over three to twelve months |
| Air mileage service | Give consumers a certain number of free miles on airlines for every W1,000 (US$1) they spend |
| Point cash | A small percentage of each settlement saved in the card user's account can be spent the same as cash, which could be used in more than two million shops This point money could be used to make political contributions or donated to a nonprofit organization |
| Pre auto financing service | HyundaiCard provides Hyundai car purchasers with a nominal discount on the price of a car. Card users must pay this amount back with accumulated mileage points. |

card bought products at the Samsung Internet shopping mall (www.samsungmall.com) and Samsung department stores run by the Samsung conglomerate. The online and offline stores used incentives such as a five percent discount or interest-free installments over three months or airline mileage points to increase consumer loyalty. In order to survive in the competitive credit card industry, companies needed to keep up with new and creative marketing incentives and promotions.

## IT Developments in South Korea

Information technology was an important growth engine for the South Korean economy and had expanded rapidly since the early 1990s. In particular, South Korea was a technology-savvy country in which electronic payment was easy and popular. The number of people using the Internet regularly was about 30.7 million as of March 2007.[1] Korea's rate of Internet usage by those above the age of six, as of June 2007, reached 75.5 percent,[2] showing a rapid growth in the number of people who were

very comfortable using the Internet. The use of credit cards was the most common mode utilized by South Koreans to pay for products and services, followed by cash and online banking services[3] (see Exhibit 8).

| Exhibit 8 | The Preference of Payments |
|---|---|

| | | |
|---|---|---|
| 1 | Credit Card | 38.70 |
| 2 | Cash | 27.76 |
| 3 | Transmitting With Cash Machine | 9.89 |
| 4 | Internet Banking | 6.98 |
| 5 | Debit Card | 6.78 |
| 6 | Telephone Banking | 4.97 |
| 7 | Giro | 4.32 |
| 8 | Mobile Banking | 0.4 |
| 9 | Electronic Cash | 0.2 |

*Source*: Korea Credit Finance Association, 2005.

Korean credit card websites had gained nationwide popularity (see Exhibit 9), resulting in various new services and goods appearing on the Internet. Generally, credit card holders checked their transaction history and processed some transactions related to products and services with their accumulated mileage points. However, credit card consumers had qualms about being treated as simply a part of a large mass, either while on the Internet or on offline channels. Korean credit card websites had been working hard to pack web pages with as many features as possible. They were spending millions of dollars on aspects of customer relation management vital to consumers. Therefore, credit card companies had taken a customer-focused view and retreated from the mass marketing approach.

In the U.S. market, many affiliated merchants were not equipped with electronic authorization and settlement technologies. Usually, it took one or two weeks to get reimbursed from the credit card companies after giving signed payment slips to the banks. This created a major inconvenience. On the other hand, Korean credit card companies, using the VAN service, developed high-end technologies and finally automated the entire process. The affiliated member stores were then reimbursed within three days. This convenience helped the issuers attract more affiliated stores.

## Active Support From the Korean Government

South Korea was one of the world's most dynamic countries encouraging credit card use (see Exhibit 10), thanks to the support and an encouraging policy by the Korean government since 2000. The Korean government encouraged consumers to use credit cards to stimulate private spending and secure more taxes. The Korean government made the acceptance of the credit card mandatory and penalized stores not accepting the credit card. There were sensational credit card lottery events and tax incentives for credit card usage. With the

---

**Exhibit 9**    The Usage Rate of Korean Financial Websites

| Domain | Unique Online Visitor | Total Page View |
|---|---|---|
| Bank | 19,931,102 | 2,120,305,390 |
| Credit Card | 14,038,598 | 664,025,739 |
| Insurance | 8,860,826 | 327,639,548 |
| Investment | 7,532,188 | 877,177,163 |
| Other Financial Service | 4,809,701 | 51,705,433 |
| Real Estate | 4,754,289 | 424,377,102 |
| Security | 4,181,004 | 320,381,728 |
| Financial Service in Portal | 5,445,323 | 50,604,349 |

*Source*: Korean Click, 2005, www.koreanclick.com, accessed December 15, 2007.

*Notes*: Unique Online Visitor: a statistic describing a unit of traffic to a web site, counting each visitor only once in the time frame of the report.

*Total Page View*: a total request to load a single page of a website.

| Exhibit 10 | Korean Population and the Number of Cards Issued |
|---|---|

Unit: 1,000

| Year | Population | Economically Productive Population | Number of Credit Cards Issued | Number of Credit Cards per Person | Membership Stores |
|---|---|---|---|---|---|
| 1995 | 45,093 | 20,845 | 33,278 (31.5) | 1.6 | 2,760 (34.3) |
| 1997 | 45,954 | 21,782 | 45,705 (11.2) | 2.1 | 4,257 (23.0) |
| 1999 | 46,617 | 21,666 | 38,993 (−7.2) | 1.8 | 6,192 (33.2) |
| 2000 | 47,008 | 22,069 | 57,881 (48.4) | 2.6 | 8,611 (39.1) |
| 2001 | 47,343 | 22,417 | 89,330 (54.3) | 4.0 | 12,627 (46.6) |
| 2002 | 47,640 | 22,877 | 104,807 (17.3) | 4.6 | 15,612 (23.6) |
| 2003 | 47,925 | 22,916 | 95,517 (−8.9) | 4.1 | 16,949 (8.6) |
| 2004 | 48,082 | 23,370 | 83,456 (−16.0) | 3.6 | 17,095 (8.6) |
| 2005 | 48,294 | 23,743 | 82,905 (−0.7) | 3.5 | 16,124 (−5.7) |
| 2006 | 48,497 | 23,978 | 91,149 (9.9) | 3.8 | 17,037 (5.7) |
| 2007 | 48,692 | 24,216 | 89,565 | 3.7 | 14,701 |
| 1/4 2008 | | 23,852 | 90,673 | 3.8 | 14,851 |
| 2/4 2008 | | 24,638 | 93,481 | 3.8 | 15,145 |
| 3/4 2008 | | 24,503 | 97,519 | 4.0 | 15,364 |

*Source*: The Credit Card Finance Association, 2008.

above-mentioned active support, the non-bank, specialized companies such as Samsung, LG (Shinhan), and Hyundai endeavored to increase their market shares through proactive marketing such as ardent sales promotions (i.e., street promotions and sales), improvement of CRM systems, and interest-free installment payments on purchases.

## Credit Card Issuers in South Korea

The Korean credit card market was characterized by rapid growth and intensified competition. The major monoline credit card issuers were Samsung Card, LG (Shinhan) Card, and HyundaiCard. The aforementioned companies issued credit cards customized for Korean individuals. There were cards such as the "Lady Card," the "Cellular Phone Card," the "Teen Group Card," the "Revolving Card" and the "Transportation Card." Another variety was credit cards issued by banks. Several banks were cooperating with BC card (a bank credit card established by several member banks). Some of these banks were with Kookmin Card and Hana Card; Gwangju was cooperating with the Korean Exchange Bank Credit Service (see Exhibit 11).

In the M&A credit card market in South Korea, Shinhan Financial Group Co. bought South Korea's largest credit card company, LG Card. LG Card was South Korea's largest credit card company, consisting of approximately 10 million card holders, which meant that approximately one out of every four and a half people in the country held an LG card. Shinhan offered at least 65,000 won ($67.30) per share for LG Card. The deal to create the credit card firm

exceeded $7.25 billion. It was the largest business deal in Korean financial history.

One of the notable competences of the Korean credit card industry was its product development ability. "LG Lady Card," "Kookmin Pass Card" and "Hyundai M Card" were benchmarked even by global issuers such as JCB. These cards developed a variety of membership programs which provided benefits associated with retail stores, popular services, etc. The diversity of the card products met the needs of the different customer segmentation groups. The proactive marketing program played a major role in the rapid growth of the Korean credit card industry.

### Kookmin Card

Kookmin Bank, the country's largest bank, launched its credit card business in 1980. With 9.3 million cardholders and total card sales of W57.3 trillion in 2008, Kookmin Card established its leadership position in the industry. Kookmin Card launched innovative cards which represented a new source of revenues. Furthermore, the Kookmin Bank worked aggressively to capture a larger share of the high-growth check card and corporate card markets, recording high growth in card usage in South Korea.

**Exhibit 11**    Korean Credit Card Companies

| Type of Credit Card | Number of Businesses | Company Names |
|---|---|---|
| Credit Cards | 7 | BC, Shinhan, Industry Bank Capital |
| • Pure Bank | 3 | Samsung, LG, Hyundai, Lotte |
| • Mono-line | 4 | |
| Bank with Credit Card Service | 15 | Kyongnam, etc. |
| • BC affiliates | 11 | Koomin, etc. |
| • Koomin Bank | 3 | Korean Exchange |
| • Korean Exchange | 1 | Jeju, etc. |
| • Shinhan Bank | 4 | |
| Retailers and Distributors | 13 | Department Stores, etc. |
| Total | 35 | |

*Source:* Credit Finance Association of Korea.

Kookmin broadened its lineup of credit cards that met customers' diverse needs, launching "SK LPG Save KB Card," "S-Oil KB Card," "KB Fn Save Card," and others. Kookmin Bank also provided enhanced services for its mainstay card product, "KB Star Card." Kookmin Card introduced a series of social service voucher cards including the "Senior Citizen Support Voucher Card," the "Housekeeping/Nursing Voucher Card," and the "Beautiful Mommy Card" for expectant mothers. Kookmin Card had its credit cards designed by renowned Korean fashion designer Andre Kim.

### Samsung Card

Established in 1988, Samsung Card was Korea's third largest card issuer. Samsung Card had launched innovative products and services, and won several awards in many customer satisfaction surveys. In 2004, Samsung Card merged with Samsung Capital, Samsung Group's financial affiliate, and expanded into commercial financing markets. In 2007, Samsung Card was listed on the Korea Exchange and was the first listing among Korean credit card issuers.

Samsung Card's core competence included its size and breadth of product offerings, advanced customer relationship management system, and extensive business network based on partnerships with Samsung Group affiliates.

Samsung Card developed new products such as the Samsung Blue American Express Card and the Shinsaegae-Samsung Card (Shinsaegae was one of the biggest Korean department stores).

The company's social contribution activities set Samsung Card apart from its peers in the industry. The company had been very active in community service, providing volunteer services and other charitable work by forming relationships with local communities. All employees joined at least one volunteer activity under the company's 365 Volunteering program.

### Shinhan (LG) Card

Shinhan Card had the strong customer base of its parent company, Shinhan Financial Group, the nation's second largest financial holding company. In 2007, Shinhan Card and LG Card were integrated as the new Shinhan Card. The integration of two card issuers resulted in a strong customer base—at the end of 2008, the number of active cardholders reached 13.6 million and market share reached 24 percent. Shinhan Card was the largest card issuer in Asia and No. 10 in the world.

Under the umbrella of the financial group, there were two kinds of distribution channels by which Shinhan Card attracted new customers—1,052 branches of Shinhan Bank and 30 credit card branches. Shinhan Card had the infrastructure of the product sales network and merchant. This great infrastructure allowed customers to easily use its credit cards almost anywhere they went. Shinhan Card boosted cross-selling between subsidiaries of the financial group, and optimized product mixture.

## HyundaiCard's Marketing Strategy in South Korea

The importance of the customer segmentation strategy and the use of websites was even greater for HyundaiCard. HyundaiCard focused on its customers' needs, developed new credit card products, and provided different online marketing campaigns in order to actively prevent the loss of customers. HyundaiCard utilized a diverse segmentation strategy using online and offline channels to create a multi-stage roadmap. The company also strengthened its internal administration regarding customer service and guaranteed safe online business. The company provided the highest level of services by utilizing customer segmentation and diverse marketing strategies to compete with other credit card companies.

In order to increase profits, credit card companies focused on the fact that customers had to be willing to use their cards often. The key to profits was frequent card usage. To achieve the goal of increasing profits, marketing strategies were employed to convert customers with low usage frequency into customers with high usage frequency.

## Customer Segmentation

The innovative marketing strategy focused on customers' lifestyles. HyundaiCard divided its card members into four categories (general, low, middle, high) according to credit card payments. Customer segmentation filtered each group's usage status and purchasing methods and helped in collecting data according to their age, gender, and the main location of purchase (shops, gas station, restaurants, etc.). Through the use of a strategic homepage and e-mail, various information and benefits (such as discount rates and bonus points) could also be offered for special cards, according to the customer's traits (gender, age, level, card type) and main usage contents. Region and location of use, usage count, and the monetary amount for which the card was used all provided more refined discrepancy data services.

HyundaiCard formulated "Alphabet Marketing." Alphabet marketing meant differentiated marketing named M, S, W, U, K, and A, based on consumer lifestyle. HyundaiCard executed the company's alphabet marketing strategy by launching HyundaiCard M, S, W, U, K, and A. For example, HyundaiCard discovered that women in their thirties represented the largest consumer group using credit cards via Internet and offline channels. Thus, the company issued the new "HyundaiCard S" for women in their thirties. Features such as "more enjoyable shopping" and "more purchases lead to more bonus points and benefits" were adopted with an aim to dramatically increase new membership. The customized marketing approaches included "Alphabet Credit Cards" having unique and creative designs.

To distinguish its services from those of its competitors, HyundaiCard diversified its product line and expanded into the premium market via the introduction of "the Black" and "the Purple" cards. HyundaiCard had moved beyond its earlier premium-level credit cards to concentrate on VIP customers. Powerful efforts were made to advance into the niche market by establishing alliances with various financial partners. HyundaiCard targeted the top 0.05 percent of credit card holders, limiting its issue to 9,999 extremely important clients.

## eCRM Strategy

Electronic Customer Relationship Management (eCRM) was introduced in the most widely used credit card websites in Korea. HyundaiCard upgraded its Internet system environments and integrated customer relationship management (CRM) capabilities to fully satisfy the ever-increasing needs and expectations of customers. To raise the eCRM quality to a higher level, HyundaiCard intended to (1) provide effective tailor-made services through its website for HyundaiCard consumers; (2) promote marketing campaigns with suitable online business strategies and competitive online services; and (3) upgrade e-mail solutions. To achieve the company's objectives, the following activities were implemented:

- Strengthened customer relationship management: HyundaiCard discovered and analyzed customer tendencies to provide customized services for individual credit card holders.
- Established themed malls in the website: mall themes, such as shopping, insurance and travel products, were based on card members' tendencies.
- Design and GUI upgraded: The company upgraded designs to connect the Hyundai Card website, family site services, and contents with ease.

The eCRM collected HyundaiCard customer information. It accurately collected and analyzed data regarding HyundaiCard customers on its family site. It analyzed customers' online activities in categories such as anonymous members, royal members, and special card members and loaded every customer's online usage information into the database. It provided data on content preferences, banner ads, and e-mail marketing. The database provided useful, accurate information about Internet customers and their transactions. Establishing an effective eCRM system could potentially strengthen Internet services and allow the company to execute effective Internet marketing strategies (see Exhibit 12).

| Exhibit 12 | An Example of 1:1 Marketing |
|---|---|

| Gender | Age | Content | | | |
|---|---|---|---|---|---|
| | | Area A | Area B | Area C | Area D |
| Female | 20–29 | a1,a2 | b1 | c1 | d1 |
| Male | 20–29 | a2 | b2 | c2,c5 | d2 |
| Female | 30–39 | a3 | b3,b5 | c3 | d3 |
| Male | 30–39 | a4,a5 | b4 | c4 | d4 |

HyundaiCard defined the marketing rules appropriate for 1:1 marketing. According to the rules, it provided different content to different customer segment groups.

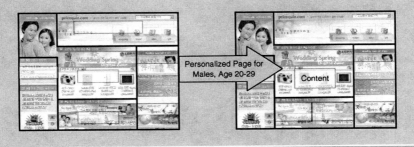

*Source:* Company files.

## Promotion Development

The finance shop (see Exhibit 13) was the place that enabled HyundaiCard customers to enjoy all-in-one service, getting financial consultation services and enjoying an ambience created by world-famous designers. HyundaiCard's first finance shop opened for business in 2006 in Seoul, South Korea, and, by 2009, the company had doubled the size of the network to 12 shops nationwide. HyundaiCard also brought a paradigm shift to culture marketing by hosting the Super Concert series with big celebrities such as musical stars Billy Joel and Placido Domingo.

## Integration of Customer Information

To capture the attention of consumers, Hyundai Card broke from tradition by deploying a unique marketing plan. HyundaiCard integrated online and

| Exhibit 13 | A Finance Shop in South Korea |
|---|---|

*Source:* HyundaiCard, 2009.

offline customer data and maximized the potential of marketing campaigns. HyundaiCard had long known of the importance of this process. It maximized the two channels (online and offline channels) to increase customer profits and strengthen customer relationships. HyundaiCard enjoyed the synergy effect of online and offline channels for customer information. Online, HyundaiCard improved customer relationships and familiarity. The recent website usage duration, frequency of visits, and history with HyundaiCard provided metrics[4] for assessing online familiarity, such as last log-in date, frequency, etc. The above evaluation of familiarity determined various stages of customer status. Thus, to carry out an effective marketing strategy and increase profits, HyundaiCard focused on customer value and online interaction.

The integration of online and offline information provided accurate customer data to CRM Business departments and related administrators. The integrated information could then be shared by the whole company. For example, after CRM department representatives produced analysis reports, every department was able to access the resources. In addition, by integrating the data analysis environment, a variety of marketing data could be shared using web log and actual channel customer data. This assisted marketers with decisions on strategies.

HyundaiCard's customer information had been converted into a marketing database available for anyone within the company to easily use and expand. Integration of customer data created new card products suitable for customer needs. Connecting marketing programs with their targets helped provide more diverse data for financial services and added value. In addition, cross-selling mechanisms for shopping, travel, insurance, and financial products could be established.

## HyundaiCard's Performance

After surpassing three million members in August 2005, with the introduction of "HyundaiCard M" in the same year, the company set new standards. HyundaiCard M had the largest subscriber base of any credit card in Korea. HyundaiCard's market

share increased more than five-fold, from 1.8 percent in 2001 to 9.96 percent in 2006 (see Exhibit 14), and its business grew six-fold in five years while posting the highest sales volume per cardholder in the domestic cards market. In 2006, the number of HyundaiCard members grew to 5.3 million (see Exhibit 15), and its Alphabet Cards continued to lead the domestic credit card market. In 2007, through an innovative marketing strategy, HyundaiCard was named Korea's Most Admired Company for the second consecutive year out of all Korean credit card companies. HyundaiCard ranked number one in the National Customer Satisfaction Index (NCSI) for the third consecutive year (2005, 2006 and 2007). HyundaiCard was also selected number one in the Credit Card category of Net Promoter Score (NPS) surveyed by Bain & Company in 2006. HyundaiCard joined Samsung Card, Kookmin Card and LG Card

| Exhibit 14 | Market Share of Korean Credit Card Companies | |
|---|---|---|
| **Rank** | **Company** | **Market Share** |
| 1 | Koomin | 16.21 |
| 2 | LG* | 16.08 |
| 3 | Samsung | 12.33 |
| 4 | Hyundai | 9.96 |
| 5 | Shinhan | 8.70 |
| 6 | Nonghyup | 7.58 |
| 7 | Woori Bank | 6.35 |
| 8 | Lotte Card | 5.82 |
| 9 | Industrial Bank | 4.47 |
| 10 | Korean Exchange Bank | 4.46 |
| 11 | Hana Bank | 3.61 |
| 12 | SC Bank | 1.33 |
| | Others | 3.11 |

Source: www.Hankyung.com. May 2007.

*Merged with Shinhan.

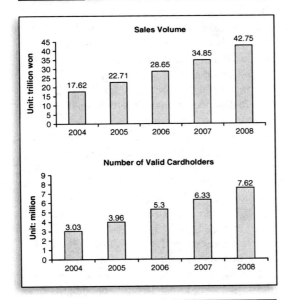

| | Exhibit 15 | Sales Volume and Number of Valid Cardholders |

*Source:* HyundaiCard, 2009.

(merged with Shinhan in 2007) as one of the four leading enterprises within the credit card market.

According to analysis reports in 2002 and 2005 by MediaChannel Inc, a professional research and consulting company based on Internet users' behavior analysis[5], the web traffic of the HyundaiCard website was low in comparison with several competitors in spite of an aggressive marketing campaign in 2003 and 2004. But its web traffic almost caught up with the top three credit card companies in 2005 and 2006. Backed by its stable financial results (see Exhibit 16), HyundaiCard was slowly becoming a brand name in the international markets.

## Market Competition and Challenges

Compared to other major credit card companies, HyundaiCard entered the Korean credit card market late. As a latecomer, HyundaiCard sustained a very low customer count. HyundaiCard, as a market follower, had to generate an aggressive marketing strategy to catch up with the market leaders. But HyundaiCard suffered a few problems such as low brand awareness, weak marketing communication, and weak card services. To cover these strategic problems and to increase its membership and credit card usage rate, HyundaiCard had to adopt a differentiated marketing strategy. However, under the strict control of the Korean government,

| Exhibit 16 | HyundaiCard's Financial Highlights |

| | 2007 | | 2006 | | 2005 | | 2004 | | 2003 | |
|---|---|---|---|---|---|---|---|---|---|---|
| Operating Revenue | 11,213 | *11,952* | 11,095 | *11,826* | 7,333 | *7,816* | 5,877 | *6,264* | 4,950 | *5,276* |
| Net Income | 2,344 | *2,498* | 2,810 | *2,995* | 863 | *920* | −2,184 | *−2,328* | −6,273 | *−6,686* |
| Total Assets | 46,452 | *49,512* | 33,834 | *36,063* | 28,968 | *30,876* | 24,584 | *26,203* | 24,707 | *26,334* |
| Total Liabilities | 35,222 | *37,542* | 25,527 | *27,208* | 26,619 | *28,372* | 23,207 | *24,736* | 23,602 | *25,157* |
| Total Shareholders' Equity | 11,230 | *11,970* | 8,307 | *8,854* | 2,349 | *2,504* | 1,377 | *1,468* | 1,105 | *1,178* |

*Source:* HyundaiCard, 2007 Annual Report.

*Note:* First column for each year is in 100 millions of Korean won. Second column is in 100 thousands of U.S. dollars.

adding new members swiftly and redistributing cards to expired members proved very difficult.

The Korean credit card market experienced a period of overheating due to a rapid expansion in the number of cards, reduced standards for issuing cards, etc. In the loan services, credit card companies began witnessing an alarming growth in the number of late payments and users with bad credit history. There was an indication that the Korean economy would face a so-called "Korean Credit Card Crisis." The Korean credit card industry was a bubble on the verge of foaming and bursting.

The industry underwent an adjustment period, with many credit card companies forced to change the way they did business. To avoid mounting losses, numerous credit card companies decided to downsize their operations and undergo reconstruction to lower their burden. HyundaiCard was no exception. In comparison to its competitors, HyundaiCard had fewer customers and sustained moderate losses.

## What Next?

HyundaiCard will face tough competition from Kookmin Card, Samsung Card and Shinhan (LG) Card, all of whom are leading players in the South Korean credit card industry. HyundaiCard will have to realize sustainable growth by further developing its differentiated marketing strategies. It will be important for HyundaiCard to continuously develop advanced marketing strategies to maintain current customer relations and attract potential customers. HyundaiCard will have to increase efforts to create new, additional value in the constantly changing domestic market.

In the auto financing sector, HyundaiCard will have to create additional value by promoting cross-selling and expand customized services that will perfectly address each customer's lifestyle and needs. Strong efforts should also be made to maintain the company's leading position in the auto financing market. HyundaiCard will also have to extend its network of alliances with major players in various industries, and strengthen its "M point"-based marketing activities.

Internationally, HyundaiCard will have to break into the foreign financial markets, thereby solidifying a base from which it can become a global player. HyundaiCard is expanding its business territory into North America, Europe, and Asia, and aligning itself with well-known global brands such as VISA, Coca-Cola, Walmart and Google. As a new brand in the international market, raising the status of the company by solidifying with GE will be vital.

## CASE QUESTIONS

1. As part of the environmental analysis, what environmental forces favor HyundaiCard, or the credit card industry in general in South Korea?

2. In a market analysis, describe how the marketing management team at Hyundai conducted its competitive/industry analysis. Do you agree with its findings and the responses the company made to the competition?

3. What product positioning did HyundaiCard hold? What position should the company seek to gain?

4. Which market segments are the most favorable for HyundaiCard? Does the company do an effective job of targeting and reaching those segments? If so, how? If not, why not?

5. As part of a customer analysis, what could the company's leaders learn from the concepts "share of mind" and "share of heart"?

6. Would a market analysis of the credit card industry yield the same results in the United States as it does in South Korea? What findings might be similar? What would be different?

# TerraCycle Inc.

*By Andrew Smith, under the supervision of Elizabeth M. A. Grasby*

It was January 2006, and Betsy Cotton, chief financial officer of TerraCycle Inc., sat in her office considering the company's future opportunities. TerraCycle, located in Trenton, New Jersey, focused on applying business practices that would allow for the creation of profit as well as help to minimize the impact on, and to even replenish, natural resources. TerraCycle's main product, All Purpose Plant Food, was an all-natural fertilizer used to foster growth in plants. TerraCycle had experienced some positive feedback for this product line, and alternatives for expansion were now under consideration. An alternative was altering the formula of the fertilizer to focus on specific types of plants. Two different product formulas were being considered: an orchid product and an African violet product. Cotton planned to first assess TerraCycle's historical performance. In addition, she wanted to project the potential financial results for the two new products as well as project the company's overall results. With this information, she would be able to determine the most appropriate course of action for the future.

## Eco-Capitalism

In recent years, there had been a trend in North America to focus more on the environment and humanity's effect upon it. There was a realization that the globe had a finite amount of resources and, as such, individuals and companies would need to rethink their impact on the environment and make a concerted effort to minimize this impact.

This point of view was taken one step further with the new and emerging concept of eco-capitalism. Eco-capitalism was a belief that not only should a business's impact on environmental resources be reduced, but also steps should be taken to renew these resources, as long as these

actions were profitable. When facing alternative methods of production, if one method created a profitable by-product, profit-oriented companies would certainly choose this method. The concept of eco-capitalism took the same point of view, with a slight twist: the by-products were considered profitable if they aided the environment and provided a return for the company.

## TerraCycle Inc.

### A Brief History

A strong belief in eco-capitalism was what led to the creation of TerraCycle Inc. in the fall of 2001 by Tom Szaky and Jon Beyer. Both men were Princeton University (U.S.A.) students, and the company concept was developed for a business plan competition. The partners had arranged with Princeton Dining Services to gather dining hall waste, which was then fed to worms in a prototype "worm gin."[1] Research and product development were performed at the Rutgers University Eco-Complex, a facility that aimed to provide real-world applications for environmentally sustainable technologies. TerraCycle operated a worm gin within the Eco-Complex's greenhouse. Through further experimentation with the process, the partners developed the end product, the All Purpose Plant Food.

In the spring of 2003, Szaky took an extended leave of absence from Princeton in order to pursue the business on a full-time basis. Operating on a relatively tight budget, the business was funded with prize money from business plan competitions and angel investors.[2]

Growth was slow in the early stages, but in May 2004, TerraCycle experienced a major breakthrough when The Home Depot agreed to begin selling TerraCycle Plant Food online. This growth

Version: (A) 2010–04–20

continued as TerraCycle's products were picked up by a number of companies across North America, including Whole Foods, Home Depot Canada, Walmart Canada, Wild Oats, and Do-It-Best.

Committed to being the "ultimate" eco-capitalist corporation, TerraCycle applied this concept to all its business practices. Its products utilized an all-natural, environmentally friendly production process and were packaged using waste, such as recycled pop bottles. This unique concept and its innovative nature, as well as TerraCycle's environmental focus, had always been a source of praise for the company. The noble concept caught people's attention, and TerraCycle routinely received public recognition and positive press coverage for its efforts. Most recently, *Red Herring* magazine named TerraCycle one of the 100 most innovative companies, and Home Depot Canada awarded TerraCycle the Environmental Stewardship Award, one of only two company-wide awards presented by Home Depot Canada.

## TerraCycle Products

The first product developed and sold by TerraCycle was All Purpose Plant Food (see Exhibit 1), an organic liquid plant food. The production of this plant food (see Exhibit 2) started with source-separated organic

**Exhibit 1**    Current and Proposed Products

*Source:* www.terracycle.net.

waste that was fed to worms. The resulting material was separated into a fine, particle-sized mixture that was then liquefied over a seven-day period. Finally,

**Exhibit 2**    Production Process

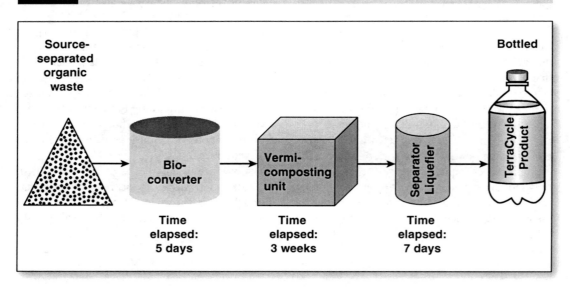

once the mixture was completely liquefied, it was packaged into recycled two-liter and 20-fluid-ounce[3] pop bottles and shipped to customers.

Unlike other competitive fertilizers, TerraCycle's Plant Food not only had a far more natural and environmentally friendly production process, but also this production process helped to eliminate organic waste and used recycled pop bottles, thus reducing the impact of this waste on the environment.

TerraCycle had also found a noble way to collect the recycled pop bottles used for packaging. In 2005, the company launched a program called the Bottle Brigade. This program allowed schools, charities and other nonprofit groups throughout North America to collect 20-fluid-ounce pop bottles and remit these pop bottles to TerraCycle. In return, TerraCycle would either give the group five cents per bottle or make a donation on the organization's behalf to the Nature Conservancy that saved one square meter of rain forest per bottle submitted. Over time, this program would provide a large supply of bottles; however, it had yet to provide the major supply of the bottles for TerraCycle.

TerraCycle developed and sold other environmentally friendly gardening products, such as Water-Less and ProFusion. Water-Less, a gel form of the All Purpose Plant Food, provided similar fertilization, but the gel would remain to absorb and release liquid over a longer period of time,

reducing the need to water. ProFusion was a fertilizer specifically formulated for soil-less hydro gardens.[4] Similar to TerraCycle's other products, these were also packaged in reused packaging, such as recycled oil containers for the ProFusion product. These products were still in their infancy and were offered on a limited basis only to fit a specific need and at the request of a customer. As a result, sales of these other products were negligible when compared to the All Purpose Plant Food sales.[5]

## TerraCycle's Historical Financial Performance

TerraCycle was still in the growth phase of the business and, as such, the financial results achieved had not yet reached the anticipated levels of success (see Exhibit 3 and Exhibit 4 for fiscal 2004 and fiscal 2005 financial statements). The eco-capitalist philosophy, however, was beginning to show a great deal of promise for the company. In addition to the moral benefits of running an environmentally forward business, TerraCycle was experiencing positive signs of growth. To date, production levels had not yet reached economies of scale,[6] resulting in disproportionately high costs and ensuing losses. The sales growth achieved more recently, however, appeared to be an indication that a more efficient level of production might be within sight.

---

**Exhibit 3**  Income Statement

| | | For the year ending December 31 (all numbers are in U.S. dollars) | | | | |
|---|---|---|---|---|---|---|
| | | **2005** | | | **2004** | |
| REVENUE | | | | | | |
| Sales | | $461,665 | 100.0%[1] | | $104,470 | 100.0% |
| Less: Cost of goods sold | | 487,524 | 105.6% | | 150,113 | 143.7% |
| Gross profit | | (25,859) | (5.6%) | | (45,643) | (43.7%) |
| OPERATING EXPENSES | | | | | | |
| Salaries | $579,887 | | 125.6% | $335,142 | | 320.8% |
| Office & administrative | 33,585 | | 7.3% | 67,342 | | 64.5% |

*(Continued)*

**Exhibit 3** (Continued)

| | 2005 | | | 2004 | |
|---|---|---|---|---|---|
| Insurance | 43,815 | | 9.5% | 13,868 | 13.3% |
| Advertising | 75,283 | | 16.3% | 26,815 | 25.7% |
| Research & development | 14,267 | | 3.1% | 20,775 | 19.9% |
| Property overhead[2] | 92,846 | | 20.1% | 36,942 | 35.4% |
| Telephone & communications | 23,632 | | 5.1% | 19,492 | 18.7% |
| Professional Fees/licenses | 47,138 | | 10.2% | 79,555 | 76.2% |
| Travel/vehicles | 74,514 | | 16.1% | 82,909 | 79.4% |
| Interest expense | 18,218 | | 3.9% | 1,643 | 1.6% |
| Amortization | 30,766 | | 6.7% | 5,098 | 4.9% |
| Miscellaneous | 1,818 | | 0.4% | 1,300 | 1.2% |
| Less: Total operating expenses | | (1,035,769) | (224.4%) | (690,881) | (661.3%) |
| Net income before taxes | | (1,061,628) | (230.0%) | (736,524) | (705.0%) |
| Income taxes[3] | | — | 0.0% | — | 0.0% |
| NET INCOME AFTER TAX | | $(1,061,628) | (230.0%) | $(736,524) | (705.0%) |

1. Totals may be off due to rounding.
2. Includes items such as rent, utilities, etc.
3. Should TerraCycle begin to generate income, Cotton anticipated paying income tax at a rate of 25 percent.

**Exhibit 4** Balance Sheet

| As at December 31 (all numbers are in U.S. dollars) | | | | | |
|---|---|---|---|---|---|
| | 2005 | | | 2004 | |
| **ASSETS** | | | | | |
| Current Assets: | | | | | |
| Cash | $120,929 | | | $83,941 | |
| Accounts receivable | 267,691 | | | 20,561 | |
| Due from shareholder[1] | 75,000 | | | — | |
| Inventory | 421,980 | | | 81,605 | |
| Prepaid expenses | 30,600 | | | 55,825 | |
| Total current assets | | $916,200 | | | $241,932 |
| Long-term assets: | | | | | |
| Fixed assets | 151,712 | | | 94,341 | |
| Less: Accum. amort., Fixed assets | (57,405) | 94,307 | | (30,577) | 63,764 |

| | 2005 | | 2004 | |
|---|---|---|---|---|
| Patents & trademarks | 42,059 | | 26,560 | |
| Less: Accum. Amort., Patents & trademarks | (4,545) | 37,514 | (2,775) | 23,785 |
| Total long-term assets | | 131,821 | | 87,549 |
| Total Assets | | $1,048,021 | | $329,481 |
| LIABILITIES & SHAREHOLDERS' EQUITY | | | | |
| Liabilities | | | | |
| Current liabilities: | | | | |
| Accounts payable | $228,020 | | $52,565 | |
| Salaries payable | 48,927 | | — | |
| Insurance payable | 21,348 | | 15,550 | |
| Demand loan[2] | 149,988 | | — | |
| Total Current Liabilities | | $448,283 | | $68,115 |
| Shareholders' equity | | | | |
| Common stock | 292,011 | | 292,011 | |
| Series A preferred stock | 1,117,000 | | 1,117,000 | |
| Series B preferred stock | 1,500,000 | | 100,000 | |
| Retained earnings | (2,309,273) | | (1,247,645) | |
| Total shareholders' equity | | 599,738 | | 261,366 |
| Total Liabilities & Shareholders' Equity | | $1,048,021 | | $329,481 |

1. Represents an amount due from the company's largest shareholder, relating to the purchase of Series B preferred shares.

2. Represents a loan from Zoltan Szaky that may be called or repaid at any time. Zoltan Szaky indicated he had no interest in calling the loan in the near future. This loan bears interest at 12 percent per annum.

## The Competition

The gardening industry was a diverse one, with a wide range of customers' needs and preferences as well as varying levels of expertise and experience. Gross sales (see Exhibit 5 for industry statistics) were significant, and this attracted a sizable number of competitors, ranging from small local businesses to large multinational companies. Large multinational companies would often operate under multiple brand names, some of which competed against each other. The plant food segment of the market in which TerraCycle operated was no different. There were a number of competitors in varying sizes, but this segment was dominated by two large competitors, The Scotts Miracle-Gro Company and Spectrum Brands.

## The Scotts Miracle-Gro Company

The Scotts Miracle-Gro Company (Scotts) offered a wide variety of gardening products under different brand names. Scotts operated globally, was a publicly traded company, and was quite large, both financially and in terms of number of employees. Scotts focused on the lawn and garden market. The products offered by Scotts were the number-one-selling products in almost every market in which they competed. In fiscal 2005, Scotts achieved net sales of $2.3 billion (see Exhibit 5 for Scotts' ratio

| Exhibit 5 | Industry and Major Competitor Ratios |
| --- | --- |

| | Industry | | Scotts Miracle-Gro | | Spectrum Brands | |
| --- | --- | --- | --- | --- | --- | --- |
| | 2005 | 2004 | 2005 | 2004 | 2005 | 2004 |
| Vertical analysis: | | | | | | |
| Gross profit to sales | 25.5% | 27.9% | 36.3% | 37.6% | 37.7% | 42.8% |
| Operating expenses to sales | 21.5% | 23.7% | 28.2% | 26.1% | 35.0% | 36.4% |
| Profit before taxes to sales | 4.0% | 3.3% | 6.7% | 7.5% | 2.7% | 2.4% |
| Current ratio | 1.2 | 1.3 | 1.6 | 1.9 | 1.9 | 1.6 |
| Acid test ratio | 0.6 | 0.8 | 0.8 | 1.1 | 0.7 | 0.8 |
| Age of accounts receivable (days) | 30.0 | 38.0 | 49.1 | 50.0 | 58.3 | 73.6 |
| Age of inventory (days)[1] | 65.0 | 61.0 | 77.5 | 79.5 | 113.1 | 117.5 |
| Age of accounts payable (days) | 24.0 | 40.0 | 36.2 | 35.7 | 70.6 | 100.4 |
| Debt to equity | 1.9 | 2.0 | 1.0 | 1.3 | 3.8 | 4.2 |
| Interest coverage | 3.4 | 3.4 | 4.8 | 4.2 | 1.5 | 2.4 |
| Fixed asset turnover | 10.0 | 5.8 | 7.0 | 6.4 | 7.6 | 7.8 |
| Total asset turnover | 2.4 | 1.9 | 1.2 | 1.0 | 0.6 | 0.9 |

1. Calculated using cost of goods sold.

*Industry Ratios Source:* The Risk Management Association (RMA) Annual Statement Studies 2006–2007.

*Competitors Ratios Source:* All competitive ratios have been derived from the companies Fiscal 2006 Annual Reports.

statistics). One of its products, Miracle-Gro, had become the dominant plant food in the industry, enjoying a tremendous amount of brand name recognition and customer loyalty. Miracle-Gro was a concentrate of which a small amount was added to water and used to feed plants. Unlike TerraCycle's plant food, but similar to most plant foods, Miracle-Gro was not derived from an all-natural production process and did not contain all-natural ingredients.

## Spectrum Brands

Spectrum Brands (Spectrum), the other major competitor in the plant food segment of the market, also provided a wide range of gardening products under different brand names.[7] Spectrum was a publicly traded company with over 10,000 employees and annual sales in the area of $2.8 billion (see Exhibit 5 for Spectrum's ratio statistics). Spectrum's product lines which posed the largest threat to TerraCycle, were the Peters Professional line and the Garden Safe line of products. The Peters Professional line was a line of granular fertilizers designed for home gardening. This brand had different fertilizer mixes that could be used for different types of plants. Variegated Violet and Orchid Plant Food were two of the fertilizer mixes being sold by Peters Professional at the time. The Garden Safe line was a naturally derived liquid fertilizer mix, a similar product to TerraCycle's All Purpose Plant Food. This product line, however, was not as well known among its direct competitors in the market, and it did not represent a very large market share.

### Do-It-Yourself Composters

Another competitor for TerraCycle's products was do-it-yourself composters. They used home composting to generate nutrient-rich soils used for home gardening, thereby reducing the need to buy fertilizers. Among a variety of reasons, these gardeners composted at least partially for environmental concerns, but they primarily used this method as a means of reducing their overall level of waste, as well as providing a useful by-product for their gardening. Although not difficult, composting took some time, space, and effort in order for it to work effectively and the result was still not generally as potent as vermicompost.[8]

## The Consumers

TerraCycle's products were not intended for commercial growers; instead, the end users for TerraCycle's All Purpose Plant Food products were individual gardeners. These customers enjoyed gardening around their home, tending to small gardens as well as potted plants within their homes. TerraCycle's products provided these gardeners with more environmentally conscious products for fertilizing their plants and gardens.

TerraCycle did not sell to these end consumers directly. Instead, TerraCycle sold to retailers that sold to these end consumers. The bulk of TerraCycle's sales came from large multi-national retailers. In fiscal 2005, Walmart U.S.A. represented 44 percent of TerraCycle's total sales; Home Depot U.S.A., 16 percent; Walmart Canada, 15 percent; and Home Depot Canada, 13 percent. The remaining 12 percent of sales were made to other retailers, including Home Hardware, Whole Foods, and True Value.

Retailers were given credit terms of net 60 days, no discounts by TerraCycle and all sales were made on credit. Often, some retailers took longer than 60 days to pay, but TerraCycle could always be assured that they would pay eventually.

Due to their size, some retailers enjoyed a great deal of negotiating power with all of their suppliers, including TerraCycle. TerraCycle often made special arrangements in order to keep these retailers satisfied, such as providing products in special displays or being lenient with regard to product returns.

## Future Expectations for Terracycle

### The New Products

Both the African Violet and Orchid Plant Foods would be sold in Canada and the United States. Based on some preliminary research, Cotton had gathered information regarding the expected results of the two new products. TerraCycle planned to launch both products or no products at all. Cotton expected 70 percent of the total projected sales of the African Violet product would come from the United States, and the remaining sales would come from Canada. Similarly, she estimated that sales of the Orchid Plant Food would be split evenly among the United States and Canadian customers. Both products would be sold in the 20-fluid-ounce bottle format. Based on TerraCycle's wholesale selling price of $2.84 per bottle for each of the African Violet and Orchid products,[9] Cotton anticipated that both products would sell in equal quantities and that the total new product sales would be between 30,000 and 110,000 bottles. Since both products would be sold to current customers, the current credit terms of net 60 days, no discounts would be extended to these two new products, and it was expected that all customers would take full advantage of these credit terms.

With such rapid growth experienced in fiscal 2005, managing customers' accounts had been an issue; however, Cotton projected that with a focus in this area, customer payments for all products would return to the results experienced in fiscal 2004. Inventory and accounts payable levels had also suffered during TerraCycle's 2005 growth period. Although she did not believe that TerraCycle could reach fiscal 2005 industry levels in the short-term, Cotton was confident that with proper attention, TerraCycle would be able to reach levels of 85 days[10] for inventory and 64 days[10] for accounts payable for all products offered.

No additional facilities or salaried employees would be required in order to produce and sell the new products; however, Cotton thought that 10 percent of TerraCycle's operating expenses should be allocated to these products. The research and development costs reported on the fiscal 2005 income statement were the only costs incurred to create the two new products.

TerraCycle did not have a great deal of excess cash available for specifically promoting the new products, so Cotton anticipated that an additional $10,000 for each of the African Violet and Orchid Plant Food could be budgeted for promotions annually. Since these promotion costs were incurred throughout the year, if sales were low, total promotions costs would be cut to 25 percent of the planned amount. Promotion costs were paid in cash.

The bottles used to package both the African Violet and Orchid products would cost an average of 35 cents a bottle. The safety cap for each African Violet product bottle would cost seven cents. Instead of the safety cap, the Orchid Plant Food would be sold with a spray head. These spray heads would cost 27 cents each. Labor costs for hourly production workers would total 85 cents per bottle and the "brewing" costs would be approximately $1.97 per gallon.[11] The cost of the packaging, which also doubled as a stand-alone shelf display, would be 40 cents per bottle.

The product sold in the United States would have an all-English label; whereas, the product sold in Canada would have an English/French label. The English labels for the African Violet product would cost 15 cents each, and the English/French labels would cost 44 cents each. The English/French label cost for the Orchid product would be the same as that of the African Violet Plant Food; however, each English label for the Orchid Plant Food would cost 44 cents.

Cotton was confident that, over time, with increased efficiency and economies of scale, some of the above costs for both African Violet and Orchid Plant Food would be reduced; however,

in the near future, Terracycle would have to manage with the costs as listed.

## Current Operations

In addition to new products sales, Cotton expected sales growth for TerraCycle's existing products. Cotton did not expect annual percentage sales growth to be as dramatic as it was from fiscal 2004 to fiscal 2005; however, she did believe it was reasonable to assume that half this level of sales growth would be achieved in fiscal 2006. With the sales of the two new products and the expanded sales of its current products, Cotton believed that TerraCycle would begin to reach economies of scale; consequently, she anticipated cost of goods sold would decrease for existing products to 65 percent of sales, and the percentage change in operating expenses between fiscal 2005 and fiscal 2006 would be similar to that experienced between fiscal 2004 and fiscal 2005.

Cotton estimated that cash on hand would remain the same, but many of the other assets would change. In addition to the expected changes in the working capital accounts, Cotton anticipated that the loan due from the shareholder would be collected. She also thought that prepaid expenses would increase by 50 percent, given the company's growth. Finally, due to the increased sales, more manufacturing facilities would be needed for increased production. TerraCycle would purchase $47,710 worth of additional manufacturing equipment. Amortization of these and other fixed assets for fiscal 2006 was expected to be $28,475. There was no change expected in patents and trademarks. Amortization of these patents and trademarks was expected to total $1,770 for fiscal 2006. This amortization had been included in the estimated increase in operating expenses.

For fiscal 2006, the only change in liabilities, other than the change in the working capital accounts, would be the elimination of the Insurance Payable account. There were no anticipated changes to the equity accounts; although, if financing was needed, Cotton would have to evaluate whether to finance through debt or through equity. If the decision was to finance through equity, the company would have to issue additional shares at 25 cents per share.

### Promotion Campaign

TerraCycle had always enjoyed a great deal of positive press coverage due to the environmentally friendly nature of its business and the youth of its founders. This press coverage was invaluable in the early development stages of the business since it provided a low-cost means of educating customers about TerraCycle's mission, as well as advertising its products. More recently, TerraCycle had spent more on advertising in order to continue to grow and develop the company presence and image even further. Cotton was considering a revamp of the organization's promotional campaign for both current and potentially new product lines.

Cotton wanted to consider the benefits and drawbacks of using either a "push" or "pull" strategy for marketing TerraCycle's products. Also, she needed to settle on the message that TerraCycle should use in any future marketing plan. Finally, Cotton wanted to consider some creative promotional ideas that would provide the best return for the cost. With the slim promotions budgets for TerraCycle's products, Cotton wanted to ensure that whatever promotion plan was chosen, it would provide the company and its new products with "the biggest bang for the buck."

### The Decision

Cotton knew this would be a difficult challenge. Although she knew history did not predict the future, she wanted to learn from TerraCycle's past performance what had led to the company's positive growth so that she could apply these best practices to future plans. She was interested in analyzing the company's past performance from profitability, liquidity, and cash flow perspectives. Cotton would also have to assess the financial potential of the two new products, Orchid Plant Food and African Violet Plant Food, before deciding whether to proceed with both new products or not to proceed at all. Since both products would be launched simultaneously, she knew this would entail an examination of the products' combined projected results, Cotton also wanted to create a set of financial projections for the company which would reflect her decisions. Cotton also wanted to develop an effective promotion plan for TerraCycle's products. Finally, if further financing was going to be required, Cotton wanted to consider the benefits and drawbacks of debt versus equity financing, as well as the likelihood of actually being able to obtain the required financing. Cotton had always enjoyed assessing TerraCycle's past performance and strategizing for the future, and she looked forward to the current task and its outcomes.

### CASE QUESTIONS

1. When conducting a competitive/industry analysis, what are TerraCycle's primary advantages? What are the company's main weaknesses when compared with the competition?

2. What is TerraCyle's product positioning? What is its target market?

3. If a share-of-mind/share-of-heart analysis were conducted, where would TerraCycle be placed relative to its main competitors?

4. Should the marketing team pursue a push or pull strategy for the new product offerings? Defend your choice.

5. What are the variable costs associated with the new products? Conduct a contribution margin analysis for the new products.

6. What qualitative factors might affect the decision to develop one or both of the new products?

CHAPTER

3

# Data Warehousing

Today's marketing managers cope with the impact of two major innovations. The first, improvements in computer technology, creates many new possibilities in the areas of storing information and analyzing the data being stored. The second, increasing competition, results from Internet usage and the expanding worldwide marketplace. Responding requires the development of a quality database program. A data warehouse holds all customer data and can be accessed by any employee who deals with customers in any capacity.

## The Data Warehouse

Many marketing managers have reached the conclusion that two key ingredients in marketing success are knowing your customers and having them know you. An effective data warehouse facilitates both of these objectives. In building a data warehouse, the first distinction to be made is between an operational and a marketing database. An operational database contains the transactions customers have with the firm and follows generally accepted accounting principles. The marketing database holds information about current customers, former customers, and prospects, as well as transactional data. It also carries records of interactions between the customer and the company.

## Data Warehouse Functions

A data warehouse serves a variety of functions. Communication with customers may be the most vital function performed by a data warehouse. The primary objectives of communication are strengthening perceptions of brand equity and building customer loyalty.

Website operations include the database technology that allows for personalization of web content. It should provide easy access to product information and collect information from customers that can be used for future communication, marketing programs, and interactions.

A data warehouse assists in designing and implementing data-driven marketing programs. Rather than sending the same marketing piece to every customer or business, specific individuals and companies can be targeted with more precise marketing offers.

Providing customer service and information to customers can be facilitated by the data warehouse. When a customer contacts a company, the employee who answers should have access to a great deal of information about the person in order to better assist him or her.

Customer information obtained for the data warehouse helps in the development of a company's website and its features. High-quality FAQs and information about the locations of brick-and-mortar stores can be provided with the assistance of effective customer information.

An effective data warehouse facilitates customer service. Marketing plans are derived from the information that has been gathered about the target market. When customers do not have face-to-face interactions with the company, the data warehouse fills part of the void by helping establish quality interactions.

## Types of Customer Data

The data in a data warehouse takes four forms: customer data, transaction data, appended data, and analytical data. Customer data includes names, addresses, and contact information for both individual consumers and businesses. The basic rule of thumb in collecting customer data remains "The more, the better." Customer data must be constantly updated, as 20% of Americans move each year.

Transaction data record purchases communications, and interactions with customers, including tracking visits to the firm's website. Transaction data may be used to generate follow-up contacts after purchases have been made. Purchasing histories are recorded. All this information helps the marketing team target specific customers with specific offers.

Appended data add demographic, geographic, and sometimes psychographic information to customer records for more targeted marketing approaches. Geocoding is the process of adding geographic codes to each customer record so that the addresses of customers can be plotted on a map for more targeted direct mail and other marketing offers.

Analytical data consist of the data and codes generated through the analysis of the data. A lifetime value analysis figure represents the monetary amount and profit stream generated by a consumer over a "lifetime," which is typically viewed as 5 years. Lifetime value figures assist the marketing team in making sure the best customers receive extra service and help turn other customers into better customers.

RFM analysis—recency, frequency, and monetary—expresses the date of the last purchase, the number of purchases, and the amount of money associated with individual customers or target markets. RFM codes note the type of customer visiting a store or being seen by a salesperson. Those with the highest RFM scores may receive the most customized and attentive service.

## Data Mining

Closely related to data analysis is data mining. Data mining includes two activities. The first is building profiles of customer segments. The second is preparing models that predict future purchase behaviors based on past purchases.

Data mining may be used to develop a profile of the company's best customers. The profile allows the marketing department to identify customers from the database who fit the profile but are making fewer than five purchases per year. The marketing team can then design specific offers to encourage additional purchases. Customer profiles also assist in locating individuals that might be in the market for a company's products.

Developing models that predict future sales based on past purchase activities has many applications. The information may be used in cross-selling, development of special marketing programs, or creating specific communications. Data mining provides the marketing manager with information that can lead to products being emphasized or de-emphasized, modifying sales tactics, and refining marketing proposals to customers.

## ⬚ Data-Driven Marketing Programs

Data-driven marketing programs include trawling, direct marketing, permission marketing, frequency or loyalty programs, viral marketing, and customization. These programs can be tested using contribution margin and RFM analyses.

Direct marketing occurs when a company sells items directly to end users. Standard mail, inbound telemarketing, television infomercial offers, catalog offers, and purchases over the Internet are the most common forms. Through database technology, direct marketing becomes more efficient and cost-effective.

Permission marketing entails sending marketing offers to individuals who have given the company permission to do so. The key is making sure the consumer has truly given permission and wants to receive the offers.

Frequency and loyalty programs encourage repeat purchases. The programs are widely used in the travel and hospitality industries. Database technology allows the marketing team to track individual purchases and manage the programs effectively.

Viral marketing is attaching or including an advertisement or marketing offer in an e-mail or some other customer correspondence, such as a blog. These programs will be most successful when consumers pass them along to family and friends.

Customization and personalization are not the same. Customization is the ability to modify marketing programs or offers to different groups of individuals within a database. Personalization refers to an individual customer's interactions with the company.

## ⬚ The Cases

### AIR MILES Canada: Rebranding the Air Miles Reward Program

The AIR MILES frequency program built its base on a distinct feature. While other airlines concentrated rewards for loyalty to a single carrier, AIR MILES expanded its customer base by offering reward miles for purchases of everyday products. The program's success was due to the links created with Sponsors, the companies that issued reward miles for purchases of products, and with Suppliers, which redeemed reward miles. AIR MILES enjoyed nearly 100% brand recognition in Canada and was in third place worldwide for reward programs. The company's marketing management team became concerned that the explosion in reward programs, from items as small as coffee shops to major product purchases, would diminish the effectiveness of AIR MILES. The vice-president for marketing, Caroline Papadatos, led the rollout of a rebranding effort designed to renew interest. She worried the effort, which was based on storytelling research rather than focus groups and was emotive rather than data driven, might not be the best fit for the company. Her problem illustrates common issues associated with frequency and loyalty programs.

## Conroy's Acura: Lifetime Customer Value and Return on Marketing

Conroy's Acura president, Terrence Conroy, was concerned that while the economy was healthy, sales at his dealership had become stagnant. The vice-president of sales, Rachel de Lima, had several ideas about how to increase business by attracting new customers through direct mail and more advertising in several media. In contrast, the sales staff believed reducing the markup per car would create more business. To retain customers, the company sent regular postcard mailings reminding them of oil change schedules and provided various marketing offers. The lifetime customer value approach could be used to compare an increase in the costs of retention from $10 per customer to a larger figure. The return on marketing statistic could be used to evaluate the values of efforts to attract new customers and retain current customers, depending on the marketing program being deployed. Each would be complicated by the length of time between purchases and not knowing whether any given marketing enticement led to a repeat purchase.

# AIR MILES Canada: Rebranding the Air Miles Reward Program

### By R. Chandrasekhar, under the supervision of Professor Niraj Dawar

Toward the end of September 2005, Caroline Papadatos, vice-president of marketing for the AIR MILES Reward Program (the Program) was reviewing a campaign, undertaken a year earlier by her team, to rebrand the Program. The campaign was to be launched nationally the following week. The anticipation was building because the rebranding campaign was more than a routine TV commercial and a radio spot. It was intended to re-energize the brand and the Program's more than nine million active household accounts, representing more than 14 million Canadians. The campaign was also meant to refocus the brand's premier position in the loyalty industry.

The rebranding campaign featured two approaches that were new for a company known for its direct marketing and data-driven loyalty strategies. The background consumer research had not followed the conventional route of focus groups, and the campaign had strong emotive elements in its design and execution. These strategies were a departure, even at a personal level, for a database-marketing career professional, such as Papadatos. "Can a campaign build on behavioral loyalty to secure a deeper emotional connection between the brand and its consumers?" she wondered.

Said Papadatos:

There are, of course, several parts of the campaign which are aligned with our corporate DNA. There is documentation at each stage of the run-up to the campaign. There is consistency in the methodology. The campaign is targeted at a specific customer sub-segment. There is organizational commitment to the goals and measurement metrics. They give us confidence in managing the uncertainties of the campaign. But, at the end of the day, a creative strategy driven by non-traditional consumer research is a new territory for us.

## The Company

The Program was owned and operated by Loyalty and Marketing Services, a wholly owned subsidiary

Version: (A) 2008–04–03

of Alliance Data Systems Corp. (ADS), which was based in Dallas, Texas. ADS had three different business segments: transaction services, credit services and marketing services (see Exhibit 1). Managing more than 105 million consumer relationships for some of North America's leading companies, ADS employed approximately 8,000 associates at more than 40 locations worldwide. Papadatos had joined the company in 1998 and assumed the marketing leadership role in 2004.

Said Papadatos:

Our business is to help clients build long-term relationships with their customers and reward consumers for loyalty. We develop insights into consumer behavior, create customized solutions for individual companies and manage all aspects of the loyalty program for them. With re-branding, we are deepening the emotional engagement that consumers have with the AIR MILES brand.

**Exhibit 1** Alliance Data Systems, Inc.'s Business Segments

| Business Segment | Products and Services | Target Markets |
|---|---|---|
| Transaction services | Issuer services | Specialty retail |
| | – Card processing | |
| | – Billing and payment processing | |
| | – Customer care | |
| | Utility services | Utilities |
| | – Hosting customer information systems | |
| | – Billing and payment processing | |
| | Merchant services | Petroleum retail |
| | – Point-of-sales services | |
| | – Merchant bankcard services | |
| Credit services | Private-label receivables financing | Specialty retail |
| | – Underwriting and risk management | |
| | – Merchant processing | |
| | – Receivable funding | |
| Marketing services | Loyalty programs | Financial services |
| | – Coalition loyalty | Supermarkets |
| | – One-to-one loyalty | Petroleum retail |
| | Marketing programs | Specialty retail |
| | – Database marketing | Utilities |
| | – E-mail communication solutions | Pharmaceuticals |

*Source*: Company reports

# The Customers

The Program had two sets of customers: Sponsors and Collectors.

## The Sponsors

More than 100 brand-name business partners, representing thousands of retail, service, marketing and promotion opportunities, utilized the coalition loyalty platform offered by the Program, by issuing reward miles to shoppers for their everyday purchases. The Sponsors included supermarkets, financial services providers, a national petroleum retailer, specialty retailers, pharmaceutical retailers, consumer services, and business-to-business services, together forming the largest coalition offering a common loyalty platform and a common currency. Canada Safeway, Bank of Montreal, Shell Canada, and Amex Bank of Canada were the four largest Sponsors, representing 44.6 percent of the Program's revenues in 2005.[1] Each AIR MILES reward mile was both a reward to the consumer for shopping at a Sponsor's location and an incentive to shop again with the same retailer. Each transaction helped Collectors accumulate reward miles that could be redeemed for rewards.

The Program offered category exclusivity to Sponsors on a regional or segment basis. For example, in the grocery category, A&P Dominion had sponsorship rights in Ontario, IGA in Quebec, and Sobey's in Atlantic Canada.

For Sponsors, the benefits of participation were many. Most important, the Program contributed to a Sponsor's effort to change consumer behavior in a manner that was beneficial to the consumer and increased the Sponsor's market share and profitability. It also provided a Sponsor with a turnkey loyalty program, enabling the business to operate a loyalty program at a lower cost than if it were implemented as a stand-alone program. In addition, the Program assigned, for each Sponsor, a dedicated account team led by a relationship manager. The team included marketing and analytical professionals focused on guiding and servicing each account.

## The Collectors

The Program's reach in Canadian households was unparalleled. Individual consumers and households signed on as Collectors and accumulated reward miles based on their purchases at Sponsor locations or by using one of the Program's credit card partners. The reward structure facilitated a quick and easy manner for Collectors to earn a broad selection of rewards. The Program had issued about 17 billion reward miles since inception in 1992.[2]

## The Suppliers

Suppliers included airlines, leisure and entertainment providers, and manufacturers of consumer electronics that provided the products and services that Collectors could receive in exchange for their accumulated AIR MILES reward miles. The Program featured more than 300 suppliers, offering more than 800 reward opportunities, in multiple categories of products and services.

# The Business Model

Most of the Sponsors were in non-discretionary staple categories, such as grocery, petroleum, and banking services.

## The Revenue Stream

The Program collected fees from the Sponsors based on the number of reward miles issued. However, issuance fees were not immediately recognized as revenue. The issuance fees became recognized as revenue when the reward miles were redeemed, or at 42 months, whichever occurred earlier.[3]

A second component of revenue was the fee for marketing and administrative services provided to Sponsors. This fee was recognized as revenue pro-rata over the estimated life of a reward mile. It was shown on the balance sheet as "deferred revenue—service."

Some reward miles went unredeemed by Collectors. The percentage of unredeemed reward miles was known as "breakage" in the loyalty industry. Breakage could occur for several reasons: a Collector moved out of the Program area, death of a Collector, or loss of interest in the Program or in the Sponsors. Breakage was factored into the revenue and cost models. If actual redemptions were greater than the estimates, the cost of "excess" redemptions (however notional) would affect the profitability of the Program. AIR MILES reward miles never expired. Some Collectors thus chose to save for big-ticket items, such as a family trip, which would take longer to accumulate.

ADS estimated the average life of a reward mile at 42 months. The provision for breakages based on historical analysis was 33 percent.[4] These two measures had remained constant over the years and had been independently validated. As of December 31, 2005, the Program had $610.5 million[5] in deferred revenue related to the reward program. It had issued 3.25 billion reward miles in 2005 (see Exhibit 2).

## The Competition

The Program competed with advertising and other promotional programs, both traditional and online, for a portion of the Sponsor's total marketing budget. It also competed against loyalty programs and services created by other companies in the market. Crucial to staying competitive was an ability to remain partnered with Sponsors that were desirable to consumers and that offered rewards consumers perceived to be both attainable and attractive. Also crucial was the Program's ability to sustain a large number of active Collectors. A reduction in Collectors' use of the Program would undermine the Program's ability to attract new Sponsors and consumers, and to generate revenue from current Sponsors and consumers. As loyalty programs became more prevalent in the Canadian market, loyalty was becoming an increasingly

| **Exhibit 2** | Alliance Data Systems, Inc.—Income Statement | | | | |
|---|---|---|---|---|---|

| In US$ millions | 2005 | 2004 | 2003 | 2002 | 2001 |
|---|---|---|---|---|---|
| Revenue | | | | | |
| Transaction services | 699.89 | 681.74 | 614.45 | 538.36 | 503.17 |
| Credit services | 561.41 | 513.99 | 433.70 | 342.13 | 289.42 |
| Marketing services | 604.14 | 375.63 | 289.76 | 231.72 | 201.65 |
| Others | (313.00) | (313.92) | (291.37) | (245.63) | (220.52) |
| Total | 1,552.44 | 1,257.44 | 1,046.54 | 866.58 | 773.72 |
| Operating Income | | | | | |
| Transaction services | 28.78 | 30.42 | 34.53 | 32.14 | 25.35 |
| Credit services | 151.12 | 112.52 | 69.41 | 31.18 | 25.69 |
| Marketing services | 56.71 | 29.15 | 26.85 | 12.45 | 3.18 |
| Total | 236.61 | 172.09 | 130.79 | 75.77 | 54.22 |
| Rewards miles issued (mn) | 3,246.55 | 2,834.12 | 2,571.50 | 2,348.10 | 2,153.55 |
| Reward miles redeemed (mn) | 2,023.22 | 1,782.18 | 1,512.79 | 1,260.00 | 984.92 |

Source: Alliance Data Systems, Inc. annual reports.

commoditized industry. Maintaining differentiation was therefore crucial.

Said Papadatos:

> AIR MILES has had a strong differentiation since the beginning. Before AIR MILES, the dominant loyalty model was frequent flyer programs that rewarded frequent travelers for choosing one airline over another. AIR MILES was the first to open up an opportunity to collect to all Canadians, by offering AIR MILES for all of their key shopping categories. Unlike other loyalty cards which are specific to a Sponsor or category, AIR MILES offers everyday rewards for everyone on every purchase. The "democratization" of loyalty rewards has always been the main plank of differentiation for AIR MILES. That has remained unchanged as the core value proposition. Rebranding is meant to reinforce the brand proposition with an emotional connection.

## Rebranding

The Program ranked among the top-three loyalty brands in the world.[6] AIR MILES was a well-known brand in Canada, with 97 percent awareness among Canadians. But the Canadian loyalty market, already limited in size because of low population density, was becoming saturated. Credit-card loyalty programs were growing in popularity: 97 percent of Canadian households participated in at least one loyalty program, 73 percent had three or more loyalty cards, and 53 percent had four or more loyalty cards.[7] Countless coffee-club cards, sandwich cards, bookstore cards and discount programs were moving in and out of the consumer mindspace. Papadatos had to find ways to sustain Collectors' activity levels in the Program, but more importantly, she had to keep the Program relevant to their needs. She also had to preserve the distinctiveness of the AIR MILES brand and communicate it in such a way as to motivate consumers.

The Program had segmented Collectors into four groups based on the intensity of their engagement with the brand: The Best, Next Best, Maintain, and Low.

Said Papadatos:

> The Best segment comprises those who are strong advocates for the brand. They collect reward miles regularly, visit the company's website, respond to its surveys and pull out their AIR MILES card at the checkout counter without a prompt. They are highly profitable, contributing significantly to the Program's bottom line. The rebranding is not targeted at them. Instead, it is targeted at the Next Best Collectors. We need to get them to lift their activity level to that of The Best segment. The Next Best will of course happily pull out their card but only on a prompt. It is not top-of-mind. That would happen when the collection of reward miles, rendered mechanical through every-day activities like buying groceries and gasoline, acquires an aspirational ring to it. The aspiration is created, not by the reward per se, but by the emotional experience that Collectors go through while spending their reward miles.

There were two other reasons for rebranding. First, Collectors were diversifying their collection across multiple categories. The Program was thus no longer earning a bulk of its revenue from air travelers; however, Collectors had limited awareness that the Program went beyond the flight reward. Second, Aeroplan, the Air Canada frequent flyer program, was indicating that its goal was to replicate the AIR MILES model.

## The Rebranding Methodology

### The Basics

In developing a rebranding strategy, Papadatos first examined the two traditional approaches to rebranding: Look outward at the competitive scenario, ascertain the gaps in the market offerings and seek differentiation by filling one or more of them; and look inward, get to the heart of what the company stands for and adjust the positioning to reflect that deeper insight. The latter, thought Papadatos, would be an opportunity for the Program to reconnect with what had made the AIR MILES Reward Program successful as an organization. Such an approach, she felt, would also provide an opportunity for AIR MILES, as a brand, to become more meaningful to consumers.

Papadatos and her team were clear about their expectations from rebranding. The rebranding campaign was not targeted at Sponsors or suppliers. Customer acquisition was not a goal, neither was creating consumer awareness. Nor were they looking for a direct increase in the issuance of reward miles or their redemption. The goal was to change the attitudes of a specific Collector segment—the Next Best—from neutral (or negative) to positive.

Focus groups had been a key source of consumer insight in past years at AIR MILES. The focus group format—in which a direct question yielded little more than a direct answer—was seen as unsuitable for an exercise aimed at exploring the basis for an emotional connection to the brand. The company looked at alternative forms of research. Storytelling emerged as a possible format.[8]

## Storytelling

The company brought together groups of about 20 Collectors for in-depth research in key consumer markets across Canada. It enlisted the help of a consultancy firm that specialized in storytelling methodology. The consultancy's chief executive officer (CEO), Edward Wachtman, acted as the facilitator. Rather than focusing on consumers' experiences with an AIR MILES card, as might have been expected in a focus group setting, consumers participated in a series of storytelling exercises that centered on the theme of "feeling rewarded."

As the members of each group shared their individual experiences of being rewarded, a commonality emerged in the participants' use of specific terms and the meanings they associated with those terms, such as *gifts*. Each group was randomly split into teams, and each team was asked to develop a story about "feeling rewarded," written as a play, a poster or a narrative. A team member was then asked to present the story in an interactive session with the group. As a wrap-up, each participant was invited to write a personal story about feeling rewarded. At that stage, the participants were free to leave but, invariably, everyone preferred to stay. The storytelling exercise—taking on the form of icebreakers, group activities and solo play—lasted three to four hours for each group. By the end of the session, the company had accumulated a portfolio of about 120 stories.

Said Edward Wachtman:

We know from a generation of neurological research that many of our so-called rational decisions are, in fact, driven by deep and powerful emotions. These emotions are difficult, if not impossible, to identify through conventional focus group methods. The StoryTellings™ process helps individuals let go of their logical guards so that they have better access to their emotions. Although the process itself never varies; the prompt—what individuals create stories about—changes from client to client. The AIR MILES prompt was "Feeling Rewarded." AIR MILES believed that understanding and repositioning its brand around a deep-seated motivation would help create enduring bonds with Collectors and provide the brand with a strong competitive advantage.

Collectors from one end of Canada to the other opened up with strikingly similar stories about the reward experience. Although each story was personal and different, they all followed the same plot. Every story Papadatos and her team heard was built around common elements. Each story began with a sense of hope for the future. A baby was born, a young woman moved to a new town to take a new job, a young man went to school to earn his degree. Then there was crisis. An unexpected, life-altering event happened. The newborn was diagnosed as being deaf. The woman who left her family behind lost her job. The university student lost his scholarship and had to drop out. In every story, the feeling of anticipation was followed inevitably by a period of despair. And then, a helping hand came along. A nurse gave a referral to a pediatric surgeon who might help restore the baby's hearing. A friendly neighbor gave the young woman a job lead. A guidance counselor suggested that the student apply for a work-study program. The arrival of unexpected help was followed immediately by goal setting and a period of hard work. The parents found time and money to find the surgeon, the young woman interviewed for jobs, and the young man balanced classes with a night job.

After a period of trial and tribulation, each story ended with a resolution. The goal was achieved. That was the reward. The baby's operation restored some of her hearing. The woman landed a higher-paying job than she had before. The student stood on the podium to receive his degree. And then interestingly, in every story, there was a second level of reward. The mother saw the child from her kitchen responding to the neighbor's query. The young woman brought her family to where she was now located. The student came home to share his pride in his degree with his parents.

There were many lessons from the storytelling research but a couple of insights stood out. First, a reward that came out of the blue was not as valuable as a reward that one had worked hard to earn. Second, the work of collecting had intrinsic value. Third, an equal exchange of value was critical to the feeling of being rewarded, in recognition of the give and take in life. Finally, it became clear that the emotions associated with "feeling rewarded" were deep-rooted and, in many cases, individuals were marked by these defining moments that gave real meaning to their day-to-day lives.

Said Papadatos:

One of the biggest lessons was the notion of the double reward. It has a lot of relevance to the direction we took with our re-branding. In each of our stories, the protagonist enjoys

the extrinsic achievement of the goal. But there is also an intrinsic, emotional connection to the reward. For the mother of the deaf child, the real reward comes long after the operation, when she looks out of the kitchen to see her daughter playing with the neighborhood kids. For the young man, the real reward occurs after he takes the midnight bus to his hometown to sit at the dining table, degree in hand, and celebrates with his family. The lesson here is that the material reward matters little in and of itself. It is what you do with it and with whom you share it that does. Interestingly, the consumer research echoes the hundreds of letters that we at AIR MILES receive from Collectors every year, thanking us for the experiences they have had with people who matter most to them.

That learning was a defining moment, in its own right, for Papadatos and her team. They realized that the AIR MILES reward experience, although effective from a functional and service perspective, was not celebratory. The company was congratulating Collectors for earning their rewards but was not addressing the inherent possibilities for celebration. It was this realization that marked the beginning of a new journey for the brand, from a functional experience to one that is emotionally engaging.

The findings of the research formed the basis for developing a new creative platform. The company hired a new brand agency to work on a two-minute brand manifesto that would serve as a talking piece to employees and Sponsors. In fact, this video became the catalyst for every employee to "participate" in the development of the new brand, and Papadatos met with all 600 call-center employees in small group settings to ascertain that the "voice of the brand" was consistent with "the voice of the Collector." The agency developed TV commercials, radio spots, employee launch materials, direct marketing materials, and a video message from the company's president to Sponsors and their employees.

Papadatos was keen that the campaign should be monitored to ascertain not only whether it was delivering results but whether there was need for mid-course corrections. She decided upon some metrics of performance to track the progress of the campaign (see Exhibit 3).

| Exhibit 3 | Performance Metrics |

| AIR MILES Brand Study 2005–06 Supporting Numbers for the Brand Re-launch Awareness and Recall Section | |
|---|---|
| | **Lift** |
| **AIR MILES Unaided awareness (total sample)** | 5% |
| Best | 15% |
| Next Best | 5% |
| Maintain | 5% |
| **AIR MILES – Measuring Attitude, Action, Engagement** | |
| **Best** | |
| **(Top Box) % Strongly Agree** | **Lift** |
| I'd rather use an AM coupon than a cents off coupon | 7% |
| I've set a goal to collect AMRM towards a specific reward | 4% |
| I plan to increase the number of AMRM I collect over the next 12 months | 6% |
| AIR MILES is making a strong effort to earn my loyalty | 4% |
| The rewards or experiences I can earn with AIR MILES are things that can be used in a meaningful way | 4% |
| I always recommend AM to friends and neighbors | 4% |
| **Next Best** | |
| **(Top Box) % Strongly Agree** | |
| I'd rather use an AM coupon than a cents off coupon | 7% |
| I've set a goal to collect AMRM towards a specific reward | 6% |
| I plan to increase the number of AMRM I collect over the next 12 months | 4% |
| I choose to shop at/use an AM Sponsor over a competing retailer/service | 5% |
| AIR MILES is making a strong effort to earn my loyalty | 5% |
| The rewards or experiences I can earn with AIR MILES are things that can be used in a meaningful way | 8% |

| | |
|---|---|
| I trust AM and its product and services | 4% |
| AIR MILES is the perfect program for people like me | 6% |
| I always recommend AM to friends and neighbors | 4% |
| **Competitive Assessment (Personality, Attributes)** | |
| **For AMRP** | |
| Exciting | 4% |
| Makes time to be with family | 12% |
| A good storyteller | 14% |
| Fun | 6% |
| Could get along with anyone | 11% |
| Optimistic | 6% |
| Feminine | 6% |
| It's simple and straightforward to be part of this program | 5% |
| I'm proud to use this program | 5% |
| Has unique rewards | 6% |
| It's a program set up to help everyday people | 5% |

*Source:* Air Miles Canada.

*Notes:* AMRP is the Air Miles Rewards Program; Lift refers to the increase over prior baseline measurement.

The campaign was set to launch in early October 2005. As she looked out of her office at Yonge Street in Toronto and at the greenery extending into the Don Valley Golf Course, Papadatos wondered, "Will this be the platform for building lasting engagement with Collectors?"

## CASE QUESTIONS

1. How would a data warehouse assist the marketing team at AIR MILES, going forward? What functions would it perform that would be most useful?

2. Which type of data would be most valuable to the Sponsors and Suppliers? Which type of data regarding the Collectors would be most valuable to the airline?

3. Would a data-mining program be useful to AIR MILES? Would it be helpful to Sponsors and Suppliers? If so, how? If not, why not?

4. The AIR MILES marketing team relied on storytelling to develop the rebranding program. Would the use of lifetime value analysis or RFM analysis have been more useful? Defend your answer.

5. How might data regarding customers who had stopped using AIR MILES be helpful?

# Conroy's Acura: Customer Lifetime Value and Return on Marketing

*By Mike Moffat, under the supervision of Professor Kyle B. Murray*

In the fall of 2006, Terrence Conroy, president of Conroy's Acura, was poring over the company's quarterly sales. Despite a healthy economy, sales at his dealership were stagnant. If the dealership were to remain profitable, Conroy needed to find a cost-effective way to increase sales. His vice-president of sales, Rachel De Lima, was continually coming up with new marketing schemes to boost sales. But Conroy had difficulty determining how successful past marketing efforts had been in increasing profitability. He needed a way to put the numbers into context.

## History of the Dealership

Conroy's Acura was founded in November 1986 by Ross Conroy, a veteran of the car industry who also owned a General Motors dealership and an American Motors (AMC) dealership. Conroy's Acura was the first Acura dealership to open in Toronto and one of the first in North America. Located in downtown Toronto, Conroy's Acura sold both new and pre-owned vehicles, and its service department was dedicated to Acura products.

In 1999, Ross's son, Terrence Conroy, became president of Conroy's Acura. Along with Terrence Conroy and De Lima, the dealership had a staff of nine salespeople, two administrative assistants/receptionists, and six technicians who worked in the service department.

Conroy's Acura was an independently owned dealership that held a franchise agreement with Honda, Acura's parent company. Conroy's Acura purchased its inventory directly from Honda's Canadian distributor and sold the cars at a markup.

Conroy's Acura also sold pre-owned automobiles, the majority of which were obtained through trade-ins from consumers.

## The Marketplace

Conroy's Acura had a number of competitors in the marketplace, the most obvious were the dozen or so other Acura dealerships within a 30-kilometer radius. Conroy's Acura competed directly with dealerships that sold cars comparable to Acura's offerings, such as Saab, Volkswagen, and, most notably, Honda. Conroy believed the four biggest competitors in the Toronto market were BMW, Mercedes-Benz, Lexus, and Infiniti. BMW and Mercedes-Benz, two German brands, tended to price their cars higher than Acura. Lexus, the luxury brand of Toyota, and Infiniti, the luxury brand of Nissan, tended to price their cars in the same range as Acura.

Competition had grown fierce over the past few years, because of the advent of the Internet, which made it much easier for consumers to comparison shop.

## The Cars

Conroy's Acura sold six models of new cars:

### Acura CSX—average sales price: $31,860

The Acura CSX was an entry-level luxury car, similar to the Honda Civic. It competed against cars such as the Volkswagen Jetta and the Nissan Sentra.

Version: (A) 2008–02–04

## Acura RSX—average sales price: $35,100

A small sporty sedan, the Acura RSX competed with cars such as the Mitsubishi Eclipse and the Volkswagen Golf GTI.

## Acura TSX—average sales price: $42,984

The Acura TSX competed in the entry-level luxury market with the BMW 3 series, the Mercedez-Benz C-Class, the Audi A4 and the Lexus IS.

## Acura TL—average sales price: $49,680

The Acura TL was a mid-sized luxury car with many competitors, including the Infiniti G35, the Lexus ES, the Saab 9–3, the Mercedes-Benz E-Class and the Volvo S60. The Acura TL was far and away Conroy's Acura's highest-selling car.

## Acura MDX—average sales price: $61,776

The Acura MDX was a sport utility vehicle (SUV), which had an SUV appearance but a unibody construction typically seen in cars. Other mid-sized crossover SUVs included the Lexus RX, the BMW X5, the Infiniti RX, and the Volvo XC90

## Acura RL—average sales price: $79,812

The oldest model of the six sold by Conroy's Acura, the Acura RL, competed with the Audi A6, the Lexus GS, and the Volvo S80 in the luxury sedan market.

## Sales and Existing Marketing Efforts

The firm was currently spending $120,000 on marketing to new clients each year, split between billboards, direct mail, radio and television spots, and newspaper and community magazine advertisements. Conroy's Acura sold approximately 650 cars each year, spread over six car classes. On each model, the firm's gross markup was approximately eight percent of the dealer cost. After fixed expenses, such as staff salaries, rent, and taxes, net profit was typically two percent of sales revenue.

The firm also spent $10 a year to maintain each of its existing customers. The bulk of this expense came from quarterly postcards reminding drivers to change their oil and the occasional letter promoting new models and specials offered by Conroy's Acura.

The dealership typically judged the success of its marketing efforts by comparing the cost of the marketing effort to the number of extra cars sold. De Lima believed this method understated the true value of her efforts, because it did not take into account that 25 percent of customers who bought a car today would also buy their next car from the dealership. To get an accurate gauge of the dealership's marketing efforts, this statistic needed to be taken into account.

Conroy was also very concerned with quantifying the return on marketing. He had seen more than his share of creative marketing ideas that did not produce a tangible financial return. Although brand building and general recognition were important to him, his dealership was now well known in the community and, at the end of the day, he wanted new marketing initiatives to provide a compelling return on his marketing investment.

Sales could be broken down into two types: sales to new customers and sales to previous customers. Conroy's Acura used a two-pronged marketing approach to gain sales from each group, but spillovers occurred; a billboard designed to gain new customers could also help the dealership to retain its existing customers.

## Increasing the Number of New Customers

Most of De Lima's ideas to increase the number of new customers were simply to do more of what they were already doing: more direct-mail post-cards, more billboards, and more advertisements on television, on radio, and in newspapers.

The sales staff, however, had a different sug-gestion. They believed the eight percent markup on cars was too high, given how easy it was for con-sumers to comparison shop. The salespeople believed that by lowering the margin they could more than make up for it in increased sales. Conroy, though, was skeptical that sales could be increased enough to make a price reduction worthwhile.

## Increasing the Customer Retention Rate

Conroy's Acura spent approximately $30,000 a year on customer retention, or approximately $10 to $12 a year for each customer that had pur-chased in the past four years. This expense was largely spent on postcard mailings to customers to remind them to change their oil or to notify them of upcoming promotions from the service department (for example, 10 percent off tire rota-tion). Because it was less expensive to retain an existing client than to acquire a new customer, De Lima believed increasing the customer reten-tion rate should be the primary focus of the deal-ership's efforts. After a brainstorming session with her sales force, they came up with the follow-ing ideas:

- Providing free oil changes or car washes with purchase of a new car
- Customer reward programs along the lines of frequent flyer miles offered by airlines. But the sales force had difficulties coming up with details. For example, who would run the program? What would the rewards be? How could consumers collect points other than buying a new car?
- Increased contact with customers (through postcard or letter mailings, phone calls, and e-mails).

- Surveys of existing customers to ask what would influence them to purchase from Conroy's Acura in the future.

Conroy was intrigued by the ideas, but needed a way to compare the costs to the benefits. How much would their retention rate need to increase if the marketing budget for existing clients were doubled?

## The Data Kept by Conroy's Acura

The dealership kept simple records of their sales and marketing efforts, including the following:

- The $120,000 spent on advertising.
- The number of sales of each car class, including the sales to first-time clients and the sales to previous Conroy's Acura customers.
- The dealer cost per car class, the average price and the markup for the firm, which historically was eight percent per car class.
- The length of time a customer kept a car before purchasing a new one. Historically, for the Acura brand, the average was four years for each class of car.
- The historic retention rate, which was the percentage of customers who purchased their next car from the dealership. Since 1999, when Terrence Conroy became pres-ident of Conroy's Acura, the retention rate had been stable at 25 percent.
- The yearly maintenance cost, or the cost of maintaining the customer relationship. Currently the firm spent $10 per year per current customer (those that had pur-chased in the past four years).

From these data, the firm could calculate the cost of acquiring a new consumer (the acquisition cost), the customer lifetime value and the return on marketing of increasing the marketing efforts (see Exhibit 1).

| **Exhibit 1** | Excel Sheet Definitions |

The Excel sheet (available on the Instructor Teaching Site for this text or see Ivey product # 7B08A001) contains two scenarios: a base case in columns H through N and a modified scenario in rows A through G. When changes are made to the modified scenario, the Excel sheet will calculate the differences between the modified and the base scenario. The cells on the sheet are color-coded as follows:

**Cyan cells**: The user enters a figure into these cells.

**Blue cells**: These parameters or figures are calculated automatically. The user does not need to alter anything in a blue cell.

**Yellow cells**: The numbers in the yellow cells are chosen from a set of options in a drop-down box.

**Green cells**: These cells show the final results of the sheet, indicating the profitability and return on marketing (ROM) of any changes made.

**Row 2—Fixed Costs**: The costs of any marketing efforts not captured by the acquisition cost and the yearly maintenance costs box. If an additional $2,500 is spent on a billboard, then this number should be increased by $2,500.

**Row 4—Car**: The model of the car.

**Row 5—Total Sales**: The total sales in a year for that particular model.

**Row 6—New Sales**: The total sales in a year for that particular model to *first-time customers*.

**Row 7—Return Sales**: Sales made to returning customers. This figure is calculated automatically as the difference between Row 5 and Row 6.

**Row 8—Avg. Markup**: The price markup for that particular model.

**Row 9—Return (Yrs)**: The average length of time a customer keeps a car before purchasing a new one.

**Row 10—Retain Rate**: The percentage of customers who will return to purchase their next car from Conroy's Acura.

**Row 11—Yr. Main Cst**: The yearly maintenance cost of keeping an existing client. This cost includes expenses such as mailings and postcards sent to existing clients, free oil changes and other promotions given to existing clients.

**Row 12—Disc. Rate**: The discount rate represents the time value of money, the fact that a dollar today is worth more than a dollar next year. The higher the number, the more the future is discounted relative to today.

**Row 14—Acq. Cost**: The per-consumer acquisition cost, calculated using the fixed costs from Row 2 and the yearly sales to first-time customers (Row 6).

**Row 15—Dealer Cost**: The dealer cost for each type of car.

**Row 16—Avg. Price**: The average price of the car. This price is calculated by Dealer Cost × (1 + Markup)

**Row 17—T Life Maint**: The total lifetime maintenance for all the cars sold of a particular class, taking into account the length of time the average customer keeps a car (Row 9) and the discount rate (Row 12).

*(Continued)*

| **Exhibit 1** | (Continued) |

> **Row 18—Tot. Acq:** The total acquisition cost, calculated by multiplying the acquisition cost of Row 14 by the number of sales to first-time customers (Row 6).
>
> **Row 19—Unit Gross:** The per-unit gross profitability of the car. This figure is the average price minus the dealer cost.
>
> **Row 20—T Gr Lifetime:** The total gross lifetime profit from the car class. This figure includes maintenance costs but does not include acquisition costs.
>
> **Row 21—T Gr Net of Acq:** Similar to Row 20, but excluding acquisition costs.

## Acquisition Cost

The acquisition cost compared the amount of money spent on marketing to the general public to the number of cars sold to first-time clients. This cost is expressed by the equation:

Fixed Marketing Cost / Total Sales to New Clients

The firm's marketing budget was currently set at $120,000, and it expected to sell 497 cars to first-time clients this year, leading to an acquisition cost of $241 per client ($120,000/497 = $241).

## Customer Lifetime Value (CLV)

The customer lifetime value related the amount the firm expected the average customer to spend over a lifetime. This amount varied from car class to car class. To calculate the customer lifetime value, the following data were needed:

- $d$: The discount rate, which represents the time value of money, the fact that a dollar today is worth more than a dollar next year. The higher the number, the more the future is discounted relative to today. Conroy's Acura used a discount rate of five percent.
- $y$: The length of time a customer keeps a car before purchasing a new one.
- $r$: The retention rate, the percentage of consumers who return to the dealership to purchase their next car.

- $m$: The yearly maintenance cost of maintaining the customer relationship.
- $p$: The sales price of the car.
- $c$: The dealer cost of the car.

The customer lifetime value (CLV) is calculated as follows:

$$CLV = ((1 - d)^y \times ((p - c - (m \times y))/(1 - r))).$$

The customer lifetime value increases as the price $p$ and the retention rate $r$ increase, but decreases as the discount rate $d$, the dealer cost $c$, the yearly maintenance cost $m$, and length of time between purchases $y$ increases.

## Return on Marketing

In order to estimate the effect of a change in marketing efforts, the new marketing efforts needed to be compared to a base case in which nothing had changed. To calculate the expected return on marketing of the marketing change, the following calculation is used:

ROM = Increased Profits in New Scenario/ Increased Costs.

To be worthwhile, the return on marketing should be at least as high as the returns Conroy's Acura could have achieved by investing in the stock market.

## The Decision

Terrence Conroy felt that the dealership should be able to do something to increase the bottom line. Although, he was glad that they had some numbers to work with, he knew that a great deal of uncertainty always surrounded any projections. Conroy wondered, "What should I be doing differently to increase customer lifetime value, return on marketing, sales and profits? What steps do I need to take to make this happen?"

### CASE QUESTIONS

1. What types of customer data would be useful when examining retention rates and costs?

2. The typical lifetime value statistic reflects a time period of 5 years. Would the statistic be useful for evaluating customers that may purchase an automobile once every 4 years? What data might make the statistic more helpful?

3. Calculate the acquisition costs for new customers if the marketing budget were raised to $150,000 annually and led to 600 new automobile purchases.

4. Calculate the return on marketing when the company's increased profits were $100,000 and the costs incurred to achieve those profits were $80,000.

5. Which data-driven marketing programs would be viable options for Conroy's Acura?

CHAPTER

4

# Building a Customer-Oriented Marketing Department

B uilding a customer-oriented marketing department incorporates a variety of leadership efforts and managerial activities. These include choosing the appropriate management style, utilizing the best leadership theories and ideas, making quality decisions, motivating employees, empowering and engaging employees, inspiring creativity, handling personal and employee stress, and fostering an ethical environment.

## ⊠ Management Styles

Four basic management styles may be found in business organizations. The authoritarian style, in which the manager gives orders and expects them to be followed without question, rarely fits with a marketing department—except possibly when a company is in crisis mode. A consultative style also may be best suited to organizations experiencing difficulties, but the manager still might find it advisable to seek counsel from some company members. Participative management leads to employee input and often a sense of engagement in the organization. An open-door policy can also create some disenchantment for members whose input is not considered or utilized. Very few organizations exhibit the democratic management style, because at least some leadership and direction is expected from those at higher ranks.

## ⊠ Leadership Theories

Effective leadership skills may be gleaned from the three approaches to understanding formal leadership, which focus on managers that are elected, appointed, or promoted to leadership positions. The traits and characteristics approach suggests that four key leadership traits likely include task maturity, emotional maturity, a human relations orientation, and intelligence. Leaders may be elected, appointed, or promoted based on these characteristics.

People versus production theories emphasize the balance needed between completing tasks and providing support and counsel to subordinates. In more recent years, the leader–member exchange models noted the value of in-group relationships between leaders and subordinates. The substitutes for leadership theory recognizes that organizational characteristics can take the place of leadership. Path-goal theory suggests leaders succeed when they are able to create a style of leadership that accounts for the follower's characteristics and the characteristics of the situation. In essence, no one best way to lead exists. Effective leaders are those who adapt to the situation at hand.

## Making Quality Decisions

Making quality decisions relies on three components. First, the decision-making environment should be ethical. Second, managers should focus on making customer-oriented decisions. Third, decisions should be made as openly as possible to prevent rumors and gossip from hindering the truth and harming morale.

## A Customer-Oriented Marketing Department

Building a customer-oriented marketing department requires several major activities. First, the marketing team works closely with the human resources department to help select, train, and evaluate the types of workers that have a keen interest in customers and customer service. Then goal-setting programs and reward systems, along with peer approval through role modeling and coaching, enhance the emphasis on serving the needs of customers. A customer-oriented culture allows employees to freely share information, encourage one another, help out others during crises or difficult periods, and build quality relationships with one another as well as with customers.

## Motivation Theories

Motivation is what starts behaviors, what maintains behaviors, and sometimes what stops behaviors. Key behaviors to start include attendance, punctuality, effort and/or productivity, supporting coworkers, and good on-the-job citizenship. Behaviors to stop are absenteeism, tardiness, gossip, unprofessional behaviors, wasting time, and unethical behaviors.

Three models of motivation appear in the literature. Need-based theories focus on the ways individuals are motivated by items they need or crave. Operant process models emphasize the role that the external environment and reinforcements play in shaping behaviors. Cognitive process models explain how employee thoughts can drive their motives and responses to various situations.

Three needs apply well to a marketing department. Those driven by the need for achievement require tangible evidence of success that is visible to others. Those motivated by needs for affiliation should be placed into social roles within the organization. Individuals dominated by the need for power may become a liability to the department unless successfully managed.

The operant process approach offers four consequences that shape future employee behaviors. Positive reinforcement takes many forms of pleasant outcomes, from simple praise to bonuses and pay raises. Negative reinforcement explains circumstances in which an employee overcomes an aversive situation through a certain behavior, such as defeating feelings of pressure associated with a deadline by completing the task on time or early. Punishment is a direct negative consequence associated with a behavior and should be limited to severe violations, such as breaking rules or laws or placing others in danger. Extinction notes that in the absence of a consequence a behavior tends to disappear. Savvy managers can utilize each of these reinforcers as means to help employees achieve higher levels of performance.

Cognitive process models include equity theory and expectancy theory. Equity theory explains that employees need and seek fair and equitable treatment in terms of workload and rewards for performance. Expectancy theory links expectancy with instrumentality and valence. Expectancy is the belief that a person can successfully complete a task. Instrumentality connects successful task completion with the reward. Valence is the value of the reward itself. An effective marketing manager understands what subordinates want, helps them successfully complete assignments, and rewards performance whenever possible.

## Empowering and Engaging Employees

Empowering and engaging employees take the forms of delegation to individual employees and decentralization on an organization-wide scale. Empowerment creates loyalty and role clarity for individual workers.

Creativity may be inspired by first selecting the types of employees that are interested in creative activities. Then, a creative environment can be built through items as subtle as open office spaces and informal and first-name relationships with employees. Creativity techniques such as brainstorming and nominal groups are more formal approaches to inspiring new ideas.

## Managing Stress

Handling personal and employee stress requires understanding of the sources of stress, how stress affects individuals, and responding with physical, psychological, and social techniques. Each individual is unique and can seek to identify ways to limit and/or manage stress. Time management is closely related to stress management.

Effective leadership of a marketing department demands a constant balance between the need for order and direction and the desire for creative, inspired workers. Leaders and managers who create customer-oriented marketing departments use all the tools of management to constantly emphasize the importance of quality relationships with all publics that interact with the company. Ethical leadership provides a sound basis for inspiring others to behave in the same way.

## The Cases

### A Difficult Hiring Decision at Central Bank

Central Bank's management team had recently dismissed a longtime, popular manager for poor performance. The employee had 3 years left to work before retirement. Three viable candidates were finalists for the position. Each exhibited some strengths and some areas that were less strong. The company's core values focused on building positive client relationships. It was possible that tension existed between serving clients effectively and maintaining a positive and satisfied workforce.

## Boman Communications

Klas Boman had developed a brand new method for delivering marketing communications to prospective client companies. Unfortunately, Boman Communications had attracted only one large client. Boman believed part of the problem was that company employees did not fully understand his innovative system and were therefore unable to communicate its advantages to others. One of his two locations experienced a substantial amount of turnover, and Boman was concerned that he was not hiring the right type of individual to work in the firm.

# A Difficult Hiring Decision at Central Bank

### By Mark S. Schwartz and Hazel Copp

## The Challenge

Martin Smith, vice-president (VP), Regional Sales at Central Bank, had recently been let go, and the search for his replacement was taking place. As part of the recruitment process, several candidates for the position needed to be ranked, while taking into account Central Bank's recently established vision, mission and values (see Exhibit 1).

| Exhibit 1 | Central Bank's Vision, Mission, and Values |

**Vision**
- To be the leader in client relationships.

**Mission (Employees)**
- To create an environment where all employees can excel.

**Mission (Clients)**
- To help them achieve what matters to them.

**Mission (Community)**
- To make a real difference in our communities.

**Mission (Shareholders)**
- To build the highest total return for shareholders.

**Core Values: Trust**
- Act with integrity, honesty, and transparency, open and candid, treat others with dignity and fairness, behave according to ethical principles, operate with integrity, and support our colleagues.

**Core Values: Teamwork**
- Work collaboratively with others; share info; respect opinions of others, listen attentively, ask for input and feedback.

**Core Values: Accountability**
- Live up to commitments, accept overall responsibility for behavior, admit mistakes and learn from them, seek clarity on roles.

Version: (A) 2009–09–15

# Background

The position would require managing a number of employees in a region just outside of Toronto (see Exhibit 2).

Through conversations with Smith's former supervisor, Central Bank's Executive Resources established the background that led to Smith's dismissal:

- "Values driven" and well liked by his staff
- Strong community ties/profile

- Lowest turnover rate in segment
- Employee satisfaction scores in middle of pack
- Region in last place; results poor/growth stalled
- Integration of new segment incomplete
- Critical new processes/procedures not bought into or implemented
- Dismissed the previous week, decision unpopular in Region
- Three years away from early retirement, 30 years with Central Bank

---

**Exhibit 2**   Job Posting—Vice President, Sales

**Business Unit Description**

With over 1,200 locations in the Canadian marketplace, our premiere Retail Banking segment represents the soul of the Central Bank brand and is the key to our long-term success. Our in-branch retail professionals provide a range of financial services to clients, from savings and chequing accounts, mortgages and loans, small business credit solutions and investment products, to complete financial planning.

**Purpose of Position**

To lead effective and profitable sales execution of multiple customer offers in the Region and to maximize the contribution generated by its retail customers. Lead the advancement of the Region's market share and profitability through delivery of an excellent customer and employee experience.

Work closely and cooperatively with internal service and operations providers and other regional colleagues to better position Central Bank as the pre-eminent financial services provider in Canada. To improve Central Bank's reputation with customers, regulators and government and create an environment where employees can excel.

Provide leadership to the design and execution of segment-wide and cross-segment initiatives.

**Accountabilities of Positions (Key Outcomes and Activities)**

Establish a vision and clear purpose for the region; inspire commitment to the vision in employees and colleagues in a manner that puts the best interests of Central Bank and its customers first.

Develop, communicate and manage an aggressive regional sales plan aligned to national strategies and based on a deep understanding of regional market conditions, customer segments and resource requirements; drive the sales, business development, and sales management processes for the region.

Build a customer-focused, high-performing sales team in the region that focuses on maximizing profitability, growth and customer loyalty; employ rigorous hiring practices/policies to ensure newly hired and current sales staff subscribe to all of Central Bank's values and professional standards.

Ensure all delegated roles, responsibilities, and accountabilities are well defined and understood; apply metrics to measure; and manage performance and foster continuous improvement.

Lead employees through periods of organizational change and maintain high levels of motivation during transition period; coach and mentor staff; actively support staff in their professional growth and personal development.

Deliver customer offers in accordance with core Central Bank business strategies, risk management requirements and Brand standards; build keen awareness of governance and regulatory requirements and closely manage process to monitor adherence.

Develop close partnerships with local leaders of all customer segments; build integrated sales plans where possible to maximize customer coverage.

Model the values of the organization internally and in the community; encourage staff to actively participate in their communities and publicly acknowledge their efforts.

## Competencies (Skills and Knowledge)

Highly developed leadership skills; experience turning around a business or managing significant business change is highly desirable.

Proven ability to develop and manage a world-class sales force in a highly competitive business environment. Candidates must have:

- a track record for delivering aggressive financial and business growth targets;
- a staffing model and experience recruiting high performing sales staff;
- a well-honed and highly successful coaching methodology;
- demonstrated sales prospecting and sales tracking capabilities.

Expert knowledge of business and financial planning processes is required; demonstrated financial discipline and cost management capabilities.

Ability to manage relationships between various customer offers, delivery channels and support/supplier groups; demonstrated ability to work collaboratively across Central Bank to achieve collective business goals and satisfy customer needs.

Ability to instill respect for risk management and compliance requirements and deliver effective processes/systems to manage all aspects of operational, regulatory, market, credit and reputational risk.

Ability to translate strategic intent into action, communicate action/direction openly and effectively up, down and across the region.

Able to represent Central Bank in various external communities of interest.

## Attributes Required

Trustworthy (e.g., Integrity); Relationship builder; Team Player/Builder; Accountability (i.e., Results orientation); Customer focus; Adaptability

Smith's former supervisor also provided a summary of "what went wrong":

- Need to be liked got in the way of critical changes
- Thought there was a trade-off between performance and values
- Couldn't make the tough people calls
- Said he bought into sales process/disciplines but didn't enforce the process
- Hadn't built appropriate relationships with colleagues in other strategic business units; no previous goodwill to help smooth integration of new segment
- Business continually left on table due to poor teamwork between segments
- Would blame others (often Head Office) for lack of success
- Should have moved on Smith earlier, *but* he'd been around for so long

Smith's former supervisor provided an indication of what he believed was needed:

- Major turnaround
- Build new team; exit players who can't deliver
- Hire well; recruit people who can deliver and have required values
- Get buy-in into new sales processes/value of a more disciplined approach
- Employ a person who can build trust/relationships with other segments to grow business

Hire a candidate who could ultimately prove to be a good "succession" candidate.

## The Candidates

Following an initial screening and interview process (see Exhibit 3) conducted by Central Bank's Executive Resources, the number of final candidates had been reduced to three. The following provides a summary of each of the final candidate's profiles.

| Exhibit 3 | Interview Questions/Responses of the Three Candidates |
|---|---|

### 1. Describe the Culture in Which You Do Your Best Work.

**Charlotte Webb:**

I'm the sort of person who likes a work environment that provides some challenges professionally. So far, Central Bank has provided that for me. What's most important to me now is the ability to grow career-wise. I like working with bright people, in an organization that is willing to take some risks. I'm not talking about recklessness, but I like working for an organization that wants to operate at the "cutting edge" with respect to conducting business, one that is attuned to the market, uses technology and analytics to the fullest, and knows where it wants to play. It's also important to me how organizations treat their people, that people are rewarded not only for achieving goals, but for how they are achieved as well.

**Scott Warren:**

I guess I can speak best about the Royal, which puts a heavy focus on being number one. That's the sort of place where I do my best work. I like everything to be fast paced, with clear deadlines to meet. As well, when the firm allows its managers and employees to take reasonable risks, and be rewarded for results, that's best for me, that's when I'm most motivated. I also like "hands-off" managers, I really don't like being micromanaged.

**James Skinner:**

The First Northern bank culture works for me, it's critical to me that employees and customers are treated with respect and dignity, where people can work as a team. I don't subscribe to the "star" system, where only the top performers receive all of the rewards. I like to think through the short- and long-term implications of what we do, and I appreciate a culture that supports that. I really dislike the "churn" that results from poor planning and last minute changes. Those sorts of twists and turns are really tough on people.

### 2. What's the Toughest Call You Have Had to Make?

**Charlotte Webb:**

While working at a Central Bank branch as a summer student, a friend of my dad's came in, and asked me for some personal information on his ex-wife's bank accounts. They were going through an ugly divorce, and it was very awkward for me given my family's connection to say no, and my desire to please an important customer. I knew that I shouldn't give him the information, and I politely refused, but he became very vocal and threatened to pull out his accounts. I knew I was doing the right thing but it was pretty tough, I was so junior at the time.

**Scott Warren:**

I can't say anything I've ever had to do was really that "tough" or "difficult." I guess I'm just the sort of person who does what has to be done, and tries not to think too much about it afterwards. But if I had to pick something, it would be when I was working as an executive director in corporate finance in Australia, and there was pressure coming from Head Office to close off our loan book, since we were beginning to close down Australia. One of our clients was in trouble could easily have been put on the watch list. He had a seasonal business and was desperate to buy more time. It was still within my discretion in terms of what to do, but it was somewhat of a tough call to let his account ride since I could have had some difficulties with Toronto, but I did think the guy deserved a chance, and in the end everything worked out and we got our money back.

**James Skinner:**

Well, it probably was last year when my wife got sick, and I had to give up an opportunity to become a senior VP in the Calgary office. It was an opportunity that I had been waiting for, for years. In the end you make the right decision for your family, but it wasn't easy, letting the opportunity that I had worked for slip through my fingers.

### 3. What Would You Be Afraid to Find if You Got This Job?

**Charlotte Webb:**

I wouldn't exactly say "afraid" is the right word, but if you're asking me what I think the biggest challenges would be, I would say winning over the staff, who will know I don't have a lot of line experience, and introducing sales discipline to the group, but it's a challenge I'm happy to accept. It's not the first time I've gone in without all the required skills, but I think my record shows I've not only met the desired targets, but exceeded them as well.

**Scott Warren:**

I'm concerned that it would take forever for me to get ahead, and that people don't really get rewarded for producing results. I'm willing to do whatever it takes, to deliver, but my expectation would be that I would be rewarded accordingly.

**James Skinner:**

This is a very important question for me, so I'm very glad you asked it. I am concerned whether Central Bank is more focused on the "numbers," than on people. I know this is perhaps the wrong perception, but I'm also concerned about teamwork issues at Central Bank; too many "silos" and "revolving doors." It's certainly perceived to be a very different culture here, but despite my concerns, I believe I'm up for the challenge.

### 4. How Do You Feel About the Recent Emphasis Being Placed on Corporate Governance?

**Charlotte Webb:**

It certainly has been a lot of work for managers throughout the organization. I used to spend 5 percent of my time on what I would loosely call governance, but in the last year that has shot up to 45 percent. No one

| Exhibit 3 | (Continued) |
|---|---|

could argue that this isn't critical, or necessary, but I certainly would hope that once we have installed the governance engine, that the time requirements will be reduced. It's not just about enforcing rules and regulations and policies, it's also about making sure you've hired the right people.

**Scott Warren:**

I guess you're referring to *Sarbanes-Oxley* and the Basel Accord stuff. I'm really not sure whether it will make a difference at the end of the day in terms of discouraging the "bad apples"—I think all of those CEOs and CFOs involved in the recent scandals knew what they were doing was wrong, but did it anyways. People always seem to find a way around laws and regulations. But at the end of the day, it's important for the banks to comply with what the regulators want, because none of us can afford to lose the trust of our customers. But hopefully as the checks and balances are built into the system, it won't continue to be as cumbersome as it has been at the front end.

**James Skinner:**

I'm very happy to see the renewed emphasis being placed on corporate governance. It's been needed for a while to remind everyone of the importance of having rules and regulations. I think that people have forgotten that firms have responsibilities to their shareholders and the public. I believe that unfortunately sometimes very ethical people can be placed into an organization with certain pressures to perform that can make them do some very bad things. We need to renew the public's faith in the corporate world, and this seems to be the best way of doing it.

**5. Describe an Ethical Dilemma You Have Faced in the Workplace and How It Was Resolved.**

**Charlotte Webb:**

I was in an awkward situation a few years ago. The department was required to dramatically reduce its expenditures. What this meant was that we could no longer sponsor things like department lunches, or have prizes for reaching certain goals. At first the managers accepted it, but then a number of people started to become upset when they saw how the VP, who enforced the rules with all of us, was continuing to spend on lavish dinners, staying at upscale hotels, and continuing to use limos. None of these expenses seemed to lead to a return on business, everyone could see the VP taking people out, he wasn't even discreet about it. When people started complaining to me, I decided to see the VP. I suggested to him that he might be setting a poor example for everyone, and that he might want to cut down on the expenses before someone decided to raise the issue with his supervisor. He became very annoyed, said he wasn't really prepared to discuss it with me further, that there was an agenda that I wasn't fully aware of. Although it appeared afterwards that he did in fact cut down on some of the excesses, unfortunately our working relationship was strained from then on, in fact sometimes he was quite verbally abusive to me, and on one occasion he even pushed me to tears in front of a group of colleagues. After that, I just took the first opportunity I could to move out of that division.

**Scott Warren:**

I'm not sure if I've every really faced a true ethical dilemma, but I did have an issue once that related to Royal's Code of Conduct. In about half my branches, I have responsibility for wealth management, we were courting some high net worth individuals, and I wanted to plan a day that they would really enjoy and differentiate us from the other banks. But that meant taking me over my approved entertainment budget. I knew Royal's code spoke about "moderate" business entertainment, but these were some pretty important potential clients. I wanted to take them golfing and for dinner at Glen Abbey, since I certainly couldn't take them to the local municipal course. I debated whether I needed to get my supervisor's approval since I suspected my supervisor would probably stick to the code, and wouldn't be able to see the bigger picture. As it happened, my supervisor was away on vacation, and I was able to get it approved by Head Office. When my supervisor returned he was very upset at first that I had gone over his head to get approval, until he found out that I managed to bring in about $30 million dollars in new assets, which he agreed justified the few thousand spent.

**James Skinner:**

I think I've probably faced many ethical dilemmas over my career. It's hard to pick just one, but if I had to it would probably be the story of how I met my wife at First Northern bank. She was my administrative assistant at the time, and I struggled with whether to disclose the relationship, particularly when it became more serious, knowing that it was "taboo," that it was frowned upon. The way we resolved it though was to hide the relationship, to the point where no one had any idea we were together. In the end the dilemma resolved itself, we ended up getting married, my wife ended up leaving the bank, and no one knew any differently.

## 1. Candidate: Charlotte Webb (Internal Candidate)

**Current Position:** Senior Director, Customer Experience, Marketing Division (Toronto)

**Status:** First round interview with VP, Executive Resources completed

### Background

Webb was the only internal candidate to be shortlisted. She worked at Central Bank during summers while in university, initially as a teller, and then in the marketing division and for one year between her undergraduate and postgraduate degrees. Webb was recruited to the World Bank from the London School of Economics, and assigned to the World Bank offices in Geneva and Washington, D.C., for a total of four years.

A desire to return to Canada prompted her to reconnect with Central Bank. Initially hired as a senior analyst in January of 1998 by the Corporate Strategy unit, she had exposure to many of Central Bank's businesses and, while in that role, led a number of strategically critical and enterprise-wide projects. In 2001, Webb was seconded into Central

Bank's Small Business Division to help implement a new go-to-market strategy she had crafted. The role was made permanent, and she was appointed general manager (GM), Small Business Sales and Operations in early 2002. In January of 2004, Webb applied for and secured her current role in the Marketing Division (see attached resume, Exhibit 4, for greater detail).

People were eager to work for Webb because of the emphasis she put on personal development. Many of her "graduates" had gone on to bigger and better roles because of the challenges/exposure she provided and her willingness to hire on potential and coach/mentor for missing skills.

Webb was currently viewed as one of Central Bank's highest potential level 10s. She sustained high performance ratings over the last six years and had been the recipient of numerous internal awards based on her superior contributions to the organization. While this new position would constitute Webb's first front-line role, this experience would fill an important development gap for her.

At her most recent performance review, Webb requested just such an opportunity to round out her experience and wondered aloud how many

**Exhibit 4**   Resumé: Charlotte M. Webb

Charlotte M. Webb
177 Roxborough Drive, Toronto, Ontario M8T 2C7
Phone: 416–376–8827
E-mail: charlotte.webb@cibc.ca

**Career Summary**

Seasoned author and executor of far reaching corporate strategies that deliver tangible business results.
Demonstrated thought, people and values leadership capabilities. Award winning corporate and community citizen.

**Education**

1994   Masters in Economics, London School of Economics, London, England
1991   Bachelor of Science, Applied Mathematics & Statistics, University of Waterloo (Ontario Scholar—full
       scholarship to university)

**Professional Experience**

**Central Bank: 1998—Present**

**February 2003—Present**
**Senior Director, Customer Experience & Communication,**
**Marketing Division**

- Led initiative to transform customer experience at Central Bank in all delivery channels. Worked across
  SBU lines to engage all relevant participants in cultural and operational changes required to position
  Central Bank as the premiere Canadian Bank.
- Diagnosed root causes of customer dissatisfaction and defection; segmented issues into employee and
  operations related challenges and recommended solutions. Received approval for 80% of suggestions,
  achieving buy-in from all business units and infrastructure groups. (Cost reduction delaying
  implementation of remaining 20%).
- Developed innovative training programs for front line staff that minimized time away from customers,
  provided a standard Central Bank customer interface across Central Bank, improving both customer and
  employee satisfaction ratings.
- Worked with product groups and front line management to reduce product "fatigue"; reduced number
  and complexity of products available, producing just-in-time interactive training modules that
  significantly increased sales volumes.
- With process re-engineering specialists, explored solutions to common customer irritants related to
  lengthy or unreliable processes/procedures; liaised with Technology & Operations Division to resolve
  existing challenges and gain support for new initiatives.

**August 2000—January 2003**
**General Manager, Small Business Sales & Operations**

- Led Small Business executives through design of new go-to-market strategy for segment; assessed
  lifetime value of small business client by conducting statistical and segmentation analysis; analyzed
  competitive environment and best practices.

- Provided strategic options and led deliberations to validate and choose optimal direction; worked with VP, Strategic Initiatives to translate strategy into operational plan for deployment across Canada.
- Implemented new sales and resourcing model for segment which included new client team configuration, revised roles and accountabilities and new sales discipline. Provided tools to assess sales versus service capabilities and introduced new compensation plan to incent sales force.
- Worked with central operations group to achieve better efficiencies and improve client service; liaised with Branch Banking group to facilitate improved in-branch service of Small Business clients and to increase cross selling opportunities.
- Achieved: 24% revenue growth, versus corporate target of 12%; ten point increase in client satisfaction ratings, grew market share by 5%.

**May 1998—August 2000**
**Senior Analyst, Corporate Strategy, Office of the Chairman**

Responsibilities included leading projects, analyzing/developing new business opportunities; providing analytical support for key business decisions.

Projects included:

- Customer Strategy Project for Business Segment: Led customer preference/conjoint statistical analysis, resulting in the divesture of unprofitable unit and increased investment in profitable business.
- Growth Strategy for E-Business venture: Worked with McKinsey to explore feasibility of moving successful banking venture into US and European markets. Helped develop detailed go forward plan, emphasizing regulatory challenges and recommending alliance partners.

**August 1994—November 1997**
**The World Bank, Washington, D.C.; Geneva**

- Supporting teams comprised of World Bank, Eastern European Development Commission and the United Nations in the financial restructuring of the Balkan States.
- Conducted preliminary needs assessment for economic reconstruction of the Ukraine. Supported commission examining banking needs/functions in various developing countries.

**Scholarships and Awards**

| | |
|---|---|
| 1999 | Present: Rated "exceeds expectation" on all performance evaluations |
| 2004, 2002, 2001 | Quarterly Achiever Award Recipient |
| 1991 | Big Sister of the Year Award |
| 1992 | Young Woman of Distinction, Toronto YWCA |
| 1987 | Ontario Scholar |
| 1987 | University of Waterloo Entrance Scholarship |

**Affiliations:**

- United Way Coordinator and Spokesperson
- Run for the Cure Campaign Manager for GTA
- Board of Directors, Centre for Family Literacy
- Chair of Fund Raising, Bayview Centre for Abused Women

more years she was destined to spend at the same level. She also voiced disappointment that Central Bank had gone outside the organization repeatedly for VP hires, overlooking talented insiders. Retaining Webb was a priority for Central Bank.

### Education

Havergal alumni. Has undergraduate degree in Mathematics and Statistics from the University of Waterloo. Graduate of the London School of Economics.

### Strengths Relative to This Role

- Highly intelligent, superior analytic and strategic skills
- Very eager to learn, had taken every opportunity to acquire new skills/perspectives
- Big-picture thinker, had long-term perspective
- Very high energy level, expected a lot of herself and others
- Positive, can-do attitude, engaging, gots things done
- Quick study, had grasped complex and diverse business equations with relative ease
- Superior knowledge of financial needs and delivery preferences of this segment's customers (currently leading initiative to enhance the quality of customer experience in all delivery channels)
- Had successfully developed strategies, objectives and sales programs for several business segments, key contributor to the sales measurement and tracking systems currently in use
- Had operationalized and executed a sales program for Small Business that resulted in aggressive growth, successfully led a roll-out of sales process across Canada
- Respected and well liked by her team, Employee Commitment Index (ECI) scores among highest in Bank
- Very principled, good examples of doing the right, rather than the expedient, thing

- Good influencing skills, successfully delivered initiatives across SBU lines despite competing agendas

### For Consideration

- Minimal front-line interaction, had "knowing" rather than "doing" perspective of sales
- Had hired several professional staff, but never exited anyone
- While her roles had clearly influenced the direction of the business, most of her interactions had been with Head Office types
- Had led "thought" turnaround, rather than "people/business" turnaround
- Could personalize issues, on occasion, cared too much and got emotional
- Thinks very quickly, question whether she could bring others (slower staff) along
- Suspect she will always do "the right thing" but occasionally came across a bit pedantic/righteous
- Once raised concerns over supervisor's seemingly improper use of his expense account, matter later resolved as a "misunderstanding"

### Of Interest

- This candidate had been very active in both Central Bank's Run for the Cure and United Way efforts. Several years ago, Webb was named "Young Woman of Distinction" by the Toronto YWCA for her work with the Big Sisters' group. Albeit junior, she was a popular member of Central Bank's informal women's network
- Webb is the niece of a Central Bank Board member. The Director commented on "Webb's great interest in this role" when he bumped into the hiring manager at a recent social gathering

Webb was five months pregnant, and it was not clear how long a maternity leave she would require.

## 2. Candidate: Scott Warren

**Current Position:** VP, Retail Bank, Toronto West & Hamilton, Regional Bank

**Status:** Interviewed by executive search firm and VP, Executive Resources, Central Bank

### Background

Warren originally planned to pursue a career in the foreign service or international law but a stint with Nesbitt Burns (between his undergraduate and law degrees) sharpened his interest in financial services. Recruited to McKinsey's Montreal office after articling with a prominent Ottawa law firm. Recruited by Regional Bank (former client) two years later to work on a high-profile new venture in Australia; Warren returned to Toronto after the venture was terminated and was put on an accelerated management program. Served 12-month stints in both Audit and Risk and was then selected from bank's high-potential pool to work as executive assistant to Regional Bank's chairman. Warren moved out of the chairman's office into his first executive posting and his first line role. He had been in this post, the smallest territory nationally, since December 2001 (see Exhibit 5).

Warren was chaffing against Regional Bank's long-term and disciplined approach to development and felt that he should have been moved to a bigger, more complex mandate or promoted to senior vice-president (SVP). He believed that he could move up the ladder more quickly here, given (in his view) Central Bank's penchant for hiring externally and promoting on perceived potential rather than experience. Warren was told by Regional Bank in March that a move was imminent but this promise seemed to have been lost in the noise around the massive restructuring of Regional Bank's senior ranks. Most troubling was the fact that Warren's sponsor had been exited.

| **Exhibit 5** | Resumé: T. Scott Warren |
|---|---|

T. Scott Warren
28 Bayview Crescent, Oakville, ON M3P 1B9
Telephone: 905-846-3321 (Home);
416-307-2215 (Business); 416-537-9856 (Cell)
Confidential e-mail address: melissaandscott@rogers.com

**Profile**

A seasoned financial services professional with broad managerial experience. Motivated by challenging environment, aggressive goals, teamwork and the opportunity to make a tangible contribution to an organization's performance.

**Professional Experience**

**Royal Bank of Canada**
**December 2002—Present**
**Regional Vice President, Toronto West & Hamilton**

Led all aspects of Regional Bank's retail business in Toronto West & Hamilton area; executed dramatic turn around of region (last to first place) within first 18 months. Sales volumes increased by 60%; significantly exceeding profitability and cost management targets. Steps to achievements:

*(Continued)*

**Exhibit 5** (Continued)

- Assessed existing branch location and resource deployment; closed branches in four unprofitable locations, piloted two new state of the art branches with enhanced physical design and front-end technology.
- Significantly upgraded Regional talent pool, exiting 35% and redeploying 15% of workforce; designed and implemented comprehensive assessment process (now adopted by Regional Bank overall) for sales ability; seeded region with top talent identified in recruitment blitz.
- Used available Customer Relationship Management (CRM) tools and Risk Management expertise to mine more affluent pockets in region, greatly increasing the number in profitable customers and reducing credit losses.
- Helped design and pilot training program for front line staff; content included advanced use of CRM tools, prospecting techniques and selling "the Regional Bank way."
- Re-segmented customer population along "share of wallet" and potential to cross-sell lines; focused efforts on high yield sales activities resulting in increased sales volume of most profitable products.
- Negotiated successful referral program with Regional Bank colleagues to grow customer base.
- Led measure and manage project for Regional Bank Branch Banking, redesigning sales metrics and rewards.

**October 2001—October 2002**
**Acting Vice President, Office of the President & CEO**

- Chosen from the high potential pool for assignment. Responsible for ensuring the smooth operation of the President & CEO's business day by anticipating needs, organizing events, undertaking strategic analysis and preparing presentations. Work with departments throughout the organization to deliver pertinent and timely information to the President and CEO's office.
- Operate as a conduit for information from the bank's various divisions to the President & CEO's office.

**June 2000—October 2001**
**Accelerated Management Program, Toronto, Canada**

- Audit Division: Participated in audits of Wealth Management and Retail Banking units in Canada, West Indies and Guernsey. Co-led project to define new Audit philosophy for Regional Bank and to enhance the effectiveness of the function.
- Risk Management: Assigned to Credit Adjudication for Commercial Bank Group; participated in initiative to re-engineer end-to-end credit processes relating to Commercial and Corporate Banking.

**February 1998—March 2000**
**Executive Director, Regional Bank, Australia**

- Crafted strategy, provided legal expertise for Regional Bank entry into Australian corporate finance market; led integration efforts with newly acquired firm.
- Originated, negotiated and executed senior debt, mezzanine and equity financings for acquisitions, leveraged buy-outs, and other structured corporate finance transactions.
- Developed valuation models and negotiated to sell Regional Bank's corporate finance business in Australia.

**January 1996—February 1998**
**Management Consultant, McKinsey & Co., Montreal, Canada**

- Created customer profitability strategy for Travel and Hospitality client. Helped reposition brand, did service profit chain analysis and recommended product and service innovations which resulted in brand turnaround.
- Helped Canadian Oil & Gas company launch new venture for European exploration and production, significantly broadening their operating base and increasing profitability.
- Performed business unit, product/channel and customer profitability studies for retail wealth management business unit, resulting in product bundling and pricing policy changes.
- Developed acquisition and integration strategy for Corporate banking arm of leading Canadian bank. Developed detailed integration plan and managed "first 100 days" project teams, including contractual negotiations, regulatory requirements and infrastructure build.

**May 1994—May 1995**
**Articling Student, Wise, Strong & Kessler, Barristers and Solicitors,**
**Ottawa, Ontario**

- Provided corporate, commercial, securities, tax, insolvency, and litigation legal services.

**Education**

1994   LLB (Bachelor of Laws), Osgoode Hall Law School, York University
1991   BA (with Honors), Government, Harvard University

**Achievements and Interests**

Fluent in French
Currently working on MBA (Richard Ivey School of Business, The University of Western Ontario)
Qualified for and completed the Boston and NYC marathons in 2003 and 2004
Competitive skier—competed with Team Canada in 1994 Winter Games
Member of the National Club (nominated to run in Presidential election 2005)

*Education*

Toronto French School Alumni; BA, Government, Harvard; LLB, Osgoode Hall Law School, York University

*Strengths Relative to This Role*

- Extremely bright, versatile player; voracious learner
- Driven, results oriented, huge capacity for work

- Executed turnaround of small, but lucrative territory, moved area from last to first place in 18 months
- Exited 35 percent of sales staff and redeployed additional 15 percent more
- Designed hiring profile/recruitment process for sales staff now adopted by the rest of the bank
- Increased sales volumes by 60 percent for the last two years, significantly exceeding profitability and cost management targets

- Worked closely with customer relationship management (CRM) area and Risk Management to hone prospecting skills and reduce losses
- Contributed to and piloted new sales training program for Regional Bank, led national initiative to "measure and manage" more effectively
- Key contributor to bank initiatives within his division and across the bank
- Moved to west end of the city to better participate in community activities

*For Consideration*

- Hinted of intellectual arrogance, a bit condescending around Regional Bank's "superiority"
- Difficult to get handle on what Warren personally accomplished in Australia; became vague when pressed for details, alluded to Regional Bank strategic gaffe
- Believe Warren cares about people but suspect he doesn't always show it
- Intense, could be overpowering for more reticent team members
- May not always give credit to others; seemed to be a one-man show on occasion
- Activity level on the job and elsewhere was awesome, but how much is too much?
- Enthusiasm engaging but candidate interrupted, wanted to speak rather than listen

Warren's tenure in any position had not exceeded two years—not sure how much success candidate can claim for projects initiated before his arrival or executed after his departure.

*Of Interest*

- Warren was working on his MBA (Richard Ivey School of Business, University of Western Ontario) and was actively campaigning to be the next and youngest president of the National Club, which he hoped to revitalize. He was also an avid runner (finishing both the Boston and

New York marathons in the middle of the pack) and longtime skier (visited his family's chalet at Mount Tremblant in Quebec as often as possible).

A preliminary and very discreet reference was obtained from a former peer (now a SVP at Central Bank) of Warren's at Regional Bank. The individual confirmed Warren's long-term potential, superior results and high-potential status at Regional Bank but described him as "overly ambitious" and "political."

## 3. Candidate: James (Jim) Skinner

**Current Position:** District Vice-President, First Northern Bank

**Status:** Interviewed by executive search firm and VP, Executive Resources, Central Bank

*Background*

Skinner grew up in Toronto's East end where his father owned a printing business. He ran the office for his father for two years after his graduation from Ryerson University. At the suggestion of the manager, Skinner joined the local First Northern Bank branch where his family banked. He progressed through the ranks to Bank Manager (including a two-year stint in the West Indies) and was moved through increasingly senior roles in Human Resources, Commercial Bank and Risk Management, returning to retail banking as a District Vice-President in 2000 (see attached resume, Exhibit 6, for more detail).

Beginning in 1996, First Northern Bank agreed to sponsor Skinner's executive MBA (EMBA) program in recognition of his strong leadership capabilities and to supplement his rather weak academic background.

Skinner was in the process of moving to Calgary to a larger and more senior District VP role (with a promise to re-evaluate the role for possible upgrading to SVP) when his wife became seriously ill. Skinner elected to remain in Toronto where family support and better treatment is available to his wife. His old role was backfilled quickly with a rising

| **Exhibit 6** | Resumé: James (Jim) Skinner |
|---|---|

James (Jim) Skinner
11 Moorecroft Road, Ajax, Ont. M4N 2S5
Home: 905–777–0456; Business: 416–437–8813
E-mail: jamess@rogers.ca

**Professional Experience**

**Bank of First Northern**
**1979 to present**
**February 2004—Present**

On interim assignment with EVP, Retail Branch Banking.
Projects include:

- Initiative examining correlation between employee and customer satisfaction.
- Macro planning for replacement of segment's aging executive population.
- Roll out of new technology/CRM tools to branch network.

**March 2000—December 2003**
**District Vice President, Toronto East**

- Assumed responsibility for troubled Toronto East Region during restructuring of GTA regional territories. Merged two smaller districts into largest mandate in Ontario, reduced FTE and rolled out new sales process concurrently.
- Formed Employee Association to ensure employee voice heard during major transition, to augment communication strategy and garner input/insight into regional dynamics and build marketing strategies.
- Assessed staff for sales versus servicing skills, finding jobs for all employees displaced in process; introduced disciplined sales process to Region, traveling to all branches at least bi-monthly to personally coach branch managers and communicate expectations to all levels.
- Initiated annual "Customer First Award" for District employee who best exemplifies customer service and monthly award (extra vacation days or gift certificates) for "Best Assist" given for teamwork resulting in new or expanded business.
- Built strong alliances with segment peers to increase business flow and provide broader market and community coverage.
- Recognized as most improved district in 2001. Received Best District Award (Ontario) 2003 and 2004 for highest sales volumes, top quartile Employee Commitment and lowest NIX ratio.

**October 1998—March 2000**
**General Manager, Credit, Ontario Region**

- Co-led initiative to re-engineer credit approving/adjudication and compliance reporting process for Small Business and Agriculture portfolios.

*(Continued)*

| **Exhibit 6** | (Continued) |
| --- | --- |

- Engaged line staff in streamlining front end credit approval processes, using behavioral scoring and technology assisted decisioning tools.
- Introduced base line accreditation requirements for Risk Managers and credit training for all front line originators.
- Dramatically reduced credit losses and significantly improved credit approval time.

**August 1996—October 1998**
**General Manager, Small Business Banking, Central Toronto**

- Implemented Small Business strategy in Central Toronto, the largest market in Canada; led the change management effort to reposition the Small Business offer, adding wealth management products to traditional credit focus.
- Chaired the GTA Risk Committee, significantly improving the region's risk profile through the development and implementation of sound risk and governance practices and policies.
- Achieved highest improvement award in Employee Index in 1997.
- Publicly recognized for strong contribution to operations and infrastructure groups.
- Partnered with external groups to develop added value programs for Small Business clients.
- Delivered on cost containment and client retention targets, exceeding sales targets by 31%.

**June 1995—August 1996**
**General Manager, Service Effectiveness,**
**Western Canada, Calgary**

Seconded to Regional Head Office to deploy successful sales & services strategies developed for Main Branch, Calgary across the Western Division.

- Developed and implemented a business retention and development plan for the Division;
- Expanded the Regional Call Centre's mandate to augment customer support;
- Aligned service response to segments, providing differentiated service to high value customers;
- Developed and implemented Local Market Management in the Division;
- Met retention objectives and exceeded sales targets by 120MM by year end.

**August 1992—May 1995**
**Director, Retail and Private Banking Services,**
**Main Branch, Calgary**

Responsible for managing Retail and Private Banking, Main Branch, Calgary

- Designed and launched a customer-centric sales and service model; differentiated high net worth customer experience from standard service.
- Restructured Main Branch to better implement new customer strategy, make productivity gains and increase profitability.
- Increased individual sales capacity by 95%, increased branch customer satisfaction ratings (in top 10 branches nationally). Won national Customer Service Excellence Award.

**June 1990—July 1992**
**Human Resources Officer,**
**Head Office, Toronto**

Seconded to Human Resources to help implement a major restructuring of Retail Banking; provided field perspective for organization design, training and recruitment specialists:

- Conducted span of control and capacity planning for realigned districts;
- Helped design and facilitate new training and orientation programs;
- Revamped roles and responsibilities for newly crafted line positions;
- Established selection criteria for senior District leaders and conducted first line interviews.

**1985—1990**
**Branch Manager**

- Managed increasingly larger and more complex branches in Ontario, Western Canada and Atlantic Canada. Key achievements: (1) The effective leadership and development of staff; (2) Continually exceeding sales and profitability goals.

**1979—1985**

- Progressed through a number of line roles to Branch Manager

**Education**

1996   EMBA, University of Toronto
1991   Fellow, Institute of Canadian Bankers
1981   Canadian Securities Course
1975   Business Administration Diploma, Ryerson

**Affiliations**

Director, Canadian Parkinson Society
Treasurer, Pickering Lions Club
Trustee, Separate School Board, Durham Region
Coach, Boys Intermediate Soccer

star, and Skinner has spent the last 10 months without portfolio, working on special assignments and getting progressively frustrated. He was open to talking to headhunters for the first time in his career.

### Education

High School; Business Administration Diploma, Ryerson University; Fellow, Institute of Canadian Bankers; Canadian Securities Course; EMBA, University of Toronto.

### Strengths Relative to This Role

- People management/motivation was a key strength
- Able to build trust, trusted advisor to senior management and staff alike

- Clearly saw the correlation between employee satisfaction and customer satisfaction
- Track record for turning around under-performing units Grounded in First Northern Bank way: doing more with less, employees for life, if humanly possible
- Didn't shoot from the hip, down to earth, honest and open
- Achieved results through people and teamwork
- Results focused, takes time to understand the variables
- Strong on process, cutting time and money where possible
- Mature, strong communicator

### For Consideration

- While capable of meeting immediate business and "values" needs, Skinner may be a less viable succession candidate
- Not clear if Skinner could take necessary tough stand without usual First Northern Bank safety net for employees
- Whether Skinner was committed to leaving First Northern Bank was unclear; Skinner's ability to adjust to/change Central Bank's culture was also questionable
- Significant front-line experience, but candidate lacked analytical/strategic depth

### Of Interest

- Skinner, a First Northern Bank lifer, was reluctant to leave but felt he needed to find a "real job" soon. He was concerned about the adverse publicity Central Bank had generated over the last few years and his perception that it "chews up and spits out executives," "eating its young," to quote Skinner.
- During the interview (his first, in 26 years) Skinner confessed he was very nervous about starting over again at 50 and was worried about adjusting to a new corporate culture.
- His wife required periodic visits to the Mayo Clinic and First Northern Bank had been very supportive with time off and professional support for him and his three teenagers. He wondered if Central Bank would be as helpful and compassionate.

## CASE QUESTIONS

1. What message does it send when a company dismisses a longtime, popular employee so late in his career? What options, rather than termination, could the company have pursued?

2. Do you believe that it would be difficult to keep employees happy while at the same time doing a better job of serving clients?

3. Outline the strongest argument for hiring each of the three candidates. Outline the strongest argument for not hiring each of the three candidates.

4. Which candidate best fits with the current opening? Explain your choice.

5. When a company consistently goes outside to hire managers and does not promote from within, what message does this send to current employees?

# Boman Communications

*By Erika Lundholm, under the supervision of Professor John Haywood-Farmer*

At the end of December 2005, Klas Boman, owner and founder of Boman Communications, a Swedish marketing communications firm, sat in his Stockholm office reflecting on the 2005 business year. He was not happy. Not only had the firm been unable to attract more than one large client, but some recent events had led Boman to believe that many of his own employees did not understand the firm's business concept. Boman knew he had to tackle these pressing issues soon, but he was unsure how to do so.

## Background

Boman founded Boman Communications in the early 1980s as a privately owned market communications agency. The firm employed approximately 25 people in its two offices. Although the offices worked closely together and shared many clients, they had different areas of competence. The head office, located in Hudiksvall, a coastal town of about 15,000 some 300 kilometers north of Stockholm, focused on printed and graphical communication. The Stockholm office did Web and information technology (IT) communication. Boman Communications tried to target long-term, business-to-business marketing communications; the firm preferred to serve a small number of large clients.

Boman founded the firm with a desire to do things differently than other Swedish marketing communications companies. Because Boman had a technical background and had spent almost 10 years working in the industry prior to his own start-up, he knew the industry well. He believed that using more logical and rational techniques than the ones generally accepted in the marketing communications industry would lead to greater efficiency. Boman realized that he could not develop his ideas further without being independent; he thus decided to go his own way. As Boman put it:

I like doing business my own way. When I know I have a good idea, I want to be able to go with it. An employer would never have allowed me to go ahead with some of the wilder ideas that I have had, and BOCS[1] would certainly not have been developed. The whole concept is not in line with how marketing communications should be carried out but challenges the very foundations of marketing communications traditions. I believe that marketing communications can be done more efficiently and create greater customer value through this new approach. That's what I'm trying to do with my company.

BOCS started in the late 1980s as a primitive embryo of how to structure and organize the marketing communications service process more logically. At that time, the ideas were housed in a cardboard box. By the mid-1990s, the ideas were digitalized in a very rudimentary form. By 2005, the concept had developed into an advanced, computerized database structure, radically different from the methods usually applied by Swedish marketing communications firms. Boman foresaw significant future development of BOCS as well.

Version: (A) 2009–09–16

## The Swedish Marketing Communications Environment

Many marketing communications companies operated in the Swedish market. Although a few large companies dominated the industry, employing several hundred people each, most of the firms employed only five to 10 individuals. Some 20 percent of the firms performed 80 percent of the marketing communications services, and vice versa. Like many Swedish industries, there was a gap in marketing communications—very few middle-sized companies existed. Although it was relatively easy for Swedish entrepreneurs to start their own ventures, moving from 10 employees to 30 was difficult, and moving from 30 to 50 was nearly impossible. Very few succeeded in growing beyond 30 employees. The increase in revenues from being a middle-sized company was simply not enough to offset the increased costs of taxation and legislated safety requirements. Virtually all marketing communications firms used essentially the same methods, regardless of their size.

## The Traditional Marketing Communications Process

According to industry sources, production costs accounted for some 80 percent of the budgets of traditional marketing communications firms; creative work made up the balance. Despite dramatic advances in technology, the industry remained strongly bound by the complex mixture of competencies of its historical professions. Copywriters, art directors, scriptwriters, graphical designers, market communicators, and production leaders were all very proud and carefully protected their handicrafts. It was still not uncommon for typesetters manually to make text into pages. Many believed that the professions' strong sense of tradition prevented the industry from evolving.

Traditionally, clients approached a marketing communications agency with a specific request, for example, the production of a product leaflet. The agency then had to identify the necessary information from the client's databases. This information was often scattered in both likely and unlikely places in the client's organization. Often, no central source existed for an official up-to-date version. The effort needed to gather accurate information often left little time for creative work, including assessments of more fundamental marketing strategy questions such as, What makes customers buy products?

Marketing communications firms might become more preoccupied with collecting information than with communicating it. The frequent need to modify existing collections of brochures for recently updated product lines was usually random and uncoordinated, creating growing inconsistencies across the company. The alternative was to start the information search all over again, thus reinventing the wheel. By tradition, printed communication was still seen as being different from digital information. This restriction created a need for clients to have several marketing communications suppliers, as agencies often focused on only one type of marketing communications. Having multiple suppliers reduced the client's risk and simplified management, as each marketing communications purchase was an individual project that was relatively easy to manage and evaluate. However, the practice made it difficult to maintain a coherent image in both printed and digital communication. Exhibit 1 compares BOCS and the traditional approach.

## The Boman Communications System Approach

Boman talked very enthusiastically about the differences that BOCS brought to the marketing communications service production:

> My favorite way to illustrate BOCS is to use a numerical example. Imagine a company marketing five product lines, carrying six to eight products each, which are updated once a year. The company needs to supply its customers with relevant, up-to-date,

**Exhibit I**    A Comparison of Traditional Versus Boman Communications Approaches

### The Traditional Approach

The traditional approach is a linear process. Information is gathered, professionals get to work producing the marketing communications and the output is delivered to the client. When the client requires a new project or needs to adapt the already produced one, the process starts all over again. The wheel gets reinvented as information is not uniformly collected and stored. The process is outlined in the following diagram:

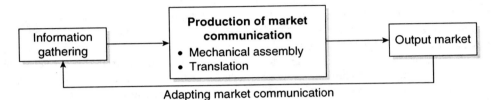

### The Boman Communications Approach

As shown in the diagram below, BOCS is based on a quite different foundation then the traditional approach. Information is gathered only once and structured into an SQL database. Once the database is created, it is used as a sole source for marketing communications. Potentially, digital as well as printed media can be assembled from the information in BOCS, which is an automated and instant process of creating updates as well as new products. As soon as a fact is changed in BOCS, all digital documents in manuals and brochures are corrected accordingly. New products are created based on information that is updated and available in the BOCS structure. Thus, the wheel gets invented only once.

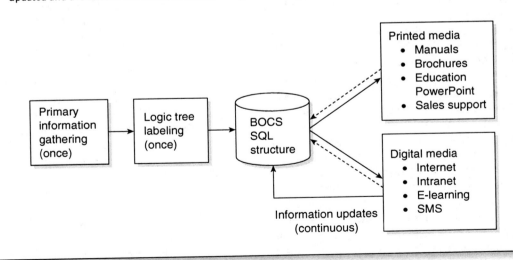

four-page-information brochures and 50-page manuals for each product. Because the products are internationally marketed, the marketing communications have to be translated into six languages. This is a complex situation. That is 420 different print works, or 11,340 pages, that have to be produced. Annually. It does not take a rocket scientist to figure out that the average production cost per page does not need to be very high for the bottom line to add up to a considerable number. And, if the company at some point should want to correct an error or change a logotype, product specification or phone number, change is extensive, since each marketing communications item has to be altered individually. These are exactly the kinds of problems that BOCS is designed to deal with. It eliminates them altogether and provides a manageable and controlled situation.

Creating a full-scale BOCS was a wide-ranging, four-stage procedure spanning the client's complete marketing communications. In the first stage, information was sorted and checked for relevance, contradictions and outdated material. At Stage 2, the crucial procedure of deciding a logic tree began. All information was structured into generic categories wide enough to include enough information, but narrow enough to be useful. At this stage, it was important to identify correctly the least common denominators and the most useful categories. In the third step, the pieces of information were labelled and entered into an SQL server database. The data formed the content of the database. Although the sorting process was time-consuming and had to be accurate, it had to be done only once. The logic tree, containing all the logical information connections between categories of related information, lay at the heart of BOCS and was derived from the information in the database. The logic tree gave structure to the information. The fourth stage was database maintenance, during which (preferably) the client updated the information as the situation changed. Content or structure could be exchanged independently of each other in real time, throughout the system. The BOCS engine provided automated, instant and complete dispersal of any type of information. Although information was stored in only one place, the logic tree connected the complete system. Boman described BOCS as the information equivalent of the network organization where information about the whole is stored in each part.

To make the system manageable, only certain key users—the Boman Communications client project managers and some carefully selected and trusted representatives from the client company[2]—could change documents. Connections between digital documents and the database were mutual. Whenever the information in a document was changed, the database source was changed accordingly and vice versa. The database could provide the client with a single complete source of marketing communications. Exhibit 2 gives some additional information on BOCS.

Boman recalled the development of the project for HIAB,[3] Boman Communications' biggest client:

> We began the HIAB BOCS project about three years ago in combination with some traditional market consulting. It was a very arduous and time consuming effort going through the available information, as it was in great disorder. Also, this was the first large-scale BOCS that we ever created, so we did not really know what we were doing at first. We had to learn through some mistakes, but eventually we were able to sort the information and reconstruct it according to BOCS criteria.
>
> The main development of BOCS for HIAB took place during 2004. During that year, one of our employees worked full time on the development, and an additional four people worked part time. We billed HIAB €105,000[4] for this work. In addition, we

**Exhibit 2**    The Boman Communications Approach—Inside the Heart of BOCS

The figure below[1] shows the logical structure at the heart of BOCS, with specific reference to the database for HIAB. Every media type carries a form of template. At the click of a button, relevant parts of the present information structure are realized, according to the specific template. The connections between the digital documents and the database are mutual. Whenever the information in a document is altered, the database gets altered accordingly and vice versa. When a new product is introduced, it is linked to the system and interconnected with already available and relevant information for that specific product, thus ensuring coherence and efficient use of available information.

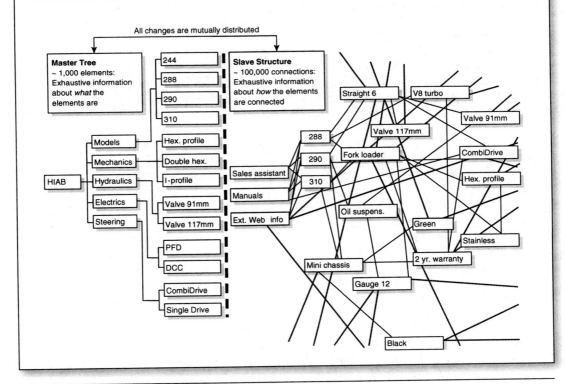

*Source:* Company files.

1. This diagram shows only a small fraction of the elements. On the right-hand side of the diagram, the solid lines show connections within the set of elements shown. Dotted lines show connections to other elements not shown in the diagram.

billed HIAB €385,000 for the production of printed matter (6,021 pages), €9,000 for the preparation of training material (115 pages) and €180,000 for photography sessions in five foreign countries. The pictures were taken as a necessary step in the process of making HIAB's market communication better. There were no good pictures before these were taken. The cost should be shared between development and operating expenses, perhaps half each. We also prepared a small amount of Web material, but we didn't charge for that. I estimate that we would have billed HIAB €1.45 million for the 6,021 pages of printed matter, €63,000 for the 115 pages of training material and €11,000 for preparing Web material had we prepared them using the traditional method.

The development figure is very low. We were lucky there. Only one person in HIAB made the decision, and he took part in the creation of BOCS. He took quite a risk. Because of his production background and knowledge of HIAB's products, he could become the sole source of information that went into BOCS. Had he done things the "proper" way, many more people would have been involved at HIAB and the process would have taken a lot longer. From our perspective, this setup cost might have been a bit on the low side, but HIAB was able to profit much more when the system was up and running.

In early 2005, things became a lot easier, as BOCS got up and running on a larger scale. It is now the single information source for all of HIAB's printed marketing communications. Before BOCS, HIAB produced 340 print works over three to five years. Now, during the short time it has been in operation, BOCS has helped generate 839 print works and 365 updates! A ketchup effect[5] has been visible, and coherence in the marketing communications has improved tremendously. We billed them about €33,000 per month through 2005. Before, the same crane could be described differently in different brochures, stressing different selling points and benefits of the same product, creating confusion. Today, BOCS emphasizes the same set of benefits per model. BOCS data are being used as a control measure. The HIAB experience has shown us not only the benefits of having BOCS for printed material, but as it now carries all necessary information, it can be used as a source for other digital types of marketing communications as well. We are currently designing an e-learning feature for HIAB's sales representatives across the world and are discussing producing Web sites, internal as well as external ones. Essentially, we have access to all the information we need. HIAB only has to give us the signal and we'll get going.

## The Current Situation

As Boman looked back on 2005, he became increasingly discouraged. Although, in some respects, it had been a very successful year, he felt very uneasy. He was certain he had a very good business idea, but so far, the market had largely failed to realize its potential. Having a successful BOCS year with one client was not sufficient in the long run. More business would be needed in the future to sustain profitability and the growth necessary to stay competitive. But how was the firm supposed to achieve this? Boman could not do it alone. He needed help from competent employees who knew BOCS and could help him communicate and sell its benefit to the market. He knew that two of the staff who had worked on this year's successful project understood BOCS thoroughly. However, they would not be able to do everything. More people would have to step in, and soon. Boman had no idea who that would be. At this point, things did not add up. He knew that he would have to do something as soon as possible.

## Client Issues

The launch of BOCS with HIAB in early 2005 marked the first large-scale use of the technology. Although, thus far, HIAB had used BOCS only for printed material, Boman Communications was already realizing BOCS's potential. Now that all necessary information was gathered in one place, it could easily be put into other marketing communications channels. HIAB had already approved a minor e-learning model for its sales representatives across the world. However, at this point, other uses of BOCS were stalled by corporate bureaucracy, and it was uncertain how long it would take for HIAB to work this through. Boman explained:

HIAB knows that we have saved them a lot of money by using BOCS. The problem is that we mainly work directly with the Hudiksvall office and not the corporate head office in Helsinki. In Helsinki, some of the people in charge are still a bit hesitant to trust us further.

Although HIAB is a big account, it is not big enough by itself to ensure that we will remain competitive, or even profitable. I think I have to attract at least one more client of HIAB's size somehow, both for financial reasons as well as to reduce our risk. On a strategic level, we are slowly increasing our focus on BOCS. I want to take this even further, making us a totally BOCS company. However, we keep getting distracted from this goal by having to find other short-term projects to generate sufficient cash flows. I have made a serious effort to get another large BOCS client, but my experiences have been very disappointing. I'll come to meetings with potential clients feeling very excited about sharing the benefits they can reap by letting us create a BOCS for them. I have really tried to explain the specifics and thoughts behind BOCS to illustrate what kind of benefits this new and untraditional approach to marketing communications can give them. But thus far, they have not been impressed enough to hire us. I realize that many simply don't understand BOCS when I explain it to them, but even those who do understand at least parts of it still seem very hesitant.

I am totally committed to BOCS. One of its attractive features is that its highly digitalized features allow for less geographical dependency. Once a BOCS is set up for a client, anyone with access, anywhere, can modify the system. If HIAB sales representatives in India, for example, found an error in a product specification, they could simply change the digital version themselves, provided they had database access, or, if they did not, they could notify someone who did. As soon as the digital document is changed, the entire HIAB corporation would have access to the new, and now correct, information, thanks to BOCS.

What I like most about BOCS is that once the structure has been created for a client, we can shift our focus from collecting to communicating information. Clients are buying our competence in communicating, so communication and design efforts should account for most of a project's billed hours. BOCS is an attempt to break time-worn industry practices. It is about time people started thinking of marketing communications as an industrial process and trying to rationalize and optimize the information flow. I think of the work we do as offering clients lean communications. Because we eliminate slack, we can focus on the essence of the service we provide—communicating effectively rather than collecting information. BOCS is not a pre-made product that a client can purchase and implement, but rather a structure that needs support from a way of thinking in terms of information flows. The increased customer value that we create comes when BOCS is up and running and automatically transforming inputs into efficient and scalable marketing communications. Before this can happen, though, a considerable investment in time and money is required.

BOCS's advantages are obvious and undeniable. It is very flexible, as the system is highly scalable. The information used for printed marketing communications can, in essence, be used for other digital types of marketing communications, such as Webpages, e-learning and sales support. BOCS has enabled us to help our clients establish coherence in their marketing communications. All design templates as well as content are centralized in the interconnected BOCS logic structure. Therefore, BOCS will never create any marketing communications that don't fit the approved graphical design and structure. If that does not create customer value, I do not know what does.

I know my ideas are groundbreaking and that some people will search for downsides and difficulties associated with the BOCS approach, in part because they don't fully grasp the idea. Some potential clients have told me that they don't want to rely on a sole supplier for their marketing communications purchases. Because BOCS is a heavy investment that depends on clients sharing all available information relevant to marketing communications, there are risks. Normally, having several suppliers of different kinds of marketing communications allows clients to protect information more easily, as it is never concentrated in the hands of one supplier. It's a risk for us too. What if the relationship didn't work? Once clients choose to go along with us and create a BOCS, it is not easy to get out of it. Also, cash flow might be a problem. It takes quite a while to set up BOCS and begin to see the benefits.

One problem many potential clients have with BOCS is that it requires a long-term commitment. A BOCS is not instantly created and in operation. Further, before any benefits can be seen, serious amounts of time and money have to be invested. Before that can realistically happen, I realize that we have to prove ourselves to potential clients. But, how can we do that, and build a business relationship to generate trust, without an opportunity to do so?

We are a relatively small firm without a substantial, proven track record among large potential clients. I know that, at present, because of BOCS, no other firm in Sweden can offer marketing communications production benefits to clients like we can. I was recently reading in an industry magazine about technology development in the marketing communications industry. The article said that despite recent technology shifts, obtaining all information needed for all types of marketing communications from one single source and by a click of a button is still a utopia. But that is basically what we have with BOCS! Clearly we have a head start over other Swedish companies.

One of my main concerns is that our current lead will not last forever. Other, and larger, firms will eventually catch up. We have to act soon to capitalize on what seems to be an arbitrage opportunity. The first-mover advantage will not be enough. As larger and more capital- and labor-intensive firms adopt more efficient marketing communications approaches, we will find it increasingly difficult to compete. Before then, we have to find a way to grow sufficiently, both in revenues and in competent labor.

## Personnel Competence Issues

During the autumn of 2005, Boman decided that it was time to educate his personnel more formally on the BOCS concept. This move was very important, as, except for two people who were actively working on the HIAB project, very few others had had anything to do with BOCS on a daily basis.

The two Boman Communications offices were very different in character. The Hudiksvall office experienced a high level of staff consistency and stability. In contrast, the Stockholm office experienced high personnel turnover; in 2005, six new people started and eight left the firm. It had proven to be difficult to find the right people for the Stockholm office and to ensure that they understand BOCS. Boman thought that some type of formal training would be a step toward increasing employee competence and BOCS understanding. Boman explained what happened:

I wanted us to have a BOCS education day for the entire company, both offices together at the same time. Not only would this present a good opportunity for everyone to learn about BOCS, but it would also be a nice office get-together and a social event. We all work for the same company and share the same goals, but so many new people have come to the Stockholm office this year, and I thought it was a good idea for both offices to get together. I let the guys that are working on the HIAB project put together a presentation, since they are the ones who truly know what BOCS is all about.

The day seemed to be very successful. The employees were all very positive about this opportunity to find out about BOCS and ask questions about it. They also appreciated the social event of an inter-office get-together. We encouraged employees to ask any questions they had about BOCS at the question-and-answer session near the end of the day. Only a few asked questions. I assumed that the presentation's message had been clear and comprehensible to all.

A while later, I asked one of our systems developers to draft a BOCS client proposal[6] for an upcoming meeting. I was going to go, and I wanted the systems developer drafting the proposal to come with me. I knew that I needed to introduce more personnel in the sales of BOCS. I, myself, was not enough and some others were busy with the HIAB project. I felt that the systems developer was smart, and I wanted to give him a chance to step up to his full potential. But when I received the draft a couple of days before the meeting, I was speechless. He clearly had not understood a single thing about BOCS from our company training day. Besides obvious errors in terms of database structure, the possible benefits of working with us and with BOCS were nowhere to be found. The draft showed a service concept that was impossible to sell! Obviously, I did not take the systems developer or the draft to the meeting.

This incident got me worried. If the BOCS concept was so difficult for our employees to understand, how would they ever be able to sell it? Although I knew that it was an untraditional approach that most other marketing communications firms would consider nonsense, I felt differently and hoped that our employees felt the same way. At this point I really began to wonder if my ideas on marketing communications approaches and BOCS are simply too different and untraditional for most people to comprehend.

There have been some other incidents too that have made me worry about the competence of our staff. One graphical designer and three systems developers worked together to create the e-learning model for HIAB. As is usual in such projects, the project manager, Hans, described the features in a specification, and then the systems developers and the graphical designer got to work. When the group presented the first version, Hans was thunderstruck. He came directly to me. He said he had never seen anything like it. It was as if they had purposely ignored the specification that Hans gave them and decided to do something on their own. Now, I am all for initiative as long as you know what you are doing, but these people didn't. After working on this first draft for two weeks, they had to start over again. What they had created was useless in every sense and certainly not in line with BOCS principles. We can't afford to lose two weeks' worth of work because people don't know what they are doing. We need and depend on professionals to do what they are hired for.

Work that should have taken two weeks to complete took two months instead. Their second draft was almost as bad as the first. In the end, Hans had to closely monitor every step the designer and system developers took in order to get a model that was compatible with the BOCS structure. We wasted valuable time because four people were unable or unwilling to understand BOCS. After this incident, two of the developers resigned. I believed I had no choice but to lay off the designer.

Because Boman Communications is still a fairly small company, each employee is a very large part of the whole. If someone is not pulling their weight or messes up, the entire company is endangered. I do feel that it was right for those three people to leave Boman Communications, as they were simply not competent enough to contribute. I am now, however, faced with the difficult situation of having to find new people. Two out of those who recently left Boman Communications joined about a year ago, and it was my mistake for hiring them. Now I have to make sure that I do not repeat that mistake, and I have to find people who not only understand but feel compassionate about BOCS.

## A Decision to Make

Boman definitely sensed that he was facing a very difficult situation, internally as well as externally. He had to decide how to manage his service concept on two equally important levels simultaneously. Solving one of the issues simply was not enough; measures were required on both fronts. Boman had to figure out how to come to terms with these issues. He wondered what options he had.

---

**CASE QUESTIONS**

1. Which management style would best serve the needs of the Boman Communications company? Why would it work best?

2. To build a customer-oriented marketing department, what types of selection criteria should be used in the future? Is it possible that the company should hire a totally different type of person from one seeking work in a traditional marketing communications company? If so, what characteristics best fit with Boman Communication's approach?

3. How could goal setting, motivation systems, and reward programs be established to make sure employees both understand the Boman system and effectively convey its advantages to prospective clients?

4. Boman Communications does not deliver a traditional marketing communications program. How could Klas Boman turn this difference into an advantage when hiring, training, and rewarding employees?

5. What tactics could Klas Boman use to empower and engage employees in ways that might lead to attracting new client customers? How might role modeling and coaching assist in this process?

# CHAPTER 5

# Customer Acquisition Strategies and Tactics

anaging customer acquisition consists of a variety of interrelated tasks and activities. Among the more important are pricing programs, advertising, alternative and direct marketing systems, sales promotions, and personal selling methods. Based on the solid foundation of developing a customer-oriented company, customer acquisition creates the lifeline of sales and return visits vital to a company's long-term success.

The product life cycle model remains an important tool for understanding how to acquire customers. The introduction, growth, maturity, and decline stages of the cycle necessitate careful responses and strategies from the marketing team.

Customer acquisition provides a key response to the challenges of competition, especially in the maturity stage of the product life cycle. At every point, companies face the demands of keeping current customers balanced with using tactics to find new customers. In general, three basic forms of customer acquisition are

1. developing existing or new markets,

2. developing existing or new products, and

3. branding programs.

## Identifying Markets

Customers are acquired through the analysis of existing markets and new markets. New customers can be located in existing markets. Some may be found through the efforts to increase brand switching. Others can be identified when new needs arise as situations change, such as when television programming shifted from analog to digital signals. Further, a product may be featured as being different and better, which is the product differentiation approach to attracting new customers in existing markets.

Finding new markets, the second approach to identifying markets, consists of geographic expansion into domestic markets and international markets. When a company does not operate nationally, domestic markets are assessed to see which will be the most viable for entry. International markets require careful study prior to setting up any kind of exporting arrangement.

## Developing Products

Acquisition of new customers often results from the implementation of a product strategy. Products attract new customers by offering new features, eliminating old problems, and solving different needs. Products will be matched with viable market segments.

Product development is a marketing strategy in which new goods and services are developed and then added to current lines. These are marketed to existing customers. Product diversification occurs when new goods and services are created for new market segments not currently served by the company. Unmet needs, cultural trends, and other developments lead to development and diversification strategies. Recent cultural trends associated with diet have led to new food products, while the desire for connectivity has been associated with the creation of new electronic devices. One key to developing products is following through with a well-designed plan of implementation that brings the whole company into the process.

Product improvements solve specific problems. Many products have been made smaller, faster, more efficient, and more user-friendly over the years. Product improvements may help a firm capture new customers and acquire competitors' customers when it appears the company is selling a "better mousetrap."

Product line extensions allow the marketing team to meet more specific consumer needs. A customer with blood pressure problems is likely to try a no- or low-sodium food product. Someone with diabetes will watch for unsweetened or artificially sweetened products.

## Branding

A strong brand can contribute to customer acquisition. Major brands enjoy the benefit of being the first considered for new shoppers or those in new situations. Gillette may be the first brand a new shaver will try. Holiday Inn benefits from a well-known brand name that might attract international travelers in foreign countries.

## Types of Brands

A brand is the name given to an item or, in some cases, an organization. Brands are assigned to individual products, lines of products, companies offering products, individual services, and companies that offer services. The term used to identify an entire company is the corporate name, which may or may not also be a brand. When the corporate name is attached to all products, it is a house mark. The primary forms of brands include family brands, flanker brands, brand extensions, private brands or private labels, cobrands, and global brands.

A family brand is the name used when a company offers a series or group of products under one brand. The primary advantage of a family brand is that consumers usually transfer the image associated with the brand name to any new products added to current lines. The transfer associations hold as long as the products are in the same product category.

A flanker brand is the development of a new brand by a company in a good or service category in which the company has a brand offering. Proctor and Gamble has launched a variety of flanker brands for products such as laundry detergent. Flanker brands may offer lower or higher priced options in the same brand category.

A brand extension is the use of the firm's current brand name on new products and new versions of current products. Successful brands continuously evolve to meet the changing needs of a diverse marketplace. When a company offers multiple brands or creates brand extensions, one concern will be that one version of the product can cannibalize the others from the same company. Also, when the extension does not fit with the company's image, problems are likely to emerge.

Private brands or private labels appear in stores that sell consumer goods, such as generic soups and vegetables in grocery stores. They are also found in retailers that launch company private-label brands, such as No Boundaries, Simply Basic, and Kid Connection in Walmart. Private labels have become increasingly popular as low-cost but relatively equal-quality options. These labels fit well with retail stores with strong brand or company names.

Cobranding occurs when two firms work together to market a good or service, such as a credit card attached to an airline or retail chain. Ingredient branding takes place when a product is featured as a key ingredient or component of another product, such as Dolby Sound or NutraSweet. These programs build on the strength of two brands rather than one and encourage cooperative advertising, data sharing, and cross-selling of additional products.

A global brand is one used by a multinational corporation. Strong global brands often possess the advantage of brand equity.

## ⬛ Developing Powerful Brands

The three steps of developing powerful brands include brand awareness, brand equity, and brand loyalty. Brand awareness is the beginning. The two levels of brand awareness include the knowledge that a brand exists followed by knowing what unique things a brand provides. Brand equity is the perception that a brand is different and better. The foundation of brand equity consists of five parts:

1. Differentiation

2. Relevance

3. Esteem

4. Knowledge

5. Emotion

Brand loyalty exists when a consumer makes a concerted effort to find and purchase a specific brand. Brand loyalty can take place between consumers and retail operations. It also links customers with specific brands or products. Brand-loyal customers are more likely to become advocates who encourage others to try a brand.

Brand parity means consumers believe there are few, if any, tangible distinctions between competing brands. It is more likely to be present in mature markets, and consumers become primarily price sensitive. Price does not always serve as a signal of quality. Brand parity may be combated through promotional and advertising programs seeking to find and promote differences, or the marketing team may simply recognize it exists and that such perceptions cannot be changed.

## ⬚ Customer Service and Customer Acquisition

Perceptions of excellence will be not only based on tangible product features but also emerge from intangibles. To acquire customers, manufacturing operations must go beyond providing superior products and make sure the items are delivered on time, in accurate amounts, with correct billing procedures, and with quality service after the sale.

Retail stores become more likely to acquire customers when best-value merchandise is offered by caring and attentive salespeople, delivery teams, repair departments, and all others who make contact with consumers.

The importance of a brand reaches a premium for companies that vend services. Services are intangible, which makes the name the primary means by which a company and its services are identified. The responsibility for strong brands spreads from the top marketing manager through the entire organization, including first-line employees both within and outside the marketing department.

A connection also exists between pricing and company service. Customers paying higher prices expect the best service. In general, any time a customer considers a new company, product, or service, several factors influence the final choice. The one common denominator for markets, products, brands, and prices is the connection to customer service. The company that delivers the most memorable quality service automatically has an advantage.

## ⬚ The Cases

### Ruth's Chris: The High Stakes of International Expansion

The Ruth's Chris Steakhouse company began with a single unit in New Orleans and had, over the years, expanded to more than 80 locations in 5 countries. Some of the locations were franchisees. The management team, led by Dan Savannah, successfully launched a public offering of stock. The marketing managers needed to sustain the organization's growth by expanding into more countries with franchise restaurants. Other potential options included opening different types of restaurants in the same locations, adding different types of restaurants in new locations, or placing more of the same types of restaurants in the same markets.

### The Ultimate Fighting Championships (UFC): The Evolution of a Sport

Mixed martial arts may be viewed as both a sport and as an entertainment venue. The Ultimate Fighting Championship (UFC) brand enjoyed the advantage of a strong domestic fan base in a growing market. International expansion opportunities also were available. Bryan Johnston, the chief marketing officer for UFC, faced the challenges of participant injuries that made some events less attractive, increasing competition, and finding ways to retain two types of fans—those who saw the sport as an athletic fighting event and those who enjoyed the entertainment aspects. After many state governments banned the original format, rules were created to protect participants and eliminate some of the more unseemly aspects of the fights. Combatants were expected to demand higher pay as the level of competition grew. In these circumstances, the goal became to defend the current fan base while reaching new market segments domestically along with international markets.

## Best Buy Inc.—Dual Branding in China

In 2002, the successful retail chain Best Buy acquired Future Shop, the largest consumer electronics firm in Canada. Bests Buy's marketing managers faced the choice of operating with two brands or consolidating. In Canada, the choice to keep two brands worked well, with little cannibalization. Based on this experience, the marketing team encountered a similar decision. Best Buy acquired Five Star, the third-largest retailer of appliances and consumer electronics in China. The primary choice was between assuming only the Best Buy brand and operating with two. Five Star was well known and established, whereas Best Buy had only recently entered the Chinese market.

# Ruth's Chris: The High Stakes of International Expansion

## By Allen H. Kupetz and Professor Ilan Alon

Well, I was so lucky that I fell into something that I really, really love. And I think that if you ever go into business, you better find something you really love, because you spend so many hours with it . . . it almost becomes your life.

Ruth Fertel, 1927–2002
Founder of Ruth's Chris Steak House

In 2006, Ruth's Chris Steak House (Ruth's Chris) was fresh off a sizzling initial public offering (IPO). Dan Hannah, vice-president for business development since June 2004, was responsible for the development of a new business strategy focused on continued growth of franchise and company-operated restaurants. He also oversaw franchisee relations. Now a public company, Ruth's Chris had to meet Wall Street's expectations for revenue growth. Current stores were seeing consistent incremental revenue growth, but new restaurants were critical and Hannah knew that the international opportunities offered a tremendous upside.

With restaurants in just five countries including the United States, the challenge for Hannah was to decide where to go to next. Ruth's Chris regularly received inquiries from would-be franchisees all over the world, but strict criteria—liquid net worth of at least US$1 million, verifiable experience within the hospitality industry, and an ability and desire to develop multiple locations—eliminated many of the prospects. And the cost of a franchise—a US$100,000 per restaurant franchise fee, a five percent of gross sales royalty fee, and a two percent of gross sales fee as a contribution to the national advertising campaign—eliminated some qualified prospects. All this was coupled with a debate within Ruth's Chris senior management team about the need and desire to grow its international business. So where was Hannah to look for new international franchisees and what countries would be best suited for the fine dining that made Ruth's Chris famous?

## The House That Ruth Built

Ruth Fertel, the founder of Ruth's Chris, was born in New Orleans in 1927. She skipped several grades in grammar school, and later entered Louisiana State University in Baton Rouge at the age of 15 to

Version: (A) 2006–11–20

pursue degrees in chemistry and physics. After graduation, Fertel landed a job teaching at McNeese State University. The majority of her students were football players who not only towered over her, but were actually older than she was. Fertel taught for two semesters. In 1948, the former Ruth Ann Adstad married Rodney Fertel who lived in Baton Rouge and shared her love of horses. They had two sons, Jerry and Randy. They opened a racing stable in Baton Rouge. Ruth Fertel earned a thoroughbred trainer's license, making her the first female horse trainer in Louisiana. Ruth and Rodney Fertel divorced in 1958.

In 1965, Ruth Fertel spotted an ad in the *New Orleans Times-Picayune* selling a steak house. She mortgaged her home for US$22,000 to purchase Chris Steak House, a 60-seat restaurant on the corner of Broad and Ursuline in New Orleans, near the fairgrounds racetrack. In September of 1965, the city of New Orleans was ravaged by Hurricane Betsy just a few months after Fertel purchased Chris Steak House. The restaurant was left without power, so she cooked everything she had and brought it to her brother in devastated Plaquemines Parish to aid in the relief effort.

In 1976, the thriving restaurant was destroyed in a kitchen fire. Fertel bought a new property a few blocks away on Broad Street and soon opened under a new name, "Ruth's Chris Steak House," since her original contract with former owner, Chris Matulich, precluded her from using the name Chris Steak House in a different location. After years of failed attempts, Tom Moran, a regular customer and business owner from Baton Rouge, convinced a hesitant Fertel to let him open the first Ruth's Chris franchise in 1976. It opened on Airline Highway in Baton Rouge. Fertel reluctantly began awarding more and more franchises. In the 1980s, the little corner steak house grew into a global phenomenon with restaurants opening every year in cities around the nation and the world. Fertel became something of an icon herself and was dubbed by her peers "The First Lady of American Restaurants."

Ruth's Chris grew to become the largest fine dining steak house in the United States (see Exhibit 1) with its focus on an unwavering commitment to

| Exhibit 1 | Fine Dining Steak Houses by Brand in the United States (2005) |
| --- | --- |

| Company Name | Number of Restaurants |
| --- | --- |
| Ruth's Chris | 92 |
| Morton's | 66 |
| Fleming's | 32 |
| Palm | 28 |
| Capital Grille | 22 |
| Shula's | 16 |
| Sullivan's | 15 |
| Smith & Wollensky | 11 |
| Del Frisco | 6 |

*Source:* Ruth's Chris Steak House files.

customer satisfaction and its broad selection of USDA Prime grade steaks (USDA Prime is a meat grade label that refers to evenly distributed marbling that enhances the flavor of the steak). The menu also included premium quality lamb chops, veal chops, fish, chicken, and lobster. Steak and seafood combinations and a vegetable platter were also available at selected restaurants. Dinner entrees were generally priced between US$18 to US$38. Three company-owned restaurants were open for lunch and offered entrees generally ranging in price from US$11 to US$24. The Ruth's Chris core menu was similar at all of its restaurants. The company occasionally introduced new items as specials that allowed the restaurant to offer its guests additional choices, such as items inspired by Ruth's Chris New Orleans heritage.[1]

In 2005, Ruth's Chris enjoyed a significant milestone, completing a successful IPO that raised more than US$154 million in new equity capital. In their 2005 Annual Report, the company said it had plans "to embark on an accelerated development plan and expand our footprint through both company-owned and franchised locations." 2005 restaurant sales grew to a record US$415.8 million from 82 locations in the United States and 10 international locations including Canada (1995, 2003), Hong Kong (1997, 2001), Mexico (1993, 1996, 2001), and Taiwan (1993, 1996, 2001). As of December 2005, 41 of the 92 Ruth's Chris restaurants were company-owned and 51 were franchisee-owned, including all 10 of the international restaurants (see Exhibit 2).

| **Figure 1** | Ruth's Chris Restaurant Growth by Decade | | |
|---|---|---|---|
| Decade | New Restaurants (total) | New Restaurants (company-owned) | New Restaurants (franchises) |
| 1965–1969 | 1 | 1 | 0 |
| 1970–1979 | 4 | 2 | 2 |
| 1980–1989 | 19 | 8 | 11 |
| 1990–1999 | 44 | 19 | 25 |
| 2000–2005 | 25 | 12 | 13 |
| | 93[2] | 42 | 51 |

*Source:* Ruth's Chris Steak House files.

Ruth's Chris's 51 franchisee-owned restaurants were owned by just 17 franchisees, with five new franchisees having the rights to develop a new restaurant, and the three largest franchisees owning eight, six and five restaurants respectively. Prior to 2004, each franchisee entered into a 10-year franchise agreement with three 10-year renewal options for each restaurant. Each agreement granted the franchisee territorial protection, with the option to develop a certain number of restaurants in their territory. Ruth's Chris's franchisee agreements generally included termination clauses in the event of nonperformance by the franchisee.[3]

## A World of Opportunities

As part of the international market selection process, Hannah considered four standard models (see Figure 2):

Product development—new kinds of restaurants in existing markets

Diversification—new kinds of restaurants in new markets

**Exhibit 2** Ruth's Chris's Locations in the United States (2005)

*Source:* Ruth's Chris Steak House files.

| Figure 2 | Restaurant Growth Paths[4] |
|---|---|

Penetration—more of the same restaurants in the same market

Market development—more of the same restaurants in new markets

The product development model (new kinds of restaurants in existing markets) was never seriously considered by Ruth's Chris. It had built a brand based on fine dining steak houses and, with only 92 stores, the company saw little need and no value in diversifying with new kinds of restaurants.

The diversification model (new kinds of restaurants in new markets) was also never considered by Ruth's Chris. In only four international markets, Hannah knew that the current fine dining steak house model would work in new markets without the risk of brand dilution or brand confusion.

The penetration model (more of the same restaurants in the same market) was already underway in a small way with new restaurants opening up in Canada. The limiting factor was simply that fine dining establishments would never be as ubiquitous as quick service restaurants (i.e., fast food) like McDonald's. Even the largest cities in the world would be unlikely to host more than five to six Ruth's Chris steak houses.

The market development model (more of the same restaurants in new markets) appeared the most obvious path to increased revenue. Franchisees in the four international markets—Canada, Hong Kong, Mexico and Taiwan—were profitable and could offer testimony to would-be franchisees of the value of a Ruth's Chris franchise.

With the management team agreed on a model, the challenge shifted to market selection criteria. The key success factors were well defined:

- Beef-eaters: Ruth's Chris was a steak house (though there were several fish items on the menu) and, thus, its primary customers were people who enjoy beef. According to the World Resources Institute, in 2002 there were 17 countries above the mean per capita of annual beef consumption for high-income countries (93.5 kilograms—see Exhibit 3).[5]
- Legal to import U.S. beef: The current Ruth's Chris model used only USDA Prime beef, thus it had to be exportable to the target country. In some cases, Australian beef was able to meet the same high U.S. standard.
- Population/high urbanization rates: With the target customer being a well-to-do beef-eater, restaurants needed to be in densely populated areas to have a large enough pool. Most large centers probably met this requirement.
- High disposable income: Ruth's Chris is a fine dining experience and the average cost of a meal for a customer ordering an entrée was over US$70 at a Ruth's Chris in the United States. While this might seem to eliminate many countries quickly, there are countries (e.g., China) that have such large populations that even a very small percentage of high disposable income people could create an appropriate pool of potential customers.
- Do people go out to eat? This was a critical factor. If well-to-do beef-eaters did not go out to eat, these countries had to be removed from the target list.

| Exhibit 3 | Meat Consumption per Capita[5] (in kilograms) |
| --- | --- |

| Region/Classification | 2002 | 2001 | 2000 | 1999 | 1998 | Growth Rate 1998–2002 |
| --- | --- | --- | --- | --- | --- | --- |
| World | 39.7 | 38.8 | 38.6 | 38.0 | 37.7 | 5.31% |
| Asia (excluding Middle East) | 27.8 | 26.9 | 26.6 | 25.7 | 25.4 | 9.45% |
| Central America/Caribbean | 46.9 | 45.7 | 44.8 | 42.9 | 41.3 | 13.56% |
| Europe | 74.3 | 72.5 | 70.5 | 70.6 | 73.1 | 1.64% |
| Middle East/North Africa | 25.7 | 25.7 | 26.0 | 25.1 | 24.7 | 4.05% |
| North America | 123.2 | 119.1 | 120.5 | 122.2 | 118.3 | 4.14% |
| South America | 69.7 | 68.4 | 69.1 | 67.6 | 64.2 | 8.57% |
| Sub-Saharan Africa | 13.0 | 12.9 | 13.1 | 12.8 | 12.6 | 3.17% |
| Developed Countries | 80.0 | 78.0 | 77.2 | 77.3 | 77.6 | 3.09% |
| Developing Countries | 28.9 | 28.1 | 28.0 | 27.1 | 26.6 | 8.65% |
| High-Income Countries | 93.5 | 91.9 | 92.0 | 92.2 | 90.9 | 2.86% |
| Low-Income Countries | 8.8 | 8.6 | 8.4 | 8.3 | 8.2 | 7.32% |
| Middle-Income Countries | 46.1 | 44.6 | 43.9 | 42.7 | 42.3 | 8.98% |

- Affinity for U.S. brands: The name "Ruth's Chris" was uniquely American as was the Ruth Fertel story. Countries that were overtly anti-United States would be eliminated from—or at least pushed down—the target list. One measure of affinity could be the presence of existing U.S. restaurants and successful franchises.

## What Should Ruth's Chris Do Next?

Hannah had many years of experience in the restaurant franchising business, and thus had both personal preferences and good instincts about where Ruth's Chris should be looking for new markets. "Which markets should we enter first?" he thought to himself. Market entry was critical, but there were other issues too. Should franchising continue to be Ruth's Chris exclusive international mode of entry? Were there opportunities for joint ventures or company-owned stores in certain markets? How could he identify and evaluate new potential franchisees? Was there an opportunity to find a global partner/brand with which to partner?

Hannah gathered information from several reliable U.S. government and related websites and created the table in Exhibit 4. He noted that many of his top prospects currently did not allow the importation of U.S. beef, but he felt that this was a political (rather than a cultural) variable and thus could change quickly under the right circumstances and with what he felt was the trend toward ever more free trade. He could not find any data on how often people went out to eat or a measure of their affinity toward U.S. brands. Maybe the success of U.S. casual dining restaurants in a country might be a good indicator of how its citizens felt toward U.S. restaurants. With his spreadsheet open, he went to work on the numbers and began contemplating the future global expansion of the company.

"If you've ever had a filet this good, welcome back."

Ruth Fertel, 1927–2002
Founder of Ruth's Chris Steak House

**Exhibit 4**  Data Table

| Country | Per Capita Beef Consumption (kg) | Population (1,000s) | Urbanization Rate (%) | Per Capita GDP (PPP in US$) |
|---------|----------------------------------|---------------------|------------------------|------------------------------|
| Argentina | 97.6 | 39,921 | 90% | $13,100 |
| Bahamas | 123.6 | 303 | 89% | $20,200 |
| Belgium | 86.1 | 10,379 | 97% | $31,400 |
| Brazil | 82.4 | 188,078 | 83% | $8,400 |
| Chile | 66.4 | 16,134 | 87% | $11,300 |
| China | 52.4 | 1,313,973 | 39% | $6,800 |
| Costa Rica | 40.4 | 4,075 | 61% | $11,100 |
| Czech Rep | 77.3 | 10,235 | 74% | $19,500 |
| France | 101.1 | 60,876 | 76% | $29,900 |
| Germany | 82.1 | 82,422 | 88% | $30,400 |
| Greece | 78.7 | 10,688 | 61% | $22,200 |
| Hungary | 100.7 | 9,981 | 65% | $16,300 |
| Ireland | 106.3 | 4,062 | 60% | $41,000 |
| Israel | 97.1 | 6,352 | 92% | $24,600 |
| Italy | 90.4 | 58,133 | 67% | $29,200 |
| Japan | 43.9 | 127,463 | 65% | $31,500 |
| Kuwait | 60.2 | 2,418 | 96% | $19,200 |
| Malaysia | 50.9 | 24,385 | 64% | $12,100 |

| Country | Per Capita Beef Consumption (kg) | Population (1,000s) | Urbanization Rate (%) | Per Capita GDP (PPP in US$) |
|---|---|---|---|---|
| Netherlands | 89.3 | 16,491 | 66% | $30,500 |
| Panama | 54.5 | 3,191 | 57% | $7,200 |
| Poland | 78.1 | 38,536 | 62% | $13,300 |
| Portugal | 91.1 | 10,605 | 55% | $19,300 |
| Russia | 51 | 142,893 | 73% | $11,100 |
| Singapore | 71.1 | 4,492 | 100% | $28,100 |
| South Africa | 39 | 44,187 | 57% | $12,000 |
| South Korea | 74.4 | 48,846 | 80% | $20,400 |
| Spain | 118.6 | 40,397 | 77% | $25,500 |
| Switzerland | 72.9 | 7,523 | 68% | $32,300 |
| Turkey | 19.3 | 70,413 | 66% | $8,200 |
| UAE/Dubai | 74.4 | 2,602 | 85% | $43,400 |
| U.K. | 79.6 | 60,609 | 89% | $30,300 |
| United States | 124.8 | 298,444 | 80% | $41,800 |
| Vietnam | 28.6 | 84,402 | 26% | $2,800 |

*Source:* World Resources Institute, "Meat Consumption: Per Capita (1984–2002)," retrieved on June 7, 2006 from http://earthtrends.wri.org/text/agriculture-food/variable-193.html and World Bank Key Development Data & Statistics, http://web.worldbank.org/WBSITE/EXTERNAL/DATASTATISTICS/0,,contentMDK:20535285~menuPK:232599~pagePK:64133150~piPK:64133175~theSitePK:239419,00.html, retrieved on June 7, 2006.

## CASE QUESTIONS

1. What decision criteria were being used in the selection of potential nations for expansion? Are there other criteria the company should have included?

2. Of the four potential options, which assumes the most risk? Which is the most risk-averse? Defend your answers.

3. Of the four potential options, which offers the best chance to attract more customers in the same areas? Which offers the best opportunity to expand the total number of company customers? Why?

4. What modifications to the company's brand might be necessary, either when operating a steakhouse in other countries or some new form of restaurant?

5. Which marketing tactics will the company have to examine and possibly change when operating in other countries?

# The Ultimate Fighting Championships (UFC): The Evolution of a Sport

*By Jesse Baker, under the supervision of Matthew Thomson*

The UFC is the most exciting combat sport in the world because there are so many ways to win and so many ways to lose. . . . Boxing is your father's sport.

–Dana White

What makes UFC so great is that every single man on the planet gets it immediately. It's just two guys beating each other up.

–Lorenzo Fertitta

We're not for everyone, and we don't try to be. If you don't like fighting sports, great, this is America, that's your right. All we ask is that people understand what we are.

–Dana White

In early February of 2010, Bryan Johnston, the chief marketing officer for the Ultimate Fighting Championship (UFC), returned to his office at Zuffa LLC, the parent company for the UFC, in Las Vegas, Nevada. He was frustrated by the numerous athlete injuries that continued to plague scheduled events, most recently UFC 108 on January 2, 2010. This situation gave him cause to reflect on some much bigger issues he had been dealing with since leaving his role as vice president of partner marketing at Burton Snowboards to join the UFC and take full control of the organization's marketing activities in June 2009. Johnston was the first senior member of the firm who did not come from a background in boxing or television.[1] He felt a great deal of pressure to ensure that the UFC continued to meet the high expectations that had been set by its phenomenal early success.

The name UFC had become synonymous with mixed martial arts across North America. Over the past decade, the company had experienced unparalleled growth in the sporting industry and was now valued at more than $1 billion.[2] However, the competitive landscape was changing quickly, and Johnston understood that he was running out of time to make important decisions on how to continue to grow the league while maintaining the UFC's competitive advantage that stemmed from its dominant position as the market leader.

The UFC had already begun to make strides in new international markets. According to the results of an Ipsos-Reid Canadian Sports Monitor Study, 22 percent of Canadian adults were interested in the UFC, which was fast approaching the Canadian National Basketball Association (NBA) fan base of 26 percent of Canadian adults.[3] Furthermore, 39 percent of those interested in the UFC said their interest had increased over the past few years, more than any of the 30 other sports surveyed in Canada, including hockey and the Olympics (see Exhibit 1).[4] Still, Johnston wondered about the long-term sustainability of the UFC's current strategy. In January 2010, a 10 percent stake in the company had been sold to Flash Entertainment, a Middle Eastern entertainment company and a wholly

Version: (A) 2010–06–16

| Exhibit 1 | Ispos-Reid Canadian Sports Monitor Study Results |

S3_11. (U.F.C. (Ultimate Fighting Championship)) Thinking about your interest in these sports and events in the past few years, would you say that you have less interest, the same interest or more interest than before? If you have never had an interest in the sport or event you can indicate that as well

Proportions/Means: Columns Tested (5% risk level) - A/B/C/D/E/F - G/H - I/J/K/L/M/N/O/P/Q/R/S - T/U*
small base

|  | Total (Age) | 18 to 34 | 18 to 49 | 25 to 54 | 35 to 54 | 45 to 54 | 55+ |
|---|---|---|---|---|---|---|---|
| Base: Casual or avid fan | 409 | 166 | 318 | 295 | 185 | 74 | 58 |
| Weighted | 431 | 208 | 354 | 315 | 176 | 64* | 47* |
| Less Interest | 60 | 27 | 44 | 39 | 24 | 11 | 8 |
|  | 14% | 13% | 13% | 12% | 14% | 17% | 18% |
| The Same | 203 | 91 | 165 | 148 | 91 | 34 | 21 |
|  | 47% | 44% | 47% | 47% | 52% | 54% | 44% |
| More | 169 | 90 | 145 | 129 | 61 | 18 | 18 |
|  | 39% | 43% | 41% | 41% | 35% | 29% | 38% |

*Source:* Ipsos-Reid Canadian Sports Monitor Study. Table 25.

owned subsidiary of the Abu Dhabi government.[5] Johnston hoped that this move would allow the UFC to develop strategic partnerships in the Middle East and throughout Asia. However, if the UFC could not even deliver on the advertised fights within the United States, how would the company be able to deliver quality fights overseas? New international markets would dramatically increase the demand for talented main-event fighters.

Johnston also wondered whether local talent would need to be identified and recruited to attract fans and fill seats in these new markets. The popularity of English-born fighter Michael Bisping was paramount to the success of UFC events in the United Kingdom. Would his popularity also hold true in other regions? Johnston was also wary of an expansion strategy that would compromise the company's core fan base, many of whom remained skeptical of the UFC's international initiatives. He remembered an interview he had seen recently, in which Marshall Zelaznik, the UFC's managing director of International Development, had reiterated the

disappointment of many UFC fans, who feared that too many international events would dilute the quality of the events held within the United States.[6] Johnston did not want to alienate the UFC's primary market by stretching the resources too thin.

## Early Development

The concept of the UFC was originally developed in 1993, as a single-elimination, eight-man tournament called War of the Worlds by Art Davie, an enthusiast with an advertising background, and Rorion Gracie, a master in the martial art of Brazilian jiu-jitsu.[7] The concept developed as a tournament that would feature martial artists from different disciplines facing each other to determine the best martial art. Davie and Gracie formed WOW Promotions and founded Semaphore Entertainment Group (SEG) as a television partner.[8] The trademarked octagon design was developed for the enclosure in which the bouts were staged, and Davie and Gracie named the show "The Ultimate Fighting Championship."[9] The first event, later to be known as UFC 1, was held in Denver, Colorado, and proved to be a success from its inception, drawing 86,592 pay-per-view (PPV) television subscribers.[10] Following UFC 5, in April 1995, Davie and Gracie sold their interests in the organization to SEG.

Despite the UFC's early success, controversy surrounding the absence of any standard set of rules to govern the sport led to the sport being banned in 36 states.[11] One of many public figures who spoke out against the sport was U.S. Senator John McCain, who declared it to be "human cock-fighting."[12] As a result, the UFC was dropped from major cable PPV distributor, Viewer's Choice, and other individual cable carriers, such as TCI Cable.[13] The controversy also was a major barrier against obtaining official athletic sanctioning from state athletic commissions.

In the early 1990s, in fact, the UFC's tagline had been "There Are No Rules!" In reality, though, a limited set of rules did exist: no eye gouging and no biting. Other techniques such as hair pulling, head butting, groin strikes, and fish hooking were frowned upon, but still permitted. These rules, or their lack thereof, were a major source of the controversy. Although the sport was appealing to some, until the sport was able to establish a clear set of rules to better protect fighters, opportunities were clearly limited for the sport's growth.

In an attempt to gain more widespread acceptance and popularity, the UFC changed some rules and decided to increase its cooperation with state athletic commissions. On September 30, 2000, the UFC held its first U.S.-sanctioned mixed martial arts event in New Jersey. UFC 28 was sanctioned under the New Jersey State Athletic Control Board's "Unified Rules."[14]

## Zuffa LLC Purchase

Attempts to have the sport sanctioned across the United States eventually drove SEG to the brink of bankruptcy. In 2001, Frank and Lorenzo Fertitta, executives with Station Casinos, and Dana White, a boxing promoter, bought the UFC for $2 million

and created Zuffa LLC (Zuffa),[15] a parent entity controlling the UFC.[16]

Lorenzo Fertitta, a former member of the Nevada State Athletic Commission, used his relationships to secure sanctioning in the state of Nevada in 2001. The UFC made its return to pay-per-view with UFC 33: Victory in Vegas. The UFC slowly began to regain popularity, and advertising and corporate sponsorships followed.[17] The UFC started generating higher live gates (i.e., ticket revenue) from hosting events at casino venues such as Trump Taj Mahal and the MGM Grand Garden Arena. The organization started to see PPV revenues as high as revenues before the political controversies in 1997.

The UFC secured its first television deal with Fox Sports Net (FSN). *The Best Damn Sports Show* aired the first mixed martial arts match in June 2002 at UFC 37.5, featuring as its main event Chuck Lidell vs. Vitor Belfort.[18] Later, FSN would also air one-hour highlights of the UFC's greatest fights.

The first major milestone came at UFC 40, when pay-per-view buys hit 150,000. The fight featured a grudge match between Tito Ortiz and UFC legend Ken Shamrock.[19] Despite this success, the UFC continued to experience financial deficits. By 2004, Zuffa had reported $34 million of losses since purchasing the UFC. [20]

## The Ultimate Fighter and Spike TV

To avoid bankruptcy once again, Zuffa decided to take the UFC beyond pay-per-view and into cable television by creating *The Ultimate Fighter (TUF)*, a reality-TV series that featured up-and-coming mixed martial arts (MMA) fighters competing for a contract in the UFC. Several different networks rejected the concept, and not until Zuffa offered to pay the $10 million production costs was a partner found—in Spike TV.[21]

The show aired for the first time in January 2005, following *WWE Raw,* and it became an instant success. The finale for the first show featured fan favorite Forrest Griffin matched up against Stephan Bonnar with the winner receiving a six-figure contract with the UFC. Dana White had since credited this event with having saved the UFC.[22] A second season was aired in August of the same year, and two more seasons were aired in 2006. The success of the show led Spike TV to pick up more UFC content in the form of *UFC Unleashed,* an hour-long show that aired select fights from previous events, and *UFC Fight Night,* a series of fight events that debuted in August 2005. Spike would also feature *Countdown* specials to promote upcoming UFC pay-per-view cards.

In 2009, the 10th season of *TUF* featured a selection of heavyweight fighters, including the YouTube-famous, Kevin "Kimbo Slice" Ferguson.[23] This episode was an enormous success, drawing the highest ratings in the show's history with a household rating of between 3.7 million and 5.3 million total viewers.[24] The difficulty for Johnston lay in whether this success could be duplicated in foreign markets. The company's expansion strategy involved airing non-live UFC content, such as *TUF* and *UFC Unleashed* and *Fight Night;* however, given what he knew about the highly fragmented nature of his target audience, Johnston wondered whether these shows, which did incredibly well in North America, would experience similar success in other countries.

UFC's strategic partnership with Spike TV proved to be the ideal opportunity for the UFC to maximize exposure. These programs became the main outlets through which the UFC promoted its pay-per-view events, which allowed UFC to spend very little on advertising while targeting its core audience effectively. UFC was also able to generate significant sponsorship revenues through its television programming. The result was a dramatic increase in pay-per-view buys and an overall explosion in growth for the sport of MMA as a whole.

## Explosion of Pay-per-View Buy Rates

UFC 52 was the first event to air after the first season of *TUF.* The event featured two future hall-of-famers, Chuck "The Iceman" Liddell and Randy "The Natural" Couture. The event doubled the last benchmark with pay-per-view audience of 300,000.[25] The second season of *TUF* was used to promote a rubber match between Liddell and Couture at UFC 57.[26] This event drew an estimated 410,000 pay-per-view buys.[27] The next big milestone came in the same year when Chuck Liddell faced Tito Ortiz in UFC 66. The event drew more than one million pay-per-view buys, and the UFC's popularity continued to skyrocket.[28] In 2006, the UFC broke the pay-per-view industry's record for the most revenues in a single year with more than $222,766,000, exceeding PPV revenues from boxing and the WWE.[29] In July 2007, BodogLife.com, a gambling website, stated that, for the first time, the betting revenues from the UFC would surpass those from boxing.[30]

Playing a huge role in UFC's success was the organization's ability to promote its pay-per-view events through its cable television outlets, along with its ability to capitalize on the hype created by these shows, with much-anticipated fighter match-ups following directly after. In the meantime, UFC had developed a self-sustaining positive feedback loop of publicly available material that served to promote the next pay-per-view event without having to draw on outside sources, resulting in favorable cost-efficiencies for the organization.

## World Extreme Cagefighting and PRIDE Acquisitions

The UFC continued to expand its reach into new markets with the acquisitions of World Extreme Cagefighting (WEC) in December 2006 and PRIDE Fighting Championships (PRIDE) on March 27, 2007.[31]

WEC was a promotional company based in California that showcased fighters in lower weight classes than those featured by the UFC. This arrangement allowed the UFC to control a broader range of mixed martial arts entertainment within the United States (see Exhibit 2).

The acquisition of PRIDE, a struggling Japanese-based league cost less than $70 million and was intended initially to be run as a separate

| Exhibit 2 | List of Weight Classes for Ultimate Fighting Championship and World Extreme Cagefighting |
|---|---|

| Ultimate Fighting Championship | | | |
|---|---|---|---|
| Division | Upper Weight Limit | Champion | Title Defenses |
| Heavyweight | 265 lb (120 kg) | Brock Lesnar *UFC 91* | 1 |
| Light Heavyweight | 205 lb (93 kg) | Lyoto Machida *UFC 98* | 1 |
| Middleweight | 185 lb (84 kg) | Anderson Silva *UFC 64* | 5 |
| Welterweight | 170 lb (77 kg) | Georges St-Pierre *UFC 83* | 3 |
| Lightweight | 155 lb (70 kg) | BJ Penn *UFC 80* | 3 |
| World Extreme Cagefighting | | | |
| Division | Upper Weight Limit | Champion | Title Defenses |
| Lightweight | 155 lb (70 kg) | Ben Henderson *WEC 46* | 0 |
| Featherweight | 145 lb (66 kg) | Jose Aldo *WEC 44* | 0 |
| Bantamweight | 135 lb (61 kg) | Brian Bowles *WEC 42* | 0 |
| Flyweight | 125 lb (57 kg) | Vacant | – |

*Source:* Case writer.

organization.[32] PRIDE had been the UCF's largest international rival and had featured many of the world's greatest fighters. Shortly after the acquisition, on October 4, 2007, the UFC closed the Japanese operations of PRIDE and began to rebrand many of the top PRIDE fighters under the UFC name.[33] When interviewed on ESPNEWS, Dana White remained vague about the reasons for closing the league, simply claiming that the model was not sustainable and that "PRIDE is a mess."[34] Many people in the MMA community understood this rebranding as another step in the company's attempts to align the UFC's brand as closely as possible with the sport of MMA as a whole. It also revealed the UFC's intentions to buy out competitors and close their doors as a strategy to ensure its market position. The league followed this decision with a series of UFC events that served to unify the leagues under one name by pitting UFC and PRIDE champions against each other.[35]

Johnston was becoming increasingly concerned with the longer-term implications of the UFC's current business strategy. The league was undoubtedly the strongest it had ever been. However, limiting the number of avenues that young fighters could take to pursue careers in the sport of MMA seemed counter-intuitive, especially while simultaneously attempting to grow the organization. This strategy would undoubtedly require access to an increasingly large pool of talented fighters. Although ultimately the UFC's strategy had worked well in terms of ensuring its dominance in market share, Johnston was beginning to wonder whether these decisions would hinder the UFC's ability to jump into international markets. Despite the huge potential market that existed in Asia, he wondered how the UFC would be perceived given its previous decisions to close the doors of PRIDE and force its fighters to compete overseas in the UFC. PRIDE fighters were generally given very little time to adapt to the UFC's different fighting styles and rules. Many PRIDE fighters refused to accept the terms of the merger and felt they were not receiving a fair opportunity to establish themselves in the UFC. As a result, many fighters left the UFC for other smaller competing organizations.

## New Competition Emerges

Mixed martial arts had reached superstar status in the world of sport, and the UFC was capturing approximately 90 percent of the industry's total revenues.[36] However, many challenging organizations were emerging, each with a unique business model in attempts to become established in the market and to steal revenues from the MMA giant. The UFC had a simple strategy for limiting the growth of its competitors; it scheduled free counterprogramming at the same time as their competitors with the intention of stealing revenues.[37] And although this approach was not profitable in itself, it worked by preventing new competitors from both achieving profitable operations and recouping their investments in high-profile fighters.

Although some competing organizations were airing live fights for free on cable television, an offering that the UFC was yet to make available on a regular basis, others were investing huge amounts to attract some of the world's best fighters. A key example was the world's number-one ranked mixed martial arts fighter, Fedor Emelianenko, who held the PRIDE Heavyweight Championship before the league was closed by the UFC, and who, despite being considered by most to be the world's best fighter, had never fought in the UFC. This situation was the result of Emelianenko's long-standing dispute with Dana White over the terms of a contract. Emelianenko was quoted as saying, "The bottom line was that the UFC was a one-sided offer, and you know, that's something that can never be acceptable."[38] Johnston recalled White's less than politically correct response to Emelianenko's accusations. "Let me put it this way. I've done fight contract with all the best fighters in the world . . . who the——is Fedor? Are you serious?"[39] Although Johnston

understood that this attitude had played a crucial role in building the UFC brand with free publicity through Dana White's constant appearances in the media, he was also concerned with how this attitude could negatively affect other important relationships as the league continued to grow. Facing increased competition, Johnston wondered whether the organization might need to start rethinking the way it negotiated contracts with the league's fighters. He knew that the UFC would not be able to continue dominating the terms of contract agreements as it had in the past.

In 2008, Affliction Entertainment emerged as a promotions company, created by Affliction Clothing. The clothing company was looking to challenge the UFC in the United States after having experienced disputes with the UFC over royalties. Affliction Clothing, which had been one of the UFC's largest clothing sponsors, had been able to secure, with the financial support of Donald Trump, Fedor Emelianenko, considered by many to be the world's number-one ranked fighter.[40] The UFC reacted by banning fighters from wearing Affliction Clothing logos. The UFC also aired a last minute, free, live event on Spike TV, featuring one of the UFC's top fighters, Anderson Silva, to compete with Affliction Entertainment's pay-per-view event, *Affliction: Banned*, on July 19, 2008.[41] One year later, on July 24, 2009, Affliction Entertainment announced that it would be closing the promotions business and Affliction Clothing would return to sponsoring the UFC.[42]

When Affliction Entertainment closed its doors, Strikeforce, a fighting league based out of California, signed Emelianenko and offered its first MMA fight on November 7, 2009, on live CBS. Strikeforce established sponsorship deals with Rockstar Energy Drink and found other partners to begin hosting fights in Japan. In June of 2009, Strikeforce also aired the first female championship on cable television.[43]

Other emerging competition included the International Fight League (IFL), which had a huge presence in overseas markets but was not well established within the United States. IFL was also not airing televised live fights. As well, EliteXC was challenging for market share, but the company had invested too much money in few main fighters and its business model did not appear to be sustainable. Mark Cuban, a well-known entrepreneur who also owned the National Basketball Association's Dallas Mavericks, was also pushing his way into the MMA market by partnering with organizations, such as Affliction Entertainment, and airing fights on his cable network, HDNet.[44]

DREAM was one of the UFC's strongest international competitors that emerged after the UFC's purchase and dissolution of PRIDE. The league contained numerous well-respected and talented fighters who would be competitive in U.S. markets but who had very limited exposure in North America. The style of the DREAM fighters and the marketing of their events differed greatly from the UFC. The league had established partnerships with HDNet, EliteXC, Strikeforce and M-1 Global, owned in part by Fedor Emelianenko.[45,46,47] Johnston expected this large network of increasingly integrated organizations would pose a serious threat to the UFC's ability to compete in new international markets.

## Fighters' Salaries

With new competition in the United States and globally, Johnston wondered whether the company was doing enough to both retain the league's top talent and attract new fighters. He reflected on what he knew about original fighter payouts that often left first-time fighters losing money from their fights. To be cleared for a fight, the average medical bills for a fighter totaled approximately $2,500,[48] which included magnetic resonance imaging (MRI) scan, computerized axial tomography (CAT) scan, blood work, an eye exam, and a full physical examination. For first-time fighters, the actual payout was set at approximately $2,000, with an additional $2,000 being awarded to the winner.[49] As a result, because of the medical bills alone, a first-time fighter who lost his fight would lose money overall. In reality, many other costs, such as training expenses, travel, and fight preparation, would further compound the situation. If a fighter

won his first fight, he might break even. If he continued to win, his earnings would increase incrementally (usually by $2,000 a fight).[50] The majority of fighters in the league, however, did not have large endorsements or high-profile contract agreements with the UFC; instead, they were barely scraping by. Johnston wondered whether this model provided enough real incentive for young athletes to join the sport. How was this model going to affect the long-term growth prospects for the sport? Did it make sense for an organization that had experienced such immense growth and success to take advantage of its talent?

Fighter compensation had been increasing along with company revenues, but Johnston realized that the UFC continued to lack significantly, compared with other major sports leagues.[51] Johnston examined an analysis of disclosed payouts and compared it with the UFC revenues over the past four years (see Exhibit 3). He wondered whether the current payout structure was enough, or did the UFC need to drastically change the way it compensated fighters?

The UFC also lacked any form of union to protect the interests of its athletes, although such unions existed in every other major sports league: the National Football League (NFL), the National Basketball Association (NBA), Major League Baseball (MLB), the National Hockey League (NHL) and the Association of Tennis Professionals (ATP). In the past, attempts to protect the athletes' interests had been actively resisted by the company's president, Dana White. The league had been criticized for refusing to negotiate contracts; as a result, in several instances, the UFC's most popular fighters had refused to fight, preferring instead to leave the UFC for smaller, competing leagues. For example, Tito Ortiz, a former light heavyweight champion and fan favorite, left the UFC over a dispute with Dana White.[52] He later returned to the league and ended up fighting for less money than he had originally been offered.[53]

Johnston was uncomfortable with the way the UFC had, in the past, exploited what was essentially a monopoly in the North American market in order to bully fighters into what many believed to

| Exhibit 3 | Ultimate Fighting Championship: Number of Fights/Event, Average GATE Revenue/Fight, and Total Bonuses Paid Out to Fighters, 2006–2009 | | | | |
|---|---|---|---|---|---|
| **Year** | **2006** | **2007** | **2008** | **2009** | **Δ 2006 – 2009** |
| Average Number of Fights, per Event | 8.9 | 9.1 | 9.9 | 10.5 | 18.3% |
| Average Gate Revenue, UFC Events | $376,406 | $614,077 | $735,000 | $898,375 | 138.7% |
| Average Gate Revenue, UFN/TUF Events | $170,250 | $245,300 | $321,833 | $434,665 | 155.3% |
| Size of Average Bonus Pool Paid Out by UFC Event to Fighters | – | $162,500 | $196,667 | $216,333 | 33.1% |

*Note:* UFC = Ultimate Fighting Championships; TUF = The Ultimate Fighter; UFN = Ultimate Fight Night.

be unfair contracts. As new leagues emerged and gained momentum, he realized that achieving such favorable payment contracts with fighters might become increasingly difficult. The UFC had already seen many of its fighters leave, but had taken little action to rebuild these relationships. He wondered whether it was time to start paying more attention to this issue, but was unsure of how to go about making changes and how to gain buy-in from the rest of the leadership team, including White, who had seriously resisted the issue in the past.

Beyond the league's contract policies, the UFC also had final say on all sponsorship deals, including all forms of individual fighter sponsorships. Until recently, the UFC had not been able to control any sponsored images that appeared on the fighter's body.[54] However, in 2009, a new rule was established that required every sponsor to pay a licensing fee as high as $100,000 to the UFC for the right to sponsor a fighter. This fee made it substantially harder for up-and-coming fighters because sponsors were not willing to fund newer fighters who were more likely to fight on the undercard, therefore providing the sponsor with only limited exposure.[55] The licensing requirement also essentially locked out smaller or new companies from sponsoring the UFC because they could not afford to pay the required fees. Johnston believed that limited sponsorship competition might be harmful to the UFC and might adversely affect its long-term opportunities for sponsorship revenue.

The league had also just finished establishing a new set of corporate sponsors, including Harley-Davidson and Bud Light. Referring to the UFC's sponsors, Dana White was quoted in an interview as having said, "We don't need anybody."[56] Johnston understood the value of establishing strategic partnerships, and he was unclear about what exactly White had meant by this. Although White had also spoken about how the UFC was seeking strategic partners rather than blue-chip sponsors, Johnston was not sure whether the UFC's current sponsorship relationships reflected this preference.[57] Should the league be pursuing more cross-promotional advertising initiatives to push the UFC into new markets? Harley-Davidson was an expensive motorcycle brand that primarily targeted an older demographic. Was this choice of a corporate sponsor in line with the UFC's target audience of males aged 18 to 36?

## International Expansion Opportunities

The UFC was looking to follow up its recent partnership with Flash Entertainment by building a new arena at the Emirate Hotel in Abu Dhabi, a city that was emerging as the cultural and entertainment mecca of the United Arab Emirates (UAE). The new building would be an outdoor arena with 10,000-plus seats and coliseum-style seating that preserved the trademark UFC atmosphere.[58] Johnston was still unsure about where to promote the event, but expected to see interest from across the UAE and planned to promote the event through the UFC's European, British and Asian partners.[59] When a UFC event had been held in Australia, fans had traveled from across the country to attend. Johnston wondered whether a similar response could be expected in the UAE, or whether the demand would be large enough within the city.[60]

Johnston also knew that the UFC had been working for years to tap into the huge boxing market in Mexico by developing young Mexican talent, such as Cain Velasquez and Roger Huerta. The UFC had also recently signed a television deal with Grupo Televisa S.A.B., the world's largest Spanish-speaking media company, and had debuted with a free, live broadcast of UFC 100, on July 11, 2009.[61] Other programming included live *UFC Fight Night* events, *UFC Countdown* shows and one-hour feature programs.[62] Johnston was eager to hold the UFC's first pay-per-view event in Mexico, but wanted to ensure that it would be a success.

The UFC had already experienced success through ESPN in the United Kingdom and Ireland, and on June 1, 2009, the UFC expanded into Portugal by showing UFC 98: MACHIDA vs. EVANS, on pay-per-view.[63] This event was followed by a Chinese TV Deal on June 29, 2009, which provided the UFC with one to four hours of UFC programming each week on Saturdays and Sundays, broadcast in languages specific to each province.[64] Inner Mongolia Television (NMTV) would air the events, which could reach a potential 240 million viewers in China.[65] Johnston was excited by the potential of this market, but he wondered what the next step would be. Was India the next frontier for the UFC? If successful, the UFC would see huge upside potential, but Johnston was not sure that the UFC had a product that was adequate to meet the needs of this market. He was not even sure he understood exactly what those needs were. The company was already busy trying to establish the UFC brand in Western Europe and America. Was the company perhaps moving too quickly?

Johnston also wondered how the UFC would market the events in new countries. He wondered whether he fully understood how the UFC was perceived in these new markets. Would it be enough to continue promoting the league in the same way as in the past? Would this approach be effective in foreign markets where the league did not receive free publicity through a huge range of media outlets? In Asia, for example, the league would be compared to Japanese fighting organizations such as PRIDE. These leagues featured different fighting styles and much more cultured traditions. Although Japanese events would still feature an elaborate show, many fans did not like the way the UFC had "Americanized" a sport that was seen in other countries to be worthy of much more elegance and respect.

The UFC's core fan base in North America resulted from converting fans from World Wrestling Entertainment (WWE) and boxing. Originally, the UFC's target audience had been perceived to be males aged 18 to 36. These assumptions were driving the organization's decisions on the sponsors to target and the event promotions to pursue. However, Johnston believed he was beginning to better understand the polarized and dynamic nature of the UFC's fan base.

In fact, not only men were drawn to the sport; Johnston also suspected that much interest was also generated in females aged 18 to 36. This female audience, he realized, would open up an entirely new sponsorship base. He wondered how he should go about examining the true nature of the UFC's audience and how he could best convey this audience sector to new potential sponsors.

The UFC also needed to consider an entirely new potential audience of fans who were neither MMA enthusiasts nor fans of boxing or professional wrestling. These potential fans were general sports fans who had been introduced to the UFC through various media. Johnston wondered where these general sports fans fit into the existing categories of fans or whether they valued something altogether different. WWE fans tended to be more interested in the "show" and less concerned with the more technical aspects of the sport as compared with the boxing segment, which valued the fighters' athleticism and talent. WWE-rooted fans enjoyed watching rivalries develop in the media between the fighters and valued high-profile fighters with well-developed media personalities. Ultimately, these rivalries had been initiated to drive buys for PPV events. Johnston had recognized that the situation was unique in that the UFC was able to appeal to different customer segments that watched for different reasons. He also understood that a delicate balance was required when trying to meet the needs of these core fan bases. Regardless of the direction the company chose to pursue, it needed to ensure it continued to meet the needs of the existing fans.

The UFC had become a master in the art of generating free publicity through almost all media outlets, including television, radio, newsprint, and social media networks. Much of the early success of the UFC could be attributed to the company's president, Dana White, who took a non-traditional role and became the organization's most crucial publicity machine. At various times, White had been scrutinized for his derogatory language and controversial comments. His loud personality and unorthodox role as an outspoken celebrity chief executive officer (CEO) was proving to be a unique and successful marketing strategy. Many fans related to his rough and aggressive attitude, which had been a strong driving force behind the growth and success of the league. In fact, many of his disputes with writers, athletes, and public interest groups such as GLAAD[66] had been well documented by White himself through his Twitter account.

Frank and Lorenzo Fertitta owned the remaining 90 percent of Zuffa LLC. They had got their start in business as casino executives, and both shared a passion for mixed martial arts. They had allowed White to function as the organization's front man. When the company was founded, they wrote a legally binding clause into their contract that stated, in the event of a dispute between the two majority owners, a three, five-minute round, mixed martial arts fight would be used to determine the winner.[67] Recently, Lorenzo Fertitta had resigned as Station Casinos' president to work full-time as chair and CEO of the UFC to help the organization focus on its global expansion, which

included "landing more big-name sponsors, particularly in countries other than the U.S."[68]

Another important personality of the league was Joe Rogan, a former martial artist and the former host of the popular TV reality show *Fear Factor*. Rogan had become one of the organization's most popular characters as the color commentator for all major UFC events. His seemingly infinite knowledge and incredibly accurate insights made him a fan favorite and one of the league's most valuable assets. In addition, Joe Silva served as the league's matchmaker and talent recruiter. He negotiated all contracts and played a key role in establishing the favorable deals the UFC was able to secure with many top fighters. Johnston wondered whether he should speak to Silva directly about his concerns.

## Financial Overview

Standard and Poor's had released its latest credit report on Zuffa LLC, which documented the corporation's most recent financing activities. Zuffa's credit rating was reaffirmed at BB– (stable but not "investment grade").[69]

The company's 75 percent event-driven business model posed some concern to Johnston from a business standpoint. The company had recently made attempts to diversify its revenue streams by releasing a new video game, *UFC Unleashed*, and improved operating margins had been experienced on the company's U.K. operations.[70] Despite tremendous growth over the past year, Johnston understood that the company had really only been profitable for the last four years. Johnston wondered whether the owners would ever be interested in taking the company public, and, if so, when would be the right time to do so. He believed that if this option was to be pursued, the company's financial structure would first need to be re-evaluated.

Because more and more American states were moving toward legalizing mixed martial arts, Johnston knew that a huge potential for growth remained within North America. Currently, the 2010 fight schedule featured more international events than ever before. He wondered whether the company was moving in the right direction. Too much focus on overseas markets could leave the UFC vulnerable to the increasing competition within the United States, and a failure abroad could be devastating.

Johnston sat down at his desk and began to prepare his recommendations for the company's executive meeting later that week. He had not been with the organization for long and needed to carefully consider how to approach many of these issues. He knew that the executive could not alienate the organization's core fan base or dilute the quality of the UFC experience for its viewers. The massive potential of the European, Middle Eastern, and Asian markets was an opportunity that could not be overlooked; however, moving into those international markets would not be as simple as

duplicating the experience offered in the United States. Despite the company's strong financial position, the UFC could not afford to make significant investments in unprofitable new markets. To further complicate his job, Johnston realized that White and the Fertitta brothers did not operate their company in a typical manner; they had become enormously successful by trusting their instincts and gambling on their emotions. Johnston was concerned about the potential for this mentality to lead the company down the wrong path. White and the Fertittas had done a remarkable job at building the UFC brand, but Johnston's experience told him how quickly their success could change if they did not take the right steps to protect it. His decisions would play a crucial role in shaping the future of the organization.

## CASE QUESTIONS

1. What are the primary challenges the UFC faces in defending its domestic market or reaching new customers in those markets? Do you believe young women, ages 18 to 36, represent a viable new target market? Why or why not?

2. When seeking to build the fan base by expanding into other countries, what aspects of each nation should be most carefully considered first?

3. How could the UFC product, the actual fights, be improved to attract a greater number of fans?

4. When a general sports fan considers the UFC brand, what aspects of the past may hurt the brand? How can the company refine the brand in order to retain current fans and reach the more general sports fan?

5. What additional branding opportunities are possible for the UFC?

# ———— Best Buy Inc.—Dual Branding in China ————

*By R. Chandrasekhar, under the supervision of Professor Niraj Dawar*

In June 2006, John Noble, senior vice president at Best Buy International, a division of Best Buy Inc. (Best Buy), the largest retailer of consumer electronics (CE) in the United States, faced a major strategic branding decision. Earlier that month, the company had acquired a majority stake in Jiangsu

Five Star Appliances (Five Star), the third-largest retailer of appliances and consumer electronics in China. Noble had been assigned to the international division just a month earlier from the company's Canadian operations, where he had held a similar position since 2002. In his new role,

Version: (A) 2010–05–11

Noble was tasked to decide and plan how Best Buy should implement a dual-brand strategy in China. The dual-brand strategy adopted in Canada four years earlier seemed to have worked well. "Will the dual-brand strategy work in China?" he wondered. "How should I make it work?"

While negotiating for a majority stake in Five Star, which had 135 stores in China, Best Buy announced plans to open its first Best Buy store in China in December 2006, to be followed by two more stores in the next 12 to 18 months. Five Star also announced its own agenda of opening 25 additional stores in China, under the Five Star banner, during approximately the same period.

## Context

When Best Buy decided to go beyond the domestic market in the United States in December 2000, the company had found neighboring Canada to be a logical first step. The Canadian CE market was fragmented, with only one dominant player, Future Shop. Best Buy's original objective was to set up its own stores in various Canadian cities to compete directly with Future Shop stores. It had planned to open the first of several stores in the Toronto area in 2003, and then embark on a three-year expansion program that would see the launch of 15 stores in major Canadian cities. Best Buy had a target of setting up 60 to 65 stores across Canada, competing with the 95 stores of Future Shop, which itself was planning to increase its stores to 120 over four years. As part of a defense strategy, Future Shop was also finalizing plans to relocate or renovate at least half of its existing stores by 2005.

In August 2001, the founders of the two companies met and decided, over the course of three weeks, that "together we could accomplish infinitely more than if we were to go our own ways and compete with each other."[1] By January 2002, Best Buy had acquired 100 percent ownership in Future Shop. Then, when the time came to finalize integration, the management of Best Buy took a surprising decision: to retain the Future Shop brand and let it compete with Best Buy as an independent brand, a strategy that had no precedent within the company. The dual-brand strategy—wherein two brands, both part of a common corporate entity, vied for market share—was an initiative being tested for the first time at Best Buy (see Exhibit 1).

In reference to whether the dual brand strategy could be implemented, Richard Schulze, the founder of Best Buy, was famously quoted for saying, at the time of the acquisition, "I'm not saying it can't be done, I'm saying it's never been done before. . . ."

| **Exhibit 1** | Best Buy and Future Shop in 2002 | |
|---|---|---|
| | **Best Buy** | **Future Shop** |
| Typical store size | 35,000 square feet | 26,000 square feet |
| Store associates | Blue Shirts | Product Experts |
| Staff mandate | Technology is fun. We make it easy for the customer | Providing Trusted Personalized Service |
| Customers | Tech enthusiasts who enjoy the interactive shopping experience and grab-and-go convenience | Tech savvy; a notch higher than the Best Buy customer; at the cutting edge of developments in technology |
| Aisles | Wide aisles to provide for grab-and-go shopping | Highlights key technologies first |

*(Continued)*

| **Exhibit 1** | (Continued) |

| | Best Buy | Future Shop |
|---|---|---|
| Service | Upon request | Attentive |
| Sales | Customer led<br>No high-pressure salesmanship | Sales-person led<br>Commission-based sales |
| Target group | Higher success rate with female customers | Male-oriented |
| Customer profile | 15 to 39 years | 25 to 44 years |
| Brand identity | "Turn on the fun" | "The place to get it first" |
| In-store experience | Relaxed | Guided |
| Product mix | Although by category the two store brands were very similar, each was able to offer a unique selection of products and brands. Product brands and depth of selection differed within product categories. On average, 45 percent overlap of the product assortment (excluding entertainment software) between the two store brands. | |
| Areas of distinction | Higher propensity towards self-service; non-commissioned sales staff; greater assortment of ready-made electronics packages; wider aisles and more interactive displays; higher ratio of female customers, seeking to integrate products into their lifestyles; customers with higher incomes and higher levels of education | Commissioned sales staff guiding the customer by providing customized, trusted and personalized approach; tech savvy, early adopters looking for the best deal; customer base more diverse |

*Source:* Company files

## Best Buy

Headquartered in Minneapolis in the United States, Best Buy was driven by a vision of "meeting consumers at the intersection of technology and life."[2] The company saw its core strategy as "bringing technology and consumers together in a retail environment that focuses on educating consumers on the features and benefits of technology and entertainment while maximizing overall profitability."[3] Best Buy was positioned to deliver new technologies at the retail level in the three segments of devices, connections, and content, enabling the company to capitalize on the progressive digitization of analog products and the accelerating digital product cycles to mobilize

consumer demand. The company was selling its products at moderate to upper moderate price points.

Growing at a rate of between 15 percent and 20 percent every year, Best Buy had attained sales revenues of US$30.9 billion for the year ending March 2006 (see Exhibit 2). The company had more than 20 percent share of the retail American consumer electronics market, which was valued at US$152 billion in 2006.[4] Globally, the CE market was averaging a growth rate of 10 percent and was expected, according to CEA/GfK Worldwide Consumer Electronics Sales & Forecast, to reach revenues of US$700 billion by 2009.[5] In planning to maintain double-digit growth rate year after year, Best Buy saw, in its international expansion, a window of opportunity.

**Exhibit 2**   Best Buy Inc.—Income Statement

| Year ending March (in US$million) | 2006 | 2005 | 2004 | 2003 | 2002 | 2001 | 2000 | 1999 |
|---|---|---|---|---|---|---|---|---|
| **Revenue** | | | | | | | | |
| Domestic | 27,380 | 24,616 | 22,225 | 20,946 | 17,711 | 15,326 | 12,494 | 10,064 |
| International | 3,468 | 2,817 | 2,323 | – | – | – | – | – |
| Total | 30,848 | 27,433 | 24,548 | 20,946 | 17,711 | 15,326 | 12,494 | 10,064 |
| Less: Cost of goods sold | 23,122 | 20,938 | 18,677 | 15,710 | 13,941 | 12,267 | 10,100 | 8,250 |
| Gross profit | 7,726 | 6,495 | 5,871 | 5,236 | 3,770 | 3,059 | 2,394 | 1,814 |
| Less: S&G expenses | 6,082 | 5,053 | 4,567 | 4,226 | 2,862 | 2,455 | 1,854 | 1,463 |
| Operating income | 1,644 | 1,442 | 1,304 | 1,010 | 908 | 604 | 539 | 351 |
| Net interest income | 77 | 1 | (8) | 4 | 18 | 37 | 23 | 1 |
| Earnings before tax | 1,721 | 1,443 | 1,296 | 1,014 | 926 | 641 | 562 | 352 |
| Income tax | 581 | 509 | 496 | 392 | 356 | 245 | 215 | 136 |
| Other (Loss)/Gain | – | 50 | (95) | (523) | – | – | – | – |
| Net earnings | 1,140 | 984 | 705 | 99 | 570 | 396 | 347 | 216 |
| **Category wise revenue** **Domestic** | | | | | | | | |
| – Home Office | 8,762 | 8,380 | 7,556 | – | – | | | |
| – Video & Audio | 11,773 | 9,609 | 8,445 | – | – | | | |
| – Ent. Software | 5,202 | 5,169 | 4,889 | – | – | | | |
| – Appliances | 1,643 | 1,476 | 1,335 | – | – | | | |
| **International** | | | | | | | | |
| – Home Office | 1,526 | 1,127 | 929 | – | – | | | |
| – Video & Audio | 1,318 | 1,155 | 930 | – | – | | | |
| – Ent. Software | 487 | 422 | 348 | – | – | | | |
| – Appliances | 139 | 113 | 116 | – | – | | | |
| Number of employees (in 000s) | 128 | | | | | | | |
| Cash and equivalents (in US$million) | 681 | 354 | 245 | | | | | |

*Source:* Best Buy annual report.

## History

Best Buy was founded in 1966, by Richard Schulze, an American entrepreneur from the mid-west. The chain, which was known at the time as Sound of Music, was retailing audio components sourced from vendors. The company struggled through the recession years of the 1970s, and with the arrival of the video cassette recorder in the early 1980s, the music chain expanded into retailing video components. In 1983, Sound of Music moved into mass merchandising by switching to a superstore format (characterized by a wide range of products and boxes of merchandise in a warehouse atmosphere) under the new, distinctive yellow Best Buy banner. Six years later, Best Buy refined its retailing techniques in three ways: the introduction of self-service, the placement of its salespersons (referred to as "Blue Shirts") on fixed pay instead of on commission, and reconfiguration of stores' formats to a discount style. The changes were made in recognition of both a trend in customers of being knowledgeable enough to choose products on their own and their preference of shopping in a consumer-friendly environment.

## Innovations

The company's decision to stop paying commissions to salespersons and put them on salary did not go well initially with vendors such as Toshiba and Hitachi. These manufacturers had long felt that a high-pressure, incentives-oriented, and results-driven approach at the store was necessary to move products. But Best Buy soon realized that its customers were comfortable in the new, informal ambience at its stores.

After entering new domestic markets, such as Chicago, Philadelphia, and Boston, Best Buy became the biggest seller of home personal computers (PCs) in 1995, in time for the Internet boom. In 1996, Best Buy surpassed Circuit City to become the top CE retailer in the United States, a position that Best Buy had since held.

Best Buy had spotted another trend. Digital devices and home networks were growing in complexity, opening up a prospect for marketing the necessary technical services to homes and small businesses. This opportunity was pegged at being worth more than US$20 billion a year in the United States. Best Buy had acquired, in October 2002, a Minneapolis-based start-up specializing in repairing and installing PCs, called Geek Squad. Within a year, Best Buy had Geek Squad precincts, staffed by newly recruited techies, in more than 20 stores. By 2005, the geeks had set up shop in all Best Buy stores. The move was an advantage over competitors, such as Walmart, which did not provide service back-up for their CE sales.

## Centricity

Best Buy had identified the technology enthusiast as its core customer. This target group was characterized by the following attributes: aged 15 to 39, male, highly educated, above-average income and eager for products and services that would render personal time both productive and enjoyable, and resonate with being fun, honest, young and techno-savvy. Best Buy was building its brand promise on those very lines: "being fun, honest, young, and techno-savvy."

In the late 1990s, Best Buy established a standard operating platform (SOP) for replication across the chain, which included procedures for inventory management, transaction processing, customer relations, store administration, products sales and merchandising. SOP had a harmonizing effect on the company, helping ensure consistency and enforcing discipline across the network of stores. Best Buy was now a process-driven organization with systems and procedures firmly in place. By early 2000, however, Best Buy was evolving from being an organization thriving on standardization to one offering, within a standard format, different value propositions appealing to different groups of customers. Thus, the company began in 2001 to test and implement a concept it called centricity.

The concept was based on four elements:

1. Identifying customers generating the most revenue

2. Segmenting these customers

3. Realigning the stores to meet the needs of these customers

4. Empowering the store sales staff, known as Blue Shirts, to steer these customers toward products and services that would encourage them to visit more often and spend more on each visit

The company's market researchers combed through reams of sales and demographic data to determine whether a particular location should be tailored to, say, empty nesters or small business owners. A store located in a geographical area characterized by a higher density of homemakers would, for example, include features such as personal shopping assistants (PSAs) who were chosen from among Blue Shirts to help a shopper with such tasks as selecting the right digital camera for her family. Blue Shirts were schooled in financial metrics, such as return on capital, so that they could ascertain for themselves the effectiveness of merchandising.

Centricity was a big investment in terms of enhancing end user experience. The company examined, in detail, everything from store fixtures and layout to the product–employee mix and staff training. Recasting a store toward affluent tech-enthusiasts would cost approximately US$600,000 alone for lighting and fixtures. The concept of centricity, which was built essentially on customer insights, was also meant to encourage employee innovations in support of a better customer experience, not just at a single moment in time but on a continuous basis. The goal was to drive customer engagement and foster repeat visits.

## Store Operations

At headquarters in Minneapolis, Best Buy store operations were organized into three divisions. Each division was divided into regions under the supervision of a senior vice president overseeing store performance through regional managers who were with responsibility for a number of districts within the region. The district managers monitored store operations closely. Each district also had a loss prevention manager, and product security personnel employed at each store controlled inventory shrinkage. Best Buy controlled advertising, pricing, and inventory policies from corporate headquarters.

## Competitors

The CE retail market in the United States was competitive at four levels. The major competitors were mass merchandisers (e.g., Walmart and Costco). These competitors were regularly increasing their portfolio of CE products, particularly of those products less complex to sell, install, and operate. Contemporary channels of distribution (such as Internet shopping, facilitated by e-commerce platforms set up by some manufacturers themselves) were the second source of competition. Also competing in the CE market and gaining market share were factory-direct shopping services (e.g., Dell Computers). Finally, home improvement retailers (e.g., Home Depot and Lowe's) were also entering into the consumer electronic product market. Lines were blurring as retailers of all kinds were widening their product assortments in pursuit of revenues and margins.

## Dual Branding in Canada

Best Buy paid Cdn$560.71 million (US$363.95 million) to acquire Future Shop, based on the offering price of Cdn$17 per share, a 47.8 percent premium over the market price of Cdn$11.50 per share. However, a little over a year after deciding to expand internationally, Best Buy experimented with a concept that was novel in the CE market worldwide. Said Noble:

There were four reasons why Best Buy veered towards a dual-branding strategy in Canada. First, the Canadian CE market was fragmented with the leader, Future Shop, having only about 15 percent share. We felt there was room for a second brand. Given that most retail sectors in the US had at least two major players—for example, Home Depot/Lowe's and Staples/Office Depot—we felt that a second major retailer in CE in Canada would be in order. Second, Best Buy had already signed, before perceiving Future Shop as a potential target for acquisition, about eight real estate leases as part of its original greenfield approach. Some of these leased spaces (as in the Heartland location at Mississauga, a suburb of Toronto) were situated right next to Future Shop stores for planned head-to-head competition. We were committed to those locations. Third, there were operational factors. Conversion of Future Shop stores into Best Buy stores would take a while, particularly in terms of store redesigns and staff transition. Not all the elements of Best Buy's SOP could simply be set up "as is" in Canada. There would be a period of time when the two brands had to be managed independently. As it turned out, it gave us a window through which to look at issues differently. But, the most important reason was the recognition that Future Shop was a well established brand, with over 95 percent unaided brand awareness among Canadians. Replacing such a hugely successful brand with Best Buy, which was unknown in Canada, seemed counter-intuitive.

Best Buy also had other reasons for pursuing a dual-brand strategy. If the senior staff at Future Shop were focused on setting up the Best Buy operation, their activities risked affecting negatively on the existing sales of Future Shop stores. Putting together a separate team at Best Buy, fully dedicated to opening the greenfield stores of Best Buy, as originally planned, would speed up the process of the company's market entry.

But the dual-brand strategy also had some downsides. Said Noble:

We had four concerns about the dual-branding strategy. Cannibalization was, of course, a major issue. It was likely that each Best Buy store would eat into the earnings of a Future Shop store and vice versa, particularly when the two were in close proximity. Since the company would have to manage two different brands, the marketing dollars in Canada would be split in half, minimizing the impact of ad-spend. Also imminent was the possibility of a blurring of brand identity in the eyes of the consumer. Finally, there would be duplication of roles at the corporate headquarters at Minneapolis, with the two brands requiring separate staff inputs.

The two brands were each headed by a vice president based in Vancouver, the location of Best Buy Canada Ltd. (BBYC), the newly formed subsidiary that maintained the two brands. BBYC took several steps to reinforce the operations of both brands at ground level: opening an automated 450,000-square-foot distribution center in Ontario and, eventually, another 500,000-square-foot distribution center in British Columbia, to support store growth for both brands; outsourcing a call center to provide 24-hour service, seven days a week; and retaining a premier insurance company to underwrite product warranties. Stores of both brands were open 60 to 75 hours per week, seven days a week. All stores used the parent company's SOP.

An average Future Shop store was staffed by a general manager, an operations manager, one to four department managers and 48 to 95 sales associates, as well as part-time sales associates. An average Canada Best Buy store was staffed by a general manager; assistant managers for operations, merchandising, inventory and sales; and 80 to 110 sales associates, including full-time and part-time sales associates.

Although Best Buy and Future Shop effectively competed for market share, the positioning for each company was different. Best Buy, with its yellow-price-tag logo continued to offer the "grab and go" option by providing an open floor plan that allowed customers to shop on their own or with the help of a no-pressure (i.e., noncommissioned) Blue Shirt product specialist if desired. Future Shop focused on offering the trusted, personalized customer service for which it was already well known in Canadian cities.

By the end of the first year of operations, there were indications that the dual-branding strategy was working in Canada. For example, the Future Shop store at Mississauga had sales revenues of $40 million in 2001/02. In 2002/03, post-acquisition, revenues were $38 million. Cannibalization was minimal because the Best Buy store, located across the street, had delivered an additional $30 million in sales for the same period. Overall, Best Buy had achieved a combined market share in Canada of 34 percent. In some places, the proximity of the two banners had created a shopping destination. The company's research also pointed out that the customer bases of Best Buy and Future Shop were different. Canadian customers viewed the two brands as distinct, not interchangeable. One indication was that only 18 percent of customers applying for a Best Buy credit card in fiscal 2004 already held a Future Shop credit card (see Exhibit 3).

The board of Best Buy was now willing to support the dual-brand strategy in Canada as long as

Best Buy entered new markets in Canada and delivered on sales targets, while Future Shop continued to deliver on its own sales targets. In negotiating with Five Star in China, the board was willing to support a similar strategy on similar expectations (see Exhibit 4).

## Entering China

A country of 1.3 billion consumers, China had been attracting the attention of overseas investors since it began liberalizing the economy in 1985. Over the next two decades, its manufacturing side boomed, with the growth in gross domestic product (GDP) averaging 10 percent per annum. The consumption side, however, was growing at a pace slower than output and not catching up. Consumption as a percentage of GDP had in fact dropped from 47 percent in 1995 to 37 percent in 2005.[6] A process of adjustment was under way, and because the Chinese economy was moving from the historical investment-led growth model to a consumption-led growth model, many multinational marketers were beginning to see an opportunity. McKinsey Global Institute had predicted that

---

**Exhibit 3**    Best Buy and Future Shop—Performance Metrics 2000 and 2006

| Metric | 2000 | | 2006 | |
|---|---|---|---|---|
| | Best Buy (in US) | Future Shop | Best Buy (in Canada) | Future Shop |
| Sales growth | 21.4% | 17.0% | 34.3% | 14.2% |
| Gross margin | 20.2% | 22.7% | 24.2% | 24.8% |
| SG&A expense ratio | 16.2% | 20.1% | 17.8% | 16.7% |
| Operating margin | 4.0% | 2.6% | 6.4% | 8.1% |
| Sales per square foot | $870 | $746 | $1,010 | $1,069 |
| Inventory turn | 7.5 | 7.4 | 6.4 | 6.4 |
| Operating ROA | 18.7% | 12.77% | n/a | n/a |

*Source:* Deutsche Banc Alex. Brown estimates for 2000 data. Company records for 2006 data.

*Note:* SG&A = selling, general and administrative; ROA = return on assets; n/a = not applicable.

| Exhibit 4 | Best Buy—Number of International Stores 2006 |

| Province/State | Canada | | China | |
|---|---|---|---|---|
| | Best Buy Stores | Future Shop Stores | Best Buy Stores | Five Star Stores |
| Alberta | 7 | 15 | | |
| British Columbia | 7 | 21 | | |
| Manitoba | 2 | 5 | | |
| New Brunswick | – | 3 | | |
| Newfoundland | – | 1 | | |
| Nova Scotia | 1 | 3 | | |
| Ontario | 25 | 55 | | |
| Prince Edward | – | 1 | | |
| Quebec | 8 | 24 | | |
| Saskatchewan | 1 | 3 | | |
| Anhui | | | – | 12 |
| Henan | | | – | 9 |
| Jiangsu | | | – | 99 |
| Shandong | | | – | 9 |
| Shanghai | | | 1 | – |
| Sichuan | | | – | 6 |
| Yunnan | | | – | 4 |
| Zhejiang | | | – | 21 |
| Total | 51 | 131 | 1 | 160 |

Source: Best Buy 2008 annual report.

China would become the third-largest consumer market in the world by 2025 (see Exhibit 5).

Best Buy's original interest in China had been flagged by China's manufacturing base. Since the 1990s, the China had become a major hub in the Asian region for the manufacture of CE components. In a little more than a decade, China was playing host to a number of manufacturers from the United States and Europe. Attracted by the country's low labor costs, these manufacturers had started relocating their domestic manufacturing operations to China. A fast-growing home market was also spurring China's CE manufacturing industry. According to Instat, an American high-tech market research firm with an office in China, the manufacturing end of the CE industry in China, which was estimated at $71.5 billion in 2006, was expected to more than double by 2010.[7]

In September 2003, Best Buy opened a 25-person sourcing office in Shanghai, China. This move complemented the company's plans to expand its existing 450 stores in the United States and 127 stores in Canada to at least 1,200 stores in North America over the long haul. The Shanghai office was seen as a means of both lowering the cost of goods sold and driving gross profit rates on individual

| Exhibit 5 | China's Economy, 2003–2005 |
|---|---|

| | Unit | 2005 | 2004 | 2003 |
|---|---|---|---|---|
| Gross National Income | 100 million Yuan | 183,956.1 | 159,586.7 | 135,174.0 |
| Gross Domestic Product | 100 million Yuan | 183,084.8 | 159,878.3 | 135,822.8 |
| Per capita Gross Domestic Product | Yuan per person | 14,040.0 | 12,336.0 | 10,542.0 |
| Population | Million | 1,307.56 | 1,299.88 | 1,292.27 |
| – Male | | 673.75 | 669.76 | 665.56 |
| – Female | | 633.81 | 630.12 | 626.71 |
| – Urban | | 562.12 | 542.83 | 523.76 |
| – Rural | | 745.54 | 757.05 | 768.51 |
| Economically active persons | Million | 778.77 | 768.23 | 767.05 |
| Number of employed persons | Million | 758.25 | 752.00 | 744.32 |
| Annual Per Capita Income | Yuan | | | |
| – Urban households | | 10,493 | 9,422 | 5,160 |
| – Rural households | | 3,255 | 2,936 | 2,090 |
| Annual Per Capita Consumption Expenditure—Urban households | Yuan | 7,943 | 7,182 | 4,186 |
| – Rural households | | 2,955 | 2,185 | 1,617 |

*Source:* National Bureau of Statistics of China, Chinese Statistical Yearbook, 2006, http://www.stats.gov.cn/tjsj/ndsj/2006/indexeh.htm, accessed December 10, 2008.

products. This office was also meant to fill the gaps in the company's product assortment with private labels from the Asian region. Said Noble:

> China was chosen as the second international expansion market primarily due to the overall market opportunity, consumer fundamentals and macro-economic factors. We did look at other markets such as Europe, especially France and Germany, but, they were mature, competitive and offered less quality retail real estate at a high cost.[8]

The Chinese CE retail market was fragmented. The top five players together held less than 20 percent of the market share. However, the Chinese market was expected to account for 25 percent of the global CE market by 2010. Taking a slice of the new

growth opportunity ranked high on the agendas of multinational corporations. Best Buy was the first, and so far the only, multinational to have entered the retail end of Chinese CE market.

China's CE retail market was, however, a complex terrain to navigate for a new entrant. Price wars were rampant. In categories such as TVs and white goods, excess capacity had squeezed profit margins to less than three percent, the lowest in the world. Although consolidation among electronics retailers had been ongoing, a new wave of mergers and acquisitions (M&As) was evident within a space of a few months in early 2006. Gome Electrical Appliances Holdings Ltd. (Gome), China's leading electronics specialty chain, had already mounted a bid on China Paradise Electronics Retail Ltd. (China Paradise), which itself had struck—and then put on hold—an alliance with the privately owned Dazhong

Electrical Appliance Co. Ltd., the fifth-largest CE retailer in China The formalities pertaining to acquisition of China Paradise by Gome were to reach closure in late July 2006. Best Buy had already acquired Jiangsu Five Star in April 2006.

The Chinese CE market had some unique characteristics. For example, approximately two-thirds of the sales staff in a retail store were on the payroll of suppliers. Also, the rate of growth of "other income" was often higher than the rate of growth in sales. The gross margin of Chinese retailers was understated without taking into account "other income," which included rebates and listing fees, often the equivalent of a retailer's gross profit. Instead of a mark-up on the cost of goods sold, the retailers received rebates.[9]

## Buyer Behavior

In 2004, approximately 36 million urban Chinese households had a disposable income of at least RMB25,000 (approximately US$3,000) a year, which was considered, by local standards, a reasonable threshold for entering the consumer class. By 2009, the number was expected to almost triple, to 105 million urban households. A massive influx of new consumers was now reaching the retail cash registers. Every year, approximately 20 million Chinese (the population of Australia) turned 18 years of age. Prosperity was lifting the incomes of tens of millions more.[10]

Chinese consumers were not prone to opening their wallets freely. The savings rate in China in 2006 was 28 percent of monthly household income, compared with three percent in the United Kingdom and two percent in Canada. Chinese consumers were also not accustomed to the concept of credit. The credit card penetration rate in urban households was less than four percent, compared with 75 percent in the United States, 78 percent in Japan and 91 percent in Germany. Less than six percent of credit card holders in China carried forward their ongoing balances.[11]

Observers had found that Chinese consumers responded better to messages focusing on functional features than those focusing on brand imagery. At one level, Chinese consumers were attracted to brand names but, on another level, they were wary

of premium prices. Brand preferences of customers did not always translate into revenues in the form of increased market share for companies. Salespersons held sway over the buying decisions of consumers who were also influenced by point-of-sale promotions to make last-minute switches. Because Chinese consumers had a sense of national pride, a multinational corporation, by seeming foreign, could lose potential customer segments.[12]

## Growth Centers

In markets such as the United States and Canada, consumers exhibited few differences between regions, which required companies to make choices only between products and segments. In China, the trade-offs had an additional dimension, requiring product-segment-region choices. Marketers had to factor in regional differences because as one moved across tiers of cities in China, a steep drop-off was experienced in infrastructure, channels and disposable income. When a mass merchandiser entered China, it evaluated the country's cities, giving each locale a tier designation on the basis of size, sophistication, purchasing habits, attitudes, and disposable income of its population and its own product offerings.[13] A typical classification is shown in Exhibit 6.

A massive increase in retail space was evidence of increasing competition in China's tier-one cities in particular. Major players were eyeing growth opportunities in tier-two and tier-three cities. The attendant risk was the longer breakeven point because, given the much lower income levels in those cities, sales would be slower. However, the costs of retail space would be lower, and given less competition, margins were likely to be higher.

China also had other limitations. Land acquisition in cities was often difficult; procedural delays meant that a new entrant would take at least six months to open a store; relationships between vendors and retailers were so close and guarded by local customs and preferences, that an outsider did not have an easy time getting a foot in the door. Manufacturers of CE were not likely to cut a new entrant such as Best Buy much slack on pricing, particularly because personal relationships (referred

**Exhibit 6**   China's Tiered Cities

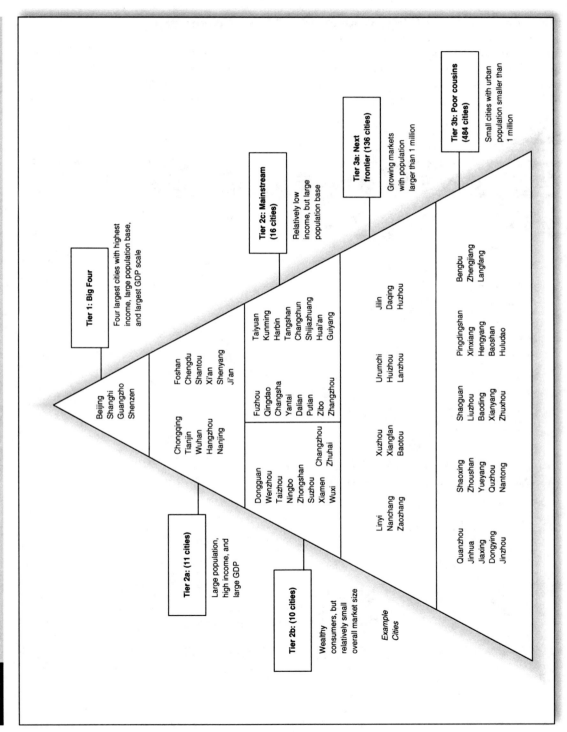

**Tier 1: Big Four**

Four largest cities with highest income, large population base, and largest GDP scale

Beijing
Shanghi
Guangzho
Shenzen

**Tier 2a: (11 cities)**

Large population, high income, and large GDP

Chongqing
Tianjin
Wuhan
Hangzhou
Nanjing

Foshan
Chengdu
Shantou
Xi'an
Shenyang
Ji'an

**Tier 2b: (10 cities)**

Wealthy consumers, but relatively small overall market size

Dongguan
Wenzhou
Taizhou
Ningbo
Zhongshan
Suzhou
Xiamen
Wuxi

Changzhou
Zhuhai

**Tier 2c: Mainstream (16 cities)**

Relatively low income, but large population base

Fuzhou
Qingdao
Changsha
Yantai
Dalian
Putian
Zibo
Zhangzhou

Taiyuan
Kunming
Harbin
Tangshan
Changchun
Shijiazhuang
Huai'an
Guiyang

**Tier 3a: Next frontier (136 cities)**

Growing markets with population larger than 1 million

Linyi
Nanchang
Zaozhang

Xuzhou
Xiangfan
Baotou

Urumchi
Huizhou
Lanzhou

Jilin
Daqing
Huzhou

**Tier 3b: 'Poor cousins' (484 cities)**

Small cities with urban population smaller than 1 million

Quanzhou
Jinhua
Jiaxing
Dongying
Jinzhou

Shaoxing
Zhoushan
Yueyang
Quzhou
Nantong

Shaoguan
Liuzhou
Baoding
Xianyang
Zhuxhou

Pingdingshan
Xinxiang
Hengyang
Baoshan
Huludao

Bengbu
Zhengjiang
Langfang

*Example
Cities*

*Source:* Diana Farrell et al., from *"Made in China"* to *"Sold in China": The Rise of the Chinese Urban Consumer,* McKinsey Global Institute, November 2006.

to as "guanxi" in local terminology) influenced the conduct of business among Chinese who were more comfortable dealing with people they knew. China was also experiencing a crunch of quality human resources because retailing, as an industry, had not yet developed in the country.

## Major Competitors

Before being acquired by Best Buy, Five Star had two major competitors, Gome Electrical Appliances Holdings Ltd. (Gome) and Suning, both publicly held (see Exhibit 7). Together, the two

**Exhibit 7**  Major Competitors in China

| Financials (in RMB million) | Gome | | Suning | |
|---|---|---|---|---|
| | 2004 | 2005 | 2004 | 2005 |
| Revenue | 12,647 | 17,959 | 9,107 | 15,936 |
| Net profit | 486 | 496 | | |
| Revenue by geography (%) | | | | |
| – Northeast China | | 5 | | 3 |
| – North China | | 33 | | 15 |
| – East China | | 9 | | 59 |
| – West China | | 23 | | 5 |
| – South China | | 26 | | 15 |
| – Central China | | 4 | | 3 |
| Sales per square meter | 25,940 | | 32,141 | 23,929 |
| Number of stores | 442 | | 94 | 224 |
| Revenue by category (%) | | | | |
| – Air conditioners | | 16 | | |
| – Audiovisual | | 28 | | |
| – Refrigerators/Washing machines | | 18 | | |
| – Telecom | | 16 | | |
| – Small electrical appliances | | 10 | | |
| – Digital/IT products | | 12 | | |
| – Service | | – | | |
| Mission | "Competitive pricing from high volume" | | "Service is the sole product of Suning" | |
| Store formats, positioning | a. Traditional (3,500 square meters): price-conscious mass market<br>b. Digital (260 square meters): high-end customer in downtown<br>c. Eagle (15,000 square meters): service-conscious, mid to high-end customers | | Flagship: in large cities<br>Central: the most common | |

*Sources:* Gome Electrical Appliances Holdings Limited website, http://www.gome.com.hk/eng, accessed December 5, 2008; Suning website, www.cnsuning.com/include/english, accessed December 5, 2008; Jean Zhou, Deutsche Bank equity research Report, dated April 7, 2006; Sandy Chen, Citigroup equity research report on Gome, dated October 12, 2005.

companies had saturated many of the country's largest cities over the past few years. Although the total market shares in 2005 of the top five in 2005 (comprising Gome, Suning, Five Star and two others) accounted for less than 20 percent of market share, Gome and Suning held a combined market share of 70 percent in some appliance product categories, such as air conditioners.

## Gome Group

The Gome Group had two companies: Gome Electrical Appliances Holdings Ltd. and Beijing Gome (an unlisted company). In 1993, Gome opened its first store in Beijing, and soon expanded into other major cities in China, gaining widespread consumer acceptance. By mid-2005, the group had 437 stores (of which 263 belonged to the listed company) in 132 cities in China, with the most extensive distribution network of all the home appliance retailers in China. It was leading in all regional markets (Northeast China, North China, Northwest China, South West China, and South China) with the exception of East China, the home market of Suning, where Gome was ranked number three.[14] Gome was the largest CE retailer in China with six percent market share, prior to its acquisition of China Paradise. The company was mounting a bid on China Paradise, likely to come through in a few weeks, for a record sum of $677 million.[15]

At the beginning of 2005, Gome had announced its four-year growth initiative aimed at enlarging its geographical coverage and raising its national market share to 10 to 15 percent by the end of 2008. Although Gome had set itself apart, to start with, on a super-store format offering the lowest prices, the differentiation had been subsequently commoditized in by its competitors. Gome had then cracked the traditional business model (of selling through intermediaries to various retail formats) by dealing directly with mega brands. In introducing category killers, the company had set a new trend in CE retailing in China. The company had also begun to focus on pre-sales service, as opposed to the industry practice of after-sales service, by advising customers on which brands to choose. Because this service was not easy to

implement at the store level, where brands had their own commission-based sales staff, Gome was examining a new store format it called Eagle (Gome had been known earlier as China Eagle). Gome opened its first Eagle store in December 2005, in Shenyang. This mega-store, which occupied 15,000 square meters differed in two ways: all sales staff at Eagle were on the payroll of Gome; and the display format was based on categories not brands. The company was planning to open six to nine Eagle stores in the next three years, depending upon how the performance of the first two.

The group was planning to expand rapidly into tier-two cities in particular, not only because of improvements in economies of scale and customer acquisition but also because, as a first mover, it could secure preferential tax treatments from local governments welcoming jobs creation opportunities. It was unlikely that the second or third movers would be entitled to the benefits offered to the first mover.[16]

## Suning

Suning had grown from a regional air-conditioning retailer to a leading CE retail chain in China in less than a decade. It was in the process of converting its stores into a customer-oriented format it called 3C (computers, communications and consumer electronics). The company was on an expansion spree, increasing its stores five fold in the last three years to 224, with more than half of them opening in 2005 alone, covering 61 cities. It was now planning to double the number of stores in two years. By the end of 2006, only 25 percent of Suning's retail space would have been opened for two years or more. In common with Gome, which also had a high proportion of new retail space, rapid store expansion and entry into less affluent tier-two cities had led to lower productivity of retail space at Suning.[17]

Suning operated three types of stores that shared the same format: flagship, central, and community. The stores differed in size and product assortment. Flagship stores were found in large cities or regional headquarters. These stores were the largest in size and sold a wide variety of products. The central stores were most common. All the stores were CE retail stores targeting the mass market.

Suning sought differentiation in two ways. It was aligning its product assortment to address the needs of what it called "3C" customer groups (computers, communications and consumer electronics). It was also using service as its key competitive advantage. The company had set up 15 regional distribution centers, 30 customer service centers, and 500 service stations of its own to reinforce the message that service was its main product.

## Five Star

Five Star was China's third-largest electronics and appliances chain. It had 135 stores located mostly in the fast-growing, second-tier cities, in eight of China's 34 provinces. Founded in 1998 and headquartered in Nanjing in Jiangsu province, it had revenues of US$700 million in 2005, a 50 percent increase over 2004. The company's founder Wang Jianguo wanted to expand internationally but was constrained by delays in official permissions for listing his company abroad. "Our scale was becoming a bottleneck to development," he said.[18] When Best Buy sounded the idea of making an investment in the company, he decided to cash out and offload 75 percent stake in the company to Best Buy for $180 million. Five Star employed more than 12,000 of its own employees (see Exhibit 8).

| **Exhibit 8** | Best Buy and Five Star—July 2006 |
|---|---|

| Metric | Best Buy[1] | Five Star |
|---|---|---|
| Store size | 86,000 square feet | 35,000 square feet |
| Customers | Middle-to upper-income young singles and couples | Middle-income families<br>Somewhat price sensitive |
| Service | Mixed-brand packaged solutions displayed by lifestyle requirements | Personal shopping assistants guiding customers through vendor booths: Attentive |
| Sales | Led by non-commissioned staff on Best Buy's payroll | Led by staff on the payroll of manufacturer |
| Customer profile | 18–42 years old | 20–50 years old |
| Brand identity | Premium full service | Good price with good services |
| In-store experience | Grab and go | Guided |
| Product mix (%) | | White goods: 16%<br>Air conditioning: 23%<br>Home entertainment: 25%<br>Digital products: 7%<br>Cell phones: 13%<br>Kitchen utensils: 9%<br>Small appliances: 5% |
| Store associates | 100% employed by Best Buy and non-commissioned | 30% employed by Five Star on non-commission; 70% employed by vendors on commission |

| Metric | Best Buy[1] | Five Star |
|---|---|---|
| Sales growth | | 44% |
| Gross margin | | 13.5% |
| SG&A expense ratio | | 11.5% |
| Operating margin | | 2.0% |
| Sales per square foot | | $230 |
| Inventory turn | | 7 |
| Operating ROA | | 5% |

*Source:* Company files

*Note:* SG&A = selling, general and administrative; ROA = return on assets.

1. Best Buy was yet to open its store in China as of June 2006.

## Issues in June 2006

In examining the prospects of dual-branding strategy in China, Noble had to make a call on whether it would serve as well in China as it did in Canada. He had to define the road map for implementing the strategy in China. In a broader context, he also had to explore the possibility of developing dual branding into Best Buy's main competence over time. Best Buy was now at a stage at which the learning it had gained from international expansion, initiated in 2002, could be used to accelerate the company's transformation in the U.S. domestic market, which it considered its core market. In his new role at Best Buy International, Noble was regularly tracking and evaluating global opportunities,

looking for growing economies with buoyant consumer demand. Turkey and Mexico were potential targets for international expansion.

Customer centricity was a home-grown competence that Best Buy had deployed in Canada, and that seemed to have a universal appeal, applicable to any new market. SOP, which the company owned, was another. Geek Squad, a company innovation, seemed to be equally pervasive. Noble wondered whether a dual-branding strategy, which had been executed in Canada, could be as readily implemented in the international markets of the future. Was there a template of dual-branding that could be deployed, with a minor tweaking where necessary, to any new market, he wondered. What would that template be?

### CASE QUESTIONS

1. What are the primary advantages of using a dual-brand strategy in China? Are they the same as what occurred in Canada?

2. What are the primary disadvantages of using a dual-brand strategy in China? Are they the same as what occurred in Canada?

3. What are the advantages of moving to a single brand name in China?

4. What are the disadvantages of moving to a single brand name in China?

5. Are there any cultural differences in Canada, as compared with China, that would affect the choice of brand strategy?

6. In terms of employees, would allowing Five Star to retain its management team and local employees create problems or opportunities for Best Buy? What happened in Canada? Does that outcome affect your answer?

# Pricing

A price is the amount charged for a good or service. Two common factors influence consumers as they consider prices: emotional factors and situational factors. Many purchases contain emotional components, with emotions ranging from fear to love to taking care of personal security or one's family. Situational factors reflect the immediate circumstance in which a purchase is made. An impulse buy, made on the spot, provides an example of how the situation can influence a decision.

A price perceptual map helps the marketing team examine brand image and brand market position relative to competing brands. Often, price and quality form the two axes of a price perceptual map graph. Marketers can examine the status of a brand relative to others along the two dimensions chosen.

A second tool used to examine pricing is the evaluation of customer value along primary and secondary factors. The primary factors are quality, brand image, price, and competitive comparisons. Perceived substitutes, uniqueness, switching costs, and availability are on the list of secondary factors. Consumers determine the values of brands using the two factors to assess various competitors.

## Pricing Strategies and Objectives

A pricing strategy indicates the basic direction the company's marketing and management team intends to take when setting prices. The pricing strategy expresses the relationship between the level of quality the company attempts to provide and the price it will charge.

Pricing objectives create the starting point for determining pricing strategies. Four common pricing objectives are sales maximization, profit maximization, market-share maximization, and competitive parity. Sales maximization may be achieved by charging higher prices to increase revenue per item or by asking lower prices in order to increase volume. Profit maximization strategies consider price along with the cost of the item in order to select the price that optimizes eventual profits. Market share maximization strategies emphasize the long term when making pricing decisions. Competitive parity may be achieved by pricing near company competitors and then competing on variables other than price.

## ◪ Setting Prices

The four basic approaches for setting prices are (1) cost-oriented, (2) demand-oriented, (3) competition-oriented, and (4) profit-oriented. Typically, more than one approach is used even though one method will be given priority.

The cost-oriented approach reflects the amount needed to cover the fixed and variable costs necessary to stay in business. The two most common methods are cost-plus pricing and markup pricing. Cost-plus pricing bases the price of the product on its fixed costs, its variable costs, and a desired contribution margin. The price that is set covers all three items. Markup pricing indicates the difference between the price of an item and the cost to produce that item, without including fixed costs. The method works well for retailers selling numerous products and for manufacturers that produce a multitude of items.

The demand-oriented approach finds an equilibrium point at which there is a balance between the amount available (supply) and what people are willing to pay (demand). Shortages drive up prices; excess supply pushes the price down. Careful market research is undertaken to determine demand levels at various prices.

Competition-oriented pricing matches the maturity stage of the product life cycle. The three basic approaches are

1. below the industry average,

2. at the industry average, and

3. above the industry average.

Below-the-industry-average pricing makes the selling price the key feature of the marketing program. At-the-industry-average pricing will be found in oligopolistic situations and in markets where brand parity prevails. Above-the-industry-average pricing emphasizes exclusivity, quality, and superiority.

The profit-oriented approach maximizes profits by setting the price at the highest possible level. Profit-oriented pricing captures start-up costs quickly, especially in circumstances in which a company will not experience new competition in the short term.

A consideration or evoked parity set contains the set of brands the consumer views as being approximately equal in all the aspects that customers value. A brand comparison perceptual map assists in identifying brands that meet the threshold of value that will be considered along with those for which inert parity exists, thereby eliminating the brands from consideration.

## ◪ Pricing New Products

Introducing a new product creates a unique pricing situation. Company leaders have some latitude when setting the price. The price ceiling will be the highest possible price; the price floor will be the lowest.

Skimming price strategies set the price near the ceiling and emphasize the exclusivity of owning a new product. Skimming also is used in dual-channel marketing when products are first introduced in the business-to-business segment at a higher price. Penetration pricing sets the first price near the price floor. The objective is to discourage the entry of competition while building market share. When deciding on the strategy to employ, marketers consider the advantages or uniqueness of the product, the similarity to substitutes, the risks of switching and switching costs, the company's corporate image, the presence or absence of copyright or patent protections, and the ease of market entry by competitors.

The initial price of a product establishes the reference price, which is what customers identify with the new product. When setting a price, marketing managers may use an incremental approach, which bases the price on the incremental costs of producing the product over the costs of producing an existing product. When a new product costs 15% more to produce than an existing product, the new item will be priced 15% higher.

## Price Discounts

One common tactic used to attract new customers is offering a price discount. Lower prices seem more attractive and pose less of a purchase risk. Price discounts are offered to consumers in the forms of sale prices (e.g., loss leaders, promotional prices, and introductory prices), seasonal discounts, quality discounts, and bundle discounts. For businesses, the discounts include sale prices, volume discounts, and early payment discounts. Price discounts can be analyzed using break-even analysis techniques.

## Changing Prices of Existing Products

When considering price changes, marketing managers examine the potential reactions of consumers, reactions of competitors, whether the company is an industry leader or follower, the impact on brand image, and the impact on the company's gross margin. Weber's Law suggests that unless a price change is more than 10%, it will not have an impact.

Price reductions result from lower production costs, increased competition, meeting a competitor's price reduction, and declines in demand. One or more of these circumstances will be present before a reduction will be considered.

Price increases are undertaken when production costs rise. In most industries, an industry leader leads the way on price increases. Prices can be raised incrementally or in one step. Marketers evaluate the potential impact on customers and competitors when choosing the price increase method.

## Legal and Ethical Pricing Issues

The Federal Trade Commission (FTC) and other agencies monitor the pricing practices of firms. When price discrimination occurs, a company sells merchandise to different buyers at different prices. Price fixing is an agreement between competitors to charge the same price for a good or service, even if the agreement has been reached informally. Deceptive pricing is any pricing practice that misleads customers. The standard is that a typical person would be deceived by the practice or that it induced the typical person to make a purchase. Predatory pricing is pricing designed to eliminate competition. In essence, a company tries to price a competitor out of business. The FTC is empowered to intervene in these issues when necessary.

## Pricing and Customer Service

A strong connection exists between prices and customer service. Simply stated, customers paying higher prices expect the best customer service. When customers consider a new company, product, or service, many factors influence the final choice. The one common denominator for markets, products, brands, and price is the connection to customer service. The company that delivers memorable, quality service automatically creates a marketing advantage.

## The Cases

### Hanson Production: Pricing for Opening Day

Hanson Productions, a theatrical production company founded by a husband and wife, had grown to moderate status in the Broadway district in New York. The most current production, which was about to open, featured some racial overtones that resonated with the 2008 presidential campaign. For Joanne Shen, president of productions, the key issues to resolve included the size of the venue for the show along with ticket prices. Pricing too low left money on the table and made it difficult to recoup the upfront investment. Prices that were too high alienated both theater patrons and critics. Lowering prices signaled a form of defeat and made raising them to regular prices extremely difficult. Joanne was facing the classic dilemma regarding quantity, quality, and price.

### Sy.Med Development, Inc.

As president of Sy.Med Development, Jim Ayers was concerned. The company's annual sales were far below projections and, as a result, the company incurred losses. Although the software to be used by physicians was innovative and would have saved most medical practices containing 20 doctors or more substantial amounts of money, it was not selling. The small, eight-person company was in jeopardy. Ayers wondered if the selling price, which was about $15,000 for the first year with relatively small maintenance costs each year after, was the problem. His primary decision was whether to lower the asking price, knowing that the marginal costs of producing additional units were extremely low.

### Arvind Mills: Re-Evaluating Profitability

Arvind Mills is a large textile and garment manufacturer located in India. The company's vice-president for operations, Mr. Bala, had a major dilemma. One of the company's strengths, cotton denim fabrics, had begun to lose significant market share to companies in China. Although the textile industry was a major force in India, Arvind Mills encountered difficulties based, in part, on national regulations that tended to favor smaller competitors. The overwhelming problems, however, were cost and price. Arvind Mills was unable to meet the prices set by Chinese competitors due to higher production costs. Governmental restrictions and other forces had kept the company from modernizing its production technologies, thereby reinforcing the cost problems.

# Hanson Production: Pricing for Opening Day

*By Peter Famiglietti, under the supervision of Professor June Cotte*

## Hanson Productions

Formed in the mid-1950s by a husband and wife team, Hanson Productions had earned acclaim with its off-Broadway shows. The company's goal was to further the advancement of the arts in New York City. Hanson's first show had been a small production of *Cat on a Hot Tin Roof,* which had played off-off Broadway to an audience of 50 people, most of whom were friends and relatives of the cast. Over time, the quality and scope of Hanson Productions' shows outgrew the off-off Broadway model, and the company began opening at some respected off-Broadway venues.

The company achieved its first major success in the 1970s, when a well-known Academy Award–winner had fallen in love with a script that the Hansons had under option. The script was a musical based on the Old West and had several great musical numbers for the two leads. The Oscar-winning actor had made an offer to purchase the script himself but the Hansons, recognizing his passion for the material (and hoping to entice him into the show), offered him a role as an executive producer. Their bet paid off, and the high-profile star helped the Hansons to secure a major theater on Broadway. This move was the beginning of a successful production that opened to remarkable reviews and a healthy advance. The show went on to win a Tony for Best Musical.

From that moment forward, the Hansons grew their name and reach as a production company. They continued to option material and to commission new work. At any one time, the company was in development on up to a dozen projects in the United States and in the West End (in London). With shows in Chicago, San Francisco, and London, the company had grown to become a global production force. Although the company grew consistently each year, the work force had expanded at a much slower pace. George Hanson recounted:

The company goal was simple; continue to develop the Arts in urban locations. We wanted quality, not quantity, so we were deliberately rigorous about developing the material. We would tolerate some of the more temperamental writers or eccentric directors because of their good work. Our sense of material was the key and there were countless story meetings where we locked horns over even the smallest of details. In the end, I think that's what set us apart. We weren't the easiest place but we certainly displayed a work ethic that showed we cared. Artists, at the end of the day, appreciated that and so it was not so difficult to work with them again on future shows. Some of my best friends in the theater are people I've screamed at and who've screamed right back at me.

## Current Production

Shen's biggest concern was what to do with her current production, a large-scale musical with a cast of 20 (see Exhibit 1 for a list of all the shows on Broadway at the time of the case). Set in 1967 Detroit, this rarely seen revival boasted some of the most beloved songs in the show-tunes canon. The musical was in development, and opening night was slated for first week in the coming March. In the meantime, a considerable amount of work still needed to be done to finalize the show: the composer had agreed to contribute two new numbers but they weren't working yet; some rewrites to the book required additional massaging; marketing materials had to be reconceived after research showed the initial materials did not successfully sell the show as a "fun night at the theater"; the costumes needed to be overhauled because the

Version: (A) 2010–05–20

**Exhibit 1** Theater Venues and Capacity

| Theater | Current Show | Address | Capacity | Opening Date | Closing Date |
|---|---|---|---|---|---|
| Ambassador Theatre | Chicago* | 219 West 49th Street | 1,125 | 1996-11-14 November 14, 1996 | Open-ended |
| American Airlines Theatre | Hedda Gabler | 229 West 42nd Street | 740 | 2009-01-25 January 25, 2009 | 2009-03-28 March 28, 2009 |
| Brooks Atkinson Theatre | Rock of Ages* | 256 West 47th Street | 1,044 | 2009-04-07 April 7, 2009 | Open-ended |
| Ethel Barrymore Theatre | Speed-the-Plow | 243 West 47th Street | 1,096 | 2008-10-23 October 23, 2008 | 2009-02-22 February 22, 2009 |
| Vivian Beaumont Theatre (at Lincoln Center) | South Pacific* | 150 West 65th Street | 1,080 | 2008-04-03 April 3, 2008 | Open-ended |
| Belasco Theatre | Joe Turner's Come and Gone | 111 West 44th Street | 1,018 | 2009-04-16 April 16, 2009 | Open-ended |
| Booth Theatre | The Story of My Life | 222 West 45th Street | 785 | 2009-02-19 February 19, 2009 | Open-ended |
| Broadhurst Theatre | Equus | 235 West 44th Street | 1,186 | 2008-09-25 September 25, 2008 | 2009-02-08 February 8, 2009 |
| The Broadway Theatre | Shrek* | 1681 Broadway | 1,752 | 2008-12-14 December 14, 2008 | Open-ended |
| Circle in the Square Theatre | | 235 West 50th Street | 623 | | |
| Cort Theatre | You're Welcome America. A Final Night With George W Bush | 138 West 48th Street | 1,084 | 2009-02-01 February 1, 2009 | 2009-03-15 March 15, 2009 |
| Samuel J. Friedman Theatre | The American Plan | 261 West 47th Street | 650 | 2009-01-22 January 22, 2009 | 2009-03-15 March 15, 2009 |
| George Gershwin Theatre | Wicked* | 222 West 51st Street | 1,933 | 2003-10-30 October 30, 2003 | Open-ended |
| Hilton Theatre | | 213 West 42nd Street | 1,813 | | |
| Al Hirschfeld Theatre | Hair* | 302 West 45th Street | 1,437 | 2009-03-31 March 31, 2009 | Open-ended |

(Continued)

**Exhibit 1** (Continued)

| Theater | Current Show | Address | Capacity | Opening Date | Closing Date |
|---|---|---|---|---|---|
| Imperial Theatre | Billy Elliot the Musical* | 249 West 45th Street | 1,421 | 2008-11-13 November 13, 2008 | Open-ended |
| Bernard B. Jacobs Theatre | God of Carnage | 242 West 45th Street | 1,078 | 2009-03-22 March 22, 2009 | Open-ended |
| Walter Kerr Theatre | Irena's Vow | 219 West 48th Street | 947 | 2009-03-29 March 29, 2009 | Open-ended |
| Longacre Theater | | 220 West 48th Street | 1,096 | | |
| Lunt-Fontanne Theatre | The Little Mermaid* | 205 West 46th Street | 1,475 | 2008-01-10 January 10, 2008 | Open-ended |
| Lyceum Theatre | Reasons to be Pretty | 149 West 45th Street | 924 | 2009-04-02 April 2, 2009 | Open-ended |
| Majestic Theatre | The Phantom of the Opera* | 247 West 44th Street | 1,655 | 1988-01-26 January 26, 1988 | Open-ended |
| Minskoff Theatre | The Lion King* | 200 West 45th Street | 1,710 | 1997-11-13 November 13, 1997 | Open-ended |
| Music Box Theatre | August: Osage County | 239 West 45th Street | 1,010 | 2007-12-04 December 4, 2007 | Open-ended |
| Nederlander Theatre | Guys and Dolls* | 208 West 41st Street | 1,203 | 2009-03-01 March 1, 2009 | Open-ended |
| New Amsterdam Theatre | Mary Poppins* | 214 West 42nd Street | 1,747 | 2006-11-16 November 16, 2006 | Open-ended |
| Palace Theatre | West Side Story* | 1564 Broadway | 1,784 | 2009-03-19 March 19, 2009 | Open-ended |
| Richard Rodgers Theatre | In the Heights* | 226 West 46th Street | 1,368 | 2008-03-09 March 9, 2008 | Open-ended |
| Shubert Theatre | Blithe Spirit | 225 West 44th Street | 1,521 | 2009-03-15 March 15, 2009 | Open-ended |
| Neil Simon Theatre | OCCUPIED December 10 | 250 West 52nd Street | 1,297 | | |
| St. James Theater | | 246 West 44th Street | 1,623 | | |
| Studio 54 | Pal Joey* | 254 West 54th Street | 920 | 2008-12-18 December 18, 2008 | 2009-03-01 March 1, 2009 |
| August Wilson Theater | Jersey Boys* | 245 West 52nd Street | 1,275 | 2005-11-06 November 6, 2005 | Open-ended |
| Winter Garden Theater | Mamma Mia!* | 1634 Broadway | 1,513 | 2001-10-18 October 18, 2001 | Open-ended |

*Source*: www.en.wikipedia.org/wiki/Broadway_theatre. as of December 18. 2009.

*denotes musical performance.

director had decided late in the game that he wanted a wind machine and real rain for the Act I finale. Shen had to revise the budget and pull funds from other areas without dipping too deeply into the contingency fund. She had decided that the natural target audience was baby boomers not only because of the familiar music from the 1960s but also because the female lead had been a child star on the Disney Channel; Shen wisely had the audience in her crosshairs.

A big question remained of whether this play would appeal to the tourist crowd because the subject matter presented its fair share of challenges. Shen wanted to attract the widest possible audience to the show, but she could not afford to alienate parents, the typical the ticket buyers, due to the relative high prices for Broadway shows. The highest weekly grossing shows in New York are included in Exhibit 2. Typical ticket prices for New York on Broadway plays and musicals is included in Exhibits 3 and 4.

Shen always conducted market research with test audiences, despite her extremely hectic daily activities. Shen stated:

A typical day during development would start at the office around 7 A.M. just so I could get some work done before the phone rang.

By about 8 A.M., I would start getting calls about the state of the set design and the orchestra selection or [would need to] deal with a "crisis" regarding an actor who was photographed in an undesirable environment that may hurt the draw of the show. Then I'd be off to the venue to sit through a tech rehearsal; meet with the director, conductor, union stewards and give them updates on ticket projections or critic concerns with the script.

In the afternoon I would meet with my boss and explain where we were in relation to the budget. By the time the evening rolled around I would have to follow up on the eight other projects either in development or production or go see other shows that we might have investments in. It was always satisfying to launch a show, but the next day it was back to the drawing board to make sure my show was still on course.

| Exhibit 2 | Attendance and Weekly Gross Revenue—Highest Grossing New York Shows |
|-----------|---------------------------------------------------------------------|

| Rank | Title | Theater | Average Attendance | Gross |
|------|-------|---------|--------------------|-------|
| 1 | *Wicked* | George Gershwin Theatre | 100.0% | $1,769,489 |
| 2 | *The Lion King* | Minskoff Theatre | 100.0% | $1,555,984 |
| 3 | *Billy Elliot the Musical* | Imperial Theater | 99.9% | $1,358,454 |
| 4 | *Shrek the Musical* | The Broadway Theatre | 90.2% | $1,268,342 |
| 5 | *Mamma Mia!* | Winter Garden Theatre | 99.5% | $1,261,939 |
| 6 | *Jersey Boys* | August Wilson Theatre | 101.1% | $1,248,236 |
| 7 | *Mary Poppins* | New Amsterdam Theatre | 97.6% | $1,225,467 |
| 8 | *The Phantom of the Opera* | Majestic Theatre | 100.4% | $1,188,823 |
| 9 | *The Little Mermaid* | Lunt-Fontanne Theatre | 96.7% | $1,159,724 |
| 10 | *In the Heights* | Richard Rodgers Theatre | 92.4% | $1,136,062 |

*Source:* www.broadway.com/buzz/broadway-grosses, accessed December 18, 2008.

*Note:* Some venues rendered as vacant in Exhibit 1 for case illustration only.

| Exhibit 3 | New York City Average Ticket Prices for Plays |

| Seat Area | Regular | Group | Cap | Notes |
|---|---|---|---|---|
| Price Code: **A** | STANDARD | | | |
| ORCHESTRA 20+ | 110.00 | 69.50 | 0 | |
| MEZZ A–J 20+ | 110.00 | 69.50 | 0 | |
| ORCH O–P 20+ | 110.00 | 49.50 | 0 | STUDENT/SENIOR ONLY |
| MEZZ K–L 20+ | 76.50 | 49.50 | 0 | STUDENT/SENIOR ONLY |
| COMP 1/20 | 0.00 | 0.00 | 0 | ONE PER 20 PAID |
| ORCHESTR A 10+ | 110.00 | 92.40 | 0 | |
| MEZZ A–J 10+ | 110.00 | 92.40 | 0 | |
| MEZZ K–L 10+ | 76.50 | 49.50 | 0 | |
| Price Code: **B** | FRIDAY(E) | | | |
| ORCHESTRA 20+ | 110.00 | 69.50 | 0 | |
| MEZZ A–J 20+ | 110.00 | 69.50 | 0 | |
| COMP 1/20 | 0.00 | 0.00 | 0 | ONE COMP PER 20 PAID |
| Price Code: **X** | SATURDAY(E) | | | |
| ORCHESTRA | 110.00 | 120.85 | 0 | NO DISCOUNT SERVICE FEE APPLIES |
| MEZZ A–J | 110.00 | 120.85 | 0 | NO DISCOUNT SERVICE FEE APPLIES |
| MEZZ K–L | 76.50 | 84.00 | 0 | NO DISCOUNT SERVICE FEE APPLIES |

*Source:* www.broadway.com/shows/august-osage-county/, ticket prices for August Osage County, accessed December 18, 2008.

| Exhibit 4 | New York City Average Ticket Prices for a Musical |

| Seat Area | Regular | Group | Cap | Notes |
|---|---|---|---|---|
| Price Code: **A** | TUESDAY–THURSDAY | | | |
| ORCHESTRA | 111.25 | 100.25 | 1176 | |
| LOGE AA–EE | 111.25 | 100.25 | 46 | |
| FRONT MEZZ A–E | 111.25 | 100.25 | 229 | |
| REAR MEZZ F–G | 76.25 | 68.75 | 104 | |
| REAR MEZZ H–M | 51.25 | 46.25 | 138 | |
| ORCHESTRA (STUDENT) | 111.25 | 56.25 | 100 | STUDENTS ONLY: ROWS Y–ZZ |
| REAR MEZZ (STUDENT) | 76.25 | 41.25 | 206 | STUDENTS ONLY: BEST AVAIL IN RMEZZ |

| Seat Area | Regular | Group | Cap | Notes |
|---|---|---|---|---|
| Price Code: **B** | FRIDAY | | | |
| ORCHESTRA | 126.25 | **113.75** | 1176 | |
| LOGE AA–EE | 126.25 | **113.75** | 46 | |
| FRONT MEZZ A–E | 126.25 | **113.75** | 229 | |
| REAR MEZZ F–G | 91.25 | **82.25** | 104 | |
| REAR MEZZ H–M | 66.25 | **59.75** | 138 | |
| Price Code: **C** | SATURDAY, SUNDAY MATINEE | | | |
| ORCHESTRA | 126.25 | **138.75** | 1176 | NO DISCOUNT / SERVICE FEE APPLIES |
| LOGE AA–EE | 126.25 | **138.75** | 46 | NO DISCOUNT / SERVICE FEE APPLIES |
| FRONT MEZZ A–E | 126.25 | **138.75** | 229 | NO DISCOUNT / SERVICE FEE APPLIES |
| REAR MEZZ F–G | 92.25 | **100.25** | 104 | NO DISCOUNT / SERVICE FEE APPLIES |
| REAR MEZZ H–M | 67.25 | **72.75** | 138 | NO DISCOUNT / SERVICE FEE APPLIES |

*Source:* www.broadway.com/shows/wicked/, ticket prices for Wicked, accessed December 18, 2008.

The story was centered on the riots in Detroit in 1967 and shared a common racial thread with the upcoming 2008 American presidential election. The script had been purchased several years ago, but the announcement of the Democratic nomination had created a new relevance to the subject matter. Timing, after all, was everything; and, according to the talk, if the Democrats should win the November 2008 election, Shen's show was poised to be a hot ticket. Should the Republicans win, however, the undertones would still exist but they would not be nearly as loud.

The cast was a coup for Hanson Productions. The lead actors were splashed all over the tabloids but they hadn't yet flamed out from over-exposure. The rest of the ensemble was played by solid performers, some of whom had television experience. Their worth to the show was indicative of their projected weekly salaries, as presented in Exhibit 5. The venue had still not been secured, which was

**Exhibit 5**  Production Costs for a Broadway Production (Musical)

**"THE DETROIT RIOTS" Estimated Production Budget – Draft For Discussion Only – Subject to Change**
**October 4, 2008**

| Physical Production | | Fees | | Rehearsal Salaries | | |
|---|---|---|---|---|---|---|
| scenery | 750,000 | executive producer | 30,000 | principals | 8 | 225,000 |
| motors/hardware/ | | directors | 50,000 | ensemble | 12 | 225,000 |
| paint | 105,000 | choreographer | 30,000 | swings | 6 | 98,000 |
| automation | 120,000 | scene design | 25,000 | standbys | 4 | 25,000 |

*(Continued)*

## Exhibit 5   (Continued)

| Physical Production | | Fees | | Rehearsal Salaries | | |
|---|---|---|---|---|---|---|
| trussing | 40,000 | costume design | 20,000 | stage managers | 2 | 70,000 |
| props | 100,000 | lighting design | 30,000 | company managers | | 60,000 |
| costumes/shoes | 800,000 | sound design | 30,000 | associate director | | 50,000 |
| hair/makeup | 60,000 | projection/video design | 20,000 | PA to the director | | 6,000 |
| lighting | 120,000 | hair/makeup design | 25,000 | design assistants | scenic - 4 | 140,000 |
| set electrics | 25,000 | special effects design | 10,000 | design assistants | costume - 6 | 120,000 |
| special effects | 50,000 | general manager | 40,000 | design assistants | lighting - 2 | 44,000 |
| projections/video | 20,000 | technical supervisor | 60,000 | design assistants | sound - 2 | 50,000 |
| sound | 80,000 | production supervisor | 5,000 | design assistants | SFX - 2 | 0,000 |
| production reserve | 500,000 | casting director | 25,000 | tutors/chaperones | | 44,500 |
| musical instruments | 25,000 | musical supervisor | 7,500 | production crew | | 527,650 |
| | | musical director | 12,000 | wardrobe | | 217,525 |
| theatre refurbished | 20,000 | musical coordinator | 5,000 | prod. assistants | 2 | 10,000 |
| | $ 2,815,000 | orchestration | 200,000 | musical director | | 52,500 |
| | | vocal arrangements | 10,000 | rehearsal musicians | | 63,000 |
| audition/rehearsal halls | 30,000 | dance arrangements | 10,000 | orchestra musicians | | 42,000 |
| | | vocal coach | 2,500 | | | |
| scenery/props/ costumes | 22,475 | press agent | 8,000 | | | 2,120,175 |
| | | marketing director | 10,000 | | | |
| script blueprints/ models | 23,750 | internet marketing | see ad budget | | | |
| stage manager | 12,000 | | $ 665,000 | | | |
| casting expense | 9,656 | | | | | |
| miscellaneous | 5,000 | | | | | |
| | $ 102,881 | | | Subtotal carried forward | | 5,703,056 |
| | $ 2,917,881 | | | | | |

| Advertising Marketing & Publicity | | Administration & General | | Out of Town – Production Period | | |
|---|---|---|---|---|---|---|
| newspaper/outdoor | | producer office | 18,000 | theater expenses | | |
| television/radio commercial | | GM office | 10,000 | local musicians | | |
| | | legal | 125,000 | AEA per diems | | |
| photography/ printing/signs | | immigration attorney | 15,000 | per diems – crew | | |
| | | accounting | 12,000 | transportation | | |

| Advertising Marketing & Publicity | | Administration & General | | Out of Town – Production Period | |
|---|---|---|---|---|---|
| artwork & mechanicals | | payroll taxes (13%) insurance | 275,619 225,000 | hauling storage | |
| direct mail | | pension/welfare/401k (20%) | 424,030 | advertising misc | |
| group sales/tourism educational programs | | vacation/sick pay transportation relocation fees | 45,000 111,545 7500 | | $3,000,000 |
| promotions/ marketing website/internet | | star housing star expenses hauling - local | 27,000 32,000 68,547 | | |
| marketing/email blast | | payroll service telephone/fax/xerox | 12,375 25,000 | | |
| press agent expense press video | | opening night | | | |
| tony award show campaign | | gifts/etc | 75,000 | | |
| post opening advertising miscellaneous | | | $1,508,616 | | |
| | $ 1,500,000 | | | | |

| Union Bonds & Deposits | | | | Reserves | |
|---|---|---|---|---|---|
| AEA | – | | | | |
| IATSE | 40,000 | | | closing costs | |
| ATPAM | – | | | potential | |
| AFM | 15,000 | | | contingencies | |
| Local 764 | 40,000 | | | | $ 1,250,000 |
| Theatre | – | | | | |
| misc | 25,000 | | | | |
| | $ 120,000 | | | | |
| | 1,620,000 | | | | |

| | | |
|---|---|---|
| Subtotal carried forward (page 1) | $5,703,056 |
| Advertising | $1,500,000 |
| Union bonds | $120,000 |
| Administration | $1,508,616 |
| Out of town | $3,000,000 |
| Reserves | $1,250,000 |
| **TOTAL CAPITAL REQUIRED** | **$13,081,672** |

*Source:* Case Writer's Estimates.

*Note:* PA = personal assistant; SFX = special effects; GM = general manager; AEA = Actors' Equity Association; IATSE = International Alliance of Theatrical Stage Employees; ATPAM = Association of Theatrical Press Agents and Managers; AFM = American Federation of Musicians.

not a catastrophe because Shen was in talks with three possible theaters: the Longacre Theater, the St. James Theater, and the Hilton Theater. Regardless of the theater, revenue expectations were expected to be between $830,000 and $1.03 million per week. The weekly costs incurred by the production are included in Exhibit 6, the royalty schedule in Exhibit 7.

---

| **Exhibit 6** | Weekly Operating Costs for a Broadway Production (Musical) |

**"THE DETROIT RIOTS"**
**Estimated Weekly Operating Budget**
**For Discussion Only – Subject to Change October 4, 2008**

| Salaries | | | Department Expenses | | Fixed Fees/ Royalties | | General Administration | |
|---|---|---|---|---|---|---|---|---|
| principals | 8 | 90,000 | general managers | 500 | executive producer | 3,500 | producer's office | 1,225 |
| ensemble | 12 | 18,000 | carpenter | 450 | marketing consulting | 1,200 | GM office | 575 |
| swings | 6 | 12,000 | props | 475 | hair design | 500 | legal | 900 |
| standbys | 4 | 8,000 | electrics | 1,750 | makeup design | 200 | accounting | 1,500 |
| child standbys | 2 | 2,000 | projections | 800 | special effects design | 300 | payroll taxes | 13,437 |
| tutor | 1 | 700 | special effects | 175 | orchestrator | 900 | insurance | 7,500 |
| stage managers | 4 | 8,000 | wardrobe/ cleaning | 2,750 | dance arranger | 500 | pension/ welfare/ 401 | 20,672 |
| musical director | | 3,000 | physio | 800 | vocal arranger | 500 | vacation pay | 4,134 |
| company crew | 8 | 14,400 | music rehearsal calls | 1,000 | music rights | 400 | star expenses | 4,750 |
| wardrobe super | 2 | 3,350 | costume accrual | 1,000 | music contractor | 635 | per diems | 1,000 |
| star dresses | | 1,800 | closing cost accrual | 5,000 | synth programmer | 250 | misc | 4,000 |
| hair/makeup super | 2 | 3,270 | | **$14,700** | casting director | 1,250 | | **$59,693** |
| stylist | 2 | 2,850 | | | technical supervision | 1,225 | | |
| associate director | | 1,800 | **Advertising & Publicity** | | electrician | 300 | **Rentals** | |
| general manager | | 4,000 | print/outdoor | | misc fees | 1,500 | automation | 7,000 |
| company manager | | 2,000 | television/radio | | | | electrics | 9,525 |
| playbill press agent | | 2,135 | talent payments | | | | projections | 1,100 |
| marketing director | | 1,550 | playbill website | | | | music rights | 2,000 |
| | | **$178,855** | | | | **$13,160** | sound instruments | 11,000 750 |

| Salaries | | | Advertising & Publicity | | Fixed Fees/Royalties | | Rentals | |
|---|---|---|---|---|---|---|---|---|
| | | | tony award accrual | | | | props | 125 |
| | | | | | | | special effects | 900 |
| | | | press agent expenses | | | | misc | 500 |
| | | | marketing expenses | | | | | |
| | | | | | | | | **$32,900** |
| | | | production costs | | | | | |
| | | | misc | | | | | |
| | | | | **$115,000** | | | | |

*Source:* Case Writer's Estimates.

---

**Exhibit 7**  Royalty Fee Schedule for Typical New York Musical (based on profit)

| | Points | Royalties | Minimums |
|---|---|---|---|
| Authors | 7.90 | 13.28% | $6,000 |
| Underlying Rights | 2.63 | 4.43% | 2,000 |
| Director | 2.00 | 3.36% | 2,000 |
| Choreographer | 1.50 | 2.52% | 1,500 |
| Set and Costume Designers | 1.00 | 1.68% | 1,000 |
| Lighting Designer | 1.20 | 2.02% | 1,000 |
| Sound Designer | 0.50 | 0.84% | 500 |
| Producers | 3.50 | 5.88% | 3,000 |
| TOTAL Weekly Royalties | 20.23 | 34.01% | $17,000 |

*Source:* Case Writer's Estimates.

## Recent Developments

Hanson Productions had been in extensive talks with the three theaters and had handshake deals—conditional offers—that followed the customary provision that the theater owner could enact an early termination clause if theater revenue (based on 6 percent of gross) fell to less than $50,000 per week. Each theater presented its own unique values and drawbacks. Shen's choice of venue would influence the pricing strategy for the show. Shen commented:

The great balancing act is to find a venue that perfectly suits the audience and the production. We could save money with a smaller theater, but fewer seats make it much tougher to recoup in a timely manner. Conversely, having empty seats in too large a theater would also be less than ideal. I wanted to be careful not to be forced into offering hefty ticket discounts during the first six months from opening. Critics are not the only ones who hate to see empty seats and the actors don't draw the same energy from a half-filled house.

The three venues that could accommodate the production were the Hilton Theater, the Longacre Theater, and the St. James Theater (see Exhibit 8). The owners of these theaters demanded the industry standard 6 percent rental fee, based on gross ticket sales. The owners of the Hilton Theater were willing to invest 10 percent of total costs in the production, which would entitle them to 6 percent of the gross revenue in addition to 10 percent of the profits after tax (pre-recoupment) and 10 percent of 50 percent of the adjusted net profits post-recoupment.

Regardless of the theater chosen, Hanson Productions would need to enter into agreement with the theater owner regarding a termination clause. Typically, if the gross receipts of the show dipped below the weekly operating costs (including rent) for two consecutive weeks, the theater owner had the option to cancel the contract. If the contract were canceled, the show's chances of launching a national tour would be seriously impinged. Shen appreciated the potential for a national tour, but

---

| Exhibit 8 | Theater Budgets for Three New York Theaters |
|---|---|

**"THE DETROIT RIOTS" Theater Budget – Weekly October 4, 2008**

| Longacre Theater | | St James Theater | | Hilton Theater | |
|---|---|---|---|---|---|
| operating budget | $414,308 | operating budget | $414,308 | operating budget | $414,308 |
| Theater Expenses | | Theater Expenses | | Theater Expenses | |
| fixed expense | 11,500 | fixed expense | 27,500 | fixed expense | 31,250 |
| fixed rent | 6% of gross | fixed rent | 6% of gross | fixed rent | 6% of gross |
| House Payroll | | House Payroll | | House Payroll | |
| 15 Local One Crew | 52,605 | 15 Local One Crew | 52,605 | 16 Local One Crew | 56,112 |
| 13 musicians | 49,257 | 17 musicians | 64,413 | 17 musicians | 64,413 |
| house manager ⎫ box office ⎬ ushers ⎪ cleaners ⎭ | 26,815 | house manager ⎫ box office ⎬ ushers ⎪ cleaners ⎭ | 39,709 | house manager ⎫ box office ⎬ ushers ⎪ cleaners ⎭ | 44,358 |
| other (taxes, energy, etc.) | 21,952 | other (taxes, energy, etc.) | 24,763 | other (taxes, energy, etc.) | 26,584 |
| **TOTAL FIXED WEEKLY** | 576,437 | **TOTAL FIXED WEEKLY** | $623,298 | **TOTAL FIXED WEEKLY** | $637,025 |

*Source:* Case Writer's Estimates.

this possibility was secondary to her desire for a long run on Broadway.

## Ticket Pricing

Setting the price correctly could influence the success of a production. Setting the price too low left money on the table and forestalled recoupment, which was the goal of any show. On the other hand, setting the price too high risked alienating a large portion of the paying audience and offending the all-powerful critics who could be unforgiving if the on-stage performance was not commensurate with the ticket price. Rolling prices back, after setting the initial ticket price, was often interpreted as admitting failure and,

thus, created negative publicity for the show. Worse, dropping the ticket price meant the road to recoupment would be that much longer. After a show started to discount its ticket prices, climbing back up to full-price tickets was almost impossible unless a major change in casting created a surge in the demand at the box office.

Shen was weighing the potential rate of return, on the basis of an average ticket price. If Shen charged at the average show price ($79.10),[1] and demand was intense, she would have left too much money on the table. If, however, she priced too high, and demand was low, audience perceptions would be lowered if the show later had to lower its prices. See Exhibit 9 for a list of typical seating for a New York show.

| Exhibit 9 | Theater Seating Charts for Three New York Theaters |

Scale: Tuesday through Saturday at 8 p.m.
   Wednesday and Saturday at 2 p.m.
   Sunday at 3 p.m.
   (8 performances per week)

| Longacre | | St James | | Hilton | |
|---|---|---|---|---|---|
| Seats* | | Seats* | 734 | Seats* | 852 |
| Orchestra | 530 | Orchestra | 212 | Orchestra | 325 |
| Front | | Mezzanine (A–K) | 208 | Mezzanine (A–K) | 104 |
| Mezzanine | 300 | Mezzanine (L–P) | 98 | Mezzanine (L–P) | 92 |
| Rear | | Rear | | Rear | |
| Mezzanine | 266 | Mezzanine | 243 | Mezzanine | 259 |
| | | Balcony A–D | 114 | Balcony A–D | 169 |
| | 1,096 | Balcony E–H | 14 | Balcony E–H | 12 |
| | | Boxes | | Boxes | |
| | | | 1,623 | | 1,813 |

*Source:* www.nytheatre.com/nytheatre/chartweb/plan_lon.htm and www.newyorkcitytheatre.com/theaters/stjamestheater/seatingchart.php and www.hiltontheatre.com/seating.php, accessed December 18, 2008, as well as Case Writer's Estimates.

*Note:* Seat layouts may require modifications due to placement and size of orchestra, lighting, set design, curtain adjustments. Some numbers have been modified for case purposes.

Shen knew she had to consider the financial situation of *The Detroit Riots* production (see Exhibits 5, 6, 7 and 8), choose a theater and make a final pricing decision. She needed to do make these decisions fast—opening day was only eight weeks away, and the play still had no home!

---

### CASE QUESTIONS

1. What should be the primary pricing objective for the upcoming production? Why?

2. Should the opening-day price be based on cost, demand/supply, the competition, or a profit target? Defend your answer.

3. What is the contribution margin for each ticket sold if the price was set at $80.00 for the best seats, $70.00 for average seats, and $60.00 for the poorest locations?

4. Describe the relationship between price, quality, and demand for theater productions such as this one.

5. How would pricing based on the competition work in this situation?

6. Determine what you believe would be the optimal price and theater size for this situation.

---

# Sy.Med Development, Inc.

### By Randle Raggio

When Jim Ayers joined Sy.Med Development, Inc. (Sy.Med) as chairman, chief executive officer (CEO) and president in 1997, he believed he was sitting on a gold mine. Sy.Med's projections, fueled by the success of its value-adding software product for the health-care industry, showed that the company would easily make money into the foreseeable future. Moreover, Sy.Med faced little direct competition and had never lost a customer on the basis of price.

Some four years later, however, as Ayers reviewed Sy.Med's results through February 2001, he grew concerned that the company would not hit its financial projections for the full year. The 2001 forecast showed that by the end of October 2001, ongoing maintenance contracts should cover all of the company's sales, operations and development costs (see Exhibit 1). The actual results in Ayers's hands revealed a different, bleaker story: two months into the year, Sy.Med was behind its unit forecast by 66 percent, behind its net income forecast by 210 percent, and had lost $40,000 (see Exhibit 2).

Sy.Med faced great challenges, and Ayers knew that he had to make important decisions regarding marketing, development, staffing and pricing that would affect the company's profitability in both the near term and the long term. Should he change the price of Sy.Med's base product or the price of the ongoing maintenance fees? Should he spend money developing additional products, scrap one or more of his current products, or stick with what he had and boost his selling effort? Should he change his marketing approach from promoting the time-saving benefits of the product to some other valuable feature? He knew that any decision he made could be irrelevant as soon as a serious competitor jumped in to the market.

---

Version: (A) 2009–05–26

**Exhibit 1** Projected 2001 Income Statement

| | Jan-01 | Feb-01 | Mar-01 | Apr-01 | May-01 | Jun-01 | Jul-01 | Aug-01 | Sep-01 | Oct-01 | Nov-01 | Dec-01 | Totals |
|---|---|---|---|---|---|---|---|---|---|---|---|---|---|
| **Sales** | | | | | | | | | | | | | |
| Software Sales | $75,000 | $60,000 | $90,000 | $60,000 | $120,000 | $60,000 | $105,000 | $90,000 | $105,000 | $120,000 | $90,000 | $120,000 | $1,095,000 |
| Software Maintenance | 15,023 | 16,023 | 17,523 | 18,523 | 20,523 | 21,273 | 23,023 | 24,523 | 26,273 | 28,273 | 29,773 | 31,523 | 272,276 |
| Install.,Train & Consult.-Payor | – | – | 7,005 | – | 7,005 | – | 7,005 | – | 7,005 | 7,005 | – | 7,005 | 42,030 |
| Ancillary Revenue & Sales | 4,613 | 1,485 | 4,933 | 1,505 | 5,290 | 1,525 | 5,573 | 1,545 | 5,930 | 1,565 | 6,288 | 1,600 | 41,850 |
| **Total Sales** | $94,636 | $77,508 | $119,461 | $80,028 | $152,818 | $82,798 | $140,601 | $116,068 | $144,208 | $156,843 | $126,061 | $160,28 | $1,451,156 |
| Operations Costs | $10,257 | $9,032 | $10,402 | $10,071 | $11,241 | $12,325 | $14,945 | $13,065 | $14,211 | $14,481 | $13,256 | $14,621 | $147,908 |
| Development Expenses | – | – | 1,500 | 11,033 | 11,033 | 11,383 | 11,033 | 11,033 | 11,383 | 15,033 | 11,908 | 10,508 | 105,850 |
| Depreciation & Amortization | 2,172 | 2,172 | 2,177 | 2,229 | 2,577 | 3,085 | 3,449 | 3,623 | 3,814 | 3,878 | 4,038 | 4,119 | 37,332 |
| Total Cost of Sales & Operations & Development | $12,429 | $11,204 | $14,079 | $23,334 | $24,851 | $26,793 | $29,428 | $27,722 | $29,408 | $33,392 | $29,202 | $29,249 | $291,090 |
| Gross Profit | $82,207 | $66,304 | $105,382 | $56,694 | $127,967 | $56,005 | $111,173 | $88,346 | $114,800 | $123,451 | $96,858 | $130,879 | $1,160,066 |

*(Continued)*

153

**Exhibit 1** (Continued)

| | Jan-01 | Feb-01 | Mar-01 | Apr-01 | May-01 | Jun-01 | Jul-01 | Aug-01 | Sep-01 | Oct-01 | Nov-01 | Dec | Totals |
|---|---|---|---|---|---|---|---|---|---|---|---|---|---|
| Selling, General & Administrative Expenses | | | | | | | | | | | | | |
| Sales & Marketing - Provider | 26,038 | 23,838 | 28,713 | 24,463 | 30,363 | 27,976 | 29,813 | 31,111 | 30,774 | 34,226 | 28,326 | 31,851 | 347,490 |
| Sales & Marketing - Payor | 6,277 | 15,497 | 13,203 | 9,402 | 12,153 | 9,540 | 12,153 | 8,277 | 15,290 | 15,290 | 10,152 | 12,153 | 139,389 |
| Corporate Expenses | 19,974 | 21,159 | 26,784 | 22,339 | 23,254 | 22,129 | 21,004 | 21,004 | 24,079 | 22,254 | 22,254 | 21,129 | 267,363 |
| Total Selling, General & Administrative Expenses | 52,289 | 60,493 | 68,700 | 56,204 | 65,770 | 59,645 | 62,970 | 60,392 | 70,143 | 71,770 | 60,732 | 65,133 | 754,242 |
| Operating Profit | $29,918 | $5,811 | $36,682 | $490 | $62,198 | $(3,640) | $48,203 | $27,954 | $44,657 | $51,680 | $36,126 | $65,746 | $405,824 |

*Source:* Company records.

**Exhibit 2**   Variance Report for January 2001

Sy.Med Development, Inc.
Calendar 2001
Operating and Capital Budget
Income Statement—Budget to Actual Variances by Category

| | Jan-01 Budget | Jan-01 Actual | Feb-01 Budget | Feb-01 Actual | Cumulative Variance |
|---|---|---|---|---|---|
| Beginning Balance—Units Installed | 52 | 52 | 57 | 54 | — |
| New Unit Sales | 5 | 2 | 4 | 1 | (6) |
| De-Commissioned Units | — | — | — | — | — |
| Ending Balance—Units Installed | 57 | 54 | 61 | 55 | (6) |
| Sales | | | | | |
| Software Sales | $75,000 | $44,000 | $60,000 | $13,500 | $(77,500) |
| Software Maintenance | 15,023 | 14,407 | 16,023 | 15,090 | $(1,549) |
| Installation, Training & Consulting— Payor | — | — | — | — | $— |
| Ancillary Revenue & Sales | 4,613 | 6,700 | 1,485 | 3,750 | $4,353 |
| Total Sales | $94,636 | $65,107 | $77,508 | $32,340 | $(74,697) |
| Operations Costs | $10,257 | $15,225 | $9,032 | $11,357 | $7,293 |
| Development Expenses | — | — | — | — | $— |
| Depreciation & Amortization | 2,172 | 5,697 | 2,172 | 5,697 | $7,050 |
| Total Cost of Sales & Operations & Development | $12,429 | $20,922 | $11,204 | $17,054 | $14,343 |
| Gross Profit | $82,207 | $44,185 | $66,304 | $15,286 | $(89,040) |
| Selling, General & Administrative Expenses | | | | | |
| Sales & Marketing Expenses—Provider | 26,038 | 27,150 | 23,838 | 28,309 | $5,583 |
| Sales & Marketing Expenses—Payor | 6,277 | 7,780 | 15,497 | 18,872 | $4,878 |
| Corporate Expenses | 19,974 | 7,422 | 21,159 | 11,209 | $(22,502) |
| Total Selling, General & Administrative Expenses | 52,289 | 42,352 | 60,494 | 58,390 | $(12,041) |
| Operating Profit | $29,918 | $1,833 | $5,810 | $(43,104) | $(76,999) |

*Source:* Company records.

# The Company

Sy.Med's website included the company's mission statement, a brief history of the company and an introduction to its products:

> Sy.Med's Mission: To develop and license software that helps simplify managed care for healthcare providers, payors and consumers.
>
> Founded in 1995 under the name Medilink, Inc. the company has not strayed from its initial mission of "Simplifying Managed Care." The company's name changed to Sy.Med Development, Inc. in November 1996 coinciding with an equity investment by State Volunteer Insurance Company (SVMIC). SVMIC is Tennessee's premier medical malpractice insurance company, insuring over 10,500 physicians.
>
> In July 1998, Sy.Med was acquired by one of its first software clients, FPIC Insurance Group, Inc. (FIG), which is publicly traded on the NASDAQ under the symbol "FPIC." FIG is a provider of medical malpractice insurance products and services to the healthcare community. In 1998, FIG was chosen as one of *Forbes* magazine's 200 Best Small Companies in America.
>
> In April of 1999, Sy.Med spun-off its credentialing application service bureau business to focus exclusively on development and licensing of software. Seeing an increasing demand for its products and tremendous growth opportunity, Sy.Med management and renowned healthcare industry investors successfully completed a private equity buyback of the company in April 2000.
>
> Sy.Med has developed products that improve the administrative processes required by healthcare facilities and managed care organizations. With revolutionary software products like OneApp, one of the most innovative products ever introduced to assist providers with the paperwork hassles of managed care credentialing, OneApp MCO, Sy.Med's answer for managed care organizations' administrative burden of gathering, maintaining, and updating provider data, or PhysicianFinder, a consolidated physician directory, Sy.Med is positioned to meet the current needs of our clients.[1]

Sy.Med arranged its products and marketing activities around two groups: first, the provider side, which included the physicians and other health-care professionals that provided medical care and, second, the payor side, which included the insurance companies and managed care organizations (MCOs) that paid for the services rendered by the providers.

Ayers felt that the Sy.Med team was one of its assets. Although Sy.Med had been in business for more than six years, it was still a small company with only eight employees. Ayers liked it that way. Fearing a disruption in firm culture, and having a relentless focus on cash flow, he generally was cautious about adding new employees. Despite his general aversion to personnel growth, in January 2001, Ayers gave Jim Stephenson, Sy.Med's vice-president for Provider Sales, approval to add one additional sales rep to the provider side in hopes that the additional staffing would help increase the company's installed base (see Exhibit 3).

# The Product

## Background

MCOs, insurance companies and other health-care organizations on the payor side would pay only for services rendered by providers[2] that they had pre-approved. To manage their own risk and that of the patients, the payors sought to ensure that a physician's training and education were current and valid through a process known in the industry as "credentialing." The merits of credentialing aside, no one could argue that the process was not cumbersome. Each payor organization that a physician dealt with had its own credentialing application and required that answers be written or

**Exhibit 3**   Sy.Med Organization Chart

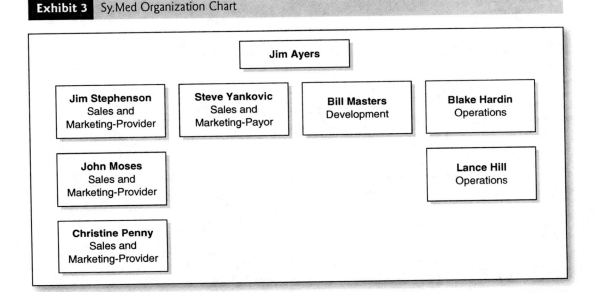

*Source:* Company records.

typed on its own unique form. A 2005 study indicates that within 10 years, physicians may fill out nearly 20 credentialing applications per year.[3]

The credentialing process could take two to three hours per application, and the payors required re-credentialing every two years (see Exhibit 4).

**Exhibit 4**   Credentialing White Paper Written by Ayers, May 29, 2001

**What Is Credentialing?**

Health plans and hospitals consider "credentialing" to be the process of making sure that a health care provider is properly trained and educated. This includes making sure that there are no sanctions by licensing boards or an inordinate number of malpractice claims. Health plans and either the National Committee on Quality Assurance (NCQA), or the Joint Commission on Accreditation of Healthcare Organizations (JCAHO) accredits hospitals. Each of these has certain standards that the health plan or hospital must adhere to, and a large part of the overall accreditation is the manner in which their healthcare providers are credentialed.

From the physician's perspective, "credentialing" means completing, by hand, multiple, lengthy applications that provide the health plan or hospital the information they need to "credential" the provider. These credentialing applications can range from 10 to 25 pages in length and can take up to two or three hours to complete per provider. Applications are required for HMOs, PPOs, hospitals, Medicare, Medicaid, specialty boards, medical societies, IPAs, and other health care organizations. Primarily, the information that is asked on these applications is very similar from application to application. That is, Acme HMO will ask virtually all the same questions as Good Health PPO, but in a different order and on a different application.

*(Continued)*

**Exhibit 4** (Continued)

Our experience has shown that physicians in the following specialties participate in the greatest number of health plans and hospitals:

- Orthopaedic surgery
- Neurosurgery
- Cardiovascular surgery
- Obstetrics and gynecology
- Ophthalmology
- Radiology
- General surgery
- Endocrinology
- Anesthesiology
- Urology

It is not uncommon for physicians in these specialties to participate with as many as 50 or more healthcare organizations that require credentialing applications. Assuming the average time to complete an application to be 90 minutes and each physician participating in 25 health plans, five hospitals and six other organizations, a ten physician practice could expect to spend 540 hours per year completing credentialing applications. Broken down further, this equates to nearly 3.5 months of 8-hour per-day labor.

**What Information Is Generally Contained on Credentialing Applications?**

Information is usually broken down into the following categories:

- Licensure
- Education
- Work history
- Current hospital privileges
- Drug Enforcement Agency (DEA) certificate validity
- Continuing education
- Board certification
- Professional liability insurance history
- Personal information
- Health history
- Office locations
- Medicare/Medicaid participation
- Professional references
- Physician extender information
- Call coverage
- Investments in other health care facilities
- Participation in managed health care plans

Most applications also require copies of the following documents:

- DEA certificate
- Specialty board certification
- State medical license
- Professional liability certificate of insurance
- Medical degree certificate
- Internship, residency, and fellowships
- Continuing medical education statements
- Curriculum vitae
- Letters of reference
- Copy of letterhead

**What Is the Typical Workflow of the Credentialing Process?**

After a physician meets with the representative of the health plan and the rates of reimbursement are negotiated, the physician must complete the credentialing application to participate in the network. Most often the office manager handwrites the applications. The physician signs the application and answers personal health and malpractice claim related questions. The application is then forwarded to the credentialing organization where the information is entered into their database. Many organizations return the entire application if information is incomplete, illegible, or if it does not include the requested attachments. Health care providers are not reimbursed by the health plan until the credentialing application is completed and accepted by the network.

The information is then forwarded to the verification unit whose responsibility is to verify the information on the application. In many cases, the organization contracts with a Credentialing Verification Organization (CVO) that verifies the information to the standards required by either NCQA or JCAHO.

Once the verification is completed a packet is prepared for the credentialing committee that meets to determine whether the physician meets the standards of the organization. Frequently, this committee meets only quarterly and, if the credentialing application and accompanying information is not complete, the application is returned to the physician and the decision is postponed until the next quarterly meeting.

*Source:* Sy.Med Development, Inc., reprinted with permission from Sy.Med Development, Inc. February 2002.

In most practices, credentialing was a back-office issue that did not attract the attention and resources of the physicians unless it was not completed properly or on time. The standard process in physicians' offices was for an administrative assistant or office manager to complete the credentialing applications. In addition, the offices would photocopy documents such as diplomas, certificates, and curriculum vitae, which were attached to the application form.

If an existing practice added a new physician, or an existing physician did not re-credential on time, the payor would refuse to pay for the services rendered. Credentialing was thus not merely a formality of confirming professional accreditation but also—and perhaps more importantly—a critical cash management process for medical practices.

Sy.Med automated the credentialing process with its OneApp software, which offered its customers greater accuracy and reduced the clerical time required, both of which saved money. Because most doctors set up their practices as partnerships, the savings produced by Sy.Med's product flowed to where it mattered most—directly into the physicians' pockets.

## Sy.Med's OneApp (Provider System)

Even aside from the sheer number of credentialing applications that each physician was required to fill out each year, the process challenged physicians on a number of fronts. Not only was each application time-consuming, but physicians would often need to fill out each application more than once to correct errors or clarify handwriting that the payor's data entry staff found to be illegible.

Sy.Med's OneApp solved the problems of time consumption, accuracy, and legibility by using a database of physician information to automatically populate electronic copies of the various application forms.

OneApp's database held a complete set of data for each physician, and its software linked these data to specific "blanks" on the various applications. To use OneApp, the user scanned all application forms into the system to convert them to Adobe (portable document format, or .pdf) files. The user then "tagged" each blank on the forms with the type of data that should be loaded. The users would then enter all physician information corresponding with all "blanks" into the database, including electronic copies of letters and scanned copies of diplomas, certificates, and other required documents. After the data were linked to the correct blanks on the forms, OneApp could process new or revised application forms automatically. With the single click of a mouse, OneApp could produce a complete set of legible application forms for all physicians, or all forms for a new physician or all physicians for a new payor. Sy.Med increased the accuracy of submissions and completed the forms in a fraction of the time required by an assistant manually completing the forms in an office. Sy.Med's sales brochure focused on the time-saving benefits of the software:

With the OneApp software solution you'll never have to complete multiple credentialing applications again! Simply input your physician's information ONCE and OneApp automatically completes any credentialing application. The next step is to simply print the completed forms for review and sign off by your physicians, then forward to the appropriate healthcare organization for verification.

OneApp saves time and money by eliminating redundant manual applications and providing laser quality applications for credentialing organizations. This results in fewer delays in getting your providers through the credentialing process, which improves cash flow.

Sy.Med estimated that compared with a manual process, its software would reduce the time to prepare an initial application by 95 percent and would reduce follow-up time by 50 percent. The system also provided alerts to notify users when forms were due, thus reducing the risk of late applications and the resulting lost revenue.

Sy.Med sold four versions of its OneApp software: eFC, Classic, PRO, and Enterprise (see Exhibit 5).

OneApp eFC, which stood for "electronic filing cabinet," included the basic database and linkable forms described above. Sy.Med recommended the eFC version for practices with fewer than 15 physicians and health-care assistants working from a single personal computer.

OneApp Classic included all the features of eFC, but additionally included ad hoc reporting capabilities and could accommodate multiple personal computers (PCs) in a single location. Sy.Med recommended the Classic version to practices with 15 to 25 physicians.

OneApp Pro and OneApp Enterprise included an application design facility that allowed users to scan and link to their own forms. For users of versions other than Pro or Enterprise, a Sy.Med rep would charge a fee to scan and link new or updated forms. The self-scan feature saved the customer from having to pay for new applications. Sy.Med specifically designed the Enterprise version for practices with multiple locations operating on a local or wide-area network.

| Exhibit 5 | Sy.Med's Four Versions of OneApp Software | | | |
|---|---|---|---|---|
| | **eFC** | **Classic** | **PRO** | **Enterprise** |
| Approximate # of providers | 1–14 | 15–25 | >25 | >25 |
| User Friendly Screens & Database | X | X | X | X |
| Canned Management Reports | X | X | X | X |
| Tracking | X | X | X | X |
| Ad Hoc Reporting | | X | X | X |
| Multi-User (Single Location) | | X | X | X |
| Application Automation | | X | X | X |
| Application Design Capability | | | X | X |
| Multi-Location (LAN/WAN) | | | | X |

*Source:* Sy.Med sales brochure.

## The OneApp MCO (Payor System)

Managed care organizations (MCOs) received credentialing applications both when a provider joined an organization and when the providers submitted their biannual reapplications. When an MCO received an application, the information was entered from the paper form into its database. In some cases, information from the same application would also be used by other stand-alone computer systems within the MCO, resulting in some information being rekeyed as many as five times.

The OneApp MCO database stored the requested provider information and included an electronic data interchange (EDI) interface to receive this information electronically. An MCO that purchased OneApp MCO would receive hard copies of credentialing applications from providers who did not have OneApp (provider system) and electronic applications from those who have the OneApp system.

Sy.Med would customize the OneApp software at the provider site to enable the system to electronically submit its data in the various formats required by an MCO's system. MCOs that installed OneApp MCO could save hours of manual data entry for each provider, even more if an MCO could avoid manual entry into multiple systems. Sy.Med hoped that MCOs that installed OneApp MCO would both encourage their providers to submit their credentialing applications electronically and recommend the Sy.Med product. As a result, Sy.Med saw its OneApp MCO system as a driver of additional provider sales. Ayers believed that each MCO sale could drive as many as five additional provider sales.

### Product Performance

In its May 2001 edition, *Health Management Technology* published a test case describing the use of Sy.Med's OneApp PRO at Fondren Orthopedic Group in Houston, Texas (see Exhibit 6).

| Exhibit 6 | Article From *Health Management Technology* Describing Successful Implementation of Sy.Med's Product |
|---|---|

**Computerized Credentialing**

Physician practice can process 30 MCO applications in one day instead of seven.

Fondren Orthopedic Group LLP is a comprehensive association of private orthopedic surgery practitioners in Houston, TX. Formed as a partnership in 1973, the group has more than 30 surgeons practicing in nearly 20 subspecialties.

**Problem**

Like many practices, we needed a long-term, cost-effective solution to the inefficiency and delays associated with the credentialing/provider data management process. Our standard practice was to manually complete individual applications; this could require as much as two hours per application.

The provider data itself resided in various spreadsheets, word documents and databases throughout the organization. Completing credentialing paperwork for 30 providers at two hours per application meant a tremendous time commitment and loss of productivity. When that amount of time is multiplied by the number of managed care organizations (MCOs) and other entities that require this information, the number of man hours is notable.

*(Continued)*

**Exhibit 6**  (Continued)

Working manually, it would take one person seven days to complete 30 applications. Multiply that by 50 MCOs and that same person could spend 375 days completing applications. Inherent in the manual process was the likelihood of mistakes and incomplete applications, which further delay a provider's ability to see patients for an MCO. We needed to do the following:

- Reduce time required to credential providers with MCOs.
- Accumulate and organize all data elements required to complete applications for MCOs.
- Automate completion of forms required using MCO format.
- Track the flow of applications once submitted.
- Monitor expiration dates, alert the staff when renewals are due.
- Build a resource for providing data to other departments or organizations in electronic or paper form.

### Solution

After reviewing several alternatives, including a trial with another vendor, we decided to license and install Sy.Med Development, Inc.'s OneApp PRO software. This software allows us to enter all the information necessary for credentialing into a simple user-friendly Windows database, then "link" the data onto any application or form.

Forms are scanned into the system using a standard TWAIN compatible scanner. We then "map" the data onto the forms. Once a form is mapped, it can be linked to each provider's data as often as necessary. This eliminates dependence on a third party vendor for mapping forms and maintaining data.

### Results

The software was installed at Fondren within 10 days of license agreement execution. Sy.Med provided on-site training for two days in addition to the installation. Our staff was able to complete applications automatically at the end of the first training day.

When Fondren signed its most recent payor contract, we were able to deliver 30 completed applications on the same day the contract was signed. This put the onus on the MCOs to get the verifications done. The credentials were verified and the group had provider numbers within 30 days.

Using the software, it takes us 10 to 15 minutes to process an automated application and collect the necessary documentation and attachments for its submission.

As new providers join the group, they provide all the information necessary to load into the database. Once loaded, our credentialing department generates all the other applications necessary to get their provider numbers and privileges with the various MCOs and facilities. The applications can all be signed at once.

Fondren recognized other benefits of OneApp as well:

- The software alerts us daily of any licenses or certifications within Fondren's parameters for expiration.
- All provider data is maintained in the OneApp database, eliminating the need to maintain records in separate spreadsheets and databases. This database has become the key point of entry for any changes in provider information.

- We can share database information with other departments including, human resources, billing and information technology.
- Provider CV's are updated automatically as data is changed or added in the database.

*SOURCE*

Karen Yates

Administrative Coordinator

Fondren Orthopedic Group, LLP

Houston, TX

*PRODUCT/COMPANY*

OneApp PRO

Sy.Med Development, Inc.

Brentwood, TN

Although no formal customer survey data existed, all of Sy.Med's customers since 1997 had renewed their maintenance contracts.

As of February 2001, no units of the payor system, OneApp MCO, had been sold; therefore, no independent test cases were available.

## Pricing

### OneApp

In addition to generating revenues from the sales of its software, Sy.Med priced a variety of services related to the OneApp, including pre-linked applications and maintenance charges.

OneApp Pro and Enterprise versions sold at a list price of $13,500 for up to 50 physicians and $2,500 for each group of 50 physicians thereafter. Sy.Med sold the Classic and eFC versions for less because these versions included less functionality and typically were sold to smaller practices. Although the Classic and eFC versions did not include the application development module, Sy.Med would sell pre-linked applications for $300

each. Most of the forms that the physician-customers requested had already been scanned and set up, requiring Sy.Med only to email the new application to the customer in an Adobe (.pdf) file. Sy.Med's marginal cost for the pre-linked application sales was essentially zero. Several provider practices had paid more for new forms than for the purchase price of the original OneApp system.

Customers paid a maintenance charge of 20 percent of the system sales price per year, including the first year (e.g., first-year charges would be $13,500 for the system plus $2,700 for maintenance). Customers also paid for all installation expenses, including travel and lodging for the installation team and $150 per hour for setup, customization, and training. A typical setup would take one person two and one-half days to complete.

Sy.Med offered few discounts from its list prices. The only regular discounts were for small practices that could join together with other small practices in a close geographical area. Those practices would share Sy.Med travel expenses and were eligible to receive a discount of up to 20 percent on each system.

For budgeting purposes, Sy.Med projected an average selling price of $15,000 per system (not including maintenance fees). As of January 2001, the historical average was $14,800. Ayers calculated that if each physician saw 250 patients per month, a medical practice would produce approximately $1 million in revenue per physician per year. At this rate, any new physicians that start providing service before the approval of their credentialing applications could cost a practice more than $80,000 per month until credential approval was received. Thus, it seemed to Ayers that he should have no problem selling to practices the potential savings from expediting the credential process—$65,000 the first month and $80,000 each month thereafter! Even for practices that were not rapidly expanding, he felt that the speed and accuracy provided by the OneApp software were well worth the price, given the potential for errors and late submissions resulting from the manual procedures used by most practices.

## OneApp Sales Process

Selling to doctors was difficult. "[Physicians] will spend millions on diagnostic equipment, but not on the back office," said Ayers.[4] Many smaller practices were still using PCs with 386 or 486 processors, and few had Internet access other than dial-up through an Internet service provider such as AOL. Ayers noted:

> It's like reverse groupthink. Instead of taking more chances when they get together to discuss their practice, they become much more conservative in front of their partners, even though what we're selling can save them thousands of dollars.[5]

Part of the hesitation to spend on back-office improvements arose from the logistics of the doctor's office: physicians who were busy with patients all day had limited opportunities to see what actually happened in the back office. As a result, physicians likely underestimated the amount of administrative work required to keep the practice running.

Additionally, profit-sharing systems created an incentive for each partner to appear to be minimizing expenses that affected the other partners' profits.

Ayers believed that $15,000 was near the upper limit that physicians would pay for any sort of administrative support software, regardless of the cost savings. He wondered whether some magic threshold might be closer to $10,000. "Maybe we could dramatically increase sales if we sold it for $10,000." He also wondered whether he should increase the maintenance fee, given that customers developed a very strong dependence on the software once it was installed.

Typically, physicians got involved in the sales process only when it came time to approve the purchase. An office manager or administrative assistant was typically the first point of contact for the sales reps. In many cases, these same people were completing the manual credentialing applications. Although Sy.Med sales reps explained that OneApp's time-saving benefit would allow the administrative staff to perform more important services for the practice, the sales reps had to be careful in their approach; the software must not be seen as a potential replacement of the buyer. Most administrative assistants earned between $24,000 and $30,000 per year plus benefits. Although office managers, chief financial officers (CFOs), and chief operating operators (COOs) liked the cost savings OneApp offered, administrative assistants were not likely to be as enthusiastic if adopting the software would reduce their hours, possibly to the point where they would not be eligible for benefits.

## Selling the Payor System—OneAPP MCO

Sy.Med found that MCO sales were even more difficult than physician sales because of the bureaucracy involved in the MCO buying process. Whereas the provider buying cycle took up to three months and might require approval of an administrative assistant or possibly a CFO or COO before gaining the final approval of the physicians, the payor buying cycle could take more than six months and typically required presentations and product demonstrations to managers of the MCO at multiple locations.

OneAPP MCO listed for $30,000. As of February 2001, Sy.Med had not sold a single system, despite the concentrated efforts of Steve Yankovic, Sy.Med's (only) payor sales rep. Ayers saw the MCO selling process as inefficient and, to date, ineffective. As a result, he considered either hiring more payor sales reps to join Yankovic (because Ayers was still convinced that MCO sales would drive provider sales) or moving Yankovic to the provider side (because sales on that side were easier to make). Although Ayers expected efficiency to improve over time, the momentum was definitely on the provider side, a market that Ayers was eager to capture before serious competition arrived.

## Incentive Compensation

Sy.Med sales reps were paid base salaries that ranged from $35,000 to $50,000. In addition, they received a 10 percent commission on sales up to $35,000 and 17 percent on sales over $35,000. As Ayers commented, "We have to sell three units a month or the lights go out. But I'll pay heavily for units four, five and six because they're mostly profit." The sales reps were budgeted to receive approximately 40 percent of their projected annual salary in incentive compensation.

Sales reps received their incentive compensation on the basis of cash received, as opposed to on the basis of systems installed. This approach encouraged the sales reps to not only to close the deal and install the software but also to help collect receivables.

## The Market

### Projected Size

According to the Medical Group Management Association (MGMA), approximately 690,000 licensed physicians practiced in the United States (see Exhibit 7). Each physician, on average, was required to submit 10 credentialing applications each year. Each initial filing required up to two hours to complete; follow-ups for incorrect or illegible forms required an additional hour. Thus, each year, the submission of credentialing applications could consume more than 20 million hours from a total of 10,000 full-time workers.

As of March 2001, Sy.Med had installed 55 units of its product at practices in 24 states (see Exhibit 8).

## Competition

### IntelliCred and IntelliApp for Windows

IntelliCred was a database system that stored all provider information. IntelliApp was a report-generation software that linked the database information to specific applications and printed the completed forms. The price for both was $6,900 for a single-user system (i.e., one computer in one location used by one person) plus 20 percent of the purchase price per year for ongoing support. The first year's support was included in the purchase price. Additional user licenses were available for $1,000 per user. A two-day training session at IntelliSoft's office was also included in the purchase price. Onsite training at a customer's location was available for $1,000 per day plus travel expenses. Users could scan in new applications and then link the provider information with each of the blanks on the application forms. At the beginning of 2001, IntelliSoft had pre-scanned applications for payors available only in New York and Texas.

### Medsite

Medsite offered online credentialing data storage and report preparation. The user would enter all provider information online into one generic application. Medsite would then automatically pre-fill any application selected from its list of insurance companies and then print the forms directly from the web. Medsite would also store all provider information for future use. At the beginning of 2001, Medsite was available only in New York and Michigan. Its yearly fee was $99 per physician for unlimited applications throughout the year.

| Exhibit 7 | MGMA Members in the United States by Number of Physicians |
|-----------|-----------------------------------------------------------|

| State | % of Total | Practices | 1–10 | 11–25 | 26–50 | 51–75 | 76–100 | 101–150 | >150 | 0* |
|-------|-----------|-----------|------|-------|-------|-------|--------|---------|------|----|
| California | 6% | 377 | 214 | 69 | 33 | 12 | 7 | 11 | 22 | 9 |
| Washington | 3% | 194 | 128 | 30 | 18 | 3 | 4 | 2 | 5 | 4 |
| Colorado | 3% | 169 | 129 | 16 | 13 | 4 | 0 | 1 | 2 | 4 |
| Oregon | 2% | 134 | 79 | 28 | 14 | 5 | 3 | 1 | 3 | 1 |
| Arizona | 2% | 109 | 76 | 19 | 6 | 3 | 1 | 0 | 4 | 0 |
| Kansas | 1% | 84 | 55 | 18 | 5 | 2 | 1 | 1 | 2 | 0 |
| Nebraska | 1% | 82 | 60 | 14 | 3 | 0 | 0 | 0 | 4 | 1 |
| Oklahoma | 1% | 69 | 43 | 18 | 3 | 2 | 1 | 1 | 1 | 0 |
| Nevada | 1% | 46 | 29 | 11 | 4 | 0 | 0 | 1 | 0 | 1 |
| South Dakota | 1% | 44 | 30 | 7 | 3 | 3 | 0 | 1 | 0 | 0 |
| Idaho | 1% | 37 | 26 | 7 | 3 | 1 | 0 | 0 | 0 | 0 |
| Montana | 1% | 36 | 26 | 3 | 4 | 0 | 1 | 2 | 0 | 0 |
| Utah | 1% | 36 | 14 | 15 | 4 | 0 | 0 | 0 | 2 | 1 |
| New Mexico | 0% | 32 | 17 | 8 | 2 | 0 | 0 | 0 | 4 | 1 |
| Alaska | 0% | 28 | 22 | 4 | 1 | 0 | 0 | 0 | 1 | 0 |
| North Dakota | 0% | 26 | 16 | 2 | 4 | 1 | 0 | 0 | 2 | 1 |
| Wyoming | 0% | 20 | 16 | 4 | 0 | 0 | 0 | 0 | 0 | 0 |
| Hawaii | 0% | 18 | 8 | 4 | 2 | 1 | 0 | 0 | 1 | 2 |
| Guam | 0% | 3 | 0 | 3 | 0 | 0 | 0 | 0 | 0 | 0 |
| Puerto Rico | 0% | 1 | 1 | 0 | 0 | 0 | 0 | 0 | 0 | 0 |
| TOTAL WEST | 24% | 1,545 | 989 | 280 | 122 | 37 | 18 | 21 | 53 | 25 |
| Texas | 6% | 377 | 235 | 62 | 35 | 9 | 8 | 6 | 16 | 6 |
| Florida | 5% | 317 | 191 | 66 | 29 | 8 | 5 | 4 | 10 | 4 |
| North Carolina | 5% | 307 | 216 | 53 | 14 | 6 | 3 | 1 | 12 | 2 |
| Tennessee | 3% | 211 | 134 | 46 | 17 | 6 | 2 | 1 | 4 | 1 |
| Georgia | 3% | 207 | 146 | 29 | 16 | 5 | 3 | 2 | 2 | 4 |
| Virginia | 3% | 197 | 132 | 39 | 11 | 2 | 2 | 3 | 5 | 3 |
| Alabama | 2% | 123 | 83 | 25 | 6 | 0 | 1 | 1 | 4 | 3 |
| South Carolina | 2% | 117 | 83 | 22 | 3 | 1 | 2 | 1 | 1 | 4 |
| Maryland | 2% | 105 | 68 | 17 | 5 | 4 | 1 | 2 | 4 | 4 |
| Kentucky | 2% | 104 | 64 | 25 | 5 | 1 | 1 | 1 | 3 | 4 |
| Louisiana | 2% | 101 | 69 | 14 | 6 | 3 | 0 | 3 | 3 | 3 |

| State | % of Total | Practices | 1–10 | 11–25 | 26–50 | 51–75 | 76–100 | 101–150 | >150 | 0* |
|---|---|---|---|---|---|---|---|---|---|---|
| Arkansas | 1% | 76 | 55 | 11 | 5 | 1 | 2 | 1 | 1 | 0 |
| Mississippi | 1% | 65 | 49 | 7 | 7 | 0 | 0 | 1 | 0 | 1 |
| West Virginia | 1% | 38 | 25 | 5 | 3 | 0 | 0 | 0 | 3 | 2 |
| Washington DC | 0% | 21 | 12 | 2 | 1 | 1 | 1 | 0 | 4 | 0 |
| TOTAL SOUTH | 36% | 2,366 | 1562 | 423 | 163 | 47 | 31 | 27 | 72 | 41 |
| Pennsylvania | 5% | 302 | 188 | 64 | 18 | 7 | 4 | 4 | 12 | 5 |
| New York | 4% | 264 | 134 | 51 | 28 | 9 | 9 | 8 | 19 | 6 |
| Massachusetts | 2% | 145 | 75 | 29 | 14 | 5 | 5 | 4 | 11 | 2 |
| New Jersey | 2% | 129 | 87 | 29 | 5 | 0 | 1 | 1 | 3 | 3 |
| Connecticut | 2% | 112 | 74 | 20 | 5 | 2 | 4 | 2 | 3 | 2 |
| Maine | 1% | 77 | 54 | 16 | 5 | 1 | 0 | 0 | 1 | 0 |
| New Hampshire | 1% | 50 | 41 | 4 | 1 | 1 | 0 | 0 | 2 | 1 |
| Rhode Island | 0% | 22 | 13 | 2 | 3 | 2 | 1 | 0 | 0 | 1 |
| Delaware | 0% | 18 | 13 | 4 | 0 | 0 | 0 | 0 | 1 | 0 |
| Vermont | 0% | 14 | 11 | 1 | 0 | 0 | 0 | 0 | 2 | 0 |
| TOTAL NORTH | 17% | 1,133 | 690 | 220 | 79 | 27 | 24 | 19 | 54 | 20 |
| Ohio | 4% | 292 | 181 | 56 | 21 | 6 | 6 | 5 | 9 | 8 |
| Illinois | 4% | 279 | 164 | 59 | 26 | 6 | 1 | 8 | 10 | 5 |
| Michigan | 3% | 225 | 152 | 36 | 15 | 5 | 2 | 2 | 7 | 6 |
| Missouri | 3% | 178 | 112 | 32 | 9 | 5 | 3 | 2 | 9 | 6 |
| Indiana | 3% | 167 | 91 | 40 | 18 | 7 | 3 | 2 | 2 | 4 |
| Minnesota | 2% | 152 | 76 | 37 | 21 | 5 | 2 | 1 | 9 | 1 |
| Wisconsin | 2% | 131 | 74 | 18 | 13 | 9 | 3 | 1 | 10 | 3 |
| Iowa | 1% | 96 | 55 | 17 | 13 | 4 | 4 | 1 | 2 | 0 |
| TOTAL MIDWEST | 23% | 1,520 | 905 | 295 | 136 | 47 | 24 | 22 | 58 | 33 |
| MGMA TOTAL | 100% | 6,564 | 4,146 | 1,218 | 500 | 158 | 97 | 89 | 237 | 119 |
| % OF TOTAL | | 100% | 63% | 19% | 8% | 2% | 1% | 1% | 4% | 2% |

*Source:* Medical Group Management Association (MGMA represented 185,000 of 690,000 licensed physicians in America or approximately 27%).

*Some members of MGMA were not physician groups (Sy.Med for example); therefore, the number of physicians was zero.

| Exhibit 8 | Sy.Med's Customers as of March 2001 |
|---|---|

| Practice Size | Units Sold |
|---|---|
| 1–14 | 0 |
| 15–25 | 13 |
| 26–200 | 33 |
| 201–500 | 6 |
| 501–1000 | 0 |
| 1000+ | 3 |
| TOTAL | 55 |

Source: Company records.

### PRIVplus for Windows

PRIVplus was software specifically designed for the reapplication process. It stored provider information, prompted the user when dates for verifications were approaching, and provided report generation capability. PRIVplus did not print the actual application form. PRIVplus sold for $6,900 plus a yearly maintenance fee.

### Visual CACTUS

In 2001, on its website, CACTUS Software billed its product as "the leading credentialing and provider management software for hospitals and healthcare organizations."[6] CACTUS Software's product was similar to Sy.Med's MCO product in both functionality and price. Its software was installed in more than 500 organizations worldwide. CACTUS Software's client list included Prudential, Blue Cross and Kaiser. Deloitte & Touche listed CACTUS Software as one of Kansas/Western Missouri's fastest-growing technology companies in 1998, 1999, and 2000.

### Vistar

The Vistar system was designed for large group practices and hospitals. In addition to the features included in the OneApp and Cactus products, the Vistar system could track quality improvement, patient satisfaction and rate disputes. It also allowed users to create in-house forms to be completed with provider data. Its base price was $10,000 for a single stand-alone user and approximately $20,000 for a networked version for 10 users. Vistar based its price on the number of users, not on the number of physicians. Its client list included large hospitals and insurance companies.

### Credentialing Service Bureaus

A provider organization could outsource its credentialing processing to a service bureau that specialized in gathering information and submitting reports. The service bureau charged a per-application fee in addition to a one-time setup fee. Larger service bureaus typically charged between $2,000 and $3,000 per physician per year for up to 20 applications, then $60 per application thereafter.

Although credentialing service bureaus provided a competitive alternative to Sy.Med's software, six service bureaus had purchased OneApp to help them manage their client information. As a result, Ayers did not see service bureaus as a competitive threat, but instead as a potential market that the other software companies were ignoring.

According to Ayers, Sy.Med had not lost a single sale of its provider system to one of these competitors on the basis of price. Ayers believed that unlike Sy.Med and its physician practice market, his competitors offered "hospital-centric" systems that focused on hospitals and health plans. He did not know the share of the market held by each competitor, but he believed that no single company had a significant share because the industry was still young and growing.

Interestingly, though Ayers felt that Vistar and CACTUS were his main competition, representatives of these companies dismissed Sy.Med as a competitor. According to one CACTUS representative, "Our application is not designed for small group practices. We are on the other end of the spectrum."[7] The Vistar representative indicated that its smallest customer was a practice in Kentucky with 30 providers and noted that it could easily match Sy.Med's prices for practices with up to 50 users, but providing services to small practices was not its focus.[8]

## Marketing

Sy.Med's marketing activities consisted of trade show booths, direct mail, live product demonstrations and its website. Sy.Med sent direct mail to all MGMA members prior to each trade show to invite them to a demonstration of the OneApp product at the Sy.Med booth. Sy.Med then followed up by calling those practices both before and after the show.

The direct mail pieces included product information and Sy.Med's website address. Cold calls to practices on its mailing list generated 70 to 80 percent of Sy.Med's sales in 2000 and required between 25 and 50 percent of a sales rep's time. Sy.Med sales reps spent the balance of their time following up on leads from these sources and traveling to customer sites to demonstrate the product to potential buyers.

The "ideal prospect" for Sy.Med's provider system was a medical practice with at least 20 physicians in a market with "lots of managed care." Because population drove the penetration of managed care, Sy.Med did not target the approximately 10 to 15 states that had few or no MCOs (e.g., North Dakota and South Dakota).

The most important trade show was the MGMA, which held its annual meeting in October. Practice managers, CFOs, and administrators who were actively involved in the credentialing process were regular attendees at the MGMA meetings. In addition, regional MGMA meetings were held throughout the year. Ayers had hoped to have at least one MCO sale completed by the 2001 show and to have a representative of that organization in the booth to help Sy.Med pitch its product.

Ayers wanted to educate the market on the benefits of back-office technology in the medical field. He was writing an article on credentialing technology that he hoped would provide additional exposure for the company and its products. The editor of *Health Management Technology* indicated that she would be interested in the article sometime during the fourth quarter. Although that publication schedule was too late for the October MGMA meeting, he knew the publication of his article would help his sales reps by leading to follow-up calls and generating additional leads.

## The Pricing Question

As Jim Ayers sat at his desk in mid-March 2001, he knew the clock was ticking. Sy.Med's board was scheduled to meet on April 2, 2001, to review year-end results and preview his plans for the upcoming year. Although increasing the sales organization seemed like an easy way to increase revenue, Ayers was careful as he grew the company:

> We've gone from four people to eight since I've been here. That fifth one [hire] was tough, because if we made a bad decision, then 20 percent of our organization was no good. It's not that extreme now, but I'm still very careful with who we'll hire.

As a result, Ayers felt that the best approach would be to get his pricing right first and then determine how to staff the company to meet his sales goals. Because the board would need to approve any substantial pricing changes, he had only two weeks to prepare his recommendation on a new pricing strategy.

Furthermore, in less than seven months, the most important marketing opportunity of the year—the upcoming MGMA trade show—would take place, which offered the opportunity to introduce new pricing to potential customers.

Ayers analyzed the projected revenues (see Exhibit 9) as he reviewed his pricing strategy. He needed to get the company back on track to achieve its numbers for the year.

*(Text continued on page 174.)*

Exhibit 9  Provider Revenue

## Sy.Med Development, Inc. Calendar 2001 Operating & Capital Budget Provider Sales and Revenues: Units & Dollars

| | 1-Jan | 1-Feb | 1-Mar | 1-Apr | 1-May | 1-Jun | 1-Jul | 1-Aug | 1-Sep | 1-Oct | 1-Nov | 1-Dec | Totals |
|---|---|---|---|---|---|---|---|---|---|---|---|---|---|
| Beginning Balance – Units Installed | 52 | 57 | 61 | 65 | 69 | 74 | 77 | 81 | 86 | 90 | 95 | 99 | 52 |
| New Unit Sales | 5 | 4 | 4 | 4 | 5 | 4 | 4 | 5 | 4 | 5 | 4 | 5 | 53 |
| De-Commissioned Units | – | – | – | – | – | (1) | – | – | – | – | – | (1) | (2) |
| Ending Balance – Units Installed | 57 | 61 | 65 | 69 | 74 | 77 | 81 | 86 | 90 | 95 | 99 | 103 | 103 |
| Selling Price Per Unit – Beginning | 15000 | 15000 | 15000 | 15000 | 15000 | 15000 | 15000 | 15000 | 15000 | 15000 | 15000 | 15000 | |
| Planned Discounts in Percent | 0% | 0% | 0% | 0% | 0% | 0% | 0% | 0% | 0% | 0% | 0% | 0% | |
| Planned Discounts in Dollars | 0 | 0 | 0 | 0 | 0 | 0 | 0 | 0 | 0 | 0 | 0 | 0 | |
| Selling Price Per Unit – Effective | $15,000 | $15,000 | $15,000 | $15,000 | $15,000 | $15,000 | $15,000 | $15,000 | $15,000 | $15,000 | $15,000 | $15,000 | |
| Software Sales – New Units | $75,000 | $60,000 | $60,000 | $60,000 | $75,000 | $60,000 | $60,000 | $75,000 | $60,000 | $75,000 | $60,000 | $75,000 | $795,000 |

Other Variable Sales & Revenues – New Unit Sales

Recurring Maintenance:

| | 1-Jan | 1-Feb | 1-Mar | 1-Apr | 1-May | 1-Jun | 1-Jul | 1-Aug | 1-Sep | 1-Oct | 1-Nov | 1-Dec | Totals |
|---|---|---|---|---|---|---|---|---|---|---|---|---|---|
| Percentage of Unit Price | 20% | 20% | 20% | 20% | 20% | 20% | 20% | 20% | 20% | 20% | 20% | 20% | |
| Annual Maintenance Revenue | $15,000 | $12,000 | $12,000 | $12,000 | $15,000 | $12,000 | $12,000 | $15,000 | $12,000 | $15,000 | $12,000 | $15,000 | |
| Monthly Approximation | $1,250 | $1,000 | $1,000 | $1,000 | $1,250 | $1,000 | $1,000 | $1,250 | $1,000 | $1,250 | $1,000 | $1,250 | $13,250 |

| | 1-Jan | 1-Feb | 1-Mar | 1-Apr | 1-May | 1-Jun | 1-Jul | 1-Aug | 1-Sep | 1-Oct | 1-Nov | 1-Dec | Totals |
|---|---|---|---|---|---|---|---|---|---|---|---|---|---|
| Recurring Maintenance From Installed Base-Beginning of Month | $13,773 | $15,023 | $16,023 | $17,023 | $18,023 | $19,273 | $20,023 | $21,023 | $22,273 | $23,273 | $24,523 | $25,523 | |
| Maintenance Revenue From New Sales | $1,250 | $1,000 | $1,000 | $1,000 | $1,250 | $1,000 | $1,000 | $1,250 | $1,000 | $1,250 | $1,000 | $1,250 | |
| Less: Maintenance Revenue Lost From De-Commissioned Units | - | - | - | - | - | (250) | - | - | - | - | - | (250) | |
| Total Recurring Maintenance From Installed Base | $15,023 | $16,023 | $17,023 | $18,023 | $19,273 | $20,023 | $21,023 | $22,273 | $23,273 | $24,523 | $25,523 | $26,523 | $248,526 |
| Installation & Training - New Unit Sales | | | | | | | | | | | | | |
| Estimated Revenue Per New Installation | $- | $- | $- | $- | $- | $- | $- | $- | $- | $- | $- | $- | $- |
| Monthly Installation & Training - New Unit Sales | $- | $- | $- | $- | $- | $- | $- | $- | $- | $- | $- | $- | $- |
| Total Monthly Revenue: | | | | | | | | | | | | | |
| New Unit Sales | $75,000 | $60,000 | $60,000 | $60,000 | $75,000 | $60,000 | $60,000 | $75,000 | $60,000 | $75,000 | $60,000 | $75,000 | $795,000 |
| Maintenance | $15,023 | $16,023 | $17,023 | $18,023 | $19,273 | $20,023 | $21,023 | $22,273 | $23,273 | $24,523 | $25,523 | $26,523 | $248,526 |
| Installation & Training | - | - | - | - | - | - | - | - | - | - | - | - | - |
| Total Monthly Revenue | $90,023 | $76,023 | $77,023 | $78,023 | $94,273 | $80,023 | $81,023 | $97,273 | $83,273 | $99,523 | $85,523 | $101,523 | $1,043,526 |

(Continued)

Exhibit 9 (Continued)

Payor Revenue

| Sy.Med Development, Inc. Payor Market Operating & Capital Budget Sales and Revenues: Units & Dollars | | | | | | | | | | | | | |
|---|---|---|---|---|---|---|---|---|---|---|---|---|---|
| | 1-Jan | 1-Feb | 1-Mar | 1-Apr | 1-May | 1-Jun | 1-Jul | 1-Aug | 1-Sep | 1-Oct | 1-Nov | 1-Dec | Totals |
| Beginning Balance – Units Installed | - | - | - | 1.0 | 1.0 | 2.0 | 2.0 | 3.0 | 3.0 | 4.0 | 5.0 | 5.0 | - |
| New Unit Sales | - | - | 1.0 | - | 1.0 | - | 1.0 | - | 1.0 | 1.0 | - | 1.0 | 6.0 |
| De-Commissioned Units | - | - | - | - | - | - | - | - | - | - | - | - | - |
| Ending Balance – Units Installed | - | - | 1.0 | 1.0 | 2.0 | 2.0 | 3.0 | 3.0 | 4.0 | 5.0 | 5.0 | 6.0 | 6.0 |
| Selling Price Per Unit – Beginning | $30,000 | $30,000 | $30,000 | $30,000 | $30,000 | $30,000 | $30,000 | $30,000 | $30,000 | $30,000 | $30,000 | $30,00 | |
| Planned Discounts in Percent | 0.0% | 0.0% | 0.0% | 0.0% | 0.0% | 0.0% | 0.0% | 0.0% | 0.0% | 0.0% | 0.0% | 0.0% | |
| Planned Discounts in Dollars | 0 | 0 | 0 | 0 | 0 | 0 | 0 | 0 | 0 | 0 | 0 | 0 | |
| Selling Price Per Unit – Effective | $30,000 | $30,000 | $30,000 | $30,000 | $30,000 | $30,000 | $30,000 | $30,000 | $30,000 | $30,000 | $30,000 | $30,000 | |
| Software Sales – New Units | $– | $– | $30,000 | $– | $30,000 | $– | $30,000 | $– | $30,000 | $30,000 | $– | $30,000 | $180,000 |
| Other Variable Sales & Revenues – New Unit Sales | | | | | | | | | | | | | |
| Recurring Maintenance: | | | | | | | | | | | | | |
| Percentage of Unit Price | 20% | 20% | 20% | 20% | 20% | 20% | 20% | 20% | 20% | 20% | 20% | 20% | |
| Annual Maintenance Revenue | $– | $– | $6,000 | $– | $6,000 | $– | $6,000 | $– | $6,000 | $6,000 | $– | $6,000 | |
| Monthly Approximation | $– | $– | $500 | $– | $500 | $– | $500 | $– | $500 | $500 | $– | $500 | |
| Recurring Maintenance From Installed Base- Beg. of Month | $– | $– | $- | $500 | $500 | $1,000 | $1,000 | $1,500 | $1,500 | $2,000 | $2,500 | $2,500 | |

| | 1-Jan | 1-Feb | 1-Mar | 1-Apr | 1-May | 1-Jun | 1-Jul | 1-Aug | 1-Sep | 1-Oct | 1-Nov | 1-Dec | Totals |
|---|---|---|---|---|---|---|---|---|---|---|---|---|---|
| Maintenance Revenue From New Sales | $– | $– | $500 | $– | $500 | $– | $500 | $– | $500 | $500 | $– | $500 | |
| Less: Maintenance Revenue Lost From De-Commissioned Units | $– | $– | $– | $– | $– | $– | $– | $– | $– | $– | $– | $– | |
| Total Recurring Maintenance From Installed Base | $– | $– | $500 | $500 | $1,000 | $1,000 | $1,500 | $1,500 | $2,000 | $2,500 | $2,500 | $3,000 | $16,000 |
| **Installation, Training & Report Development – New Unit Sales** | | | | | | | | | | | | | |
| Estimated Consulting Hourly Rate per New Installation | $– | $– | $150.00 | $150.00 | $150.00 | $150.00 | $150.00 | $150.00 | $150.00 | $150.00 | $150.00 | $150.0 | |
| Estimated Report Development Hours Per New Installation | 6.7 | 6.7 | 6.7 | 6.7 | 6.7 | 6.7 | 6.7 | 6.7 | 6.7 | 6.7 | 6.7 | 6.7 | |
| Estimated Consulting Hours Per New Installation | 40 | 40 | 40 | 40 | 40 | 40 | 40 | 40 | 40 | 40 | 40 | 40 | |
| Monthly Installation, Training & Report Development - New Sales | $– | $– | $7,005 | $– | $7,005 | $– | $7,005 | $– | $7,005 | $7,005 | $– | $7,005 | $42,030 |
| **Total Monthly Revenue:** | | | | | | | | | | | | | |
| New Unit Sales | $– | $– | $30,000 | $– | $30,000 | $– | $30,000 | $– | $30,000 | $30,000 | $– | $30,000 | $180,000 |
| Maintenance Revenue | $– | $– | 500 | 500 | 1,000 | 1,000 | 1,500 | 1,500 | 2,000 | 2,500 | 2,500 | 3,000 | 16,000 |
| Installation, Training & Report Development | $– | $– | $7,005 | $– | $7,005 | $– | $7,005 | $– | $7,005 | $7,005 | $– | $7,005 | $42,030 |
| Total Monthly Revenue | $– | $– | $37,505 | $500 | $38,005 | $1,000 | $38,505 | $1,500 | $39,005 | $39,505 | $2,500 | $40,005 | $238,030 |

*Source:* Company Records.

**CASE QUESTIONS**

1. Do you believe Sy.Med Development had set its initial price near the price ceiling (skimming) and that this was the cause of the low amount of sales?

2. What type of pricing objective should Jim Ayers and Sy.Med Development set? Why?

3. The Sy.Med system is one that adds value to a physician's practice by cutting costs, while the actual physical product is inexpensive to copy and deliver after the initial software system has been developed. How does this feature affect the pricing program?

4. With marginal costs being very low, should Sy.Med set prices based on some other factor, such as demand/supply, competition, or profits? Why or why not?

5. Are any discounting programs appropriate for Sy.Med? If so, what type should the company offer?

6. Would you lower the price for the Sy.Med product or seek some other method to increase sales and revenues? Defend your answer.

---

# Arvind Mills: Re-Evaluating Profitability

*By Rajeev Khera, under the supervision of Professor Murray J. Bryant*

It was a typical, tropical June summer afternoon in western India. The temperatures outside were soaring to 45°C, and in his climate controlled environment, Mr. Bala, vice-president of operations, knitwear division, at Arvind Mills Limited, had been thinking hard about a trial order from one of the world's major ready-to-wear apparel retailers. The initial developments leading up to this trial order had gone smoothly, and the company was confident that it had more than adequately addressed all the major concerns of this customer. The continued communications to and from the customer reflected this sentiment. In fact, the success of this trial order was taken as a given, and management was planning for the large volume of business that would, in all probability, come their way. The entire deal hinged upon the premise that the customer would accept the prices that were going to be quoted on June 22, 1999, the following Monday.

The importance of the "right" price was not in the least bit underestimated by Bala. He had carefully

monitored each and every elemental cost of raw materials and process, and had suggested tremendous innovations on aspects that provided a considerable reduction in costs, without compromising on the quality; delivery schedules; and other critical metrics. And yet, the numbers he was looking at today were not globally competitive—a fact borne out of the company's own market study. Any further reduction in prices would render the entire business un-profitable.

The choices to be made were stark and difficult. On the one hand was the option of quoting the prices that had been worked out by the current costing system—and lose the business to the competition (mainly China) (see Exhibit 1). The other option was to accept the business at the price of the competition (ignore what your own costing is telling you), ensure continuing revenues and take a hit on profitability—and hope that in due course, the company would be able to negotiate better prices and recover some of the lost profits.

Version: (A) 2009–10–08

**Exhibit I**   Textile Exports (in millions of dollars)

|                      | 1990   | 1995   | 1999   | 2000   | 2001   |
|----------------------|--------|--------|--------|--------|--------|
| China                | 16,889 | 37,967 | 43,121 | 52,206 | 53,476 |
| Hong Kong (China)    | 23,619 | 35,112 | 34,642 | 37,656 | 35,660 |
| India                | 4,709  | 8,468  | 10,240 | 11,929 | 13,897 |

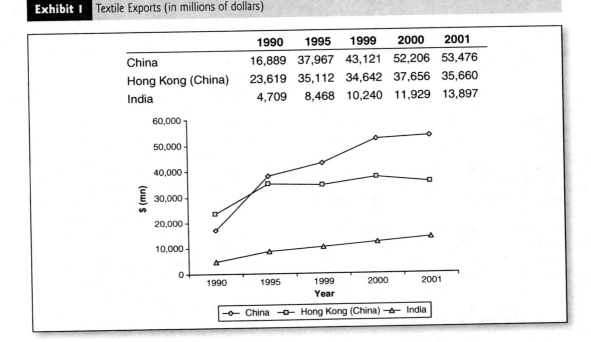

# Textile Industry in India—An Overview

From the day India achieved its independence on August 15, 1947 (after about 200 years of the British Raj), until about 1986–87, the industrial policies of each successive government were guided by the principles of socialist form of governance. The governments enacted a labyrinth of laws, rules and regulations, ostensibly to promote industrial growth in a market environment that was protected to the greatest possible extent from external competition.

The textiles and clothing industry is the largest manufacturing sector in India, accounting for around four percent of GDP, 20 percent of India's industrial output and 37 percent of total exports (WTO, 1998). Textiles (i.e., yarn, cloth, fabrics and other products not made into garments) constituted 25 percent of India's total exports, over half of which consisted of cotton fabrics.[1] As the second largest employer after agriculture, the textile industry provided direct employment to 35 million people including substantial segments of weaker sections of society. Its growth and vitality, therefore, had critical bearings on the Indian economy at large.

The dominant concerns of government policies towards the cotton textile industry centered around import substitution (the credo of self-sufficiency). Exports were considered a marginal outlet for surpluses, protection of existing employment in the organized (big business) sector, support of the decentralized (small scale) sector, and protection of the cotton farmers' interests. These pre-occupations were reflected in the major government policies for this sector such as:

- extensive quota restrictions on various product categories,
- strong exit barriers, even for unviable operations (to ensure continued employment),
- general discouragement of automation, even for exports,
- stringent price regulations to ensure the poorest were able to afford to clothe themselves, and

- stringent licensing for the organized sector at the expense of small and medium-scale manufacturers.

These strict policies led to an extremely skewed development of the Indian textile industry. The large-scale industries were restrained at the expense of the small-scale industries that prevented modernization, quality investments, scale adoption, and change in product mix from exclusive reliance on cotton garments to mass clothing items based on synthetic and man-made fibers. Indian fiscal and customs policy too discriminated against development of synthetic base in India in line with the government belief that "synthetic is for the classes and cotton is for the masses." As a result, while cotton prices were not allowed to move up (trade control, and buffer state operations), synthetic fibers were deliberately priced at uncompetitive levels (viewed as a luxury fiber for higher income groups) against cotton.

In its development policies, the state discriminated against the mill sector in favor of the power-loom sector, which was perceived as an engine of growth. This was done through preferential import and export quotas for the powerloom sector. As a result, the powerloom sector flourished at the expense of the other two.

Between 1977 and 1986, the powerloom sector more than doubled its capacity, reaching 800,000 looms, while the mill and handloom sectors lagged behind. Government controls on scrapping obsolete equipment and restrictions on imported machines resulted in further under-used capacity, poor productivity, and loss in profitability.

Strong resistance from workers fearing job losses prevented any technological changes and internal restructuring in these two state-owned textile sectors. This led to a loss of competitiveness, rising operational costs, and a weak and sickly industrial structure.

The degree of skewing became apparent in the fact that the Indian textile and clothing industries had one of the longest and most complex supply chains in the world, with as many as 15 intermediaries between the farmer and the final consumer. Each contributed not only to the lengthening of lead times, but also to additional costs. By the time cotton worth INR100 reaches from farmer to the spinning unit, its cost inflated to INR148. By the time it reaches the final consumer, it costs INR365.

The spate of broken links, exemptions available to various segments such as small scale industrial units that compete with excise and duty paying segment, and disproportionate excise duty incidence across the chain had become major impediments to developing competitiveness in the industry. Market structures were distorted, creating unhealthy competition among the segments themselves, and succeeding in creating a diverse variety of vested interests that are (even today) opposed to any reform in the sector.

The global trade in textiles was also regulated to a considerable degree, and access to markets in the developed countries was not free of protective tariffs and artificial barriers usually in terms of quantitive restrictions. From 1974 and up to the end of the Uruguay Round in 1994, textile and clothing quotas were negotiated bilaterally and governed by the rules of the multi-fiber arrangement (MFA). Though this system had its fair share of drawbacks, it did help transfer the demands from the developed countries like China and India.

With the Indian industry crying for reforms to essentially ensure its survival, and sensing a whiff of the opportunities in the markets abroad, manufacturers met with the government to embark on a long-term policy of liberalization and earning export revenues became a key thrust area. The years 1986–87 marked this key turning point. The initial forays into the international market were made by the first generation, entrepreneurial apparel (clothing) manufacturers. Their abilities and resourcefulness brought a number of international clothing majors such as Levis, Benetton, Lacoste, and Pierre Cardin to the Indian stores. Their gains also percolated downstream, and the large-scale manufacturers began making huge capital investment to maximize potential gains.

The textile industry's restructure was helped in large measure by the rapid devaluation of the Indian rupee, and for the most part, it camouflaged the lack of industry competitiveness and ensured a steady growth.

The MFA was later replaced by Agreement on Textiles and Clothing, a more rationalized system that came into effect in 1995 at the Uruguay round of General Agreement on Trade and Tariff (GATT), giving further boosts to exports.

## Arvind Mills Limited

With the current revenues at US$550 million,[2] Arvind Mills Limited is the flagship company of Lalbhai Group (Exhibit 2). It was incorporated in 1931 to manufacture cotton textiles. Operating in a highly regulated and protected market, the company grew to become one of the leading cotton manufacturing companies in the country, producing conventional suiting fabrics, shirting fabrics, and sarees (traditional Indian robe).

Cashing in on its technical skills and managerial capabilities, Arvind Mills undertook its first expansion to manufacture denim. In 1986, the company started to look for textiles that had global demand, high margins, high entry level barriers, (either of technology, expertise or set-up costs) and, very importantly, low "fashion volatility." The company wanted to focus on fabric that would never go out of style. From within the possible products, denim proved to be most suitable. From 1987 (at annual production levels of three million meters), within 10 years, Arvind Mills expanded to become the world's third largest producer of denim cloth at 120 million meters.

In 1993, a study of seven countries found that the price of cotton yarn per kilo was cheapest in India at $2.79, compared to $3.30 in Brazil, $4.19 in Japan, and $3.10 in Thailand. This was the result of overall labor and raw material costs being cheaper in India.

Spurred on by the successes in the denim industry, Arvind Mills undertook substantial

---

**Exhibit 2**   Sales and Profitability

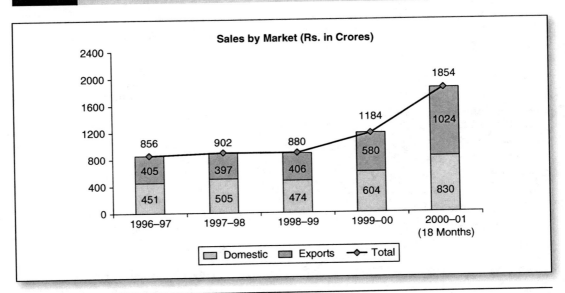

**Exhibit 2**   (Continued)

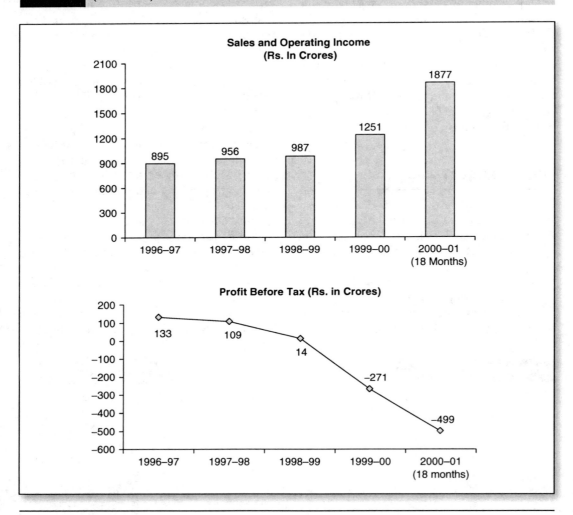

**Sales and Operating Income
(Rs. In Crores)**

**Profit Before Tax (Rs. in Crores)**

*Source:* Company files.

Conversion:

1 Crore = 10 million

US$1 = INR36

investments of millions of dollars into manufacturing other textile fabrics as:

- bottom weights (fabrics used to make trousers) $275 million;
- shirting (fabrics used to make shirts) $100 million;
- knitted fabric $120 million; and
- apparel.

The company organized itself along these product lines and imaginatively named the respective divisions as bottom weights, shirting, knit and apparel division. Apart from these, the company had other business interests in related and non-related industries. One of the group's companies, Atul Limited ($130 million), manufactured chemicals and intermediaries for the textile, paper, and leather industries. Another, Amtrex Appliances Limited, manufactured and marketed household air conditioners and had joint ventures with Hitachi (Japan) and Fedders (United States).

## Market Dynamics—Increase Toward Complexity

The fashion and textile market worldwide had witnessed an immense transformation since 1990. Moving from constant, non-volatile fashion trends, major retailers, working with textile designers in the fashion centers of the world, continually added complexity to the products they retailed in terms of fabric color, composition, structure and styling of the garments. The customer therefore was no longer buying out from the inventory they associated with the manufacturers and the very initial stages in the process of fabric manufacture. Tough competition placed further pressures on the lead time to market and development cycles; in fact, the entire end-to-end logistics of the value chain was bearing the pressures of such transformations.

Arvind Mills' expansion kept pace with the increasing complexity of the marketplace. The process of manufacturing denim was relatively simple. It had fewer variables, a less complex product mix and relatively easy logistics in terms of process and workflow (see Exhibit 3). The company was able to successfully exploit the economies of scale, (thereby reducing per unit overhead), the low price of cotton, and the power in its supply chain. The growth was therefore relatively smooth, controlled, and predictable. But the early gains were being eroded due mainly to the increase in cotton prices that more than doubled between March 1989 and March 1993. Also, the worldwide demand in denim reached a plateau, and the margins were being squeezed out.

The product structure, the product mix, and the logistics involved in the manufacturing processes the other divisions were, however, much more involved.

The apparel retailers and designers looked to fabrics other than denim that offered more possibilities in terms of color and structure to manufacture trousers. Bottom weights became the next logical step forward. Whereas the manufacturing processes remained essentially similar, the logistics had to address many more variations, production run switches, different lot sizes, etc.

A recent addition to the range of fabric and clothing came in the form of knitwear. The technology, equipment, processes, material inputs, product mix, and logistics were entirely different from those currently followed to manufacture woven fabrics such as denim, shirting or bottom weights.

The fabrics came in both tubular and open widths, in single knits as jersey, pique, textures,

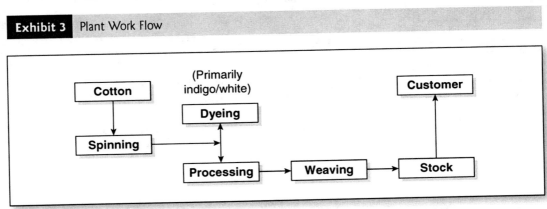

**Exhibit 3** Plant Work Flow

*Source:* Company files.

pointells, fleece, French terry, jacquards in solids, feeds, and automatics, and in double knits such as interlocks, needle-outs, ottomans, thermals, pointells, textures, reversible, jacquards, ribs in solids, feeds and automatic collars, plains, and jacquards (see Exhibit 4). These fabrics had applications from casuals to formals, from active wear to sleepwear for men, women, children, and infants.

With so much variation and range, the one thing that stood out was the immense necessity to understand and manage all specifications pertaining to each and every order from the customer, and more importantly the need to have fast and clear communications with the customers across the world. Arvind Mills, sensing this need, set up a high-tech design center. The centre was networked globally with designers to create corpus of the finest international design. That linked the designing facility to a "pilot mill," and the designs created on-screen were duplicated on fabric in a matter of hours. This ensured that the customer got an exclusive, world-class design in a very short time. This process not only helped shorten design-to-market

lead-time; it also allowed the retailers and designers to watch the trends closely and design and launch the products close to the start of a season.

The potential order that Bala was looking at was as follows:

- Twelve shades (five dark, three medium, and four light colors)
- Overall quantity
  - Dark shades— 6 EoQ /color
  - Medium shades—2.5 EoQ / color
  - Light shades— 6.25 EoQ /color

    Total = 180 EoQ
    1 EoQ = 350 kgs
    => total kgs = 63,000 kgs

  - Rejection rate—3% (overall)
  - Program anticipated in peak season
- Installed capacity = 3,500 kgs/day (in three eight hour shifts)
- Therefore total program books about 20 days worth of production; very lucrative

---

**Exhibit 4**    Production Process Flow

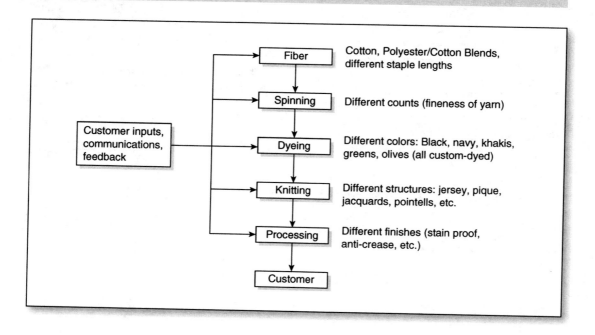

- Target price = 250–275/kg
- Probability of this order coming through = 0.80

*So and So* was confident that the company could meet the target price. The central issue, to his mind, was to propose a system of costing an order that was more reflective of the current business process (see Exhibit 5), and then re-evaluate the quote to be sent to the buyer. He asked the process managers to work out different scenarios using SAP, and come up with the numbers (see Exhibit 6).

| **Exhibit 5** | Cost Flow |

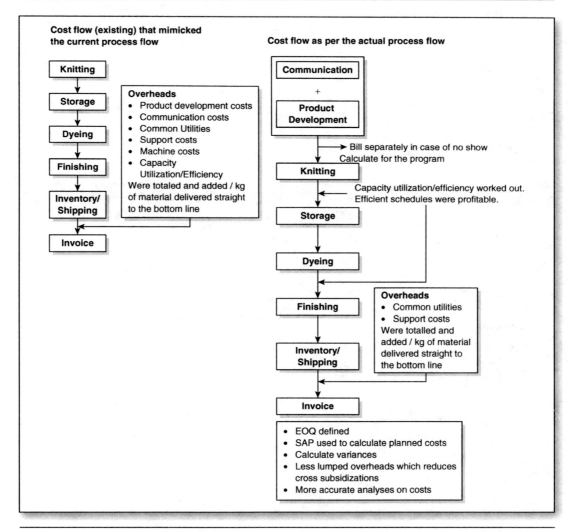

**Exhibit 5** (Continued)

| Cost Data | |
|---|---|
| Cotton yarn costs (seasonal variation) | Rs170/kg (10 – 15%) |
| Machine costs knitting (perEoQ) | Rs5/kg |
| Machine costs dyeing (per EoQ) | Rs12/kg |
| Direct labor | Rs12/kg |
| Communication costs/color EoQ | Rs2/kg |
| Product development/color/EoQ | Rs6/kg |
| Dyeing costs | Rs65 – 80/kg |
| Finishing costs | Rs15/kg |
| Shipping costs | Rs3/kg |
| Overheads | Rs30 – 40/kg |
| Total | Rs300 – 340/kg |

**Exhibit 6** Cost Methodologies Compared

| Traditional Method | Elemental Costing |
|---|---|
| 1. Direct costs:<br><br>  a. Raw cotton yarn @ 150/kg<br>  b. Dyes and chemicals @ 80/kg<br>  c. Finishing costs @ 30/kg<br>  d. Packing costs @ 3/kg<br>  e. Shipping costs @ 3/kg<br><br>2. Conversion costs:<br><br>  a. Yarn to knitted fabric<br>    i Installed capacity (depreciated) / projected capacity utilization for the season<br>    ii Direct power costs (per order)<br>    iii Direct labor costs (per order)<br>    iv Departmental salaries and overheads / projected capacity utilization for the season<br><br>  b. Dyeing of knitted fabric<br>    i Installed capacity (depreciated) / projected capacity utilization for the season | 1. Communication costs:<br><br>  a. Employee costs of the persons corresponding with the buyers<br>  b. Actual communication bills (international fax, phones, etc.)<br>  c. International courier charges at different stages of product development for approvals from the buyers<br><br>2. Product development:<br><br>  a. Design development costs at the knitting stage (structure specific, pattern specific if required)<br>  b. Shade development<br>  c. Multiple iterations taken to get to the sample as per the requirements of the buyers<br>  d. Collating the costs and calculation the EoQ and the projected cost/kg<br><br>3. Order costing:<br>  a. Direct costs<br>    i Cost of yarn (reflecting the seasonality of cotton prices)<br>    ii Dyes and chemicals<br>    iii Finishing costs<br>    iv Shipping costs |

| Traditional Method | Elemental Costing |
|---|---|
| ii  Direct power costs (per order)<br>iii Direct labor costs (per order)<br>iv Departmental salaries and overheads / projected capacity utilization for the season<br><br>c. Common costs<br>  i  Development costs<br>  ii Communication costs<br>  iii Support costs<br>  iv Utilities etc are divided over the projected order bookings<br>3. Did not use centralized system of managing operations | b. Operational costs<br>  i  Efficiencies in capacity utilization based on the order mix (shades, fabric types, etc.)<br>  ii Machine costs<br>  iii Labor costs<br>  iv Calculating the transfer costs between the knitting and dyeing processes<br><br>c. Overheads<br>  i  Allocated for the division based on the output / day for the program<br>  ii Eliminated cross subsidies between orders of differing sizes, nature, seasonality, etc.<br><br>SAP installed and used to manage Operations (BOMs, routings shop floor planning, etc.) Materials (purchasing, inventory levels, price rationalizations, etc.) Order costing and pricing among other aspects of the business. |

## CASE QUESTIONS

1. What pricing objective should be set for Arvind Mills? Why should it be chosen?

2. Which concept—sales maximization, profit maximization, market-share maximization, or competitive parity—best applies to the situation at Arvind Mills?

3. Should Arvind Mills resort to competition-based pricing, utilizing a meet-the-industry-average strategy? Why or why not?

4. Are any discounting tactics available to Arvind Mills that might help fight the competition? Why or why not?

5. Should the marketing management team at Arvind Mills attempt to resolve this problem by changing the products being offered, the methods of production, and the delivery systems? If so, how would the pricing program affect these changes?

# Advertising, Alternative and Direct Marketing

**A**dvertising management is the process of developing and overseeing a company's advertising program. The tasks involved are (1) establishing advertising objectives, (2) creating an advertising budget, (3) choosing an advertising agency, (4) overseeing the advertising program, and (5) assessing advertising effectiveness. These activities take place in an environment that changes radically and dramatically each year.

## ✕ Establishing Advertising Objectives

Advertising objectives will be based on the nature of the product, the stage of the product life cycle, the target audience, the activities of the competition, and other factors. The primary advertising objectives include creating brand and product awareness, building brand image, providing information, making persuasive arguments, supporting other marketing efforts, and encouraging action.

## ✕ Creating an Advertising Budget

To achieve the marketing objectives, the advertising budget must be sufficient. The primary forms of advertising budget creation are

1.  percentage of sales,

2.  meet the competition,

3.  arbitrary allocation, and

4.  objective and task method.

The percentage of sales method allocates funds to advertising and promotion based on either a percentage of the previous year's revenues or a projection on the upcoming year's sales. An arbitrary allocation occurs when company leaders set the budget at a level they think should be spent or believe the firm can afford. The objective and task approach begins with the company's marketing objectives as the basis for the budget estimate of dollars needed to achieve those objectives. An effective marketing manager reviews not only how much has been spent but also how well the money has been used.

## ◩ Choosing an Advertising Agency

The first choice to be made as part of this function is between an in-house advertising program and an outside advertising agency. In-house advertising is cheaper, and the marketing manager maintains greater control. Outside agencies offer a fresh perspective and expertise, including creativity.

When retaining an outside agency, selection criteria play a key role. The criteria of agency size, relevant experience, creative ability, and services offered are reviewed along with any existing or potential conflicts of interest. The company's creative reputation and capabilities merit careful consideration. When agencies are called in to make formal presentations (the creative pitch or shootout stage) the marketing team gains face-to-face insights about each firm and its proposed approach. Finally, the agency selected begins work and others are notified they did not win the contract.

## ◩ Overseeing an Advertising Program

The role of the marketing manager in advertising is overseeing the advertising process, including the methods used to design ads. The actual commercials or advertising pieces are prepared by creatives and advertising agency employees. Effective oversight of an advertising campaign program consists of (1) reviewing the advertising design and (2) confirming the media selection choices that are made.

A creative brief outlines the major elements of an advertising campaign. It consists of the objective for the campaign, the target audience, the message theme to be conveyed, the support for the message theme, and any constraints that should be considered. The account executive for the advertising agency works in concert with the client's marketing department to achieve the desired objectives in a manner agreed to by all parties.

Media selection combines the selection of a primary medium with all secondary media to be used. The traditional list of advertising media consists of television, radio, magazines, newspapers, outdoor/billboards, direct mail, and the Yellow pages. Currently, these media join with nontraditional or alternative media to complete a fully integrated advertising and marketing program. Nontraditional media include websites, social media forums, and placement on Internet search engines.

## ◩ Assessing Advertising Effectiveness

To fully assess advertising success requires deployment of several tools, not the least of which is reasoned judgment by the marketing team. A typical advertising campaign lasts between 4 weeks and 3 months. Those with continuous formats run advertising uniformly throughout the year.

Campaigns with pulsating formats feature advertisements throughout the year with a spurt of additional advertising during major seasons, such as Christmas. A discontinuous format includes periods when there are no advertisements and others when advertising is heavily used. Diet and exercise programs tend to focus on the New Year and the start of summer. Assessments of all these campaigns center on attitudinal effects and behavioral effects.

Attitudinal effects are measured using surveys and interviews via various media. Focus groups assist in evaluating messages prior to and after being released. Attitudes to be evaluated include recall of the ad, recognition of the brand, attitudes or feelings, brand positioning, perceptions of loyalty, and brand equity or parity. These variables are aligned with brand awareness, brand liking, and brand preferences.

Behavioral effects provide identifiable and immediate results from a marketing effort. Some of the standard behavioral measures include increases or decreases in store traffic; telephone, mail, and Internet inquiries; website visits; direct marketing responses; redemption rates of consumer and sales promotions; and sales by units or total volume. Marketers are aware that competitor actions and random events can influence these numbers. Normally, a direct relationship between an advertising campaign and subsequent sales does not exist. The campaign requires support from other marketing activities such as free samples, coupons, bonus packs, premiums, and a contest or sweepstakes.

To fully understand the relationship between advertising expenditures and sales, lag effects, threshold effects, carryover effects, and decay effects should be considered. Lag effects indicate that sales tend to rise some time after advertising expenditures have been made. When sales match expenditures, the threshold effect point has been reach. When a company stops advertising or a campaign ends, the sales curve tends to continue to rise but the rate of growth slows, which illustrates carryover effects. Over time, when advertising expenditures end, sales level off and begin to decline, which is the decay effect. The impact of advertising has worn off or decayed.

Marketing managers attempt to estimate when threshold effects for individual campaigns will take place in order to meet the need for increases in units of sales. They also try to identify the point at which carryover will end and decay will begin in order not to waste advertising dollars.

## Alternative Marketing Programs

Traditional and nontraditional advertising programs are often insufficient. They should be accompanied by alternative marketing programs that reach customers in new ways. The most common methods include guerrilla marketing, lifestyle marketing, and buzz marketing.

Guerrilla marketing seeks to obtain instant results with limited resources using tactics that rely on creativity, quality relationships with customers, and the willingness to try unusual approaches. Guerrilla marketing emphasizes quality rather than quantity. Reaching a carefully targeted audience becomes the goal of the planning process. Effective timing is a key factor in the success of a program. The message should reach the target market at the right time to gain maximum impact.

Lifestyle marketing involves tapping into a target audience's core lifestyle, music, culture, or fashion venues. The approach features engaging with customers at places where they relax and enjoy leisure activities. Farmer's markets, bluegrass festivals, citywide garage sales, flea markets, craft shows, stock car races, fashion shows, and 4H events present potential lifestyle marketing opportunities.

Buzz marketing, or word-of-mouth marketing, involves consumers passing along information about a product. It is one of the fastest-growing areas in alternative marketing. Buzz can be generated by customers who like the brand and tell others, consumers who like a brand and are sponsored by a company to tell others, and company or agency employees. Those who truly enjoy the brand are the best candidates to generate believable buzz. Employees posing as advocates raise ethical questions, especially when they do not identify themselves during interactions with others.

## Direct Marketing

Direct marketing programs connect the company directly with customers without the use of a middleman or intermediary. Direct marketing helps companies acquire and retain loyal customers. The key to an efficient program is a quality prospect list and a complete understanding of the needs of the target audience. The most common forms of direct marketing continue to be direct mail, catalogs, direct radio, television programs, Internet contacts, e-mail, and telemarketing systems. Internet microsites are efficient, make tracking simple, and allow for customization of offers.

## Implications for Entry-Level Employees

Entry-level workers should be fully apprised of all marketing and advertising campaigns so they can effectively deal with customers in contact with the company. Most of the interactions that take place in guerrilla marketing, lifestyle marketing, and buzz marketing programs are between customers and entry-level employees. Employee training regarding effective and positive ways to meet and greet potential customers is crucial. Supervisors carefully monitor events to make sure those involved create positive interactions with others.

## The Cases

### La Hacienda del Sol

La Hacienda del Sol is a Mexican hotel located in the Baja Peninsula that caters primarily to American tourists, most notably from Los Angeles and San Diego. Juanita Garcia, a member of the family that owned the hotel, served as the vice-president of administration. Her primary concern was that the hotel achieved full bookings each summer during the vacation season but had far less occupancy during the winter months. Perceptions by local Mexicans that La Hacienda del Sol was primarily an American hotel and that locals would feel less welcome would need to be overcome. Also, room prices eliminated many potential guests. Ms. Garcia knew the hotel would have to develop a successful advertising and promotions program in combination with price discounting to reach a new potential market—local Mexican tourists and guests.

### Shoppers Stop—Targeting the Young

The nation of India holds a unique marketing position in the world economy. As an emerging economy, the number of consumers with funds to make more elaborate purchases rose annually. At the same time, however, most of these newly affluent consumers were younger citizens. Nearly 70% of the nation's population was under the age of 35. Shoppers Stop had achieved its success in the highly fragmented retail market by focusing on customer service geared to urban consumers with disposable income. In order to sustain growth in the coming years, the company's marketing managers recognized that the chain would need to find ways to attract and retain the younger segment over time while not alienating current customers.

### Eat2Eat.com

Eat2Eat.com was developed as an Internet-based restaurant reservation service. It was located in the Pacific Rim. The company's technology, business model, and relationships with restaurants were well established. Owner and founder Vikram Aggarwal was concerned that his company had not been able to grow past the 12,000 registered users that it maintained. He was looking for cost-efficient ways to attract new registered users in order to continue to grow the company. The promotions needed to convince prospects that they would have access to a wealth of information about restaurant choices and would be able to make reservations online, receive discounts, and participate in loyalty programs. His revenues came from commissions on booking. The market consisted of corporate customers and private individuals that were registered users. The primary challenges included raising capital and then spending it in ways that would build the customer base.

## La Hacienda del Sol

*By Neeta Khera, under the supervision of Professor Elizabeth M. A. Grasby*

It was the morning of January 7, 2004, and Juanita Garcia, vice-president of administration of La Hacienda del Sol, a resort hotel in San Felipe, Mexico, was reviewing the fiscal 2003 financial records. The hotel catered primarily to American tourists during the country's hot summer months, but it had experienced another winter of low sales levels. Garcia had this problem each winter season and wondered how to better promote the hotel. Garcia considered targeting the Mexican market to improve sales levels in the off-season.[1]

### San Felipe

La Hacienda del Sol (Hacienda) was located in San Felipe, Baja California. San Felipe was approximately 230 miles[2] from the United States/Mexican border. See Exhibit 1 for a map of Baja California. Due to its location in the northern part of the California Gulf, San Felipe attracted tourists who sought and enjoyed a beach vacation of two to four days in length. The city was known for its

| Exhibit 1 | Map of Baja California |

Version: (A) 2009–09–24

green-blue waters, clean beaches, and comfortable climate and, as a result, was the most popular tourism spot, offering 1,600 hotel rooms, in Baja California. With a population of 25,000, the city attracted approximately 250,000 tourists each year.[3] See Exhibit 2 for a breakdown of the resort accommodations available in San Felipe.

| Exhibit 2 | Accommodations Available in San Felipe |
| --- | --- |

| Type of Accommodation | Number of Facilities |
| --- | --- |
| Resorts | 4 |
| Hotels/motels | 8 |
| Condominiums and Apartments | 15 |
| Bed and Breakfasts | 1 |
| RV and Campgrounds | 2 |
| Total | 30 |

*Source:* Company files.

## La Hacienda Del Sol

### Activities and Events

Hacienda offered a wide range of activities to tourists of all ages including swimming, surfing, jet-skiing, parasailing, jogging, and whale-watching. On the beach itself, there were many independent vendors who sold hair braiding services, horseback rides, ATV[4] rentals, and souvenirs. The hotel's premises included two outdoor swimming pools, children's playgrounds, pool tables, table tennis, racquetball courts, gardens, and shopping facilities. Additional activities during the summer months included bingo games, contests, and arts and crafts, to name a few.

### Dining Facilities

There were two restaurants and three dining halls located on-site. One of the restaurants offered both American and Mexican food, with the focus mainly on traditional Mexican meals. This restaurant served food in two locations: a full-service sit-down room and a buffet-style room with both rooms providing a wide variety of foods. The sit-down location had a casual atmosphere, and customers could come in and out of the restaurant at their convenience. The buffet-style location had specified hours for breakfast, lunch and dinner. During the summer months, there were often regular performances on a stage during dinner (e.g., traditional Mexican dances) and, on some nights of the week, the room served as a nightclub after dinner. Consequently, it characteristically exhibited a fun and energetic atmosphere.

The second restaurant, adjacent to the hotel's main building, focused on a fine-dining experience and served French and Continental cuisine for lunch and dinner only. The restaurant was located in the founder's original mansion, with most of the mansion's original drapery, carpets, floors, lighting and furniture originating from the 1920s. Occasionally, a pianist would play on a grand piano to create a mellow ambiance.

In addition to the two restaurants, the hotel had three bars. The bars were the second-largest source of income, representing 25 percent of revenue.[5]

### The Spa

The hotel's European-style spa offered a variety of services, which were growing in popularity even though many customers were unaware of the hotel's spa prior to arrival. Garcia recently introduced a promotional offering that included a room and spa deal which helped encourage the growth in spa sales. The spa, located in the second half of the founder's mansion, offered hairstyling, waxing, over 10 different types of body treatments, reflexology, manicures, pedicures, and facials. The pleasant service, pastel-colored walls and furniture, and soft music playing in the background added to the spa's relaxing atmosphere and sophisticated ambiance.

Many wedding packages were made available by the hotel to suit customers' needs. For example, a package that included a three-course meal for 50 guests, champagne, a reception site by the garden or ocean, soft drinks, linens and seat covers, waiters, and flower arrangements for the reception tables cost $1,260.[6] Between the months of July and October, the hotel held, on average, one wedding per week. Many brides and their bridal parties took advantage of the spa before their wedding ceremony at the hotel.

## Hotel Rooms

The price of the rooms changed each season depending on the expected demand. See Exhibits 3 and 4 for a breakdown and prices of the rooms. Each room included a full bath, telephone, cable television, and bottled water. The price of the room also included one margarita per person and dinner for two from the hotel's Special Getaways menu. For families with up to two children, the children were given free accommodations and three meals each day from the children's menu. Rates were also lowered for seniors. Parking was available on-site to customers at $3 per car per night.

The hotel operated at a 90 percent to 100 percent occupancy rate from the last week of June to the first week of September. The weekends were generally fully booked, while some rooms were available during the weekdays. Due to the seasonality of the business, the hotel depended on its success in July and August to carry it through the rest of the year. After Labor Day weekend,[7] occupancy levels dropped dramatically, reaching 30 percent on weekdays and between 60 percent to 80 percent on some weekends. From November to March, occupancy averaged 20 percent all week. The hotel would reach 90 percent occupancy only during the weeks that college students had their spring break holiday (typically in late February); the hotel continued to average an occupancy rate of 20 percent between the end of spring break and the last week of June. U.S. holidays typically put the resort at full capacity regardless of the time of year.

## Juanita Garcia

The hotel had been a private, family-run business for over 75 years. Juanita Garcia was the third

| Exhibit 3 | Breakdown of Hotel Rooms |

| Type of Room | Number Rooms Available | Number of People/Room |
|---|---|---|
| Garden view rooms | 40 | 2 |
| Ocean front rooms | 134 | 2 |
| Junior suites | 26 | 2 |
| One bedroom suites | 42 | 2 |
| Apartments | 4 | 4 |
| Two bedroom suites | 11 | 4 |
| Master suite | 18 | 4 |
| Presidential suite | 1 | 4 |
| **Total** | **276** | |

*Source:* Company files.

| **Exhibit 4** | 2003 Hotel Rates[1] |
|---|---|

| | Summer Rates | |
|---|---|---|
| **Type of Room** | **Sunday to Thursday** | **Friday and Saturday** |
| Garden view rooms | $97.30 | $125.30 |
| Ocean front rooms | $111.30 | $160.30 |
| Junior suites | $125.30 | $174.30 |
| One bedroom suites | $132.30 | $188.30 |
| Apartments | $139.30 | $209.30 |
| Two bedroom suites | $160.30 | $237.30 |
| Master suite | $174.30 | $244.30 |
| Presidential suite | $300.30 | $370.30 |
| | Autumn, Winter, Spring Rates (off-season) | |
| **Type of Room** | **Sunday to Thursday** | **Friday and Saturday** |
| Garden view rooms | $69.30 | $118.30 |
| Ocean front rooms | $90.30 | $139.30 |
| Junior suites | $111.30 | $153.30 |
| One bedroom suites | $125.30 | $174.30 |
| Apartments | $139.30 | $195.30 |
| Two bedroom suites | $160.30 | $209.30 |
| Master suite | $174.30 | $230.30 |
| Presidential suite | $307.30 | $349.30 |

*Source:* Company files.

1. All prices are in U.S. dollars per night (regardless of occupancy).

generation family member to operate the business, with her father holding the position of chief executive officer (CEO) for over 20 years. Garcia's father, his two daughters, and his three sons were the only shareholders of the business.

Garcia and her siblings were approached by their father to take over the family business in the summer of 1999. Juanita Garcia was the only one interested, since the other children knew how difficult the task would be from witnessing the number of hours worked by their father. She stepped into the role of vice-president of administration and was initially responsible for promoting the hotel, creating new marketing strategies and managing communications between the company and its shareholders. Juanita knew that if she was going to take over the business one day, she needed to understand the company and what would make it successful.

Running a family business provided the flexibility needed to make quick operational decisions; however, all recommendations had to be approved by Garcia's father. If her father was not convinced initially or was remotely skeptical, he completely dismissed any recommendations. All proposed recommendations had to be well supported.

## Hotel Guests

From late June to early September, Hacienda targeted families who spent, on average, $500 during their stay at the hotel (typically three days and two nights). During the off-season, the hotel attracted seniors and couples who were looking for a peaceful getaway. The highest spending consumers were between the ages of 28 and 49, primarily due to their liquor purchases.

At one time, the hotel attracted a large number of college students during the spring break season. Garcia wondered if this market was suitable given the hotel's reputation.

Ninety-five percent of the hotel's customers were from the United States, half from Los Angeles and the other half from San Diego. See Exhibit 5 for selected information on the two cities. Of the remaining five percent, two percent were from the state of Baja California with the remaining three percent from the other parts of the United States.

## The Mexican Market

Garcia was hopeful that targeting the Mexican market during the off-season would help boost sales. Hotel management had never considered entering this market since it was believed that Hacienda's rates would be too high. Furthermore, it was well known that Hacienda catered to the American market, leaving Mexicans with the perception that they were not welcome. Garcia knew that if the company were to enter this market, she would have to address this perception.

| **Exhibit 5**  Los Angeles and San Diego Demographics | |
|---|---|
| **Los Angeles** | |
| Total population (2003) | 3,819,951 |
| Average personal income per capita | $26,773 |
| Unemployment rate | 6.8% |
| % of family households | 16.4% |
| % of families with children under the age of 18 | 53.5% |
| % of people 65 years and older | 9.7% |
| Distance from San Felipe | 6.5 driving hours |

*Source:* City of Los Angeles: www.ci.la.ca.us, February 7, 2005 and U.S. Census Bureau: www.census.gov/statab/www, February 7, 2005.

| San Diego | |
|---|---|
| Total population (2003) | 1,266,753 |
| Average personal income per capita | $27,657 |
| Unemployment rate | 3.0% |
| % of family households | 16.4% |
| % of families with children under the age of 18 | 53.4% |
| % of people 65 years and older | 10.5% |
| Distance from San Felipe | 4.5 driving hours |

*Source:* City of San Diego: www.sandiego.gov, February 7, 2005 and U.S. Census Bureau: www.census.gov/statab/www, February 7, 2005.

## Mexicali

Mexicali, the capital of Baja California, was 124 miles from Hacienda and was well known for its agriculture and Maquiladoras;[8] however, half the working population was employed in the tourism industry with 44 percent employed by hotels and restaurants. Of Mexicali's 813,853 population, 14 percent lived in rural areas. See Exhibits 6 and 7 for additional information on the Mexicali population.

Mexicali was also known for its extreme climate. See Exhibit 8 for typical annual temperatures.

| Exhibit 6 | Age Distribution of Mexicali Residents |
|---|---|

| Age Bracket | Percent of Population |
|---|---|
| 0 to 14 | 32 |
| 15 to 24 | 20 |
| 25 to 54 | 38 |
| 55 and over | 10 |

*Source:* California Center for Border and Regional Economic Studies: www.ccbres.sdsu.edu, July 19, 2004.

| Exhibit 7 | Annual Household Income of Mexicali Families |
|---|---|

| Annual Household Income | Percent of Population |
|---|---|
| Less than $1,174 | 1.4 |
| $1,174 to $1,388 | 2.3 |
| $1,389 to $2,669 | 7.1 |
| $2,670 to $3,949 | 7.7 |
| $3,950 to $5,337 | 14.8 |
| $5,338 to $10,674 | 25.1 |
| $10,675 to $16,011 | 22.5 |
| $16,012 to $21,349 | 9.7 |
| More than $21,350 | 9.4 |

*Source:* California Center for Border and Regional Economic Studies: www.ccbres.sdsu.edu, July 19, 2004.

*Note:* Converted from pesos to U.S. dollars on December 31, 2002, at a rate of $0.08895/peso.

| Exhibit 8 | Annual Weather in Mexicali 2003 |
|---|---|

| Month | Temperature |
|---|---|
| January | 75°F |
| February | 73°F |
| March | 84°F |
| April | 80°F |
| May | 93°F |
| June | 105°F |
| July | 116°F |
| August | 96°F |
| September | 105°F |
| October | 98°F |
| November | 69°F |
| December | 64°F |

*Note:* The maximum temperature on the 15th of each month.

Residents were always looking to get away during the hot months. Those who could afford it generally owned a second home where the climate was not as uncomfortable.

## Hotel Rates

Mexicans viewed the hotel as overpriced, so Garcia knew that she needed to come up with a package deal to attract these customers to the hotel; nevertheless, she was uncertain whether a lower rate should be offered just to Mexicali residents. A marketing manager who used a similar strategy in another hotel suggested advertising at a rate equal to half the season's average monthly temperature (in Fahrenheit) for a garden view room. The rates of all other rooms would have to be priced accordingly. Garcia wanted to consider this pricing strategy due to the hotel's vacancy rates. She did not want to limit her analysis to this pricing strategy and was open to any alternatives.

## Promotion Timing

Garcia also needed to decide when to offer such a promotion. She wanted to focus only on one of the seasons initially: summer (June to August), autumn (September to November), winter (December to February), or spring (March to May). Consideration would need to be given to the $20 daily cost to maintain each room, regardless of size, which included employee wages, linens, electricity, water, sewage costs and any other amenities. These costs were only incurred while the room was occupied.

## Promotion

The hotel spent, on average, $150,000 to $200,000 on advertising during its off-season each year. Currently, Hacienda promoted through newspaper, press releases, radio and on its website. The hotel could not afford the expensive television advertising in the United States.

The hotel's website was the first of its kind to be listed on the Internet in Mexico. Although the site was not aesthetically appealing, it was known as being user-friendly and received approximately 1,000 hits per day. It had been the most up-to-date hotel website in Mexico until December 2003 when one of its competitors had upgraded its site. Garcia suggested to her father on numerous occasions that the website should be upgraded, but he remained unconvinced. He thought that since the hotel reached 100 percent capacity during the summer months, the website upgrade could not be justified from a financial perspective.

Approximately five percent of the Mexicali population had access to a computer. Garcia estimated that only one percent of the population in Mexicali had access both to a computer and to the Internet and, of those who had access to the Internet, 0.5 percent of targeted consumers would visit the hotel by viewing the hotel's Web site, per season.

Television was very common in Mexicali, regardless of the income level of the household. Garcia estimated that 85 percent of Mexicali residents had access to a television and watched regularly.

She predicted that 15 percent of targeted television viewers would visit the hotel in the summer months and 2.5 percent would visit during the off-season. There were two local television stations in Mexicali. If Hacienda were to advertise on television, Garcia thought it would be best to pay for airtime during the peak times of the day: 7 A.M. to 8 A.M. and 7 P.M. to 9 P.M. During these time periods, the cost was at its highest: $41.25[9] for each 30-second advertisement.

There were also two popular radio stations to consider. Each 30-second ad cost $10.50. Statistics indicated that 45 percent of the population listened to the radio. Garcia predicted six percent to 8.5 percent of targeted listeners would visit the hotel in the summer, and one percent would visit the hotel in the off-season.

Although newspaper was a popular form of advertising to Americans, Garcia believed distributing flyers in a local mall would be a more viable option. Since there was only one air-conditioned mall in Mexicali, a large portion of the population shopped at this mall during the hot months. The cost to produce 1,000 flyers would be $2.30. For every 1,000 flyers, there was an additional distribution cost of $27.50. A response rate between two percent and three percent of the target market was expected per season.

Garcia needed to estimate a reasonable budget in order to promote to this market segment, and she wanted to initially use one type of promotional medium for one season to test the new market. She knew that her father would not agree to spend more than $50,000 per season on additional promotions. She had to assess how best to spend the budget—all on radio ads, all on television ads, or $10,000 per season on flyers.

## Decision

Garcia knew that the hotel needed a solution to its low sales in the off-season. She wondered whether it was viable to target the Mexicali market and whether it was a good fit with the company's marketing strategy. If so, she needed to decide on the room rates, the type of promotional media to use and when to start advertising. She knew she had to give some incentives to the Mexicans to entice them to come to the hotel in addition to heavily promoting specific services that would cater to this new market. She had to have a convincing argument to give to her father if some positive changes were to be made to the company's current financial position.

### CASE QUESTIONS

1. Should Juanita Garcia consider the possibility of promoting La Hacienda del Sol to U.S. "snowbirds" wishing to travel south during winter months rather than promoting to local Mexicans, using the logic that the hotel could charge higher prices to U.S. citizens looking for a warm place to spend some time? What cost considerations would be involved in such a strategy?

2. Assuming La Hacienda del Sol offered major discounts during the off-season, should they be given to both locals and any U.S. citizens wishing to visit the hotel during the off-season? Why or why not?

3. Which traditional advertising media do you believe would be most effective in reaching the local Mexican market and potential hotel guests in that market? Which would be the least? Defend your response.

4. If asked to develop an advertising and promotions campaign directed at the local Mexican market, what would be the size of your budget? What would be the theme of the campaign?

5. What types of alternative media would be most effective in enticing the local Mexican market to visit the hotel during the winter? Explain your choices.

# Shoppers Stop—Targeting the Young

*By R. Chandrasekhar, under the supervision of Professor Shanker Krishnan*

In June 2006, Govind Shrikhande, chief executive officer (CEO) of Shoppers Stop, India's biggest chain of large-format department stores (in terms of retail space), was reviewing the Brand Navigator study that had landed on his desk. This study was conducted periodically to measure customer perceptions of the Shoppers Stop brand compared with its closest competitors. According to the 2006 study, Shoppers Stop was perceived as a "caring" brand. This perception seemed to harmonize with the characteristics of its core customer group, adults aged 25 to 45. But the study also showed

disengagement with younger customers. The lack of connection was evident in how customers perceived the three competitors' brands: Lifestyle, Pantaloon, and Central, which were described as "fashionable," "trendy," "flashy," "modern," "sporty" and "lively" (see Exhibit 1).

Shrikhande had been appointed CEO two months earlier, after having joined Shoppers Stop in April 2001 as director of Buying and Merchandising. Previously, he had worked at Bombay Dyeing & Manufacturing Co. Ltd., a branded apparel maker and a Shoppers Stop vendor. Since Shoppers

**Exhibit 1** Brand Perception Study of Shoppers Stop Compared With Lifestyle, Pantaloon and Central

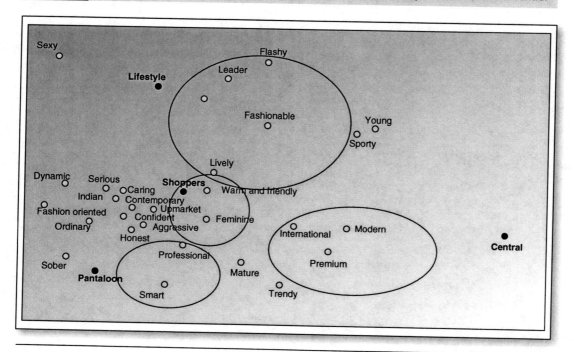

*Source:* Company.

Version: (A) 2009–05–05

Stop's inception 15 years earlier, the company had sustained its focus on the department store format. The retailer had also built up a loyal customer base, which had become a source of competitive advantage over its peers.

Shrikhande needed to establish a fit between the company's strategic goals and the necessity to connect with younger consumers. The company's major competitors were all weighing their options for pursuing the youth market although none had yet formulated any specific, long-term plans. Shrikhande had to ensure that any attempt on the part of Shoppers Stop to connect with younger consumers would neither detract from the Shoppers Stop's business focus, dilute its brand identity, nor alienate existing customers.

## Indian Retailing

The Indian retail market was valued at INR12,781 billion[1] (see Exhibit 2). With approximately 12 million retail outlets spread across the country, India was home to the world's highest number of retail outlets per capita. The fragmented nature of the Indian retail industry was evident in Pantaloon, an apparel retailer that opened in 1993. Pantaloon, despite having sales of INR35.63 billion (US$0.87 billion) in 2006, the highest revenue among retailers on India's stock exchange, had a national market share of only 0.3 percent. More than 85 percent of India's retail outlets were so-called mom-and-pop establishments.

In 2006, India's share of organized retail—characterized by customer requirements being met by trained staff in an ambience of comfort, style and speed[2]—was INR530 billion. At 4.1 percent of total retail, the percentage of organized retail contrasted sharply with not only the United States (at 80 percent) but also with neighboring markets, such as China (at 20 percent), Indonesia (at 30 percent), Thailand (at 40 percent), Malaysia (at 55 percent) and Taiwan (at 81 percent).[3] India's share of organized retail was expected to grow to 10 percent by 2010 and 20 percent by 2020. The imminent rise was

| Exhibit 2 | Indian Retail Industry, 2006 |

| Category | (in INR billion) | | % |
| --- | --- | --- | --- |
| | Total Retail sales | Organized Retail Sales | Share of Total Organized Retail |
| Food and beverages | 9,510 | 93 | 0.98 |
| Clothing and textiles | 1,190 | 195 | 16.39 |
| Consumer durables | 622 | 106 | 17.04 |
| Home décor and furnishing | 388 | 34 | 8.76 |
| Jewelry and watches | 549 | 34 | 6.19 |
| Beauty care | 281 | 10 | 3.86 |
| Footwear | 134 | 44 | 32.84 |
| Books, music and gifts | 107 | 14 | 13.08 |
| Total | 12,781 | 530 | 99.14 |

*Source:* "Retail – Market and Opportunities," by Ernst & Young for India Brand Equity Foundation, 2008, p. 4.

mainly because India was in the middle of a retail revolution that had no parallel in economic history.

Elsewhere in the world, the development of a country's retail industry was usually spread over 30 to 40 years, with customers savoring each experience methodically, as it was introduced. Thus, consumers first became accustomed to convenience stores, which were followed by department stores and shopping centers, then large shopping malls. Big-box retailers, hypermarkets, discounters, and specialty stores followed at their own pace. In India, however, all retail development was coming together at the same time. All retail formats, which were commonplace in the developed markets of Europe and North America, were appearing simultaneously in India. The retail phenomenon, already evident in Tier 1 and Tier 2 cities, which comprised the major and mainstream cities of India, was percolating progressively into Tier 3 and Tier 4 towns (see Exhibit 3) and further into India's vast rural areas. Simultaneously, consumers themselves were

undergoing a change in profile, which was as sudden and dramatic as the changes in external environment. Indian consumers were becoming rich, youthful and aspirational, all at the same time. They now also had an unprecedented choice of product offerings.

At a more basic level, four factors were driving the retail revolution in India: changing demographics, an upward migration of income, easy availability of credit, and government impetus.

## Changing Demographics

India had the second-highest population of all countries in the world. Against the backdrop of an aging world, however, India had the advantage of a large young population. For example, 35 percent of Indians were younger than 15 years of age, and 70 percent were younger than 35 years of age (see Exhibit 4). Because young customers had a high propensity to consume, the lucrative consumer

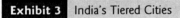

**Exhibit 3**    India's Tiered Cities

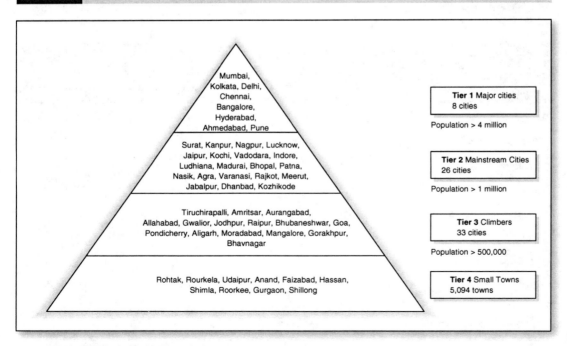

*Source: The "Bird of Gold": The Rise of India's Consumer Market,* McKinsey & Company, November 2007, page 74.

| Exhibit 4 | India's Demographic Profile, 2006 |
|---|---|

| | Brazil | Russia | India | China |
|---|---|---|---|---|
| Age in Years | Percentage of the Population | | | |
| 0–14 | 29 | 16 | 35 | 25 |
| 15–34 | 37 | 26 | 35 | 35 |
| 35–59 | 26 | 36 | 23 | 30 |
| 60 and over | 8 | 23 | 7 | 10 |

*Source:* Shoppers Stop Equity Research Report, B&K Securities, February 2007.

base had positioned India as a promising destination for global retailers.

## Upward Migration of Income

Of India's 204 million households, 22.0 million households (amounting to 10.8 percent) were defined as "rich" because they had annual incomes greater than INR180,000. Just below the rich households was a population of 50 million households that formed the consuming class who earned between INR90,000 and INR180,000. This middle-income class, known as the real consumers, currently comprised 24.5 percent of the total households, but was

expected to increase to 32 percent of the total households by 2010 (see Exhibit 5). This large and growing consumer class was also witnessing a shift in attitude from saving money to spending money. As a result, a consumption boom was in the offing in India, fueling the growth of Indian retail for the next few decades.

## Easy Credit

Indian consumers had been under-leveraged for decades, having financed all their purchases through cash payments. During the mid-1990s, leading commercial banks, led by Citibank, started promoting credit cards. Going forward, with falling

| Exhibit 5 | India's Growing Middle Class |
|---|---|

| Annual Household Income | 2002 | 2006 | 2010 (Estimate) |
|---|---|---|---|
| (INR) | (Percentage of the population) | | |
| Up to 45,000 | 35 | 26 | 16 |
| 45,000–90,000 | 37 | 39 | 35 |
| 90,000–135,000 | 14 | 17 | 22 |
| 135,000–180,000 | 7 | 8 | 10 |
| Above 180,000 | 7 | 10 | 17 |

*Source:* Shoppers Stop Equity Research Report, B&K Securities, February 2007.

or stable interest rates, consumer credit was expected to grow, providing an impetus for both consumer spending and the growth of organized retail. Penetration of credit cards was low, at 18 to 20 cards per 1,000 consumers, which indicated a major opportunity for expansion.

## Government Impetus

A major driver for retail revolution was the Indian government's decision in February 2006 to allow 51 percent ownership by a foreign enterprise in a local retail venture of a "single" brand. Thus, "multi-brand" retailers, such as Walmart, did not have an easy time establishing a direct presence in India. Global apparel brands, however, could now enter India and establish a local business with majority ownership.

From the perspective of global retailers seeking new markets, retail businesses in India fell into three categories: Ready-to-Go, Shape/Adapt, and Wait-and-Watch (see Exhibit 6). The first category, Ready-to-Go, consisted of several sub-categories in which determined retailers could quickly build their positions. New entrants did not need to make a major

investment. Ease of sourcing, proliferation of brands, and consumer acceptance in this category had reached levels that permitted, from day one, the exploitation of both economies of scale and economies of scope. The second category, Shape/Adapt, required investments both in back-end operations, such as building the supply chain, and in front-end operations, such as developing the sales force. The third category, Wait-and-Watch, consisted of underdeveloped businesses that provided no immediate opportunities for market development. The businesses were largely regulated by federal and provincial governments, making market entry difficult for a foreign company.

## Demographic Dividend

The population of India was forecast to stay young for the next two decades (see Exhibit 7). The country was on the cusp of what economists referred to as "a demographic dividend." This rare social phenomenon led to opportunities for economic growth because of a confluence of factors, such as a decline in the birth rate, an increase in the number of working adults, and a

**Exhibit 6**  Indian Retail Categories

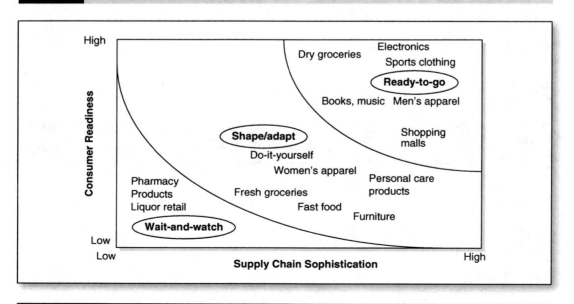

Source: Michael Fernandes et al., "India's Retailing Comes of Age," *McKinsey Quarterly*, December 2000.

| Exhibit 7 | Young India |

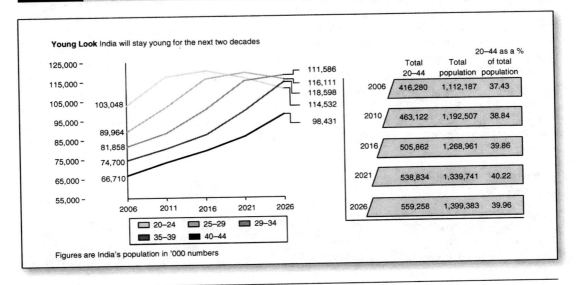

**Young Look** India will stay young for the next two decades

| | Total 20–44 | Total population | 20–44 as a % of total population |
|---|---|---|---|
| 2006 | 416,280 | 1,112,187 | 37.43 |
| 2010 | 463,122 | 1,192,507 | 38.84 |
| 2016 | 505,862 | 1,268,961 | 39.86 |
| 2021 | 538,834 | 1,339,741 | 40.22 |
| 2026 | 559,258 | 1,399,383 | 39.96 |

20–24   25–29   29–34   35–39   40–44

Figures are India's population in '000 numbers

*Source:* Indian Census population projection report.

decrease in the dependent population. Demographic dividend would provide India with a competitive advantage over not only the developed countries of the world but also emerging economies in Brazil, Russia, and China. Experts widely acknowledged that the Indian economy could achieve consistent growth of approximately 9 percent each year for the next two decades.

The concept was explained by economist Kaushik Basu:

> Consider that in the year 2004, India had a population of 1,080 million, of whom 672 million people were in the age-group 15 to 64 years. This is usually treated as the "working age population." Since outside of this age group very few people work, it is reasonable to think of the remainder, that is, 408 million people, as the "dependent population." A nation's "dependency ratio" is the ratio of the dependent population to the working-age population. In the case of India, this turns out to be 0.6. On this score, India does not look too different from many other developing countries. Bangladesh's dependency ratio is 0.7, Pakistan's 0.8, Brazil's 0.5.

> What is different about India is the prediction that it will see a sharp decline in this ratio over the next 30 years or so. This is what constitutes the demographic dividend. India's fertility rate—that is, the average number of children a woman expects to have in her life time—used to be 3.8 in 1990. This has fallen to 2.9 and is expected to fall further. Since women had high fertility earlier, we now have a sizeable number of people in the age-group 0–15 years. But since fertility is falling, some 10 or 15 years down the road, this bulge of young people would have moved into the working-age category. And, since, at that time, the relative number of children will be small (thanks to the lowered fertility), India's dependency ratio would be lower.

> It is expected that, in 2020, the average age of an Indian will be 29 years, compared to 37 for China and 48 for Japan. By 2030, India's dependency ratio should be just over 0.4.[4]

By increasing the percentage of young people in the population, the demographic dividend would bring additional benefits: a rise in the relative number of breadwinners, an increase in the number of women joining the workforce, and a decline in the dependency ratio. Together, these benefits would lead to higher savings. The rate of savings in India as a percentage of gross domestic product (GDP), was already much higher than developed countries at 33 percent and would increase further over the next few decades.

The demographic dividend would come into play only for a period of time. In a progressive cycle, each demographic dividend phase would be followed by a "demographic echo," characterized by a rise in the dependency ratio as the working population moved into retirement. Therefore, reaping as much as possible from the demographic dividend and investing in social capital would ensure the social foundation of a community (i.e., education, skill levels, employability, health care and civic infrastructure) was robust enough to withstand the effects of an echo (see Exhibit 8).

| **Exhibit 8** | India's Demographic Dividend |

| (Population in Millions) | | | |
|---|---|---|---|
| **Age Group in Years** | **2001** | **2011\*** | **2021\*** |
| 0–4 | 110.45 | 115.58 | 110.96 |
| 5–9 | 128.31 | 115.43 | 112.69 |
| 10–14 | 124.85 | 120.43 | 113.07 |
| 15–19 | 100.21 | 119.99 | 114.31 |
| 20–24 | 89.76 | 116.21 | 119.10 |
| 25–29 | 83.44 | 103.84 | 118.23 |
| 30–34 | 74.27 | 92.33 | 114.23 |
| **YOUNG POPULATION (15–34)** | **347.68** | **432.38** | **465.88** |
| 35–39 | 70.57 | 83.62 | 101.85 |
| 40–44 | 55.74 | 74.09 | 90.19 |
| 45–49 | 47.40 | 63.51 | 80.96 |
| 50–54 | 36.58 | 52.43 | 70.58 |
| 55–59 | 27.67 | 41.82 | 59.03 |
| 60–64 | 27.52 | 32.58 | 47.02 |
| **WORKING POPULATION (15–64)** | **613.16** | **780.43** | **915.51** |
| 65–69 | 19.81 | 24.92 | 35.56 |
| 70–74 | 14.71 | 18.74 | 25.71 |
| 75–79 | 6.55 | 12.55 | 17.53 |
| 80 plus | 8.03 | 8.46 | 15.99 |
| Age not stated | 2.74 | – | – |
| **TOTAL POPULATION** | **1,028.61** | **1,196.55** | **1,347.02** |

| (Population in Millions) | | | |
|---|---|---|---|
| **Age Group in Years** | **2001** | **2011\*** | **2021\*** |
| Median age of the population (years) | 22.51 | 25.47 | 29.33 |
| Working population as % of total population | 59.6 | 65.2 | 68.0 |
| Dependent population as % of total population | 40.4 | 34.8 | 32.0 |
| Percentage of young population (15–34 years) | 33.8 | 36.1 | 34.6 |
| Percentage of population below the age of 35 | 69.1 | 65.5 | 59.6 |

*Source:* Adapted from "Youth in India — Profiles and Programmes," the Ministry of Statistics and Programme Implementation of the Government of India, October 2006, Table 2(a) "Distribution of population by age and sex, 2001–2021," page 37, http://www.mospi.gov.in, accessed November 12, 2008

*Note:* The government of India conducts the official census once in a decade. The most recent census was in 2001.

\* Projected population.

## Customer Segmentation

When identifying customer target groups, Indian companies relied on data from two basic sources: the periodic analysis of consumers' income levels by the National Council of Applied Economic Research, an Indian market research agency (see Exhibit 9), and the socio-economic classification (SEC) of consumers, provided by the Market Research Society of India, another premier market research agency (see Exhibit 10).

**Exhibit 9**   India's Income Classes and Number of Households, 2005

| Income Classes | | Number of Households (in 000s) | |
|---|---|---|---|
| **Category** | **Annual Income Range (INR 000s)** | **Urban** | **Rural** |
| Super rich | >10,001 | 46 | 6 |
| Sheer rich | 5,001–10,000 | 87 | 16 |
| Clear rich | 2,001–5,000 | 360 | 94 |
| Near rich | 1,001–2,000 | 842 | 280 |
| Strivers | 501–1,000 | 2,301 | 911 |
| Seekers | 201–500 | 8,889 | 4,923 |
| Aspirers | 91–200 | 25,158 | 28,118 |
| Destitutes | < 90 | 23,156 | 109,093 |
| Total | | 60,839 | 143,441 |

*Source:* The Great Indian Middle Class, the National Council of Applied Economic Research, www.ncaer.org, accessed November 12, 2008.

| Exhibit 10 | India's Socio-Economic Classes and Number of Households, 2006 |
|---|---|

| Socio-Economic Class | Estimated Number of Households (in millions) |
|---|---|
| A1 | 2.2 |
| A2 | 4.1 |
| B1 | 5.3 |
| B2 | 5.3 |
| C | 12.8 |
| D | 14.2 |
| E1 | 6.7 |
| E2 | 10.8 |
| R1 | 5.8 |
| R2 | 15.9 |
| R3 | 56.7 |
| R4 | 67.3 |
| Total | 207.1 |

Source: Market Research Society of India.

Note: The top band of purchasing power in India, Urban A1A2, comprised a little more than 6 million households. The next band, which would qualify for the "middle-class India" label, comprising B1R1B2C, included approximately 30 million households. These two groups together formed the ABCR1 target group, the broadest possible target group for most consumer goods, at approximately 36 million households. The lower middle-class comprised DE1R2 at approximately 37 million households.

The SEC system, India's most widely used consumer classification system, had two categories: urban and rural. SEC Urban used demographics as a combination of occupation and education, both of which shaped not only the earning capacity of the "chief wage earner" (the term used for the purpose of classification) in an urban household but also the self-image and social status of the household (see Exhibit 11). The system was based on the assumption that consumption behavior of an executive with a professional qualification working in the corporate sector differed from the consumption behavior of a self-employed store owner even when both shared the same income level. SEC Urban comprised eight segments (A1, A2, B1, B2, C, D, E1 and E2), whereas SEC Rural comprised four segments (R1, R2, R3 and R4).

The retail advisory group of Ernst & Young India, a management consultancy firm, published a study of Indian youth, whom it referred to as "the main architects of Indian retail." The study classified India's youth into three segments: Dabblers, aged 13 to 21; Aspirers, aged 22 to 28; and Thrivers, aged 29 to 35 (see Exhibit 12).[5]

## Company Background

Promoted by K Raheja Corp., a real estate and hospitality enterprise based in western India, Shoppers

| Exhibit 11 | India's Socio-Economic Classification (Sec)—Urban |
|---|---|

| Education/ Occupation of the Chief Wage Earner in a Household | Illiterate | Up to Grade 4 | Grade 5–9 | Grade 10 | Pre-University | Grad/PG (General) | Grad/PG (Professional) |
|---|---|---|---|---|---|---|---|
| Unskilled workers | E2 | E2 | E1 | D | D | D | D |
| Skilled workers | E2 | E1 | D | C | C | B2 | B2 |
| Petty traders | E2 | D | D | C | C | B2 | B2 |
| Shop owners | D | D | C | B2 | B1 | A2 | A2 |

| Education/ Occupation of the Chief Wage Earner in a Household | Illiterate | Up to Grade 4 | Grade 5–9 | Grade 10 | Pre-University | Grad/PG (General) | Grad/PG (Professional) |
|---|---|---|---|---|---|---|---|
| Entrepreneurs (Nil employees) | D | C | B2 | B1 | A2 | A2 | A1 |
| Entrepreneurs (<10 employees) | C | B2 | B2 | B1 | A2 | A1 | A1 |
| Entrepreneurs (>10 employees) | B1 | B1 | A2 | A2 | A1 | A1 | A1 |
| Self-employed professionals | D | D | D | B2 | B1 | A2 | A1 |
| Clerical/Salesmen | D | D | D | C | B2 | B1 | B1 |
| Supervisory level | D | D | C | C | B2 | B1 | A2 |
| Officers/ Executives (Jr) | C | C | C | B2 | B1 | A2 | A2 |
| Officers/ Executives (Mid and Sr) | B1 | B1 | B1 | B1 | A2 | A1 | A1 |

*Source:* Market Research Society of India.

*Note:* Socio-economic classification (SEC) indicates the affluence level of a household. The SEC of an urban household is defined by the education and occupation of the chief wage earner of a household. The classification system has eight categories: A1, A2, B1, B2, C, D, E1 and E2, rated in descending order of affluence.

Stop pioneered modern retailing in India when it opened its first, 2,800 square foot store in suburban Mumbai in 1991. By 2006, its operations had grown to 20 stores across 10 cities, covering a total retail space of 950,000 square feet. Sixteen stores were located in the Tier 1 cities of Mumbai (seven stores), Bangalore (two stores), Kolkatta (two stores), Pune (two stores), and Hyderabad, Chennai, and Delhi (one store each). For the year ending March 2006, the company had a sales turnover of INR6.6 billion and after-tax profit of INR271 million (see Exhibit 13).

Shoppers Stop's target was to cover 22 cities with 39 stores by March 2008, occupying an area of 2.5 million square feet. The company was also planning to extend its footprint into the country's Tier 2 and Tier 3 cities. By regularly expanding its vendor portfolio, the company had partnered with more than 200 brands, both local and global, for distribution in India. Shoppers Stop also had an active private-label program that in 2006 contributed 23 percent of its overall revenues and approximately 40 percent of its overall margins. The pursuit of private labels conflicted with the need for recognition as a national-branded retailer that stocked the best of brands.

Driven by the vision of "being India's number one global retailer in the Department

**Exhibit 12** Indian Youth as Consumers, 2006

| Segments | Dabblers | | | Aspirers | | | Thrivers | | |
|---|---|---|---|---|---|---|---|---|---|
| Age Group | 13–21 | | | 22–28 | | | 29–35 | | |
| Segment size (in millions)<br>- All India<br>- In Tier 1 and 2 Metros | 174.0<br>17.0 | | | 129.0<br>10.3 | | | 105.0<br>12.2 | | |
| Consumption Attributes | – Children of liberalizing India<br>– Into their early years of discretionary spending<br>– 10 percent have graduated and are working<br>– Spend seven hours a day with friends at a movie, gym, class, or just "hanging out" where they form consumption-related opinions | | | – Coming of age with more than 90 percent receiving their first pay check<br>– 60 percent get married during this phase<br>– Steady growth in incomes<br>– Driven by middle-class values<br>– Price-conscious but also prone to impulse purchases and a need for instant gratification | | | – Time is a major constraint<br>– A large part of household expenses is spent on stores providing customization, relationship-based service and flexible hours<br>– Seek efficiency and convenience | | |
| Media/Leisure Habits | – Quality time at home limited to commercial breaks on sports or music channels<br>– Although they pay little attention to commercials, dabblers do not forget witty advertising | | | – Major time spent in commuting, leaving little time for leisure or shopping on week days<br>– Tend to splurge, however, on weekends<br>– Extensive users of the Internet | | | – TV is the main source of news and entertainment<br>– Drawn to prime-time sitcoms and serials | | |
| Monthly Discretionary Spend on Lifestyle Products (Metros) | INR 4,000–5,000 | | | INR 5,000–8,000 | | | INR 6,000–9,000 | | |
| Largest Share of Spend | Apparel and footwear | | | Apparel and eating out | | | Apparel and health-care products | | |
| Attitude<br>- toward shopping<br>- toward malls | A by-product of hanging out with friends<br>A place for a bite and to be with friends | | | "The" purpose, with or without friends<br>Meets all my shopping needs in one place | | | A necessity<br>A good place for my family to shop | | |
| Sub-segments (Income) | Very well-to-do | Well-to-do | | Very well-to-do | Well-to-do | | Very well-to-do | Well-to-do | |
| Present in Tier 1 and Tier 2 | 3 million | 7 million | | 3 million | 6 million | | 2 million | 5 million | |
| SEC classification | A1, A2 and B1 | | | A1, A2 and B1 | | | A1 and A2 | | |

*Source:* "YouSumerism: Youth in India — Opportunity Knocks." Ernst & Young India Retail Advisory Group. 2007. http://www.ey.com/Global/Assets.nsf/India/Youth_Final/$file/Youth_Final.pdf. accessed April 20, 2009.

**Exhibit 13**    Shoppers Stop Income Statements, 2002–2006

| Year Ending March 31 (in INR million) | 2002 | 2003 | 2004 | 2005 | 2006 |
|---|---|---|---|---|---|
| Income | 2, 402 | 2,949 | 3,953 | 5,001 | 6,660 |
| Gross retail sales | 9 | 25 | 100 | 114 | 311 |
| Less: Value-added tax | 2,393 | 2,924 | 3,854 | 4,887 | 6,349 |
| Net retail sales | 93 | 81 | 91 | 79 | 191 |
| Other income | 2,486 | 3,005 | 3,945 | 4,966 | 6,540 |
|  |  |  |  |  |  |
| Less: Cost of goods sold | 1,757 | 2,077 | 2,712 | 3,421 | 4,322 |
| Employee costs | 158 | 172 | 224 | 288 | 403 |
| Operating and | 467 | 560 | 764 | 920 | 1,249 |
| administrative expenses | 54 | 32 | 40 | 39 | 24 |
| Interest and finance | 49 | 58 | 75 | 90 | 139 |
| charges | 1 | 106 | 130 | 207 | 402 |
| Depreciation | 1 | 106 | 120 | 190 | 271 |
| Profit before tax |  |  |  |  |  |
| Profit after tax |  |  |  |  |  |

*Source:* Company annual reports.

Store category,"[6] the company's strategy had three elements:

> Delivering higher levels of sensory experience by offering fashionable merchandise, great store layout and ambience, educated staff, food, and events for a complete shopping experience; contemporizing the product basket to offer premium value; and sustaining leadership in the department store format through pan-India presence, efficient processes and excellent service standards.

For more than a decade, Shoppers Stop's focus on a single format had led to better operational metrics and higher profitability than its competitors, which were not only late entrants but were experimenting with different formats simultaneously. Of late, Shoppers Stop had begun to leverage its learning to new formats, such as hypermarkets and specialty stores. Each new format, however, was being planned and executed as a separate strategic business unit (SBU) within the group. The diversification had not led to any shift in the positioning of Shoppers Stop, which had not only remained as a premium, lifestyle departmental store but had continued to contribute the maximum to the company's revenues and margins. Within each Shoppers Stop store, however, a progressive list of offerings was available, from apparel (for men, women, and children) to non-apparel (e.g., personal accessories, perfumes, cosmetics, home leather, watches, jewelry, and electronics).

The majority Shoppers Stop offerings were standardized, and the scope for customization was limited. In 2005, however, the company had launched a "do-it-yourself" program as a special service: customers could purchase fabric from the store and in-house fashion designers, who were recruited from leading fashion schools, could design an outfit according to individual requirements.

As of March 2006, the company had 2,509 employees. Nearly 65 percent of the front-end sales staff comprised university graduates who received higher than average pay. This remuneration was in contrast to the North American retail industry, where most front-end jobs were held by high school graduates receiving minimum hourly rates.

Shoppers Stop was a conservative retailer, wary of the risks of inventory pile-up (which would increase costs) and low inventory turns (which would reduce cash flow). The risk aversion stemmed from its grounding as an apparel retailer that purchased goods largely on an as-needed, consignment basis. The company had an initial public offering (IPO) in May 2005, which raised INR1.53 billion. Unlike other listed retailers in the country, Shoppers Stop believed in funding expansion from internal accruals. Some analysts believed the company could "easily leverage its balance sheet to fund expansion plans without impacting cash flow in a significant manner" and that it could be more aggressive in pursuing growth.[7]

Shoppers Stop's strong back-end systems provided real-time information to managers and had helped them to achieve operating metrics often considered the benchmarks for Indian retail (see Exhibit 14). Shoppers Stop was becoming a preferred partner for global brands seeking to do business in India. It had also become a poaching ground for new entrants to Indian retail seeking managerial talent.

The company had adopted a customer-centric marketing campaign as opposed to the conventional product-based campaign (see Exhibit 15). Together with promotions that coincided with the seasonal fashions, the advertisements had helped to drive footfalls (i.e., the number of people entering the stores) at a compounded annual rate of 16 percent and to maintain the conversion rate (i.e., the number of customers making a purchase) at about 27 percent.

Shoppers Stop had contrasting experiences with men's and women's clothing. Men's clothing was a growth area. Valued at US$3.5 billion in 2006, the men's clothing segment was growing at 30 percent per annum. The branded ready-to-wear category, in which Shoppers Stop led its competitors, comprised 40 percent of the market for men's clothing. However, the market for women's clothing in India was uncertain, particularly outside two particular outfits distinctive to Indian women: the sari and the salwar kameez. Western clothing was likely to remain a niche market, restricted to college students in urban markets and a relatively small number of women executives. Standardization, which was typical of ready-to-wear dresses, was not favored by Indian woman, who preferred the cloth, cut, and finish of their clothing to be unique. Thus, the manufacture of women's clothing in India was dominated by small-scale businesses offering an array of fabric designs and patterns and an army of tailors who catered to individual tastes. The difficulty of building a strong retail business in women's clothing was the single largest bottleneck in the development of clothing superstores and of department stores in general because women were often the main buyers of all clothing, including men's clothing and accessories.

Shoppers Stop viewed the young adult apparel category to be medium on supply chain sophistication and very high on consumer readiness. This category included not only casualwear that young adults wore to college—T-shirts, jeans, denims, and casual shirts—but also partywear. The fashion quotient was high among the young adult target group. Their clothing was most likely to feature colors, patterns and designs that were the latest in vogue. The company had also found that young adults were high consumers of accessories. Although young adult rarely splurged on high-end

**Exhibit 14**    Shoppers Stop Performance Indices, 2003–2006

| | 2002 | 2003 | 2004 | 2005 | 2006 |
|---|---|---|---|---|---|
| Number of Stores | 9 | 12 | 14 | 16 | 20 |
| Operating Profit (%) | 4.2 | 6.5 | 6.1 | 6.6 | 8.4 |
| Dividend Payout (%) | Nil | Nil | Nil | 10.0 | 15.0 |
| Retail Space (millions of square feet) | | 0.56 | 0.67 | 0.77 | 0.95 |
| Inventory Holding Period (number of days) | | | | 107 | 94 |
| Gross Margin Return on Inventory (INR/ Inventory) | 2.69 | 2.41 | 2.41 | 2.23 | 2.35 |
| Gross Margin Return on Floor Space (INR/Unit of retail space) | 1,775 | 1,910 | 2,000 | 2,330 | 2,353 |
| Gross Margin Return on Labor (INR/ Employee) | 594,971 | 676,509 | 636,690 | 899,045 | 1,046,768 |
| Same Store Growth (%) | (4) | 9.1 | 12.0 | 9.1 | 17.0 |
| Footfalls[1] | 6.5 | 7.1 | 12.2 | 14.6 | 18.3 |
| Conversion Ratio[2] (%) | 33 | 34 | 26 | 27 | 27 |
| Sales per Square Foot[3] (INR) | 5,923 | 6,238 | 6,898 | 6,903 | 7,576 |
| Sales Mix[4] (%) | 70.5 | 70.1 | 67.6 | 64.7 | 61.0[5] |
| | 29.5 | 29.9 | 32.4 | 35.3 | 39.0 |
| Average Selling Price[6] (INR) | 477 | 535 | 591 | 605 | 647 |
| Transaction Size[7] (INR) | 1,109 | 1,280 | 1,258 | 1,278 | 1,366 |
| Shrinkage[8] (%) | 0.66 | 0.54 | 0.41 | 0.41 | 0.41 |
| Associate Satisfaction Index | – | – | 4.0 | 4.03 | – |
| Customer Satisfaction Index | – | – | – | 61 | 60 |
| Number of First Citizens | | | 254,000 | 429,000 | 632,000 |

*Source:* Company annual reports.

1. Number of people entering the stores.
2. Number of entrants making a buy.
3. Sales per square foot of built-up area.
4. Consists of Apparel and non-apparel.
5. In 2006, apparel sales were further divided into men's apparel (35.5%), women's apparel (18.8%) and kids' apparel (6.7%).
6. Sales divided by the number of units sold.
7. Sales divided by the number of invoices.
8. Loss of inventory (due to pilferage).

| Exhibit 15 | Shoppers Stop Print Advertisements |
| --- | --- |

*Source:* Company files.

apparel, they preferred to have the best brands of fashion accessories, such as sunglasses, shoes, and handbags.

## Customers

Shoppers Stop had one of the most successful loyalty programs among Indian retailers. First Citizen, which was introduced in 1994, had enrolled 630,000 members by March 2006. Membership had been growing by 10 to 15 percent every year. The amount spent by the First Citizen card members was approximately twice the amount spent by other customers. The loyalty program provided the company with the competitive edge of a solid customer base and business certainty. The loyalty program had also generated a perception, strengthened over time, that Shoppers Stop was a "caring" brand, more reminiscent of a mature adult than a young adult.

Internal data had generated a demographic profile of First Citizen members: 75 percent were in the 25- to 45-year-old age group; 70 percent were married; 30 percent were independent, working women; and 90 percent belonged to the SEC-A classification of the Indian urban consumer. Most were high net-worth individuals (HNWs) with high disposable income in terms of their shopping habits. Of all Shoppers Stop's revenue, 65 percent came from its First Citizens. The number of First Citizens was approaching one million, of a total number of 20 million customers. First Citizens were the most valued among Shoppers Stop customers.

The loyalty card was available in three categories: Classic, Silver and Gold as shown in Table 1.

A common characteristic of Shoppers Stop customers was their aspiration quotient. They wanted to see themselves shopping with others of the same ilk and mindset. This characteristic was in contrast to typical luxury customers in India, who, based on the belief of having arrived in life, wanted to differentiate themselves from people around them. Shoppers Stop catered to the high-end consumers but saw itself as a bridge to luxury.

The typical Shoppers Stop customer belonged to SEC A urban, was between 15 and 40 years of

| **Table 1** | Shoppers Stop Loyalty Cards |

| Tier | Number of Visits per Year | Average Spend per Year (INR) |
|---|---|---|
| Classic | 2 | 6,000 |
| Silver | 5 | 25,000 |
| Gold | 7 | 45,000 |
| Overall | 4 | 15,000 |

age, earned a household income of INR30,000 per month, owned a car, shopped in groups (with family or friends), visited Shoppers Stop at least once a month and spent between INR2,000 and 2,500 per month on apparel and accessories.

On the basis of the findings of a sample survey by Customer Satisfaction Management & Measurement (CSMM), an independent, specialist unit of IMRB International, the company had classified its existing customers into three categories: premium-conscious, value-conscious, and time-conscious (see Exhibit 16).

| **Exhibit 16** | Shoppers Stop Customer Segmentation |

| | Premium-Conscious | Value-Conscious | Time-Conscious |
|---|---|---|---|
| Percentage of Shoppers | 26 | 46 | 28 |
| Socio-Economic Classification | A1 | A1 and A2 | A1 |
| Age Group (years) | 15–40 | 15–35 | 15–40 |
| Profile | Males and females in almost equal numbers; married and single people in almost equal numbers | Single males | Single males |
| Shopping Habits | Visits with family and friends. 80 percent are First Citizens | Visits with friends and family; most likely walk-in customers | Visits with friends and family, 70 percent are First Citizens |
| Spend | High | Average | Average |
| Shopping Statements | * Shopping helps me buy the latest * I want to be the first to buy the latest * I buy only brands* I do not mind paying extra for quality * I don't like designs which are common * I like to check out new outlets * I prefer a mall because you can do other things as well * I prefer exclusive outlets offering premium products * I often buy on impulse * I don't mind spending time while shopping * Shopping is like an outing with friends * We don't just shop, we also like to eat and drink at the mall * Shopping is a way of spending quality time with the family | * I do most of my shopping during the sales * I shop where there are special offers or sales * I like to browse around and may not always buy * I don't think brands are worth the price * When I buy items at full price, I feel I am paying too much | * I don't care about the ambience as long as the store is conveniently located * I like to finish my shopping quickly * I do not like sales people disturbing me * I compare prices before deciding to buy * Shopping frees me from daily tensions of life * I first buy what was planned and then, if I have time, browse |

*Source:* Company.

More than half the individuals in the premium-conscious segment earned more than INR50,000 a month. The time-conscious and value-conscious segments were predominantly male and single. Half of the individuals in the value-conscious segment were walk-in customers; in contrast, the other two segments had a high proportion of loyal customers.

## Net Generation

The United States and other countries had classified their ongoing demographic pool into four broad categories: the Baby Boom Generation, Generation X, the Net Generation, and Generation Next. The Baby Boom Generation consisted of those born between January 1946 and December 1964. Generation X comprised those born between January 1965 and December 1976. The Net Generation, the focus of most youth marketing initiatives, consisted of those born between January 1977 and December 1997. The most recent generation, born after January 1998, was called Generation Next.[8]

Each generation had been exposed to a set of events that characterized its place in history and varied with each country. For example, the Vietnam War was a defining moment for the Baby Boom Generation in the United States. However, some universal forces shaped the Net Generation's outlook in most countries, including India. The three most common drivers were the rise of the personal computer, the arrival of the Internet, and the availability of digital technologies. These drivers cut across geographies. In India, the Net Generation had an additional stimulus—they had grown up with the process of economic liberalization begun in early 1980s. The Net Generation comprised a large share of the population in most economies although its rate of growth varied with each country. India had topped the list on both indices (see Exhibit 17).

Net Geners, as the members of the Net Generation were called, had unique shopping

---

| Exhibit 17 | The Net Generation's Share of Population, 2005 |

| Country | Population Younger Than Age 25 | Percentage of Population Younger Than Age 25 | Growth in Population Younger Than Age 25 Since 1980 |
|---|---|---|---|
| India | 593,293 | 52 | 46 |
| China | 501,558 | 38 | (9) |
| United States | 105,246 | 35 | 11 |
| Brazil | 87,437 | 47 | 22 |
| Mexico | 50,986 | 49 | 14 |
| Russia | 46,209 | 32 | (15) |
| Japan | 31,846 | 25 | (27) |
| Germany | 21,655 | 26 | (20) |
| France | 19,029 | 31 | (7) |
| United Kingdom | 18,676 | 31 | (10) |
| Spain | 11,500 | 27 | (27) |
| Canada | 10,004 | 31 | (4) |

*Source:* UN Department of Economic and Social Affairs, Population Division World Population Prospects: The 2006 Revision; and World Urbanization Prospects: The 2005 Revision, http://esa.un.org.unpp, accessed December 10, 2008.

behaviors, which were common across geographies. Before going to a store, they went online to scrutinize the product they wanted to buy. They were not satisfied with one-size-fits-all items that could be bought only in certain places and at certain times: they wanted something that fit them where, when and how they wanted it. They expected plenty of choice and high-speed service. They believed that fun should be embedded into the product. They were not easily influenced by commercial advertising the way that baby boomers were (see Exhibit 18).

| **Exhibit 18** | Net Generation's Buying Behavior |

| | Attribute | Underlying Statement | Articulation |
|---|---|---|---|
| 1 | Freedom | "Give me choice." | They value the freedom to be who they are. They are not overwhelmed by the proliferation of sales channels, product types and brands. They leverage technology to cut through the clutter and find the marketing message that fits their needs. They love the freedom of choice and the challenge of finding the perfect fit. |
| 2 | Customization | "Make it my own." | They have grown up receiving the kind of media they want, when they want it, how they want it and being able to change media for greater customization. They want to customize everything in the world around them — their desktop, their website, their ring tone, their screen saver, their news sources, their entertainment. |
| 3 | Scrutiny | "Let me check out." | They are skeptical, scrutinizing what they see and read in the media, including the Internet. They turn to their friends for advice on shopping instead of trusting company executives or advertisements. |
| 4 | Integrity | "Do you deserve my money?" | They see through public relations and "spin." They are honest, considerate, and abide by their commitments. Whether they are researching a future employer or exposing a flawed viral campaign, Net Geners ensure the company's values align with their own. Transparency, in the form of gaining access to pertinent information about companies and their offerings, seems natural to them. |
| 5 | Collaboration | "Let us talk. Let me help." | They are great collaborators, both with friends online and at work. They develop what is called N-Fluence networks via the Internet, especially through social media channels. |
| 6 | Entertainment | "Make it fun." | Having fun with the product is as important as using it. From their experience with video games, they know there is always more than one way to achieve a goal. They are less structured. The interactive experiences they are exposed to help them both to think outside the box and to be irreverent. |

*(Continued)*

| | Attribute | Underlying Statement | Articulation |
|---|---|---|---|
| 7 | Speed | "Serve me now." | They are quick on the uptake. Net Geners assume that companies can respond with the same kind of simplicity, speed and directness that they respond with when they exchange instant messages with their friends. |
| 8 | Innovation | "Give me the latest." | They want to be current and contemporary with whatever they buy. Buying the latest is their way of indulgence and self-gratification. |

**Exhibit 18** (Continued)

Source: Adapted from Don Tapscott, *Grown up Digital: How the Net Generation Is Changing Your World*, McGraw-Hill, Columbus, OH, 2009.

Some people, particularly parents and employers, had expressed concerns and criticisms regarding the general behavior of Net Geners. According to some critics, Net Geners were shallow and distracted, lacking an ability to focus. They lacked social skills and had no time for reading, sports, or healthy activities. They had no sense of privacy; instead, freely divulged their personal information online. They regularly violated intellectual property rights on peer-to-peer networks, by sharing anything they could, such as music, with no respect for the rights of its creators. They were violent and narcissistic. They had no work ethic and they didn't care.[9]

According to Mark Bauerlein:

The 21st century teen, connected and multi-tasked, autonomous yet peer-mindful, makes no great leap forward in human intelligence, global thinking, or netizen-ship. Young users have learned a thousand new things, no doubt. They upload and download, surf and chat, post and design, but they haven't learned to analyze a complex text, store facts in their heads, comprehend a policy decision, take lessons from history or spell correctly. Never having recognized their responsibility to the past, they have opened a fissure in our civic foundations, and it shows in their halting passage into adulthood and citizenship.[10]

## Issues in June 2006

As CEO, Govind Shrikhande knew that he had to set the tone for the company's overall strategy. In his mind, the youth market could be the future of the company. Yet, he had seen countless cases where others had failed with this segment because their targeting efforts had been imprecise. Further, Shoppers Stop had limited experience catering to the younger generation and would require a shift in mind-set to be able to appeal to this consumer group. In approaching this decision, Shrikhande thought he should run the numbers first and then assess whether any change made sense from a business perspective. Despite having decided how to approach this decision, Shirkhande continued to be preoccupied by the following questions.

- Were young adult Indians a market force that Shoppers Stop needed to factor into its long-term growth plans? Or could Shoppers Stop ignore this segment?
- Although the demographic dividend was a major driver of growth in Indian retail, Shrikhande needed to identify the target audience that was relevant for Shoppers Stop. Because the company catered to premium-end lifestyle products, the addressable audience would be limited to urban centers. How should Shoppers Stop

zero in on young adults in the country's tiered cities?

- After it had decided to focus on the young consumer, Shoppers Stop needed to create new categories, discover new segments, unfold new formats, develop new distribution channels, experiment with new media and advertising vehicles, form new

stores structures, and rewire the entire organization to make it more responsive to younger customers. How could this enormous task be implemented?

- Given the shopping behavior of Net Geners on eight different attributes, how should Shoppers Stop reorient its retailing to be relevant to the young?

## CASE QUESTIONS

1. What advantages does Shoppers Stop hold due to governmental regulations and other in-country factors? Will these advantages continue in the future?

2. Should Shoppers Stop target premium-conscious, value-conscious, or time-conscious consumers with its promotional program? Defend your choice.

3. The youth of India hold many similarities to young people in developed nations, with access to new technologies and with a strong cultural divide based on generations. How can Shoppers Stop develop advertisements and promotions that attract young people without alienating its current customer base?

4. The strong customer-centric approach employed by Shoppers Stop has been featured in advertisements and promotions over time. Should the company maintain this approach or move to a more product-oriented promotional program? Why or why not?

5. Which alternative media might best appeal to the new, younger generation of Shoppers Stop customers? How can the marketing team take advantage of those opportunities?

## Eat2Eat.com

By Nigel Goodwin, under the supervision of Professor Kenneth G. Hardy

## Eat2eat.Com

Eat2Eat.com was the most highly rated Internet-based restaurant reservation service covering major cities in the Asia Pacific region. It was the principal business of Singapore-based Eat2Eat Pte Ltd (Eat2Eat). Eat2Eat.com had firmly established its technology, business model- and industry

relationships. However, after five years of operation, the website's registered user base remained at approximately 12,000 customers. In January 2006, founder and Chief Executive Officer Vikram Aggarwal was considering new ways to promote the company and the website. Eat2Eat had limited resources, so Aggarwal knew his methods would have to be innovative, efficient and effective.

Version: (A) 2009–09–11

The Richard Ivey School of Business gratefully acknowledges the generous support of the Lee Foundation in the development of this case as part of The Lee Foundation Asian Case Series.

## Company Origin

In the late 1990s, Aggarwal had been an investment banker specializing in the high-technology sector at Chase Manhattan in Tokyo. He had seen many entrepreneurs launch their own companies and was confident he could do the same. When Chase Manhattan merged with JP Morgan in 2000, Aggarwal's group was dissolved. He accepted an exit package, voluntarily left the bank, and decided to launch his own Internet company.

Aggarwal saw an opportunity in online restaurant bookings. He noticed that airline bookings, hotel reservations and car rentals were highly automated processes, with customers frequently searching for information and transacting business online. However, there was little or no similar automation for restaurant reservations. The technology discrepancy was particularly noticeable in the case of hotel restaurants: a consumer could reserve a room at a hotel online, but not a table at the hotel's restaurant.[1] Many corporations—particularly large ones—negotiated special room rates for employees at preferred hotels, but did not negotiate discounts at preferred restaurants. Given that business dinners were a common occurrence, Aggarwal wondered why corporations had not extended their purchasing power to restaurants in the same way they exercised it with hotels.

Aggarwal believed there was a value proposition in connecting diners—both corporate and personal—with restaurants. He believed diners could benefit from accessing a wealth of information on restaurant options, conveniently reserving tables online and receiving loyalty points or discounts. Moreover, he believed restaurants could benefit by having a presence on the Internet, an increasingly popular medium.

## Establishment and Business Model

In 2000, Aggarwal relocated to Singapore, registered Eat2Eat Pte Ltd and began running the company out of his home. He hired a chief technology officer and a programmer, both based in India, to develop the website and the supporting technology. Aggarwal himself signed up the first participating restaurants. The English version of the website was launched in July 2001. Aggarwal wanted to retain full ownership and control, and subsequently financed the company himself. He invested US$1 million from his personal savings and his exit package from Chase Manhattan. Aggarwal eventually hired two other people to help with the workload, one in Singapore and one in Sydney.

Eat2Eat.com was an Internet-based restaurant portal promoting fine dining in the Asia Pacific region. The website was a guide to the region's best restaurants with an online reservation service. Features included restaurant reviews, recipes, interviews with leading chefs, and lists of top establishments in various categories. By January 2006, Eat2Eat.com covered more than 800 restaurants in Bangkok, Hong Kong, Kuala Lumpur, Shanghai, Singapore, Seoul, Sydney, Taipei, and Tokyo. The company was also launching in Kyoto, Melbourne, and Phuket. The original website appeared in English, but equivalent sites had also been launched in Japanese and Korean to cover the restaurants in Tokyo and Seoul, respectively.

## Core Business: Restaurant Reservations and Advertisements

Eat2Eat.com allowed diners to reserve tables through the Internet, conveniently and with a wealth of supporting information. Aggarwal met with restaurant managers in cities across the Asia Pacific region and encouraged them to participate. (See Exhibit 1 for participating restaurants by city.) He negotiated discounts for corporate customers and commissions for Eat2Eat, and then listed the restaurants on the website. A registered customer wishing to make a meal reservation visited the website and used a simple booking interface to select a restaurant, date, time, and party size.[2] See Exhibit 2 for registered customers by city. The restaurants could be searched by various criteria, including location, ambiance, accessibility for disabled diners, smoking preference, cuisine, price range, quality rating, and hotel affiliation (if applicable). Customers received loyalty points that could be redeemed during future restaurant visits.

| Exhibit 1 | Eat2eat.com Participating Restaurants by City, 2000–2005 |

| | Participating Restaurants (Cumulative) | | | | | |
|---|---|---|---|---|---|---|
| | 2000 | 2001 | 2002 | 2003 | 2004 | 2005 |
| Bangkok | – | – | 12 | 32 | 58 | 98 |
| Hong Kong | – | 18 | 42 | 84 | 97 | 112 |
| Kuala Lumpur | – | 6 | 30 | 54 | 66 | 72 |
| Shanghai | – | – | 6 | 48 | 60 | 62 |
| Singapore | – | 24 | 84 | 102 | 120 | 174 |
| Seoul | – | – | – | 4 | 18 | 72 |
| Sydney | – | 30 | 66 | 94 | 98 | 137 |
| Taipei | – | – | – | – | – | 23 |
| Tokyo | – | – | 6 | 14 | 44 | 73 |
| Total | – | 78 | 246 | 432 | 561 | 823 |

*Source:* Company files.

*Note:* Actual figures have been disguised for the purpose of confidentiality.

*Note:* Figures do not include Kyoto, Melbourne, or Phuket. Eat2Eat was in the process of launching in those cities.

| Exhibit 2 | Eat2eat.com New Customer Registrations by City, 2000–2005 |

| | Registered Users (Annual) | | | | | | |
|---|---|---|---|---|---|---|---|
| | 2000 | 2001 | 2002 | 2003 | 2004 | 2005 | Total |
| Bangkok | – | – | 30 | 18 | 48 | 100 | 196 |
| Hong Kong | – | 300 | 324 | 94 | 576 | 804 | 2,098 |
| Kuala Lumpur | – | 60 | 126 | 30 | 324 | 509 | 1,049 |
| Shanghai | – | 30 | 65 | 14 | 54 | 70 | 233 |
| Singapore | – | 126 | 204 | 42 | 391 | 778 | 1,541 |
| Seoul | – | – | – | 84 | 204 | 402 | 690 |
| Sydney | – | 48 | 222 | 90 | 120 | 204 | 684 |
| Taipei | – | – | – | – | – | 300 | 300 |
| Tokyo | – | 152 | 466 | 694 | 1,176 | 2,580 | 5,068 |
| Total | – | 716 | 1,437 | 1,066 | 2,893 | 5,747 | 11,859 |

*Source:* Company files.

*Note:* Actual figures have been disguised for the purpose of confidentiality.

*Note:* Figures do not include Kyoto, Melbourne, or Phuket. Eat2Eat was in the process of launching in those cities.

Eat2Eat contacted the restaurant the day after the reservation date, confirmed that the customer had actually eaten there and invoiced the restaurant for the agreed-upon commission.[3] Commissions varied depending on the restaurant in question, but typically were between seven to 10 percent of the customer's bill. In 2005, these reservations contributed 40 percent of Eat2Eat's total revenue of US$478,000. (See Exhibit 3 for annual revenue, profit and loss figures.)

The company also sold website banner advertisements to restaurants wanting additional promotion. In 2005, advertisements on Eat2Eat.com contributed an additional 20 percent of the company's total revenue.

Eat2Eat.com had received considerable recognition. A poll taken by the Smart Diners Organization in the United States had rated Eat2Eat.com as the top restaurant information and reservation site in the world. In addition, Google and Yahoo! search engines

| **Exhibit 3** | Eat2Eat Revenue, Profit and Loss by City, 2000–2005 |

| | | Revenue, Profit and Loss (Annual, in US$000s) | | | | | | |
|---|---|---|---|---|---|---|---|---|
| | | 2000 | 2001 | 2002 | 2003 | 2004 | 2005 | Total |
| Bangkok | Revenue | – | – | – | 4 | 6 | 8 | 18 |
| | Cost | – | – | 18 | 30 | 17 | 30 | 95 |
| | Profit / (Loss) | – | – | (18) | (26) | (11) | (22) | (77) |
| Hong Kong | Revenue | – | 8 | 24 | 6 | 54 | 66 | 158 |
| | Cost | 6 | 28 | 41 | 30 | 24 | 32 | 161 |
| | Profit / (Loss) | (6) | (19) | (17) | (24) | 30 | 34 | (2) |
| Kuala Lumpur | Revenue | – | 18 | 31 | 8 | 34 | 56 | 148 |
| | Cost | 4 | 18 | 30 | 30 | 36 | 37 | 155 |
| | Profit / (Loss) | (4) | – | 1 | (22) | (2) | 19 | (7) |
| Shanghai | Revenue | – | – | 20 | 2 | 24 | 22 | 68 |
| | Cost | – | 41 | 66 | 18 | 34 | 44 | 203 |
| | Profit / (Loss) | – | (41) | (46) | (16) | (10) | (23) | (134) |
| Singapore | Revenue | – | 12 | 36 | 18 | 70 | 91 | 227 |
| | Cost | 162 | 180 | 156 | 114 | 144 | 144 | 900 |
| | Profit / (Loss) | (162) | (168) | (120) | (96) | (74) | (53) | (673) |
| Seoul | Revenue | – | – | – | – | 12 | 42 | 54 |
| | Cost | – | – | – | 18 | 66 | 36 | 120 |
| | Profit / (Loss) | – | – | – | (18) | (54) | 6 | (66) |
| Sydney | Revenue | – | 18 | 60 | 48 | 48 | 46 | 220 |
| | Cost | 12 | 96 | 96 | 42 | 36 | 48 | 330 |
| | Profit / (Loss) | (12) | (78) | (36) | 6 | 12 | (2) | (110) |
| Taipei | Revenue | – | – | – | – | – | 18 | 18 |
| | Cost | – | – | – | – | – | 48 | 48 |
| | Profit / (Loss) | – | – | – | – | – | (30) | (30) |

| | | Revenue, Profit and Loss (Annual, in US$000s) | | | | | | |
|---|---|---|---|---|---|---|---|---|
| | | 2000 | 2001 | 2002 | 2003 | 2004 | 2005 | Total |
| Tokyo | Revenue | – | – | 30 | 54 | 90 | 128 | 302 |
| | Cost | 6 | 30 | 70 | 90 | 98 | 114 | 408 |
| | Profit / (Loss) | (6) | (30) | (40) | (36) | (8) | 14 | (106) |
| Total | Revenue | – | 56 | 202 | 140 | 337 | 478 | 1,213 |
| | Cost | 190 | 392 | 476 | 372 | 455 | 534 | 2,419 |
| | Profit / (Loss) | (190) | (336) | (275) | (232) | (118) | (56) | (1,206) |

*Source:* Company files.

*Note:* Actual figures have been disguised for the purpose of confidentiality.

consistently ranked Eat2Eat.com first in search results for Asian restaurant reviews and reservations.

There were other restaurant portals on the Internet, covering Asia Pacific and other regions, but Eat2Eat.com was different. Most of the other portals derived revenue from advertising alone, and subsequently depended on hits and click-through statistics. Also, the other Asia Pacific portals were city-specific, whereas Eat2Eat.com offered regional coverage.

In 2004 Aggarwal adapted Eat2Eat.com to make its content and booking function accessible through WAP-enabled mobile phones.[4] He believed this added accessibility would significantly extend the company's reach and utilization, considering the high penetration of mobile phones in the region. The service became popular in Tokyo and Seoul, but lagged elsewhere. Aggarwal was disappointed the service had not found greater acceptance in cities such as Hong Kong and Singapore. In the latter cities, virtually every person carried a multi-function mobile phone and people were very savvy about applications such as customized ring tones, photographs and games. Aggarwal suspected people in these cities were uncomfortable in actually making transactions using the new technology.

## Complementary Business: Third-Party Sourcing

Aggarwal also engaged in another, complementary business: negotiating preferred arrangements between credit card companies and restaurants for the benefit of credit card holders. Credit card companies typically offered special deals and perks for cardholders, including discounts at preferred restaurants, spas, sporting venues, and retail stores. The card companies' motivations were to attract and retain cardholders by offering superior value, and to encourage cardholders to use the cards, thereby bolstering loyalty and increasing transaction volume.

The credit card companies did not negotiate the arrangements themselves; instead, their marketing teams outsourced the job to third parties. Because Aggarwal already negotiated with restaurants to sign them up for the website, he found it was a natural extension to source restaurants for credit card companies as well. In 2005, third-party negotiations contributed the remaining 40 percent of Eat2Eat's revenue.

## Segmentation and Approach to Market

### Reaching the Restaurants

Aggarwal dealt exclusively with what he described as first-tier restaurants. First-tier restaurants were typically those that accepted reservations, were moderately expensive, or were very popular and busy. Second-tier restaurants did not accept reservations and therefore were of no concern to Aggarwal.

Aggarwal approached the restaurants himself to sign them up as suppliers. This task typically involved traveling to the 12 cities covered by Eat2Eat.com and personally meeting with restaurant managers. In some cities, the restaurants were predominantly chain organizations, while in other cities they were predominantly independently owned. A single chain might have many restaurants, so at first glance a chain-focused approach seemed more efficient. However, it usually took much more time and effort to sign up a chain than a single independent restaurant.

The restaurant reviews posted on Eat2Eat.com were written by Aggarwal and his two employees. He had considered adding reviews by professional restaurant critics, but had decided against it since critics and their publications typically demanded payment for reprinting their reviews. Also, many restaurant reviews in Asia were actually written as promotional pieces on the restaurants' behalf, and Aggarwal felt such reviews were neither independent nor objective. He did consider adding user reviews, as Asia-Hotels.com did for hotels, but had not yet taken any action in that direction.

## Market Characteristics

As he traveled, Aggarwal gathered information on the different markets. He was particularly interested in population density, dining habits, the presence of first-tier restaurants, broadband Internet penetration, and receptivity to new marketing and distribution tactics. The information helped him select new restaurants to pursue as suppliers. See Exhibit 4 for some of Aggarwal's market observations.

| Exhibit 4 | Market Observations |
| --- | --- |

| City | Description |
| --- | --- |
| Bangkok | • Fragmented restaurant industry with broad range of dining options<br>• Opportunities primarily in the mature hotel industry, particularly with established chains that E2E has worked with elsewhere<br>• Low Internet penetration<br>• Language issues<br>• Difficult to gain customer acceptance |
| Hong Kong | • High Internet penetration but low transaction volume<br>• High population density with easy movement around the island<br>• Many corporate head offices<br>• Many restaurants, but choice normally based on proximity to office<br>• Free local phone calls made it easy to reserve by phone<br>• Language issues |
| Kuala Lumpur | • Broad restaurant base and large dining population<br>• Tendency to choose restaurants by the type of food<br>• High restaurant turnover, which encouraged marketing innovations<br>• Customers willing to try new technology<br>• Growing market of visitors from the Middle East<br>• Spontaneity in dining leading to no-shows and multiple bookings<br>• Low Internet penetration |
| Shanghai | • Rapidly growing local market<br>• Strong business from overseas, with visitors to Shanghai willing to book tables in advance<br>• Unscrupulous restaurant managers posing difficulties for E2E<br>• Busy restaurants not requiring any promotional support<br>• Language issues<br>• Low Internet penetration |

| City | Description |
|------|-------------|
| Singapore | • Vibrant dining scene, with hotel restaurants and many new eateries opening outside hotels as well <br> • Tendency for restaurants to cluster in common areas <br> • Willingness to try any restaurant at least once <br> • Government initiatives to support Internet business <br> • High Internet penetration but reluctance to transact business online <br> • Restaurateurs' resistance to new promotion / distribution channels |
| Seoul | • High WAP acceptance <br> • Busy city with many dining options, so restaurant managers valued the promotional assistance <br> • Many international visitors willing to book tables <br> • Language issues |
| Sydney | • Dining well-established as a pastime <br> • Many new restaurants <br> • Many visitors from overseas <br> • Higher margins for Eat2Eat.com <br> • Reluctance to provide personal information over the Internet |
| Taipei | • Busy city with established dining scene <br> • High Internet penetration <br> • Web-based reservations new and considered trendy <br> • Relatively low number of first-tier restaurants |
| Tokyo | • High Internet penetration <br> • Widespread WAP use, and marketing on mobile phones widely practiced and accepted <br> • Huge city with established dining culture and countless restaurants <br> • Widespread acceptance among local population <br> • Major foreign presence in the city as well <br> • Difficulty in growing fast enough and keeping up with the ever-changing environment |

*Source:* Company files.

*Note:* Information unavailable for Kyoto, Melbourne, and Phuket.

## Promotional Strategies

In the beginning, Aggarwal focused his promotional efforts on corporate customers. People who planned business dinners invariably made reservations; by contrast, timing and restaurant choice for personal dining were often spontaneous. Also, Aggarwal thought personal diners were too numerous and, consequently, too difficult and expensive to reach. He thought the corporate approach would bring more value for his efforts and would be the best way to reach customers.

Aggarwal approached large corporations and asked them to encourage their employees to sign up for the service. Because corporations reimbursed their employees for business lunches and dinners, the discounts available for meals reserved through Eat2Eat.com essentially offered the corporations a cost reduction. The service was easy for clients to find, preview and reserve at good restaurants, and users received loyalty points that could be redeemed for free meals in the future.

Aggarwal was pleased with the adoption rates from the targeted corporations. Roughly 80 percent of the companies he approached endorsed the program. At those companies, typically 15 percent of employees would register as Eat2Eat.com users with

10 percent becoming active users. Most of the active users were secretaries and personal assistants to executives because they were the people typically tasked with arranging business functions. They spent most of the workday at their desks with broadband Internet connections, so it was easy for them to access Eat2Eat.com. Also, Eat2Eat.com simplified the task of finding and reserving at an appropriate restaurant.

This approach worked well in most of the cities in question, but Aggarwal found a different strategy worked better in Tokyo. In his opinion, Japanese corporations were reluctant to try new ideas. Also, many first-tier restaurants in Japan had their own websites. Those websites provided information to customers, but did not support online reservations because the required technology was too complex. Eat2Eat.com enabled the reservations for the restaurants' websites, so when a customer viewed a restaurant website and wanted to reserve a table, that customer was redirected to Eat2Eat.com's own booking engine. This model proved to be popular among Tokyo's personal diners.

The adaptation of Eat2Eat.com for mobile phones also bolstered the website's success in Tokyo. As with Korean customers in Seoul, Japanese customers in Tokyo were comfortable finding information and transacting business through that medium.

By the end of 2005, Eat2Eat.com had almost 12,000 registered users. Approximately 43 percent of those users lived in Tokyo, and most of them were personal customers making reservations for their own dining. The remaining 57 percent of registered users lived in other markets, and most of them were secretaries or personal assistants reserving tables for corporate dining.

## Expanding in the Personal Market

Although Aggarwal had built a solid user base through the corporate market, he knew he would have to tap the personal market (beyond Tokyo) if Eat2Eat were to reach its potential. However, the company did not have the employees or financial resources needed to pursue such a vast market. Aggarwal believed Eat2Eat would have to partner with other companies that already had large, established user bases and "piggyback" with them.

There were many possible options, including airlines, hotel chains, and local and regional newspapers. "There is no end of possible partners we could work with," he commented, "if we only had the time to approach them, convince them and develop the partnerships."

In May and June of 2004, Eat2Eat partnered with leading regional newspaper, *The Asian Wall Street Journal,* for the first Eat! promotion. The promotion tied in with a regular feature of the paper's Friday section in which food critics sought and reviewed the most authentic and exciting eateries in Asia's culinary capitals. This promotion was one of the paper's most popular features, with readers regularly contacting the paper to request more information or suggest additional eateries.

The three-week promotion featured 70 participating restaurants in Hong Kong, Kuala Lumpur, and Singapore, with cuisine ranging from Mediterranean to Asian to fusion. The restaurants offered special set menus for lunch and dinner, featuring more variety and value than their regular offerings. Some restaurants also offered complementary glasses of wine or champagne. Diners could view restaurant details and menus and could make reservations online at www.eat2eat.com/awsj. The promotion was held for a second time in September 2005, when, in addition to the original cities, it was expanded to include Seoul and Taipei for a total of 101 participating restaurants.

The Eat! promotion had little immediate impact on Eat2Eat.com reservations and revenue, but it did give the website a great deal of publicity that would likely attract more users and reservations in the longer term. Also, it allowed Aggarwal to expand his restaurant base in current cities and establish his business in new cities, such as Taipei.

Aggarwal thought credit card companies would be another natural avenue for reaching personal customers. He had already negotiated restaurant deals on the companies' behalf so he had the necessary contacts and credibility. He thought it would be logical to extend the arrangements to cover online bookings.

When credit card companies sent monthly statements to cardholders, they often included brochures of benefits for cardholders, including discounts at restaurants, spas, hotels, and entertainment venues. The credit card companies also maintained websites with the same information, but they were basic information websites and were rarely visited by cardholders. Aggarwal wanted to enhance the websites by tying them to Eat2Eat.com and providing booking functionality.

Credit card companies would benefit from such arrangements by driving more cardholders to their websites. Such interaction would build customer loyalty and also increase transactions on the credit cards, which would be the reason for offering such deals in the first place. Restaurants would likewise benefit by attracting more customers. Finally, Eat2Eat would benefit by leveraging the credit card companies' large user bases. A partnership with a single credit card company might expose Eat2Eat .com to millions of new customers.

The idea made sense to Aggarwal, but he admitted it was hard to convince the credit card companies to buy into it. It required a shift in their thinking, which he was finding difficult to achieve. The marketing teams at credit card companies turned over quickly. Just when Aggarwal made headway with them, the representatives changed and he had to start over with new people. Aggarwal had been trying to negotiate such arrangements for five years and still had not closed any deals, although he felt he was close with at least one company.

## Raising Additional Capital

Eat2Eat had established a strong presence with Aggarwal's initial investment, but additional funding would be required to reach the next level. Aggarwal and his two employees spent practically all their time managing the company's day-to-day operations and had little time for additional strategic developments or promotional activities. Aggarwal thought this lack of strategic focus inhibited Eat2Eat's growth and put the company at a competitive disadvantage. As he commented:

> I feel like I'm in a Formula One race with a private entry car. I compete with professional teams with major funding, and I'm always one or two laps behind, just trying to keep up.

Aggarwal hoped to raise US$2 million in additional capital. Roughly 50 percent of those funds would be allocated to establishing three or four new sales representatives throughout the region. The sales representatives would add more restaurants to the company's inventory. Each representative would be paid US$5,000 to US$6,000 per month and would incur related costs, including computers and travel expenses. It was difficult to estimate the return for investing in new sales representatives, but Aggarwal hoped the additional revenue would outweigh the additional costs by a factor of two to one.

Roughly 40 percent of the new capital would be spent on public relations and marketing activities to reach the personal dining market segment. Aggarwal planned to hire a well-known public relations firm with regional influence and expertise in the hospitality sector. A public relations campaign would begin in a single market, as a test of its effectiveness, before being rolled out to the rest of the region.

The remaining 10 percent of the new capital would be spent on a technology upgrade. The Eat2Eat.com website and the supporting software were currently hosted by a third party; Aggarwal wanted to set up his own server and support the website in-house. He also wanted to enhance the company's mobile phone functionality to enable more reservations. While the technology upgrade would not have a direct impact on Eat2Eat .com's revenue, it would support the company as a whole and improve operational efficiency.

## Potential Sources for Additional Capital

Aggarwal considered debt financing but quickly dismissed the idea. He believed it would be difficult to obtain bank loans because Eat2Eat had not yet established a profitable track record. In fact, he believed it would be difficult for practically any early-stage Internet company to obtain bank loans for this reason. "If I were a banker," he mused, "I wouldn't loan money to this company."

He also contemplated a public stock offering, but likewise dismissed the idea. Eat2Eat simply did not have a big enough profile to make a public offering feasible or worthwhile.

Aggarwal thought he might find another Internet company willing to purchase a stake in Eat2Eat. He pointed to the recent example of Yahoo! purchasing a major stake in Alibaba.com, the Chinese online business-to-business marketplace.[5] The deal had received a great deal of publicity, and Aggarwal hoped it would galvanize the Asian Internet investment scene and inspire more deals in the sector. However, no other Internet companies had yet expressed an interest in buying into Eat2Eat.

Venture capital was a more likely option, although not necessarily a more favorable one. Aggarwal had been approached by several venture capital firms in recent months, but he had low expectations. He believed venture capitalists and entrepreneurs had inherently opposing objectives. The former wanted to buy into companies cheaply while the latter wanted to maximize investment value, so the two parties would naturally dispute the true value of a company's equity. Furthermore, a venture capitalist typically wanted to crystallize a profit from an investment within five years and wanted a return on investment in the 30 percent range. The venture capitalist would also impose a set of conditions (covenants) regarding the company's management and financial performance, and Aggarwal believed that in most cases those conditions might be difficult to meet.

Aggarwal had received telephone calls from other Asian restaurant website entrepreneurs trying to sell their businesses to him. Their companies were specific to certain cities, whereas Eat2Eat.com covered the entire region. Aggarwal considered buying or merging with another company to increase his restaurant inventory and user base, but only if such an amalgamation could be accomplished at a reasonable price. However, each of the companies concerned expected several million U.S. dollars for their equity, and Aggarwal was confident he could build or expand his business in any given city organically with a lower investment.

Aggarwal thought he would have to make a decision about new funding in the first half of 2006. He also thought it would be difficult to raise the money. Not only would it be hard to find the right investor, but the task would require more of his time, and his time was already in short supply.

## Aggarwal's Challenge

Aggarwal was proud of what Eat2Eat had achieved in its first five years, including its technology, industry recognition and value to both diners and restaurants. However, he knew the company would have to significantly expand its user base in 2006 and beyond. Such growth would be a difficult challenge, considering his limited time and financial capital. Aggarwal reviewed his current promotional strategies and tactics and wondered what he should do in the year ahead.

### CASE QUESTIONS

1. One of Eat2Eat.com's most popular programs was Eat!, which consisted of a set of reviews of various restaurants in the participating cities. While customers enjoyed it, the promotion did not seem to attract new patrons. Can you explain why?

2. Are there any opportunities to build a guerrilla marketing program? If so, what could the company do? If not, why not?

3. Some individuals who dine out consider the activity to be a major component of their social lives. Would a lifestyle marketing program attract new customers, based on this characteristic?

4. How might Eat2Eat.com take advantage of buzz marketing?

5. How could Eat2Eat.com take advantage of social media and placement in Internet search engines to build its base of customers?

6. Should Eat2Eat.com focus on attracting additional corporate customers or individual consumers? Defend your answer.

CHAPTER

8

# Sales Promotions

Sales promotions consist of two types: consumer promotions and trade promotions. Consumer promotions are incentives directed toward end users of a product with the goal of pulling that product through the market channel. Trade promotions are used by channel members and directed to other channel members to push the product through the channel. Manufacturers offer trade promotions to wholesalers and wholesalers offer them to retailers.

## ▧ Objectives of Promotions

Consumer and trade promotions are routinely designed to accomplish four objectives. First, promotions can stimulate sales or demand. Sales promotions tend to generate quicker results than most other marketing activities. Second, consumer promotions help a firm acquire new customers. New product sales may be induced through programs such as sampling and contests or sweepstakes. Third, repeat purchases may be produced by effective sales promotions programs. Consumers return to take advantage of price-offs, bonus packs, and premiums. Effective trade promotions encourage retailers to restock items. Fourth, companies offer sales promotions to counter competitive actions.

## ▧ Managing Consumer Promotions

Consumer promotions entice individuals to move beyond the interest and knowledge created by advertising to actually make purchases. Consumer promotions can persuade consumers to switch brands, sample a new brand, and keep current customers from considering competitive brands. The factors to consider when choosing consumer promotions to offer to the target market include the primary objective, promotional approach, distribution method, accompanying advertising or marketing communications, the break-even point, and potential non-sales benefits.

## ◫ **Types of Consumer Promotions**

Consumer promotions assist in attracting new customers and retaining current customers. A coupon is a price-reduction offer to a consumer or end user. A coupon may state a percentage off the retail price or an absolute amount. Coupon forms include print media, on- or in-package, in-store, sampling, bounce-back, scanner-delivered, cross-ruffing, online, and those delivered by the sales staff. Coupons can stimulate sales and match a competitor's offer. They often lead customers to make additional purchases. Disadvantages occur when coupons are often misredeemed or are counterfeited.

Premiums are the prizes, gifts, or special offers consumers receive when purchasing products. Fast-food restaurants offer prizes or toys in children's meals. Cereal companies also offer small prizes in the various boxes of product. The primary advantage of a premium is that consumers pay the full price for the product. The disadvantages arise from the costs of the gift and advertising the promotion.

Contests require participants to perform an activity to win a prize. Sweepstakes do not require a purchase, and prizes are granted in a random fashion. A contest offers the intrinsic value of participating, such as picking the winners of the NCAA basketball tournament. Both contest and sweepstakes prizes should have extrinsic value, the value associated with content of the actual prize. These promotions create excitement and buzz. Unfortunately, at times they merely stimulate store traffic without raising sales.

Refunds are cash returns on soft goods such as food or clothing. Rebates are returns on hard goods, such as automobiles and appliances. These promotions create interest in brands that otherwise might not draw attention and can lead to purchases. Rebates are attractive to retailers because they are funded by the manufacturer. The disadvantages of refunds and rebates begin with the costs of lost revenues combined with record-keeping and mailing costs.

Sampling is the delivery of a good or service for trial use. Samples target both consumers and businesses with goods or services. Sampling reduces purchase risk for the customer, which makes it an effective tool for acquiring first-time customers. Sampling is expensive, with little or no return on items given out.

Bonus packs offer an additional or extra number of items in a special package. Bonus packs attract consumers who are not loyal to a particular brand. They also encourage greater use of the product. The disadvantages of bonus packs include the cost of a different package plus the loss of revenue for extra items in each pack.

A price-off is a temporary reduction of the price of a product to the consumer. It can be physically marked on the package to ensure the retailer actually grants the discount. Price-offs attract new customers by reducing purchase risk. They also can increase the sales of an existing product. They reduce revenues per item, which should be considered in light of additional sales to be gained.

## ◫ **Types of Consumers**

When planning consumer promotions programs, the marketing team considers the types of individuals who are likely to respond. Promotion-prone consumers regularly react by using coupons, premiums, or price-off programs. Price-sensitive consumers use price as the only purchase criterion. Brand-loyal consumers do not use promotions unless they are being granted for their favorite brands. Preferred-brand consumers have a set of brands they enjoy and use promotions to purchase the item that is on-deal. Preferred-brand consumers are the best targets for consumer promotions.

## International Considerations

Various promotions are perceived in different ways, depending on the country involved. Coupons may be less popular in nations where using them creates the perception of being poor rather than prudent. A cultural assimilator should be commissioned to assist in selecting the best consumer promotions for a specific country.

## Trade Promotions

The most common trade promotions are offered to retailers by manufacturers. Trade promotions represent the second-largest expense for manufacturers, after the cost of goods sold. Trade promotions can be divided into (1) trade allowances, (2) trade incentives, and (3) trade shows.

Trade allowances provide financial incentives to other channel members to motivate them to purchase products for resale. The most common trade allowance, the off-invoice allowance, is a financial discount given to a channel member per item, case, or pallet ordered. The allowance normally consists of a percentage reduction in price. Trade allowances are popular with retailers that can purchase products at lower prices and generate greater profits as a result. Forward buying occurs when a retailer purchases extra amounts of a product while it is on-deal from the manufacturer and stockpiles it for the future. Diversion means the retailer purchases a product on-deal in one location and ships it to another location where it is off-deal.

The most controversial form of trade allowance, a slotting fee, is a charge for stocking new products on shelves. The large number of new products released each year necessitates the fees, from the retailer's perspective. Manufacturers complain they are practically a form of extortion.

Trade incentives are programs in which retailers must perform a marketing function in order to receive funds. The three most common are (1) cooperative merchandising agreements, (2) premium or bonus pack programs, and (3) cooperative advertising. A cooperative merchandising agreement takes the form of a formal agreement between the retailer and manufacturer to undertake a two-way marketing effort. One version, a calendar promotion, maps out promotional campaigns the retailers plan for customers through manufacturer trade incentives. A bonus pack or premium plan is an offer where merchandise is given as a form of discount. Cooperative advertising plans result from agreements between manufacturers and retailers to share the costs of advertising the manufacturer's product in combination with the retail outlet. Many retailers prefer trade allowances over trade incentives because a similar price discount is being given in the trade allowance and the retailer does not have to perform an activity to receive the lower price.

Trade shows are gatherings of buyers and sellers for the purpose of making contacts, inducing sales, and building relationships. Trade shows are prevalent in business-to-business marketing programs. Beyond presenting the manufacturer's products, company leaders can see what the competition is doing. Few deals are finalized at trade shows in the United States; however, purchases are much more common at international shows.

## Implications of Sales Promotions Programs

Building a strong brand produces the best weapon available to a manufacturer for reducing trade promotions expenditures. Without differentiation, retailers expect price to be the primary purchase criterion. In essence, a bidding war using trade promotions emerges.

Most consumer promotions are handled by entry-level employees. Consequently, customer service plays a crucial role in the success of a promotions program. Supervisors should be sure the program being offered is thoroughly understood by those who come in contact with the public. The same holds true for trade promotions. Any sales representative authorized to give a trade discount or trade allowance should be able to clearly explain the benefits of the promotion. Those who run the booth at a trade show become the face of the company. Cordial, professional behavior becomes the key to success in that environment.

## ⊠ The Cases

### SC Johnson: Planning Coupon Promotions

SC Johnson's Glade brand experienced a large variance in coupon redemption rates and coupon return metrics. A young intern, Dave Unipan, wanted to prove that the company's couponing program could be improved. To do so, the program would need to account for the range of retail outlets and associates involved in the delivery and redemption of coupons.

### Phillips Foods, Inc.—Introducing King Crab to the Trade

Phillips Foods is one of the largest seafood businesses in the United States with sales of more than $160 million annually. The company is known for its chain of restaurants and its food service and grocery blue swimming crab products. The company's marketing manager, Ron Birch, was expanding into sales of pasteurized King Crab products in the refrigerated and frozen self-service sections of grocery stores. The product had been heavily advertised to buyers in the food service and restaurant channels. Having already committed much of the annual marketing budget, Birch considered how to allocate the remaining dollars to promote the new product.

### Boots: Hair-Care Sales Promotion

Boots offers a well-accepted line of professional hair-care products in Great Britain. Marketing manager Dave Robinson was planning a consumer promotion program for the upcoming year. The primary goals of the promotions would be to drive up sales volume and to move consumers from lower-value brands to those with a higher price. The competition included several well-known hair-care companies, including the Proctor & Gamble lines, Alberto-Culver, and L'Oreal, as well as generic products. His promotions choices included coupons, bonus packs, and a premium gift program. While the costs of these promotions were significant, Robinson's ultimate objective was to maintain the Boots line over time, especially in terms of the company's standing in the professional hair-care market.

## SC Johnson: Planning Coupon Promotions

*By Dave Unipan, under the supervision of Professor Peter C. Bell*

In late May 2005, Dave Unipan requested a meeting with his boss, Brad Hause, to discuss a new initiative he wanted to pursue during his summer internship at SC Johnson. After spending the better part of May analyzing coupons for SC Johnson's Glade brand, Unipan had identified

Version: (A) 2009–09–17

a large variance in coupon redemption rates and coupon return metrics. Inspired by his Management Science Class during HBA1, Unipan wanted to discuss the possibility of developing a better way to plan coupon promotions with Hause.

## SC Johnson

SC Johnson was one of the largest and oldest companies in North America with a 119-year history and annual sales of more than $6.5 billion. SC Johnson was a global leader in markets for household cleaning, insect control, home storage, air care, and personal care products. Some of SC Johnson's most reputable brands were Glade®, Raid®, Shout®, OFF!®, Ziploc®, and Windex® (see Exhibit 1).

SC Johnson was still a privately held company with offices and production facilities in 20 countries around the world. Five generations of Johnsons had led the company, including the current CEO, Fisk Johnson.

| **Exhibit 1** | SC Johnson Canada Brand and Sample Product Listing |
|---|---|

**Drano®**
- Drano® Max Gel
- Drano® Dual-Force™ Foamer

**Pledge®**
- Pledge® Multi-Surface
- Pledge® Furniture Care

**Edge®**
- Edge® Advanced™

**Raid®**
- Raid® House & Garden
- Raid® Double Control Ant Baits
- Raid® Spider Blaster

**fantastik®**
- fantastik® All-Purpose Cleaners
- fantastick® Bathroom and Toilet Care

**Saran™**
- Saran™ Premium
- Saran™ Cling Plus®

**Glade®**
- Glade® Scented Oil Candles
- Glade® Wisp®
- Glade® PlugIns®
- Glade® Air Infusions®

**Skintimate®**
- Shave Gels

**Grab-it**
- Grab-it® Cloths
- Grab-it® Go-Mop™

**Shout®**
- Shout® Action Gel™
- Shout® Trigger & Liquid
- Shout® Carpet

**OFF!®**
- Deep Woods® OFF!®
- OFF!® Skintastic®
- OFF!® Mosquito Lamp

**Windex®**
- Windex® Original
- Windex® Mountain Berry®
- Windex® Multi-Task Wipes

**Oust®**
- Oust® Aerosol
- Oust® Bathroom
- Oust® Fan
- Oust® Mini

**Ziploc®**
- Ziploc® Bags
- Ziploc® Containers

## SC Johnson Canada

SC Johnson Canada was consistently ranked as one of the top 50 employers in Canada by *Report on Business*. By continually winning this award, SC Johnson Canada was able to attract and retain top talent, keep a highly engaged workforce, and maintain an entrepreneurial and flexible corporate culture with a great work-life balance.

SC Johnson Canada maintained a degree of autonomy from the U.S. parent company and acted as an independent profit center. Canadian Brand Managers designed and executed their own country specific strategies, and had their own promotions budget to manage. Therefore SC Johnson brand managers were always seeking innovative marketing strategies to improve their sales and to better use their limited promotions budget. Brand managers also had the power to set their own product retail prices, which could range anywhere from $1 to $10 for one well-known SC Johnson brand.

## Dave Unipan

Dave Unipan had a passion for business ever since his participation in Junior Achievement in high school. Unipan had been pre-admitted to the undergraduate business program at the Richard Ivey School of Business and, during his first two years of undergraduate studies, had worked part-time as a marketing assistant for a national non-profit organization. After completing the first year of the Ivey business program (his third year of university), Unipan was excited to accept a corporate position as a summer intern in the marketing department at SC Johnson where he reported to Brad Hause.

## Brad Hause

Brad Hause was the Brand Manager for Oust®, SC Johnson's market share leader in the odor eliminator marketplace. Hause had graduated with an MBA from the Richard Ivey School of Business in 2000 and started at SC Johnson as a sales associate immediately after graduation, working his way up to his current position. Prior to completing his MBA, Hause obtained a diploma from Fanshawe College in London, Ontario. He had also been a competitive ski racer which led to his first full-time job as a sales representative for a sporting goods company.

Unipan found Hause to have a charismatic and open leadership style, which provided his interns with invaluable learning experiences by constantly challenging and encouraging them to take initiative (within reason). Unipan also saw Hause as an analytical "fact-based" decision maker, and the Oust® brand had flourished under his guidance because of his ability to understand market conditions and make decisions accordingly.

## Coupon Promotions

SC Johnson Canada spent millions of dollars annually promoting their products using in-store coupon advertisements. In-store coupons usually provided customers with a discount (10 percent to 50 percent) off the retail price of a product and generally ran for one to two months. Typically coupons were printed in packs of 50 with eight packs delivered to each store that had been selected to receive coupons.

SC Johnson believed that these coupons could be one of the most cost effective forms of promotion, but could also be unpredictable since redemption rates varied considerably depending on market conditions, competitor promotions and in-store sales efforts. Roughly one to six percent of all coupons distributed were redeemed, costing SC Johnson the face value of the coupon. This redemption cost made up 30 percent to 70 percent of the total cost of a coupon promotion, with printing and design costs accounting for the remainder of the expense. The high variability in the redemption rate meant that SC Johnson's brand managers had a difficult time adequately budgeting for coupons.

SC Johnson used coupon promotions to serve three strategic purposes: to promote trial use of a new product, to create incremental sales of an existing product, and to attempt to reduce the impact of competitors' promotions.

### Promoting Trial Use of a New Product

SC Johnson launched dozens of new line extensions[1] each year. Brand managers used coupons to substantially discount these new products in order to encourage first-time users, thereby establishing an initial customer base that was essential for new products to reach desired levels of profitability.

### Creating Incremental Sales of Existing Products

SC Johnson had several products that had reached the mature stage of their life cycle.

Brand managers would often use coupons (two products for the price of one were common) to flush out store inventory, and perhaps make room for new line extensions. Additionally, coupons created impulse buying reactions from customers, resulting in immediate incremental sales, above and beyond monthly sales expectations.

## Reducing the Impact of Competitor Promotions

Most SC Johnson brands were sold in highly competitive markets where there were very low switching costs between products. In markets with such high price elasticity, brand managers were essentially forced to match discounts offered by competitors' coupons in an effort to ensure their product sales levels were maintained. Essentially, coupons provided a temporary way for consumer packaged goods companies to engage in price wars.

## Coupon Politics

At some of SC Johnson's larger accounts, not having a coupon promotion offering a temporary price decrease could create a competitive disadvantage. These companies purchased substantial volumes of SC Johnson products and controlled product placement on store shelves. SC Johnson's brand managers were therefore limited by what companies they could exclude from a coupon program. It was generally felt that Loblaw, Metro,

Sobeys, A&P, and Shoppers Drug Mart had to be included in all SC Johnson coupon promotions.

## Marketing Source and Promospace

Companies wishing to do any form of in-store advertising had to purchase advertising space from either Marketing Source or Promospace. These companies acted as advertising representatives for most grocery, wholesale, and drug markets and, in addition to coupons, offered a variety of in-store promotional opportunities including shopping cart advertisements, shelf billboards, and talking floor displays. Brand and marketing managers often worked with sales associates from Marketing Source and Promospace to try to build integrated[2] yearly promotional campaigns.

### Promospace Coupon Pricing

Promospace, which owned the rights to all Loblaw and Metro chain stores, offered advertisers a fixed base rate for every 1,000 customers estimated to visit a store chain in a given week. All prices were based on a one-week program and the entire store chain had to be included. Premiums were charged for regional and/or chain specific coupon programs. Customer volume estimates were provided by a third party and in no way reflected coupon users. Exhibit 2 summarizes prices, store availabilities and estimated coupon redemption rates based on 2005 Glade® coupon analysis at Promospace sites.

| Exhibit 2 | Promospace Coupon Pricing | |
|---|---|---|
| **Base Rate: $1.85 per 1,000 Customers/Week[1]** | | |
| **Pricing Breakdown** | | |
| National | All 14 stores | Base Rate |
| Regional | All stores within a specific region | 5% |
| Chain Specific | Less than 100% of a region | 25% |

*(Continued)*

**Exhibit 2** (Continued)

| | Store Count | Circulation/Wk | Redemption Rate |
|---|---|---|---|
| **Ontario** | | | |
| Loblaws | 55 | 1,234,567 | 3.50% |
| Zehrs | 60 | 1,176,964 | 3.20% |
| RCSS | 35 | 506,807 | 3.70% |
| Fortinos | 27 | 632,705 | 2.60% |
| Valumart | 61 | 467,321 | 2.70% |
| YIG | 54 | 590,311 | 3.80% |
| Freshmart | 39 | 173,604 | 4.70% |
| No Frills | 111 | 1,777,629 | 4.10% |
| **SUB-TOTAL** | **442** | **6,559,908** | |
| **Quebec** | | | |
| Loblaws | 43 | 763,587 | 3.40% |
| Metro | 569 | 41,520 | 3.10% |
| Provigo | 125 | 1,269,042 | 4.10% |
| **SUB-TOTAL** | **737** | **2,074,149** | |
| **Atlantic** | | | |
| Superstores | 62 | 643,096 | 2.70% |
| Save Easy/IGA | 38 | 532,087 | 2.80% |
| Dominion/Dave Easy (NFLD) | 31 | 238,974 | 3.20% |
| Freshmart | 42 | 93,628 | 4.10% |
| **SUB-TOTAL** | **173** | **1,507,785** | |

1. Production and design costs are an additional four percent of redemption and distribution expense of Promospace coupons.

## Marketing Source Coupon Pricing

Marketing Source owned the rights to such well known chains as Shoppers Drug Mart, Zellers, Sobeys, Canadian Tire, and A&P, and offered three levels of pricing based on how many stores, within a given market, a potential advertiser wanted for coupon distribution. Pricing was not based on the overall percentage of stores purchased for couponing and all prices were for a one-month program. Marketing Source allowed advertisers to choose to advertise in less than 100 percent of a chain's stores. Marketing Source's detailed pricing, store availability and estimated redemption rates based on 2005 Glade coupons analysis are summarized in Exhibit 3.

| Exhibit 3 | Marketing Source Coupon Pricing[1] |
| --- | --- |

| Pricing Breakdown | |
| --- | --- |
| **Tier Breakdown by Market** | **Price/Store** |
| Tier 1 – National (80–100%) | $26.35 |
| Tier 2 – Regional (50–79%) | $31.78 |
| Tier 3 – Chain Specific (less than 50%) | $37.60 |

| | | |
| --- | --- | --- |
| Canadian Tire | 544 | 2% |
| Zellers | 326 | 6.30% |
| SUB-TOTAL | 870 | |
| Market 2: Drug Stores | | |
| Guardian Drug Stores | 24 | 2.20% |
| IDA Drug Stores | 28 | 4.10% |
| Le Groupe Jean Coutu Inc. | 320 | 3.30% |
| Lawtons Drug Stores Limited | 43 | 1.50% |
| Pharma Plus Drug Marts LTD. | 225 | 1.70% |
| Pharmasave Drugs Limited | 201 | 2.30% |
| Shoppers Drug Mart | 773 | 1.60% |
| Les Pharmacies Uniprix | 438 | 3.70% |
| SUB-TOTAL | 2,052 | |
| Market 3: Grocery Stores | | |
| A & P Food Stores LTD. | 121 | 5.20% |
| Food Basics Stores | 109 | 3.40% |
| Price Chopper | 88 | 3.70% |
| Canada Safeway Limited | 229 | 2.80% |
| Sobeys Inc. | 187 | 3.50% |
| Overwaitea Foods | 76 | 2.30% |
| Commisso's Food Markets LTD. | 23 | 1.20% |
| Federated Co-Op | 93 | 2.30% |
| Hy & Zel's | 64 | 5% |
| Sobeys (West) | 125 | 3.10% |
| Sobeys (Quebec) | 211 | 2.40% |
| Sobeys (Ontario) - IGA | 111 | 2.90% |
| Longo Brothers Fruit Markets | 17 | 1.70% |
| SUB-TOTAL | 1454 | |

1. Pricing does not include design and production costs. Design costs are a fixed rate of $3,000 per coupon program and production costs are an additional $11.30/store.

## The Decision

As Unipan sat in his cubicle, he realized he had reached the crossroads of his internship. In theory, he believed the coupon optimization had great potential within the highly innovative brand team. Unipan knew he had the time necessary to complete the model before his internship ended in August. He wondered, though, how he would demonstrate to Hause that he had the technical and analytical expertise to pull it off. More importantly, Unipan questioned how he would be able to prove to the entire brand team that the way they had been purchasing coupons was inefficient. He obviously had a lot to think about before his meeting with Hause.

Unipan had four hours to prepare for the meeting and wondered how he should go about explaining his idea. He knew he had all the data necessary to create a model, but was unsure at this point as to the general functionality of the model and how exactly it would improve the coupon selection process at SC Johnson.

### CASE QUESTIONS

1. What were the goals of the SC Johnson coupon program? Were these the most advisable goals? Why or why not?

2. Should SC Johnson offer coupons only to selected retail outlets? Defend your answer.

3. Which forms of coupons would be best for SC Johnson products? Are there any new formats (e.g., electronic coupons, Internet-delivered) that would be valuable to the company?

4. Should SC Johnson use coupons to play "defense" or "offense"? If for offense, describe additional advertising and promotional programs that should accompany the couponing program.

# Phillips Foods, Inc.—Introducing King Crab to the Trade

*By Professor Frédéric Brunel, with the assistance of Deborah Utter*

On a hot Baltimore day in August 2006, Phillips Seafood Restaurants were full of tourists lunching on local seafood specialties. Among them, Cherry Stockworth, vice-president of marketing for Phillips Foods, Inc., and Ron Birch, product manager for the new pasteurized King Crab, were discussing the upcoming phase II of the launch of King Crab (see Exhibit 1). In phase I, Birch had targeted foodservice buyers and had spent almost half of his $160,000 King Crab launch budget for ads in foodservice trade magazines. For phase II, Stockworth was advocating a different strategy. She summarized:

Ron, King Crab is one of the most important launches we have done in years. We are the leaders in blue swimming crab and our pasteurization process is arguably the best in the business. However, if we want to maintain our double-digit growth, we need to leverage the product diversification that King Crab provides. In phase I, you have advertised the product in restaurant and institutional foodservice magazines, and the response has been good and the trade ads have worked well. Now, for this second phase, we must ensure

Copyright © 2009, Ivey Management Services                    Version: (A) 2010–04–29

The authors recognize the assistance and support of the Society of Independent Show Organizers and the Exhibition Industry Foundation.

**Exhibit 1**  King Crab Package—Eight oz. Size for Foodservice and Retail

A. Foodservice packaging

B. Retail packaging

an equally successful launch in the other two markets: food retailers and wholesale distributors. I know that your phase II plan is to stick with the proven trade advertising strategy but I think that we can generate more sales leads if we make King Crab the centerpiece of our booth at the IBSS (International Boston Seafood Show) in March. This will generate buzz and give King Crab the needed exposure to distributors and retail buyers. If we go that route, I will charge your budget for half of Phillips' cost for the trade show. Please take a few days to consider this idea; work up the numbers on the two options and let's talk next week to finalize the decision.

## Phillips Foods, Inc.

Founded by Augustus E. Phillips in 1914 on Hoopers Island, Maryland, Phillips Foods Inc. had grown into one of the largest seafood businesses in the United States ($160 million for 2006 sales[1]) and was the number one U.S. brand for crab meat. The company was made up of three business units: (1) a restaurant division which operated eight full service restaurants in the Baltimore region and a growing franchise division along the East Coast (e.g., airport locations), (2) a foodservice products unit that sold to restaurants and foodservice institutions, and (3) a retail products division which sold directly (or indirectly via wholesalers and distributors) to grocery stores and other retail food merchants.

Phillips was renowned for its crab products and the brand image remained closely associated with its Maryland origins. Yet, the company had actively diversified its supply sources and production, and had 14 manufacturing sites (one in Baltimore and 13 overseas) and three sales offices outside the United States. Unlike most of its competitors, Phillips owned and operated all of its plants. It believed that this strategy ensured greater food safety and quality.

Phillips had also differentiated itself on at least two other fronts. Phillips was the first to perfect a method to pasteurize and can crabmeat while preserving a fresh-like product taste and texture. Once canned, the crabmeat needed to be refrigerated, but it enjoyed an 18-month shelf life. In retail stores, pasteurized crab was typically sold in self-service refrigerators that were located in proximity to the seafood counters (see Exhibit 2). To support these product innovations, Steve Phillips (CEO Philips Foods, Inc.) also implemented a bona fide branding strategy. Instead of selling crabmeat as a commodity, he invested in brand-building activities for the Phillips brand. In 2006, Phillips' products could be found in over 10,000 retail stores in the United States. To sell to these stores, Phillips relied on its own direct-to-retailers sales force and on a network of food brokers, distributors, and wholesalers who acted as intermediaries between the company and some retailers.

In recent years, Phillips' product strategy had centered on developing value-added products (e.g., ready-to-eat products) that offered higher margins than plain seafood. According to Bob Goldin, executive VP with Technomic Inc., a food research and consulting firm, profit margins for commodity food items ranged between one percent and three percent, whereas margins for value-added products could be eight times as large.[2] By 2007, Phillips expected to derive most of its revenues from sales of value-added items. In the retail channel, its product line included refrigerated crab meat, crab dip, frozen appetizers, frozen crab cakes, assorted frozen seafood (e.g., shrimp, salmon, tilapia,

| Exhibit 2 | Examples of Refrigerated Seafood Displays |
|---|---|

A. Open merchandiser refrigerator

B. Open display case

C. Display on ice

D. Icelator bin used for in-store promotions

mahi-mahi), a line of frozen Asian-inspired products, and also a line of seasonings and cocktail and tartar sauces (see Exhibit 3).

Phillips' latest innovation was King Crab. In 2006, no other company had a pasteurized King Crab product with the same fresh-like quality. The pasteurization technique allowed Phillips to position the product as an alternative to fresh or frozen King Crab. The product was available in two packages: one targeted at restaurant and institutional foodservice markets, and one for retail consumers (see Exhibit 1). For phase II of the launch, Birch was looking into the best way to secure retail distribution for the consumer market version of the product.

## King Crab

While blue swimming crab might conjure images of family fun, summer days and sandy Maryland beaches, King Crab was "synonymous with the raw, rugged beauty of Alaska."[3] Most King Crab was fished in the rough Northern Pacific waters off the coast of Alaska and Russia. Fishing for King Crabs was often a dangerous and epic affair, and had been the subject of a popular program (*Deadliest Catch*) on the Discovery Channel. *Seafood Business* magazine stated that "during the show's rise to prime-time prominence, king crab became a seafood spectacle."[4]

The crabs themselves were spectacular. Depending on the sub-species, mature specimens

**Exhibit 3**  Selection of Phillips' Retail Products

| Crab Cakes (Frozen) | Blue Swimming Crab (Refrigerated) | Seafood (Frozen) | Asian Rhythms (Frozen) |
|---|---|---|---|
| • Boardwalk Crab Cakes<br>• Crab & Shrimp Cakes<br>• Crab Cake Minis<br>• Maryland Style Crab Cakes | • Jumbo Crab Meat<br>• Lump Crab Meat<br>• Backfin Crab Meat<br>• Special Crab Meat<br>• Claw Crab Meat | • Coconut Mahi Mahi<br>• Lemon Peppercorn Ahi Tuna<br>• White Wine & Herb Mahi Fillet<br>• Salmon Cakes<br>• Crab-Stuffed Shrimps<br>• Stuffed Salmon<br>• Stuffed Tilapia | • Crab & Shrimp Fried Rice<br>• Hot & Spicy Shrimp Soup<br>• Shrimp Green Curry<br>• Shrimp Pad Thai<br>• Shrimp Red Curry<br>• Spicy Coconut Shrimp Soup |

| Appetizers & Dips (Frozen) | Shrimp (Frozen) | Condiments & Seasonings | Seafood Soups (Frozen) |
|---|---|---|---|
| • Crab & Shrimp Spring Rolls<br>• Crab & Spinach Dip<br>• Crab Pretzel<br>• Crispy Dim Sum<br>• Jalapeno Crab Slammers<br>• Party Pack<br>• Maryland Style Crab Dip (Refrigerated) | • Breaded Shrimp<br>• Buffalo Shrimp<br>• Coconut Shrimp | • Blackening Seasoning<br>• Seafood Seasoning<br>• Tartar Sauce<br>• Cocktail Sauce | • Crab & Corn Chowder<br>• Crab & Shrimp Chowder<br>• Cream of Crab Soup<br>• Lobster Bisque<br>• Maryland Style Crab Soup<br>• New England Clam Chowder<br>• Shrimp Bisque |

*Source:* Company material.

weighed up to eight pounds for golden king crabs and up to 20 pounds (with leg spans of five feet) for blue King Crabs. King Crab was considered a delicacy and a luxury seafood product, and was mainly consumed in restaurants. Most King Crab meat was shipped cooked and frozen in bundles of legs and claws still in the shell (some was shipped fresh or live). Restaurateurs said that consumers enjoyed King Crab "because of its sweet and succulent taste" as well as "the wow factor" of the large legs. "You crack open a leg, and there's a huge piece of meat . . . you don't have to fight with it to get a little teeny piece."[5]

King Crab legs used for Phillips' product were cooked, chilled, and brine-frozen at sea. They were then transported to Asia, where the meat was extracted from the shell, pasteurized and packaged in 8-ounce containers (16 ounce for warehouse clubs). The product had no additives or preservatives. Advantages to retailers were the 18-month shelf life and the potential for retail margins in the 35 to 45 percent range. The suggested retail price was $16.99 for an 8-ounce container. Besides Phillips' brand reputation, advantages for consumers were: a reasonable price in comparison to fresh or frozen; the convenience of 100 percent usable crab meat; and the high-quality taste of fresh without the mess of cracking and removing the shell. Phillips expected that a sizeable number of U.S. consumers would buy this new retail product.

## Seafood Retail Market

U.S. seafood retail sales ($14.4 billion in 2006[6]) had been fueled by increased health concerns of U.S. consumers, the introduction of innovative seafood products, and the growth of warehouse clubs. Over the next six years, five percent to six percent annual growth was predicted. Fresh seafood (chilled or refrigerated) represented 54 percent of seafood retail sales, frozen represented 33 percent, and shelf-stable seafood (non-refrigerated) accounted for 13 percent.[7] These relative shares were not expected to change significantly.

Seafood consumption patterns varied greatly across products and situations. Among the 110 million U.S. households, 90 percent of them ate seafood; however, 43 percent of these households ate seafood mainly when they dined out. Further, only 27 percent of U.S. households reported buying frozen seafood and 18.5 percent buying fresh seafood, with crab (all forms) being purchased by eight percent of U.S. households.[8] Generally, most U.S. homemakers were not confident in their ability to properly cook seafood, thus resulting in this low penetration of seafood for home-cooking. As a result, experts agreed that direct-to-consumer advertising campaigns and cooperative promotional programs (e.g., in-store signage, sampling, demonstrations) were necessary to achieve successful new seafood product launches.[9] According to the CEO of Blue Horizon Organic Seafood Co., when seafood was cooked at home, "consumers want approachable flavors similar to those they've experienced in restaurants or on vacation . . . they are looking for something tasty and nutritious that they can put on the table in minutes."[10] In response, manufacturers had introduced products that emphasized "convenience," "natural," "premium" or "microwaveable" as the main product benefits.

The retail side of the market had been marked by (1) a considerable industry consolidation within supermarkets (grocery stores with annual sales over $2 million) and (2) the growth of warehouse clubs (see Exhibit 4). In 2006, seafood products were sold through 34,000 supermarkets (75 percent were part of chains), 1,100 warehouse clubs, and 13,000 smaller independent food stores[11] (including 3,800 specialty seafood markets[12]).

Seafood sales accounted for four percent of supermarket sales, with packaged seafood representing one third of that amount and bulk seafood representing the rest. It was also estimated that sales of packaged seafood in supermarkets accounted for 25 percent of total U.S. seafood retail sales.[13] Most retailers purchased either directly from the manufacturers or through food brokers. Brokers were used for their relationships with retailers and their geographic coverage. They sold the products to retailers and visited the retail outlets frequently to maintain the presentation of the products on the shelves. Food brokers were typically paid a three to five percent commission based on the manufacturer's selling price.

| Exhibit 4 | Top 100 US Supermarket Chains and Wholesale Club Stores |
|---|---|

| Number of Stores per Chain | Number of Chains | Chain Names (partial list) |
|---|---|---|
| >1,000 stores | 5 | Delhaize, Kroger, Safeway, Supervalu, Walmart |
| 500–999 stores | 6 | Ahold USA, Aldi, B.J.'s, Publix, Sam's Club, Winn-Dixie |
| 100–499 stores | 33 | Albertsons, Costco, Great Atlantic & Pacific, Hannaford Bros, H-E-B, Price Chopper, Roundy's, Shaw's/Star, Smart & Final, Whole Foods, Weis Markets |
| 50–99 stores | 28 | Big Y Foods, DeMoulas/Market Basket, Wegman's, WinCo |
| < 50 stores | 28 | Gristede's, King Kullen, Roche Bros, Stew Leonards, United Supermarkets |

*Source:* Food Marketing Institute Data, 2007.

Most retailers were ambivalent about new products. On one hand, they sought them to gain a competitive advantage or improve margins, but on the other hand, they were resistant because of limited retail shelf space and a desire to minimize risk. To carry a new product, retailers would routinely eliminate another SKU (stock keeping unit) in order to make room for the new one. New products were selected based on their bottom line potential and their potential inventory turn rate. It was common when negotiating with retailers to offer a promotion calendar, which included discounts and promotional events during the year. To support the retailers and educate consumers, Phillips had developed a King Crab recipe booklet that would be available for free at the point of purchase, shelf signage and an icelator display bin to hold the products during promotional events (see Exhibit 2).

Two main trends were expected to shape the future of seafood retail. First, consumers were expected to purchase a greater share of their weekly food basket in warehouse clubs and large mass merchandisers; thus, the share of seafood sold through these channels would increase. Second, there was a trend toward greater emphasis on self-service selling for seafood. For example, loose seafood counters were being phased out by several grocery chains (e.g., Stop & Shop, Giant). In these instances, the traditional counters were replaced with prepackaged seafood in refrigerators or freezers. The Food Marketing Institute estimated that, by 2007, less than 60 percent of supermarkets would still have a full-service seafood counter. Chains following this strategy were mainly motivated by cost savings and a desire to align their operations more closely with the models used by mass merchandisers and warehouse clubs. Although consumers might enjoy more competitive prices thanks to these changes, they had also lost a key source of seafood information and home-cooking advice: the counter employees. Though, there were some notable exceptions to this trend. Some up-market chains such as Whole Foods had gone in the opposite direction: hiring more personnel in their seafood departments and offering more education and premium items.[14]

## Trade Show Marketing

In the United States and Canada, over 14,000 trade shows (a.k.a. exhibitions, expos, fairs) would be held in 2006. A typical show ran for two or three days and had about 35,000 square feet of exhibition space and over 100 exhibitors.[15] Smaller shows were typically held in hotels or conference facilities and larger ones were held in large exhibition and convention centers. Most of these face-to-face events were aimed at business audiences. Although consumer shows (e.g., a local boat show) tended to have more visitors, they only accounted for 18 percent of all shows.

Exhibition professionals argued that shows were a unique sales and marketing medium because (1) they brought the most active prospects and customers to the exhibiting company, (2) companies could demonstrate products, answer questions, overcome objections and interact face-to-face with their current or potential customers, (3) companies could build on all five human senses in order to deliver impactful and memorable messages and (4) multiple marketing goals could be pursued at once (e.g., from long-term relationship-building to immediate sales lead generation).[16]

However, there were limitations to the marketing power of this medium. A small number of trade shows might not always deliver on the promises made to the exhibitors and attendees. Occasionally, attendees and exhibitors had reported that some shows felt too cramped. There were also isolated anecdotes of keynote speakers being disappointing or even failing to show up. It was thus important that attendees and exhibitors selected well-managed shows with a strong reputation and a positive track record. Also, because most attendees wanted to be able to see the key industry players for one industry under one roof, the absence of some important exhibitors had contributed to the downfall of several shows. Conversely, while some shows failed to attract enough exhibitors or attendees, others might fall victim to their own success. Trade shows could be so large that exhibitors had problems standing out among all exhibiting companies and attendees had problems finding the companies or products they sought. As attendance grew larger, exhibitors found it challenging to properly staff the exhibits or make sure that their exhibit space was large enough to accommodate the volume of visitors. Irrespective of overall show size or exhibit design and staffing, there was one common complaint from attendees and exhibitors: shows were tiring and it was hard to be "on" for 12 or more hours per day, for two to three days at a time.

In 2005 in the United States, firms spent $7.5 billion on trade show exhibit space and 42 million visitors attended.[17] In addition to renting floor space, companies spent money on exhibit design (e.g., design and construction of display, refurbishment, storage, display material), show services (e.g., electrical, plumbing, carpet, janitorial services, security, lead retrieval information system), shipping (e.g., freight and material handling), travel and entertainment (e.g., travel and lodging of personnel, meals, hospitality and client events), and advertising and promotion (e.g., sponsorship of events at the show, ads in programs, pre-show marketing, print material, giveaways and prizes) (see Exhibit 5). As a rule of thumb, total trade show costs were about three times the cost of floor space for small exhibits that did not require extensive setup and show services. However, if the exhibit was larger and required more services, a better rule of thumb was five times the cost of floor space.

A comparison of the effectiveness and usage of face-to-face events versus other marketing tactics suggested that B2B marketers viewed face-to-face events as the most effective tactic for generating leads and building brand image (see Exhibit 6). These results could be reinforced by the fact that

| **Exhibit 5**  How the Exhibit Dollar Is Spent | |
|---|---|
| Exhibit space | 28% |
| Travel and entertainment | 21% |
| Show services | 19% |
| Exhibit design | 13% |
| Shipping | 9% |
| Advertising and promotion | 6% |
| Other | 4% |

*Source:* Center for Exhibition Industry Research, SM22, 2001.

**Exhibit 6**    U.S. Business to Business (B2B) Marketing Practices (2005 data)

| Types of Marketing Tactics | Tactic Effectiveness for Brand-Building* | Tactic Effectiveness for Lead Generation* | % of Companies Using** | % of Marketing Budget** |
|---|---|---|---|---|
| In-person events (e.g., trade shows, conferences) | 60.9% | 62.6% | 78.9% | 22.2% |
| Public relations | 51.7% | 45.4% | 36.8% | 3.1% |
| Industry trade magazines (e.g., *Progressive Grocer*) | 50.2% | 47.4% | 63.2% | 12.6% |
| Custom publications (e.g., brochures) | 44.6% | 41.3% | 56.1% | 5.6% |
| TV | 42.9% | 36.3% | 35.1% | 9.2% |
| Online marketing | 39.8% | 42.1% | 52.6% | 14.4% |
| Direct mail | 39.7% | 42.0% | 56.1% | 8.3% |
| Printed newsletter | 39.0% | 35.3% | 54.4% | 5.3% |
| General business magazines (e.g., *Forbes*) | 37.9% | 34.6% | 49.1% | 7.2% |
| Newspapers (e.g., *Wall Street Journal*) | 37.4% | 33.3% | 49.1% | 6.4% |
| Radio | 31.8% | 30.7% | 22.8% | 1.8% |
| Printed directories (e.g., *Yellow Pages*) | 29.9% | 31.7% | 28.1% | 1.2% |
| Other | – | – | – | 2.6% |

*Source:* Forester Research, 2005.

*Percentage of respondents who selected one of the top two boxes (5 or 6), where 1 = "very ineffective" and 6 = "very effective" N = 867, companies from all B2B sectors.

**N = 57, manufacturing and processing sector companies.

most attendees had not been called on by a salesperson in the 12 months preceding a show.[18] Yet, the majority of attendees were planning a purchase in the next 12 months and had some direct buying influence (e.g., final say in purchase decision, specify products, or make recommendations).[19]

The number one reason buyers attended trade shows was to see new technology or products. Other motives included building relationships, comparing brands, getting insights in the industry, and interacting with salespeople without the obligation to make a purchase.[20] When buyers were asked to identify the most useful sources of product information, exhibitions were the most often mentioned (90 percent), followed by direct sales and field sales (75 percent), public relations (75 percent), the Internet (63 percent), direct mail (58 percent), trade advertising (55 percent) and telemarketing (50 percent).[21] Besides their informational value, exhibitors and attendees also pointed to the shows' usefulness in building and maintaining vendor/customer relationships (see Exhibit 7). Most attendees went to only one or two shows per year and selected which one to attend based on word-of-mouth and trade magazines.[22]

Trade show interactions had an impact beyond the show itself. Estimates suggested that show attendees would share the information they had received at the show with other people in their own companies.[23] It was therefore important that exhibitors created positive and memorable show experiences. Exhibit 8 summarizes the top reasons (other than exhibit size) that make an exhibit memorable. Jefferson Davis, a prominent trade show consultant, argued that exhibitors should measure outcomes with hard and soft metrics (e.g., visual impact of the booth, quality versus quantity of interactions, number of leads generated, cost per lead and return on expenditure). Second, exhibitors should be prepared to leverage the fact that at a trade show, "customers come to you with an open mind, looking for products and ready to engage in discussions." Therefore, it was crucial that companies be properly staffed, have an appropriate exhibit size, and have processes to capture client information at the show.

Following up on trade show leads could be effective and efficient. Research had shown that sales leads from trade shows were more likely to yield sales and have lower costs than regular sales calls. In the absence of a prior trade show interaction, it took on average one initial field sales meeting and 2.7 follow-up field sales meetings (at an average cost of $308 for each) to close a sale. However, if the initial sales meeting took place at a

| **Exhibit 7** | Importance of Face-to-Face Interaction During the Purchase Process | |
|---|---|---|
| | **Percentage of Respondents Who Find Face-to-Face Interaction Important** | |
| **Purchase Process Stage** | **Show Attendees** | **Exhibitors** |
| Awareness-building | 76% | 86% |
| Evaluation of product or service | 67% | 74% |
| Narrowing choice | 50% | 59% |
| Purchase | 32% | 48% |
| Implementation of product or service | 37% | 45% |
| Maintaining vendor/customer relationships | 51% | 76% |
| Upgrading/repurchasing | 40% | 51% |

Source: Center for Exhibition Industry Research. Report F03.03. 2003.

| Exhibit 8 | Top Reasons for Remembering Exhibits | |
| --- | --- | --- |
| Product interest | | 64% |
| Well-known company | | 51% |
| Product demonstrations | | 43% |
| Stage/theater presentation | | 26% |
| Exhibit color/design | | 19% |
| Exhibit personnel | | 18% |
| Giveaway | | 15% |
| Literature | | 13% |

*Source:* Center for Exhibition Industry Research, MCRR 5040, 2000.

trade show (average cost of a trade show sales lead was $212), it took 1.6 follow-up field sales meetings to close a sale.[24]

## The International Boston Seafood Show

The IBSS was held annually in early March at the Boston Convention & Exhibition Center and was the largest seafood show in the United States. The show lasted for three days and is open from 10 A.M. to 5 P.M. on the first two days and 10 A.M. to 3 P.M. on day three. Attendance for the 2007 show was expected to be about 18,000, with a net attendance of 12,000 (this excluded exhibitors, show organizers, and the press). With 175,000 square feet of exhibit space and over 800 exhibitors promoting products ranging from wild Alaskan salmon to farm-raised fish from Vietnam to refrigerated display cases and ice machines, the show covered the full range of industry players.

The show drew decision makers from food retailers, foodservice providers and distributors (see Exhibit 9). Visitors represented companies with median annual seafood purchases of $3.4 million (see Exhibit 10). Most visitors had purchasing authority and were looking for new products; 81 percent said that they had found new products at the show, 73 percent had planned purchases after attending the show, and 88 percent wanted to return from year to year.

Floor space was $30 per square foot and exhibits were available in many sizes (multiples of 100 square feet) and configurations. The minimum size was 10 feet by 10 feet. There was an extra charge of $500 per corner. At the time of the case, Phillips had not committed to a specific space; however, the company was trying to decide the size and location that it needed to reserve (see Exhibit 11).

| Exhibit 9 | IBSS Net Attendance Breakdown | |
| --- | --- | --- |
| **Segment Represented** | | **% Attendees** |
| Suppliers (processors, importers, exporters, aquaculture, etc.) | | 41% |
| Services (packaging, research, transportation, etc.) | | 16% |
| Seafood distributors, brokers and wholesalers | | 15% |
| Foodservice (hotels, restaurants, institution food services, catering, etc.) | | 10% |
| Retailers (supermarkets, warehouse clubs, seafood markets, etc.) | | 8% |
| Others | | 10% |

*Source:* Diversified Business Communications.

| Exhibit 10 | Partial List of Key Buyers Typically Attending the International Boston Seafood Show |
|---|---|

According to registration data from previous shows, this is a partial list of some key buyers who traditionally attend the show. It is not exhaustive, but rather illustrative of the types of attendees.

**Foodservice**

- Aramark Corporation
- Avado Brands
- Applebees
- Bonefish Grill
- California Pizza Kitchen
- Captain D's Seafood
- CKE Restaurants
- Compass Group
- Darden Restaurants
- Friendly's Ice Cream Corp
- Golden Corral
- Ground Round
- Harrah's Entertainment
- Houlihans Restaurants
- Isle of Capri Casinos
- J Alexanders Corp
- Legal Seafoods
- McCormick & Schmicks
- Outback Steakhouse
- Perkins Family Restaurants
- Popeye's Chicken
- Princess Cruises
- Red Lobster
- Rubios Fresh Mexican Grill
- Ruby Tuesday
- Sonny's Franchise Co (Sonny's BBQ)
- Subway
- Sushi Shop

**Retail**

- Ahold USA
- Aldi Inc
- A&P Supermarkets
- BJ's Wholesale Club
- Costco
- Giants Foods
- Hannaford Bros
- HEB
- Price Chopper/Golub
- Roche Bros Supermarkets
- Roundy's
- Shaw's/Star Markets
- Smart & Final
- Stew Leonards
- Target
- Walmart
- Wegman's
- Weis Markets
- Whole Foods Market

**Distributors**

- C&S Wholesale Grocers
- SYSCO
- US Foodservice

*Source:* Diversified Business Communications.

**Exhibit 11**  Booth Spaces Under Consideration by Phillips

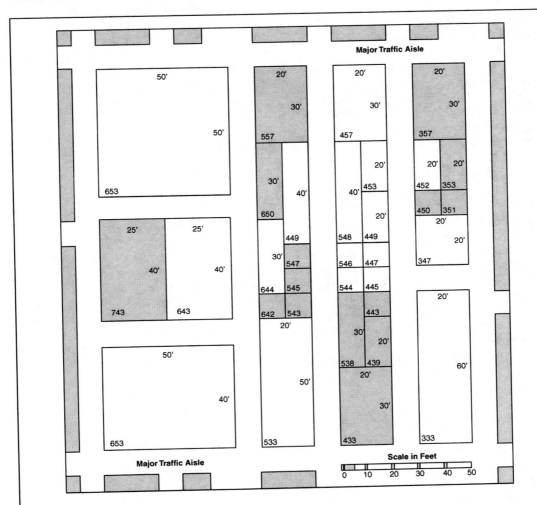

**Partial Floor Plan – Boston Convention & Exhibition Center**

- Space shown in the Exhibit represents about six percent of the total floor space of the International Boston Seafood Show.
- White-colored booths are available for lease. Grayed-out booths have already been leased.
- Booth types:
  - *Linear* or *inline* booth: only one side of the booth is exposed to the aisle and the booths are arranged in a series along a straight line (e.g., #546; 10 × 10 minimum)
  - *Peninsula*: exposed to the aisle on three sides (e.g., #533; 20 × 20 minimum)
  - *Island*: Exposed to the aisle on four sides (e.g., #633; 20 × 20 minimum)

*Source:* Diversified Business Communications.

# Phillips' Trade Show Strategy

Phillips exhibited at several trade shows and had recently built an exhibit that could be shipped to any show. It was modular and made up of multiple elements that could be assembled based on different booth sizes (from 600 to 2400 square feet) and shapes. The main visual theme was reminiscent of an old-fashioned seaport crab shack. The exhibit used large wooden pilings, wooden shelves for product displays and zinc lighting fixtures. However, the exhibit also included hi-tech details such as large flat-panel TVs (see Exhibit 12). The dominant colors reinforced Phillips' brand identity: red carpet and black for most of the furniture, and counters shaped as oversized cans of Phillips crab. The exhibit elements needed 250 square feet for set-up. For larger shows such as the IBSS, Phillips also included a kitchen where food samples were cooked. The kitchen area occupied 350 square feet and three staff members were needed to run it. Because of its large size and number of elements, it cost $9,000 each way to ship out and then return the exhibit to storage in Maryland. Exhibit 13 gives the breakdown of Phillips' cost estimates.

Phillips tended to limit pre-show marketing expenses and instead used its resources for the elaborate exhibit and prominent locations where its brand name and samples it served were used to draw visitors. In addition, during each show, it was Stockworth's policy to organize a VIP party where Phillips' staff could foster relationships with the most important accounts. VIP parties were usually held in the evening in one of the hotels adjoining the conference center. Typically, a VIP party cost $20,000 (including rental of venue, food, beverages, entertainment and decoration).

One of the main decisions that Stockworth and Birch would need to make was to determine the size of the exhibit and the number of staff that would travel to the show. Phillips wanted its exhibit to look busy but not be overly crowded. Decisions on space and staffing were based on the traffic expected. In the open floor area of the exhibit (total size minus kitchen and space taken by exhibit elements), an average density of four people per 100 square feet was comfortable and ideal for most shows. It was important to note that most show attendees would not spend time in the actual exhibit; most would walk the show aisles and grab food samples from the outward-facing displays. However, potential target customers would typically enter the exhibit and spend some time with staff members.

Based on past experience and industry averages, Phillips estimated that an average interaction with a potential customer lasted six minutes,[25] long enough for them to express some interest in the products, share contact information (attendance badges were scanned), and request some literature. It was Phillips' goal to have one Phillips staff member to accommodate every potential client who stopped in during the three days of the show. However, it was also important to realize that some potential customers might not have enough time or sufficient interest to stop at every exhibit in a show. Based on initial attendee registration data, Phillips estimated that 65 percent of its target attendees (retailers, distributors, and foodservice) were looking for products that matched Phillips' offerings. Among that group, 16 percent of them were looking for King Crab. Further, based on past trade show experience and the draw of the Phillips' brand, Phillips believed that over the duration of the show, it could typically attract and interact with 70 percent of these target customers who had an actual interest in Phillips' products. This was slightly better than the industry average of 57 percent.[26]

Although certain times of day were a bit busier than others, variations were not very large and customers tended to come throughout the duration of the show. However, Phillips believed that it was a good practice to have two extra staff members above the minimum needed in order to accommodate potential peaks, plus also have two more people whose sole job was to manage the displays, refresh the samples and attend to the general good state of the exhibit.

**Exhibit 12** Phillips' Trade Show Booth (overall layout and specific elements)

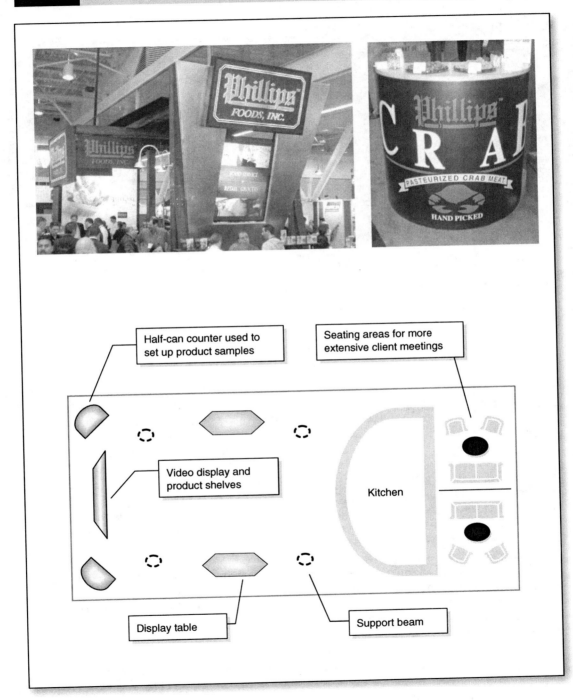

| Exhibit 13 | Phillips' Expected Trade Show Costs (excluding exhibit space) |
|---|---|

| | |
|---|---|
| **Exhibit design** | |
| Booth design (maintenance, updates, wear and tear) | $16,000 |
| Display materials (food to be cooked in kitchen) | $10,000 |
| Set-up & tear-down | $7,000 |
| **Transportation & freight** | $18,000 |
| **Show services** | $27,000 |
| **Travel & entertainment** | |
| Travel and lodging | $1,400 per staff |
| Meals & entertainment | $300 per staff |
| VIP party | $20,000 |
| **Advertising & promotion** | |
| Print advertising and mailing | $2,000 |
| Collateral material | $2,000 |

*Source:* Company.

## Phillips' Trade Advertising Strategy

Industry specific (trade) magazines were critical information sources in most major industries. These publications provided up-to-date business news, research, and insights to managers in key decision-making positions. Many managers tended to read several trade publications, often including vertical publications which were specific to their industry as well as horizontal publications which cut across industries but were specific to their job functions. For example, a human resources manager at a grocery retailer might read *Progressive Grocer* and *Employee Benefit News.*

In 2005, B2B magazine advertising spending reached $10.7 billion.[27] This amount of spending was a testimony to the value that vendors placed on this type of marketing communications. In addition to the magazines' articles, the advertisements were a valued source of information for readers. Forrester reported

that business decision makers rated industry-specific magazines as one of their most important information sources.[28] In fact, 44 percent of business decision-makers spent three or more hours reading trade magazines per week, a rate that had more than doubled from 2001. Importantly, 80 percent of the Forrester study's respondents agreed with the following statement about their advertising involvement: "When reading or interacting with industry-specific magazines, I find that I spend more time reading or thinking about the editorial content and product/service messages than with other general business media."

Birch believed that trade advertising was particularly effective in generating sales leads and reaching large audiences: "Trade shows may allow you to interact one-on-one with a few prospective buyers over three days, however trade ads reach broad audiences and can build your brand twelve months per year." During the six months of phase I of the launch, Birch had run a total of 12 full-page color ads (placed across four monthly foodservice publications). Birch was pleased by the results. In response to each ad, an average of 0.30 percent of the foodservice readers had called Phillips to inquire about more product information. This response rate was consistent with average response rates for trade magazines.[29] Based on these direct response leads, subsequent field sales meetings (2.7 on average) had yielded substantial sales for the product. Birch expected a similar response amongst retail and distributor audiences in phase II. He had identified three trade magazines that could potentially reach retailers and distributors (see Exhibit 14), and he felt that the two ads that had been developed for phase I could be used again for phase II (see Exhibit 15).

## Three Days Later

Three days had passed since the lunch with Stockworth, and Birch was still uncertain about what to do for phase II. He had reviewed the trade show information but was wondering if Stockworth's idea was the right thing for the retail launch. Stockworth had asked him to make a decision quickly because she wanted to offer the trade show opportunity to another product manager if Birch were to turn it down. Was the best strategy to focus his remaining budget on the March trade show or spread it across a series of trade advertisements? This was going to be a difficult choice. He knew how to evaluate advertising buys in magazines and he had a good sense of the potential return that these buys could generate. However, trade shows were another beast. Trade shows were large one-time expenses with hard-to-gage results. After supporting half of the cost of the trade show, would he have any money left for other marketing activities? Would he be able to reach enough buyers during the three days of the show? His instincts were telling him that he would be able to reach a larger audience through mass media. But what about actual sales leads and overall return on marketing expenditure? What was the most cost-efficient way to obtain sales leads and ultimately sales in the retail channels?

| Exhibit 14 | Trade Publications for Food Retailing Industry |
|---|---|

| Publication | Industry Focus | Monthly Circulation | Number of Issues per Year | Cost of 1 Full Page Color | Readers by Sector | | | Percent of Readers Involved in Seafood Buying |
|---|---|---|---|---|---|---|---|---|
| | | | | | Foodservice | Distribution/ Wholesaling | Retailing | |
| *Progressive Grocer* | Food retailing | 43,000 | 14 | $12,200 | n/a | 13% | 65% | 4% |
| *Seafood Business* | North American seafood industry | 15,000 | 12 | $4,500 | 32% | 37% | 21% | 90% |
| *Refrigerated and Frozen Food Retailer* | Food retailing | 12,000 | 11 | $4,400 | n/a | 16% | 78% | 35% |

*Source:* Data from SRDS (2007) and industry interviews.

**Exhibit 15** Creative for King Crab Advertising Campaign

SMASH.

SMASH HIT.

BREAK.

BREAKTHROUGH.

## CASE QUESTIONS

1. What should be the objectives for the sales promotions program for King Crab products?

2. Which trade promotions should Phillips Foods offer to make sure grocers stock King Crab products? Defend your choices.

3. Which consumer promotions should Phillips Foods use to attract retail grocery store customers to buy King Crab products? Explain your reasoning.

4. Trade promotions push products onto the shelves of retailers. Consumer promotions pull them through the channel. Describe an effective combination of both to launch the King Crab products to grocery stores and grocery store customers.

5. What quantitative and qualitative variables should be used as metrics to assess the success of the promotions program?

6. How much emphasis should the marketing team of Phillips Foods place on trade shows, relative to other promotional efforts? Defend your answer.

# Boots: Hair-Care Sales Promotion

By Pankaj Shandilya, under the supervision of Professors
Robert Fisher and Murray Bryant

In early November 2004, on a cold winter afternoon in Nottingham, England, Dave Robinson was planning his sales promotion strategy for a line of professional hair-care products at Boots. The professional hair-care line consisted primarily of shampoos, conditioners and styling products (gels, wax, mousse, etc.) developed in collaboration with United Kingdom's top celebrity hairdressers. Robinson's challenge was to select one of three promotional alternatives—get three for the price of two ("3 for 2"), receive a gift with purchase ("GWP"), and an on-pack coupon worth 50p[1]—for the Christmas season. He realized that the alternative he selected would have immediate effects on both costs and sales as well as long-term implications for the brands involved. His primary objective was to drive sales volumes and trade-up consumers from lower-value brands, while retaining or building brand equity.

## The Company

Boots, one of the best-known and respected retail names in the United Kingdom, provided health and beauty products and advice that enhanced personal well-being. The company owned global differentiated brands in the self-medication market such as Nurofen, Strepsils, and Clearasil. It employed around 75,000 people and operated in some 130 countries worldwide in 2004. Besides retailing, Boots had international sales and marketing operations and also developed and manufactured its own products.

### Early Days

John Boot, born in 1815, spent his early life as an agricultural laborer on local farms, where herbal remedies were popular with the laboring poor. John Boot's mother used herbs for healing, and he was familiar with the remedies. In 1849, Boot opened "The British and American Botanic Establishment" in Nottingham, hoping to provide physical comfort to the needy as well as a reasonable living for his family. However, after years of hard work and ill health, John Boot died in 1860, and his wife, Mary, took over management of the shop, with the help of her 10-year-old son, Jesse.

Jesse took sole control of the shop in 1877, and, in 1883, established it as a private company "Boot and Company Limited," with himself as chairman and managing director. He was determined to cut prices and asked customers to pay cash rather than offering them credit. Additionally, the company adopted its own logo (see Exhibit 1).

The company began to expand with more stores in Nottingham. In 1884, Boots opened its first store outside Nottingham in Sheffield. Jesse wanted the company to be fully self-contained so that he could

| **Exhibit 1** | First Logo Adapted in 1883 |
|---|---|

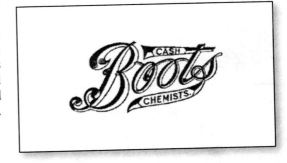

*Source:* Company files.

Version: (A) 2009–09–24

control not only prices but also quality. He wanted to be the "Largest, Best and Cheapest" and, by 1913, sales in the 560 Boots stores across the United Kingdom amounted to over £2.5 million a year.

## Post-War Regeneration and New Development, 1945–1968

A program of factory development in Nottingham was begun following the war, the major part being completed by 1953. This included a new power house, printing works, and, in 1959, a new pharmaceutical research building. In 1949, a factory for the manufacture of cosmetics was opened at Airdrie in Scotland. The company adopted a new black and white logo (see Exhibit 2).

## The Modern Era

Boots continued to develop product ranges, many of which became household names. "17" cosmetics, aimed at the teenage market, was launched in 1968. In 1969, the analgesic Ibuprofen was introduced and was launched as the OTC brand, Nurofen, in 1983.

With time, Boots also introduced new services. Boots Opticians, formed in 1987, became one of the United Kingdom's leading chain of opticians. Insurance services and initiatives in dentistry, chiropody, "Boots for Men" stores, and "Internet Services" were introduced in 1999. International expansion in operations was conducted by Boots Healthcare International (formed in

| Exhibit 2 | New Black and White Logo Adapted in 1949 |

Source: Company files.

1991), which exported healthcare products to more than 130 countries round the world. Boots Health and Beauty stores were established in Ireland, Thailand and Taiwan.

## United Kingdom Hair-Care Market

In the mid-'90s, the consumer market for hair-care comprised brands such as Pantene Pro-V and Head and Shoulders by Procter and Gamble, Alberto V05 by Alberto-Culver, and Elvive by L'Oreal. These national brands were widely available in supermarkets such as Tesco, Sainsbury's, and Morrisons, and at drug retailers including Boots and Superdrug. The sales of these brands were directly proportional to the amount of advertising expenditure.

In 2000, over 60 major brands of hair care products were available in the U.K. market. None of these brands had more than a nine percent market share. The overall market was expected to grow by between one percent and three percent per year for the next five years. However, severe price competition meant that volume would grow more quickly than value. In some instances, notably shampoo, the use of price promotions to secure volume would see an overall decline in prices of approximately one percent. Significant price discounting through promotional activity and competition from low-cost private label alternatives were expected to continue into the foreseeable future.

Boots saw an opportunity to be the retail hair-care expert and to offer the latest ranges. Additionally, Boots desired to build a new market by using celebrity endorsements to create awareness and create an emotional attachment between consumers and the brand. Celebrity hairdressers had their own branded products, but distribution was limited to their own salons. No celebrity-endorsed products were available in retail stores. Boots began to cultivate relationships, beginning 1996, with well-established hairdressers in the United Kingdom. In particular, they sought hairdressers located on High Street in London that had high consumer awareness and a premium positioning.

The relationship with Boots was lucrative for the hairdressers because it gave them access to a large percentage of U.K. consumers through Boots'

1,300 stores. Research indicated that over 85 percent of female adults in the United Kingdom visited a Boots store within the past week.

Boots developed a critical mass of professional hair-care brands. Some ranges were developed and launched in partnership whereas others (existing products) were launched through a beneficial supplier and retailer partnership (e.g., John Freida). Using its superior technological capabilities and significant production capacity, Boots worked with the celebrities to design formulations that were functionally better than existing brands. Under the agreement, Boots manufactured the products and paid a per-unit licensing fee for use of the celebrity's brand name.

In the more than five years since the first celebrity brand was introduced, Boots felt that it had not been able to sufficiently link its name with these products and hence missed on maximizing profitability. Boots and the brand owners (hairdressers), between them, currently undertook the management of the licensed brands. The brand owners, given their contacts with the media, specifically managed the public relation activity. Boots managed all other activities in consultation with the brand owners.

## The Professional Hair-Care Brands

Exhibit 3 gives details about associated celebrities and the brands. Exhibit 4 gives a summary of the brand's product ranges. Exhibit 5 shows their distribution and introduction dates.

**Exhibit 3** Brand Descriptions

| Name | Description | Specifics | Market Awareness |
|---|---|---|---|
| Charles Worthington[1] | One of the most influential and creative hairdressers. His name is synonymous with style, innovation, and success. | Five prestigious London[2] salons tending to more than 2,000 clients a week. Celebrity following on both sides of the Atlantic | Medium |
| John Frieda[3] | Entrepreneurial in spirit, global in impact, John Frieda's team of celebrity stylists (the "House of Experts") fuels the company's new product initiatives with the inside track on hot, new celebrity hair trends. | Three salons in London, two in New York and one in Los Angeles. The product range is targeted for specific hair types. | Strong |
| Nicky Clarke | A popular hairstylist to the stars from the film, television, fashion, and music industries. | Salons in London and Manchester | Medium |
| Umberto Giannini[4] | One of the most esteemed and influential names in British hairdressing. His company's philosophy is simple—creating sexy, contemporary catwalk looks within its salons alongside a salon performance range of hair-care products to recreate catwalk glamor at home. | Eight salons in the United Kingdom | Low |

*(Continued)*

**Exhibit 3**   (Continued)

| Name | Description | Specifics | Market Awareness |
|---|---|---|---|
| Toni & Guy[5] | "At Toni & Guy we create wearable, catwalk-led hairstyles for people who want easy-care, trend-setting hairstyles. Be an individual; be ahead in the style stakes with Toni and Guy." | 250 salons in the United Kingdom | Strong |
| Trevor Sorbie[6] | Trevor Sorbie, is considered as the showman of all hairdressers. His pioneering techniques and cuts—the Wedge, the Chop, and the Scrunch are now part of everyday salon parlance. | Two salons in the United Kingdom | Medium |
| Lee Stafford[7] | He is known for hairstyle and hair care. | Three salons in the United Kingdom | Low |

1. Charles Worthington home-page http://www.cwlondon.com
2. All references to London in United Kingdom
3. John Frieda home-page http://www.johnfrieda.com
4. Umberto Giannini home-page http://www.umbertogiannini.com/
5. Toni & Guy home-page  http://www.toniandguy.co.uk/start.html
6. Trevor Sorbie home-page  http://www.trevorsorbie.com/index.htm
7. Lee Stafford home-page  http://www.leestafford.com/

**Exhibit 4**   Product Categories

| Product Categories | Styling Products | | Brands | | | | | | |
|---|---|---|---|---|---|---|---|---|---|
| | | | Charles Worthington | John Frieda | Nicky Clarke | Umberto Giannini | Toni & Guy | Trevor Sorbie | Lee Stafford |
| | | | 1996 | 1996 | 1998 | 1999 | Jan-01 | Sep-01 | Sep-01 |
| | | Shampoo | X | X | X | X | X | X | X |
| | | Conditioner | X | X | X | X | X | X | X |
| | | Spray | X | X | X | X | X | X | X |
| | | Balm | X | | X | | X | X | X |
| | | Shaper | | | | | | | X |
| | | Mousse | X | X | X | X | X | X | X |
| | | Jelly | | | | X | | | |
| | | Glosser | X | X | | X | | X | |
| | | Hair cream | | X | | X | X | X | |
| | | Serum | X | X | | X | X | X | |
| | | Gel | X | X | | | | X | |
| | | Styling Foam | | X | | | | | |

| | | Brands | | | | | | |
|---|---|---|---|---|---|---|---|---|
| | | Charles Worthington | John Frieda | Nicky Clarke | Umberto Giannini | Toni & Guy | Trevor Sorbie | Lee Stafford |
| | | 1996 | 1996 | 1998 | 1999 | Jan-01 | Sep-01 | Sep-01 |
| | Hair lotion | | X | | | | | |
| | Putty | X | | | | | | |
| | Wax | X | | | X | X | | |
| | Makeover kit | X | | | | | | |
| | Hair powder | | | | X | | | |
| | Hair color | | | | X | | | |
| | Hair dryer | | | X | | | X | |
| | Hair brush | X | | | | X | X | |
| | Hair comb | | | | | X | X | |
| | Barber's clipper | | | | | | X | |
| | Straightning iron | | | | | | X | |
| | Heat rollers | | | | | X | | |
| | Hair band | | | | | | X | |
| | Face wash | X | | | | | X | |
| | Face scrub | X | | | | | | |
| Men's Range | Beard softener | | | | | | X | |
| | Shave oil | | | | | | X | |
| | Shave foam | X | | | | | | |
| | Shave gel | X | | | | | X | |
| | After shave | X | | | | | X | |
| | Shower gel | | | | | | X | |
| | Deodorant | X | | | | | X | |
| | Eau de toilette | | | | | | X | |
| | Hair wipe | | | | | | X | |
| | Lip balm | | | | | | | |

*Source:* Company files.

**Exhibit 5**  Distribution and Introduction Dates

| Brand | Introduced | Distribution |
|---|---|---|
| Charles Worthington | 1996 | Only Boots |
| John Frieda | 1996 | Widely Available |
| Nicky Clarke | 1998 | Widely Available |
| Umberto Giannini | 1999 | Widely Available |
| Toni & Guy | January 2001 | Only Boots |
| Trevor Sorbie | September 2001 | Only Boots |
| Lee Stafford | September 2001 | Only Boots |

**Exhibit 6**  Price Comparison Chart

| Category* | | | | | Price** | | | | |
|---|---|---|---|---|---|---|---|---|---|
| | Charles Worthington | John Frieda | Nicky Clarke | Umberto Giannini | Toni & Guy | Trevor Sorbie | Lee Stafford | Pantene | L'Oreal |
| Shampoo | 1.7–2.2 | 1.4–2.5 | 1.6 | 1.6 | 1.5–2.0 | 2.0 | 1.6 | | 0.5 |
| Conditioner | 1.7–3.3 | 1.7–2.5 | 1.8 | 1.8 | 2.0 | 2.0 | 1.6 | | 0.5 |
| Gel | 3.30 | 2.43 | | | | 3.33 | | 1.86 | |
| Mousse | 2.0–3.5 | 1.8–2.5 | | 2.3–3.0 | 2.2–2.4 | 1.8–2.0 | | 1.86 | 1.4–1.8 |
| Hair-spray | 1.9–3.5 | 1.3–6.5 | | 2.7–7.6 | 2.0–4.0 | 1.5–4.0 | 2.5 | 1.12–1.90 | |
| Wax | 9.0–11.0 | | | 5.0–10.0 | 10.0 | | | | |
| Serum | 9.2–11.0 | 11.4–15.6 | | 12.0 | 14.0–26.7 | 12.0–21.7 | | | |
| Hair Brush | 4.8–8.5 | | | | 2.8–8.5 | 2.3–8.0 | | | 7.0 |

*All products are normally available in 250 ml sizes. Their smaller Take-Away versions are normally 75 ml.

**All prices are in British pounds and per 100 ml unless otherwise stated. These prices are only applicable at Boots stores. Within a product category the prices vary because of their formulations.

## The Major Competitors (Mass-Market Brands)

### Procter & Gamble

Swiss drug company Hoffman-La Roche developed Pantene as a shampoo and launched it in Europe in 1947. The name "Pantene" refers to the product's origins, from "Panthenol," which is another name for pro-vitamin B-5. Richardson-Vicks acquired Pantene in 1983, by which time Pantene had developed into a fragmented business with more than 100 products, sold mainly in department stores and salons.

Procter & Gamble acquired Richardson-Vicks in 1985, and in 1991, the product was reformulated as the Pantene Pro-V (Pro-Vitamin) line and rolled out as a global brand. By 1995, it became the best-selling hair-care brand in the world with a lineup that included shampoos, conditioners, and styling products for all different hair types. The consumer awareness for Pantene was very high, and the brand was widely available. It held a 8.4 percent share of the U.K. hair care market in 2001.

Apart from Pantene, Procter & Gamble offered other complete ranges of hair-care brands including Clairol, Head & Shoulders, Daily Defense, PERT plus, and Herbal Essences.

## Alberto-Culver (United Kingdom)[2]

Over 60 years, beginning in 1955, Alberto Culver grew into a multibillion-dollar company. The company's head office was located in Illinois, but its products were sold globally. Alberto-Culver's acquisition of Sally Beauty Company in 1969 has grown from a handful of franchised stores to over 2,000 store locations today in United States, United Kingdom (150), Canada, Germany, and Japan. The company's most famous claim to fame was when, in 1971, its founder, Leonard Lavin, forced television networks to abandon their 60-second commercials with the introduction of 30-second ones. In the recent past, the company, in order to increase its product base, has globally acquired diverse firms.

Alberto-Culver offered a variety of products for hair-care, skin-care and home-care. Some of its top brands included St. Ives, V05, Consort hair care for men, and FDS, etc. Alberto-Culver's hair-care range offered a broad assortment of shampoos, conditioners, and styling agents.

## L'Oréal

L'Oréal began in 1907 when a young French Chemist, Eugene Schueller, developed an innovative hair-color formula. He called his new perfectly safe hair dye "Auréole." In 1909, he registered the company, the "Société Française de Teintures Inoffensives pour Cheveux," the future L'Oréal. The company started exporting its products as early as 1912 when they could be found in Italy, Austria and Holland. A few years later, via agents and consignments, they were distributed in the United States, South America, Russia, and the Far East. Today the group is present worldwide through its subsidiaries and agents.

L'Oréal's nearly century-old history was marked with major successes, with landmark products that offered women new ways and means to enhance beauty. The group marketed over 500 brands and more than 2,000 products in all sectors of the beauty business: hair color, permanents, styling aids, body and skincare, cleansers, and fragrances. These products were found in all distribution channels, from hair salons and perfumeries, to hyper-super markets, health/beauty outlets and direct mail. Communications became the other key in the company's history. Back when advertising was still in its infancy, L'Oréal commissioned promotional posters from graphic artists like Colin, Loupot, and Savignac to publicize the company's products. The product range consisted of shampoos, conditioner, and styling products. It held a five percent share of the U.K. hair care market in 2001.

## Hair-Care Product Retailers

Most major retailers carried a variety of professional and mass market hair-care brands. The major competitors in the supermarket segment were Tesco, Sainsbury's and Morrisons. Tesco was the largest supermarket chain in the United Kingdom with more than 1,800 stores and 45,000 employees. Sainsbury's was the second largest with 700 stores. Both Tesco and Sainsbury's offered a wide product assortment that included traditional supermarket items and online shopping, as well as CDs, books, DVDs, wine, flowers and gifts, kitchen appliances, banking services, and mobile phones. Morrisons had 400 stores and prided itself on providing quality products at the same low price across all of its U.K. stores. Morrisons had taken over Safeway in the United Kingdom in 2004.

A second major hair-care competitor was Superdrug. Started in 1966, Superdrug had grown to become one of the largest health and beauty retailers, with almost 700 stores in the United Kingdom. The company's value offering was that of a value retailer with a wide assortment of around 10,000 products, ranging from essentials to premium products. Superdrug stores layout, lighting, and color, allowed customers to move at their own pace in an attractive setting, thus providing a welcoming and relaxing environment.

Superdrug launched hundreds of private label products each year. Working with its suppliers, Superdrug identified trends (including catwalk fashion) and transformed them into an affordable reality. More than 25 percent of the company's stores featured a pharmacy.

## Consumers

Research indicated that consumers were not very brand loyal for a variety of reasons. First, there was a general belief by U.K. consumers that changing shampoo brands produced better results than continually using a single brand. Second, trends in buying behavior led to changing preferences. Whereas in the '70s consumers wanted shampoos that were gentle, the '80s saw a greater emphasis on detangling, and in the '90s, shiny hair became more important. Third, it was difficult for consumers to identify meaningful differences between the various brands available in any given store. Consumers had a large number of choices that varied not only on brand name, but also packaging, advertising, price, ingredients, consistency, fragrance, and so forth.

Consumers who purchased professional brands were largely fashion-conscious women in the 20–35 age category. These purchasers tended to be more affluent than buyers of mass-market brands. However, most Boots consumers bought both basic and premium brands. In some cases, the female head of household would buy basic products for her kids and husband, and premium for herself. Other customers bought basic products for everyday use and premium products for special occasions such as weekends or social outings. These customers used premium brands as a "treat" when consumers wanted to look and feel their best.

## The Decision

Current Boots consumers and existing purchasers of mass-market brands were the primary target for the promotion, which was to run for one month starting December 1st. Due to efficiency considerations and ongoing management of stock, Boots was not considering any variation in product-sizes because of the added cost and complexity involved. No media advertising budget was allocated for this promotion, although it would be highlighted in flyers distributed by the store. Stock would be placed in a dedicated end of aisle or mid-aisle display during the promotional period. There would also be signage within the store to promote the offer, and approximately 400 Boots stores would include signage visible on the exterior of the store.

Average bottle size (shampoo/conditioner) was 250 milliliters (ml)—with an average pre-promotional price of £3.99. Industry average retail margins on premium brands averaged 40 percent. Mass-market brands had an average retail price of £2, with retailer margins of approximately 25 percent. The manufacturer's typical margin was between eight percent to 12 percent on their cost for both types of products.

The following alternatives were being considered.

### "3 for 2"

This offer would enable consumers to buy two hair-care items at regular price and receive one free. Customers could combine any three items they liked (e.g., shampoo, conditioner, and styling gel, etc.), but the three items had to be the same brand. The free item would be the one that was the least expensive of the three items selected by the shopper. An interesting aspect of this promotion is that most competitors did not yet have the technology at point of sale to imitate this promotion. They could implement only a 3-for-2 offer when the prices for the three items were the same.

Robinson estimated that sales per day would increase to 300 percent of pre-promotion sales during the deal period. In other words, if 100 units of hair-care product were sold per day before the promotion, 300 bottles would be sold per day during the promotion (including the free bottles). Approximately 60 percent of these sales would be to customers who would not otherwise have purchased a hair-care product from Boots during the promotional period.

### GWP (Gift With Purchase)

A GWP was an offer in which customers were given a product sample along with a regular purchase. For example, a sample size of conditioner would be packaged with a regular bottle of shampoo. An existing sample product would be used to avoid the need to design and produce additional packaging. Adding the sample would cost approximately 90p per unit for the product plus 3p per unit to secure the sample to the featured product. Robinson expected that sales during the promotional period would be 170 percent of sales that would have occurred without the promotion. He estimated that 40 percent of sales would be to Boots shoppers that would not have otherwise purchased a hair-care product from Boots during the promotional period.

### On-Pack Coupon (50p off)

The 50p off option was a more conservative approach to promoting the brands. All customers would be able to redeem the coupon during their current store visit. Robinson estimated that sales would increase to 150 percent of non-promotion sales because December would be a heavy promotional period for mass market brands. Also, most competitors tended to use price discounts or GWP's as their promotional method. Fifty percent of sales would come from Boots customers who would not have otherwise purchased a hair-care product within the promotional period.

Under all three promotional tactics, the vast majority of sales would be for shampoo, conditioners, and gels. Based on market research, Robinson expected low levels of stockpiling because of the promotions.

## Conclusion

Boots' aim was to secure market leadership in the United Kingdom in the hair-care segment. The celebrity hair-care brands were clearly an important component of their strategy. Competitors could not easily copy their strategy because Boots had contracts with some of the most prestigious salon brands in the United Kingdom. He wanted to ensure that the promotions were profitable, but the importance of maintaining and enhancing the professional hair-care brands could not be understated.

## CASE QUESTIONS

1.  Beyond coupons, premiums, and bonus packs, what other consumer promotions programs are available to Boots?

2.  Many women purchase the lower-end Boots products for the rest of their families and the higher-end products for themselves. Others buy the high-end product as a "treat" for special occasions. Given these two situations, which consumer promotion is most advisable? Why?

3.  If the ultimate goal is to maintain brand prestige, even when brand parity exists, which consumer promotions program is most advisable? Which is least advisable? Why?

4.  Typically, of the four types of consumers—promotion-prone, price-sensitive, brand-loyal, and preferred-brand—a company will target preferred-brand consumers with promotions. Is this the ideal course of action for Boots? Why or why not?

# CHAPTER 9

# Personal Selling

The essence of customer service takes place in personal selling situations. An effective salesperson may at times be a counselor, advisor, consultant, and even an advocate for the customers he or she serves. Retail and business-to-business selling activities are vital functions that bring sales to the company.

## Retail Selling

Retail sales jobs range from simple cashier-type positions to much more intricate and personal contacts with customers. The primary forms of retail sales are order taker, commission-based, and service sales. An order taker works near the cash register and may stock shelves, answer questions, and finalize sales. Commission sales are normally jobs in which employees sell bigger-ticket items. Many times, the salesperson receives a base salary plus all commissions earned. A service salesperson provides the services offered by the company. Various forms include financial services as well as personal services. Varying degrees of emphasis are placed on customer acquisition in these jobs.

## The Business-to-Business Selling Function

Missionary salespeople make contact with businesses to deliver samples, leave information, and make sure things are in order. Telemarketers either make calls to potential customers (outbound) or receive calls from prospective customers (inbound). Field salespeople call on businesses, following a relatively standard series of steps related to customer acquisition.

The first step in customer acquisition is producing or generating leads. The sales staff obtains them from customer referrals, vendor referrals, channel referrals, networking, and various directories. They are identified by the marketing department through the application of the company's database, from inquiries, from sales promotions feedback, and at trade shows.

Leads are then qualified based on the potential income the company might generate and the probability of acquiring the prospect as a customer. The leads with high scores on both aspects (income and odds of acquisition) receive the greatest attention. Others merit lesser amounts of effort.

The third step in selling to new customers, knowledge acquisition, begins with gathering the information needed to make an effective sales presentation. Key information comes from the prospect's business, customers, and needs; from purchase criteria used by the prospect; the level of satisfaction with a current vendor; risk factors and switching costs that would accompany changing suppliers; and the names of the prospect's decision makers and influencers.

Fourth, the actual sales presentation will be prepared. A sales call can be used to gather information, to discuss bid specifications, to answer questions, or to close the deal with a final pitch or offer. A stimulus-response sales presentation uses specific statements (stimuli) to elicit specific responses from customers, similar to a canned sales pitch. Telemarketers, retail salesclerks, and new sales reps often rely on this method. A need-satisfaction presentation places emphasis on discovering a customer's needs and then providing quality solutions to meet those needs. A problem-solution sales approach requires employees from the selling organization to analyze a buyer's operations, usually by deploying a team of experts from various departments. The mission-sharing sales approach combines the efforts of two organizations into one shared mission and can lead to the sharing of resources to achieve common objectives, similar to a joint venture.

The fifth step of a sales presentation, overcoming objectives, takes several forms. The head-on approach means that the salesperson handles any objections directly. The indirect denial method allows the salesperson to never say the customer is wrong but, rather, to sympathize and then provide correct information. A compensation method allows the customer to raise an objection. The salesperson responds with a "yes . . . but" followed by an explanation of the product's benefits that allays the objection. The "feel, felt, found" method is normally directed at anxious customers. The salesperson relates to the experience and explains how the product calms those fears and makes the purchaser feel less nervous. A boomerang approach turns the objection into the reason a person should make the purchase. In essence, someone who says, "I can't afford this," is told, "You can't afford *not* to buy this."

Closing the sale, the sixth part of a sales presentation, can be difficult for the salesperson, who may be told "No." Methods used to close sales vary. A trial close means the salesperson solicits feedback that provides a clue about how the client will respond without directly asking for the sale. A direct close is an outright request for the sale. Using a continuous-yes close allows the salesperson to ask a series of questions that will receive responses of "Yes" before finally asking for the sale. The salesperson may also simply assume the customer wishes to make a purchase and go directly on to the final details of the sale.

The follow-up is the final crucial element of an effective sales presentation. Keeping a customer happy following the purchases often leads to repeat business and customer loyalty. Motivating salespeople to follow up sales can be difficult. The marketing manager should make sure it occurs through incentives, role modeling of successful salespeople, and feedback provided during the performance appraisal process.

## Relationship Selling

Relationship selling turns initial transactions into stronger partnerships over time. When the salesperson fosters a positive purchasing experience, commitment begins to grow. Strong relationships create advantages for both the seller and the buyer.

# ▨  International Personal Selling

Language, slang, culture, methods of introduction, eye contact, body language, gestures, physical distance, giving and receiving gifts, the use of business cards, table manners, and directness in tone constitute some of the challenges associated with selling in international markets. A cultural assimilator helps with the training of salespeople traveling to foreign lands. Motives vary by country, which means the company's compensation system may require some adjustment as well.

# ▨  Managing a Sales Force

Effectively managing a sales department relies on a unique combination of activities and relationships, with members of the department and with other departments. Five key aspects of sales for management are (1) recruiting and selection, (2) training, (3) compensation, (4) motivational programs, and (5) performance evaluation. Each should be geared to assisting members of the sales force in achieving their goals.

Recruiting and selection begins with basic selection criteria such as the applicant's level of education, degree of experience, personality and personal characteristics, and all issues associated with legal compliance. Then those involved in the selection process assess each individual's aptitudes and talents, skill levels for individual tasks, and personal traits. Aptitude refers to natural ability, verbal intelligence, mathematical ability, and reasoning skills. Skill levels include product knowledge, interpersonal communication skills, and presentation skills. Personal traits make individuals unique and should be matched with the type of sales position being offered.

Sales training takes place on and off the job. The on-the-job training methods of demonstration and sink-or-swim are used in actual selling situations. Off-the-job training can be delivered by providing simulations of sales calls or film and classroom exercises and through interactions with professional trainers.

Sales force compensation consists of a salary, commissions, salary-plus-commission systems, and the use of bonuses. Benefit packages help the company in the areas of recruiting new employees and retaining successful salespeople. Benefits are costly and should be carefully managed. The pay system should be perceived as being fair, should create opportunities to succeed, and should be helpful in creating long-term relationships with the company and with the company's customers.

Motivation programs are made up of financial and nonfinancial incentives. Financial incentives include promotion and pay-raise systems as well as contests providing quality prizes. Nonfinancial incentives may be delivered in the form of recognition, praise, and special privileges to high performers.

Performance evaluation starts with the development of quality criteria. These include input measures and output measures. Input measures consist of presales activities, selling activities, postselling activities, and nonselling activities. Output measures are the actual results obtained, such as capturing accounts and generating orders. Financial measures of performance include the sales volume generated by the salesperson, gross margin on those sales, and the contribution margin produced by each salesperson. Careful consideration will be given to how these items are measured and the potential organizational and environmental factors that influence sales performance. Organizational factors include the company's culture and its incentive system. Environmental factors range from actions by competitors to natural disasters and shifting economic conditions.

A performance appraisal meeting commences with notice of the meeting to allow the salesperson time to prepare. At the meeting, the individual should be made comfortable. The meeting should start with a discussion of the person's accomplishments and strong points. Next, weaknesses and problem areas are identified. Then, goals can be set for the next evaluation period.

Personal selling has been called the "last 3 feet" of the marketing function. The 3 feet represent the distance between a customer and a sales clerk in a retail store and the distance between a salesperson and a business-to-business prospect across a desk. It is the face-to-face contact between a company and its most important constituent—the company's prospective and ongoing customers. Quality customer service should be a primary area of concern for every marketing manager from the first-line supervisor to the company's CEO.

# ▨ The Cases

## Global Source Healthcare: Allocating Sales Resources

Global Source Healthcare provides domestic and international staffing services to healthcare facilities. The company charges fees for placing healthcare workers with various organizations. The environment for these services became increasing volatile due to increasing competition, consolidation of healthcare organizations, fluctuations in demand for healthcare workers based on shifting economic conditions, and suspicion of the companies providing the services because of the actions of a few unscrupulous organizations. Shamail Siddiqi, the founder and CEO of Global Source Healthcare, was forced to make decisions regarding his company's sales activities. He could emphasize the acquisition of new accounts or seek to provide additional services to existing accounts. His domestic staffing accounts had been designed to generate cash flow and stability but instead began consuming time and resources. Part of the decision to be made included the choice of focusing on domestic health organizations, international healthcare companies, or a balance between the two.

## Spectrum Brands, Inc.—The Sales Force Dilemma

The Rayovac Corporation, which had primarily focused on batteries, grew and expanded through the acquisition of other companies, leading to the new company name Spectrum. Product lines now include batteries (Rayovac), shaving and grooming products (Remington), lawn and garden (Nu-Grow and Spectrum), and the specialty pet supply market (Tetra). The issue facing Bob Falconi, vice-president of sales and marketing, was how to manage the sales force. Various options included a separate sales force for each brand, a merged sales force, or greater utilization of distributors to conduct selling activities. Falconi recognized the advantages and disadvantages of each approach, knowing that the ultimate goal was to build and maintain each brand but also to create synergies and potential cross-selling opportunities for retailers and consumers.

## BioMed Co., Ltd.: Designing a New Sales Compensation Plan

BioMed's parent company, Thai Drugs, was dissatisfied with sales by the brand. The leaders at Thai Drugs were considering dropping the line if sales and profitability figures were not improved. Ponlerd Chiemchanya was charged with finding ways to improve the division's numbers. The strategic decision was made to reduce the company's target market by one-third. Instead of selling to hospitals, pharmacies/drug stores, and doctor's clinics, only the latter two would receive attention.

Further, while the company offered about 100 products, to achieve profitability the new focus would be to emphasize only 15 to 20 products, seeking larger orders by providing significant discounts. The role of salesperson would also change. Instead of primarily traveling around to take orders, sales representatives were charged with making effective sales presentations about the main products to be sold. Differences in training, methods of compensation, and performance appraisals would likely occur. Ponlerd knew that if these tactics failed, the company was at risk—as well as his own personal career.

## Global Source Healthcare: Allocating Sales Resources

*By Shamail Siddiqi, under the supervision of Professor Donald W. Barclay*

It was the summer of 2003, just over a year since Global Source Healthcare (Global Source) became operational. Shamail Siddiqi, the company's founder and chief executive officer (CEO), was at his desk in the company's New York City office, thinking about how rapidly the healthcare staffing industry had changed over the past year. He was trying to figure out how the industry had gone from explosive growth to consolidation in such a short period of time, and what the implications were for Global Source. His most immediate concern was a growing trend among his company's client hospitals to rationalize their outsourced nursing recruitment by drastically cutting the number of staffing vendors, and slashing external recruitment budgets.

Over the past year, Global Source's strategy had been to capture as much market share as possible. The company had acquired a few lucrative contracts with both small and large hospitals. However, an increasing number of hospitals were putting new contracts on hold, and because of their rationalizing, the window of opportunity to acquire new clients was rapidly diminishing. After the next few months, it might not be possible for Global Source to acquire new contracts for a long period of time. Also, given the limited resources of the company, existing contracts were being serviced at a moderate level. With hospitals now choosing to retain only the best-performing vendors, there was an immediate need to increase the level of service for existing clients.

Siddiqi had exhausted all options to raise additional financing. Given the company's current financial situation, it would be impossible to hire additional sales personnel. Siddiqi wondered how he should allocate the company's sales efforts in order to meet at least modest growth targets. He wanted to make sure that the company was resilient enough to get through the difficult times ahead.

## Healthcare Staffing

Healthcare staffing involved the recruitment and placement of clinicians at healthcare facilities, including nursing staff, such as Registered Nurses (RNs), and Licensed Practical Nurses (LPNs), as well as allied healthcare professionals, such as occupational and speech therapists. Healthcare staff could be placed on a temporary or permanent basis.

Healthcare staffing in the United States represented a tremendous outsourcing opportunity. Nurses accounted for 25 percent of total hospital expenditure. Acute-care hospitals spent approximately $60 billion on RN staffing in 2001. Hospital expenditure on RN staffing was projected to grow at 10 percent per year. Ninety percent of these funds were spent on hiring full-time employees, while 10 percent was outsourced to staffing companies. The healthcare staffing market had been growing at a robust rate of 20 percent per year for the last several years.

Version: (A) 2009–09–24

The most common temporary staffing alternatives available to hospital administrators were *per diem staffing* and *travel staffing*. Per diem staffing composed 75 percent of the temporary staffing market, while the travel staffing segment comprised 25 percent. Per Diem staffing involved placement of locally based healthcare professionals on very short-term assignments, often for daily shift work. For example, an unexpected absence of a permanent employee, or a sudden rise in emergency room patients, would create a need for per diem staffing. Per diem staffing often involved little advanced notice by the client, and therefore, it required a sizable database of local healthcare personnel.

Travel staffing involved placement of healthcare personnel on a contracted, fixed-term basis. Travel staff provided a long-term solution to a staff shortage, presented hospitals and other healthcare facilities with a pool of potential full-time job candidates and enabled healthcare facilities to provide their patients with continuity of care. Assignments could run from several weeks to one year, but were typically 13 weeks long. The healthcare professional temporarily relocated to the geographic area of the assignment. The staffing company generally was responsible for providing travel staff with customary employment benefits and for coordinating travel and housing arrangements. Exhibit 1 provides a summary of the healthcare staffing market.

The demand for healthcare staffing was influenced by demographic drivers and the trend towards outsourcing. While the overall economy had experienced a considerable slowdown over the past two years, healthcare staffing had been enjoying double-digit growth as a result of favorable industry dynamics:

- Increasing demand for healthcare services as a result of the aging population
- A severe shortage of nursing staff due to a large number of nurses retiring and not enough new nurses entering the profession
- Increased outsourcing of staffing services by hospitals to reduce the costs associated with permanent staff

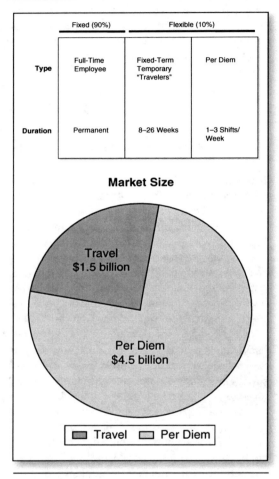

**Exhibit 1** Temporary Staffing Market

*Source:* Company files.

- Seasonality in the demand for healthcare services
- New legislation requiring minimum nurse-to-patient ratios

Healthcare staffing was a supply-driven business. The opportunity existed in the massive unmet demand for healthcare personnel. Even as numerous staffing companies were entering the industry, the staffing situation for healthcare facilities was not improving. Two-thirds of all job orders continued to be left unfulfilled, because every staffing company was competing for the same domestic pool of nurses, therapists and other allied health professionals. This pool was not just limited, but diminishing. The key to tapping the potential of this industry was not to compete for the same source of supply as everyone else, but to explore and develop alternative sources of healthcare personnel, perhaps internationally.

## Healthcare Clients

Acute-care facilities, that is facilities that provide critical care in specialty units, such as surgery, emergency room and cardio-thorasic, were often faced with persistent staff shortages. These shortages were concentrated in major urban and metropolitan areas.

There were two types of acute-care hospitals in the United States: independent facilities, and facilities that were part of large healthcare networks. While some of these were not-for-profit, most were run on a for-profit basis. Small- and medium-sized independent facilities (50 to 500 beds) typically had few layers of management. It was possible to develop relationships at higher levels in the organization at such facilities, typically with the vice-president of nursing, or the director of human resources. While the sales cycle for such facilities was fairly short (about one to three months), the staff requirements could be limited. Also, smaller hospitals had more restrictive budgets and were more price-sensitive. Pricing was usually negotiated aggressively, and contracts were awarded based largely on the lowest billing rates.

Larger healthcare facilities (more than 500 beds) could be fairly bureaucratic, and the sales cycles could be lengthy, sometimes as long as six to 12 months. The most time was typically spent during the contract negotiation phase since many of these facilities had an extensive contract review process. Relationships for domestic staffing were typically established at the Nurse Recruiter level. Relationships for international recruitment could be established with VP-level personnel, even though the initial point of contact was typically the Nurse Recruiter or a mid-level HR manager. Some large hospitals had entire departments dedicated to international personnel and used a combination of in-house and outsourced recruitment. Larger hospitals had a much greater need for international personnel, and typically allocated a substantial budget to this resource. They typically assigned more weight to the staffing company's track record and ability to deliver, rather than awarding contracts based solely on pricing.

There were a number of large healthcare corporations in the United States, some owning several hundred hospitals nationwide. Many of these large networks used a request for proposals (RFP) process to award contracts for staffing services. A single network contract could increase the client base dramatically, and expand the staffing company's reach nationwide. However, these RFPs were typically awarded through an extensive process, and required an established track record. So far, Global Source had been unsuccessful in meeting the criteria to obtain a contract through an RFP process.

## The Company

Global Source was a comprehensive healthcare staffing company providing both domestic and international staffing services. Shamail Siddiqi's vision for the company was to continue to diversify its services and eventually position Global Source as the one-stop shop for every hospital's outsourcing needs.

Shamail Siddiqi had graduated from the HBA program at the Richard Ivey School of Business, London, Ontario, Canada in 1999. He started his career working as an equity trader for Goldman Sachs. Siddiqi had always aspired to be an entrepreneur and after spending three years at Goldman, he decided to leave his job and start Global Source to tap what he saw as a tremendous outsourcing opportunity in healthcare. He started the business with his wife, Tania Siddiqi, who had a background in recruitment. Although roles were very fluid in the new company, Siddiqi decided to focus on sales and marketing, while Tania would focus on the recruitment side of the business.

By targeting international markets and developing a steady stream of international healthcare personnel, Global Source was able to fulfill unmet demand and provide a long-term solution to hospitals for their staff shortages. Siddiqi's initial strategy for the company had been to focus on international recruitment to supply domestic hospitals and to stay out of the domestic staffing market altogether. However, he had not been able to raise enough capital when he started the company a year ago. The cash flow shortage had forced him to enter both markets simultaneously. The domestic staffing business was meant to generate quick cash flow to support the primary international recruitment business.

Global Source's clients were mainly located in the Northeast, mostly in New York. They consisted of both small and large hospitals. Eighty percent of revenue was derived from the top three accounts, all of which were large New York hospitals. Currently, most client relationships were either for international recruitment or domestic staffing. Only a handful of clients were utilizing Global Source's complete staffing services comprising both domestic and international staffing.

## Domestic Travel Staffing

Competition to recruit U.S. nurses was fierce, and nurse pay rates and benefits had been rising sharply. As a result, staffing company margins were under pressure. Global Source's typical margin for travel staffing was 10 to 15 percent, which translated into an average net profit of $4,000 for every 13-week assignment. Since invoicing was done on a biweekly basis, and most healthcare facilities made payments within 30 to 60 days, this business helped generate cash flow for the company.

The travel staffing business had become very saturated. Global Source did not have a distinct competitive advantage in domestic travel staffing. It had only been able to obtain travel staffing contracts by offering discounted billing rates, or by

offering travel staffing as part of a complete staffing solution, including both international and domestic staffing.

## International Recruitment

There were many fewer companies offering international recruitment because this process required considerable expertise and resources. Most healthcare facilities were very keen to seek out companies that could successfully deliver international nurses.

International recruitment involved the recruitment of foreign nurses from countries such as the United Kingdom, Australia, New Zealand, Philippines, and India for placement in U.S. hospitals. Besides immigration, foreign nurses had to complete an extensive credentialing process. They had to appear for an intensive international examination administered by the Commission on Graduates of Foreign Nursing Schools (CGFNS), have their degrees and other certifications authenticated by the CGFNS, and apply for a license in the state in which they intended to practice. Some tasks could be completed concurrently with immigration processing, while others, like CGFNS certification, had to be completed prior to applying for immigration. The process was highly complex and required a considerable amount of expertise on the part of the staffing company. The turnaround time varied between 10 and 14 months. The key was effective planning to ensure that a large number of nurses were in the pipeline at different stages of processing to ensure a steady revenue stream after the initial lag. The average cost of processing each international nurse was $7,000, but could vary depending on country of origin and the volume.

There were different international recruitment models being used by different companies. Global Source was using a flat-fee model, placing international nurses on a permanent basis with a healthcare facility on a two- to three-year employment contract. The flat fee varied between $15,000 and $20,000 per candidate. Margins were about

50 to 60 percent. Some contracts allowed Global Source to collect half the payment from the healthcare facility after final selection of the candidate (three to four months after the process was initiated), and the remainder after the candidate arrived in the United States. This schedule enabled Global Source to recover the cost of processing the candidate at the beginning of the process and thus was very favorable in terms of cash flow. However, some hospitals did not pay any fees up front, and the entire amount was invoiced after the candidate arrived in the United States.

## Sourcing International Nurses

Global Source established its international recruitment infrastructure through strategic alliances with local companies around the globe. This strategy enabled Global Source to rapidly build up its international recruitment capability in various countries, including United Kingdom, Canada, Philippines, Australia, and New Zealand.

As a result of extensive recruitment by U.S. hospitals and staffing companies, countries like the United Kingdom, Philippines and South Africa were now facing their own nursing shortages. As a result, it was becoming increasingly competitive to recruit in these markets, and some ethical questions were being raised about further depleting these countries of already scarce healthcare staff. The European Union had recently banned the recruitment of nurses from South Africa.

The industry was seeking a new recruiting market, and the answer was India. India was one of the few countries in the world with an abundant supply of qualified nurses. Furthermore, the market was still largely untapped. Many large companies had tried to recruit in this market but failed since they did not have an understanding of local dynamics. Global Source had just established a strategic alliance with a CGFNS test-preparation company in Bangalore to source Indian nurses. Siddiqi knew that not only would this alliance establish a reliable supply of international nurses,

but it would provide him and his sales team with a much needed edge in the sales process. The prospect of Indian nurses had created a lot of buzz in the industry, and hospitals were very eager to explore this source.

## Sales Strategy

The sales strategy involved presenting Global Source to a potential client as an international recruitment specialist, and then offering domestic travel staffing as an add-on service to complete the total staffing solution.

Global Source could differentiate itself in the international recruitment market by offering a consistent supply of international nurses, especially from India. This positioning also enabled the sales staff to approach a prospect at a higher level in the organization. Even when a different person at the facility was responsible for domestic staffing, being referred by a senior person made the sales process much easier. At the contract negotiation stage, discounted billing rates for domestic travel staff were offered if the hospital signed both international and domestic staffing contracts.

While Siddiqi felt that this strategy was effective, it had only been intermittently successful. The main issue was that often different people, or even different departments, were responsible for international and domestic staffing. The people responsible for international staffing had nothing to gain by negotiating better billing rates for domestic staff. Furthermore, while Global Source wanted to position itself as a comprehensive staffing provider, most hospitals were accustomed to dealing with separate companies for international and domestic staffing. They did not seem comfortable dealing with one company for both, which made it very difficult to obtain domestic travel staffing contracts without offering deep discounts.

## Sales Process

While salespeople generated some prospects by means of referrals and personal relationships, most prospects were approached by means of cold calling from a nationwide database of healthcare facilities. Sales personnel were always trying to find inroads to potential clients. Trade shows provided a great vehicle for meeting potential clients.

Every contact with a prospect was recorded in the company's contact management software. The sales process started with an initial call to qualify the prospect. The salesperson acquired basic information about the hospital, such as size, whether it was private or public, and whether it was unionized. Only non-unionized hospitals with more than 100 beds were qualified. Private hospitals usually made better prospects, however this was not always the case. The most important purpose of this call was to determine the possible points of contact. The next step was to contact the relevant person in the organization, briefly introduce Global Source and its services, and ask permission to mail or e-mail information about the company's services. Exhibits 2 and 3 show some of the brochures that were mailed to clients.

A few days after the brochure was sent, the salesperson made a follow-up call to make sure the prospect had received the brochure, and used this opportunity to ask about the hospital's needs and describe how Global Source could fulfill those needs better than its competitors. If the prospect was interested, pricing often came up in this conversation. The salesperson then asked for a brief meeting to have a further discussion of the client's needs. During the meeting, the salesperson explained Global Source's services and got a sense of the facility's needs and price-sensitivity. The meeting also served as an opportunity to cross-sell domestic travel staffing. Based on the outcome of the meeting, a formal proposal was sent out that detailed the services that Global Source would provide, as well as the pricing structure. The proposal was often reviewed by a senior manager at the hospital, such as the vice-president of nursing or the director of human resources. Once the proposal was approved, a contract was prepared. This was the longest part of the sales process. Facilities often took a very long time to review contracts. Even though the contract was standard for all clients,

some hospitals requested certain changes in the language. It was the responsibility of the salesperson to continue to follow up with the client until the contract was signed.

## Sales Organization

Sales personnel reported directly to Siddiqi, who served the dual role of CEO and director of sales and marketing. Given the small size of the organization, the structure was fairly simple (see Exhibit 4). Sales personnel were assigned geographic territories such as cities and boroughs. Salespeople were required to make at least 100 new sales calls each day, with many of these being short cold calls. In addition, salespeople were expected to follow up prospects in the pipeline. The target was to achieve a one percent conversion rate. However, even this sometimes turned out to be too optimistic. Siddiqi frequently met with salespeople to analyze sales techniques and determine what was working best. He worked with salespeople who were unable to obtain contracts over an extended period of time. Global Source was a small company with limited resources, and salespeople had to justify their salaries. Salespeople who were unable to perform consistently were asked to leave. Turnover had been fairly high.

Sales personnel also acted as account managers. It was their responsibility to maintain a relationship with the client, which involved taking clients out for meals and occasionally providing sports tickets. They also managed the job order process whereby the client placed a job order with Global Source committing to hiring the requested number of nurses, an important step in the international recruitment process. The salesperson continued to liaise with the client at every step of the recruitment and selection process.

Siddiqi handled the most important territories, and managed the relationships with the most important accounts himself. Besides overseeing the sales staff, he also stayed involved in the sales process once contracts were sent out. He often accompanied sales staff to meetings and lunches once the relationship had been established. In fact, there

**Exhibit 2**  International Recruitment Brochure

# GLOBAL SOURCE
# HEALTHCARE
# International Recruitment

*Global Source* is the leader in Foreign Nurse Recruitment. We have international recruitment platforms in nearly every region of the world, including Canada, U.K., New Zealand, Australia, South Africa, Philippines, and India.

## What Does Global Source Offer?

- **Reliable and Consistent Supply** — The only company with a strong recruiting platform in India
- **Expedited Delivery Time** — Our streamlined process, and the recent dramatic reductions in immigration processing times ensure delivery of Nurses within 8 to 12 Months
- **Exceptional Quality** — Stringent screening of candidates, including localized background, criminal and reference checks
- **Complete Solutions** — We manage every aspect of the process, including recruitment, training, certification exams, immigration, licensing, relocation and orientation support upon arrival in the U.S.
- **Total Flexibility** — Since we control the process from start to finish, we can customize every aspect of our international recruitment program
- **Tremendous Cost Savings** — With our streamlined program and flexible fee structures, we can help you maximize your cost savings
- As hospitals prepare for an unprecedented Nursing shortage, they are faced with tighter budgets and skyrocketing costs of domestic staffing methods like Travel and Agency staffing. International recruitment is the only logical step to meet your long-term staffing needs while dramatically reducing your labor costs!

*Global Source — Take A Slice Of The Best The World Has To Offer!*

**Exhibit 3**   Travel Staffing Brochure

## Global Source — Where the Best Want to Work and the First Choice of Where Hospitals Want to Do Business!

*Global Source Healthcare* is a comprehensive healthcare staffing solutions provider. We strive to develop a close relationship with our clients, and to gain an understanding of the unique needs of each client. We understand that the rising costs of contracted labor are on your mind, and we are working hard to offer you **Greater Value and the Most Competitive Billing Rates in the Industry!**

### *Why work with Global Source for your staffing needs?*

- The most competitive billing rates in the industry!
- Performance Guarantee — If you are not satisfied with a *Global Source* healthcare professional within 2 weeks of a travel assignment or 90 days of a permanent placement, we will credit you for the total billing related to that professional!
- Interviewing & Applicant Management Services to reduce your administrative burden.
- Consultancy services to develop recruitment and retention strategies for your facility.
- Complete staffing solutions, with an equal emphasis on Travel Staffing and Permanent Placements.
- A consistent supply of Nursing and Allied Health professionals, varying from fresh graduates to experienced healthcare professionals.
- International recruiting platforms in every region of the world. International recruitment is our specialty!
- Consistent emphasis on risk management and regulatory compliance.
- Above all, *Global Source* prides itself as a company with the highest standards of ethics, integrity, and respect for the healthcare profession.

were few accounts with whom Siddiqi did not have a direct relationship.

Most salespeople were young with three to five years of experience. Some had experience in healthcare. Every new hire was required to attend two sales seminars conducted by a company called "Foot in the Door." The seminars were "Cold Calling for Cowards" and "From Cold Call to Appointment."

The sales staff was currently compensated on a salary basis. Salaries averaged $40,000 per year, which was inline with the lower range of industry standards. Siddiqi believed that he needed to provide some sort of performance-based incentive

| Exhibit 4 | Organizational Structure |

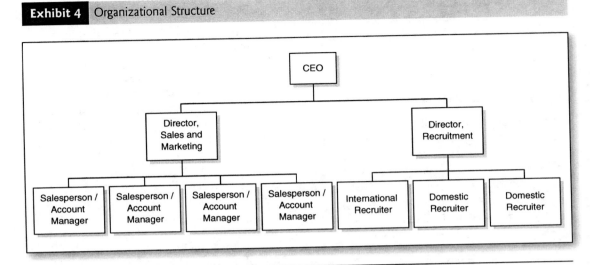

*Note:* The roles of both chief executive officer and director, sales and marketing were being filled by Shamail Siddiq.

down the line. At this time, however, the company lacked the resources to provide any additional compensation. He was also struggling with how he would structure any kind of bonus system. It was difficult to gauge the value of a staffing contract. Long turnaround times for international recruitment meant that the revenue was not immediately realized. Some of the salespeople primarily had clients that utilized domestic staffing services, while others had clients that primarily utilized international recruitment, which produced much greater revenues. How could an incentive system be designed that would be perceived as fair and equitable? He had thought about giving every employee a small equity piece in the company but wasn't sure if this would be the best route to take.

## Current Market Situation

The dynamics in the healthcare staffing industry had changed drastically over the past year. While the healthcare industry was not directly influenced by general economic conditions, it was being impacted in indirect ways that Global Source had not anticipated.

## Amelioration of the Nursing Shortage

The prolonged recession had produced an indirect effect, which was the short-term alleviation of the nursing shortage. Nursing was typically a mid-life career, and a large number of nurses required only part-time or shift work to supplement the family income. However, many nurses found their spouses without work for an extended period of time and started picking up more shifts or even accepting permanent positions with hospitals. Thousands of nurses came out of retirement to earn income for their families. As a result, staffing situations for hospitals improved. While everyone in the industry recognized this as a short-term dynamic, it created a perceived if not real challenge for the sales team. It was much easier to sell a staffing contract when a hospital faced a staff shortage. Some hospitals put international recruitment on hold altogether, especially smaller facilities. However, most of Global Source's top clients continued to recruit international personnel based on expected future requirements. Siddiqi expected that the number of personnel being recruited by each client would decline in the short term, and Global Source would need more good accounts to maintain volume.

## Competitive Situation

Over the last year, there had been a massive influx of start-up staffing companies looking to capitalize on the healthcare opportunity. Healthcare staffing was especially gaining attention as most other industries suffered in a recessionary environment. Many information technology (IT) recruiters were expanding into healthcare staffing. Many of these companies were willing to settle for slim margins, and had started offering higher hourly wages and lavish benefits in order to attract nurses. The benefits included generous housing and travel allowances, large sign-on and completion bonuses, and additional perks, such as free cellular phones and even laptops. In doing so, they were driving up the cost of recruiting healthcare staff and exerting pressure on industry margins, especially since there was a limit to the cost increases that could be passed on to clients. Many healthcare professionals started demanding similar benefits from larger companies such as Cross Country and AMN or threatened to leave. In fact, these large companies had lost market share to start-ups in recent months.

## Credibility Issues

The influx of new companies had also created credibility issues for the industry. Many unscrupulous players had created suspicion among both hospitals and healthcare staff. The biggest problem for Global Source were the recent high-profile scandals where fraudulent companies claiming to be international recruiters collected large deposits from hospitals and then disappeared. As a result, many hospitals were becoming very resistant to paying fees up front, creating a potential cash flow issue for Global Source.

## Budget Cuts

U.S. hospitals were highly dependent on medical insurance companies for their revenues. As medical insurers became increasingly powerful, they put immense pressure on doctors and hospitals to reduce their fees. After 9/11, medical insurance companies who were already suffering due to the recession, started drastically cutting payments to healthcare providers. At the same time, the U.S. federal government was running a record deficit, and cut back on Medicare payments on which hospitals were heavily dependent. In the past, most hospitals had enjoyed liberal budgets. There was very little price-sensitivity in healthcare facilities, and staffing companies had been able to pass cost increases on to clients fairly easily. These hospitals now found themselves in a sudden budget crunch. Many smaller hospitals were forced to close entire wards because they were unable to cover their operating costs. A surprisingly low patient census in 2003 further deteriorated the revenue situation. Most outsourced services were being substantially reduced or even eliminated. The largest impact was on nurse staffing, which was one of the largest expenditures incurred for outsourced healthcare services.

## Vendor Rationalization

Most healthcare providers dealt with a number of staffing companies with a wide range of billing rates, especially for domestic staffing. Besides the inconsistency in billing, administration of these contracts was very costly for the hospital. Hospitals started rationalizing their vendors, and this trend was accelerating. Some larger healthcare providers hired consultants to help with the process. Hospitals were canceling contracts for companies that had not been performing and choosing to retain a handful of top-performing contracts. Furthermore, hospitals started exerting pressure on staffing companies to reduce billing rates. As a result of the intense competition and the current environment, hospitals were in a strong bargaining position.

Many hospitals standardized their rates and expected companies to adhere to the new billing system or they would refuse to renew their contracts. An increasing number of hospitals were putting new contracts on hold.

Staffing companies were unable to reduce nurse pay rates to counteract the billing reductions. Companies that had existing contracts with hospitals were locked into higher billing rates until year end. In the short term, this situation gave them a competitive advantage since they could continue to offer high pay rates to attract nurses. Unfortunately for Global Source, additional new contracts could only be acquired at lower billing rates, making it very difficult to attract U.S. nurses. Siddiqi expected that this rationalization trend would accelerate into 2004 as more staffing contracts came up for renewal. However, once all contracts had been renegotiated at lower rates, nurses would be forced to accept lower pay.

Companies that stood to gain the most from the rationalization were large, established travel staffing companies, such as Cross Country and AMN. These companies were typically providing a high level of service to most of their clients. Hence they became the logical choice for hospitals looking to retain only the best vendors. Many were able to negotiate exclusive contracts with hospitals. Furthermore, these large staffing companies enjoyed economies of scale that would allow them to better withstand lower billing rates.

Some large companies started offering vendor management services for travel staffing. This service was free to the hospitals, while all secondary vendors were required to pay a service fee to the management company. Vendor management allowed large companies to become even more entrenched in client hospitals.

## Internalization

There was a growing trend among hospitals to internalize nurse recruitment and remove staffing companies from the chain altogether. This approach, seemingly a reversal of the earlier trend to outsourcing, was emerging in both domestic and international recruitment markets. In some cases, hospitals had created entire departments to handle nurse recruitment. However, the trend to internalization was developing more rapidly in domestic staffing since international recruitment required a great deal of expertise that many hospitals did not possess.

## The Decisions

Siddiqi thought about the above recent and how they would affect the company. He knew it was time to make some hard decisions. The company was overextended in terms of both sales and financial resources. While his sales force was focused on obtaining new contracts, there was a lot of room to further penetrate existing accounts. With the first international nurses due to arrive shortly, he knew that much of his own time in the next few months would be taken up by managing the logistics for the newly arrived nurses. He thought about his options and wondered which option or combination of options to pursue.

### Continue Aggressive Account Acquisition

With an increasing number of hospitals putting new contracts on hold, there was a very small window of opportunity within which to acquire new accounts. With the volume of placements at existing clients expected to decline, there was good reason to expand the account base quickly. In New York state alone, there were about 300 hospitals. In the combined tri-state area of New York/New Jersey/Connecticut, the number was closer to 500. However, many of these hospitals had not yet been qualified as prospects.

If Global Source were to continue with aggressive account acquisition, there would need to be a refocusing of the sales effort. What type of hospitals should be targeted: small, medium, or large hospitals and healthcare systems? Should the sales strategy be to focus on domestic staffing, international recruitment or both? What geographical area should be the focus? Currently, Global Source was following a nationwide account acquisition strategy, which made sense for domestic staffing since a nationwide client base would allow the company to offer a wide range of placement options to attract nurses. There were currently 5,764 registered hospitals[1] in the United States. Thus, a nationwide approach also enabled Global Source to pursue a much larger pool of potential prospects.

Siddiqi wondered if this approach would be the most efficient use of sales resources, especially since successful sales had largely been achieved in the tri-state area where salespeople could easily visit client facilities. For hospitals outside the company's local area, most of the sales process was conducted on the phone. Although hospitals were accustomed to conducting negotiations for domestic staffing contracts by phone, due to the complexity involved in international recruitment and the greater value of the contract, hospitals did not seem comfortable conducting the entire sales process on the phone.

One of the most important contracts for domestic travel staffing that Siddiqi was working on was with the Department of Veterans Affairs (VA). The VA owned a network of 163 hospitals nationwide that served the medical needs of the nation's veterans. The U.S. federal government was the largest customer in the country, and Siddiqi was excited about the possibility of obtaining this contract. VA hospitals, like private hospitals, suffered from a nursing shortage. In recent years, they increased their pay scales to compete with the private sector, and retained staffing companies to obtain contracted labor. With the United States engaged in two armed conflicts, the demand for veterans' healthcare services was expected to increase.

The VA awarded contracts through an RFP process. However, a certain number of contracts were reserved for small businesses. Realistically, this was the only large hospital network that Global Source could potentially access. This contract was exactly what Global Source needed to expand its struggling domestic staffing business. It would immediately provide Global Source with a national client base and enable travel staffing to reach the critical mass necessary to be lucrative. The VA would also serve as an excellent reference account.

Siddiqi had already spent six months trying to obtain the VA contract. The process was extremely laborious and bureaucratic, and could end up taking several more months. Simultaneously, he was getting ready to launch a direct-mail and print ad campaign directed at U.S. nurses as soon as this contract was finalized. The management team felt that by appealing to their sense of patriotism, Global Source would be able to recruit a large number of nurses for the VA system. Even though Siddiqi wanted to see this opportunity through, he knew it would be at the expense of drawing effort away from international recruitment.

## Penetrate Existing Accounts

Global Source was, at best, a secondary vendor for most hospitals. The relationships were still very new, and there was much room to develop them further. Hospitals typically went to their preferred vendors with job openings first, and only contacted secondary vendors if these positions could not be filled. As a result, Global Source only received a fraction of the job listings that actually existed. A few hospitals had a streamlined system for disseminating openings, such as e-mail or fax. However, most of them had to be contacted on the phone on a regular basis to obtain openings. Salespeople contacted their accounts about once a week for new openings, but most of their time was spent making sales calls to new prospects.

On the supply side, the company's recruitment resources were also spread thin. A small pool of nurses had to be divided among the 20 or so domestic staffing clients. As a result, salespeople were not always able to fill the openings that came up. Approximately one to three domestic nurses were placed on travel assignments at each client hospital every quarter. This number varied widely and some hospitals went for months without any placements.

The vendor rationalization process was of great concern to Siddiqi. Global Source could easily be replaced as a vendor for domestic travel staffing. A much greater emphasis needed to be placed on increasing the number of placements at each hospital in order to service clients at a higher level and to increase revenues. If the number of placements could be increased to a steady rate of five placements per hospital each quarter, this increase would generate substantial revenue and enable Global Source to improve its position with clients. Siddiqi felt that this growth could be accomplished by placing greater emphasis on relationship-building. Salespeople would have to allocate much more time to contacting hospitals on a daily basis for job openings and for regularly meeting clients in person. Simultaneously, it would be critical to ramp up the domestic recruitment effort so that salespeople had personnel available to fill job openings.

On the international recruitment side, job orders received to date were fairly small since most clients wanted to test the company before commiting to a large order. For the four contracts for international recruitment, the job orders varied between five and 10 international nurses. Siddiqi felt that a volume of 15 to 20 nurses per hospital was attainable. Once the client facility had been through the initial steps of international recruitment involving interviewing and selection, it would reach some level of trust in Global Source. The sales team could build on this trust and grow the relationship to try to obtain a larger order. Since high-level hospital executives were involved in international recruitment, this task required a big investment of time and entertainment expenses. Furthermore, the logistics of international recruitment were quite complex and needed constant attention. Any distraction could result in a fiasco that could destroy new fragile client relationships. Siddiqi wanted to service these clients better to try to position Global Source as a primary vendor for international recruitment.

## Cross-Selling Existing Accounts

Since most clients were either using Global Source's domestic or international staffing services, there was an opportunity to cross-sell the other service to these clients. Obtaining international recruitment contracts with these facilities would especially help entrench Global Source in these accounts and reduce the likelihood of being eliminated from domestic staffing. It would also maximize the revenue potential from each client and fully leverage any existing relationships. Even if a small job order of five international nurses could initially be obtained from 50 percent of existing domestic staffing clients, this addition would provide a big boost to company revenues. However, many clients had not yet explored international recruitment, and some were even intimidated by the complex process. These clients would have to be educated as to the benefits of international recruitment and what Global Source could do to simplify the process. While it could be fairly easy to up-sell existing international recruitment clients on domestic staffing, Siddiqi wondered how realistic it was to expect domestic staffing clients to adopt international recruitment.

A company had recently expressed interest in establishing a strategic alliance with Global Source. The company provided a technology-based vendor management system and proposed that Global Source introduce the system to its clients in return for a profit-sharing agreement. While such a vendor management system would help Global Source entrench itself in its clients and provide an additional source of revenue, Siddiqi was hesitant about pursuing this relationship. Client relationships were too new and fragile, and pursuing this venture would further dilute the company's resources, time, and focus.

As Siddiqi thought about his options, he knew that whatever path Global Source chose, it would have to be implemented quickly to adapt to the changing market dynamics.

## CASE QUESTIONS

1. What are the primary intangible elements of the Global Source Healthcare service the salespeople should emphasize?

2. Should the sales force emphasize price, discounting, or service quality when making cold calls on healthcare companies?

3. With the domestic market experiencing problems, should Global Source move to an exclusive focus on international service? Why or why not?

4. What type of sales presentation should the sales representatives make to potential new customers? To existing customers? Explain why the presentations might be different.

5. What role should relationship selling play in Global Source Healthcare's strategic, long-term plan?

# ─── Spectrum Brands, Inc.—The Sales Force Dilemma ───

*By Joe Falconi, under the supervision of Professor Don Barclay*

We are in the business of building our strengths by managing brands. . . . As retailers get bigger, . . . we get bigger to fight fire with fire. I'm now in the business of managing BRANDS, not simply PRODUCTS!

It was November 2005, and Bob Falconi, vice-president of sales and marketing for the Canadian division of Spectrum Brands Inc., was sitting in his new Brantford, Ontario, office, pondering his next steps regarding his sales force. During the course of the last year, the company had gone through a number of changes at the global level. Spectrum Brands (Spectrum), a global consumer products company formerly known as Rayovac Corporation, had made a number of acquisitions to diversify and expand its product and brand portfolio. With these changes, Spectrum had become a leading supplier of consumer batteries, lawn and garden care products, specialty pet supplies, and shaving and grooming products.

Falconi, charged with the task of creating a national sales force from the teams of the newly merged companies, sat in his office trying to make sense of the new business. He knew that creating an effective sales team—one which would capitalize on the synergies across the various businesses—would be very difficult, since these companies each operated differently with regard to the role of their sales forces, customers targeted and products sold. Knowing the importance of the sales function to each of these companies, Falconi wanted to ensure, despite the differences among the diverse groups, that he still maintained a team that would effectively and efficiently continue to increase the sales of each business unit.

The task ahead of him was big, but Falconi knew that a plan needed to be implemented immediately to avoid disrupting the growth momentum of the company's individual brands, to maintain customer relationships, and to preclude competition

Version: (A) 2007–02–21

from taking advantage of any perceived disruptions during this time of change.

## The Context

The consumer brands industry had become highly competitive on a global basis. Numerous acquisitions and mergers had taken place over the past decade, resulting in a select group of large companies with extensive brand portfolios. These companies had developed numerous product lines that allowed them to compete in a variety of markets and product categories, and also strengthened their relationships with retailers.

With the growth of large retail chains across North America through retail consolidation, the balance of power had shifted away from manufacturers. Small players could no longer compete effectively, as strong relationships with retailers had become essential in order to compete for limited and valuable shelf space within stores. Manufacturers built alliances with other consumer brand companies in order to gain strength and power in the retail market. As a result, companies such as Procter & Gamble (P&G), Unilever, S.C. Johnson, and others with large portfolios of popular consumer brands, dominated the shelves in traditional retail channels including Grocery (e.g., Loblaw, Dominion), Drug stores (e.g., Shoppers Drug Mart, Katz Group), Hardware retailers (e.g., Home Hardware), Home and Garden retailers (e.g., RONA, The Home Depot), and Mass Merchandisers (e.g., Walmart). Internet and direct-to-consumer sales had not proven to be valuable alternate channels for these companies, as retailers would retaliate by de-listing products of those manufacturers who tried to go in this direction.

Companies competing against the brands under the umbrellas of these large companies continued to struggle for position and, ultimately, for market share, mainly because of the established relationships that these large firms had with the retailers. The trend was toward companies such as Spectrum Brands who had a presence in batteries,

shaving and grooming products, lawn and garden products, and specialty pet supplies.

## Consumer Brands Markets

### Battery Market

North American consumers of household batteries (AAA, AA, C, D and 9-volt standard batteries) sought convenience and quality when purchasing batteries and tended to gravitate towards the brand names they knew and trusted. Duracell and Energizer continued to dominate the market due to their brand recognition, their relationships with distributors and retailers, and their established presence in the large one-time-use alkaline battery category. These two firms were leaders in this market for decades because of their ability to adapt to consumer needs and to merge with other consumer goods companies to create brand portfolios, thus gaining valuable negotiating power with retailers. For example, the Duracell battery brand was owned by the largest and most recognized consumer products company in the world—Procter & Gamble (P&G)—while the Energizer battery brand was owned by Energizer Holdings Inc., which also owned the Shick Razors brand. Each company held a 40 percent market share within the battery industry.

Household batteries were sold through wholesalers, distributors, professionals and OEMs, but the large majority were sold through traditional retail channels. Of these retailers, mass merchandisers, home and garden centers and niche electronic stores accounted for more than 60 percent of sales.

As of 2005, the alkaline battery was the predominant type of household battery in North America, and was offered by all major competitors in all sizes. The growth within this segment had become relatively flat, at only one to two percent annually, yet, due to its size, it was expected to dominate the market for the next five to 10 years. In 2005, the overall battery market in Canada was estimated to be $300[1] million, with the alkaline category representing 70 percent, the rechargeable category making up 10 percent, and other battery chemistries, including zinc, representing 20 percent.

The market for household batteries was highly seasonal. The large majority of sales occurred during the months leading up to and following Christmas sales of electronics and other battery-operated devices. Close to 70 percent of battery sales occurred during this period.

## Shaving and Grooming Products Market

The shaving and grooming products industry was dominated by a select group of companies selling electric shavers and accessories, electric grooming products, and hair care appliances. Electric shavers included both rotary and foil designs for men and women, and accessories included replacement parts, pre-shave products and cleaning agents for shavers. Electric grooming products included beard/moustache trimmers, nose and ear trimmers, haircut kits, and related accessories. Hair care appliances included hair dryers, setters, curling irons, crimpers, straighteners, and hot air brushes.

The shaving and grooming products market was growing at a rate of three to four percent annually, and this trend was likely to continue. The market for electronic shaving and grooming products was highly seasonal with peaks during the months leading up to and following the Christmas holiday season and around Father's Day and Mother's Day weekends. The majority of these products were purchased as gifts, and thus the sales cycle followed these gift-giving seasons.

The primary competitors in the shaving market included Norelco, Braun, and Remington. Norelco was a division of Koninklijke Philips Electronics (Philips), which was one of the world's biggest electronics companies and the largest one in Europe. Braun was a member of the Gillette family of products which was now part of P&G, while Remington was part of Spectrum. Norelco only sold rotary shavers, Braun only offered foil shavers, while Remington was the only company competing in both segments. Quality, price, and brand awareness were the main factors influencing sales in this segment.

The major competitors in the hair care market were Remington, Norelco, Conair Corporation and Helen of Troy Limited. Each company offered a complete line of hair-care products and accessories and competed on quality and price within this category.

Competitors within both of these segments sold their products largely through traditional retail channels with a heavy emphasis on mass merchandisers and specialty retailers such as salons and hair and body care shops. Like all consumer product companies, those firms able to maintain or increase the amount of retail shelf space allocated to their respective products could gain share of mind and, potentially, a share of the market.

## Lawn and Garden Market

The lawn and garden market was a US$4 billion industry in North America, with an additional US$1 billion in sales of household insect control products. Companies manufactured and marketed fertilizers, herbicides, outdoor insect control products, rodenticides, plant foods, potting soil, grass seeds and other growing media. The lawn and garden industry had been driven largely by affluent baby boomers who enjoyed gardening and also by increasing home ownership levels. Growth in this market had been between four and five percent annually and was expected to continue at this pace. In North America, more than 80 percent of households were participating in at least one lawn and garden activity in 2004.

The main competitors within the lawn and garden segment included United Industries (United)/Nu-Gro, Scotts Miracle-Gro Company (Scotts), and Central Garden & Pet Company (CGPC). Scotts marketed products under the Scotts and Miracle-Gro brand names. They led this market with a 30 percent market share. CGPC sat behind United with a 17 percent market share.

They sold garden products under the Amdro, Image, and Pennington Seed brand names.

Growth in the insect control market had been generated by population growth in the insect-prone Sunbelt region and the heightened awareness of insect-borne diseases such as West Nile virus. Growth in this market had been slightly higher than historical levels since 2002 with a seven to eight percent annual growth rate.

In the insect control market, the major competitors included United, Scotts, and S.C. Johnson & Son, Inc. Scotts, once again the market leader, sold products under the Ortho and Roundup brand names, while S.C. Johnson marketed their insecticide and repellent products under the Raid and OFF! brands.

Competitors within both of these markets sold mainly through mass merchandisers, home centers, independent nurseries, and hardware stores. Home centers and mass merchandisers typically carried one or two premium brands and one value brand on their shelves. Obtaining and maintaining share of shelf within these retailers was critical as 50 to 60 percent of sales passed through these two channels.

The lawn and garden market was also highly seasonal. Products were shipped to distributors and retailers beginning as early as March in preparation for the spring season. Demand for products typically peaked during the first six months of the calendar year. This seasonality created a major risk within this industry, as there was a heavy dependence on weather to drive sales. A poor season greatly hindered the bottom line.

## Specialty Pet Supply Market

The specialty pet supply industry had historically been one of the fastest-growing consumer product categories with annual growth between six and eight percent. This category consisted of aquatic equipment (i.e., aquariums, filters, pumps), aquatic consumables (i.e., fish food, water treatments, conditioners) and specialty pet products for dogs, cats, birds, and other small domestic animals. In North America, this was an US$8 billion market in 2004, and was expected to grow to over US$11 billion by 2007.

Much of this growth could be attributed to the increasing levels of pet ownership. On average, households with children under the age of 18, and adults over 55 (who were typically "empty nesters"), tended to keep pets as companions and had more disposable income and leisure time to spend with them. In North America, both of these categories have expanded rapidly with the aging of the baby boomer population. As of 2004, 62 percent of households in the United States owned a pet, and 46 percent owned two or more pets. In addition to these trends, the growing movement toward pet humanization—the tendency of pet owners to treat pets like cherished members of the family—had also factored greatly into this market expansion.

The specialty pet supply industry was highly fragmented. There were over 500 manufacturers in North America, consisting of both small companies with limited product lines and larger firms. No company held a market share of greater than 10 percent. The largest competitors included CGPC, United Pet Group/Tetra, and the Hartz Mountain Corporation. CGPC led the market with a nine percent market share.

Products within this segment were sold through specialty pet stores, independent pet retailers, mass merchants, grocery stores, and through various professional outlets. Mass merchandisers, supermarkets, and discounters increasingly supplied pet products, but they focused mainly on a limited selection of items such as pet food. The majority of sales were made through pet supply stores, of which there were over 15,000 in the United States and more than 5,000 in Canada. There were only two national retailers in this industry: PetSmart and PetCo. PetSmart accounted for 10 percent of North American pet product net sales in fiscal 2004. PetCo reflected similar statistics, but no other retailer accounted for more than eight percent of industry retail sales.

Sales in this segment remained fairly stable throughout the year since pets needed to be maintained continuously.

## Competitive Context

In all of these industries, some competitors had gained significant market share and had explicitly committed significant resources to protecting share and/or stealing share from others. In some product lines, competitors had lower production costs and higher profit margins, enabling them to compete more aggressively through advertising and by offering retail discounts and other promotional incentives to retailers, distributors and wholesalers. This aggressive strategy obviously provided additional strength in attracting retailers and consumers. The ability to retain or increase the amount of retail shelf space allocated to their respective products provided competitive advantages in each of these market spaces.

## Spectrum Brands, Inc.

Spectrum brands products were available through the world's top 25 retailers, in over one million stores throughout North America, Europe, Asia Pacific, the Middle East, Africa, Latin America and Brazil. Overall, the company was generating US$2.8 billion in annualized revenues from its brand portfolio (see Exhibits 1 and 2 for Spectrum pre-merger and consolidated financial information).

Similar to its competitors, Rayovac had acquired other consumer brand companies to enhance its ability to gain retail presence. Beginning in 2003, Rayovac acquired Remington Products Inc., a company specializing in consumer shaving and grooming products. In February 2005, Spectrum Brands was created when the Rayovac Corporation acquired United Industries Corporation (a leading U.S. manufacturer of consumer lawn and garden care and insect control products), Nu-Gro Corporation (the Canadian subsidiary of United, specializing in lawn and garden care products) and Tetra Holdings Inc. (a leading supplier of fish and aquatics supplies). Continued growth and strategic acquisitions allowed the company to leverage global distribution channels, purchasing power and operational processes. These mergers

provided the company with an extended brand portfolio. This allowed all of the brands to access a number of new retailers where they had not previously been able to gain shelf space. In turn, this increased the ability for each brand to compete within its given markets. Spectrum became the global leader in aquatic supplies; the number two player in the lawn and garden industry, the household insect control market, and the shaving and grooming supplies industry; and the third-largest global company in the battery industry (see Exhibit 3 for a list of brand names under the Spectrum label).

### Rayovac

Rayovac was the third-largest global consumer battery manufacturer in the world—third largest in North America and second largest in Europe. The company sold batteries and flashlights for various household and industrial uses and was the largest worldwide seller of hearing aid batteries. Their battery product line included one-time-use alkaline and Nickel Metal Hydride (NiMH) rechargeable batteries available in all standard sizes (AAA, AA, C, D, 9-Volt) to compete in the highly saturated but lucrative household market. Globally, Rayovac held a 14 percent market share, with a 20 percent share of the Canadian market. The division generated US$1.5 billion in annual global revenues in 2004.

The company began operations in 1906, but did not introduce the Rayovac name until the 1930s. Their initial focus was on manufacturing specialty batteries for use in such devices as their patented vacuum tube hearing aids. The company expanded and grew through their continued development of state-of-the-art flashlights and non-traditional batteries, including their successful hearing aid battery line. They eventually entered the competitive household battery market through key acquisitions and by capitalizing on existing distributor and retailer relationships. This was long after the market leaders, Duracell and Energizer, had become well established within this market. Rayovac made great strides over its last few years in an attempt to gain ground.

| Exhibit I | Numbers Based on Fiscal Year Ending September |
|---|---|

| Rayovac Corporation Net Sales Breakdown | | |
|---|---|---|
| Consolidated Net Sales by Product Line (US$ millions) | 2005 | 2004* |
| Batteries | $968 | $939 |
| Lights | $94 | $90 |
| Shaving & Grooming | $271 | $272 |
| Personal Care | $143 | $116 |
| Lawn and Garden | $447 | N/A |
| Household Insect Control | $150 | N/A |
| Pet Products | $286 | N/A |
| Totals | $2,359 | $1,417 |

*United/Nu-Gro was acquired by Rayovac mid-2005.

| Rayovac & Remington | | | | |
|---|---|---|---|---|
| | Rayovac | | Remington | |
| (US$ millions) | 2004 | 2003 | 2004 | 2003* |
| Net Sales | $1,029 | $922 | $388 | N/A |
| Gross Profit | 42.8% | 38.1% | 47.0% | N/A |
| Operating Income | $109 | $60 | $47 | N/A |
| Net Income | $39 | $15 | $17 | N/A |

*Remington was acquired by Rayovac mid-2003.

| United Industries and Tetra | | |
|---|---|---|
| North America (US$ millions) | United 2005 | Tetra 2005 |
| Net Sales from External customers | $787 | $96 |
| Segment Profit | $79 | $10 |
| SP as % of Net Sales | 10.0% | 10.4% |

Acquisitions had been made to gain access to international markets including Europe (Varta Battery Corporation acquired in 2002), China (Ningbo Baowang acquired in 2004), and Brazil (Microlite acquired in 2004).

The leaders in this industry had leading brands and thus greater control over distribution channels, retailers and prices. Rayovac had only been able to secure shelf space in a small number of retailers, including Walmart (making up 40 percent of sales),

| Exhibit 2 | Spectrum Brands, Inc. and Subsidiaries Consolidated Statements of Operations (years ended September 30, 2005, 2004) (US$000s) |
|---|---|

|  | 2005 | 2004 |
|---|---|---|
| Net Sales | $2,359,447 | $1,417,186 |
| Cost of goods sold | $1,465,096 | $811,894 |
| Restructuring and related charges | $10,496 | $(781) |
| Gross Profit | $883,855 | $606,073 |
| Operating Expenses: |  |  |
| Selling | $473,834 | $293,118 |
| General and Administration | $160,382 | $121,319 |
| Research and Development | $29,339 | $23,192 |
| Restructuring and related charges | $15,820 | $12,224 |
|  | $679,375 | $449,853 |
| Operating Income | $204,480 | $156,220 |
| Interest expense | $134,053 | $65,702 |
| Other income, net | $(856) | $(14) |
| Income from continuing operations before taxes | $71,283 | $90,532 |
| Income tax expense | $24,451 | $34,372 |
| Income from continuing operations | $46,832 | $56,160 |
| Loss from discontinued operations, net of tax benefits | $– | $380 |
| Net Income | $46,832 | $55,780 |

**Spectrum Brands, Inc. and Subsidiaries Consolidated Balance Sheets**
**(years ended September 30, 2005, 2004) (US$ 000s)**

|  | 2005 | 2004 |
|---|---|---|
| **Assets** |  |  |
| Current Assets: |  |  |
| Cash and cash equivalents | $29,852 | $13,971 |
| Receivables: |  |  |
| Trade A/R, net of allowances | $362,399 | $269,977 |
| Other | $10,996 | $19,655 |
| Inventories | $451,553 | $264,726 |
| Deferred income taxes | $39,231 | $19,233 |
| Assets held for sale | $108,174 | $9,870 |
| Prepaid expenses and other | $45,762 | $51,262 |

| | 2005 | 2004 |
|---|---|---|
| Total Current Assets | $1,047,967 | $648,694 |
| Property, plant and equipment, net | $304,323 | $182,396 |
| Deferred charges and other | $47,375 | $35,079 |
| Goodwill | $1,429,017 | $320,577 |
| Intangible assets, net | $1,154,397 | $422,106 |
| Debt issuance costs | $39,012 | $25,299 |
| **Total Assets** | $4,022,091 | $1,634,151 |
| **Liabilities and Shareholder's Equity** | | |
| Current Liabilities: | | |
|   Current maturities of LT debt | $39,308 | $23,895 |
|   Accounts payable | $281,954 | $226,234 |
| Accrued liabilities: | | |
|   Wages and benefits | $47,910 | $40,138 |
|   Income taxes payable | $40,468 | $21,672 |
|   Restructuring and related charges | $16,978 | $8,505 |
|   Accrued interest | $31,529 | $16,302 |
|   Liabilities held for sale | $22,294 | $– |
|   Other | $76,935 | $60,094 |
| Total Current Liabilities | $557,376 | $396,840 |
| Long-term debt, net of current maturities | $2,268,025 | $806,002 |
| Employee benefit obligations, net of current portion | $78,510 | $69,246 |
| Deferred income taxes | $208,251 | $7,272 |
| Other | $67,199 | $37,368 |
| **Total Liabilities** | $3,179,361 | $1,316,728 |
| Minority interest in equity of consolidated subsidiary | $– | $1,379 |
| **Shareholders' equity:** | | |
|   Common Stock | $666 | $642 |
|   Additional paid-in capital | $671,378 | $224,962 |
|   Retained earnings | $267,315 | $220,483 |
|   Accumulated other comprehensive income (loss) | $10,260 | $10,621 |
|   Notes receivable from officers/shareholders | $– | $(3,605) |
| | $949,619 | $453,103 |
| Less treasury stock, at cost | $(70,820) | $(130,070) |
| Less unearned restricted stock compensation | $(36,069) | $(6,989) |
| **Total Shareholders' equity** | $842,730 | $316,044 |
| **Total Liabilities and Shareholders' equity** | $4,022,091 | $1,634,151 |

*Source:* 2005 Spectrum Brands Inc. Annual Report.

| **Exhibit 3** | Spectrum Brand Names |
|---|---|

Canadian Tire (15 percent of sales), Home Hardware (10 percent of sales), and other chains and smaller niche retailers such as Toys "R" Us, Radio Shack, and others (35 percent of sales).

## Remington Products Company

Remington was a leading designer and distributor of consumer shaving and personal care products in North America and the United Kingdom. They marketed a broad line of electric shaving and grooming products for both men and women, as well as hair-care products and other personal care items.

Beginning operations in 1936 as a division of Remington Rand, Remington captured a strong position as a global player in the market by developing new innovative shaving products. Before being bought by Rayovac Corporation in 2003, the Remington Electric Shaver Division had been involved in various mergers: merging with the Sperry Corporation in 1955; being bought by entrepreneur Victor Kiam in 1979; and then acquiring Clairol Inc.'s worldwide personal care appliance business in 1993. Through all of these moves, Remington was able to command a 30 percent market share in North America and a 21 percent share in the United Kingdom, with the number one position in men's foil shavers, women's foil shavers, and men's grooming products, and the number two position in men's rotary shavers globally. Remington had become an established name in the industry, achieving global revenues of US$350 million in 2003.

Remington, like Rayovac, sold its products largely through traditional retail channels. The breakdown of retailers was similar to that of Rayovac, with the niche retailers being salons and specialty hair and body care shops.

## United Industries Corporation

United Industries Corporation was a leading manufacturer and marketer of professional and consumer lawn and garden care and insect control products. It produced a wide variety of products, including brand name items and private label products for individual retail chains. United also produced and distributed controlled release nitrogen and other fertilizer technologies to the consumer, professional and golf industries worldwide under various brand names.

United competed in the United States under the United name. In Canada, the company operated under the Nu-Gro Corporation (Nu-Gro) name. United, which began operations in the early 1950s, acquired Nu-Gro in April 2004 to serve as the Canadian arm of the company. Nu-Gro was established in 1988 as an exclusively Canadian lawn and garden company. Both were leaders within their marketplaces, maintaining a number of top-selling brands including Vigoro, Shultz and CIL.

Within the lawn and garden industry in North America, United/Nu-Gro was the number two company, holding a 23 percent market share. The company targeted consumers who wanted products comparable to and at lower prices than premium-priced brands, and thus positioned their brands as the value alternatives. In 2004, United/Nu-Gro together generated sales of US$550 million in this market.

In the household insect control industry, United/Nu-Gro generated US$150 million in sales in 2004. With their insect control brands, it was again the number two company, with 24 percent market share in North America.

The consumer division for both of these categories sold its products through various retail outlets, including home and garden centers, large home supply retailers, and general mass merchandisers.

The sales breakdown was as follows: Canadian Tire (13 percent), Home Depot (nine percent), Rona (seven percent), Lowe's (six percent), Home Hardware (five percent), Walmart (three percent), independent garden retailers (five percent), other small retailers and garden stores (12 percent), and their professional division made up 40 percent.

The United/Nu-Gro professional division served two major markets: Professional Turf Care Products for golf courses and lawn care companies, and Professional Pest Control Products and Animal Health Products for pest control operators and farms (making up 25 and 15 percent, respectively, of the company's overall sales). This division had its own dedicated sales force and marketing team to manage the diverse needs of the professional customers.

United was also a leading supplier of quality products to the pet supply industry in the United States, under the United Pet Group (UPG) name. UPG operated in the fragmented U.S. pet supply market, manufacturing and marketing premium-branded pet supplies for dogs, cats, fish, birds, and other small animals. Products included aquarium kits, stand-alone tanks, filters, and related items, and other aquarium supplies and accessories, as well as pet treats and supplies. This division was number two in North America, with an eight percent market share and annual revenues in 2004 totaling US$250 million (figure includes Tetra sales). This division sold its products through large mass merchandisers, while also targeting the larger pet supply chains of PetsMart and PetCo, and the considerable number of independent pet supplies stores.

## Tetra Holdings

Tetra Holdings was a global supplier of fish and aquatic supplies, operating in over 90 countries worldwide and holding leading market positions in Germany, Japan, the United States, and the United Kingdom. They manufactured, distributed, and marketed a comprehensive premier line of foods, equipment, and care products for fish and reptiles, along with accessories for home aquariums and ponds.

Tetra was founded in Germany in the early 1950s, pioneering the development of flake fish foods. The company grew into one of the most recognized global brand names in the pet supplies industry. In addition to the products they offered, they also published hundreds of books on aquarium fish keeping, reptile and amphibian keeping, and water gardening.

Tetra was acquired by United Industries in early 2004, joining the UPG division. Despite the merger, United maintained separate operations for each brand with the exception of combining administrative functions. UPG only operated in the United States, while Tetra operated globally. These groups together held the number two position in the North American pet supply market, with eight percent market share. Like UPG, Tetra sold its products through large mass merchandisers, while also targeting the larger pet supply chains (PetsMart and PetCo) and smaller pet supplies stores in the countries in which it operated.

## Bob Falconi

Bob Falconi completed his Executive MBA program at the Richard Ivey School of Business in 1990. He had been involved in the battery business for 27 years, working his first 16 with Duracell, where he became vice-president of sales. He left Duracell in 1995 for a new start-up battery company, Pure Energy Battery Corporation, which introduced a revolutionary new rechargeable alkaline battery system. He left Pure Energy in 1999 to serve as country manager for Rayovac Canada, and had then taken on the role of vice-president of sales and marketing for Spectrum. Throughout his career, he had developed a keen understanding of brand management and had been given the responsibility within Spectrum to leverage his experiences.

## Reasons for the Acquisitions

Through the evolution into Spectrum Brands, Rayovac had become a channel marketer, and

purveyor of specialty brands. The Rayovac Corporation had been painted into a corner in the competitive battery market due to its lack of retail strength. In order to compete on a larger scale, greater power within retail channels was required. The company had continually looked for potential acquisitions where it felt that it could add value to the company's operations while at the same time creating a larger and more powerful combined company. Rayovac's goal was to grow through acquisitions that diversified and increased its revenue base while leveraging its strengths and capabilities in global merchandising and distribution.

With the Remington merger, there were many similarities between the two companies in terms of marketing and channel strategies. However, the systems Remington had in place to manage logistic processes were outdated and inefficient. Rayovac saw this as an opportunity to add value to this company through the sharing of best practices. Rayovac acquired Remington and was able to update the company's logistic processes and systems and improve the overall operations of the firm. Through this merger, Rayovac was able to drive US$35million in annual costs out of the combined enterprise while adding the Remington revenues to Rayovac's top line.

With the recent United/Nu-Gro/Tetra acquisitions, Rayovac was looking to continue its growth and expand into new product categories. New products would provide increased negotiating strength with the larger retailers while diversifying the company's revenue base. For example, with this merger, worldwide battery sales represented approximately 40 percent of revenue as compared to the 2004 level of 67 percent. More importantly, the merger served to balance out the sales cycle for the firm given the different seasonalities of the various categories—this meant no down time for the sales force. Finally, Spectrum Brands had at least one brand in all of the major retailers in the world, a situation they hoped to leverage into having other brands in many retailers (see Exhibit 4 for annualized revenues by product category).

| Exhibit 4 | Annualized Revenues by Product Line |
| --- | --- |

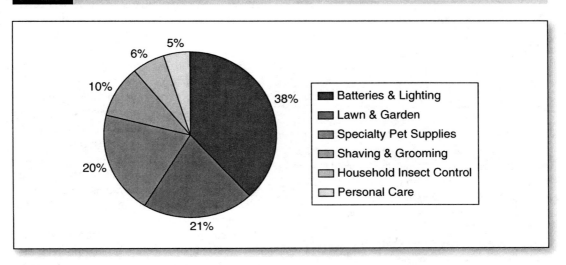

## The Issue

As Falconi looked through his notes on his individual Canadian business units and their competitive markets, he questioned how best to organize the new sales force in order to capitalize on the strengths of each brand, given the similarities and differences between them. He knew that with the recent acquisitions, the company was looking to leverage any synergies created and reduce costs where possible. However, as overarching objectives, he wanted to make sure that customers would be serviced in the same fashion, if not better, and that sales would not be affected. Falconi decided to take a look at how each business unit currently operated, and how some of their major competitors were organized (see Exhibit 5 for a post-merger organizational chart).

| Exhibit 5 | Spectrum Brands Sales Division Organizational Chart |
| --- | --- |

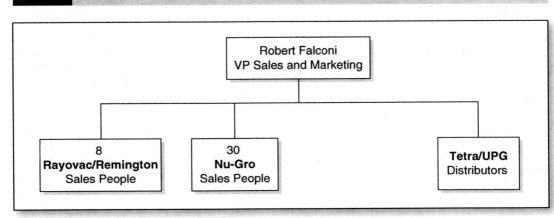

# The Current Sales Forces

## Rayovac and Remington

In Canada, the Rayovac/Remington sales force was currently organized by distribution channel. The eight sales representatives serving this division were responsible for selling all products under both the Rayovac and Remington brand names to their assigned retailers. This was a small sales team, but it had tremendous support from the U.S. office for large accounts, as well as for marketing and trade promotion campaign design. Sales targeted toward hearing aid professionals and industrial and OEM distributors were handled from the U.S. office.

These sales representatives were organized geographically as well. The allocation was as follows: six in Toronto, and one in each of Vancouver and Montreal. Each representative was responsible for the retailers in their regions. Toronto had a greater number of corporate head offices, thus requiring more representatives to service these accounts.

The average base salary for these sales reps was approximately $70,000, with an overall employee expenditure budget of around $900,000 annually, including bonuses. With these representatives, this division was able to generate a 2004 sales volume of over $50 million in Canada.

Overall, this sales force had worked well for the company. The division had been able to minimize the size of the sales force while still achieving their sales goals in an effective and efficient manner.

## Nu-Gro

In a similar fashion, Nu-Gro operated customer-focused teams made up of 30 consumer sales reps. Logistics were a very important element within the lawn and garden industry, as shipping costs for these products were significant. For example, a trailer shipment of fertilizer could have a maximum of 1,500 bags valued at $3 a bag, while the same trailer could ship $1 million worth of batteries. As a result, sales reps for Nu-Gro needed to plan carefully with customers in order to minimize costs by ensuring full truck shipments.

As with Rayovac/Remington, sales representative were distributed geographically to service key Canadian locations: 17 in Ontario, six in Vancouver, three in Montreal, and two in each of Calgary and Winnipeg.

The average base salary for these sales reps was slightly lower than for Rayovac/Remington representatives at $60,000, with an overall employee expenditure budget of approximately $2 million annually, including bonuses. With these sales reps, this division was able to generate a 2004 sales volume of more than $105 million in Canada.

Nu-Gro, however, had been struggling as the company's operations and product offerings were extremely unfocused. Over the past five years, the company had acquired a large number of their smaller competitors and had accumulated their associated brands under the Nu-Gro umbrella. As a result, Nu-Gro experienced a proliferation of products and brands (see Exhibit 6). There were strong arguments to stay in under-performing categories, including contribution toward fixed manufacturing costs, improved transportation economics and account control. On the other hand, the significant working capital required to support these under-performing products could not justify keeping them. Brand and SKU rationalization was needed, and a target of up to a 50 percent reduction over a one-year period was being considered. Ultimately, a more focused product portfolio would facilitate the efforts of the sales force.

In addition to the large SKU offerings, the sales team was forced to target a wide variety and large number of customers with these brands, including both the large mass retailers and the small "mom and pop" garden stores. These efforts were very time-consuming and uneconomical for the sales team, as the majority of stores were of the smaller garden shop variety that ordered limited quantities.

The professional division that served the two major lawn and garden markets had been fairly successful in the past through its strong established relationships. The sales force for this division had and would continue to remain independent from

| Exhibit 6 | Nu-Gro Products |
|---|---|

| Major | #SKU's | Revenue | | Contribution | |
|---|---|---|---|---|---|
| | | By Type/Category | | Margin % | |
| | | $M | % Total | $M | % Sales |
| Fertilizers | 752 | 29.8 | 36.40% | 3.9 | 13.20% |
| Pesticides | 234 | 21.9 | 26.80% | 5.5 | 25.20% |
| Soils | 176 | 12.3 | 15.00% | 0.2 | 1.30% |
| Seed | 143 | 9 | 11.00% | 0.2 | 1.80% |
| Other | 92 | 8.8 | 10.80% | 0.3 | 10.40% |
| Grand Total | 1,397 | $82 | 100.00% | $10 | 12.30% |

Spectrum's consumer (retail) sales division. Nu-Gro maintained a separate sales force beyond the 30 consumer representatives exclusive to this division.

Overall, Nu-Gro's consumer sales operations needed adjustment. A strategy that refocused the sales team's efforts on their large and more important areas, while still finding a way to reach their current customer base, was required to turn this division around.

## Tetra/United Pet Group

The sales force for this division in the United States was regionally based so that each sales rep could ensure an ample supply of product for their distributors and dealers. These sales representatives were responsible for the large accounts such as PetsMart and PetCo, mass merchandisers such as Walmart, and the large number of smaller specialty retailers.

However, in Canada, sales for this division were handled by distributors. These distributors were responsible for the sales to the highly fragmented Canadian specialty pet retailer market. They offered the same services that an internal sales force could provide, including organizing special promotions and setting up in-store displays. Ultimately, they

were able to generate sales from a large number of smaller players more economically than a small internal sales team could. The sales managers for Rayovac/Remington and Nu-Gro were responsible for managing these distributors. The larger retail accounts were managed by the U.S. sales team but serviced by these distributors.

## Sales Management

Of the 38 sales reps between the Rayovac/Remington and Nu-Gro divisions, four of them filled the roles of sales manager, two managers for each division. Each rep/manager was responsible for the various representatives in their specific geographic regions. They spent 65 percent of their time selling to their own individual accounts. The remaining 35 percent was spent managing reps, managing distributors, forecasting, strategic planning, and analyzing their market. For each division, one rep/manager was responsible for the sales reps in the large Ontario market, while the other managed the sales reps in the rest of the country. Regardless of structure of the sales operation going forward, Falconi would likely organize around three regions: the West, Ontario, and the East, with one manager responsible for the sales reps within each region. This, of course, raised the issue of the surplus manager and would provide an opportunity to reconsider the incumbents.

## Competitor Organizations

Falconi wanted to look at how some of Spectrum's competitors organized their sales forces within Canada. He decided to select a few of the major players from each industry as comparison points. Koninklijke Philips Electronics and P&G operated their sales divisions by product category. Each category had its own dedicated sales force further divided by specific retail channels and/or customer, depending on the size of the retailer. For example, Norelco's sales force was responsible exclusively for shaving and grooming products and did not cross-sell other Philips brands such as televisions. Similarly, Braun sales reps would sell both the Braun and Gillette shaving brands, Duracell would have its own sales team, but neither group would cross-sell other P&G brands. In certain circumstances, one purchasing manager for a retailer such as Walmart might deal with a sales rep from each product category but these sales reps would deal exclusively with Walmart as a customer. In other circumstances, the sales reps would interface with different purchasing managers in those retailers where the purchasing function was organized by category.

Both Scotts and CGPC operated their sales divisions in a different manner. Their sales forces were organized by product category, but covered all retail channels. Thus, they had specific sales reps for categories such as fertilizers, soils and seeds, insect control products, and pet supplies (CGPC only), but each sales rep would service clients across multiple channels. Like Philips and P&G, these companies had developed a sales force with product category expertise, yet they did not concentrate an individual sales rep on a specific retailer.

Due to the size and strength of each of these companies, they had been successful at developing a "pull" strategy with the consumers. Retailers were almost mandated to support and sell these companies' products because of the consumer demand created. In addition, the sales forces had developed strong relationships with retailers, the "push" component.

## Sales Force Options

Looking forward, Falconi wanted to evaluate his options regarding how to organize his sales force to see what alternatives or combinations made sense to Spectrum's operations and the market characteristics.

### Separate Sales Forces

Maintaining a separate sales force for each brand line would offer Spectrum the greatest degree of expertise on each brand. These sales reps were already familiar with, and had extensive knowledge about, their brands and would require little, if any, additional training. Sales reps could continue to operate as they already did, and maintain the momentum they had already generated for their product lines. Ultimately, such an organization would allow for a more focused sales force in that representatives would be in a better position to answer product-related questions and offer product educational services.

On the other hand, maintaining separate sales forces would not take advantage of the synergies that the recent merger had created for the company. There would be little to no expense reduction, as the existing sales rep levels would likely be maintained. In addition, this organization would not offer any efficiency improvements in the use of sales reps during slower seasonal periods. Finally, there would be a significant duplication of efforts as Spectrum would have multiple sales reps calling on the same retailer at any given time.

### Merged Sales Force

With a merged sales force, Spectrum would essentially move to a "one bag" sales rep approach, in that each representative would be responsible for becoming an expert on all product lines and selling every brand to their specified customers. With this option, Falconi would have to define each sales rep's responsibilities relating to whether or not the representative would cover all customers in a geographic area, or be responsible for a specific retail group or nationwide chain.

As with the separate sales force option, the "one bag" sales rep would offer Spectrum numerous benefits. First, Spectrum would be able to capitalize on the potential synergies of the merger as Rayovac did with the Remington acquisition and integration. With each representative selling the entire Spectrum product line, there would be the opportunity to cross-promote brands, leveraging the strong relationships that certain brands have with particular retailers to sell and promote the other lines. This is especially important as Spectrum tries to gain presence for all their lines within each major retailer across the country.

Additionally, Falconi would be able to consolidate the existing teams into a smaller unit. Responsibilities for individual retailers could be handled by one or two sales reps selling the entire portfolio of brands, rather than one representative for each individual brand. For example, there are certain customers to whom each business unit has been selling products, including Walmart, The Home Depot, RONA, Canadian Tire, as well as many others across the country. Overall, by merging the sales force, it is estimated that Spectrum would be able to reduce the salaries and bonus expense to approximately $2 million for the entire Canadian sales division.

Finally, a merged sales force would create a more efficient team to cope with the seasonality issues inherent in the industries in which Spectrum operates. Sales reps would always have something going on with one of the portfolio brands, allowing them to be in constant contact with retail purchasers.

While there are many benefits to this approach for a diversified company like Spectrum, there could be great difficulty in creating an effective and efficient merged team. First, with the addition of numerous new brands to the company's portfolio, sales reps would need to develop an expertise for a large number of brands and products. In addition, the new products they would be selling are completely different from the current brand category they have experience with (i.e., a battery sales rep selling fertilizer). Additional training would be required for all sales reps to educate them on the unfamiliar brands. This training could ultimately be costly and take a substantial amount of time.

Given the variety of products and brands under the Spectrum name, a merged sales force may prove to be highly unfocused. A representative may be incapable of attaining a sufficient knowledge base about every product line, or have too much going on to give each brand the necessary focus needed to sustain its current sales levels. This could hinder sales and effectively kill the existing momentum of the brands.

## Distributors

Distributors provide sales and logistic services to firms in exchange for commission fees. Such firms are typically hired by smaller companies with limited sales reach, or by companies who are entering new geographic markets but do not yet have a sales team in place. They usually have an advantage over these types of companies as they are well established, they have existing relationships with retailers, and they operate large sales groups that can service a large number of customers. They typically serve a variety of manufacturers, and thus are able to operate such a sales process in an efficient manner. As a result, distributors are typically given the task of reaching the large number of smaller retailers that prove to be too costly for a small sales force to target, while the manufacturer's internal sales team targets the smaller number of large customers that contribute greater individual sales.

Though there are many benefits to using professional distributors as the company's sales force, there are drawbacks as well. The costs associated with these services can be substantial relative to an internal sales force. The cost of sales through a distributor is approximately 15 percent against revenues, while it is two to three percent with an internal sales person. As a result, successful firms that are able to establish large sales teams can ultimately generate sales at a lower cost.

## Other Alternatives and Considerations

While each of these alternatives would provide Spectrum with benefits in particular areas, Falconi knew that creating a sales force based on a combination of one or more of these elements might generate greater returns for the company. For example, one option would be to use a combination of a merged sales force and distributors in order to reach both large and small retailers more effectively. Another option could be to create "platform teams," where one business manager would be responsible for maintaining the relationships with the retailers, while a group of product experts support the manager during sales pitches. Falconi wanted to further explore these opportunities, and others, to see what benefits might be derived.

Falconi knew that before any changes could be made to the sales strategy, selecting his sales managers would be the first essential step. He would need to ensure that he had the right people in this role, whether they were the current managers or new ones. These individuals would serve as the leaders for the overall sales force, ensuring continued momentum and performance of the representatives. They would also be the "change agents" responsible for implementing the plans developed by Falconi for any reorganization. If there was a new strategy implemented, Falconi would have to decide how to judge these managers and how best to use them given the chosen system.

Falconi realized he would have to consider the impact that this major change would have on the current employees. The employees recognized that, with such a merger, the company would look for potential synergies to reduce overall company expenses. Other companies in similar situations have typically looked to consolidate employee positions as one option to reduce costs. If there was to be a merger of the sales teams, Falconi would be responsible for selecting the best candidates for the new organization, meaning that nobody's job was safe. As a result, employees from both the Rayovac/Remington and Nu-Gro divisions would be feeling very apprehensive at this point. People are often averse to change, and the sales reps would be concerned about their future employment status and the implications of any forthcoming changes to the company.

Falconi knew that dealing with the sensitivities of his employees would be crucial to achieving a successful implementation of a new sales strategy, if, indeed, the company chose to proceed with that option. Changes would need to be made while the company was still in operation; thus, care needed to be given to these issues in order to avoid potential disturbances and to preserve the current momentum of the business. Falconi realized that change management skills would definitely be required to implement a new structure, or to alleviate concerns if no changes were planned, but he wondered how best to deal with these issues moving forward.

Finally, Falconi needed to decide how many sales reps should be kept if a new strategy was to be implemented and by what criteria he should be judging his representatives. He knew that the sufficient number of sales reps would depend on the chosen direction of the sales force strategy, but he wondered what his team would look like once the dust had settled.

## Decision

Given the nature of the new company, and the industries each business unit competed in, Falconi was unsure what sales force structure would offer the company the greatest benefits, at the same time allowing it to grow its sales and gain a greater retail presence for the entire Spectrum brand portfolio. How should the new company be structured in terms of reporting, responsibilities, and the size of the sales force? Should Spectrum try to structure itself similarly to its competitors, or did its operation require a different approach?

Additionally, depending on which sales force structure was selected, Falconi would have to consider how to organize the teams relative to Spectrum's retail customers. He could organize them by geography, by retail channel, by individual retailers, by some combination of these or by another method altogether. Falconi would have to explore the benefits of the options and determine what made the most sense.

The board of directors was meeting next week, and Falconi wanted to present them with a full report outlining his proposed strategy regarding the sales force and why the other alternatives were dismissed. Overall, Falconi knew that a decision would need to be made quickly in hopes that the new sales force strategy could be implemented prior to the peak period for the lawn and garden industry. Falconi knew that sufficient time would be needed to implement changes and initiate any training that might be required for the sales team.

## CASE QUESTIONS

1. Would the sales process and sales activities be the same for each main brand, largely different, or have some similarities and some differences? Outline why these might be important to managing the sales force.

2. Explain the primary advantages and disadvantages of maintaining a separate sales force for each of the brands.

3. Explain the primary advantages and disadvantages of merging the sales force within the larger company.

4. How might "turf wars" between the formerly independent companies now operating under the Spectrum corporate name affect relationships between salespeople?

5. What types of criteria should be used to evaluate members of the sales force as the company enters this new era?

# Biomed Co., Ltd.: Designing a New Sales Compensation Plan

### By Ponlerd Chiemchanya, under the supervision of Professor Don Barclay

Ponlerd Chiemchanya had just completed his MBA at the Ivey Business School in May 2006. On the one hand, he was excited about rejoining Biomed Co., Ltd. (Biomed), the family business in Thailand. On the other hand, as the new general manager of Biomed, he had some concerns about the first major decisions he was about to make and implement upon his return. Biomed's parent company, Thai Drugs Co., Ltd. (Thai Drugs), had just revised Biomed's market strategy, a change that created the need to realign the sales compensation system to fit with the new strategy. Chiemchanya was charged with this responsibility. Since Biomed was fundamentally a sales organization working on behalf of Thai Drugs, he knew that getting this right could be the making of Biomed. Of course the opposite also held true. Chiemchanya saw high company risk and high personal risk in this situation.

Version: (A) 2009–09–14

## The Current Situation at Biomed

Thai Drugs, a family-owned business, was one of the 170 small to medium-sized local Thai pharmaceutical manufacturers. It was overshadowed by the five large firms that accounted for over 50 percent of local manufacturers' sales, and also by foreign manufacturers that accounted for 65 percent of the Thai pharmaceutical market. Thai Drugs' main strength was in the over-the-counter market, selling to drugstores. In 1990, Thai Drugs started to use existing manufacturing capacity to expand into the generic pharmaceutical market. Overall, it provided more than 100 items of prescription and non-prescription drugs to hospitals, drugstores, and clinics.

Biomed was set up as a subsidiary of Thai Drugs and acted as Thai Drugs' sole agent to sell generic pharmaceuticals to the market. Biomed was basically a sales organization, comprising a sales manager, 11 sales representatives, and several sales administration clerks. Despite the total market size of THB14 billion[1] for locally manufactured generics, Biomed sales had been hovering around THB10 million (.07 percent market share). When compared to the over-the-counter arm of Thai Drugs, Biomed sales were minimal. Due to the unsophisticated information systems at Thai Drugs, it was not possible to determine whether these sales were even profitable. This had been of concern to Thai Drugs' management for the past few years.

This concern was exacerbated when changes in GMP (Good Manufacturing Practice)[2] requirements were expected to be effective in 2008, leading to a massive investment to upgrade manufacturing facilities. Most of this investment was to be tied to the manufacturing of Biomed products. Biomed's cost of capital, at 10 percent, had to be considered here. Biomed also knew that it had to cover THB4 million annually in fixed overhead. Given the small market share and small margins in the generics market and the upcoming investment required, management was starting to question the viability of Biomed.

Would it be worth investing in the manufacturing facilities when Biomed may not sell the products? Was Biomed's sales volume actually generating profits?

Could Biomed do better, given the market size? Would it be better to close Biomed altogether? These were the questions that management was asking while Chiemchanya was away completing his MBA.

Management did decide to make an effort to increase Biomed's sales and profitability. To accomplish this, management evaluated the situation and changed Biomed's market strategy. If this was not successful over the next one to two years, Thai Drugs might close down Biomed and abandon the generic pharmaceutical market altogether. Chiemchanya needed to understand what was behind this management decision. He needed to examine the industry, the old market strategy and the existing sales compensation plan, and the new market strategy before he could design an appropriate sales compensation plan.

## The Thai Generic Pharmaceutical Market

### Market Size

With a population of 65 million people in Thailand, the total domestic market for pharmaceuticals (local and foreign companies combined), in 2002 figures, was around US$900 million or THB40 billion at wholesale prices. Foreign companies and their original products accounted for 65 percent of the market. Local Thai companies accounted for the remaining 35 percent of the market. Since all of the Thai manufacturers were formulating drugs but were not involved in the research and development (R&D) of new drugs, 35 percent was a representative figure for the local generic market. This resulted in a THB14 billion market for generics.

### Manufacturers

Beyond the top five generics manufacturers, the market was fragmented. There were 175 Thai manufacturers, providing drugs to the THB14 billion market. Five companies accounted for more than 50 percent of the market (see Exhibit 1). The remaining 50 percent of the market was shared among 170 manufacturers, which were small private or family-owned businesses.

## Market Segments

### Hospitals

According to 2002 figures, hospitals accounted for 70 percent of the market for domestically manufactured pharmaceuticals. In April 2001, the government implemented the "30-baht universal health care" scheme whereby everyone received universal health care at hospitals by paying THB30 per visit. This new scheme put pressure on public hospitals. Under this scheme, hospitals received funding on a per-capita basis, as opposed to having 100 percent funding of a hospital's annual expenditures. Public hospitals were forced to find ways to cut costs in order to manage and service patients within budget. This led to a dramatic increase in generic substitution. Most hospitals automatically substituted all original products with generics whenever there was a generic version available.

There were two major implications for generic manufacturers resulting from the 30-baht scheme. First, the new government scheme favored generic manufacturers due to the substitution of branded products by generics. However, the second implication worked against these manufacturers. Hospitals in the same province and region collectively formed buying groups to bargain for the lowest generic prices. The process started with sellers proposing their price in a bidding process. The provider with the lowest price would win the bid and then became the primary provider of the drug throughout the province or region. The second and third runners-up would be back-up providers. The result was that only those few providers with the lowest costs could sell to public hospitals and make a profit. Manufacturers that did not have low-cost structures, or who were not interested in pursuing low-cost strategies, could sell only those low-volume products that did not end up in a bidding process. They could also decide to simply abandon this market.

### Drugstores

From 2002 figures, drugstores accounted for most of the remaining 30 percent of the market for domestically manufactured pharmaceuticals. There were an estimated 11,000 drugstores in Thailand, most of which were privately owned by pharmacists

| Exhibit I | Top 5 Thai Drug Manufacturers |
| --- | --- |

| Manufacturer | Sales (million THB) | Market Share |
| --- | --- | --- |
| Siam Bhaesaj | 1,975 | 14% |
| GPO | 1,702 | 12% |
| Biolab | 1,468 | 10% |
| Berlin Pharm | 1,261 | 9% |
| Thai Nakorn Patana | 963 | 7% |
| Total of top 5 | 7,369 | 53% |
| Total generics market | 14,000 | 100% |

*Source:* epsicom business intelligence, World pharmaceutical markets: Thailand, March 2004.

or were "mom and pop" style pharmacies. Although there were foreign drugstore chains (e.g., Boots, Watson's), these chains were geared more toward selling beauty products and food. When drugs were prescribed in chains, most of the time, the original-version drug would be used. Most generics were prescribed through privately owned drugstores.

Patients viewed drugstores as a cheap and convenient alternative compared to a visit to the hospital or a doctor's clinic. Pharmacists in drugstores had the autonomy to prescribe prescription drugs without a prescription from a physician. This latitude made drugstores a good choice for people with lower incomes, since they could receive an immediate diagnosis and prescription while avoiding waiting times and doctors' fees. Generics were widely prescribed in drugstores due to their lower cost. Drugstores purchased generics either through distributors or directly from a manufacturer such as Biomed.

### Doctor Clinics

The market for drugs in clinics was relatively small when compared to hospitals and drugstores. Doctor clinics held drug inventory to service their patients. Patients were diagnosed and given medicine at the clinic. Most clinics were privately owned by the attending doctor. Generics were also widely used in clinics due to their lower cost. Generics were purchased through either distributors or directly from the manufacturer.

## Biomed's Market Strategy

Management looked at Biomed's existing market strategy and found a disconnect between the strategy and the changing market environment.

### Existing Market Strategy for Generics

Biomed's overall value proposition to customers was to provide high quality drugs backed by excellent service.

### Market Focus

Biomed targeted all three markets (hospitals, drugstores, and clinics) throughout Thailand. There was no specific strategy to emphasize one market segment over another.

### Products

Biomed offered more than 100 items of generic products covering almost all types of drugs, e.g., analgesics, antibiotics, vitamins, allergy and respiratory drugs, electrolytes and supplements, gastrointestinal drugs, topical agents, and pediatric drugs. Most Biomed products were undifferentiated, commodity-type products. A typical example was Amoxycillin 500 mg × 1,000 capsules packaged in a plain plastic container. However, a small percentage of Biomed's product line was geared more towards drugstores and clinics. These products had some degree of differentiation, mostly in the unique color and shape of tablets or capsules. Due to the low education level of the general population, drugstores and clinics that prescribed drugs with unique appearances could have a competitive advantage in the community, since the patient would come back to the drugstore/clinic asking for "the drug," which he or she could not find anywhere else.

### Price

Biomed products were priced in the medium-high to high range of the generics market. Volume discounts were offered on a case-by-case basis. Biomed seldom used aggressive price promotions with its customers. It could not afford price discounts because of its lack of economies of scale in production, which led to a high unit cost, based on full cost accounting.

### Distribution

Biomed utilized third-party transportation companies to deliver products directly to customers. Biomed was not in a position to incur additional costs by using distributors.

### Communications

The Biomed sales force was the single contact and means of communication with the customer. No other means of advertising (journal ads, television ads, radio ads) were employed.

## Existing Sales Strategy

### Sales Role

Given that the sales representative was the only person who touched the customer, the role of the salesperson was complex. The current role and goals could be described as

- Generate sales according to quota.
- Find new accounts.
- Build and maintain relationships between customers and Biomed.
- Negotiate prices with customers within a given range.
- Decide whether customers should receive 30-day credit or 60-day credit.
- Take orders.
- Listen to customer complaints and provide feedback to management.
- Gain and share market intelligence.

### Existing Compensation Plan

The existing compensation plan had three components:

*Salary:* The current salary was THB5,000 per month (THB60,000 annually).

*Commission:* Sales reps received 1.5 percent of sales volume with a progressive ramp. Sales above 100 percent of targeted annual sales were compensated at three percent. Targeted annual sales per rep were THB2 million, on average.

*Quarterly bonus:* A bonus was paid at the end of each quarter if the year-to-date sales quota was achieved for the quarter. This bonus was retroactively paid whenever year-to-date sales reached quotas.

Overall, the compensation package was on par with the rest of the industry (see Exhibit 2).

### Expenses

Each sales representative received a basic allowance of THB380 per day. This was to cover all costs, e.g., fuel, hotel costs, entertainment expenses and cell phone. This level of allowance typically covered a basic hotel room and daily meals. No additional expenses were reimbursed. The expense allowance had an incentive portion.

---

**Exhibit 2**  Existing Compensation Plan

| Component | Base Salary With Commission and Bonus | | |
|---|---|---|---|
| Base Salary | THB60,000 | | |
| Commission on sales volume* | Performance To Goal | | Commission rate |
| | To 100% | | 1.5% |
| | Beyond 100% | | 3% |
| Quarterly bonus | Performance | | Bonus |
| | Q1  Achieve 100% of Q1 YTD Goal | | THB3,000 |
| | Q2  Achieve 100% of Q1-2 YTD Goal | | THB4,000 |
| | Q3  Achieve 100% of Q1-3 YTD Goal | | THB5,000 |
| | Q4  Achieve 100% of Q1-4 YTD Goal | | THB6,000 |
| | *Bonus for previous quarters are retro-backed when YTD goal is achieved | | |

---

*Sales were credited when money was collected.

Regardless of territory, if year-to-date sales reached a certain level, the daily allowance would increase as follows:

| Sales Volume YTD (THB) | Allowance/day |
|---|---|
| 0–500,000 | THB380 |
| 500,000–1,000,000 | THB420 |
| 1,000,000–2,000,000 | THB460 |
| 2,000,000 and above | THB500 |

### Other Benefits

Sales reps were entitled to the same basic benefits as other Thai Drugs employees. This included a medical insurance plan and a company contribution of seven percent of salary to the provident (retirement) fund.

## Strategy Review

In assessing the existing strategy against the current environment, management found two major flaws. The first concerned a lack of direction in terms of product/market focus, and the second concerned price.

There was no discipline in approaching the three different market segments (hospitals, drugstores, doctor clinics). Sales representatives called on any customer where they thought they could generate sales. Management came to believe that Biomed's products were not suitable for hospitals. Since most hospitals used a bidding process to purchase drugs, only the lowest cost providers could win in this segment. Given Thai Drugs' limitation in terms of increasing manufacturing efficiency, and given management's preference not to compete solely on price, it was felt that the hospital segment should not be a target.

Complementing this view was that Biomed actually had strength in the drugstore segment. Since Biomed sales representatives could also sell Thai Drugs' leading over-the-counter products, which were in demand in drugstores, Biomed sales representatives could leverage this to get in the door and start a conversation with the owner. Moreover, some of Biomed's products were already designed for drugstores. Thus, it would be sensible, both from a product standpoint and a sales standpoint, to focus more on drugstores and clinics.

As to the second observation, Biomed's existing strategy was to price at a medium-high to high price point. This was based on the belief that customers would pay a premium price in exchange for good service and a rewarding relationship with Biomed. Management was becoming concerned that this was no longer a compelling argument. In selling commodity-type products, having a competitive price is the No. 1 key success factor. This did not mean that Biomed would have to have the lowest price, since some customers were willing to pay more as long as the price was not too high, the seller had a good relationship, and good service was provided. However, if the price was out of the acceptable range, no matter how good the relationship or service level were, the value to the customer would not justify the higher price.

## New Market Strategy

Although management decided on changes in market focus, products and price, the overall value proposition would remain the same, i.e., high-quality products backed by excellent service. The key changes inherent in the new market strategy were:

### Product Market Focus

From the strategy review, management decided that Biomed's products could not compete in the low-price hospital market. The new product market focus was to be on drugstores and doctor clinics.

### Product

Instead of selling more than 100 items, the new strategy was to focus on only 10 to 15 items and to reduce the prices on these select items. The rationale was that by focusing on the right items at the right price, it would be possible to gain larger orders with two subsequent benefits. First, Biomed would lose fewer orders because of price. Second, combining large orders of fewer items would make it possible to have longer production runs.

This would yield economies of scale and lower the unit cost of these selected products. This would lead to more contribution and provide more room if further price cuts were required.

The items selected would have three main characteristics. From a cost perspective, there must be enough room to be able to lower the price to the same range as competitors. Since Thai Drugs had strength in manufacturing sugar coated tablets and formulating multivitamins, which were skills that not all manufacturers had, these drugs would be preferred over other basic tablets and capsules. Finally, products that had sold well in the past were also good candidates, since it meant that customers valued these products as high-quality products.

### Price

Selling prices would be reduced to the low-medium to medium price range. However, not all prices would be reduced. Price reductions would tie into the reduced set of products upon which Biomed decided to focus.

## The New Market Strategy and Biomed's Sales Strategy

After digesting the new strategy, Chiemchanya was in a position to think about the implications for Biomed's sales strategy. Before jumping into redesigning the compensation system, he knew that it made sense to review the overall implications for the sales strategy, and then to revisit the role of the sales rep under the new strategy. (See Exhibit 3 for a visualization of the new market strategy.)

### Implications for the Sales Strategy

In the new market strategy, the biggest changes included reducing market scope, lowering selected prices, focusing on 10 to 15 items, and the resulting

---

**Exhibit 3**  New Market Strategy

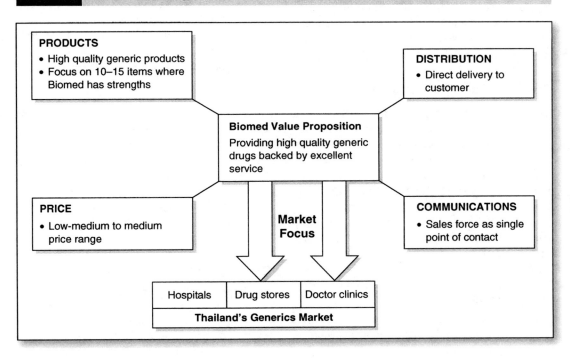

challenge of generating both volume and THB contribution from this sharper product/market focus. Chiemchanya thought that instead of focusing on sales volume, looking at each sale on a contribution basis might make sense. This would mean that reps would have to consider the cost of the products, transportation costs and ordering costs before deciding to accept an order. This would require training.

In addition, each sales representative would have to promote the same selected 10 to 15 products so that, collectively, the sales volume for each item from all territories would increase dramatically. This would lead to economies of scale in production and lower unit costs. Sales representatives would have to learn how to convince customers to purchase the items upon which Biomed wanted to focus. This would change the conversation when visiting customers. Sales reps would have to sell versus simply taking orders for any products that the customer wanted.

Finally, hospitals would not be targeted. This change would have minimal impact on sales reps, whose volume came from drugstores. However, there were some sales reps who had a lot of sales activity within the hospital segment. How could Chiemchanya encourage these reps to change their planning and working style to focus away from hospitals?

### The New Sales Role and Goals

The sales force would remain as the single point of contact with the customer. Sales reps would still have a complex set of tasks, and many of the tasks in the old strategy would transfer to the new. As Chiemchanya reflected, he thought the new sales role would have as its overarching purposes: being the single point of contact with the customer, and being the THB contribution generator for the company. He thought the following tasks would make up the sales role.

- Generate THB contribution, which included the tasks of
  - o Price negotiation—sales representatives would have autonomy to negotiate prices with customers within a range.
  - o Credit evaluation/provision—sales representatives would have autonomy to decide whether a customer should receive a 30-day or 60-day credit.
  - o Taking orders.

Focusing on contribution margin would fit perfectly with the new strategy. Biomed's new market strategy had prices going down, so reps need to combine these decreases in unit contribution with increased volumes on an order-by-order basis to ensure company profitability. Reps would be informed of the "loaded" cost of goods, including the variable cost of the product, the transportation cost for each order, and the ordering costs. They would be responsible to negotiate with the customer to reach the price and order quantity that maximized THB contribution.

- Focus selling efforts in drugstores and doctor clinics.
- Find new accounts.
- Build and maintain relationships between the customer and Biomed.
- Focus selling efforts on 10 to 15 items selected by management.
- Listen to customer complaints and provide feedback to management.
- Gain and share market intelligence.

Chiemchanya was still not comfortable jumping to a compensation system that would encourage the accomplishment of the tasks inherent in the new sales role. He thought it was important to set explicit goals against each of these tasks. In the past, only one goal had been set: a sales volume goal. He wanted to be much clearer under the new sales strategy and came up with a specific list of tasks and their associated goals (see Exhibit 4).

## Designing the Compensation System and Next Steps

Chiemchanya believed that he was now set to revamp the sales compensation system at Biomed to reflect the new market strategy. He knew that he

| Exhibit 4 | Sales Tasks and Goals |
|---|---|

| Task | Goal |
|---|---|
| Generate THB contribution | THB contribution against a quota which might vary by territory |
| Focus selling efforts on drugstores and clinics | At least 60% of contribution derived from drugstores and clinics (with allowances for reps who currently have a large number of hospital accounts) |
| Find new accounts | Number of new accounts/year, which might vary by territory |
| Build and maintain relationships between customer and company | Volume of repeat sales |
| Focus selling efforts on 10 to 15 items selected by management | 75% of contribution derived from the focused items (derived from management's estimate of what is required to achieve economies of scale) |
| Listen to customer complaints and provide feedback to management | Monthly report of customer complaints, feedback |
| Gain and share market intelligence | Monthly market intelligence report |

was following a logical path since he had translated the market strategy into a new sales strategy with a revised sales role and associated goals. He wondered how he would judge the new system as he designed it. Although Chiemchanya was confident that he had developed a logical approach to redesigning the compensation system, he knew that his task did not end with the compensation system documented on a piece of paper. Two other issues still dogged him.

The first was the implementation of the new plan. Anytime a manager makes decisions that potentially have an impact on someone's wallet, careful thought needs to be given to the communication of the proposed changes. There also has to be consideration of any protection that might be given to reps as they move from one system to the next. In addition, if the new plan required the use of territory-specific targets or quotas, deriving these would have to be done in a manner deemed to be fair and equitable by the sales reps. The first person to get on board would be the sales manager.

He could act in concert with Chiemchanya to sell the new approach, although Chiemchanya surmised that the initial reaction of the sales reps would be negative. The new plan required changes in behavior, and the sales reps may feel that their income would be at risk as a result.

The second issue that kept Chiemchanya awake at night was the sense that, although important in supporting the new strategy, there were many other things required from the sales program in order to ensure the success of the new market strategy. Chiemchanya needed to think through any training interventions that would be required. He also had to think through whether or not all the sales reps were suited to the new sales role. It is different selling on volume than selling on contribution to a focused market segment with a focused set of products. What if some reps could not make the switch? He also needed to determine whether or not there was a place for recognition, in addition to rewards, to encourage the desired behaviors under the new strategy.

The fun was about to begin.

## CASE QUESTIONS

1. The current compensations system was salary plus commission, plus bonus. Should the compensation system shift to accommodate the change in sales methods and primary target markets? If so, how? If not, why not?

2. Previously, the sales force served primarily as order takers. The new role would be to conduct actual selling activities. How should the company train its sales representatives to make the adjustment?

3. When revising the performance evaluation system, what input measures would be affected by the change in selling strategy? How would they be affected?

4. When revising the performance evaluation system, what output measures would be affected by the change in selling strategy? How would they be affected?

5. When revising the performance evaluation system, what nonselling activities would be affected by the change in selling strategy? How would they be affected?

6. How can the climate of the company, especially in the sales department, be altered to facilitate the implementation of this new selling approach?

CHAPTER

10

# Internal Communications

Communication is the process of transmitting, receiving, and processing information. Business communication has been compared to the glue that holds a company together, the electricity that gives it energy, and the oil that lubricates smooth functioning. Business communication takes two forms: (1) individual communication and (2) communication systems.

## Individual Communication

Individual communication occurs when one person addresses another person or group of people. Individual communication models suggest a two-way process by which ideas are sent and received. The sender is the person preparing a message or idea. Encoding is forming the verbal and nonverbal cues designed to relay the idea. A transmission device carries the message from one person to others. Decoding occurs when the receiver attempts to understand the message through the use of the five senses. The receiver is the person for whom the message was intended. The receiver provides feedback, such as agreement, disagreement, confusion, and other reactions, to the sender through verbal and nonverbal signals.

## Barriers to Individual Communication

Three sets of barriers to communication, or noise, distort or disrupt messages. The first group consists of differences between the sender and the receiver. Age, gender, status, culture/subculture, and personality differences can all interfere with message transmission and reception.

Situational factors are a second form of noise. In various settings, communication becomes difficult, such as what follows the announcement of the death or retirement of a popular employee. Emotions also affect communication quality. Anger and depression often keep messages from being clearly sent or understood.

Mechanical problems such as language, slang, problems with transmission, and nonverbal contradiction of verbal messages further inhibit quality communication. Persons from foreign countries cope with both the new language and local slang. Transmission problems occur in numerous ways, some as simple as a dead battery in a cell phone. Nonverbal messages are often more powerful than the words being transmitted.

## Overcoming the Barriers to Individual Communication

In any conversation, both the sender and the receiver are responsible for effective communication. A failure by either can lead to a message not being correctly understood. The sender should be careful to consider potential barriers, speak with empathy, maintain awareness of all nonverbal cues being transmitted, and seek confirmation that the message was correctly interpreted. The receiver's duties are to listen attentively and to ask for clarification of any confusing message.

## The Value of Individual Communication

Individual communication strongly links with success in marketing and management. Individual communication quality affects interactions with coworkers within the marketing department, interactions with other departments, internal marketing programs, interactions with clients and customers, and career success paths of individual employees. An internal marketing program is an ongoing process through which leaders can align, motivate, and empower employees. Quality communication facilitates the process.

## Communication Systems in Organizations

Communication in organizations takes many forms. It flows in various directions. Organizational communication moves through two channels. Formal communication travels through channels that are chosen or designated by the organization. Informal communication emerges in the form of gossip, rumors, and what travels over the grapevine. As communication systems continue to evolve through forums such as social media, the distinction between formal and informal communication becomes increasingly blurred; however, both elements deserve consideration by marketing managers.

Formal communication channels may be divided into traditional and newly developed channels. Traditional channels are a direct address from one employee to another, meetings, memos, letters, the company's manual or handbook, the bulletin board, and all company magazines and newspapers. Newly developed channels consist of cell phones, satellite transmissions, teleconferencing, e-mail, the company's website, fax transmissions, and a firm's intranet.

## Barriers to Formal Communication

Just as noise can distort or disrupt individual communication, many barriers to formal communication exist. System overload means that the formal channel is so swamped that messages become lost. Selective filtering occurs when a message that is being passed from one person to another is altered in some way. Messages sent by the wrong or an inappropriate channel are at risk of not being seen or heard. Company transmission failures include any breakdown of machinery, such as a website crash. Many times, rumors are more persistent than the truth and lead to formal communication problems. Also, any individual communication barrier represents a potential barrier to formal communication.

## Overcoming the Barriers to Formal Communication

Building an internal communication system requires two processes. The first is to establish an efficient and effective management information system. The second is to identify and eliminate the barriers to formal communication.

A management information system consists of the people and machinery used to collect and process organizational information. Effective systems employ quality individuals to collect and distribute information, including the sales force, management team, and others that make contact with the public. Management information systems need effective machinery, including phone systems and computer applications, to work properly. Also, effective systems generate quality information that is timely, accurate, relevant, concise, and stored for future use.

Eliminating barriers to formal communication begins with carefully selecting the proper channel for each message. Important messages should be transmitted through multiple channels. Then informal communication should be managed. This involves understanding that gossip travels quickly, is accurate or partly accurate about two-thirds of the time, and tends to center on things that are important to employees. Next, the manager should tap in, or have a pipeline regarding current rumors. Finally, the marketing manager should use the channel to pass along messages, especially compliments to successful employees and trial balloons, where ideas are tested out before being implemented.

## Internal Communication and Customer Service

Traditional thinking suggests that a satisfied workforce will produce satisfied customers. Recent research now suggests that satisfied and loyal customers cause employee satisfaction. Creating a customer-centric culture yields positive benefits for customers and produces long-term employee benefits as well. Several issues must be addressed to create a customer-centric culture.

First, the company's vision and mission should be clearly reinforced. A mission statement outlines the overall, most general purpose an organization serves. The firm's vision explains how the mission will be achieved. When a company's mission and vision are clearly understood, everyone from the CEO to first-line employees knows something about the type of marketing experience the company seeks to provide.

Second, effective marketing managers understand and adapt to the company's culture in order to achieve a customer-centric environment. The company's culture consists of the symbols, rituals, language, myths, stories, and jargon present in the organization. Most of the time, a founder story establishes the first elements of culture. Effective managers recognize that culture evolves over many years and becomes difficult to change. At first, the manager can work only within the parameters of the culture that exists. Building a customer-centric environment in a company that does not have one will take patience and time.

The third aspect of establishing a customer-first attitude is adjusting the firm's or department's climate. The climate is the prevailing atmosphere within a company and will be strongly affected by the organization's external environment, its strengths and weaknesses, and the preferences and activities of managers. Changing a climate involves engaging employees through empowerment and building relationships through open and honest communication.

Creating a customer service orientation requires employees to "buy in." They must be engaged in the process. They must understand and believe in the company's mission and vision. Employee engagement contributes to employee empowerment. Employees with the authority to make customer-related decisions on the spot sense greater empowerment. The process takes time, but when employees believe the company they work for is "their" company, customers are often the beneficiaries.

Honest and open communication combat obfuscation, which is the attempt to obscure, disguise, or confuse a message. Individuals who are able to send and receive constructive criticism fare better in the short and long term. Employees should resist the temptation to engage in inclusive/exclusive language whereby one set of workers develops its own lingo and patterns of communication. Exclusive language is used to discriminate and make some workers feel uncomfortable and unwelcome. Marketing managers should also be aware of and correct objectionable language, especially any type of harassment, hazing, or discriminatory statements.

Other key components of a positive, customer-oriented company are its rewards and recognition systems. Managers should remain cognizant of what they reward and how. Showing appreciation is easy and has no cost.

## International Internal Communications

The proliferation of international conglomerates and the expansion of small businesses into foreign locations creates many opportunities and challenges for internal communication systems. The opportunities include nearly instantaneous contact with employees and partners around the world, which facilitates more efficient and effective marketing and management activities. The challenges start with the barriers to communication, most notably language, slang, and technical difficulties. A successful international marketing program adapts to the intricacies of local languages and customs and adjusts to technological challenges.

## Implications for Marketing Managers

Three activities summarize the impact of communication on entry-level employees and first-line supervisors in the marketing department. First, one should work to improve personal communications skills, especially the avoidance of current lingo, such as overuse of the word "like" and "ya know." Second, successful marketers are careful listeners. Listening skills can be practiced and perfected. Third, a marketing manager wishing to achieve learns how communication takes place in an organization and adjusts his or her approach to fit the style exhibited in the company.

## The Cases

### Retail Execution: Linens 'n Things

As an organization grows, communication systems can be expected to evolve. In the case of Linens 'n Things, the changes needed did not occur in a timely fashion. Centralized decision-making processes had led to inventory decisions being made for the entire chain, rather than store by store. The consequence was stock-outs of popular items in some stores and overstocks in others. The marketing managers at Linens 'n Things found the company lagging behind Bed Bath & Beyond—both in terms of growth and sales and in setting industry practices, such as return policies and the use of coupons. Norman Axelrod, chairman and chief operating officer, decided to test a program he titled GOLD—or Guest Oriented, Locally Driven management of individual units. He encountered resistance and wondered whether the program would succeed or die.

### GDR Versus Kodak—Bart Film Scanner

Emerging technologies create a variety of problems and opportunities, both in the areas of product innovation and development and for the internal company communication system. In the dental imaging world, the transition from analog to digital technologies was taking place. Products were needed to facilitate the switch. Georginelli Dental Research (GDR) held a strong position in the marketplace that might erode as the industry moved away from film to digital imaging. The company's key manager, Angelo Bella, with the help of an original equipment manager partner, B. T. Wang, had developed a product carrying the code name Bart to ease the shift. Unfortunately, previous attempts at developing similar products had failed. Angelo and B. T. had to overcome negativism and cynicism to bring the product to market.

## Retail Execution: Linens 'n Things

*By Adenekan (Nick) Dedeke*

## Introduction

Norman Axelrod, chairman, president and chief operating officer of Linens 'n Things (LNT), reflected on the next steps that he should take to keep LNT competitive. In the early 2000s, Axelrod felt that the market and the competitive landscape were changing again. Specifically, the firm's closest competition, Bed Bath & Beyond (BBB), was extending its lead ahead of LNT. BBB had higher sales and higher profits. Axelrod recognized that LNT probably needed to change its merchandising process and the product assortment in order to cut down the advantages of BBB. The business had become more complex to manage because of the growth in number of stores, the increase in product categories, and the proliferation in the number of store-keeping units that had to be managed. Axelrod had brought in an executive to investigate what LNT should do to catch up with BBB. The executive, Bill Emerson, had introduced a successful pilot and had initiated the rollout of an assortment improvement initiative that gave store managers more decision rights for replenishment orders. Due to dwindling interest and internal resistance to the initiative, Axelrod had to decide what he would do with the Guest Oriented, Locally Driven (GOLD)

rollout. Should he stand by Emerson and the program or should he side with the opponents of the program and shut it down? If he chose to continue the program, he had to decide if he had to change it somehow. Should he put a time limit on the program? Should he limit its use to specific districts? Should he force the central buying staff to participate in the program by executive mandate?

## Company Beginnings

Eugene Wallace Kalkin, at the age of 22, laid the groundwork for Linens 'n Things, Inc. during his seven-year tenure in the buying office of Allied Purchasing Corp., which was the second largest department store chain in the United States in the late 1950s. In 1958, he collaborated with the retail discount chain known as Great Eastern Mills, Inc. by setting set up the leased-linen departments for the company's stores. Then Daylin Inc. bought a controlling interest in Great Eastern Mills Inc. in 1970 and it later went into bankruptcy. In 1975, Kalkin bought back, from a Daylin bankruptcy court, the seven specialty stores that he had helped develop. This seven-unit retail chain, which had

     Version: (A) 2010–02–26

annual sales of $2 million, was the beginning of Linens 'n Things, Inc. Kalkin applied a novel set of merchandising techniques to develop LNT into a chain of specialty retail stores. Under Kalkin's leadership the company grew from seven to fifty-five stores. In 1983, Melville Corporation (later known as CVS Corporation) bought LNT, then a 55-store chain with more than $85 million in annual sales. Kalkin left the firm shortly after the acquisition. Robert Karan, Kalkin's close associate, was chosen to succeed him. Before he left the firm, Kalkin adapted retailing practices of European hypermarchés, which reduced operating costs by piling goods on storage cubes that were piled up to the ceiling, thereby saving space and reducing expenses. Kalkin opted for stores with high ceilings in order to save space and he installed 10-foot-high, warehouse-type shelving for piling up storage cubes. He could then display in a 7,000-square-foot space the quantity of merchandise that traditionally required 12,000 to 13,000 square feet of area. The primary drive of Kalkin, and Karan after him, was to drive costs down and to invest money only in the necessary resources.

Kalkin and Karan's leadership resulted in a failure to deploy money for information technologies and even delays in the implementation of the larger store format that they had tested. The strategy involved cutting costs and earning a profit by selling quality products at discount prices. As the number of stores increased, the manual processes and the low-cost approach began to create poor retail execution and performance. Owing to problems that the firm faced under Karan, Melville Corporation's chairman, Stan Goldstein, asked Axelrod to become LNT's chief executive officer in 1988. He was elected to the additional role of chairman of the board of directors effective January 1997. From that time in recurring manner, Axelrod held concurrent positions in the firm, namely, chairman of the board, chief executive officer (CEO) and president.

Axelrod implemented major changes in his initial years. In September 1988, under his leadership, LNT opened its first superstore, which was a store with a size that varied between 35,000 to 40,000 square feet, in Rockville, Maryland. In 1989, the company started the conversion of its traditional store base to superstores and began the closing of all but the most profitable traditional-format stores The traditional stores averaged approximately 10,000 square feet in size. During the period of 1988 through 1995, LNT introduced more than 100 superstores and closed 85 traditional stores. The company's gross square footage more than quadrupled, going from 1.4 million square feet on January 1, 1992, to 5.49 million square feet by the end of 1997 (see Exhibit 1). As LNT aggressively expanded stores nationally, its closest competition, BBB, expanded into new cities too (see Exhibit 2). Axelrod also initiated the strategy of expanding LNT beyond its focus on the linens business into the "things" business. He set an aggressive goal of increasing the proportion of revenues contributed by the "things" department by up to 50 percent. LNT expanded into products such as house wares and home accessories. On November 26, 1996, LNT effected an initial public offering (IPO) of its common stock; CVS retained approximately 32.5 percent of the shares, but sold them in 1997. In 1998, LNT sales topped $1 billion for the first time in its history. Sales climbed to $1.07 billion, up 22 percent from 1997. The company operated 176 stores (153 superstores and 23 smaller, traditional-format stores) in 37 states. The stores carried brand name "linens," such as bed linens, towels, and pillows, and "things," such as house wares and home accessories.[1]

## Transforming Operational Management Practices

When Axelrod took over at LNT, he discovered that most business processes were manual and that managers made their decisions intuitively. For example, in the late 1980s inventory management and sales management were done by phone conferencing. Each morning, the senior vice-president for merchandising called store managers to get reports about what sales were on the previous day. The executive, at the headquarters, did not know what was selling and what was not selling. In those days,

**Exhibit 1**  Quantitative Analysis of Performance Data for Linens 'n Things (1997–2007)

| | 2007 | 2006 | 2005 | 2004 | 2003 | 2002 | 2001 | 2000 | 1999 | 1998 | 1997 |
|---|---|---|---|---|---|---|---|---|---|---|---|
| # of employees | 17,500 | 18,500 | 18,300 | 17,200 | 16,900 | 14,700 | 12,200 | 12,200 | 11,900 | 7,700 | 6,800 |
| # full-time employees | 6,600 | 7,300 | 8,000 | 8,000 | 7,100 | 6,500 | 5,600 | 5,600 | 5,000 | 3,300 | 3,300 |
| # of suppliers | 1,000 | 1,200 | 1,200 | 1,000 | 1,000 | 1,000 | 1,000 | 1,000 | 1,000 | 1,000 | 1,000 |
| # of closed stores | 0 | 2 | 5 | 2 | 9 | 7 | 3 | 4 | 9 | 12 | 18 |
| # of new stores at year end | 18 | 31 | 55 | 54 | 58 | 55 | 63 | 57 | 43 | 32 | 25 |
| # of stores open at year end | 589 | 571 | 542 | 492 | 440 | 391 | 343 | 283 | 230 | 196 | 176 |
| # of distribution centers | 3 | 3 | 3 | 3 | 3 | 3 | 3 | 3 | 3 | 2 | 2 |
| Gross sq. ft. store space (end period) | 19,423,000 | 18,928,000 | 18,071,000 | 16,702,000 | 1,510,600 | 13,607,000 | 11,980,000 | 9,836,000 | 7,925,000 | 6,487,000 | 5,493,000 |
| Gross sq. ft. all distribution and storage locations | 1,200,000 | 1,200,000 | 1,200,000 | 1,200,000 | 1,200,000 | 1,190,000 | 1,190,000 | 1,190,000 | 1,190,000 | 351,000 | 334,000 |

*(Continued)*

**Exhibit 1** (Continued)

| | 2007 | 2006 | 2005 | 2004 | 2003 | 2002 | 2001 | 2000 | 1999 | 1998 | 1997 |
|---|---|---|---|---|---|---|---|---|---|---|---|
| Net sales ($000) | 2,794,776 | 2,534,365 | 2,694,742 | 2,661,469 | 2,395,272 | 2,184,716 | 1,823,803 | 1,572,576 | 1,300,632 | 1,066,194 | 874,224 |
| Cost of goods / Cost of sales ($000) | 1,747,904 | 1,557,011 | 1,595,394 | 1,589,700 | 1,428,706 | 1,308,524 | 10,77,867.57 | 934,110 | 780,379.2 | 639,138 | 527,924 |
| Gross profits ($000) | 1,046,872 | 977,354 | 1,099,348 | 1,071,769 | 966,566 | 876,192 | 745,935 | 638,466 | 520,253 | 427,056 | 346,300 |
| Merchandise inventories ($000) | 795,371 | 793,002 | 787,283 | 715,184 | 700,406 | 615,256 | 492,307 | 437,258 | 342,681 | 271,389 | 223,188 |
| Total assets ($000) | 1,740,387 | 1,857,934 | 1,650,834 | 1,591,884 | 1,467,456 | 1,277,123 | 1,046,305 | 919,504 | 676,916 | 560,844 | 472,099 |
| Working capital ($000) | 414,390 | 428,043 | 537,516 | 519,686 | 458,519 | 369,221 | 218,163 | 219,571 | 181,380 | 154,893 | 123,375 |
| Increase in comparable store sales | −0.034 | −0.007 | 0.06 | 0.018 | 0.013 | 0.031 | −0.024 | 0.037 | 0.054 | 0.083 | 0.066 |
| Capital expenditures | 37,022 | 66,280 | 128,912 | 110,443 | 113,571 | 85,200 | 100,000 | 70,500 | 70,100 | | |
| Total liabilities ($000) | 1,417,603 | 1,313,191 | 800,971 | 4,661,548 | 399,491 | 399,491 | 359,716 | 305,956 | 249,298 | 200,515 | 166,517 |
| Net advertising costs ($000) | 157,000 | 127,000 | 114,000 | 103,500 | 95,000 | 59,800 | 49,700 | 39,600 | 35,600 | 28,913 | 25,161 |

*Source:* Company Annual 10K Reports.

| Exhibit 2 | Retail Outlets Count |

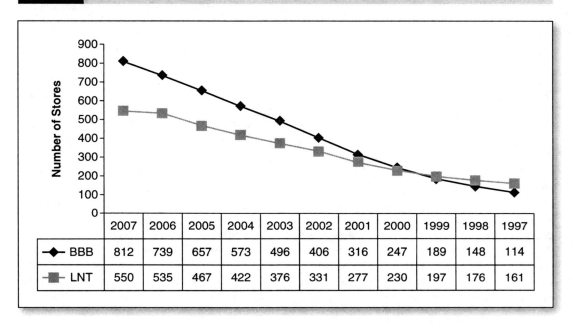

| | 2007 | 2006 | 2005 | 2004 | 2003 | 2002 | 2001 | 2000 | 1999 | 1998 | 1997 |
|---|---|---|---|---|---|---|---|---|---|---|---|
| BBB | 812 | 739 | 657 | 573 | 496 | 406 | 316 | 247 | 189 | 148 | 114 |
| LNT | 550 | 535 | 467 | 422 | 376 | 331 | 277 | 230 | 197 | 176 | 161 |

buying was done centrally, but the store managers had the authority to determine what should be replenished and in what quantities, within the limits of authorized corporate product assortment. The central buyers had the authority to set the corporate product assortment, while the store managers, by their replenishment decisions, controlled the store assortment.

After he became the CEO, Axelrod authorized the first deployment of information technology at LNT. He also hired Steven Silverstein to lead the transformation of the merchandising organization. Matt Meany, vice-president of management information systems, guided the first deployment of information systems technologies. In 1991, the firm implemented its JDA® enterprise system, specifically the order management module. This enabled headquarters to know the sales of the previous day without having to call store managers. However, the merchandising organization still did not have the technology that enabled it to know inventory levels at the stores. To deduce store-level inventory information, Silverstein, vice-president for general merchandising, introduced a sampling methodology. Once a week, on Mondays, he and his team telephoned store managers of a sample of 20 to 30 stores. These stores were required to physically count inventory for pre-selected store-keeping units (SKUs) in key product categories of their stores. The stores reported these inventory counts to Silverstein's office and he used these numbers to estimate the level of inventory across all stores.

The merchandise replenishment process remained largely dependent on reported data, which caused errors. For example, during a scheduled phone conference call to discuss an upcoming promotion drive, a store manager reported to Silverstein that he had run out of the "bed in the bag" product, the target of the fast-approaching product sales promotion. As soon as he spoke up, several other store managers spoke up too, requesting that Silverstein organize special orders from the supplier on their behalf. Apparently, several stores needed the product. The vice-president for merchandising made hurried calls to the supplier and placed a rushed order before the promotion. The supplier supplied thousands of products to the stores. After the delivery of the products, it was discovered that most of the stores had the product. Therefore, these stores were overstocked and they had to mark down products at the end of the season.

## The Era of It-Enabled Replenishment

In the mid-1990s, LNT deployed modern Point of Sales (POS) systems in all its stores. LNT bought more JDA enterprise modules that enabled the merchandising organization to automatically track both sales and inventory levels of items by stores. The POS technologies were integrated with an electronic data interchange (EDI) system that enabled the data from each store to be sent to a central database. The JDA software modules were used to manage the inventory and the merchandising processes. Given that timely sales data were made available to planners, the merchandising organization began to develop and use demand forecasting for decision making.

The forecasting tools of the acquired merchandising software module permitted the use of historical sales data to forecast demand for a class of product at the chain or aggregated level. This caused a number of surprises. Each year, LNT ordered a large number of the popular extra-long bed sheets to cover its huge demand during the "back-to-school" season. During the first back-to-school season, after the deployment of the merchandising module, Silverstein's group discovered that the replenishment plans that were suggested by the system for beddings were wrong. For example, though the extra-long bed sheets were the popular item during the season, the system, which was configured to forecast demand at the class level, predicted a rise in sales for every bed sheet in the class. Hence, it recommended comparatively high replenishment levels for all beddings. A similar effect also occurred whenever unique items within a class were included in the sales promotions. To solve the problem, LNT created separate classes, also called forecast profiles, for such seasonal items and promotions within the forecasting software.

Though the merchandising software system enabled Silverstein and the merchandising organization to reduce inventory levels and to make replenishment quantities more efficient across all product departments, he was not completely satisfied with the accomplishment. This was because he understood the weakness of chain-level forecasts. They required the use of average inventory levels of each product class for forecasting. This meant that the use of the scheme requested too few replenishment quantities for stores with the highest demand/sales, while authorizing the delivery of too many units to stores in which product sales were low. In the stores with high demand, it created early season lost sales and stock-outs, while in stores with low demand, it created over-stocking and excessive end-of-season markdowns. In the early 2000s, Silverstein and Steinhorn, then the senior vice-president and chief information officer respectively, and a third-party software provider, worked together on a pilot that tested the use of store-level forecasting. The pilot included 78 SKUs within the bedding product department. The pilot confirmed that such a methodology would optimize in-stock inventory levels at stores and make replenishment more responsive to actual store requirements. In 2002, the new forecasting approach was deployed to manage the entire 150 SKUs that were in the bedding department. The third-party software was implemented to ensure that data from the merchandising system were transferred into it once a week for analysis. The new module generated store-level-based replenishment quantities and uploaded the results into the merchandising system once a week. Steinhorn and Silverstein extended the use of store-level forecasting incrementally, on a department-by-department basis, to most of the 35 store categories. LNT carried 25,000 to 28,000 SKUs, in six product departments and across 35 store categories.

Planners reviewed the automatically generated replenishment plans and made changes to them as needed, before they centrally created product purchase orders. All replenishment orders were processed and sent to suppliers, mostly via an EDI network, by Sunday night each week. The suppliers shipped the merchandise to one of the three distribution centers (DCs) once a week. The DCs were not warehouses, but rather cross-docking zones. When the replenished deliveries arrived at the DCs, the workers broke them down by store deliveries. Thereafter, trucks transported the goods to each store. Sometimes, goods were first transported by train and then by trucks to the store. Each store had one delivery per week.

## Evolution of Customer Coupons and Product Returns Practices

Up until the late 1990s, LNT had well-defined policies about the use of store coupons and returns. However, in the 1990s, BBB adopted a policy of accepting LNT coupons, and the firm also championed the use of generic coupons in its stores. LNT decided to adopt both policies. The use of 20 percent off coupons by customers became the norm. BBB also began the practice of the no-questions-asked returns policy. LNT management felt that it also had to respond in kind. Hence, the product returns policies at LNT matched those of BBB. Items were returned to the stores with no questions asked. Stores were authorized to permit returns of items that the company carried even if the customer had no receipt to show that the item was bought from an LNT store.

## Corporate Management Context and Practices

LNT employees described Norman Axelrod as an individual who was a gifted leader, communicator, and a shrewd merchandiser/merchant. A close associate described him as being thoughtful, respectful and a motivator. Axelrod was known to be a candid CEO. He could effusively praise good work in one moment only to strongly criticize an executive for a poor decision or outcome in the next breath. People who worked closely with Axelrod cared strongly about his views, and they would go out of their way to do things that they knew or

believed would make him happy. Axelrod was known to have fired executives who did not do things his way. Furthermore, he was extremely loyal to his associates. In a few cases, some believed that he may have held on to some of his loyal associates for too long. Generally, Axelrod hired smart people who could work well with him.

Performance control was centralized at LNT. The general managers of the stores had no access to the profit and loss statements of their stores. They reported revenues and labor hours to the corporate office and the upper management worried about the issue of creating adequate store profit margins. Axelrod instituted corporate visits to stores as part of his performance monitoring practice. He held two types of corporate visits. First, there was the weekly trip to the largest LNT store and to the largest BBB store. Axelrod took these trips with the merchandisers and the purpose of the visits was to encourage learning. Second, there was the corporate visit to LNT stores across the nation. The purpose of these latter visits was to inspect poorly performing stores with district managers, regional managers, zone vice-presidents, and other executives. The corporate visits were not surprise events. Rather, the visits were announced to the zone vice-presidents and other senior executives.

## Merchandising Practices

The presentation of merchandise in LNT stores was centrally determined. Once a month, each store across the nation received a planogram from the vice-president of stores planning. The planogram described how products were displayed on shelves in each store and also in the central aisle of each store. In addition, each store adopted the assortment plan that was centrally determined by the merchandisers in the corporate office. LNT differentiated six general merchandising departments, including Bath, Home Accessories, House Wares, Storage and Cleaning, Bedding, and Window Treatment. The merchandisers at LNT determined what would be stocked in these product departments. There was little input from the regions during the assortment decision making. This contrasted with the process used by BBB, whereby merchants, planners and regional planners were included in the process of creating a floor set and planograms. Among other things, the regional planners added localized views to the process. The outcome of the BBB process was that it created a global planogram that was customized by the regional planners for each region. A further difference between these two approaches was in the kind of information that was considered. LNT merchandisers designed the planogram around the products that were selling the most across all stores. In contrast, the BBB approach accommodated the possibility that products that were top sellers nationally would not be top sellers in each individual store. Hence, the BBB planograms were customized by the consideration of regional selling patterns. Furthermore, the store spaces that were leased by BBB had a consistent layout, whereas those that were leased by LNT exhibited store layout variations. Hence, while BBB could send out a single planogram to all stores for customization, LNT had to send several versions of the planogram to its stores and store managers had to figure out which one to use for their stores.

The assortment selection and space-planning philosophies of LNT were different from those of BBB. LNT buyers bought SKUs with the purpose of covering a broad range of assortment. A typical department had between 200 and 300 SKUs. Of these items, 18 to 20 SKUs accounted for more than 50 percent of the department's sales. In contrast, BBB buyers limited the assortment selection in each department to the top-selling items. Hence, BBB carried a smaller number of SKUs per item than LNT did. BBB store managers were expected to monitor what customers bought in their stores and to ensure that those items had high in-stock levels.

Also, in the space-planning area BBB followed a different strategy than LNT. Whereas LNT assigned similar or uniform space allocations or facings to most SKUs in a department, BBB allocated more facings to more productive SKUs in the planogram (see Exhibit 3). Hence, BBB's planograms communicated the best sellers to its customers.

| Exhibit 3 | Example of a Bed Bath & Beyond Planogram |

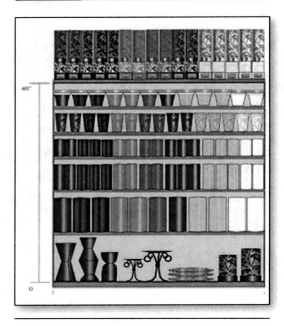

*Source:* www.joeyseemandesign.com.

## Should Assortment Decisions Be Decentralized?

There were a number of questions that every specialty retailer had to answer, including the following: How should it go about determining what to stock before the season? How should it decide what to promote during the season? How should it select the product assortment for each store? At LNT, the answers to these questions were provided by the centralized merchandising organization. The premise of the structure was that the merchandisers had the competence, knowledge, and skill set to know the products that customers desired.

This contrasted with the approach of a few specialty firms, such as BBB, which utilized a decentralized decision-making structure for assortment decisions. Under such arrangements, the store staff were expected, encouraged, empowered and trained to be merchandisers for their stores.

In stores that deployed decentralized decision structures, such as BBB, the answers to the questions listed above were informed by the knowledge and inputs of those individuals who were the closest to customers. Most of the time, these were the store staff. It is worth noting that in firms that adopted decentralized structures, such as BBB, a central merchandising group was still used. However, this central group shared the responsibility for merchandising decisions with store and regional staff. One advantage of the decentralized approach was that it enabled the delegation of decision authority from the central merchandising to the stores, with a potential for creating motivation and involvement at the store level.

The opponents of decentralization believed that merchandising decisions could not easily be done by or taught to everyone. They maintained that centralized merchandisers, when properly trained and equipped with sophisticated technologies, were the best suited for this task of assortment selection, management and development.

## Structure of the Merchandising Organization

The merchandising function at LNT was centralized in the company's headquarters (see Exhibit 4). The unit was responsible for product development, assortment design, pricing, planning, purchasing, and supply chain and distribution functions. The merchandising organization transformed the firm's mission into a merchandise strategy and plan that were executed to meet the financial goals of the enterprise.

The merchandising manager's function was organized by product categories/departments. Each department consisted of several product classes and each product class consisted of SKUs. For example, towels were classified as a product department, whereas colored towels were assigned to a class under the towel department. A class was defined as a subset of products that a customer viewed as substitutes during a purchase decision. Lastly, each class consisted of several SKUs.

For example, each unique towel size constituted an SKU under the class of colored towels.

Axelrod was aware of the arguments for and against decentralization of merchandising. However, he was of the opinion that there was a middle ground. He sought an opportunity to test what would happen if he retained the centralized merchandising organization but delegated limited replenishment authority to the stores.

## Challenges of the Existing Organizational Structures

The centralized LNT merchandising organization produced a number of challenges. There was a tendency for merchandisers to focus on reducing the number of activities that they had to do. This meant that they favored simplicity and predictability in decision making. This caused many of them to focus their attention on continuing products rather than on exploring new or test products. The merchandising group also made decisions that created a high degree of assortment similarity across stores. This meant that regional customization of assortment was rarely achieved. This yielded lost sales opportunities for some product departments. The centralized merchandising approach also meant that product promotions were executed in stores where products were selling well and in places where they were not selling. Furthermore, the centrally determined uniform inventory levels policy also increased the likelihood that more stores would end up with inventory that had to be marked down at the end of the season.

The centralization of merchandising and buying meant that most LNT stores had the same level and depth of assortment. Moreover, replenishment decisions were based on chain-level forecasts. This meant that product replenishments were based on average demand for the chain rather than on store-level averages. This created lost sales and early stock-outs in locations where a product was popular and over-stocking in locations where the product was not popular. The division of labor between merchandising and store managers also implied

**Exhibit 4** Headquarters Chart

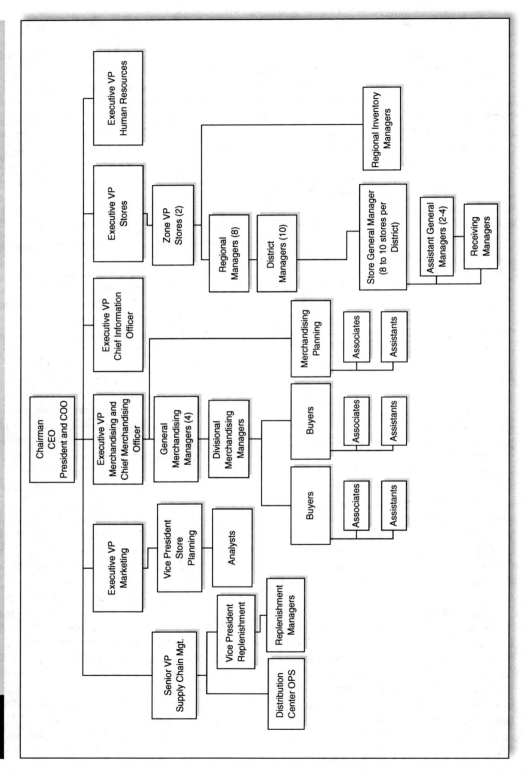

*Source:* Case interviews.

that the employees at the store level actually had little incentive to increase their product knowledge or to develop merchandising skills. The growth in the number of brands and product categories carried by each store also increased the amount of effort that a store staff must invest in order to be competent in the product knowledge sphere.

In addition to these issues, LNT stores were experiencing growing pains. It was increasingly difficult to achieve consistency of product presentation. It was becoming more challenging to ensure that the stock rooms were well organized. Also, it was no longer a given to assume that store staff were effective in filling stock-outs on the sales floors, that they were friendly and helpful to customers and that they were efficient in making floor moves.

The Home Accessories department of LNT had a mixture of about 60 to 70 percent basic replenishment items (core items) with the balance being made up of new items, seasonal items, and promotional buys. This LNT department faced a number of assortment-related challenges. (1) It struggled to find the right balance of replenishment and "fashion" items. (2) LNT did not have a rigorous lifecycle management approach for all items. This meant that it had no systematic process for introducing new core (fashion) items and for retiring old core (fashion) items in a timely and strategic manner. This resulted in a constant struggle to maintain a balanced mix of in-stock replenishment (basic) and newness (fashion) items. (3) The retailer also struggled to find an appropriate breadth of assortment, including an adequate number of sizes, colors and product selections, to carry in order to facilitate high in-stock levels for core replenishment items. (4) LNT lacked a formal process for identifying, funding and assigning store space for regionally appropriate merchandise with a specific geographic/demographic customer (e.g., western motif merchandise in the Southwest). BBB executed each of these four elements extremely well.

LNT had a very weak lifecycle management approach that yielded broad and shallow assortments. The central merchandising organization had an aversion to timely liquidation of slow-moving merchandise, and a high level of reluctance to spend time on regional and/or demographic buys.

# A New Initiative

BBB kept increasing the gap between itself and LNT, and Axelrod grew increasingly uncomfortable with the trend. He motivated his managers to explore ways to improve the competitive advantage of LNT. Internally, several vice-presidents and senior executives introduced improvement initiatives, mostly with limited success. Though most of the initiatives proved successful as projects, they failed or were discontinued after a few months of the organization-wide rollouts. After these failed attempts, Axelrod determined to try another approach. He would bring into LNT an external executive who would be charged to systematically evaluate the differences between BBB and LNT and required to make recommendations. Axelrod discussed the position with Emerson in late 2000. Emerson agreed and joined LNT as a special assistant to the chairman in January 2002.

Emerson was given full access to address the issue. There was no specific charter or job description for him and the CEO was very supportive, both privately and publicly, of the initiative. Initially, Emerson worked alone. He spent time studying the similarities and differences of both firms. As the project progressed, Axelrod assigned additional staff to Emerson's special office. The project grew so that he had two full-time assistants. Later, two senior managers and, eventually, an individual from each of the eight operating regions reported to Emerson on a dotted line basis.

Emerson discovered that LNT had done some prior work studying BBB. He spent time studying the information that had been synthesized. He also conducted independent interviews with ex-BBB employees who were working for LNT, including an ex-BBB regional inventory manager and an ex-BBB buyer. They provided a lot of insight about the inner workings of BBB. Furthermore, Emerson undertook site visits and observations of selected BBB stores and had conversations with BBB store managers. Emerson had extensive experience in retailing so he was capable of identifying possible unique strategies, if there were any. When the research was concluded, he found that BBB was not really doing anything that could be considered unknown or secret. Rather, BBB was doing several important things differently.

He identified four central differences that impacted its competitive advantage. (1) BBB manifested a system-wide focus on sales per square foot as the primary performance metric, whereas LNT focused on gross sales as the main metric. (2) BBB maintained a very decentralized decision-making and organizational structure. These decentralized practices required robust and systematic two-way communication between headquarters, the stores, and merchandising staff. On the other hand, LNT was very centralized and it manifested a top-down, mostly one-way communication pattern. (3) The employees of BBB placed great attention and focus on collaborative teamwork between corporate staff and store staff for simplifying and standardizing store layouts and operations, products fixtures, number of floor moves, and early notifications about upcoming promotions. LNT staff spent little energy in analyzing the store-level impacts of the decisions of its central merchandising organization. LNT's corporate office had very little interest in communications and feedback from the stores. The corporate decision makers gave the stores little detailed advance information on floor moves or upcoming promotions. (4) Lastly, BBB was more focused and rigorous on item lifecycle management and in editing merchandise offerings according to market and customer response and demand, whereas LNT was not.

In regard to areas of strengths, Emerson established that LNT was stronger than BBB in its logistics and supply chain management areas, which was worth something in the order of 100 basis points in the cost of goods sold line. This was due to LNT's use of several centralized DCs and its competent logistics staff. BBB did not use DCs to the same degree that LNT did. Hence, its suppliers made most deliveries directly to its stores. This created a relatively higher level of transportation cost. Emerson also identified information technology deployment as another area in which LNT was stronger than BBB. LNT was superior to BBB in its use of analytical tools and in the level of sophisticated tools used.

## Rolling Out a Pilot Program

Emerson presented his results and his recommendations to the chairman and to the board of directors in 2002. After a review of the recommendations the chairman authorized Emerson to set up a pilot program to test one of his recommendations. The pilot program was designed to authorize individual store managers and district managers to set inventory levels and product presentations as they saw fit. However, store managers were still restricted to ordering only inventory within the LNT corporate assortment. After initial results from test/pilot stores were evaluated, Emerson presented the pilot to the board with a recommendation to expand it. The pilot was given the name Guest Oriented, Locally Driven or "GOLD" program.

Under the GOLD program, store managers and individual district managers were given greater latitude in increasing order quantities and making individual floor presentations. Prior to the program, the store managers could only alter order quantities on the highest-selling items within each department on a rotating basis. However, there were strict limits on the number of SKUs and the quantities they could order, and, in some cases, these modifications were cancelled by the central staff without notification. Under the new program, the store managers were authorized to change quantities on any SKU in the assortment to any level they wanted and they had wide latitude in the area of merchandise presentation and cross-merchandising.

To introduce localized assortments, the CEO authorized the creation of the role of regional inventory manager in each of LNT's regions. The position was authorized to gather specific information on items that were the best selling for the specific region. The CEO also set apart funding for the purchase of such goods. However, it was stipulated that the central merchants should do the actual buys for such merchandise for reasons of skill set and vendor leverage. Several successful buys occurred under this program. However, the program introduced some complexity in store space management and space allocation. Furthermore, the central merchants did not wholeheartedly embrace the special buys. They preferred the leverage of chain-wide buys and had little appetite for the energy and time spent on negotiating deals on a small buy. Consequently, the program never reached a sustainable level.

Initially, the rollout of the program to stores was implemented one district at a time. The store managers and involved employees of a converted district underwent extensive training and they also signed a pledge to abide by a set of standards in their decision making. The district managers had the responsibility of managing the new process, with support from Emerson's group. In the first year, Emerson's office supervised the rollout of the program in 10 districts or roughly 30 percent of the chain districts. Emerson's office measured results throughout all districts using a single metric—change in productivity per square foot for the entire store. The metric was measured and reported to the chain weekly. The metric was measured and reported for each store within one month of its conversion to the program. Improvements in store performance typically showed up quickly. Initially, the results were impressive, running in a 10 to 30 percent or greater increase in store productivity. As the rollout expanded into more stores, the degree of gains was not as pronounced. As the addition of more stores diminished the overall productivity gains, enthusiasm for the program began to wane.

This waning interest emboldened the opponents of the program, specifically the central merchants, central inventory managers, and a few senior store personnel, who began a campaign to convince the chairman to abandon the program. A number of project requirements fueled the opposition of many to GOLD. This program required store managers, district managers and regional managers to take on new responsibility as well as authority. Only about a third of the field population was comfortable with this. Many of the central merchandising staff were hostile to the idea that stores should set product quantities and influence product displays.

## Decision Time

Norman Axelrod had to decide what he would do with the GOLD rollout. Should he stand by Bill Emerson and the program or should he side with the opponents of the program and shut it down? If he continued the program, what should he change? Should he put a time limit on the program? Should he limit the adoption to a few districts? If so, which ones? Should he mandate the central buying staff to participate in the program? If he discontinued the program, what should he do to catch up with BBB?

### CASE QUESTIONS

1. The use of a centralized decision-making system led to barriers to the formal communication process. What were the barriers present?

2. Linens 'n Things required an update of the formal communications system while at the same time encountering the problem of informal gossip and fraternization that opposed the GOLD program. What should Norman Axelrod do to address these problems?

3. How had the communication system at Linens 'n Things inhibited quality customer service? How could the system be improved to facilitate customer service instead?

4. What role did the organization's climate play in the difficulties encountered at Linens 'n Things?

5. What roles could improved information technology and more advanced communication systems play in helping Linens 'n Things compete with Bed Bath & Beyond?

# GDR Versus Kodak—Bart Film Scanner

By Donald A. Pillittere

## Introduction

Angelo Bella had every reason to celebrate as he relaxed at a fine restaurant, sipping from a glass of Reserve Cabaret Sauvignon, courtesy of his company expense account. He had started the morning with a long run to prepare him for a presentation to senior management about a new dental film scanner that had been months in planning. Running was his way to relax, give himself time to collect his thoughts, and prepare for the barrage of questions common to these meetings. The afternoon meeting was a huge success as Bella and his original equipment manufacturer (OEM) partner, BT Wang, demonstrated a working prototype of a low-cost film scanner. With management approval to move forward, what Bella had been pushing for was now a reality. So even as he enjoyed the dry cabaret, he struggled to keep his mind from racing about all the activities required to actually develop and launch in a mere nine months a saleable dental film scanner he had fought so hard for—code named Bart. He thought about that saying, "Be careful what you wish for."

Georginelli Dental Research (GDR) was starting to see digital advances in dental imaging take share away from its bread-and-butter film. This trend was most evident in teaching institutions, where the ease of using digital images in PowerPoint presentations was taking over the old school slide projector for research and instruction. GDR knew that eventually digital imaging could be a huge threat to the overall profits of the corporation. The project team named the scanner Bart for the precocious son in *The Simpsons* and his rebellious nature and zest for life. Team members would be allowed to take a unique approach to developing a new scanner—going outside the confines of the company. Could this group somehow develop a low-cost

scanner that could provide a bridge to digital and keep the very profitable film portfolio viable?

A major challenge for the Bart project was previous failed attempts by other teams at GDR to develop a low-cost but profitable dental film scanner. Many of Bella's managers had been part of these past train wrecks. Or they had been observing in peripheral departments and just did not believe the internal cost structure of GDR was conducive to designing anything inexpensive. Shaking the "Etch A Sketch" of Bella's manager's brain to erase these painful memories was going be another road block for the project team.

Regardless, as project manager, Bella was now on the clock to commercialize his scanner in nine months, working with an overseas partner, and launch the product at the dental industry's most prominent trade show—the Chicago Midwinter Dental Show, the best trade show for introducing new products. The launch of Bart was to coincide with the introduction of a new line of dental films and was intended to allow GDR to generate needed cash that could be used for future digital products. Designing and launching a scanner in less than a year was going to be a far greater challenge than creating a single prototype. Additional pressure was also on the Bart team, given the dental film launch. As the day ended, Bella asked himself, "How can the Bart team meet time-to-market and cost goals, and prove to management that it could succeed where the others failed?"

## GDR Imaging

GDR designed, manufactured and sold leading-edge dental products for use in dental offices and education and research institutes. It was one of numerous small companies in the dental industry fighting

Version: (A) 2009–09–02

for customers against giants like Kodak (now Carestream Health), Agfa, and Fuji. GDR placed much of its marketing emphasis on education and research. It was able to move into dental offices due largely to the loyalty former dental students had towards the company and its products. Many of the research-related sales led to customer suggestions that GDR adopted to continually improve its products to stay competitive.

The company wanted to continue to use profits from film sales to fund ongoing digital research and development (R&D), but feared market dynamics might not allow adequate time to transition. Being able to sell a low-cost scanner that could bridge both the analog and digital worlds was a strategic play to gain more time to launch new digital products. As much as the company wanted to invest money in scanners, there was a corporate edict to manage for cash—to gently land the film plane while the digital one readied for take off. With the uncertain market window regarding customers' continued reliance on film, any scanner had to get to market in less than a year and work flawlessly out of the box. A poorly designed and built scanner would only accelerate customers' move toward digital products.

## Products

The founder of GDR, Julie Georginelli, had been a dental student at Cornell University. Her research in dental imaging led to the company's first film product. She graduated with honors from Cornell and within three months had venture capital to start GDR. Through her reputation as an up-and-coming dental imaging researcher and her college connections, Georginelli quickly exploited the education and research markets with her patented film. GDR sold the majority of its products through dealers that called on dental customers.

Eventually GDR expanded beyond film and developed processing equipment, light boxes, film dispensers, and scanners for dentists. Thanks to high-margin film products and Georginelli's vision, GDR constantly experimented with new imaging methods—both through partnerships with Cornell and thanks to its own highly skilled staff. Therefore, the images from GDR's film and scanner products provided far more critical detail than the competitors. As much as Georginelli enjoyed and succeeded in the role of CEO, it was not unusual for her to throw on a lab coat and work alongside the research team. She was as comfortable in the lab as in the boardroom.

## Organization

GDR was a global company with production facilities in the United States, Europe and China. All design was located in the United States, with marketing and sales dispersed geographically to support the international regions. As the company grew, its structure evolved from a small entrepreneurial business to a matrix organization. Even though the rapid expansion of the company required a more definitive organizational structure, including the implementation of "phases and gates," Georginelli tried to keep the entrepreneurial spirit alive. Her goal was to do everything possible to keep the company agile so new ideas could be rapidly commercialized and launched. This was a necessity given the likes of competitors Kodak and Fuji, who could afford to throw more time, money, and people at product development.

However, as the first signs of the pending demise of film started to appear, GDR managers lost some of their zeal and began to over-analyze programs. Scrutiny of programs was not an unusual behavior, but sometimes market windows were missed as leaders literally analyzed projects to death. What was once a company with an abundance of energy became a slow-moving, cautious entity that held on dearly to dental film and anything nostalgic. The Bart team saw its project as an opportunity to get back to the way GDR was when Georginelli started the company—a group of people with a competitive spirit, clear heads, and efficient, practical processes, where no challenge was impossible and satisfying the end customer was the only goal.

## Product Development

GDR's commercialization process was world-class, with five phases and gates. The first phase was product concept, followed by technical feasibility, product design and testing, production (product launch) and, last but not least, discontinuance. Each phase ended with a gate review, at which team members were required to provide project status with an updated business case and issues to the gatekeepers. Approval from all gatekeepers was needed before a project could continue to the next phase. In years past, most of GDR's projects made it through the commercialization process—even if some of them were dogs. However, with the current manage-for-cash strategy, "thumbs downs" on projects became a more common occurrence.

The concept phase required a marketing requirements document (MRD), business case, competitive assessment and input from all of the worldwide regions. Bella had provided all of these documents to management for a possible gate review, only to be rejected by his manager, Joseph Namath. As it happens, Namath had been part of one of the previous film scanner programs that was unceremoniously canceled when an Excel error of enormous proportions was uncovered. Even though the corrected spreadsheet yielded a positive net present value, the management team cut funding and shifted the dollars to one of the film programs. Namath was impressed with the work Bella and his team had done, such as leveraging some of the graphical user interface (GUI) design from his cancelled program. But he did not have the backbone to agree to a gate review. So Bart ended up stuck in limbo, with no sponsorship from management to proceed even through the first concept phase and attendant gate.

## The Big Idea

Being a stubborn sort, Bella did not take no for an answer. He enjoyed the challenge of doing what others said could not be done. So he met with his quasi-project team to figure out a way to move the program forward. The team wrestled with ideas to pass through the initial concept gate, but ended its first meeting with no tangible ideas. Bella walked back to his desk, frustrated by the lack of ideas, and decided to catch up on phone calls and email. There was no way he wanted to let Bart die. Plus he knew his colleagues in film were pushing for him to succeed. Scanners turned film into digital images and would help ease the inevitable transition to digital.

One phone call would change the whole direction of the program. It was a message from Lynn Tseng, who represented an OEM in Taiwan—Dental Imaging Systems (DIS)—that manufactured low-end scanners. Puzzled by Tseng's message, Bella called her back and they made time to meet the following day. She wanted to know if there was an opportunity to work with GDR after reading a quote by Bella in a company press release. The conversation went well, with Bella thanking Tseng for her time and promising to get back to her if there was an opportunity to work together.

The following day, Bella called another meeting with his team and talked at length about his meeting with Tseng. In parallel, he had invited Dwayne Turner from purchasing, who worked closely with international OEMs that had partnered with GDR to provide low-cost solutions for other business units. The team quickly realized that a partnership with a low-cost OEM could be the way to quickly launch a new dental film scanner and meet the extreme cost pressures of Bart. Since all of the specifications, with volumes and cost targets, had been prepared for a gate review, the team decided to have Turner use these for request for quotes (RFQs) with several OEMs in Taiwan, Japan, and China. Many of these same companies had built scanners for GDR's competition, so their names and reputations were well known except for DIS.

## OEM Selection

Turner worked fast and had all RFQs out to OEMs within two weeks of the team meeting. GDR had very well-defined supplier selection criteria that included the items listed below:

- Previous experience with the supplier and positive past performance
- Sophistication of quality system (for example, ISO 9001:2000 certification)
- Ability to meet potential capacity requirements
- On-time delivery
- Financial stability
- Technical support
- Willingness to participate as a partner (developing optimized design)
- Total cost (material cost, inventory requirements, and incoming verification)
- Capabilities (skill level, training, education of workers)
- Track record for business improvement

Once OEMs provided quotes, financial reports would be obtained through Dun & Bradstreet or other publicly available statements. A visit by key members of the Bart team would assess the quality system, production capacity, capabilities, and willingness of the OEM to partner with GDR.

Within two weeks of sending out the RFQs, all OEMs expressed an interest in working with GDR. However, many requested a face-to-face meeting to better understand the specifications before finalizing their quotes. Given the magnitude of the task at hand and GDR's worldwide reputation for superior imaging, clarifying questions about Bart made sense for both GDR and the OEMs. Turner took the lead and arranged for Bella, the lead engineer and himself to visit each OEM to go over the specification and start the qualifying process. As part of the trip to the Far East, Bella arranged several visits to California dental dealers to share ideas about the Bart concept and gather feedback.

## On the Road

The first stop of the journey landed the team in San Francisco on a whirlwind tour of dental dealers.

The dealers were loyal to any company product that could generate revenue. Even with GDR's long-standing presence in the industry, as the saying goes, you're only as good as your last product. And GDR's dental scanner products were perceived as long in the tooth, even by those formerly loyal to the brand. Each dealer presented competing scanners, GDR's current product and a concept scanner from an unnamed company (Bart) to groups of dentists while the project team remained quiet on the sidelines.

Many praised some of the competitive low-end scanners whose capabilities had long surpassed GDR's products. Much was made of GDR abandoning the scanner market it once dominated to low-cost competitors, which in turn hurt the company's film sales—something that made the team cringe. However, there was a very positive reception to Bart, with many guessing that one of the low-cost companies had to be behind the concept. Most of what was discussed was not new, but a painful reminder of what the team already knew. Clearly, GDR had some work to do to gain back customers.

The next leg had the team traveling to the various OEMs to meet their counterparts and discuss in painstaking detail Bart's specifications, time-to-market goals and cost targets. These meetings were all very cordial, with days ending with the consumption of local cuisine and beverages. Bella enjoyed these meetings. During his morning runs he used some of the ideas raised during the meetings to come up with ways to further differentiate Bart. Of all the OEMs the team met, no one was more willing to partner with GDR than—you guessed it—Dental Imaging Systems, the one represented by Lynn Tseng.

DIS's president, BT Wang, and Bella hit it off as soon as they met. Unlike other OEMs that tried to talk GDR out of some of its exacting imaging specifications, BT agreed that DIS could meet them and still achieve the cost targets. BT's confidence in his engineering staff and company in general was a welcome change. In fact, very early on it seemed as if BT was not some distant OEM, but another member of the Bart team. Others from GDR had the same sense, but not as strongly as Bella. Bella felt that he could trust BT, a rare commodity in the business world.

## RFQs

After the Bart team's excellent adventure, it was a waiting game as Turner and others anticipated which of the six OEMs would provide a quote for the product. Two weeks after the trip, two OEMs "no quoted" based on Bart's sales volume (which was much lower than they expected) and GDR's unwillingness to back down on its imaging specifications. Most OEMs promised quotes within four weeks, but Turner and Bella started to worry that no one might be willing to partner with GDR on Bart.

That worry dissipated when DIS and three other OEMs sent in quotes. Each varied in terms of non-recurring engineering (NRE) charges, tooling cost, volume pricing, and delivery. It was now up to the Bart team, with Turner's help, to put together a decision matrix based on these quotes and data collected from the trip. All of the above-mentioned supplier selection criteria were ranked from 1 (worst) to 5 (best) for each OEM. The most difficult part was going to be ranking financial stability for the competing OEMs.

After tallying the scores, DIS and another OEM—Prime Imaging—were in a virtual tie. Major concerns centered on the finances of DIS and the true willingness of Prime Imaging to adhere to GDR's specification (based on footnotes on its quote regarding several imaging requirements). Bella and Turner followed up with both companies to get clarification. BT said he would quickly get his owner's commitment to support the Bart program. Prime Imaging questioned the reasons for the strict imaging requirements; Turner and Bella replied that they were the result of customer research. The conversation with Prime Imaging ended with the OEM requesting another week to revisit its quote to determine any additional NRE charges to meet project specifications.

## Let's Roll

While the team waited for Prime Imaging to re-quote, Bella had another heart-to-heart talk with Namath to try to understand what else could be done to move the program forward. Namath was aware of the trip and selection work regarding OEM suppliers, but this whole process—even if successful in terms of time-to-market, features and cost—made him nervous. As much as he liked Bella's drive and creativity to partner with an OEM to get Bart to market, DIS was an unknown commodity. The time, distance and potential communication issues with DIS concerned Namath, because he knew how difficult it had been to manage the project when all the resources were under GDR's control—and the results were disastrous. How could a partnership between GDR and DIS be successful?

Soon after, Bella received a call from BT, who wanted an update on the selection process. Bella mentioned that GDR was waiting for one more quote in order to make a decision. When BT pressed for a firm decision date, Bella said that even if the quotes were in line with time-to-market and cost targets, the biggest challenge was convincing management to proceed. Bella educated BT on GDR's commercialization process, plus the fact that Bart was stuck in limbo between concept and technical feasibility phases and needed some magic to proceed. Towards the end of the conversation, Bella said if he could show management a working prototype—that is, something tangible—then maybe management would see that Bart could be a reality.

BT wasted no time responding, saying that DIS could develop a prototype with the Bart interface by modifying one of its existing products and have it ready within three months—just in time for a regional trade show that was a precursor to the Chicago Midwinter Dental Show. BT said working with GDR was so important to enhancing DIS's reputation in the dental market that he would be willing to do this even if Bella's managers decided not to move forward with an OEM solution. Since Bella did not have the authority to approve BT's idea, he simply stated that taking the risk to build a prototype was solely BT's decision. Even though Bella could not verbalize his opinion, deep down he very much wanted to show his managers a working Bart film scanner.

## Trade Show

The three months were passing by rapidly. With the trade show right around the corner, Bella anxiously awaited word from BT about the Bart prototype. If BT was a man of his word (and Bella felt he had every reason to think so), a call or e-mail would arrive soon. Bella not only had to convince Namath about Bart's viability, but also win the approval of a corporate gadfly and the skeptical head of engineering, two individuals Bella knew could convince Namath to fund the project. GDR had a series of backrooms at the trade show for customer or business meetings, and Bella wanted to set aside a time and date to demonstrate the prototype.

One week before the trade show, Bella's home phone rang. The caller was none other than BT. With his ever-jovial personality, he said the Bart prototype was working and asked what would be the best time to demonstrate the product for GDR's managers. Bella said he would arrange a time and date once his administrative assistant checked each of the managers' calendars. After hanging up the phone, Bella's daughter said, "You must like BT, because every time he calls you have a smile on your face." Bella thought about the growing, genuine friendship developing between him and BT, and his growing realization, and appreciation, of how much hard work BT had been putting into helping GDR.

"I do," he replied.

**CASE QUESTIONS**

1.  In the case, one-on-one personal communication in person or by phone, combined with meetings, led to the eventual development of a successful venture. Why would such interpersonal communication become so important in this situation?

2.  Many of the challenges in this case resulted from the barriers to communication between individuals. What were they, and how did they disrupt the communication process?

3.  Part of the process of developing Bart included partnering with an outside organization. What communication challenges did these interactions create?

4.  Discuss the role of formal and informal organizational communication in the development of the Bart product.

CHAPTER

11

# External Communications

The distinction between internal and external communication may be largely artificial. Most company messages, such as advertisements and press releases, reach both company employees and external groups. In any case, what is termed *external communication* takes place with two groups: (1) non-customers and other groups and (2) customers and potential customers.

## Communications With Non-Customers

A great deal of communication results from interactions between members of an organization and various publics that are not customers or potential customers. These publics include suppliers, governmental agencies, members of the local community, labor unions, competing businesses, special interest groups, and people in mass media. Of these, the marketing team is most likely to have contact with members of the local community, media, and, to some extent, competing businesses. The two primary channels of communication with these groups are (1) messages and statements made by the management team and (2) messages transmitted through the public relations department. Each deserves careful attention as contacts are made.

## Communications With Customers and Potential Customers

Customer contact points are the interactions between a company, its customers, and its prospective customers. A case can be made that the essence of marketing is communicating with these groups. Members of the marketing team try to identify every potential contact point and consider each one from the viewpoint of the customer in order to understand how messages are transmitted and received in those situations. Contacts are made through personal communication channels (e.g., face-to-face, telephone conversations) and impersonal channels (e.g., advertisements, letters, brochures). Beyond marketers and salespeople, contacts are made with a wide variety of employees, including the company's delivery team, repair department, credit department, those who answer inquiries by e-mail or through the firm's website, the complaint department, company managers and others making public appearances, and the public relations department. Numerous methods of external communication are used. Each merits careful management.

## ⬚ Institutional Statements

Both customers and non-customers learn a great deal about a company from its institutional statements, including those found in the company's mission statement and its reports to stockholders. At times, company leaders prepare special messages about a change in strategic vision or strategic activities. Each message should speak with a consistent voice about how the firm conducts business and interacts with the larger public.

## ⬚ Product Appearance and Package Design

Another marketing component that communicates to customers is the product's appearance, which makes a first impression and might influence subsequent purchases. A product's aesthetic value, symbolic value, functional value, and attention-drawing value compose its appearance. Aesthetic value comes from anything that is pleasing or that the consumer likes. A product that is pretty or soft or one with a pleasant scent or attractive design has aesthetic appeal. Symbolic value occurs when a person's self-image, desires, or values match the product's appearance, such as the pride a person feels when driving a newly purchased Mercedes-Benz, because it fits with the individual's persona.

Functional value means that product looks as though it will work properly. Attention-drawing value emerges when a product or package stands out from competing brands. Many purchase decisions are made while in the retail store. The various aspects of product appearance may tip the scale toward one company's product over another's.

## ⬚ The Business Facility

A building can have an impact on customers, employees, and a company's bottom line. Most business facilities employ three design features in various combinations, although one will be emphasized more than the others. First, customization emphasizes a focus on customers by making them feel comfortable and welcome. Second, cost-efficiency accommodates a firm's operational needs. Third, quality may be enhanced in the form of the products or services being made available. Careful consideration should be given to the building's focal point and how the other aspects support the primary feature.

## ⬚ Personal Contacts

Two-way communication takes place only in some marketing efforts. Consequently, when someone from the company visits face to face with customers, quality communication becomes vitally important. In those settings, employee dress, grooming, and personal appearance are often factors customers use to judge a person's character, honesty, trustworthiness, and ability. Marketing managers should pay attention to the details on personal contacts between employees and customers.

Telephone communications offer a two-way channel; however, factors such as gestures and facial expressions are not germane. Quality telephone etiquette creates a major marketing advantage for the individual employee and the company that employee serves.

Web communications have been steadily increasing. Marketing managers work to ensure that the firm's website is easy to navigate, provides multiple methods of communication, and makes those methods easy to use and that employees working with the website respond quickly to customers and strive for excellent customer service. The database manager tracks correspondences to help build effective FAQ systems. Communications can be followed up with automated technology in order to ensure the customer has a satisfactory experience.

## Marketing Communication Tactics

Advertising and sales promotions are two of the most common methods used to communicate with customers. While advertising does not have a personal, face-to-face element, marketing messages can become "conversations" with the public over time. Consumer and trade promotion offers send messages that can be used to reinforce the firm's primary message, especially when delivered or redeemed by an engaged and concerned sales force.

## In-Store Communications

Many consumers are influenced by in-store signage, a display, or a point-of-purchase offer. Many manufacturers have increased budgets that support in-store marketing materials. In-store displays should present a theme consistent with the retailer's image. They should be unique, colorful, and present merchandise in an interesting and entertaining fashion. Retailers will ask for changes in displays frequently in order to keep a store's appearance fresh and inviting.

Point-of-purchase displays are often located near cash registers in retail stores, at the ends of aisles, in a store's entryway, or any place where they will be noted. The displays include signs, structures, and devices used to identify, advertise, or merchandise an outlet, service, or product. New displays incorporate digital technologies. The purpose of these displays is to entice a consumer to stop, pick up the merchandise, and then purchase it. Manufacturers spend considerable time and energy to develop successful displays so that retailers will be more likely to use them.

## Public Relations

In order to maintain quality relationships with customers and the larger public, quality public relations departments and programs become essential. The three primary areas covered by public relations are monitoring messages, damage-control activities, and publicizing image-enhancing events.

The public relations department monitors contacts between the company and non-customer publics. It can become the key listening post for all communications that take place. Gathering this type of information provides the organization's management team valuable insight regarding public perceptions of the firm and helps them take proactive steps to build or maintain a positive image.

Negative publicity occurs when a company faces a story based in fact or due to some unusual circumstance. At times, the firm creates problems such as defective products, pollution, tax fraud, false or misleading advertising, discrimination, unfair pricing, or other acts. At other times, the negative publicity is beyond the company's control, such as when a key endorser encounters problems that shed a negative light on the organization (e.g., Tiger Woods and Nike). Dealing with negative publicity can include an apology, defending the company's innocence, providing justifications, Internet interventions, or offering other explanations.

An apology begins with the acknowledgement that the company did something wrong, whether by choice or by accident. It continues with a statement of regret and the promise not to engage in the inappropriate behavior. Then, the company offers to compensate the injured party.

Defending the company's innocence relies on evidence and proof the company was not at fault. Providing justifications includes creating reasons for the inappropriate behavior that lessen the negative impact. Internet interventions involve monitoring of what circulates online, including discussions in chat rooms or on social media such as Twitter, to set the record straight when false information is being passed along by social media or other outlets. Other explanations are those that suggest a negative event was a single-time occurrence, such as one due to the actions of a disgruntled employee or an act of God, and will not happen again.

The public relations department further communicates with customers and non-customers by publicizing image-enhancing events. Press releases, press conferences, letters to constituents, and postings on the company's website assist public relations officials in sending out positive stories. An entitling takes place when the company makes sure it has been given credit for a favorable event. An enhancement involves increasing the value of that favorable outcome.

## Image-Building Programs

Marketing managers often take advantage of programs that combine the efforts of the sales force, public relations personnel, advertising specialists, and others from the company. Four such programs are sponsorships, event marketing, cause-related marketing, and green marketing.

Sponsorship marketing involves the company paying money to sponsor someone, some group, or something that is part of an activity. Sponsorships range from Little League Baseball and soccer teams to national music tours. Event marketing is similar to sponsorship marketing, but instead the company supports a specific event, such as an art festival, a local rodeo, or a concert in the park. Sports attract the largest sponsorship and event marketing dollars.

Sponsorships and event marketing programs require similar steps and activities. The marketing team first determines the objectives of the program. The sponsorship's or event's audience profile must match the target market. The event is then promoted. The sponsoring company or brand will appear prominently in promotions for the event. The sponsor tracks results to make certain the program achieved its goals.

Cause-related marketing is a situation in which a firm ties a marketing program to a charity in order to generate goodwill. In the current environment, companies carefully choose charities, making sure the beneficiary matches the company's image and theme. When a charity seems unrelated to the company, the program may experience consumer backlash based on the perception that no true altruistic intentions are present but, rather, that the firm seeks to capitalize on the charity's activities.

Green marketing is the development and promotion of products that are environmentally safe. A green marketing strategy should align with the wishes of the firm's target audience. Some companies maintain low profiles, even though the organizations are environmentally friendly, because the marketing team has concluded no real benefit would be associated with publicizing the green activities. Greenwashing occurs when a company sends out false information about its environmental efforts in an effort to deceive the public.

## ⊠ Implications for Marketing Managers

Most of the external communications described here are guided by first-level managers working with entry-level employees. Personal contacts are handled by entry-level employees. This makes the task of effectively managing those interactions a crucial element of a company's marketing program. Institutional statements, product design issues, selections of buildings, and other more sweeping decisions are made by managers at higher ranks. Even these decisions should be clearly communicated to both members of the organization and external publics.

## ⊠ Relationship to Customer Service

When everything communicates, the activities involved in external contacts should be closely aligned with a firm's mission and vision. Customer service relies on quality communication to build positive relationships with customers and non-customers.

## ⊠ The Cases

### Walmart Puerto Rico: Promoting Development Through a Public–Private Partnership

Sowing the Development of the Country (SDE) was an initiative begun by Walmart to assist local farmers in Puerto Rico to become entrepreneurs by developing small agribusinesses. The original program was designed as a cooperative effort between Walmart and the government of Puerto Rico. When the government's leaders lost the next election, Walmart became the program's champion. The challenges present included poor channels of communication with farmers in the program, the political shift, difficulty in finding funding for individual farmer projects, and problems meeting schedules and delivery dates for produce. To successfully continue this project designed to enhance the corporate social responsibility standing of Walmart, these obstacles would require attention and correction.

### "Hips Feel Good"—Dove's Campaign for Real Beauty

The Dove brand of products was in need of rejuvenation. Through careful market research, Kerstin Dunleavy discovered an opportunity: How do women define beauty? The answers to that question touched personal feelings of self-worth, well-being, and societal concepts about women. The Campaign for Real Beauty that emerged generated a tremendous amount of buzz and wide acceptance by women both in the United States and in other countries. Dove made strong in-roads against competing brands. The only question remaining was how long the positive results could be sustained.

### New Balance: Developing an Integrated CSR Strategy

New Balance is a privately held company that has been in existence for more than 100 years. The company became the fourth-largest provider of athletic shoes in the world. Throughout its history, the management team has emphasized "doing the right thing." Among the aspects of this approach were the dedication to keeping the workforce in the United States; seeking to provide a quality, safe work environment; and making strides toward the environmentally friendly products and production methods. Previously, New Balance assigned the responsibility of directing these activities to one social responsibility manager. Recent demands by governments, consumers, and interest groups have made corporate social responsibility (CSR) practices not only advisable but also sound competitive tactics. The next generation of New Balance leadership seeks to incorporate socially responsible practices into the strategic planning for the company.

# Walmart Puerto Rico: Promoting Development Through a Public–Private Partnership

By Dr. Myrna Comas and Dr. Julia Sagebien

Luis Valderrama, project manager of the program Sowing the Development of the Country (Siembra el Desarrollo del País), had just finished a meeting with farmers in the Coloso Valley of Puerto Rico (the island) when he noticed that he had a voice mail message from Ivan Baez, corporate director of Walmart Puerto Rico.

> Hola Valderrama. When you are done with the Valle del Coloso quality control meeting for the January delivery, can you please head right back to San Juan? I need to meet with you A.S.A.P. so we can prepare a presentation for Mr. Casillo [Renzo Casillo, president of Walmart Puerto Rico]. He would like us to submit a report that he can use for two meetings. One of the meetings is next week—with Walmart corporate in the United States—and the other is the meeting with the incoming government administration so we can negotiate a new alliance. As you know, changes in the political party in power here in Puerto Rico can change everything! Plus we have to show corporate what we are doing down here. We already have 300 farmers involved in the project. It's exciting stuff. Call me as soon as you are done. Thanks. See you soon.

Sowing the Development of the Country was a public–private partnership between Walmart Puerto Rico (Walmart PR), the island's Department of Agriculture and its Economic Development Bank, an NGO named Caborrojeños Pro Salud y Ambiente (Caborrojeños Pro Health and Environment), and a group of farmers. ConectaRSE, a local CSR consultancy, had facilitated the project development. The objective of the project was to promote sustainable development on the island by encouraging entrepreneurship among farmers and the development of small and medium agribusinesses. Walmart PR would provide the market demand, the government would provide technical support and micro-loans, and the farmers would grow farm products to be sold under the Del País brand name, a brand created by the government to promote local produce consumption. From Walmart's standpoint, the goal of the program was to reduce the 70 percent to 30 percent ratio of imported foodstuffs versus local food products available in Walmart's Puerto Rico stores. In this way, it could demonstrate Walmart PR's commitment to locally adapted corporate social responsibility programs. The company was determined to guarantee the continuity and expansion of the project.

As soon as he got into his car, Valderrama called Baez and left a message.

> Ivan, it's about ten in the morning. I can be at your office by noon if I don't run into

Version: (A) 2010–04–26

much traffic. For the report we can use a lot of the information we gathered for the recent presentation at the 2008 Inter-American Development Bank's annual CSR Conference.[1] It basically spells out what we did, with whom, and why we did it the way we did it. It also does a SWOT. And for the government, we have all that public–private partnership information too. OK, see you soon.

# Walmart PR[2]

In 1992, Walmart began its international expansion by opening its first store outside of the United States in Mexico City. That same year, the first Walmart store and the first Sam's Club store opened in Puerto Rico (see Exhibit 1). In 2001, the first Walmart Super center on the island was inaugurated. Although Puerto Rico is part of the United States, the international division, headquartered in Bentonville, Arkansas, managed operations. By 2006, Walmart Puerto Rico sales had reached $650 million[3] (see Exhibit 2).

The purchase of Amigo Supermarkets in 2003, a local chain of supermarkets with 33 stores and more than 40 years of service in Puerto Rico, increased Walmart sales by more than $520 million a year. This expansion strategy consolidated the company as the leader of the retail market in Puerto Rico (see Exhibit 3).

By 2008, Walmart operated 57 establishments in the island, including eight Walmart stores, six Walmart Supercenters, nine Sam's Club stores, 31 Amigo Supermarkets, and three distribution centers. Walmart Puerto Rico was the largest private employer of the island, with more than 14,000 employees.

Walmart PR received numerous awards for its contributions to the island's economy and, more recently, for its commitment to economic, social and environmental sustainability goals. In 2009, the Department of Agriculture, the Puerto Rico Farmers Association and the Puerto Rico College of Agronomists recognized Walmart for its support of local agro-foods. The company was also recognized by the Puerto Rico House of Representatives for its environmental programs. Furthermore, it received recognition from the Red Cross for assistance offered during floods as well as other awards for community service. In 2009, Casillo was chosen for the second time as one of Puerto Rico's top 10 business leaders in a poll conducted by Caribbean Business Magazine. Casillo was also known for his commitment to

---

**Exhibit 1**   Puerto Rico[1]

Puerto Rico is located in the Caribbean Sea and is the smallest of the Greater Antilles. The "Estado Libre Asociado" is a self-governing Commonwealth of the United States, which has authority over internal affairs. Interstate commerce, foreign relations, immigration affairs, citizenship, currency, maritime regulations, military service, constitutional law, legal procedures, agriculture, mining and other areas are governed by U.S. laws. In 2007, Puerto Rico had an estimated population of 3,912,000 distributed in an area of 8,959 square kilometers (2,184,591 acres). Official languages are Spanish and English. Puerto Rico is known to have one of the most dynamic economies of the Caribbean. The industrial sector surpassed agriculture as the main source of income and economic activity. The gross domestic product of the island was $72.61 billion and the GDP per capita was $18,400 (both estimated for 2007).

---

*Source:* Puerto Rico Planning Board, 2007.

1. See map of Puerto Rico and the Caribbean at: http://fis.ucalgary.ca/AVal/321/caribe.gif, accessed April 5, 2010.

| Exhibit 2 | Number of Stores and Gross Sales of Walmart PR, 2001–2006 | |
| --- | --- | --- |
| **Year** | **Number of Stores** | **Gross Sales (US$)** |
| 2001 | 10 | 411,600,000 |
| 2002 | 12 | 590,000,000 |
| 2003 | 12 | 540,000,000 |
| 2004 | 12 | 540,000,000 |
| 2005 | 13 | 620,000,000 |
| 2006 | 13 | 650,000,000 |

*Source: Caribbean Business, "The Book of Lists," 2002–2007.*

| Exhibit 3 | Main Department Stores in Puerto Rico, 2006 |
| --- | --- |
| **Company** | **Gross Sales (US$)** |
| Walmart | 650,000,000 |
| Kmart | 395,000,000 |
| Sears Roebuck of PR, Inc. | 390,000,000 |
| Almacenes Pitusa, Inc. | 190,000,000 |
| JCPenney PR, Inc. | 142,500,000 |
| Tiendas Capri | 140,800,000 |
| Marshalls | 130,000,000 |

*Source: Caribbean Business, "The Book of Lists," 2007.*

supporting small local businesses, buying local products, promoting entrepreneurship, and caring for the environment.

## Impact of Walmart International and the Company's CSR Response

In 2009, Walmart registered sales of $401 billion in 15 countries. The company achieved significant market penetration in the United States, Canada, Europe, Japan, China, Argentina, and Brazil, with more than 8,159 retail units around the world. By 2009, Walmart was the largest public corporation in the world in terms of revenues and the largest employer in the world, with more than 2.1 million employees globally.[4]

According to company critics, Walmart stores had serious negative impacts on the neighborhoods, cities and countries in which they were established. For example, Walmart was severely criticized by NGOs for its large supply chains of foreign products, bad working conditions at suppliers' factories, resistance to unions, alleged sexism, displacement of local businesses to foreign countries like China,[5] throwing thousands of people out of work in the United States, and for causing the disappearance of urban centers and small and medium businesses (SMEs).[6] According to 2004 estimates, in Puerto Rico, for every $1.7 million in Walmart sales, one SME (Pequeña y Mediana Empresa or PyME in Spanish) went out of business.[7]

Walmart executives and advocates defended the company's record by stressing that Walmart created jobs and offered low prices to customers. In addition, they pointed out that the company had received international recognition for a number of proactive environmentally and socially responsible programs in its stores and supply chains such as energy saving and recycling programs, local purchasing programs, and a Supplier Diversity Program for women and minorities.[8] In 2005, Walmart began implementing strategies aimed at achieving the use of 100 percent renewable energy sources and creating zero waste in the organization.[9]

Walmart's supply chain, a network of thousands of suppliers from small local companies to multinational corporations, was a major contributor to the company's success.[10] Thus, coordination with members of its supply chain played a prominent role in the company's CSR strategies. For example, the company fostered innovations in packaging systems and logistics throughout its supply chains, and programs such as the Walmart Local Purchase Program helped smaller local businesses qualify as suppliers authorized by both local stores and the Walmart Home Office. The company was also a supporter of Fair Trade products, and it established a food and agriculture network aimed at fostering sustainability in agro-products supply chains[11] by reducing the miles food traveled from the farm to the consumer's table. The food and agriculture network brought together buyers, suppliers, NGOs, academics, and business representatives in an effort to sell local products, reduce the distance food traveled (e.g., in the United States, food traveled an average of 1,500 miles), reduce gas emissions and transportation costs, use innovative packaging requiring fewer trees and less water in its manufacture, use packaging made of renewable resources, and remove links from the supply chains.[12] Walmart's logistics and supply chain expertise had also been helpful in disaster relief efforts (e.g., Hurricane Katrina).

## Search for a CSR Banner Project

Walmart Puerto Rico was actively involved in a number of philanthropic programs. For example, in 2008, the enterprise and its employees contributed more than $3 million to more than 100 local non-profit organizations. In keeping with its corporate-level sustainability strategies, the company implemented operational energy efficiency initiatives and recycling projects to divert waste from Puerto Rico's landfills. Sustainability programs included numerous alliances with government agencies, community organizations, schools, and suppliers.

Despite these efforts, Walmart felt a need to develop a Puerto Rico-specific signature CSR project. For this purpose, in November 2007 the enterprise hired Ms. Lilimar López, president of ConectaRSE Inc., a local organization dedicated to promoting CSR and developing CSR strategies. As part of her situation analysis, López attended a meeting held in Guatemala where several of the CSR projects that Walmart was developing in Latin America were discussed. One of the projects—Programa Tierra Fértil—caught her attention. That evening, López sent an e-mail to Baez:

Hola Ivan. I think I've got something we can work with. As you know, there is widespread public concern over the island's food supply chain and this has become even more of an issue since the local media began coverage of the global food crisis. Combine this with concern over the island's economy and increasing unemployment, and the government's efforts to foster a culture of entrepreneurship, and I think we have a number of very critical issues that we can address with a targeted CSR program. I just saw a presentation on the Programa Tierra Fértil, a project aimed at promoting agricultural enterprises in Guatemala and in Central American countries. I think it might be possible to develop a similar program for Puerto Rico. When I get back, let's start looking at Walmart corporate local product support programs. Also, let's take a look at Puerto Rico's statistics on agricultural production and food imports. OK—thanks. Let me know when we can meet next week. Saludos, Lilimar.

As soon as López returned from Guatemala, she and Baez devoted themselves to gathering research on local agriculture, food imports and existing national and international Walmart local food purchase programs. The research revealed some interesting possibilities.

Since the 1950s, Puerto Rico's economic development had veered away from agricultural production. In 2007, the total value of agricultural production was calculated at $733.3 million or one percent of GDP. Livestock enterprises were the top contributors to the agricultural gross income. That year, there were 15,745 farms on the island, a decline of 11 percent compared to the year 2002. The average farm's size was 39.1 acres.

Eighty-four percent were selling less than $20,000 worth of produce per year. Most farmers lived on their farms, did not always consider agriculture as their main occupation, and often had to supplement their income with other work. A farmer's average age was 58.2 years and more than a third were more than 65 years old. They were essentially men with an education level of high school or less (see Exhibit 4).

Agricultural production in Puerto Rico was also affected by extreme weather events such as hurricanes (the season ran every year from June to November), which could devastate crops.

In 2007, only 20 percent of the food and beverages consumed in Puerto Rico were produced in the island (see Exhibit 5). Practically all the cereal, oils and fats, sugar, vegetables, fish and soups consumed were imported, as were more than three-quarters of fruits, vegetables, and meats. Most imports came from the United States. Local production consisted mainly of milk, eggs, plantains, and coffee. Though Walmart PR purchased more

than 83 percent of basic supermarket products from more than 300 local suppliers, these suppliers imported most of the products they then re-sold to Walmart.

Puerto Rico's dependence on imported products increased its vulnerability to external factors. Globalization of the food supply chain had offered many competitive advantages for businesses since it offered a greater variety of products at lower prices. However, it also increased dependence on imported foods. Globally, a combination of record-high crude oil prices, the use of agricultural products as bio fuel, and higher demand for food in emergent economies like China and India, as well as uncertainty over climate change's impact on agriculture and supply flows, had raised the price of food, resulting in fears of a global food crisis. All together, the island's food supply chain, local as well as imported, was extremely vulnerable.

There were a number of Walmart-sponsored U.S.-based local food purchase programs (e.g., *Salute*

| **Exhibit 4** | Profile of Puerto Rican Farmers, 2007 |

| Variable | Major Characteristics | Amount | Percentage of Farmers |
|---|---|---|---|
| Years in charge of farm | 10 or more years | 9,427 | 60 |
| Residence | On farm | 9,818 | 62 |
| Main occupation | Non-agriculture | 8,947 | 57 |
| Retirement status | Non-retired | 8,696 | 55 |
| Age | Average – 58.2 years More than 65 years | 5,301 | 34 |
| Gender | Male | 13,471 | 86 |
| Education level | High school or less | 10,596 | 67 |
| % income from the farm | Less than 25% | 9,631 | 61 |

*Source:* USDA 2007 Census of Agriculture.

| **Exhibit 5** | Food Production and Imports in Puerto Rico, 2007 |

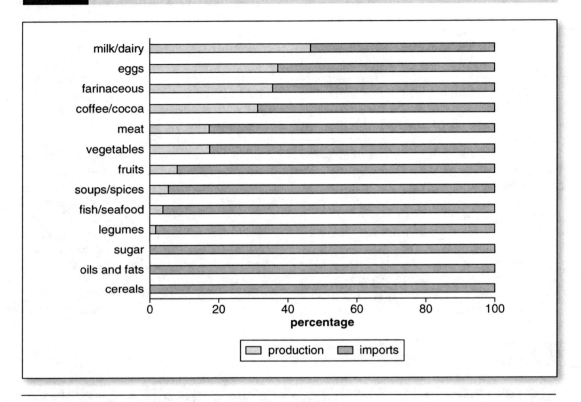

*Source:* External Trade Statistics and Office of Agricultural Statistics, 2008.

*to America's Farmers),* as well as international local food purchase programs (e.g., Fertile Land Program or *Programa Tierra Fértil).* These programs had been developed after extensive consumer research (e.g., on preference for fresher products and willingness to pay for the benefit), as well as store efficiency and transportation logistics cost-effectiveness studies (e.g., estimates of the costs of buying local products versus products that travel long distances). For example, in Illinois, fruits and vegetables were purchased from family businesses, while in countries like Guatemala the company bought herbs and aromatic plants from small farmers. Walmart International had also launched a campaign to sell produce from small and medium farms at its supermarkets. As well, the company promoted the sale of Fair Trade Certified products.

Since Walmart headquarters in Arkansas gave every country where the company operated the autonomy to establish its own social responsibility program within corporate guidelines, Baez and López presented the idea of a local agro-foods project to Casillo. Casillo quickly gave the green light to launch a project with the island's farmers. He also challenged Walmart PR's buyers to begin the process of buying goods at each store instead of doing all purchases through Walmart PR's headquarters in Caguas.

## Auspicious Coincidence— Public Sector and Civil Society Project Partners

In January 2008, López and ConectaRSE were hired by the Economic Development Bank (EDB) of the island as a consultant with the mandate of assisting with the bank's CSR efforts.[13] López was pleasantly surprised to find that, while Walmart PR was searching for a local agro-foods banner project, the Economic Development Bank (EDB) and the Department of Agriculture (DA) of Puerto Rico were looking for companies willing to provide a market for local agro-products. The EDB had been offering farmers financing through the The Key to Your Agro-Enterprise Program (Programa de la Llave para tu Agro-empresa) and helping them to solve marketing problems, while the Department of Agriculture had been providing production incentives and promoting agricultural development. However, since many of the farmers lacked managerial know-how, they often faced a number of difficulties selling their products and running their small businesses. To attend to this need, the EDB and the DA instructed the Commerce and Export Company (Compañía de Comercio y Exportación—CEE) and the Agricultural Extension Service (Servicio de Extensión Agrícola) to develop training programs for farmers. What was missing, though, was a reliable, volume-driven buyer. Walmart PR fit the bill perfectly.

The project team felt that the inclusion of an NGO was needed in order to provide stability and organizational skills to the project, and to facilitate fund raising. The NGO would also act as the liaison among all members of the group. A search was started to find an NGO that had 501C3 certification (NGO tax status so the project could request and receive U.S. federal funding) and a market orientation. Following suggestions from López, the NGO Caborrojeños Pro Health and Environment (Caborrojeños Pro Salud y Ambiente) was invited to join in the alliance. Caborrojeños Pro Health and Environment (CPSA) met the above requirements, worked with microcredit projects and was located near the Coloso Valley in Aguada, where the pilot project would be developed. The organization's president was Luis Valderrama.

## What the Partners Brought to Sowing the Development of the Country

On August 13, 2008, a collaboration agreement was signed at the Walmart Super center in Caguas. The Sowing the Development of the Country alliance involved a private company (Walmart PR), the Government of Puerto Rico (Department of Agriculture and Economic Development Bank), and a non-profit organization (Caborrojeños Pro Health and Environment).[14] ConectaRSE, a CSR consultancy, assisted the project development. Though the project was perhaps not ready to be launched in terms of logistics and management, all partners felt the need to launch it before the local gubernatorial elections of November 2008.

Besides the collaboration agreement, the project involved a number of agreements and contracts among stakeholders. These included (1) contracts between the farmers and the Land Authority of the Department of Agriculture establishing the basis for land rental; and (2) a sales agreement between the Department of Agriculture and Walmart establishing all terms, conditions and penalties for non-compliance. Each partner had a particular competence to bring to the project (see Exhibit 6).

The project's partners also contributed knowledge through a training program for farmers. The objective of the mandatory 25-hour training program was to develop managerial abilities and business skills among farmers and to provide basic farm administration skills (see Exhibit 7).

The project had benefits for all partners involved:

- It would position Walmart as a driving force in the agricultural development of Puerto Rico, since it would create agricultural businesses, increase the quantity and

| Exhibit 6 | Sowing the Development of the Country—Partner Contributions |
|---|---|

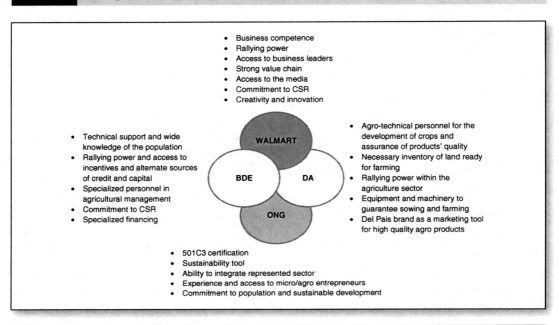

- Business competence
- Rallying power
- Access to business leaders
- Strong value chain
- Access to the media
- Commitment to CSR
- Creativity and innovation

- Technical support and wide knowledge of the population
- Rallying power and access to incentives and alternate sources of credit and capital
- Specialized personnel in agricultural management
- Commitment to CSR
- Specialized financing

- Agro-technical personnel for the development of crops and assurance of products' quality
- Necessary inventory of land ready for farming
- Rallying power within the agriculture sector
- Equipment and machinery to guarantee sowing and farming
- Del Pais brand as a marketing tool for high quality agro products

- 501C3 certification
- Sustainability tool
- Ability to integrate represented sector
- Experience and access to micro/agro entrepreneurs
- Commitment to population and sustainable development

*Source:* Walmart PR Internal Report, 2008

| Exhibit 7 | Training Program for Sowing the Development of the Country |
|---|---|

| Subject | Entity in Charge |
|---|---|
| Production Techniques | College of Agronomists of Puerto Rico |
| Product Quality Criteria | Walmart Stores Inc. |
| Hiring Process | Walmart Stores Inc. and Department of Agriculture |
| Orders and Billing | Walmart Stores Inc. |
| Del País Brand | Department of Agriculture |
| Financing | Economic Development Bank |

*Source:* Walmart PR Internal Report, 2008

quality of local food production (especially fresh produce), reduce the dependence of the island on imported goods, and reduce food miles.

- The EDB would get a good return on investment and somewhat lower risks and would meet its social responsibility commitments.

- Farmers could generate some $2.3 million in sales for the year 2008–2009 (estimate given by the Secretary of Agriculture).
- CPSA could obtain considerable funds to help it meet its mandate.
- ConectaRSE would further its CSR impact on the island in multiple ways.

## How the Project Worked

The partners would coordinate their activities in a variety of ways (see Exhibit 8):

- Around 24 farmers from the Coloso Valley participated in the first stage of the project. The goal for the first year was to increase that number to 41 farmers. The farmers were already working 600 acres and another 400 were ready to be planted. This first set of farmers had been chosen by the Department of Agriculture and had met a set of criteria including participation in the joint DA and EDB program titled "The Key to Your Agro-Enterprise" (Llave para tu Agroempresa)[15] and legal ownership of the land to be developed.
- The CPSA would provide the organizational structure of the project and would lead the search for U.S. federal funds.
- The Department of Agriculture (DA) provided support for production and the marketing of products. Farmers delivered their products to collection centers run by the DA where they were classified, packed and branded with the Del País brand. The agency then delivered the goods to Walmart stores. The Del País brand (meaning "from the country") had been previously created as a way to identify products made by Puerto Rican farmers. The brand was administered by a special fund within the Department of Agriculture.

**Exhibit 8** Sowing the Development of the Country—Partners' Relations

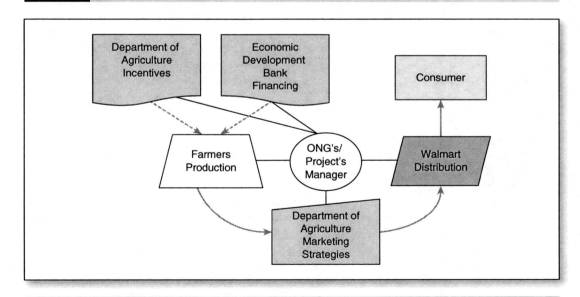

*Source:* Developed by the authors.

- The Economic Development Bank supplied financing. Though the EDB was one of the few lenders that served both the agricultural sector[16] and the island's more disadvantaged communities, it did not offer microcredit nor did it have the necessary managerial and operational structure to manage this kind of loan. In order to address this need, the bank considered a number of different options such as developing an in-house microfinance capability, establishing a separate public corporation, and creating an alliance with a private sector provider. Since the first two options entailed the creation of more government jobs (the public sector already accounted for 22.1 percent of all employment on the island) and did not especially send a message of entrepreneurship, the third option was chosen. The BBVA (Banco Bilbao Vizcaya) Foundation was approached, since its mission was to create social capital through microcredit.[17] In October 2008, the EDB signed an agreement with the BBVA Foundation[18] in order to create the "Corporación para las Microfinanzas—Puerto Rico."
- Walmart guaranteed a negotiated volume of purchases, as well as a price that avoided middlemen charges. Products were sold at Walmart, Sam's Club, and Amigo Supermarkets. In essence, the company linked farmers to its value chain. The budget for the first year included a $160,000 contribution from Walmart that would pay for the manager's salary ($60,000) and for advertising ($100,000). Since the success of the project depended to a great extent on the commitment of all participants, on clarity in their roles, obligations and commitments, and on good communication among them, Baez coordinated frequent project meetings. He visited farmers regularly and established a biweekly teleconference call where participants could share opinions and resources, and balance influence and

responsibility levels, and where the commitment, participation, trust, respect and transparency of each party could be promoted.[19] Baez also visited prospective farmer participants.

## Challenges During the First Year of Operation

Despite the best efforts of all participants, and especially those of Baez and ConectaRSE, the project encountered a number of difficult challenges in its first year of operations.

## Communication

The biweekly conference calls and farm visits were not sufficient in providing adequate communication and building trust between stakeholders. Only a few months after the project was launched, farmers from the Coloso Valley complained that there had not been sufficient follow-up. They reported that they felt abandoned because they were having difficulties obtaining the necessary financing from the Economic Development Bank and they did not have essential resources for agricultural production like machinery and irrigation systems. They also thought that the communication with government agencies and Walmart was not effective, and they were unsure about a real commitment to the agricultural development of the valley.

## Organization

The weakest link in the alliance proved to be Caborrojeños Pro Salud and Ambiente. The NGO was small and was soon overwhelmed by the magnitude of the project. After a relatively brief negotiation, the NGO withdrew from the project. In December 2008, the Collaboration Agreement was amended—CPSA was taken out of the alliance and ConectaRSE was incorporated as part of a formal project participant. Valderrama resigned the presidency of Caborrojeños Pro Health and Environment and soon afterwards joined the Sowing the Development of the Country (SDC) project. As the SDC project manager, Valderrama was directly responsible for the strategic planning of the project, as well as its day-to-day operations (see Exhibit 9). He reported to Walmart.

## Irregularities in Meeting Delivery Schedules

Farmers had not been asked to make specific production commitments or set quality control standards in the original project collaboration agreement.

| Exhibit 9 | SDC Project Manager Duties |
|-----------|----------------------------|

- Act as project spokesperson
- Lead the development of training programs for agribusiness management and for agricultural production
- Develop a project participation flowchart
- Provide economic advice to agro-entrepreneurs
- Act as coordinator of all project activities
- Ensure follow up and continuity
- Prepare budgets and cost analysis
- Provide information for project evaluation

*Source:* Interview to Luis Valderrama. October 2009.

Moreover, the sales agreement had been signed between the Department of Agriculture and Walmart. These kinds of agreements between the farmers and Walmart were supposed to develop over time as the project's potential became clearer and better defined. Unfortunately, overall volume was not as good as original delivery schedules programmed for Walmart (see Exhibit 10).

One of the contributing factors was the seasonality of the agricultural production, but there were other issues involved. One weakness of the partnership was the lack of an agricultural production feasibility study. This was perhaps the result of the need to rush the agreement before the national elections took place. A new agricultural production study would be needed in order to establish production and marketing estimates that addressed the seasonality of production and solved some of the logistics issues (e.g., delivery process with or without the DA) and administrative difficulties (red tape delays) with the Coloso Valley farmers' deliveries.

## Changes in Government Administration

In November 2008, the island's general elections resulted in a change in the party in power. In Puerto Rico, these changes usually brought

| Exhibit 10 | Department of Agriculture's FIDA Collection Center's Sales to Walmart of Sowing the Development of the Country Production |
|------------|---|

|  | Oct-08 | Nov-08 | Dec-08 | Jan-09 | Feb-09 | Mar-09 | Apr-09 | May-09 | Jun-09 | Jul-09 | Aug-09 | Sep-09 |
|--|--------|--------|--------|--------|--------|--------|--------|--------|--------|--------|--------|--------|
| Yucca | 0 | 0 | 490 | 600 | 0 | 0 | 0 | 0 | 0 | 0 | 0 | 0 |
| Yautia | 0 | 0 | 1,360 | 220 | 1,927 | 7,300 | 0 | 0 | 0 | 0 | 0 | 0 |
| Plantains | 0 | 0 | 0 | 0 | 0 | 19,500 | 18,200 | 14,650 | 98,550 | 107,700 | 74,358 | 42,250 |
| White Beans | 0 | 0 | 0 | 74 | 0 | 0 | 0 | 0 | 0 | 0 | 0 | 0 |
| Sweet potatoes | 0 | 0 | 1,680 | 3,000 | 1,598 | 7,332 | 5,120 | 3,784 | 1,800 | 0 | 0 | 0 |
| Yams | 0 | 0 | 0 | 0 | 2,350 | 8,900 | 0 | 0 | 0 | 0 | 0 | 0 |

*Source:* Walmart Net Ship Suppliers, 2008–2009.

major changes, not only in public administration, but also in the projects that were in some way financed and supported by the government. Moreover, the state's budget was in the red and all projects and agencies were at risk. Fortunately, the platform of the new governor, the Honorable Luis Fortuño, was focused on greater private sector participation in the economy, and it had even adopted the term public–private partnerships as part of its policy.[20] Therefore, the ideas behind the Sowing the Development of the Country project were not hard to sell to the new government, even though the project had been developed during the previous administration of the now-defeated political party. Nevertheless, a project partner would have to step into a project champion role. Walmart was the most likely candidate.

In 2009, the incoming administration started a review and adjustment process of existing projects in the Department of Agriculture. The Department of Agriculture's new administration disagreed with some of the established conditions of the Sowing the Development project, such as the amount of incentives granted to the project, the participation of the Department as an intermediary in the marketing process, and the use of the Del País brand. Due to these government concerns, deliveries to Walmart had become slower and more irregular. The project was also threatened by government agencies interested in acquiring parts of the land for road construction and public facilities. Continuation of the project depended on the signing of a new Collaboration Agreement with the new incumbents before the end of 2009.

## CASE QUESTIONS

1. One of the major criticisms of Walmart is that the organization causes problems for local communities. How should Walmart combat this negative publicity?

2. How could the marketing management team better equip on-the-ground managers who work closely with farmers to ensure effective communication and build trust?

3. What steps should Walmart take to improve communications with the incoming government and other publics to ensure cooperation and support in the future?

4. Should Walmart publicize its efforts to assist local farmers in an environmentally friendly fashion in Puerto Rico? In the United States? What methods should the company use if the goal was to benefit from the positive publicity that could accompany the SDE program?

## —— *"Hips Feel Good"—Dove's Campaign for Real Beauty* ——

*By David Wesley, under the supervision of Professors Thomas Gey and Nick Nugent*

Kerstin Dunleavy, brand manager for Unilever's Dove line, was both excited and concerned about her meeting the next morning with Unilever's senior management. She was about to make one of the most important presentations of her career, one that involved taking the successful re-launch of Dove beauty products to the next level.

Dunleavy had already helped mastermind the original turnaround of Unilever's Dove line, which some believed had already been a career-maker for

Version: (A) 2009–02–24

her. She, however, knew that the real test would come as phase two became operational. Only then would she truly be able to establish her reputation as a premier brand manager in the ultra-competitive beauty industry.

Without doubt, Unilever had placed a heavy load on Dunleavy's shoulders. As she gathered her thoughts, she wondered what the next month would hold as Dove rolled out the second phase of the re-launch in September 2006. She placed a call to her assistant executive brand manager and marketing advisor, Michael B. Allen. "Tomorrow I will be laying out the specifics of phase two of the re-launch," she reminded him.

> Things are looking good right now. The self-esteem issues we have focused on have resonated with our target audience. I want it to continue, but I am not so sure about our next move. I want it to continue in the right way.
>
> If the competition copies our strategy, we will just become one of them. Remember that a difference that doesn't stand out is not a difference. Let's go over what has happened in the past two years one more time to make sure we understand how we got here.

Allen agreed that societal marketing had both benefited the brand and helped customers feel good about themselves, he replied.

> Our business has been to sell products, not to satisfy our customers or cure society's ills. But now we know that we can do both. As long as we keep listening to customers, there is no reason why we can't continue to stand out and distinguish ourselves from our competitors.

## Background

Unilever was one of the largest consumer products companies in the world with annual revenues of approximately $50 billion and a staff of 250,000. The company's product lines were organized into four main areas: Cooking and Eating, Beauty and Style, Healthy Living, and Around the House.

Unilever employed a global marketing strategy that was adapted to suit individual cultures and the unique requirements of its subsidiaries. The company's branding policies had been considerably modified in recent years. In 2004, its "Path to Growth" strategy saw the number of products reduced from 1,600 to 400. The company's brand strategy was also modified to emphasize product brand names, while a newly designed Unilever logo adorned its packages (see Exhibit 1).

Along with the new public image came a new corporate mission. Titled "Vitality," it proclaimed:

> We meet everyday needs for nutrition, hygiene, and personal care with brands that help people feel good, look good and get more out of life.[1]

## Development of Dove

Dove was originally developed in the United States as a non-irritating skin cleaner for pre-treatment use on burns and wounds during World War II. In 1957, the basic Dove bar was reformulated as a beauty soap bar. It was the first beauty soap to use mild, non-soap ingredients plus moisturizing cream to avoid drying the skin, the way soap can.

In the 1970s, an independent clinical study found Dove to be milder than 17 leading bar soaps. Based on the results of that study, the company launched a promotional campaign that highlighted the soap's mildness.

Between 1990 and 2004, Dove expanded its product line to include body wash, facial cleansers, moisturizers, deodorants and hair care products. In 2005, revenues from Unilever's Dove product line reached $3 billion.

## Competition

The beauty industry was highly competitive with many well-supported brands and products.

| **Exhibit 1** | Unilever Logo and Symbols |

**Sun**

Our primary natural resource. All life begins with the sun—the ultimate symbol of vitality. It evokes Unilever's origins in Port Sunlight and can represent a number of our brands. Flora, Slim Fast, and Omo all use radiance to communicate their benefits.

**Hand**

A symbol of sensitivity, care and need. It represents both skin and touch. The flower represents fragrance. When seen with the hand, it represents moisturizers or cream.

**Bee**

Represents creation, pollination, hard work, and bio-diversity. Bees symbolize both environmental challenges and opportunities.

**DNA**

The double helix, the genetic blueprint of life and a symbol of bio-science. It is the key to a healthy life. The sun is the biggest ingredient of life, and DNA the smallest.

**Hair**

A symbol of beauty and looking good. Placed next to the flower it evokes cleanliness and fragrance; placed near the hand it suggests softness.

**Palm tree**

A nurtured resource. It produces palm oil as well as many fruits—coconuts and dates—and also symbolizes paradise.

**Sauces or spreads**

Represents mixing or stirring. It suggests blending in flavors and adding taste.

**Bowl**

A bowl of delicious-smelling food. It can also represent a ready meal, hot drink, or soup.

**Spoon**

A symbol of nutrition, tasting and cooking.

| | |
|---|---|
| | **Spice & flavors**<br>Represents chili or fresh ingredients. |
| | **Fish**<br>Represents food, sea or fresh water. |
| | **Sparkle**<br>Clean, healthy, and sparkling with energy. |
| | **Bird**<br>A symbol of freedom. It suggests a relief from daily chores and getting more out of life. |
| | **Tea**<br>A plant or an extract of a plant, such as tea. Also a symbol of growing and farming. |
| | **Lips**<br>Represent beauty, looking good, and taste. |
| | **Ice cream**<br>A treat, pleasure and enjoyment. |
| | **Recycle**<br>Part of our commitment to sustainability. |
| | **Particles**<br>A reference to science, bubbles and fizz. |
| | **Frozen**<br>The plant is a symbol of freshness, the snowflake represents freezing. A transformational symbol. |
| | **Container**<br>Symbolizes packaging—a pot of cream associated with personal care. |
| | **Heart**<br>A symbol of love, care and health. |
| | **Clothes**<br>Represent fresh laundry and looking good. |
| | **Wave & Liquid**<br>Symbolizes cleanliness, freshness and vigor. A reference to clean. |

There were few secrets within the industry, and products were in many ways similar. As such, marketing and communications were as critical to a product's success as new product development. For example, the Body Shop line of beauty care products emphasized social and environmental responsibility as well as all-natural products, thereby appealing to the psyche of the emotionally influenced buyer. As the importance of situational influences increased, marketers began to shift their emphasis from product-related variables to consumer-related variables.[2]

## Modernizing the Brand Image

In 2003, the management of Unilever met to discuss the future of the Dove brand. Even though the company's growing product line was available in 40 countries, sales of its flagship Dove brand were in decline since market share was being lost to competitors.

To understand the reasons for the decline, the company undertook a focused brand analysis under the direction of the Ernest Dichter Institute, a Zürich-based market research firm. The result of the brand audit was revealing. Consumers appreciated Dove both for its natural ingredients and its reliability as a moisturizer. However, on a more emotional level, the brand felt dated and old-fashioned.

Although Dove's brand image did not resonate with consumers, those who used it recognized the quality of the products. For Unilever it was clear that the Dove brand needed a new image, and to that end, management laid out the following targets:

- Increase market share through improvement of the brand image
- Develop an outstanding marketing campaign
- Retain the functional strengths of the brand

Dove needed to evolve into a modern and desirable brand, while at the same time standing out against the myriad other products offered by Unilever's competitors (see Exhibit 2). With that goal in mind, Unilever created a global team under the direction of Kerstin Dunleavy, global brand manager for Dove, to develop a new brand strategy for Dove beauty care products.

## The Dove Research Study

Before setting out to design a new marketing strategy, Dunleavy's team sought to first understand the relationship of women to beauty, without

---

**Exhibit 2**   Examples of Competitor Advertisements

*Sources:* Garnier, Nivea and Jergens (Center for Interactive Advertising, University of Texas, Austin), L'Oreal Communication.

specifically focusing on beauty care products. They wanted to answer four basic questions:

- What do women mean by beauty?
- How happy are they with their own beauty?
- How does a woman's sense of her own beauty affect her well-being?
- What influence does mass media and pop culture have on the perception of ideal beauty?

To find answers for these questions, the company turned to StrategyOne, a global research firm that worked with experts from Massachusetts General Hospital, the Harvard University Program in Aesthetics and Well Being, and the London School of Economics.

Between February and June 2004, StrategyOne surveyed 3,200 women from Argentina, Brazil, Canada, France, Italy, Japan, the Netherlands, Portugal, Spain, the United Kingdom and the United States. The results of the survey were presented in a paper titled, "The Real Truth about Beauty: A Global Report."[3] The report showed a wide disparity between the ideal of beauty portrayed in the media and the perception of beauty as understood by women themselves. The following were the most notable observations.

- Only two percent of women described themselves as beautiful.
- 47 percent said they were overweight—a trend that increases with age.
- 68 percent believed that the media and advertising set an unrealistic standard of beauty that most women can never achieve.
- 75 percent wished that the media would portray more diverse measures of physical attractiveness, such as size, shape, and age.
- 77 percent said that beauty could be achieved through attitude, spirit, and other attributes that have nothing to do with physical appearance.
- 48 percent strongly agreed with the statement: "When I feel less beautiful, I feel worse about myself in general."

- 45 percent believed that women who are more beautiful have greater opportunities in life.
- 26 percent have considered plastic surgery, a result which varied considerably by country. For example, 54 percent of Brazilian participants have considered cosmetic surgery.

Aside from the perceived need for cosmetic surgery, the results were remarkably consistent from country to country. For Susie Orbach, a feminist psychotherapist and writer who co-authored the report, the problem was clear. She explained:

Most of the images we see of women bear little relationship to reality. Overwhelmingly, beauty is defined as tall, thin and young. It is a very limited definition that is presented as the norm, although it is anything but—it excludes most women and encourages them to be unnecessarily self-critical as most of us fall far short of the images of perfection that we are bombarded with daily.[4]

Based on the results of the report, Dunleavy's team perceived an opportunity to redefine beauty in a way that had been ignored Unilever's competitors. The team presented its findings to Unilever's executive board along with a strategy to re-launch Dove using new and unconventional ideals of beauty. True beauty could be found in many forms, sizes, and ages, they explained. Dove had to integrate this idea in its own brand image and spark discussions by attention-seeking campaigns. The team wanted to choose "real" women for the ensuing advertising campaigns, women who were not "treated" via retouching, the type of women one might encounter every day.

The functional advantages of a high-quality product were to be retained. At the same time, it was considered essential to differ significantly in the emotional positioning from Unilever's main competitors. In contrast to competitors such as Nivea, L'Oreal and Garnier, emphasis was not to be placed on perfect looks of top models but on the ethical aspect of beauty. The moral concern was to boost the self-confidence of women. The products were to be derived from this starting point. According to Dunleavy, the brand and not the single products were to be in the foreground. The emotional ties to the target group needed to be strengthened.

Some members of the executive board expressed concern that taking such an unconventional approach to beauty might expose the company to unnecessary risk. After all, if portraying regular women in beauty advertising was such a good idea, why hadn't anyone tried it? Eventually the board decided to support the effort noting that the risk was outweighed by the need to turn around the flagging Dove brand. In Dunleavy's mind, it was the strength of the supporting data presented in the StrategyOne report that finally swayed the vote of the more reticent board members in favor of the real women campaign.

## The Campaign for Real Beauty

The campaign was launched with a mandate from Unilever to increase revenues by a lofty 80 percent, an undertaking that would be supported by an advertising budget of approximately $27 million in Europe alone. Unilever worked closely with the advertising firm Ogilvy & Mather to re-brand Dove.

The "Campaign for Real Beauty" began in earnest in September 2004, with the launch of the website campaignforrealbeauty.com. Women went online to cast their votes and join the beauty debate in chat rooms. Confessions, philosophical questions and rants showed that nerves were being struck.[5] Statements such as "My mommy taught me to believe in myself and to feel good about who I am" were prominently displayed on the site, along with opportunities for potential customers to share their views about the concept of beauty (see Exhibit 3).

The main target group was 30- to 39-year-old women, who had not yet tried any skin-firming products. Although the broader target group included any women who used body lotions and creams, Dove expected to experience significant gains among women over age 30, a time when signs of age appear, skin is increasingly less firm and cellulite forms.

Based on the results of the StrategyOne research, the Dove team believed that beauty could be reflected in different shapes, sizes, and ages, and that "real beauty can be genuinely stunning." Dunleavy explained:

> With the Dove beauty philosophy, we're not saying that the stereotypical Claudia Schiffer view of beauty isn't great—it is, we simply want to broaden the definition of beauty.

That definition was reflected in a new brand mission statement, "to make more women feel beautiful every day, by widening today's stereotypical view of beauty and inspiring women to take great care of themselves.

## The Advertising Campaign: What Is Beauty?

When Unilever launched its ground-breaking advertising campaign in Europe, the core message stated, "No models—but firm curves." Ads featured a group of women of different ages, shapes, and racial backgrounds, dressed only in bras and knickers, animated and laughing among themselves and clearly happy to be themselves. Models for the ads were chosen by well-trained assistants in a "street casting," in order to achieve a great acceptance among the observers. When the campaign was later rolled out in other countries, different models were chosen to reflect local cultural differences.

Some ads asked viewers to make a choice. For example, one featured a 96-year-old woman named Irene and asked "wrinkled or wonderful?" followed by the question "Will society ever accept the beauty of old age?" Another ad featured a heavy-set woman named Tabatha, and asked "oversized or outstanding?" followed by the question, "Does true beauty only squeeze into a size 6?"

**Exhibit 3**    Campaign for Real Beauty Online Discussion Forum

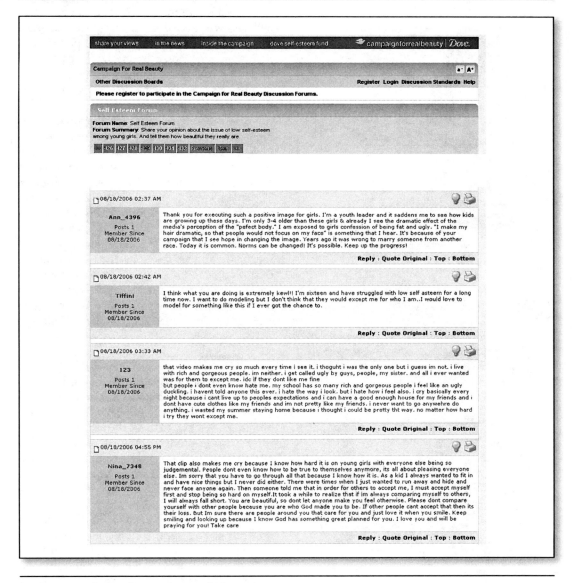

*Source:* www.campaignforrealbeauty.com, accessed February 26, 2007.

(See Exhibit 4 for two other ads in the series.) At the campaignforrealbeauty website, Internet users could cast votes for the ads or join online debates in the forums section.

The company supplemented traditional television and magazine-based beauty advertising with outdoor advertising, such as billboards, posters, and signs. Billboards specifically provided a presence

**Exhibit 4**    Tick Box Ads

44 and hot?
44 and not?

grey?
gorgeous?

*Source:* Unilever.

**Exhibit 5**    Outdoor Advertising

*Source:* Unilever.

that made it easy for journalists to report about the campaign (see Exhibit 5). When the campaign was later rolled out in the United States, an electronic billboard was erected in Times Square that asked bystanders to text message their responses to a beauty question posed by the Dove ads and see their votes counted instantly in the debate. It was the first-ever outdoor mobile marketing event in the United States.

The promotional mix was supported by an unprecedented amount of public relations that built as Ogilvy & Mather coaxed the news media to cover the launch of the campaign and to create debate around Western society's concepts of beauty. The objective was to provoke public attention with a controversial message. To foster discussion, Unilever partnered with American Women in Radio and Television, a non-profit organization that sought to advance the impact of women in the electronic media by educating, advocating and acting as a resource to its members. "It was to be the talk of town," noted Sebastian Munden, managing director for Home and Personal Care of Unilever.

## The Results

Early results were dramatic. Massive media coverage that included as many as 800 newspaper and magazine articles, many of which featured high-profile debates, helped to nearly quadruple sales of Dove-branded products. Market share increased in six European core markets from an average of 7.4 percent in 2003 to 13.5 percent by the end of 2004.[6] Traffic on the company website quickly reached 4,000 visitors a day.

In 2005, a new brand audit by Millward Brown, a market research company, showed a significant image shift. The brand gained attributes such as "open," "active" and "self-confident," and existing characteristics for the skin-firming series, such as "fun," "energetic" and "confident," strengthened further (see Exhibit 6). The turnaround was no less than remarkable. Dove was seen not only as a top-quality brand but also as an industry expert in cosmetics and beauty. Moreover, for the first

**Exhibit 6** Brand Audit 2005 by Millward Brown

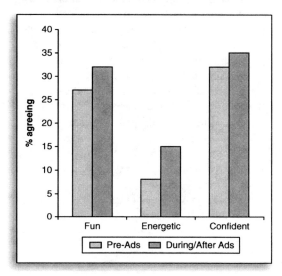

*Source:* Millward Brown International Research, Agreeing Before and After Dove Communications Strategy, "Firming Lotion."

*Note:* Pre-Ads were surveyed from November to December 2003. During/After Ads were surveyed from March to July 2004.

time, the brand was able to break into the premium segment of the market. For its part, Ogilvy & Mather won the Grand Effie Award from the New York American Marketing Association in 2006, for the "most significant achievement in marketing communications."[7]

## Realbeauty

Many girls developed low self-esteem from insecurities about their looks. As a direct result, some failed to reach their full potential later in life. To help these girls, Dove simultaneously established a "Self-Esteem Fund" to support local initiatives. "We've made it mandatory that every country launching the campaign links up with an association that's in line with the Dove Self-Esteem Fund," explained Dunleavy.[8] For example, one program titled "uniquely ME!" partnered with U.S. Girl Scout troops to help build self-confidence in girls

aged 8 to 14, largely in economically disadvantaged communities.

Unilever also sought to address eating disorders in young females, which research had shown to be directly linked to low self-esteem. The company focused on girls between the ages of 8 and 17. Unilever hired Ogilvy & Mather to develop a 45-second commercial for the 2006 Super Bowl football championship, considered by many to be the most important television advertising event of the year. The commercial suggested ways adults could make a difference in how girls felt about themselves. "All throughout the spot, the voices for the members of the Girl Scouts of Nassau County Chorus from Long Island, New York can be heard singing a version of True Colors."[9]

In Canada and Germany, similar projects were launched under the name "Body Talk," "a program to inform and educate young schoolgirls about perceptions of beauty, helping boost their self-esteem."[10] Further ideas for projects were collected in seminars with teachers in order to include Body Talk messages effectively into teaching subjects.

Another activity was a mother–daughter workbook, designed by the U.S. Girl Scout troops, in cooperation with the team that developed the original "Real Truth about Beauty" report. The free workbook could be used together by mother and daughter, and supported mothers in their efforts to encourage communication in the family and to help their daughters improve their self-esteem.

Finally, Unilever needed to improve communication about Dove products so that statements in advertisements appeared more sincere.

## Next Steps

Dunleavy's mind was working at warp speed. The more she thought, the more questions she had. While the first steps of the re-launch were clearly successful, she knew it would not be enough to satisfy Unilever. She sincerely believed that customer-based marketing was paramount. Unilever had quality, well-positioned products. Keeping them there would be the real test.

The next step of the re-launch was set to commence in September. Dunleavy wondered how to maintain the brand's momentum while continuing to take advantage of the stubborn portrayal of flawless beauty by competitors. She also wondered whether the competition would try to imitate Dove's success by launching similar campaigns. In the world of marketing, the reward for success is typically more and better competition. What should Dove do to prepare for the next phase?

## Conclusion

Dunleavy and Allen joked about how much was riding on their next series of strategic moves. "I believe we are doing what needs to be done," noted Allen.

Our customers are our customers. That may sound a little silly, but I know that we are making a difference beyond just making good products. We make good products and we sell them in a manner that is fair and honest. Our promotional work has been cutting edge and I believe it has changed the industry's approach to the portrayal of what is real beauty. Let's listen to the research and combine it with what we have learned in the past two years.

"Tomorrow morning I am going to be asking for some substantial resources to keep this thing going," Dunleavy added.

We need to be aware of what we need and why we need it. Do me a favor. Be ready with specifics as we lay out the plan. You can brief me later.

### CASE QUESTIONS

1. In many cases, companies advertise the results of positive events through entitlings and enhancements. In this instance, the positive results emerged from the advertising itself. How was the marketing team at Dove able to take advantage of this outcome?

2. Describe the role played by the Internet and social media in the success of the Real Beauty campaign.

3. Describe the role of sponsorships and event marketing in the campaign. Are there additional opportunities to build and expand on the Real Beauty theme through these venues?

4. Is a "backlash" toward Dove possible? If so, what would be the nature of the complaints about the Real Beauty approach?

5. Would a similar approach work for products made by Unilever and geared toward men? Why or why not?

## —— New Balance: Developing an Integrated CSR Strategy ——

### By Dr. Vesela Veleva

Katherine Shepard, social responsibility manager at New Balance, understood that New Balance faced new challenges in terms of corporate social responsibility (CSR):[1] how to maintain its social responsibility culture when acquiring new brands,

how to become more transparent and thus increase stakeholder trust and support, and how to position itself as a responsible leader in the industry to obtain business benefits without having to "chase" peers, as Nike and Timberland. She was struggling

Version: (A) 2010–01–28

with some issues due to her intimate familiarity with the company, and she recognized its high potential and the changing operating environment for business. Shepard also knew that New Balance needed someone outside the company to look at the current level of CSR management and performance and provide an independent and credible evaluation and list of recommendations. The Boston College Center for Corporate Citizenship (BCCCC)[2] came to mind as it was an organization with which New Balance was familiar and comfortable.

Both chief executive officer (CEO), Rob DeMartini, and vice-chairman and co-owner, Anne Davis, liked the idea and, in December 2008, the company engaged the BCCCC research team to conduct an assessment and provide recommendations for developing an aligned CSR strategy to the Responsible Leadership Steering Committee and senior leadership. That strategy could also serve as the basis for developing New Balance's first publicly available CSR report. In 2009, New Balance began a process to assess, redefine and integrate its CSR strategy with the core business strategy.

## New Balance Mission

> "Demonstrating responsible leadership, we build global brands that athletes are proud to wear, associates are proud to create and communities are proud to host."

## Introduction

In October 2008, Shepard was driving to the Burlington, Vermont, area to spend the weekend with her family. As she was enjoying the beautiful foliage, she recalled her first experience with New Balance 18 years earlier. It was an uncomfortably hot August day in Boston, but Shepard was determined to get her father a birthday present. Since he wanted some running shoes, she took him to a nearby retail outlet. Being surrounded by hundreds of sneakers that all looked very much the same was an overwhelming experience for her father, and for

her as well. After a moment of silence, Shepard's father said to the salesman, "Tell me which ones are made in the U.S." The salesman immediately suggested New Balance shoes. They had never heard of the brand before but Shepard's father liked the fit and style and they walked out with a birthday gift—a pair of New Balance sneakers. That "made in USA" label made it an easy decision and became something that Shepard remembered.

A year later, in the spring of 1991, Shepard was looking for a new job. She saw a newspaper advertisement from New Balance looking for a corporate communications manager. The job description seemed a perfect fit, and she already knew one thing about the company that was very important to her and her family: New Balance was committed to domestic manufacturing. She applied for the job and, after an extensive interview process, joined New Balance later that year. A few years later she was promoted to senior corporate communications manager and in 2007, she became the social responsibility manager for New Balance (see Exhibit 1).

Since its founding more than 100 years ago, New Balance had followed its mission and demonstrated social responsibility to its employees and communities where it had operations. A strong culture of "doing the right thing" was developed and maintained over the years, as New Balance remained the only large footwear manufacturer with production in the United States. With rapid growth in the late 1990s, however, the company turned into a global brand, which required moving CSR to the next level—from "doing what's right" to fully integrating CSR into the business strategy.

## New Balance: History and Business Overview

New Balance was founded in Boston in 1906, when a 33-year-old waiter named William J. Riley began building arch supports to alleviate pain for people who spent all day on their feet. In 1925, Riley designed his first running shoe for a Boston running club, known as the Boston Brown Bag Harriers. The shoe was so successful that in the 1940s, New Balance began making custom shoes for running,

| **Exhibit 1** | Responsible Leadership Organizational Chart, April 2009 |

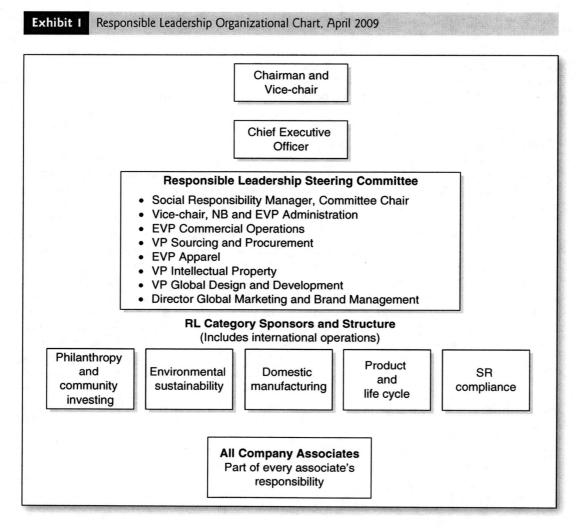

baseball, basketball, tennis and boxing. In 1960, it began manufacturing running shoes in multiple widths and significantly expanded production.

In 1972, New Balance was purchased by James Davis, who remained the owner together with his wife Anne (in 2009, James was New Balance chairman and Anne was vice-chairman and executive vice-president, administration: see Exhibit 2). After graduating from Middlebury College in 1964, James Davis worked as a sales representative for an electronics firm, but his long-term objective was to own and manage his own business. A friend told him about New Balance, whose owner at the time,

Paul Kidd, was looking to sell the business. After doing some research on the company, talking with athletic coaches in New England and trying the New Balance sneakers himself, he was convinced of the high potential for the company: "I felt leisure-time products would be a high-growth market, and I found that New Balance had a good product," he recalled. "After running in them myself I was very impressed with the shoe."[3] Using his own savings and taking a long-term bank loan, Davis purchased New Balance for $100,000.[4]

Sports shoes remained the focus of New Balance business operations, and the company

**Exhibit 2** Senior Executive Staff

A hierarchical organization chart showing the Senior Executive Staff structure:

- **Chairman**
  - CEO
  - President Emeritus/adviser
  - Executive Vice-president and CFO
  - Vice-chair and Vice-president Administration (····· Admin)

Under CEO / President and COO:
- Executive Vice-president Apparel
- President and COO
  - Executive Vice-president Manufacturing
  - Executive Vice-president Commercial Operations
    - Vice-president Sourcing and Procurement
- Executive Vice-president International
- Vice-president Intellectual Property

Under Executive Vice-president Global Footwear, Product and Marketing:
- Vice-president Global Design and Development

Under Executive Vice-president Sales, North America:
- Vice-president Key Account Sales

Under Vice-president Consumer Experience:
- Vice-president NB St. Louis

Under Executive Vice-president and CFO:
- Vice-president and treasurer
  - Vice-president Finance

Under Vice-chair and Vice-president Administration:
- Vice-president Corporate HR

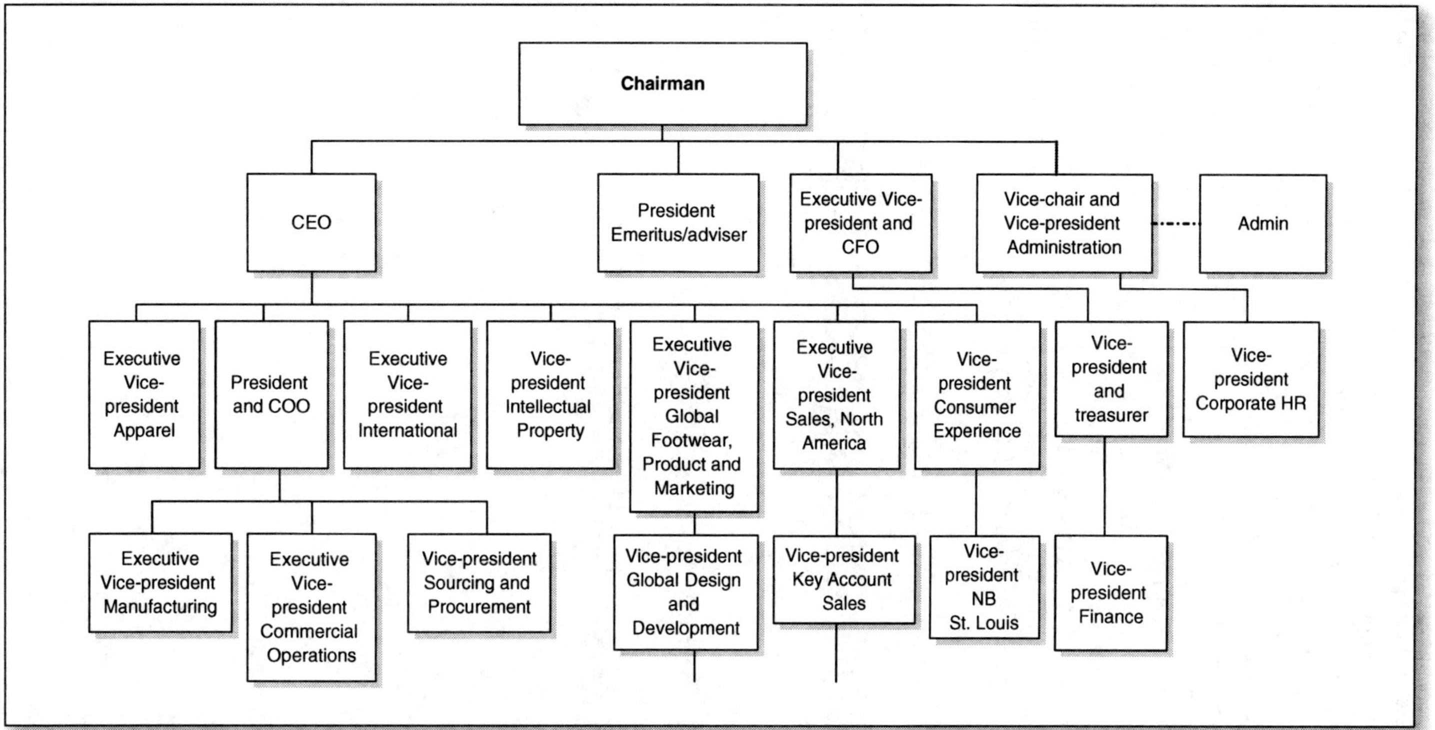

experienced tremendous growth over the next 37 years. This growth was especially significant in the late 1990s, when the company began a series of acquisitions involving various brands, such as Dunham, Warrior and Brine,[5] among others. In 2009, New Balance was a global company with 4,100 employees worldwide (2,634 of them in the United States) and sales of $1.61 billion in 2008 (see Exhibit 3). It was the second-largest manufacturer of athletic footwear in the United States after Nike, and the fourth largest in the world (see Exhibit 4). The company was the only global footwear manufacturer with production in the United States (about 25 percent of production). It had five company-owned factories in the United States—Boston and Lawrence, Massachusetts, and Norridgewock, Norway, and Skowhegan, Maine—and one in the United Kingdom. It had approximately 200 footwear suppliers in the United States, the United Kingdom, China, Vietnam, Indonesia, Mexico, Japan, Taiwan, and Cambodia.

In addition to footwear, New Balance had a small but growing apparel and accessories business (less than five percent of sales in 2008). The apparel and accessories were manufactured through suppliers and licensees from 27 countries around the world, including the United States, China, and Taiwan.

| Exhibit 3 | New Balance Worldwide Sales Growth (US$), 1991–2008 |

| 1991 | 1999 | 2005 | 2008 |
|---|---|---|---|
| $210 million | $890 million | $1.54 billion | $1.61 billion |

| Exhibit 4 | Athletic Footwear Market, 2008 |

| # | Company | Sales (in millions of US$) | Market share (%) |
|---|---|---|---|
| 1 | Nike (incl. Nike Golf, Converse) | $5,192 | 41.70 |
| 2 | Adidas (incl. TMaG, Reebok) | $1,531 | 12.30 |
| 3 | Skechers | $1,084 | 8.71 |
| 4 | **New Balance** | **$920** | **7.39** |
| 5 | VF Corp. (1) | $570 | 4.58 |
| 6 | ASICS | $449 | 3.61 |
| 7 | Collective Brands (2) | $415 | 3.33 |
| 8 | Puma | $404 | 3.24 |
| 9 | Quiksilver (3) | $275 | 2.21 |
| 10 | Crocs | $261 | 2.10 |

*Source:* Sporting Goods Intelligence, www.sginews.com, April 20, 2009, Vol. 26, No. 16.

Notes: (1) VF Corp. includes Vans, Reef Brazil and The North Face. (2) Collective Brands includes Keds, Hilfiger, Sperry and Saucony. (3) Quiksilver includes DC, Roxy, and Quiksilver brands.

New Balance was probably best known among consumers for its "Endorsed by No One" campaign. While it saw athletes as its critical market segment, in contrast with much of the industry, the company chose not to spend money on endorsements from individual professional or "celebrity" athletes or use them in advertisements.

In 2006, New Balance implemented a lean production system[6] (modeled after Toyota's lean manufacturing) in all domestic operations, which led to significant productivity improvements and reduced waste, worker exposures and costs; for example, the time it took to make a pair of shoes in the Lawrence facility was reduced from eight days to three hours. Between the years 2005 and 2009, productivity improved 49 percent as a result of waste reductions. Associates were trained and encouraged to make suggestions for continuous improvements. In 2007, a new CEO from the consumer product industry, Rob DeMartini, was brought on board to lead the company on the journey to becoming a truly global brand.

## Footwear Industry Overview and CSR Drivers

In 2009, the U.S. footwear industry consisted of approximately 100 manufacturers, 1,500 wholesalers and 30,000 retail outlets with a combined annual revenue of $25 billion.[7] Major brands, such as Nike, Reebok, Brown Shoe and Timberland, were mainly owners of brand names that sourced their shoes from independent manufacturers. The retail chain market was highly concentrated: the largest 50 chains represented approximately 80 percent of the market.

One extremely important factor in the footwear business was the logistics of delivering product to retailers. Manufacturers had to be able to respond to requests within days or even hours; therefore, most footwear companies had several distribution centers, typically 500,000 to one million square feet, and sophisticated computer systems to track inventory, orders and deliveries.

Footwear demand was driven by fashion and demographics. The industry had three main segments: athletic shoes, women's shoes, and men's shoes, which represented 30 percent, 25 percent and 15 percent, respectively (the remaining 30 percent was miscellaneous). Domestic manufacturing of shoes had been rapidly declining and in 2009, it was estimated at less than $3 billion annually. The typical U.S. manufacturer was small, with an annual revenue of $10 million and fewer than 100 employees, and able to compete with larger companies through superior design or marketing. U.S.-made products were mostly private-label men's shoes. Average revenue per employee was $100,000. Materials, mainly leather, amounted to 50 percent of costs. Over the past two decades, footwear manufacturing had been rapidly moving overseas to countries, such as China, because of the large labor cost savings. Despite technological advances, footwear was still largely assembled by hand.

As a result of moving operations to developing countries with known human and labor rights violations, the footwear and apparel sectors faced significant social and environmental challenges, underlining the urgency of implementing an integrated CSR strategy. Companies such as Nike, Adidas, Timberland, and Gap had long recognized the costs and reputational risks of poor CSR management and had devoted staff and resources to developing clear strategies to not only mitigate risks, but also take advantage of emerging opportunities related to regulatory changes and consumer preferences (see Exhibit 5). Four areas of existing or emerging issues with high potential to affect New Balance or any other company in the footwear/apparel industry included:

- **Human and labor rights issues in the supply chain**: While this was the first major CSR issue that the industry had to face (e.g., boycott of Nike products in the 1990s), it still remained an area of top focus in 2009. Over the years, there had been a shift in the specific issues. The initial non-governmental organization (NGO) campaigns focused on development of codes of conduct and implementation of supplier monitoring. In 2009, issues such as maximum work hours, health and safety in overseas factories, use of temporary workers, transparency, responsible purchasing practices and "exit strategies" when closing factories overseas dominated the agenda.

- **Increasing demands for transparency**: While privately held companies such as New Balance did not face the same disclosure pressures as publicly held peers, "size invites scrutiny" and demands were growing from NGOs and other stakeholders for greater transparency (e.g., the 2008 Play Fair campaign at the Beijing Olympics[8]). While not every company would be ready to disclose all suppliers as Nike and Timberland had done,[9] a greater transparency could build trust and mitigate unexpected reputation risks from recalls or incidents in the supply chain. It also could help build an emotional bond with ethical consumers and lead to greater customer loyalty.

- **Greenhouse gas (GHG) emissions regulation**: With fast changes in the United States in this area, regulation was just around the corner. Massachusetts, where New Balance was headquartered, introduced mandatory GHG reporting by companies effective January 2009.[10] The U.S. Senate and House of Representatives were drafting a federal climate change regulation. Some of New Balance's peers, such as Timberland and Patagonia, had already begun to prepare for the forthcoming regulation (and also attract ethical consumers) by measuring and reporting their GHG emissions and product carbon footprint.

- **Health, safety and product stewardship**: Adoption of REACH[11] (Registration, Evaluation, Authorization and Restriction of Chemical substances) by the European Union in 2006 changed the way chemicals were regulated. REACH imposed greater responsibility on companies to assess environmental, health and safety impacts of their product ingredients and to identify safer alternatives. The potential for liability from using dangerous chemicals or materials significantly increased. Nanotechnology in particular could bring a new level of health and safety concerns for workers and consumers as traditionally safe materials like carbon and silver, for example, can become toxic to human health and aquatic life when their molecular structure is changed (e.g., carbon nanotubes and nano silver). With growing pressures to reduce waste, regulatory changes were also expected at the end of products' useful lives (e.g., requiring manufacturer product take-back or imposing a fee for product disposal).

All of these social and environmental issues for the footwear and apparel industry necessitated a process aligned with the core business in which product design, operations, communications, marketing, sourcing and procurement and other functions in companies work together to address challenges and identify new opportunities for business growth and meeting social and environmental responsibilities.

## CSR at New Balance: The Right Thing to Do

In 2006, as New Balance celebrated its 100th year, owners James and Anne Davis made a commitment to corporate responsibility as a central part of the organization's values and mission. Corporate responsibility was seen as a way of differentiating a company that "thrives" from a company that just "survives." While the explicit commitment brought new focus to corporate responsibility, the notion of responsibility was not new at New Balance: ever since the Davises became the owners, the company had strongly supported corporate philanthropy, encouraged employee volunteering, and ensured compliance in factories overseas that made New Balance products.

The company did not have a CSR department, but instead had one social responsibility manager, Shepard, who reported to the vice-president of Intellectual Property. Its most formalized CSR structure was the CSR Steering Committee, which was established in 1997, the aim of which was to focus on overseas footwear suppliers and elevate overall working conditions in those factories. In 2007, it was renamed the Responsible Leadership Steering Committee (RLSC) and included four areas of responsible leadership (RL):

- Philanthropy and community investing
- Environmental sustainability
- Socially responsible compliance
- Product life cycle[12]

*(Text continued on p. 365.)*

**Exhibit 5**  Footwear and Apparel Industry: Selected CSR Benchmarks, 2008

| | Business Structure | | | | | Operations | | | | | | Structure | | |
|---|---|---|---|---|---|---|---|---|---|---|---|---|---|---|
| Company | Status | # of Employees (2008) | Revenue 2008 (in US$ mil.) | Priority Issues | | Annual CSR Report | Independent Human Rights Monitoring | Disclosing Supplier List | Steps to Reduce Energy/ Footprint | Restricted Substance Policy | % of Products With Recycled Content | CSR Dept. Home | Title of CSR Head | CSR Reports to: |
| New Balance | Private | 4,100 (2,634 in the U.S.) | $1,540 | Breast cancer, obesity | | No | Yes-footwear only | No | Improved energy efficiency; renewable energy in the U.S. facilities – 30% | No policy but in compliance with REACH. Continuous improvement & "eco score card" for footwear | All | Intellectual property Corporate | Social responsibility manager | VP of Intellectual Property |
| Adidas Group | Public | 39,000 | 10,799 Euro | Health (reproductive & HIV/AIDS), education, youth, disaster relief | | Yes | Yes (Fair Labour Association) | Yes | Reducing use of air freight; environmental guidelines and training for suppliers; energy audits of own sites & retail stores | Yes – goal of average VOC emission of 20 g/pair of shoes | Unknown. "experimenting" with use | Legal | Global director Social & Environmental Affairs | General Council |
| Nike | Public | 30,000 | $16,325 | Sport for youth inclusion – Let me Play; refugees; disaster response | | Yes | Not consistently – in FY05-06 researchers from MIT investigated factories | Yes | Sustainable design guide-lines; Climate neutral by 2011; participation | Aim for 100% of Nike footwear to meet baseline; Considered standards | Not reported | Stand alone | VP Corporate Responsibility | CEO |

*(Continued)*

**Exhibit 5** (Continued)

| Company | Business Structure | | | Operations | | | | | | | Structure | | |
| | Status | # of Employees (2008) | Revenue 2008 (in US$ mil.) | Priority Issues | Annual CSR Report | Independent Human Rights Monitoring | Disclosing Supplier List | Steps to Reduce Energy/Footprint | Restricted Substance Policy | % of Products With Recycled Content | CSR Dept. Home | Title of CSR Head | CSR Reports to: |
|---|---|---|---|---|---|---|---|---|---|---|---|---|---|
| | | | | | | | | in WWF Climate Savers program | by 2011, all apparel by 2015, and all equipment by 2020. Plan to maintain current VOC g/pair (95% reduction from a 1998 baseline) | | | | Corporate Culture officer |
| Timberland | Public | 6,300 | $1,436 | Environment, community greening | Bi-ennial, quarter-ly KPIs | No | Yes (posted on Just Means website) | Increasing renewable energy; Green Index™ rating; Env. Code of Conduct; Green Building principles for new stores; $3,000 employee bonus for hybrid car | Working on completely phasing out PVC across entire footwear line | 79.5% | Corporate Culture | VP of CSR | |

| | Business Structure | | | | | Operations | | | | | | Structure | | |
|---|---|---|---|---|---|---|---|---|---|---|---|---|---|---|
| Company | Status | # of Employees (2008) | Revenue 2008 (in US$ mil.) | Priority Issues | | Annual CSR Report | Independent Human Rights Monitoring | Disclosing Supplier List | Steps to Reduce Energy/Footprint | Restricted Substance Policy | % of Products With Recycled Content | CSR Dept. Home | Title of CSR Head | CSR Reports to: |
| Levi Strauss | Private | 11,550 | $4,200 | Disaster relief found.. bldg. assets (poverty), preventing spread of HIV/AIDS, workers' rights, environ. sustainability | | No | No | Yes | Environmental provisions in sourcing guidelines, use of organic cotton. "Cradle-to-cradle" life cycle assessment of select products, completed GHG inventory and Facilities Environmental Impact Assessment | Unknown | Unknown | Unknown | Unknown | Unknown |
| Gap | Public | 25,000 | $15,763 | Youth (developed world) & women – work and life skills (developing world) | | Yes | Yes (SAI & Verite) | No | Three focus areas: 1) energy conservation. 2) cotton/ sustainable design. | Yes – have developed "Restricted Substance List" that dictates | Working to include recycled material in packaging & labels - not discussed for products | Legal and Administration | Senior VP of Social Responsibility | Chief Legal and Administrative officer |

(Continued)

**Exhibit 5** (Continued)

| Company | Business Structure | | | | | Operations | | | | | | | Structure | | |
| | Status | # of Employees (2008) | Revenue 2008 (in US$ mil.) | Priority Issues | Annual CSR Report | Independent Human Rights Monitoring | Disclosing Supplier List | Steps to Reduce Energy/ Footprint | Restricted Substance Policy | % of Products With Recycled Content | CSR Dept. Home | Title of CSR Head | CSR Reports to: |
| Gap (con't) | | | | | | | | 3) output/ waste reduction. Pledged to reduce U.S. GHG emissions by 11%/sq. ft. from 2003-2008. Monitoring energy consumption in about 40% of U.S. stores. Env. procurement guidelines into RFP process for all non-merchandise suppliers. EMS training for factories. | which chemicals cannot be used when producing their clothing. Restricts several chemicals, including formaldehyde, lead and carcinogenic dyes. | | | | |

The committee was chaired by Shepard and included senior executives from key functional areas. In April 2009, as part of the process for greater alignment and integration with the core business, a fifth area of responsible leadership was added—New Balance domestic manufacturing—and a few additional executives were included from key divisions, such as marketing and branding (see RLSC chart in Exhibit 1). For each RL area there was a sub-team, which met on average every six weeks and focused on specific issues and tangible outcomes; for example, the team working on environmental sustainability made significant progress toward identifying restricted materials, ensuring compliance with the European Union REACH initiative and exploring how recycled, recyclable and renewable natural resources-based materials could be incorporated into product design and packaging.[13]

Throughout the years, the company's private ownership status had allowed it to take risks and make choices that publicly held companies might not have been able to do; at the same time, private ownership also meant lower pressures to disclose social and environmental performance. Strong believers in "doing what's right for employees and communities," the owners were always very "humble" and hesitant to talk aloud about social responsibility; thus, despite its numerous initiatives, very little information had been made available publicly about New Balance's work in this area.

## CSR as a Business Imperative for a Global Company

As a global player in the footwear and sport apparel industry in 2009, the challenge for New Balance became to move CSR to the next level and fully integrate it into the core business. For global companies, CSR was a critical tool for safeguarding and maintaining brand reputation in a world where up to 50 percent of a company's value could be dependent upon reputation and intangibles. A 2008 survey by the BCCCC and the Reputation Institute showed that CSR was the second most important

driver of reputation at 16.3 percent, following the quality of products and services at 17.6 percent.[14]

Global companies faced much greater scrutiny and demands for transparency than domestic brands, particularly in regards to CSR issues, such as supply chain practices (e.g., the Play Fair campaign); at the same time, CSR could be a powerful tool for improving brand awareness, increasing customer loyalty and differentiating from competitors, as companies such as Starbucks, Gap, and Nike had demonstrated. Studies had continued to demonstrate the increasing numbers of ethical consumers.[15] In this context, it was a strategic concern that both internal and external surveys of consumers showed New Balance at the bottom of its peer group on CSR performance. Internally, the New Balance marketing department was conducting such surveys of 2,000 consumers annually; externally, Rice University's Brand Management Study in 2004 came up with similar findings and concluded that "as a person is more aware of New Balance, has good feelings about the brand, and likes the brand's personality, the more willing he or she is to purchase a New Balance running shoe."[16]

In 2009, the challenge for New Balance was to build on the strong implicit values and culture of corporate responsibility and develop a comprehensive and publicly visible global CSR strategy. This strategy had to be able to support the development of New Balance as a highly successful global business capable of making a significant and meaningful contribution to global social development through its core business as well as its community investment and philanthropic programs.

To address this challenge and move toward a more integrated CSR strategy, New Balance began two initiatives in early 2009:

**1. Assessment of CSR management and performance:**[17] The purpose of this initiative was to evaluate the company's strengths, weaknesses, and opportunities in CSR management in order to identify a few areas to focus on and align with core business strategy;

**2. Development of a CSR report:** This involved the compiling of information, goals, and indicators on social and environmental performance in order to develop New Balance's first publicly available CSR report (in 2007 the company published a CSR report that was available only internally).

The company engaged a research team from BCCCC to conduct an in-depth CSR assessment and provide recommendations, as well as the Center for Reflection, Education and Action (CREA) to help develop the CSR report.[18]

## Corporate Citizenship Management Framework

In order to assess its current understanding, organizational readiness and performance in CSR, New Balance used the Corporate Citizenship Management Framework[19] (see Exhibit 6). The CCMF was developed to help companies better understand and manage corporate citizenship as

| Exhibit 6 | Corporate Citizenship Management Framework |
|---|---|

Corporate Citizenship Management Framework™

Source: Vesela Veleva, "Managing Corporate Citizenship: A New Tool for Companies." *Corporate Social Responsibility and Environmental Management*, 2009, DOI: 10.1002/csr.206, www3. interscience.wiley.com/cgi-bin/fulltext/122456956/PDFSTART, accessed January 13, 2010.

an integrated part of the business. It involves assessing and managing business practices in four closely interrelated domains[20]:

- **Overall governance—Values, mission, principles and policies:** Embedding corporate citizenship in the governance and management structure of the company. This dimension addresses how a company's core values, mission, vision, and governance structures support or prevent the company from understanding and managing corporate citizenship as an integrated part of business strategy.

- **Community support—Addressing social challenges:** Mobilizing the company's assets to address social issues and support social well-being beyond creating jobs and paying taxes. This can range from simple philanthropy to participation in multi-stakeholder social issue partnerships, engaging a range of corporate resources.

- **Operations—Responsible business practices:** Utilizing responsible business practices to minimize potential negative impacts on employees, environment and society, and maximize positive impacts. This dimension addresses how a company manages a broad range of operational issues, from business ethics to health and safety, sustainable environmental practices and human rights in the supply chain.

- **Products and services—Market strategy:** Addressing societal needs with marketplace solutions that return a profit to the company. This can range from adaptation of existing products and services to be more eco-efficient or socially beneficial, to a fundamental reinvention of a company's product line or services, as well as their marketing and delivery.

## Assessment of CSR Management and Performance

Using the CCMF framework, the research team conducted industry research, visited the Lawrence, Massachusetts, factory and interviewed 29 internal and external stakeholders between January and

April 2009. Internal stakeholders included senior executives across all key functions, factory workers and supervisors; external stakeholders included an NGO and a retailer. What follows are the key findings from the assessment.

## I. Overall Governance: Values, Mission, Principles, and Policies

New Balance's top strengths, according to almost all interviewees, included its history, values and integrity. Before CSR became a "buzz word" almost 30 years ago, the company was committed to being responsible to its employees and the communities in which it had operations. People were proud to work at New Balance, stating that "management is responsive" and "takes things very seriously." Employees felt personal accomplishment and pride in what the company was doing. As one supervisor at the Lawrence factory summed it up, "This is an exceptional company; there is no other company like New Balance, with focus on people and domestic manufacturing."

The interviews with senior management at New Balance revealed a strong basic support for CSR. The company commitment to corporate responsibility as a central part of the organization's values and mission was well understood; at the same time, there appeared to be no clear consensus or understanding of what this should encompass. Few understood what New Balance's current RL priorities or goals were. Some believed that RL was about philanthropy and volunteering; for others it was about compliance in overseas factories. Most executives still saw CSR as a cost rather than a strategic business driver with measurable social and business benefits.

While the RL platform covered many key aspects of CSR, it left out critical areas, such as transparency and accountability, employee support and domestic manufacturing; therefore, it did not provide sufficient guidance for managers on how to identify potential business risks and opportunities. New Balance's commitment to retain a portion of its manufacturing base in the United States and

avoid layoffs in the economic recession of 2007–2009, for example, were clear demonstrations of social responsibility that were not captured in the RL framework. In response to this finding, New Balance focused on strategy and initiatives in the domestic manufacturing aspect of its RL platform, an area that clearly differentiated the company from competitors.

The CSR assessment found that New Balance lacked a clear process for setting CSR goals that were linked to the core business strategy. Four of the company's six strategic business priorities could easily be linked to responsible leadership:

- Inspire an engaged and committed workforce
- Transform New Balance into a top-tier global brand
- Build an emotional bond with athletic consumers
- Practice continuous improvement

Overall communication appeared to be a challenge for New Balance and a key barrier to positioning itself as a responsible leader. "Capturing all the good things" that associates were doing in the United States and abroad and communicating on an ongoing basis was critical if the company wanted to embed CSR into the core business, further empower associates and create an emotional bond with consumers. Pressures for external reporting were growing both from inside and outside the company. Organizations such as the Maquila Solidarity Network[21] wanted to see more disclosure on supplier factories, whereas New Balance associates wanted to see more about the "wonderful work" they did. While James and Anne Davis were very "humble," they also admitted they "need to be transparent and report—we owe it to our associates and our consumers."[22]

While the assessment revealed numerous impressive CSR initiatives (e.g., worker conditions in supplier factories, greening of U.S. facilities and significant reductions in volatile organic compounds emissions domestically), these were not well connected and aligned, nor were they always measured and communicated to top management; for example, domestic manufacturing, use of renewable energy and greening New Balance stores and factories all contributed to a lower company carbon footprint, but this had not been measured or communicated internally or externally. RL was not seen as an "umbrella" initiative and "thus got a little silo'd," according to one interviewee. Initiatives were often driven by personal passion and interests rather than top-level policy or mandate. The lack of clear policies on how to address the tension of cost versus sustainability presented a challenge in some segments as employees had to balance costs, profitability and aesthetics.

The company assessment found a significant difference between the footwear and apparel divisions' experience and capability to manage CSR, particularly on the operational side; New Balance had good monitoring and control of its footwear manufacturers to ensure compliance to labor practices and restricted materials. This was not the case for apparel, where factory orders were small, suppliers were changed frequently and resources were limited.[23] There was also a gap between the level of CSR management in the U.S. facilities and overseas supplier factories (for more information about this, see the Operations section).

Many executives indicated in interviews that the lack of clear leadership was a major obstacle to developing an integrated CSR strategy, and that unless there was a senior-level champion for CSR on the leadership team, there was little possibility for CSR to advance significantly. In contrast to most peers, New Balance did not have a CSR department or a vice-president-level executive in charge of CSR. Some commented on the "lack of focus" of the RL Steering Committee, and the need to change its mission and purpose if it was to play a leadership role in developing an integrated CSR strategy.

## 2. Products and Services

Through its products, New Balance had the greatest opportunity to bring positive social and environmental changes as well as bottom-line benefits. With the 46.2 million pairs of sneakers sold around the world in 2008, as well as a growing array of apparel and accessories, the company had a truly global reach. This area included issues concerning how New Balance designed its products, sourced materials and worked with suppliers, marketed and delivered products, and how it took responsibility at the end of products' useful life. This category also included measuring and reducing the carbon and toxicity footprint of products.

From product design to marketing and delivery, this domain should include strategic innovation and "out of the box" thinking on what the next generation of footwear and apparel would look like, and how to minimize negative environmental and social impacts and maximize social benefits along the supply chain. This area was of critical importance for achieving a win-win case, with environmental, social and business benefits; however, the research team's analysis revealed that there was still a lack of complete understanding of how this domain linked to CSR and how the company could better leverage its existing environmental and social initiatives to generate business benefits.

While most footwear and apparel companies aimed to have one or two product lines that were considered "green" or "sustainable," New Balance had taken a different approach—to include recycled content and environmentally preferable materials in all footwear. This started with 20 percent in 2008, and aimed to increase to 25 percent of product weight by the end of 2009. The Outdoor Group division of New Balance had been particularly active in incorporating sustainable design criteria in the development of new footwear: it developed and implemented an "eco score card" to evaluate all new products (considering cost-effectiveness, functionality and other design criteria in addition to environmental impacts). Clearly, the impact from such an approach was much greater from an environmental point of view; the business benefits were less clear but could include cost savings and attracting ethical consumers.

New Balance appeared to be the first among peers to completely eliminate polyvinyl chloride (PVC) from all footwear[24] (both Timberland and Nike were still using PVC in 2009, albeit in very small amounts). While there was no regulation in 2009, pressures had been growing worldwide (from NGOs, regulators, socially responsible investors, etc.) to eliminate PVC from all consumer products. Retailers such as Target and Walmart had agreed to stop selling products that contained PVC. New Balance's proactive effort to eliminate this potentially harmful substance was not just a good environmental decision but a smart business move as well.

New Balance's retail group had worked to implement a "green" store design, even though there was no top management mandate. The project, which was strongly supported by James Davis, had slightly higher upfront costs but a short payback period. With the growth of environmentally conscious consumers, such steps could positively impact how consumers viewed New Balance, since retail locations were often seen as the "face of the company."

While the footwear division, and particularly the Outdoor Group, had been very active in the area of developing and introducing more sustainable products (e.g., the 070 shoe, which came to market in the third quarter of 2009 and was New Balance's first "green" shoe[25]), the apparel and accessories division had limited resources, faced a high degree of business growth pressures and was "trying to keep . . . afloat." Apparel faced much greater and more complex environmental and social challenges as production lines and factories changed quickly. It also relied on many licensees and a greater variety of materials. Although apparel represented a small fraction of the business at the time of the assessment, it could expose the company to significant risks or liabilities, even from promotional items; for example, in response to increasing media attention and consumer concerns over polycarbonate bottles containing Bisphenol A, in 2009 the company had to remove them from store shelves.

New Balance did not have a system in place to assess the life-cycle impacts of products (both footwear and apparel/accessories), a system which could help position it as an industry leader; for example, its practices of domestic manufacturing and use of rail instead of trucks for shipping products or parts significantly reduced products' carbon footprint, but this was not measured or communicated. Much more education was needed to "push design teams toward using environmentally preferred products and manufacturing."

More research was also needed on new materials and their performance. Sometimes environmentally preferred materials used in footwear and apparel did not provide good performance and durability: in the past coconut shells were found to be cost effective, but consumers did not like the material because it was too hard.

With the increasing amount of waste and shrinking landfill capacity, there was a growing trend toward product stewardship or implementing policies that would require manufacturers to take back their products at the end of their useful life;[26] for example, Germany instituted a landfill fee on footwear in 2008. While competitors such as Nike had been taking back and recycling old products for some time, this was an expensive undertaking. Developing industry collaboration was one possible approach, although historically New Balance had been unsuccessful in developing such a partnership with other footwear manufacturers. Other possible approaches included partnering with NGOs or regulators to find a cost-effective solution.

## 3. Operations

Integration of CSR into operations was one area where New Balance was particularly strong and could provide leadership for the entire industry. Most of the initiatives had demonstrated clear business value in terms of dollar savings, reduced costs or increased productivity. Intangible benefits included improved worker safety and morale. New Balance had a robust environmental program and good restricted materials program in its footwear division. It had achieved compliance with the European Union REACH regulation—a safeguard against potential fines, market exclusion or damaged reputation. The ability to reduce the number of suppliers from almost 400 to 200 had allowed New Balance to increase its control, reduce costs and improve efficiency. Partnering with organizations, such as the British Leather Group, provided the benefit of a third-party certification standard for selecting materials suppliers with good environmental compliance and safety.

One of the best examples of a win-win approach was the "spectacular reduction in volatile organic compounds" in domestic factories. According to John Wilson, executive vice-president of manufacturing, the program was "really a poster child for sustainability." It began in the late 1990s as a partnership with Henkel, New Balance's German supplier and one of the sustainability leaders in the chemicals/materials sector. The result was a process called "moisture cured reactive hot melt," which as of May 2009 was 98 percent implemented in domestic footwear production. This process eliminated the use of solvent cements, which resulted in 2.7 to 5.0 percent cost savings, translating to more than $6 million in savings from increased productivity and reduced emissions and waste. Productivity went up from 9.5 pairs per team person/hour to 19.3 pairs per team person/hour. Compared to its peers, who used water-based adhesives, New Balance had achieved much lower volatile organic compounds (VOCs) emissions per pair in its U.S. facilities—0.33 grams per pair, compared to a former 14 grams per pair.

Another example of responsible leadership was the adoption and enforcement of a maximum 60-hour workweek for Chinese suppliers, down from more than 70 hours. According to Jim Sciabarrasi, vice-president of Sourcing and Procurement, the initiative led to increased productivity in the range of 35 percent in the first year. In 2009, New Balance agreed to work with the Maquila Solidarity Network to help publicize these productivity improvements as a way to get more companies to adopt responsible supply chain practices.

Waste reduction was another strong area for the company and a good example of cost savings. In 2008, New Balance recycled 99 percent of its waste, which together with the reduced emissions of VOCs from manufacturing and cleaners led to a change in its status to a "small quantity hazardous waste generator," and thus reduced the costs for disposal, worker training and insurance.

In 2007, New Balance implemented a new job coaching program in the United States to reduce work-related injuries. The program used early symptom intervention and included ergonomic evaluation (840 evaluations were completed in 2008). Setting a goal of less than eight work-related injuries per 200,000 hours of work (or 100 full-time workers), New Balance achieved an actual rate of 6.2 to 6.3, which translated into improved productivity, reduced absenteeism and lower insurance costs; in addition, the program had improved morale among associates as they felt that management truly cared about them.

Switching to green cleaners in all U.S. facilities in 2008 had proved to be another win-win initiative that put New Balance ahead of its peers. Working with a green janitorial product company, it identified four green chemicals that replaced the previously used 20 conventional cleaners. At the end, the program saved New Balance $240,000 compared to the previous year, according to John Campbell, corporate manager of Corporate Services. This number did not include the additional benefits of improved worker health, safety, and morale.

Improving energy efficiency was identified as another strong area for New Balance. Replacing lighting, servers and improving processes were among the actions that allowed the company to reduce energy use and therefore lower costs by $340,000 in 2008 alone; as a result, New Balance was able to increase its portion of renewable energy to 30 percent in all domestic facilities at no additional cost. This was a smart business move considering the forthcoming GHG emissions regulation in the United States.

One unique operational area for New Balance was its commitment to employees. Despite the difficult economic times in 2008 and 2009, the company avoided layoffs. This focus on domestic manufacturing and protecting jobs in the United States could have won it a particularly strong reputation among U.S. consumers and helped further differentiate the brand. Studies had shown that 86 percent of American consumers wanted to see companies manufacture their products in the United States.[27] Treating employees well also improves associates' morale, engagement, and productivity.

While the footwear division had made some remarkable strives in the operations domain, apparel, accessories (done mostly through licensees) and promotional items were found to pose significant risks. According to one interviewee, New Balance did not have the same leverage with suppliers as it did for footwear. Since these items carried the New Balance logo, the company could potentially be blamed should a problem arise. The cost of compliance was a challenge, as the batches were very small: for example, the company spent $2,000 to test 400 promotional lip balms before the 2008 Olympic Games).

Another challenge in the operational domain was the gap between CSR management in domestic operations compared to supplier facilities overseas. While there were business reasons for this discrepancy (e.g., low-skilled work force, high employee turnover, and technical issues), they had to be addressed or the gap could expose the company to some potential reputational risks.

To keep domestic jobs, New Balance was considering closing some of its overseas factories. The question then became, was the company going to take measures to minimize the negative social impacts on the workers overseas (e.g., through compensation and retraining)? Organizations such as the Maquila Solidarity Network provided guidelines for responsible transitions for multinational companies forced to close down production in countries such as China. Use of contract labor in overseas factories was an area that "raise[d] a red flag," according to Sciabarrasi. While New Balance monitored for any violations and took corrective action, it did not have a standard on short-term contracts used to hire temporary workers overseas, a concern voiced by stakeholders, such as the Maquila Solidarity Network. The situation was also complicated by different cultural perceptions; for instance, some migrant workers in Asian countries may prefer to work longer hours in order to earn more in a short period of time before returning to their homes.

## 4. Community Support

A key part of New Balance's mission included supporting the communities where it had operations. Philanthropy and volunteering were an important factor in employee retention and job satisfaction. As one interviewee pointed out, "New Balance employees feel highly empowered to help others and engage in the community to do our part, inside and outside our work hours." New Balance had a "sincere and deep belief in philanthropy which came from the top—its owners Anne and Jim Davis." Between 1997 and 2007, the New Balance Foundation's giving increased from $142,750 to $6,494,388 annually.

Volunteering was very active and people were proud of the company's involvement. Studies have demonstrated that volunteering also helps improve public relations, branding and reputation, employee team and skill building, recruitment and sales.[28] In 2007, 614 associates in the United States contributed more than 3,847 hours of service to local communities, which was a 25 percent increase compared to the previous year. The 2008 job satisfaction survey demonstrated that 96 percent of employees "[felt] good about the way they contribute[d] to the community."

The community support strategy "received strong support across all levels in the company and in all geographies." There was good awareness about the programs, such as the Susan Komen breast cancer initiative, which had become a 20-year tradition. New Balance had developed a good system to measure the return on investment (ROI) for this social marketing initiative: it assigned dollar value and calculated ROI based on the cost of the event, shoe sales, expected value from shoe "try-ons," giveaways, and advertising impressions. Shoe sales at events were easy to track and drove ROI. For a $100 pair of shoes, with a profit of $30, 100 percent of the profit would contribute to the ROI for the event. Another level of the hierarchy was a "try-on." New Balance estimated the value of "try-ons" based on internal marketing benchmarks; for example, it knew that approximately 10 percent of customers who try on shoes actually buy them. If the profit on a $100 pair of shoes is $30, then the value of a "try-on" would be $3.

Despite its strong community involvement culture, New Balance community involvement strategy (including New Balance Foundation giving) was not aligned with the business strategy: it was mostly U.S.-centered and insufficiently communicated both internally and externally (to customers and other stakeholders). Employees felt that the brand did not get enough recognition for all the great work that had been done. The community support strategy was also poorly focused. Areas of involvement included childhood obesity, breast cancer, Boys and Girls Clubs, and the YMCA, among others; however, these were not issues that were relevant to all people worldwide, and employees did not always feel passionate about them.

## Opportunities and Challenges in Building an Integrated CSR Strategy

The assessment revealed that New Balance had many of the key elements required for the development of an effective CSR strategy to address the challenges that the company faced as a global business. It identified several key **strengths:**

- Strong commitment to corporate responsibility as a central part of the organization's values and mission
- Readiness to support the development of an integrated CSR strategy by key leaders from across the company, as well as the CEO and the owners
- Good range of practical knowledge and experience in CSR initiatives distributed across the organization from supply chain management to community involvement and employee volunteering

Identified **weaknesses** that had to be addressed in order to move forward included the following:

- Lack of clear and effective leadership either in the form of executive leadership or the RL Steering Committee
- Lack of a comprehensive definition and organizational understanding of what RL meant for New Balance
- Lack of a framework for systematically identifying CSR risks and opportunities that were material to the business
- Lack of a strategy for aligning and integrating CSR into the core business and measuring the business and social value from various initiatives under way
- Lack of communication and reporting systems to create awareness and measure progress in CSR and communicate progress with internal and external stakeholders

As the fourth-largest footwear brand in the world, New Balance had the opportunity and responsibility to take CSR to the next level and give new meaning and value to responsible leadership. As a growing global brand in an environment of high consumer expectations, public awareness and concerns about social and environmental issues in the footwear and apparel industry, the time was right for New Balance to create a "breakthrough" strategy on CSR; however, developing and implementing such a strategy required addressing some key questions and challenges:

- What was the right structure for adopting a unified, company-wide approach to CSR? To what extent should such a structure be formalized? Should New Balance create a CSR department or continue to rely on the RL Steering Committee for driving CSR?
- What should New Balance focus on to have the greatest impact in terms of both social and business results? Should it concentrate on two to three areas where it is particularly strong or address two to three areas identified as posing the highest risks?

- How should New Balance maintain its culture and values of social responsibility given its fast growth through acquisitions of different brands? Is it possible to promote growth and social responsibility at the same time?
- What does an industry leader look like? Is leadership about continual internal improvement or about being a strong public champion? Should the company partner with industry peers, NGOs and governments to address issues beyond its reach today?
- What are the roles of the CEO and the owners—James and Anne Davis—in moving forward with an integrated CSR strategy? Who should be leading the process?
- What is the role of senior management? Is it sufficient for senior management to fire the starting pistol and expect that people will feel empowered to move forward?

Or should it take a more active role in mapping the direction, providing goals, guidance, recognition and continuous communication?[29]

From its strong values of ethical responsibility and community support to the way it addressed key social and environmental issues, such as preserving U.S. jobs and "greening" its manufacturing processes and products, New Balance had a strong foundation on which to build this strategy. With the CSR assessment, engagement of key executives, and the work on the first CSR report, New Balance had begun the transformation. The challenge for the company going forward was to discern how to make CSR and responsible leadership a powerful force for driving global business success while increasing the contribution of New Balance to developing a just and sustainable world. Building the business case for an integrated CSR strategy was the next critical step for moving forward.

## CASE QUESTIONS

1. As a "Made in the USA" company, New Balance enjoys an advantage with some domestic consumers. Is this also an advantage in the international marketplace?

2. New Balance is privately held. Consequently, pursuing socially responsible practices, such as maintaining a local workforce and developing environmentally friendly products and production methods, which may take away from the company's bottom-line profit figures, draws less scrutiny than it would in a publically held company. Discuss how this feature might be an advantage to New Balance but also present some challenges in terms of transparency.

3. What role should entitlings and enhancements play in the publicity sent out by New Balance?

4. If New Balance discovers one of its major competitors has become involved in greenwashing, how should the company's marketing managers respond?

# CHAPTER

# 12

# Distribution and Supply Chain Management

The argument can be made that most of marketing involves spending money on various activities such as advertising, sales promotion programs, and so forth. Conversely, many marketing managers look to distribution and supply chain management as the places to try to cut costs. To some extent this may be true, but, at the same time, efficiently and effectively delivering goods and services should not be viewed as cost cutting only or something that might lessen the impact of the company's other marketing efforts. The major issues in supply chain management are (1) selecting a distribution system, (2) establishing channels of distribution, (3) managing the supply chain, and (4) overseeing the physical distribution of products.

## ▧ Distribution Systems

The first decision a marketing manager makes in terms of distribution is about the level of distribution desired. When the goal is full market coverage, an intensive distribution system in which the product is made available to consumers in as many places as possible will be chosen. The opposite, exclusive distribution, limits the number of distributors to only one or two in each geographic area in order to develop the image of exclusivity and prestige. Selective distribution means that a carefully chosen set of outlets carries the product to give the manufacturer better control over the marketing channel.

The decision variables used to select the level of distribution include the type of product, the price, the degree and type of competition, the brand's image, the desired product position, the level of brand equity or brand parity, and the image of the distributors. Successful distribution results from a partnership between the manufacturer's brands and the retail outlet. Developing partnerships can be challenging. Most manufacturers work hard to build strong relationships with retailers in order to receive the most favorable treatment in the store.

## Establishing Channels of Distribution

Channels of distribution are the paths goods and services take from the producer to the end user. Both direct and indirect channels are available. When a producer sends a product directly to the consumer or end user, a direct channel is being used. The systems fit with individuals who sell personally made merchandise, those who offer personal services such as hair care, some financial service companies, and business-to-business settings in which sales representatives visit client companies without the use of a middleman or intermediaries.

Indirect channels utilize intermediaries, including retailers, wholesalers, distributors, industrial agents, and industrial merchants. For years, the most common approach had been the traditional marketing channel (producer to wholesaler to retailer to consumer). Now, many times one step or more is bypassed.

In business-to-business markets, an industrial agent represents goods without taking title to them. Industrial merchants buy and then resell merchandise. Taking title assumes some risk, as the item may not be resold.

Dual channels are present when a manufacturer sells directly to major retail outlets and employs wholesalers or distributors to reach smaller retailers. Dual-channel marketing is also known as a multichannel distribution system, or a hybrid marketing system. Dual-channel marketing also refers to the use of both direct and indirect channels, such as when a record company sells music in music clubs or over the Internet to some buyers and in retail stores to others. Finally, dual-channel markets include merchandise sold to both individual consumers and business-to-business customers.

Intermediaries offer several advantages. They tend to reach a wider number of customers. Intermediaries provide a wider assortment of products to retailers and customers. Intermediaries provide convenience to customers and may reduce the total cost of distribution. Finally, intermediaries share some of the marketing functions, including inventory control, granting credit, and storage.

The primary disadvantages of using intermediaries include time, cost, and loss of control. It takes longer for products to move to marketing when intermediaries are employed. The cost rises due to intermediary markups. The manufacturer loses control when the retailer makes the final sale to the consumer.

In international settings, distribution systems vary widely. Distribution, warehousing, credit terms, and shipping systems will be different. The types of companies serving as intermediaries also vary. Before expanding into international sales, the marketing team carefully analyzes the types of distribution channels that are available and which ones will be favored by companies and customers in other countries.

## Managing the Supply Channel

Another major element of a supply chain management program is managing the supply channel. One approach, a pull strategy, means the manufacturer focuses on stimulating consumer demand through extensive advertising and consumer promotions so that individuals will ask for the product, thereby pulling it through the channel. A push strategy focuses on providing intermediaries with the kinds of incentives that will lead them to cooperate in marketing the product. Some manufacturers use both strategies to maximize sales and exposure of products.

Another major strategic choice is whether to use traditional intermediaries or work to create an in-house distribution channel. The management team of a manufacturing company considers three common alternatives to traditional channels. The first, vertical integration, results from the acquisition of an intermediary in the channel. Forward vertical integration occurs when a manufacturer opens a distribution system or its own stores. Backward vertical integration means the retailer creates a distribution system or begins to manufacture items to be sold in the store. A second alternative, horizontal integration is an acquisition or merger at the same level of the distribution channel. Examples would include wholesalers acquiring other wholesalers or retailers purchasing other retail outlets. The third option, vertical marketing systems, consist of manufacturers, wholesalers, and retailers within the same channel acting as a unified whole.

Successful channel management programs develop channel arrangements with key partners in the distribution system. The channel arrangement guides the administration of the marketing functions that must be performed as part of the distribution program. A contractual channel arrangement means that a binding contract identifies all the tasks to be performed by each channel member with regard to production, delivery, sorting, pricing, and promotional support. An administered channel arrangement approach has a dominant member in the distribution channel in terms of size, expertise, or influence. The dominant member, or channel captain, can emerge from any level of the channel. A partnership channel arrangement allows members to work cooperatively together for the benefit of all firms involved. Each approach leads to a different degree of channel control and varying levels of cooperation between channel members.

When choosing channel partners, a series of steps will normally be followed. Establishing objectives and selection criteria comes first. All qualified channel members are then identified, and each is encouraged to share needs and wants. The management team evaluates the potential channel partners and develops an integrated supply chain system that aspires to be a win-win for all partners. Finally, the program establishes criteria for performance. When arrangements between partners are successful, they continue. If problems emerge, the management team will try to rectify them or may look for a new arrangement system.

Channel members sometimes disagree on channel activities, the relative roles played in the channel, and the level of rewards or profits each should receive. One of the keys to successful management of the marketing channel is to understand the nature of channel power and use it properly. Expert power refers to power over channel members based on the experience and knowledge a channel member possesses. Referent power increases when a manufacturer, wholesalers, or retailer is well liked or respected. Legitimate power takes the form of a contractual relationship in which duties and responsibilities of channel members are clearly delineated. Reward power comes from the ability to influence channel members with financial rewards and other enticements. Coercive power refers to power based on the ability to remove privileges or punish channel members for noncompliance. Power for power's sake should not be the goal. Channel power should be viewed as a tool to achieve marketing objectives.

## ▧ Physical Distribution

The term *logistics* applies to materials handling, inventory location, inventory control, and transportation systems. It covers all activities from the physical movement to the storage of goods from the producer to the consumer. Materials handling programs manage the inflow of raw materials. Costs are measured in terms of delivery fees versus storage costs.

Inventory location begins with identifying the most efficient and effective methods for storing finished goods before they are shipped to wholesalers, retailers, other businesses, and consumers. One storage facility, a private warehouse, will be owned or leased and operated by a firm storing its products. Public warehouses are independent facilities that provide storage rental and related services for companies. They tend to be lower-cost options for many small companies. Third-party warehouses involve a company outsourcing the warehousing function to a company that specializes in inventory and warehouse management. The selection criteria used to analyze the options include costs, the size of the facility, access to transportation, closeness to the customer base, and closeness to the production facility.

A distribution center is not a warehouse, because it is not designed to store products but rather to facilitate the flow of goods, thereby reducing storage costs. The just-in-time inventory control system works well in the distribution-center system. Most distribution systems rely on a hub-and-spoke system similar to those used by airlines and package delivery companies, such as UPS and FedEx.

Order processing of the paperwork that follows a purchase order from the manufacturer to the final destination is a key element of quality customer service. Order processing tasks include credit, order forms, the physical movement of goods, providing purchase information to all relevant parties, verification, documentation of missing items, and submitting the final bill for payment.

Inventory control is the process of identifying the level of inventory that is needed to meet demand at a reasonable cost. When too little inventory is on hand, lost sales, frustrated customers, complaints, and other problems result. When too much exists, funds are tied up with excess product on hand. The stock turnover figure signifies the number of times per year the average inventory on hand has been sold. In dealing with inventory and stock turnover, retailers make decisions concerning how much merchandise to place on store shelves, how much to carry in a warehouse or distribution center, and how much to hold in a back room, if one is used.

Inventory management systems are designed to keep ordering and storage or carrying costs as low as possible. The traditional formula employed to make this calculation was the economic ordering quantity. Currently, many firms have moved to just-in-time inventory control to order materials more efficiently and to reduce inventories of finished goods. The retail equivalent of just-in-time, the quick-response inventory system, creates a supply flow that approximates customer purchasing patterns.

## Methods of Transportation

The final task associated with physical distribution is establishing methods of transportation. Controlling transportation can mean the difference between a profit and a loss. The choice of a method determines how quickly goods arrive at a destination and the flexibility of loading and unloading shipments. The primary modes of transportation include trucks, rail, water, and pipelines. Intermodal transportation involves using more than one transportation mode. Freight forwarders are specialized firms that collect shipments from different businesses, consolidate them into one truckload or railcar, and then deliver them to a destination.

## Evaluation of Physical Distribution

Company leaders periodically examine warehousing and physical distribution costs with an operational audit program. It studies the procedures and processes used in operating the warehouse or distribution system, layout and usage of the facility, staff productivity, and freight analysis. The goals are to lower costs per order, increase storage capacity, reduce inbound and outbound freight costs, improve service levels, and improve turnaround time.

## ⊠ Implications for Customer Service

Distribution systems affect both customer acquisition and customer retention. Stock-outs can influence customer acquisition and increase complaints. Efficient and effective product and service delivery probably does not attract a great deal of attention, but failures in this area are readily apparent.

## ⊠ Implications for Marketing Managers

Many of the tasks performed in the area of physical distribution are carried out by entry-level workers and first-line supervisors. First-line supervisors make sure items are moved carefully without breakage and that order forms are filed and processed correctly. Middle and top-level manages make decisions about distribution patterns, channel arrangements, warehouse forms, methods of inventory control, and forms of transportation. An effective distribution system informs workers at all levels of the outcomes of these decisions.

## ⊠ The Cases

### YvesCreations LLC: Alex Goes to Hollywood

Alex Yves faced a major dilemma. He had created a Hollywood-style movie titled *Movin' In* that seemingly had everything needed to become a successful project. It included a fun, romantic story, a strong international cast, and top-rate production. The story took place in part in Switzerland, making the film a candidate for both the U.S. and European markets. In spite of these advantages, Yves was not able to obtain a distribution deal from either a U.S. or a Swiss distributor. Recovering the nearly $1 million investment was going to be difficult. Yves wished he had spent more time understanding the market channel prior to investing 4 years of his life in a film that might not make it to local movie theaters.

### Eureka Forbes Ltd.: Growing the Water Purifier Business

AquaGuard, the brand name for Eureka Forbes, Ltd., was a water purification system that had become highly successful in India. It had reached the point of widespread brand name recognition. Rapid economic expansion in India created a new opportunity: Greater numbers of customers outside urban areas were now interested in owning systems. Also, increasing understanding by consumers of the health benefits of pure water led to greater demand, especially in light of diminishing water sources. The marketing team at Eureka Forbes set three goals: (1) create products for various consumer needs and situations, (2) limit cannibalization between those products, and (3) stave off the entry of new competition. Effective implementation of strategies designed to achieve these goals would lead to long-term, stable growth for the company.

## Kraft Foods: The Coffee Pod Launch

Single-serve coffee pods are widely accepted and used in Europe. Kraft, noting this acceptance, considered launching the product in the United States and Canada. In Canada, the company spent considerable effort promoting the new items to consumers, without waiting for results in the United States. Unfortunately, while Kraft gained a substantial market share, sales were highly disappointing. One primary cause of the slow rate of use was the coffeemakers, which did not work well. The marketing management team at Kraft knew that dramatic steps would need to be taken to turn the situation into a more profitable operation.

# ——— YvesCreations LLC: Alex Goes to Hollywood ———

*By David Wesley, under the supervision of Professor Chris Robertson*

Alex Yves felt disheartened as he left the office of Zurich-based Digital Film Cooperative (DFC) without a deal to distribute his recently completed independent film, *Movin' In*. Yves had spent the past year trying to negotiate an agreement with a reputable distribution company, first in the United States and later in Switzerland. DFC had been his last hope.

To date, the only distributors willing to even consider his film had made offers of a percentage commission that Yves knew were unrealistically low or that required him to relinquish his rights to the film without any compensation whatsoever. Even in the most optimistic scenario, signing over film rights for a commission would mean that his company would be lucky to recover a fraction of the nearly $1 million it had invested in the film. To Yves, both types of offers were unacceptable.

*Movin' In* had all the ingredients of a successful motion picture. It had star power, top-rate production value and a likeable story about a Swiss immigrant who falls into a series of comedic mishaps when he attempts to connect with a Los Angeles woman he met on the Internet. More importantly, Yves believed that the film's well-known international cast would attract viewers on both sides of the Atlantic. In limited private showings, most viewers seemed to enjoy the film.

After devoting almost four years of his life to the project, Yves had become increasingly frustrated with distributors who were unwilling to promote *Movin' In* on reasonable terms. Yves thought he might have better luck in his native Switzerland, but he soon discovered that most Swiss and German distributors were just as reluctant as their American counterparts. DFC was the last distributor on his list because of its focus on low-budget local productions. When the owner of DFC refused to make Yves an offer, he felt disappointed and discouraged.

Later that evening, he discussed his frustrations with Sonja Mehnert, a childhood friend who had recently moved to Zurich. "I thought I would have sold this film a year ago and I still have nothing to show for it," he lamented. He wondered whether his approach toward distributors made sense. "Perhaps I ought to try something different?" he asked, almost rhetorically.

As he recounted the last four years of his life, and the many challenges he encountered along the way, Yves hoped that his friend would be able to offer some constructive advice. For example, could he have been a better leader? Had he done enough to motivate crew members and resolve conflicts?

Version: (A) 2010–02–26

# Background

At age 18, Alex Yves had made his first film, a short feature about snowboarding in Switzerland. The film had been shown exclusively at local snowboarding events, and some clips had been uploaded to video-sharing websites, which was a new trend at the time. The project taught Yves some valuable lessons about filmmaking:

> As soon as the filming ended, people lost interest because they realized how much work had to go into editing, music and all that. People are always interested in being part of the exciting stuff, which is the filming, but they are not interested in the hard work.

The value of the film was short-lived "because new stars came up on an almost monthly basis." Within a year, Yves's film was all but forgotten.

After high school, Yves took a position at IBM as a strategic outsourcing proposal team leader. For the next two years, he provided information technology services to international companies that had offices in Switzerland and wanted to outsource their internal information technology (IT). After two years of working 80 to 90 hours a week, Yves decided to leave IBM to attend college in the United States.

> When I was very young, maybe 12 years old, I already knew I wanted to study in the U.S. I don't know why. There are just certain things in life I know I want to do, and studying in the U.S. was one of them.

After visiting several colleges, Yves decided on Northeastern University because of its emphasis on "real-world experience." Unfortunately, his test scores were not high enough for admission to the full-time business program. Undaunted by the rejection, Yves enrolled in the open evening program and, after a year of strong academic performance, he was able to transfer into the full-time business program.

Yves had always wanted to study fine arts, but he believed that the career opportunities available to BFA graduates were too limited.

I wanted to make money and be successful in life. The best way to do that is to be business savvy. I thought to myself, "Why not do the business degree and then build on that knowledge and learn the creative stuff on the side."

For Yves, Northeastern University's real-world experience was not real enough when he compared it with life at IBM. To keep himself "grounded in the working world," he started a Web design company that he operated concurrent to his studies. Despite the heavy workload, Yves managed to complete the maximum allowable course credits per semester. After fewer than three years, he graduated near the top of his class.

After graduation, Yves wanted to do something different with his life. "What is the *most exciting* thing I could possibly do?" he asked himself.

> The more I thought about it, the more I thought about taking the rest of my savings and going all out. I could always go back to Switzerland and get a job if things didn't work out. I should take some risk now, because I am probably not going to be able to later.

Yves decided to travel across the United States and to use the time to work on a novel about his experiences in America. He liked the idea of telling a story, but soon realized that the format of a novel wasn't right for him. Although he had experience writing business proposals, novels required much more descriptive content. By the time he reached the Grand Canyon, he began to feel discouraged. Then, as luck would have it, he met a Hollywood screenwriter who was dining at the same roadside restaurant. After explaining the difficulties he was having, she suggested that he try writing feature-film scripts. "Writing a script is different from writing a novel," she told him. "Novels often get overwhelmed in details, whereas scripts are straightforward. They are usually only about 100 pages long and every dozen pages or so, something interesting has to happen to drive the story and keep things moving."

As he continued his travels, his conversation with the screenwriter kept coming to mind. Eventually he landed in Los Angeles.

I was so green, it is not funny. L.A. is nothing like Switzerland. There are so many crazy people here and the traffic is horrendous. I have never experienced anything like it before in my life.

He also soon realized that opportunities for business school graduates to work in the film industry were few and difficult to find. Instead, most of the available jobs were for low-paying, unskilled positions.

I could go to an agency and they would have stuck me in the mail room. Then, maybe after a couple of years, I could work my way up. I was too impatient for that. Also, it would not have given me the opportunity to work on scripts or actual film sets, which is what I really wanted to do.

Instead, he decided to focus strictly on script writing. However, without any personal contacts, he did not know where to go for support. He knew that the best way to become familiar with L.A. and the film industry was to meet people. For that reason, he began to take acting classes and to volunteer on student film projects.

Anywhere there was an opportunity to work on a set, in any capacity, I was there, watching and learning. I would hold a boom, or position a light. Basically, I would take any job I could get. I really just wanted to learn through hands-on experience. In L.A. there are plenty of opportunities, especially if you are willing to work for free, but it's not something you can make a living at in the short run.

To support himself, he worked in restaurants and in various unskilled day-labor jobs. "They certainly weren't the kind of jobs you might expect for an educated person with a business degree."

One day, Yves received a call from his younger brother in Switzerland, who told him that one of his classmates was related to renowned cinematographer Ueli Steiger.[1] Through this contact, Yves was able to meet Steiger and a number of other Swiss expatriates. Gathering with other Swiss proved to be the tonic that Yves needed. More importantly, it opened doors to opportunities to work in film.

Steiger separated his personal and professional life. Therefore, when Yves presented him with a script version of his book, Steiger was candid. "It sounds like an interesting story, but I don't know what to do with this," he said. He told Yves to show it to Swiss documentary filmmaker Reto Caduff.[2] Caduff read the script, but wasn't interested in the story. Nevertheless, Caduff saw potential in Yves and offered him a job as a scriptwriter. For the first time, Yves had a film industry position that paid well enough to cover his cost of living, at least for a few months.

## *Movin' In*: The Movie

### Preproduction

Meanwhile, Yves continued to promote his script, titled *Movin' In*. He approached several distributors with proposals to fund the film, but none showed an interest. Most would not even look at the script unless Yves was represented by an agent. Some told him to come back when the film was finished. When Yves told Caduff about the distributors' responses, he was not surprised. Los Angeles had too many potential filmmakers for a distributor to take a chance on someone with no experience, he explained.

Undaunted, Yves decided to approach the film as if it were a startup company. "I'm not the kind of person who gives up easily," he told Caduff. "When someone says 'no' to me, it just makes me want to work harder to make it happen."

With little money of his own, Yves decided to approach private individuals with investment offers. He phoned every relative, friend and acquaintance, but found few backers. The main challenge was convincing potential investors that, despite his lack of experience, he could produce a film and find a distributor for it.

In the beginning, I didn't get any help at all, because all I had was the script. I would give potential investors a summary of the story. I told them who I wanted to get involved in the film and how much money I was going to need.

The first few investors were the hardest to convince. However, once he overcame that hurdle, others became less reluctant. The more money he raised, the easier it was to attract additional investors. Some were convinced by promises that their money would be returned within one year of completing the film, a promise that any experienced filmmaker knew would be nearly impossible to keep. But Yves believed in himself and his ability to deliver on his promise.

By October 2006, Yves had raised $180,000, enough to cover the cost of planning and production. He would eventually need to raise another $70,000 to meet the film's total projected budget of $250,000 (see Exhibit 1). That figure was considered to be at the lower end of independent film production costs. Although many independent films cost less than $1 million to make, budgets of up to $10 million were not uncommon.[3]

| Exhibit 1 | *Movin' In:* % Budget Overview—U.S. Shoot (created prior to production start) |
|---|---|

| Acct. No. | Description | Total % |
|---|---|---|
| 1100 | Development | 0% |
| 1200 | Story & Other Rights (Note: owned by producer) | 0% |
| 1300 | Continuity & Treatment | 0% |
| 1400 | Producers Unit | 4% |
| 1500 | Directors Unit | 3% |
| 1600 | Talent | 15% |
| 1700 | Travel/Living | 1% |
| | **TOTAL ABOVE-THE-LINE** | **23%** |
| 2100 | Production Staff | 4% |
| 2200 | Art Direction | 1% |
| 2300 | Set Construction | 0% |
| 2400 | Set Decoration | 1% |
| 2500 | Property Department | 1% |
| 2600 | Camera Operations | 6% |
| 2700 | Electric Operations | 5% |
| 2800 | Grip Operations | 5% |
| 2900 | Production Sound | 2% |
| 3000 | Mechanical Effects | 0% |
| 3100 | Special Visual Effects | 0% |
| 3200 | Set Operations | 6% |
| 3300 | Wardrobe Department | 1% |
| 3400 | Makeup & Hair Department | 4% |
| 3500 | Location Department | 5% |
| 3600 | Transportation Department | 6% |
| 3700 | Videotape Department | 0% |
| 3800 | Studio Facilities | 0% |
| 3900 | Atmosphere | 0% |
| 4000 | Production Fiim & Lab | 0% |
| 4100 | Tests | 0% |
| | **TOTAL PRODUCTION** | **47%** |
| 5100 | Editing | 3% |
| 5200 | Post-Production Film/Lab | 0% |
| 5300 | Post-Production Sound | 5% |
| 5400 | Music | 2% |
| 5500 | Titles | 0% |
| 5600 | Opticals | 0% |
| 5700 | Post-Production Video | 1% |
| 5800 | Facilities | 1% |
| 6200 | Legal Costs | 1% |
| 6300 | Publicity | 5% |
| 6500 | Contigency | 9% |
| 6600 | Insurance | 2% |
| | **TOTAL POST & OTHER** | **29%** |
| | Total Above-The-Line | 23% |
| | Total Below-The-Line | 77% |
| | Total Above- and Below-The-Line | 100% |
| | **GRAND TOTAL** | **100%** |

The first step was to hire a director. However, few had the qualities Yves was looking for.

They had traits that threw you off. Either they were completely inexperienced, didn't make a professional impression or they had other things about them that bothered me. Also, I knew I had to find a person I could connect with because I was going to be spending a lot of very intensive time with that person.

Eventually, a friend introduced Yves to Griff Furst. Furst had directed two independent films and had played supporting roles in numerous television and film productions. Furst was also the son of Stephen Furst, an established actor and director with many successful film credits, including starring roles in *Animal House, St. Elsewhere*, and *Babylon 5*.

Because *Movin' In* was going to be a low-budget film, Yves was doubtful that Furst would agree to work with him. "I never thought I would have enough money to get someone like Griff," Yves admitted. By accepting the project, Furst seemed to offer the first professional validation that *Movin' In* was a worthwhile script.

The next step was to find actors and crew members to fill the many roles needed to make a film. Some positions were filled through online advertisements on Craigslist and through acting and production websites. Yves and Furst reviewed résumés and work samples and then invited selected candidates to interviews and casting sessions. One of the first positions to be filled was the sound engineer.

When I hired my sound engineer, he was a person that made a really good impression on me. All the reels he showed me were great and sounded really clear. His references from previous films were also very positive.

Another critical crew member was the unit production manager (UPM). Much like a chief financial officer (CFO), the UPM had critical financial planning responsibilities that included cost management, equipment procurement and negotiating salaries and benefits with the cast and crew. The UPM also monitored the performance of each unit and resolved any problems or complaints. The director, producer and UPM comprised the film's senior executive team. Yves was impressed with the UPM he hired for *Movin' In*. Not only did she have a strong résumé, her professional attitude instilled confidence that she would be a capable and trustworthy financial manager.

Finding lead actors proved a challenge. As the filming date approached, the male roles remained unfilled. Finally, Furst suggested that Yves play himself in the movie. "You are Swiss and you know the script better than anyone," he said.

By this time, I was looking for anyone with a foreign accent who could play the role of someone coming to the U.S. for the first time. In the process of casting people, I would read the part of the script the foreign actor was supposed to play, and Griff just liked the way I did it. After that, I went home and thought about it. Then I realized that if I did it, we wouldn't have to pay another actor.

Once Yves accepted the idea of playing the lead, they decided that Furst would play the other lead role of an American who befriends Yves' character and helps him on his journey.

Furst began to call on industry colleagues to fill other important roles. One was Christy Carlson Romano, who studied acting with Furst and had gone on to star in a number of Disney programs.[4] In 2004, Romano starred as Belle in the Broadway version of Disney's *Beauty and the Beast*. Other female cast members included Estelle Harris[5] and Yangzom Brauen, both of whom had appeared in well-known films and television programs. Harris, for example, was a regular guest on *Seinfeld*, and Swiss-Tibetan actor Yangzom Brauen[6] was renowned for her work in German-language films and American sci-fi movies.

The quality of the casting went far beyond anything Yves had hoped for with the funds available to him.

Christy agreed to work for a lot less than she would usually get. She did us a big favor because she has known Griff for such a long time. I don't think I could have ever paid Christy a fair amount for her work. The same goes for Estelle Harris. They usually earn in one day what I paid them for the entire time we were filming.

Having a cast of well-known actors would later prove valuable when Yves needed to raise additional funds for post-production.

## Filming

By November 2006, YvesCreations, LLC was ready to begin filming. With a crew of 70, the production had to run like clockwork. Makeup, wardrobe, and other support positions proved far more important than Yves had anticipated. When someone was late or failed to do a proper job, the entire production had to be stopped. With limited time and funds, Yves could not afford many delays. California labor regulations and union guidelines ensured generous compensation to anyone required to work more than eight hours a day. To ensure that all the requirements were met, Yves kept detailed compliance records (see Exhibits 2, 3 and 4).

The most difficult members of the cast turned out to be those with the least experience. For some, *Movin' In* was their first movie. "I thought they would be happy to be in a film," Yves explained.

| **Exhibit 2** | Script Supervisor's Daily Report, Day One |
| --- | --- |

---

**SCRIPT SUPERVISOR'S DAILY REPORT**

PRODUCTION: _Movin' In_    SHOOTING DAY: _1_    DATE: _11/30/2006_

|  | SCENES | PAGES | MINUTES | SETUPS |
| --- | --- | --- | --- | --- |
| TODAY: | 6 | 2 | 8:25 | 16 |
| TAKEN PREVIOUS: | 0 | 0 | 0 | 0 |
| TOTAL TO DATE: | 0 | 0 | 0 | 0 |
| TOTAL IN SCRIPT: | 110 | 104 4/8 | N/A | N/A |
| TO BE TAKEN: | 104 | 102 4/8 | N/A | N/A |

CREW CALL 5:00 AM
1ST SHOT AM 7:20 AM
MEAL 1 11:30 TO 12:15 PM
1ST SHOT PM 1:00 PM
MEAL 2 0 TO 0
WRAP TIME 5:00 PM

TIME ON SET 12 HRS.
TIME SHOOTING 9:10 HRS.

SCENE NUMBERS TAKEN TODAY: 1, 124, 128, 129, 123, 12

SETS / LOCATIONS PER SCENE: 1, 124, 128 (INT-HOLLYWOOD THEATER)
123, 129 (EXT-HOLLYWOOD THEATER)
12 (TRASHY BEDROOM)

CAST / CHARACTERS PER SCENE: 1 (Young Marc + kids, audience), 124 (Marc, Allie, audience)
128 (Marc, Allie, 2 actors + audience), 129 (Ann, Marc, Gabby)
123 (ext Theatre Sign), 12 (Tad + Obese Woman)

SCHEDULED SCENES NOT TAKEN: 2, 3, 7, 8

SPECIAL NOTES: 128 is mismarked as 124 A1

**Exhibit 3**  Series Report, Day One

## SERIES

PRODUCTION: _Movin' In_   SHOOTING DAY: _1_   DATE: _11/30/0_ .

|  | SCENES | PAGES | MINUTES | SETUPS |
|---|---|---|---|---|
| TODAY: | 6 | 2 | 8:25 | 16 |
| TAKEN PREVIOUS: | Ø | Ø | Ø | Ø |
| TOTAL TO DATE: | Ø | Ø | Ø | Ø |
| TOTAL IN SCRIPT: | 110 | 104 4/8 | N/A | N/A |
| TO BE TAKEN: | 104 | 102 4/8 | N/A | N/A |

CREW CALL 5:00 AM
1ST SHOT AM 7:20 AM
MEAL 1 11:30 TO 12:15 PM
1ST SHOT PM 1:00 PM
MEAL 2 Ø TO Ø
WRAP TIME 5:00 PM
TIME ON SET 12 Hrs.
TIME SHOOTING 9:10 Hrs.

| # | SLATE | PRINT | TIME | PAGES | TOTAL |
|---|---|---|---|---|---|
| 1 | 1 1 | | | (2/8) | |
| 2 | 1 2 | | | | |
| 3 | 1 3 | | | | |
| 4 | 1 4 | | | | |
| 5 | 1 5 | | | | |
| 6 | 1 6 | P | 0:30 | | 0:30 |
| 7 | 1 A 1 | | | | |
| 8 | 1 A 2 | | | | |
| 9 | 1 A 3 | | | | |
| 10 | 1 A 4 | P | 0:10 | | |
| 11 | 1 A 5 | P | 0:10 | | |
| 12 | 1 A 6 | P | 0:10 | | 0:40 |
| 13 | 1 B 1 | | | | |
| 14 | 1 B 2 | | | | |
| 15 | 1 B 3 | | | | |
| 16 | 1 B 4 | P | 0:15 | | |
| 17 | 1 B 5 | P | 0:15 | | |
| 18 | 1 B 6 | P | 0:15 | | 0:55 |
| 19 | 1 C 1 | | | | |
| 20 | 1 C 2 | P | 0:15 | | 1:10 |
| 21 | 1 D 1 | | | | |
| 22 | 1 D 2 | | | | |
| 23 | 1 D 3 | | | | |
| 24 | 1 D 4 | | | | |
| 25 | 1 D 5 | | | | |
| 26 | 1 D 6 | | | | |

| # | SLATE | PRINT | TIME | PAGES | TOTAL |
|---|---|---|---|---|---|
| 27 | 1 D 7 | P | 0:25 | | 1:35 |
| 28 | 1 E 1 | P | 0:15 | | |
| 29 | 1 E 2 | | | | |
| 30 | 1 E 3 | P | 0:15 | 2/8 | 1:50 |
| 31 | 1 D 1 | | | (4/8) | |
| 32 | 1 D 2 | P | | | |
| 33 | 1 D 3 | P | 1:15 | | |
| 34 | 1 D 4 | P(ING) | 1:20 | | |
| 35 | 1 D 5 | P | 1:15 | 4/8 | 2:05  4/8 |
| 36 | 1 B | | | (1/8) | |
| 37 | 1 B 2 | P | 0:30 | | |
| 38 | 1 B 3 | P | 0:40 | | |
| 39 | 1 B 4 | P | 1:05 | | 2:40 |
| 40 | 1 B A 1 | P | 0:25 | | |
| 41 | 1 B A 2 | P | 0:25 | 1/8 | 3:05  7/8 |
| 42 | 1 B 1 | | ? | | |
| 43 | 1 B 2 | P | 1:20 | | |
| 44 | 1 B 3 | P | 1:25 | | |
| 45 | 1 B 4 | P | 1:20 | | 4:25 |
| 46 | 1 B A 1 | | | | |
| 47 | 1 B A 2 | P | 0:35 | | |
| 48 | 1 B A 3 | P | 0:25 | | 4:55 |
| 49 | 1 B B 1 | | | | |
| 50 | 1 B B 2 | P | 0:25 | | |
| 51 | 1 B B 3 | | | | |
| 52 | 1 B B 4 | P | 0:35 | | CONT'D → |

Copy: Script Supervisor

But people would complain, "My hair is not right, my clothes aren't right, my makeup is not right." They acted like they were accomplished stars even though they have never been in a movie.

Once they are in a shot, it is very difficult to replace them, and they know it. Especially if they are in a shot with Estelle Harris or some other famous person, they know we are going to have a hard time bringing Estelle back to do it again.

Once filming started, replacing cast members was particularly difficult, as it often meant retaking shots. Therefore, on many occasions, Yves felt he had little choice but to accommodate their requests.

Yves' other problem was the sound engineer. After several days of shooting, he began to be

| **Exhibit 4** | Day One Production Records |
| --- | --- |

### MOVIN' IN

| Producer: Alex Yves | | Date: | Thursday, November 30th, 2006 | |
| --- | --- | --- | --- | --- |
| Director: Griff Furst | | Day | 1 of 18 Days | |
| Line Producer: | | Crew Call: | | Shooting Call: |
| Production Supervisor: | | **5:00 AM** | | **6:30 AM** |
| 1st AD | | | Hot Breakfast served 30 Minutes before call | |
| | | | Please see back of call sheet for individual call times | |

| RISE: | 6:40 AM | | Weather: | |
| --- | --- | --- | --- | --- |
| SET: | 4:44 PM | | Sunny | |
| | | | High 70, Low 45 | |
| Production Office: | | Winnetka, CA 91306 | Phone: | |

**Set Contact: 2nd AD**

NO FORCED CALL W/O PRIOR APPROVAL FROM PRODUCER & 1st AD. NO GUESTS W/O PRIOR APPROVAL

| SET DESCRIPTION | SCENES / DAY | CAST #'S | D/N | PAGES | LOCATION INFORMATION |
| --- | --- | --- | --- | --- | --- |
| INT SMALL SCHOOL THEATER | 1 | 63 | E | 2/8 | The Elephant Theater |
| *Young Marc plays Wilhelm Tell in school play* | | | | | |
| INT SMALL SCHOOL THEATER | 124 | 1,10 | D | 4/8 | |
| *Marc and Allie perform before a live audience* | | | | | |
| INT SMALL SCHOOL THEATER | 128 | 1,10 | D | 1/8 | |
| *The audience applauses, as the camera pans the audience* | | | | | |
| EXT SMALL HOLLYWOOD THEATER | 123 | | D | 0 | |
| *"Movin' In -"Final Show"* | | | | | |
| EXT SMALL HOLLYWOOD THEATER | 129 | 1,3,8,18 | D | 1 1/8 | |
| *"The cabby picks up Marc, "surprise" Ann's in the taxi.* | | | | | |

### COMPANY MOVE

| | | | | | Apartment Complex |
| --- | --- | --- | --- | --- | --- |
| INT MARC'S BEDROOM; DREAM; 18 | 2 | 1,43 | M | 1/8 | |
| *Mark's dream scene of Cary Miller* | | | | | Los Angeles, CA 90038 |
| INT MARC'S BEDROOM; DREAM; REALITY | 3 | 1 | M | 5/8 | |
| *Marc wakes up from his dream, alone.* | | | | | |
| INT MARC'S ROOM | 7 | 1 | D | 0 | |
| *Marc in front of his computer* | | | | | |
| INT MARC'S ROOM | 8 | 1 | D | 7/8 | |
| *Marc is on his computer: E-Mail, Myspace, Cheap flights* | | | | | |
| INT TRASHY BEDROOM | 12 | 2 | N | 2/8 | |
| *Tad's cell phone rings* | | | | | |
| | | | | | **NEAREST HOSPITAL** |
| | | | | | Hollywood Community Hospital |
| | | | | | |
| | | | | | Los Angeles, CA 90038 |
| | | TOTAL PAGES: | | 3 7/8 | |

### TALENT

| # | CAST PLAYERS | ROLE | WORK | RPT @ | RPT H/MU | SET CALL | REMARKS |
| --- | --- | --- | --- | --- | --- | --- | --- |
| 1 | Alez Yves | MARC | SW | 6:00 AM | | | |
| 2 | Griff Furst | TAD | SW | 3:30 PM | | | |
| 3 | Cristy Romano | ANN | SW | 8:30 AM | | | |
| 8 | Aalok Mehta | CABBY | SW | 8:30 AM | | | |
| 10 | Yangzom Brauen | ALLIE | SW | 6:00 AM | | | |
| 43 | Allie McCulloch | CARY | SWF | 10:00 AM | | | |
| 63 | Joshua Schlegel | YOUNG MARC | SWF | 5:30 AM | | | |

ND Bkfst:

| ATMOSPHERE | SPECIAL INSTRUCTIONS PER DEPARTMENT |
| --- | --- |
| **BACKGROUND:** RPT @ 5:30 AM | **PROPS:** Wooden Arrow & Apple (sc1), Glass of Milk& Vitamin Pills (sc3). |
| 25 Audience | Desk Top computer (sc7), Wilhelm Tell Costume (sc8) |
| Stage actors | Piece of Paper (sc8), Tad's cell phone(sc8,12), plane ticket(sc129), luggage(sc129) |
| Young actors on stage | |
| | |
| | **VISUAL EFFECT** |
| | **VEHICLES:** Cab (sc129), Ann's car(sc129) |
| | **SET DRESSING:** Desk(sc8), Sign "Movin' IN ~ Final Show"(sc123), red curtain (sc128) |
| | **SOUND:** |
| **SPECIAL INSTRUCTIONS** | **MAKE UP/HAIR:** Messed up hair(sc3) |
| **PRODUCTION/LOCATIONS NOTES:** | **WARDROBE:** Wilhelm Tell Costume (sc1,8), Jeans (sc12), Modesty Provisions (sc2,12) |
| | **GRIP/ELECTRIC:** |
| | **NOTES:** |

### ADVANCED SHOOTING SCHEDULE

| SET DESCRIPTION | SCENES / DAY | CAST #'S | D/N | PAGES | LOCATION INFORMATION |
| --- | --- | --- | --- | --- | --- |
| INT TAD'S CAR | 24 | 1,2 | E | 1/8 | |
| EXT TAD'S HOUSE | 25 | 1,2,15 | E | 7/8 | |
| EXT CAR DEALERSHIP | 39 | 1,59 | D | 1/8 | |
| EXT CLOTHING SHOP | 42 | 1 | D | 1/8 | |
| INT HOLDING CELL | 116 | 1,41 | D | 2/8 | |
| EXT PRISON | 118 | 1 | D | 3/8 | |
| EXT VAN NUYS BLVD | 119 | 1 | D | 0 | |
| EXT RESIDENTIAL STREET LOS ANGELES | 121 | 1 | D | 1/8 | |
| | | Total Pages: | | 2 | |

| Producer: Alex Yves | | 1st AD: |
| --- | --- | --- |

consistently late for shoots, argued with other crew members, and complained about trivial issues, such as the quality of the food. Yves was livid. "On a Hollywood production, you are usually lucky to get snacks and here you get full meals," he protested.

Confronting the engineer seemed to produce the opposite effect from what Yves had intended. Instead of improving his behavior, the sound engineer became even more problematic. After a while, Yves became convinced that the engineer was deliberately seeking to disrupt the production. Finally, on the ninth day of shooting, the sound engineer was dismissed, which caused a crisis because the senior members of the crew had to scramble to find a replacement on short notice. Although Los Angeles had its share of unemployed sound engineers, not everyone had the skills to work on a feature film. Yves had to rely on word of mouth and hope for the best.

When the new sound engineer arrived the next day, Yves was impressed. He arrived on time, followed directions and had an assistant who worked with him at no extra cost. After the first few shoots, Yves and Furst reviewed the recordings and seemed pleased with the results. "As long as we have decent sound we can work on it in post-production," they agreed.

After filming was finished, Yves returned to the set to meet with the UPM and arrange payment for any outstanding invoices and paychecks. The UPM, however, had disappeared, along with some cash, the checkbooks and most of the production documents. Calls to her home were not returned. One crew member accused the UPM of hiding a drug problem and told Yves that she may have stolen the money to support her addiction.

Yves became concerned. Without the documents, no one could be certain how much the production had cost, how much money was left and how much money was owed to third parties. To make matters worse, Yves was scheduled to return to Switzerland the next day for a complicated eye surgery.

While in Switzerland, Yves remained in contact with his co-producer. After a few days, Yves became desperate. "If we don't act quickly, we could lose the production," he said. "You are going to have to break into her apartment and get the documents yourself." Later, Yves was relieved to learn that his co-producer had successfully recovered the company files and most of the missing funds. However, some of the money was still missing, and the UPM was never heard from again.

## Post-Production

As soon as Yves returned from Switzerland, he devoted himself to editing and post-production. He began by reviewing the raw footage and immediately noticed significant background noises and humming in many of the takes. Yves had reviewed the footage during filming, but between the background noise of the set and the inferior headphones, the interference had not been noticeable. However, in a quiet studio with high-fidelity playback, every piece of unwanted sound became painfully obvious. And those unwanted sounds were everywhere.

> The actors had all gone on to other films and I couldn't bring them back to redo the film, even if I wanted to. I always knew that the sound engineer was important. After all, films are picture and sound. But never in my wildest dreams did I think it was as important as it turned out to be. Sound engineering, as I have painfully learned, is an art.

Although most films required some cleaning up or redubbing, more than 90 percent of the sound for *Movin' In* was unusable. Yves asked a sound studio to filter out the noise, but nothing worked. Whenever the sound was turned up to theater levels, the background noise became clearly noticeable. The studio finally told Yves that it was hopeless. His only option would be to dub the film.

By this time, Yves' financial situation had become precarious. Investor funds had run out, leaving Yves with no option but to use credit-card debt to finance the remaining post-production expenses. That created new problems when debt collectors began demanding payment of the loans. Yves was on the verge of a nervous breakdown when he called a close friend for advice.

"What am I going to do?" he asked. "I am out of money, and if I declare bankruptcy I am going to lose a lot of money for a lot of people."

Yves' friend tried to reassure him. "The first thing you should do is go back to the investors and tell them what is going on. Tell them, if you don't get more money you won't be able to finish the film."

"It's worth a try," Yves replied.

That night, Yves fell asleep and didn't wake up until two days later. When he awoke, he immediately sought the advice of a doctor. "You are suffering from exhaustion," the doctor explained. "Whatever you are doing, it has to stop." However, by this time he had reaffirmed his commitment to the film. "I am going to do whatever it takes to finish it, even if it kills me," he said.

Later, in conversations with investors, Yves tried his best to explain the situation. "When I had my original budget, I really thought 'This is it,'" he told one investor.

> We had a contingency budget, we had insurance, we had just about everything you can imagine. But then bricks kept getting thrown in the way. I really believe in this film and I think it will make money one way or another.

Some investors questioned Yves' ability to complete the project. "I had to do a lot of apologizing," he noted. In the end, the effort paid off because he was able to raise an additional $200,000, enough money to forestall bankruptcy and to continue post-production work. However, because most of the addition money he raised went to pay existing debts, he had little left over to pay actors to rerecord their lines. Instead, he pleaded with them to do the work voluntarily without any promise of remuneration. To his surprise, all but one agreed.

About 75 percent of the dubbing was completed when Yves learned that the U.S. studio was about to go out of business. He then turned to Nadin Hadorn, a manager for Hastings Audio Network, one of the largest sound studios in Europe. Yves knew Hadorn through a mutual friend. When she saw the film, she liked it enough that she agreed to do the work on credit. Yves arranged for the U.S. studio to forward the sound files to Switzerland for further dubbing and processing.

By the time the film was complete, post-production costs had reached $630,000, including $250,000 for sound editing. When added to original production costs, the total cost of the film came close to $1 million (see Exhibit 5), most of which was still owed to investors, supporters and creditors. "Even though it ended up costing much more to complete this film, I still believe that it can be done with the budget we had available initially. Unfortunately, too many things went wrong along the way and I made too many mistakes," he admitted.

> Still, I know people who had $2 million to start with and they ran into the exact same issues I did, and ended up spending $3 million. It's definitely nothing to brag about, but I had to learn that it happens and not kill myself over it.

| Exhibit 5 | Expense Summary |
| --- | --- |

| Preproduction and Production | |
| --- | --- |
| United States (18-day shoot) | $200,000 |
| Switzerland (2-day shoot) | 80,000 |
| Total Preproduction and Production | 280,000 |
| **Post Production** | |
| Sound | 250,000 |
| Legal expense | 80,000 |
| Compensation (cast and crew) | 200,000 |
| Rights to music, additional footage | 10,000 |
| DVD Production | 10,000 |
| Advertising and Administration | 80,000 |
| Total Post Production | 630,000 |
| TOTAL | $910,000.00 |

Note: Production costs include equipment, travel, and compensation.

## Distribution

With the finished product in hand, Yves went back to distributors.

> A few offered me a contract, which would basically disown me of my film. They wanted to take the film from me without giving me anything for it, not even a guarantee for distribution. For example, one of the biggest international pay-per-view networks wanted me to sign the rights away and, on top of that, make me dub the movie into 11 different languages at my own expense. That's how they get young filmmakers who don't have legal representation. The filmmakers get super excited about getting a contract with a major distributor, sign it and get screwed. Compared to that, a five percent profit commission would actually have been a great deal, but the pay-per-view network never even offered me five percent.

Ever since he began working on the film, Yves had become wary of distributors. He knew producers who had lost the rights to their movies. They warned Yves that if he signed over the rights, he might never be compensated. One told him that he had been promised a commission once his movie had become profitable. A year later, he went back to the distributor to request payment after seeing his film in a local Blockbuster video rental store. The distributor told him that the movie had been sold to another distribution company. The only way to recover his money would be to sue the distribution company. "What could he do?" Yves asked.

> Producers usually don't have any money. I have many friends who are attorneys, so I could fight a battle like that for a little while. But I would have to cash in a lot of favors to do it and that was not something I was prepared to do.

Yves expressed regret for not having understood the business of film distribution prior to starting the film.

Nobody will ever give you money for a product that you make, unless they were involved from the beginning, which usually only happens if you are already well connected. It is a really hard business to break into and you have to take risks.

In recent years, the independent film industry had become even harder to break into. "There's a glut of films," explained Mark Gill, chief executive officer (CEO) of The Film Department, an independent movie finance and production company. Gill noted that 5,000 movies were made in 2006. "Of those, 603 got released theatrically here. And there's not room in the market—as there used to be—for even 400 of those." Even so, Yves was not about to surrender the rights to the film.

> I would rather sell DVDs on my own and make a couple thousand dollars than get $10,000 from a distributor and lose the rights to the film. But I know that most producers eventually get so frustrated that they do sell out.

After failing to find any American distributors to agree to his terms, Yves decided to approach distributors in Switzerland. He was sure that a Swiss-American production with well-known American and Swiss actors would be well received in his home country. Therefore, it came as a shock when every distributor he approached rejected the film.

In fact, Yves was not alone. American independent filmmakers found it harder to win an overseas audience. "The international marketplace may be growing dramatically, but all of that growth is eaten up by studio movies," observed Mark Gill.

> Most American independent films don't sell at all overseas. I've never seen more depressed people in my life than I did in Cannes last month. The phrase "worst market ever" could be heard from every corner. A lot of film market veterans were musing about never coming back. It's that bad out there.[7]

Still, Yves was unfazed by the poor reception American filmmakers received in Europe. Not only was *Movin' In* partly filmed in Switzerland but it was produced, funded and edited by Swiss people. It also featured several well-known Swiss actors. "This is basically a Swiss film," he said.

At the end of his trip, he visited his old friend Sonja Mehnert and told her of his frustrations. "I don't understand what is going on," he said.

> I went to theatrical distribution and DVD distribution. I showed the film to all of them, even the ones I originally was not going to consider. I went to the big distributors first and then the smaller ones. Sometimes the smaller ones would not even give me an answer. Just having these well known actors on a movie poster would draw people in, which is why I don't understand why they are not accepting it.

He was reluctant to approach TV distributors. "One should never give away TV rights before at least DVD rights are settled," he explained, "because once TV rights are gone there is no going back to other distribution channels.

As his prospects continued to diminish, Yves began to wonder whether he should begin distributing the film himself. He already had a website where visitors could view trailers, television interviews, and film outtakes (see Exhibit 6). Perhaps he could use the site to promote and sell DVDs of the film.

The problem, according to Yves, was that once the DVD was made available for purchase, distributors might look less favorably toward the film, especially if the DVD had sold poorly. As long as some hope remained that a distribution deal could be reached, Yves did not want to take the risk of making the movie available to the public. "I've had really positive feedback," he told Mehnert. "The film has even begun to be accepted at film festivals."

One such festival was the FESTIVUS, an annual independent film festival held in Denver, Colorado. Billed as "the film fest for the rest of us," FESTIVUS included more than 50 films. "We're not

**Exhibit 6** *Movin' In* Promotional Website

Sundance and we never will be," noted a FESTIVUS announcement to filmmakers.

> Too many film festivals do all they can to attract D-list celebrities and fancy-pants foreign filmmakers that nobody has ever heard of. Then they brag about it. If you're trying to sign Kirstie Alley for your next picture then this isn't the festival for you. If you've sold plasma to help fund your next film, then you'll fit right in at Festivus. No red carpet, no celebrities, no fluff. Just real INDIE flicks for real INDIE fans.[8]

Although film producers viewed festivals as important venues for promoting independent films, getting accepted into one did not guarantee success. Even pictures shown at Sundance, the most popular film festival in the United States, had no more than a 5 percent chance at winning a distribution deal.[9]

Mehnert had always been a good listener, and Yves trusted her advice. As they discussed the challenges of finding a distributor, he hoped she might have some ideas about what he could do next. Yves was willing to consider all the distribution options that were open to him, provided he did not lose full control over his film.

Alex, have you considered a less traditional approach? Maybe looking into some of the recent distribution efforts in the music industry will trigger some ideas. Also, I know authors are beginning to use the Internet more to promote their books. I know of at least one who published her book on the Internet and it became so popular that a big publisher picked it up and it went on to be a *New York Times* bestseller. Could you do something like that with your film?

"What you are saying makes complete sense," he replied. "The problem is that the production is completely out of money."

I would have to raise an additional $5,000 to $10,000 to produce DVDs and create a marketing campaign that will help sell this film; otherwise nobody will even find the website. I know the amount seems small compared to what I have raised, but after having more than exhausted all my resources, it will be tough to get more money. I'm currently trying to make some money to get the independent distribution of *Movin' In* going.

## CASE QUESTIONS

1. The two main forms of distribution, direct distribution to movie theaters and employment of a distributor, present major challenges. Describe how each makes it difficult to obtain a limited or wide release of an independent motion picture.

2. Attempting to recapture production costs by selling directly to the DVD market was an option. Describe the advantages or disadvantages of such an approach.

3. In the case of *Movin' In*, the distributors held a great deal of channel power relative to film producers. Explain the sources of that power.

4. How have economic conditions affected the film industry, especially in terms of small, independent projects? Should those conditions have influenced Yves' decision to make a movie?

## —— Eureka Forbes Ltd: Growing the Water Purifier Business ——

By R. Chandrasekhar, under the supervision of
Professors Srinivas Sridharan and S. K. "Bal" Palekar

In mid-March 2007, Suresh Lal Goklaney, vice chairman and managing director of Eureka Forbes Limited (EFL), a company that pioneered the market for domestic water purifiers in India and long-time market leader, was looking forward to SMART—the most important annual event in the firm's business calendar. SMART was an acronym for the key drivers of the company's business (sales, marketing, advertising, research, and training) and was scheduled in the first week of April, the beginning of the financial year for most Indian companies. It would provide an opportunity for Goklaney to discuss the future of the business with the company's top 150 managers.

The strategic marketing issue dominating his thoughts was how utterly different the market

Version: (A) 2010–03–26

conditions were now, compared to when EFL began selling water purifiers in India in 1984. Back then, market experts and even company insiders cast grave doubts about whether the concept of home water purifiers could be sold in India at all; however, by the 1990s these doubts were dispelled as AquaGuard— EFL's water purifier brand—became a household name in the market and its sales even overtook the company's initial and main product category— EuroClean vacuum cleaners. Having created believers, all the attention subsequently focused on the growth of AquaGuard as a premium UV-based[1] water purification brand catering to urban India.

In the 2000s, the market took yet another turn: (1) On the economic side, the Indian economy grew considerably and rapidly. Accordingly, whereas originally the company was addressing a "latent need" for water purifiers, now there was actual demand. Also this demand moved beyond major cities to smaller towns, creating new consumers with different needs and buying habits than those to whom AquaGuard originally catered. With purification technology diversifying as well, it also became clear that the market had attracted significant new competitors. (2) On the ecological side, the world noticeably woke up to the alarm bells of increasing pollution and decreasing fresh water resources, with renewed beliefs that drinking pure water was a key component of

good health and disease prevention. With this awareness came the business realization that the market potential in India, which housed 16 percent of the world's population, was huge. A national survey of water purification habits in 2003 revealed that a mere 18 percent of urban Indian households were drinking water that could be considered pure. Goklaney described this market potential in the following:

> Although we pioneered the Indian market for water purifiers and own a lion's share of the market (63 percent in 2006), the fact is that we have only touched the tip of the proverbial iceberg. In 25 years, we have installed four and a half million residential water purifiers in a country of 207 million households. So, on the one hand, Eureka Forbes still faces fundamental start-up issues like how to reach its market. On the other hand, however, we are also newly facing intense competition as befits a mature market.

As he mulled over these issues, Goklaney knew, of course, that EFL had long been preparing for this new reality. Over two decades, it had painstakingly developed a business platform comprised of three technologies, two brands and three marketing channels (see Exhibit 1); however, the worry

---

**Exhibit 1**   Eureka Forbes Strategic Platform: Technologies, Brands, and Marketing Channels

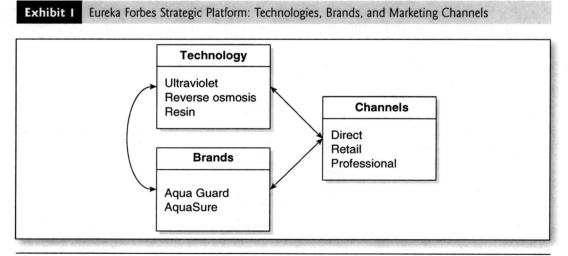

*Source:* Company records.

was that beneath the surface and at its core, the company was still largely dependent on one brand (AquaGuard), one marketing channel (direct sales channel) and one technology (UV purification).

Any new strategy would need to simultaneously meet three criteria: (1) yield good incremental growth given the huge market potential; (2) minimize internal cannibalization between brands, technologies, and channels; (3) effectively stave off the emerging competition. It was incumbent upon those who would assemble at SMART 2007 to discover the best balance between these three priorities, and to decide how to best execute an imminent change in strategic marketing direction.

## Company Background

Eureka Forbes was formed in 1982 as a 40:60 joint venture (JV) between Electrolux AB of Sweden and Forbes Forbes Campbell Ltd. of India. The name "Eureka" came from a product brand name which was in use by Electrolux. Both parent companies were very old and established. Electrolux was nearly a century old at the time, operated in many countries around the world, and was mainly in the business of home appliances (washing machines, refrigerators, and vacuum cleaners). Its initial success came through the tactic of selling vacuum cleaners to households door-to-door, but over time it also began selling through retailers. During the initial days of the Eureka Forbes JV, the new company came to rely heavily on Electrolux's direct selling unit for support, thus adopting its parent's direct selling methodology for the Indian market.

A part of the diversified Forbes and Company group, Forbes Forbes Campbell was one of very few companies surviving from the early days of the British colonization of India in the 18th century. In its long history, the group ran a diverse range of businesses: engineering, textiles, shipping, liquor, etc. In 1957, the famed Indian business group Tata acquired significant stake and also played a key role in the 1982 partnership with Electrolux to spawn Eureka Forbes.[2] The Indian parent contributed local knowledge and management, complementary to the product expertise and selling methods of Electrolux.

Goklaney, who joined the company as head of marketing and sales in its early days, described the beginning of EFL:

> Eureka Forbes began its journey in an unusual way (even by today's standards). It was an unknown company, and yet began selling an unknown product category (vacuum cleaners) under an unknown brand name (EuroClean) through an unknown system of marketing (direct sales). As if this were not enough, selling a vacuum cleaner was a daunting task in itself because the alternative—the broomstick—was the Indian tool of choice for cleaning and came at a mere five percent of the price of the vacuum cleaner!!"

At EFL's inception in 1982, a leading Indian market research agency, after observing this selling method and seeing so many odds stacked against it, recommended that the company's products not be marketed. "Boy, are we happy we did not heed their advice!" said Goklaney; in 2007, EFL was the number one direct-selling Asian business major, after having pioneered the vacuum cleaner and water purifier markets in a continent-sized country like India.

## Evolution of Business Divisions

### Direct Sales Division: Successful Growth

Goklaney continued:

> The mandate for the 20 young men who gathered on that fateful early morning in February 1982 to begin Eureka Forbes operations was to make cold calls. They would knock on the doors of perfect strangers and persuade them to give them a second appointment on a suitable evening, when all family members would be home, to witness a demonstration of their product; and then

on the appointed evening, they would carry the six kilogram vacuum cleaner to the prospective customer's home and in a most charming and interactive manner, demonstrate its applications and various accessories. They would have to progressively generate interest, overcome hesitations and objections and finally get an order at an appropriate price. The very next day they would have to personally deliver the product to the customer and collect payment in cash.

Although unique, the "direct sales" model quickly took roots in EFL after yielding profits in the very first year of operations; progressively, the company expanded its direct selling activities and sales force (fondly called "EuroChamps") across more cities. By 2007, it had 180 direct selling offices in over 100 Indian cities and had a direct sales force of 6,000 EuroChamps; EFL also had a base of six million customers, each starting with a mere cold call!

Buoyed by the initial success of its EuroClean vacuum cleaners and the unique direct selling model, EFL launched its AquaGuard line of home water purifiers in 1984. In time, the AquaGuard brand steadily gained reverence and reputation in urban India and became synonymous with water-related health and hygiene. From the company's viewpoint, AquaGuard's objective was simple: to educate consumers that "water that looks clear is not the same as being pure."

Both EuroClean and AquaGuard were pioneering appliances in India and went on to become bestsellers for EFL, earning healthy annual profits and invaluable brand reputation in a growing market. In the 1990s, EFL followed up these twin successes with a portfolio of about 20 models of electric home appliances, catering to widespread needs ranging from cleaning and water and air purification to the home security needs of urban, middle-class Indian consumers. Through product innovation, EFL achieved the positioning of a trusted provider of home appliances promoting health and safety, and through the "customized dialogue" and "magic of the demonstration" inherent to the direct sales process, the products sold through the direct sales division fetched premium prices and handsome margins for EFL.

## Retail Sales Division: Evolving Directions

Throughout the 1980s, EFL had no physical presence in the form of retail stores: its sales offices in the major cities of the country were limited to providing administrative and logistical support to the EuroChamps—the main selling engine. A. V. Suresh, senior vice president of the Direct Sales division, described the challenge of placing EFL products in retail stores:

> At the time of their introduction, these products were at a nascent stage of their category life cycle in India. Virtually no one knew of such products and what benefits they could offer. As such, retailers were unwilling to stock and display them as they were perceived as unlikely to bring customers into stores.

But over time, the situation inevitably changed. S. K. "Bal" Palekar, senior vice president of Marketing, explained why at one point it became worthwhile for the company to add new channels:

> A big challenge in direct selling is the ratio of conversion of product demonstrations into actual sales: only one of every four prospective customers buys the product even after seeing a great demonstration and having all their objections addressed satisfactorily. The other three are perhaps convinced of its utility but prefer to postpone the purchase until they are certain. When they feel ready to buy at some later point however, our salespeople are naturally no longer in their homes to close the deal! These potential customers would go to a nearby appliance retailer and inquire about our product. Hence for every sale achieved through direct selling, we generate three inquiries in retail stores, creating the perfect opportunity for our competitors to come in via the retail route and enjoy the

fruits of *our* labor! Well, so we preempted this by launching our own retail division.

In addition to the loss of potential sales from customers already approached by the EuroChamps, top management also became concerned that direct selling in a small set of exclusive cities may not be enough to maintain market leadership in the long-run. In a huge country like India, it would be prohibitively expensive and practically impossible to expand and manage a sales force in an increasing number of geographically dispersed locations; also, with a broader geographical base, the sales force would have to overcome the challenges of dwindling product awareness, purchase intentions, and willingness to pay.

These key triggers motivated EFL top management to develop a separate business division focused on the retail-marketing channel (in 1988). The direct sales division, however, was still considered the star performer, and top management was keen on avoiding potential conflicts between the direct and retail channels; as a result, the company distinguished the products sold in each channel. The newly-established retail channel got its own separate brands—Tornado (a vacuum cleaner) and AquaFlo (a water purifier)—and its models tended to be more basic, required less explanation and were typically priced 20 to 30 percent lower than their feature-rich, demonstrable, and premium-priced direct channel counterparts .

Although the direct sales approach continued to dominate the company's revenues, the retail channel showed increasing promise; over the years, the consequent brand management attention resulted in prominent "umbrella" brands Forbes and AquaSure being sold exclusively through retail. By 2007, the retail channel showed significant growth (see Exhibit 3), prompting Aslam Karmali, senior vice president of the Retail division, to become far more ambitious about the division's future prospects. He expanded the accessibility of EFL to a network of nearly 7,000 retail outlets in 500 Indian cities by instituting a dedicated sales force of over 120 people.

| **Exhibit 2** | Eureka Forbes—Financials |

| Year Ending March 31 (in INR million) | 2007 | 2006 | 2005 | 2004 |
|---|---|---|---|---|
| Sales of products | 5,909 | 5,155 | 4,518 | 4,142 |
| Service income | 1,323 | 990 | 815 | 616 |
| **Total revenue** | **7,232** | **6,145** | **5,333** | **4,758** |
| Cost of sales | 3,787 | 3,279 | 2,903 | 2,657 |
| Gross margin | 3,445 | 2,866 | 2,430 | 2,101 |
| Expenses | 3,129 | 2,631 | 2,215 | 1,944 |
| Operating profit | 316 | 235 | 215 | 157 |
| Depreciation | 90 | 84 | 60 | 56 |
| Interest | 4 | 2 | 3 | 4 |
| Other income | 167 | 190 | 169 | 164 |
| **Profit before tax** | **389** | **339** | **321** | **261** |

*Source:* Company records.

| Exhibit 3 | Eureka Forbes Revenues (by marketing channel) | | | |
|---|---|---|---|---|
| **(in INR million)** | **2003–04** | **2004–05** | **2005–06** | **2006–07** |
| **Direct Sales Division** | | | | |
| – Sales | 3,725 | 4,057 | 4,548 | 4,994 |
| – Service | 560 | 742 | 888 | 1,139 |
| **Consumer Division (Retail Channel)** | | | | |
| – Sales | 273 | 292 | 400 | 623 |
| – Service | 37 | 48 | 71 | 137 |
| **Industrial Division** | | | | |
| – Sales | 144 | 169 | 208 | 292 |
| – Service | 19 | 25 | 31 | 47 |

*Source:* Company records.

## Professional Division: New Demand

As urban Indians began using vacuum cleaners and water purifiers at home in the 1980s, they also began looking for the same benefits in the workplace. Human resources departments of various corporations began inquiring if EFL made industrial-grade and high-output vacuum cleaners and water purifiers for use in their factories and offices. Marzin Shroff, senior vice president of Business Development and Professional Business, explained:

> In the late 1980s the company initially responded in piecemeal fashion by developing a few high-output models, but pretty soon we realized it was a separate business with great potential. By the early 1990s we had become exclusive distributors of Nilfisk, a Danish company and the world's largest maker of a complete range of industrial cleaning equipment—vacuum cleaners, high pressure jet cleaners, scrubbers, etc. We also

ourselves developed a range of water purifiers for professional applications, including purifiers that could be connected to existing water coolers and cooler-purifier combos. We appointed separate distributors to reach the professional segment of the market and also set up a separate sales force to cater to these distributors and reach customers directly.

Thus, top management at EFL also set up a Professional Division around the same time frame in the late 1980s, which later paved the way for the evolution described by Shroff. By 2007, the professional business had grown to a sales force of 100 salespersons servicing over 9,000 workplaces—a sizable business by any yardstick. In this segment, the company treated its two major product categories a little differently, taking on a partnering and co-branding role in vacuum cleaners (made by Nilfisk and sold and serviced by EFL), while developing in-house competence and branding in water purifiers (branded Pureguard).

# Indian Water Purifier Market

## Infrastructure, Water Impurities, and the Purification Market Opportunity

Being a developing country and the second-most populous in the world, India had all the major pollution problems that characterize quickly-industrializing countries: this presented major water purification challenges as well as opportunities. Although a major part of drinking water in the country was treated at central treatment plants before being pumped into homes, the miles of travel and the number of storage points enroute created many opportunities for contamination and hence potentially unsafe to drink. Aging water pipes cracked. Sometimes water pipes were laid in the same trench as sewage pipes and this created potential contamination risks if pipes cracked or burst. Without continuous power supply, which was a real risk in India because of frequent power outages, pipes could crack from lack of uniform water pressure. Also the water eventually stored in water tanks at the community

and building levels, if not inspected, cleaned and serviced often, created further potential contamination points. Therefore, in spite of having been properly treated, the water was often no longer clean when it flowed out of taps at homes.

There are essentially three kinds of impurities in water: physical, chemical, and bacterial, each presenting a different challenge in terms of consequences for human health as well as technology and feasibility of removal (see Exhibit 4). Eighty percent of the diseases in the country were caused by unsafe drinking water: such diseases included gastroenteritis, typhoid fever, cholera, and diarrhea, among others.

Thus, when EFL first introduced AquaGuard in the 1980s, making water relatively safer to drink, it really struck a chord in the market. It gave urban Indian consumers a new sense of empowerment, as they perceived an enhanced ability to control the quality of their water and care for the health of their families. By March 2007, the water purification market in India was worth INR8 billion, corresponding to a volume of 1.6 million units: a far cry from the infancy days of this market in the mid-1980s.

| Exhibit 4 | Water Impurities, Health Effects, and Method/Technology of Removal |

| Type of Impurity | Source of Impurity | Effect of Impurity on Human Health | Method/Technology of Removal |
|---|---|---|---|
| **PHYSICAL** | Floating sediments (dust, sand, mud) originating from silt in river bottoms, streams and pipes. "Surface water" from rivers, lakes, streams and open wells generally will have acquired more of these impurities en route compared to "ground water" from bore wells. | Sediments carry bacteria and chemicals but are otherwise not very harmful to the human body. | As physical impurities generally discolor water and are visually unappealing, Indians have long adopted the practice of clarifying the water—using alum, sand filtration, cloth filtration (oldest and simplest method), settling tanks, etc. In the last few decades, candle filters were used extensively (basically two stacked storage drums—the upper drum, upon filling, passes raw water through a candle filter; water thus filtered then drips into the lower drum by gravity). There are also |

*(Continued)*

**Exhibit 4** (Continued)

| Type of Impurity | Source of Impurity | Effect of Impurity on Human Health | Method/Technology of Removal |
|---|---|---|---|
| | | | qualities of tap attachments available in the market. The technology in such devices is defined by the size of pore through which water is filtered—the finer the pore, the better the filtration. As water passes through, impurities get caught in the filtration medium and eventually choke it: this creates the need for regular maintenance. In India a common tendency is to seek service from the device manufacturer or marketer. |
| CHEMICAL | Innumerable chemicals can come into contact with municipal water supply: inorganic minerals from soil (e.g., salts of calcium), disinfectant chemicals added by municipalities (e.g., chlorine), industrial effluents and wastes, organic biological matter (e.g., leaves, animal wastes), residues of human medications, etc. Some chemicals react with lead pipes and iron tanks that transport or store water. Generally speaking, 'surface water' from rivers, lakes, streams and open wells is more vulnerable to organic impurities, and 'ground water' from water tables (drawn up through bore wells) contains more inorganic impurities. | Organic impurities of decomposing biological matter create offensive smells. Inorganic salts in excess of 500 mg/L create a brackish taste. Hard water leaves white residues in utensils, which when ingested could be harmful. Heavy metals (nickel, cadmium, mercury) slowly seep into organs (brain, kidneys and liver), causing negative long-term effects. | Chemicals called resins made from halogens (iodine, chlorine, bromine) can convert hard water (excess calcium) into soft water. Reverse osmosis membranes can eliminate brackish taste from inorganic salt-heavy water. Special purpose cartridges (also using resins) can remove excess metals (iron, arsenic). In reverse osmosis, pore sizes are minute (measured in microns) and also halt bacteria, an added benefit. Overall, despite proliferation of purifying technologies, hundreds of contaminants remain, for which products and markets (and even perceived consumer needs) do not yet exist. Generally speaking, the science of removal of chemicals from water lags behind the creation of new chemicals and the diagnosis of more harmful chemicals in the human body. |

| Type of Impurity | Source of Impurity | Effect of Impurity on Human Health | Method/Technology of Removal |
|---|---|---|---|
| **BACTERIAL** | Bacteria can rapidly proliferate in water, as there is oxygen, warmth and organic matter like plant and animal wastes. Again, generally "surface water" is more likely to carry bacterial impurities. | Bacteria incubate in human bodies with low resistance levels and cause diseases such as cholera, typhoid fever, diarrhea and hepatitis. Most such diseases need medical intervention and can sometimes become fatal if left untreated. | The cultural standard in India for bacterial elimination from drinking water is boiling. Newer technologies include irradiation of water with ultraviolet rays and passing water through very fine membranes. These technologies were slowly gaining acceptance in urban India: the boiling process is time-consuming and thus a hindrance in the new, time-starved economy. The most recent method for eliminating bacteria is by use of resins, which have disinfecting properties. The technology involves creating a device through which resin is released in the flow of raw water in a controlled fashion.—The chemicals dwell in the water for a sufficiently long period, which kills bacteria, and are subsequently drawn back out of the water using polishers, thereby releasing disinfected water ready for consumption. |

## Technology

Overall, traditional purification strategies predominated—boiling, settling, straining, filtration using tap attachments or otherwise, and removal of choking. However, newer technologies were slowly gaining acceptance in urban India, as the time-consuming and intensive traditional processes became increasingly difficult for urban professionals in the new, time-starved economy. People increasingly purchased equipment to aid in purification, which used technology such as alums, candle filters, ceramic candles, drum filters, reverse osmosis membranes, softener resins, special resins, UV rays, and antibacterial membranes.

In fact, technology quickly became a key differentiator in the Indian water purification market. Generally speaking, the choice of technology from a customer viewpoint would depend upon the type of impurity that needed to be removed from the water. Although numerous technologies existed, the water purification market in 2007 was dominated by three primary product categories: ultraviolet (UV), reverse osmosis (RO), and resin (see Exhibit 5 for financial details on these three product markets).

| **Exhibit 5** | Water Purifier Market by Technology Category |
| --- | --- |

| UV Market | 2001–02 | 2002–03 | 2003–04 | 2004–05 | 2005–06 | 2006–07 |
| --- | --- | --- | --- | --- | --- | --- |
| Eureka Forbes (INR Mn) | 1,337 | 1,660 | 1,767 | 1,891 | 1,997 | 2,190 |
| Eureka Forbes units (in '000s) | 297 | 357 | 372 | 394 | 416 | 447 |
| Major Competitor 1 (INR Mn) | 54 | 63 | 67 | 72 | 79 | 98 |
| Major Competitor 1 units (in '000s) | 12 | 13.5 | 14 | 15 | 16.5 | 20 |
| Major Competitor 2 (INR Mn) | 68 | 74 | 78 | 86 | 91 | 88 |
| Major Competitor 2 units (in '000s) | 15 | 16 | 16.5 | 18 | 19 | 18 |
| Major Competitor 3 (INR Mn) | 63 | 70 | 74 | 77 | 79 | 93 |
| Major Competitor 3 units (in '000s) | 14 | 15 | 15.5 | 16 | 16.5 | 19 |
| All others (INR Mn) | 482 | 516 | 537 | 552 | 622 | 622 |
| All others units (in '000s) | 107 | 111 | 113 | 115 | 129.5 | 127 |
| Total UV market (INR Mn) | 2,003 | 2,383 | 2,522 | 2,678 | 2,868 | 3,092 |
| Total UV market in units (in '000s) | 445 | 513 | 531 | 558 | 598 | 631 |
| **RO Market** | | | | | | |
| Eureka Forbes (INR Mn) | 11 | 35 | 176 | 252 | 450 | 925 |
| Eureka Forbes units (in '000s) | 1 | 3 | 15 | 21 | 36 | 74 |
| Major Competitor 1 (INR Mn) | – | – | 294 | 360 | 500 | 875 |
| Major Competitor 1 units (in '000s) | | | 25 | 30 | 40 | 70 |
| Major Competitor 2 (INR Mn) | – | – | 59 | 120 | 250 | 375 |
| Major Competitor 2 units (in '000s) | | | 5 | 10 | 20 | 30 |
| All others (INR Mn) | | | | | | |
| All others units (in '000s) | | | | 60 | 60 | 70 |
| Total RO market in (INR Mn) | 11 | 35 | 529 | >732 | >1,200 | >2,135 |
| Total RO market in units (in '000s) | 1 | 3 | 45 | 121 | 156 | 244 |
| **Resin Market** | | | | | | |
| Eureka Forbes (INR Mn) | | | | 10 | 130 | 176 |
| Major Competitor 1 (INR Mn) | | | | 65 | 130 | 390 |
| Major Competitor 1 units (in '000s) | | | | 50 | 100 | 300 |
| Major Competitor 2 (INR Mn) | | | | 73.5 | 84 | 94.5 |
| Major Competitor 2 units (in '000s) | | | | 210 | 240 | 270 |
| Major Competitor 3 (INR Mn) | | | | 57.6 | 60.8 | 64 |
| Major Competitor 3 units (in '000s) | | | | 36 | 38 | 40 |
| Total Resin market (INR Mn) | | | | 206.1 | 404.8 | 724 |
| Total Resin market in units (in '000s) | | | | 304 | 478 | 745 |

*Source:* Company records.

## Ultraviolet

UV was the most common technology used in Indian water purifier brands and had the longest market history, starting from the launch of Aqua-Guard in 1984. A UV purifier irradiated water using UV rays, eliminating bacterial micro-organisms. It was convenient to use and had instantaneous impact; however, it also posed some practical challenges. Consumers needed to (a) purchase special equipment such as an AquaGuard, (b) get it installed by a plumber as a part of the water line, and (c) seek out after-sales service when exhausted consumables like candles and UV lamps needed replacements. UV equipment also needed reliable running water and power. In a developing country like India, these were luxuries accessible only to upper-middle class segments of society. There were other cultural issues concerning UV use: for example, some vegetarian communities complained that UV rays passing through the water rendered the bacteria inert, but did not actually "remove their bodies." A newer issue was that the quantity of total dissolved salts (TDS) remained, because while UV could remove bacteria, it did not make any chemical change to the composition of water. Excess TDS made the water taste brackish. Thus in recent years, newer technologies began to appear and dent the market dominance of UV systems. UV products were priced in the INR5,800 to INR9,190 range; a mature technology, UV was growing at five to six percent per year.

## Reverse Osmosis

Reverse Osmosis (RO) was a newer technology that gained momentum in the early 2000s. It used the medium of a semi-permeable membrane to remove chemical impurities (especially dissolved salts) from water. Although very effective because of extremely fine pores, a high water pressure was required in the RO process, thus necessitating electricity, which put the pricing out of reach of the mass market; additionally, the process rejected a lot of water and was quite inefficient—a significant impediment in cities where water was scarce. There was a high cost of after-sales maintenance

because the manufacturer or retailer had to periodically remove salt deposits and regenerate the membrane; if beyond repair, the membrane had to be replaced. Being manufactured by only a small set of companies in the world, this was an expensive proposition. As a result, RO technology in India was deployed largely in commercial applications where demand for industrial-use pure water was greatest, as was ability to pay (e.g., micro-electronic, food and beverage, power and pharmaceutical sectors). Nevertheless, despite being a more expensive technology, retailing at prices of INR15,000 and above, RO grew rapidly in the 2000s.

S K Bal Palekar, senior vice president of Marketing, commented on the uses of UV and RO systems:

> Drinking water supplies have to originate from either surface water or ground water. Most cities in India have evolved around a source of surface water nearby—a lake or a river—fed by rains or glacial ice. This water gets contaminated with mud and decay. Affected also by agricultural and industrial activity around it, the water carries sediments which reduce clarity, organic matter which makes it odorous and viruses which cause diseases. However, despite such high amounts of suspended impurities, surface water is normally tasteless. When taste is not a problem, UV remains a very effective technology.
>
> Ground water, on the other hand, is stored deep within the earth through the process of seepage over centuries. In passing through several strata such as rock and soil, it accumulates a lot of minerals, giving rise to high dissolved salts, though not affected by suspended impurities as in the case of surface water. Drawn up by individual households or communities digging borewells with a view to either bypass or supplement municipality-provided water, this ground water tastes brackish and is not easy to drink. UV does nothing

to enhance taste, whereas RO does, and hence RO is more useful in the case of ground water.

## Resin

Resin, the newest of the three technologies, was targeted at removing microbial contaminants as well as some types of chemicals (e.g., iron). The technology amounted to releasing certain types of chemicals called resins into water in a controlled fashion, letting them dwell in the water for a period of time—disinfecting the water—and then drawing them out again, making the water suitable for consumption. Resin water purifiers were relatively inexpensive, with prices starting at INR1,800; however, water-softening resins did involve extensive replacement requirements (every few weeks or months) and thus involved higher total costs of ownership. As resin-based devices did not require electricity, it was attractive to a much broader range of customer segments with lower incomes and housing standards; as a result, resin was the fastest growing water purification technology in the Indian market.

## Marketing Water Purifiers at Eureka Forbes

### Brands

#### AquaGuard

Being the flagship brand of EFL, AquaGuard was historically targeted at the premium segment of the market (see Exhibit 6), consisting of approximately 18 million households in the major cities of India. The typical AquaGuard customer belonged to a relatively affluent urban household, with above-average education and disposable income. This was a customer who felt the need to proactively do something to make her/his household drinking water safer, as well as someone who possessed the purchasing power to acquire the best product in the market. This target customer was a perfect fit with the direct sales process: AquaGuard customers liked the personal attention afforded in the direct sales approach, and it created a powerful impression.

| Exhibit 6 | Eureka Forbes—Brand Positioning by Demographics |
|---|---|

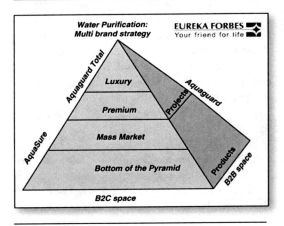

*Source:* Company records.

Based primarily on UV technology, the AquaGuard product line had prices ranging between INR5,800 and INR14,500 (see Exhibit 7).

### AquaSure

In the 2000s, after two decades of dominance by the AquaGuard brand, EFL management saw enough market signals to convince them that it was time to develop a new high-quality brand. For one thing, AquaGuard continued to be most conducive to the direct sales mode of selling, leaving open the need for a stellar brand for retail channels. Although the original Aquaflo and subsequent Forbes brands—both created specifically for retail sales—had done a reasonable job over the years, they did not have the mass market potential.

In 2004, after careful market research, EFL launched a new brand of water purifier, AquaSure. Simultaneously, the company deployed a careful brand-delineating exercise, which involved investing in separate marketing communication as well as channel resources for the two brands. Generally speaking, AquaSure was targeted at a more mass-market customer segment (lower purchasing power and less or unreliable access to electricity and running water). Accordingly, for this price-sensitive

| Exhibit 7 | Eureka Forbes Product Line Sample (by brand) |
|---|---|

| Product | Technology | Key Features/Differentiators | | Price (INR) |
|---|---|---|---|---|
| **AquaGuard UV** | | | | |
| AquaGuard Booster | UV | Inbuilt pressure pump and voltage stabilizer ensure pure water in absence of running water and under varying voltage. | | 7,940 |
| AquaGuard Hi-Flo | UV | Higher flow rate; Ideal for large families and small businesses. | | 9,190 |
| **AquaGuard RO** | | | | |
| AquaGuard Total RO | RO | Superior service network. | | 14,500 |
| **AquaSure UV** | | | | |
| Aquaflow | UV | 3-stage UV purifier with basic features. | | 5,573.2 |

*(Continued)*

**Exhibit 7** (Continued)

| Product | Technology | Key Features/ Differentiators | Price (INR) |
|---------|-----------|------------------------------|-------------|
| Crystal Water Purification System | UV | 3-stage UV purifier with advanced features; E. | 7,254.2 |
| **AquaSure RO** | | | |
| Aquacare RO Water Purification System | RO | Online RO water purifier | 9,203.3 |
| Spring Fresh (Water filter and purifier) | RO | Storage, RO based 5 stage purifier with advanced features. | 14,000 |
| **AquaSure Resin** | | | |
| AquaSure Storage Water Purifier – 18 lt jar | Resin | Gravity based 18 lt resin purifier, no electricity, no boiling. | 1,600 |

*Source:* Company records.

and affordability-driven market, AquaSure was priced at INR1,600.

The key distinguishing facet of the new brand was that it did not require electricity or running water, which meant greater convenience and access to a larger mass-consumer segment. The absence of electrical parts also meant lower costs of production. Despite the "low-tech" feel, however, Aqua-Sure was technically sound: its resin products had a two-stage purification system housed in a single cartridge, and removed physical and chemical impurities in turn (as well as odor). The purification cartridge was easy to install (requiring no changes in plumbing) and easy to replace.

### AquaGuard Total

By 2006, the premium positioning of the Aqua-Guard brand had come under considerable strain. AquaGuard was the pioneer when it was established in 1986, but in two decades competitors had grown considerably and also used the same bacteria-killing UV technology for which AquaGuard became famous; hence, there was a need for some new point of differentiation. As before, the technological leadership of EFL offered a solution. In recent years, water in India was being polluted with vastly different chemical pollutants than was the case in the 1980s, and EFL had adapted by making significant improvements in its carbon block technology. The growth of AquaSure, since its launch in 2004, also necessitated that AquaGuard's positioning should be made much sharper. Based on these threat/opportunity situations and aided by additional evidence from market research of evolving consumer needs and market conditions, the company decided to relaunch AquaGuard as Aqua-Guard Total in 2006. The retention of AquaGuard in the brand name signalled to consumers that the brand was still the same trusted name of the past two decades, while the addition of "Total" to the brand name communicated an impression that something fundamental had changed and improved in the scope of the brand—allowing the company to subsequently explain this change in a blitz of marketing communications.

## Technology

Over the years, the technological backbone of EFL water purifiers also needed continuous revisiting. As it happened, the market cache of AquaGuard was to last quite long, but EFL management surmised early that technological conditions would eventually change. AquaGuard was based entirely on UV technology, whereas the water conditions in India were continuously evolving. Palekar addressed these changing conditions:

> EFL built its business on the basis of UV technology partly because that was the technology of the time when we started, and also because most of the urban population in India got their drinking supply from municipalities, sourced from surface water, which did not have a taste problem. Even as recently as five years ago, hardly eight percent of the urban areas of the country had a taste problem. But that can no longer be said. Recently, with rapid development, the demarcation between towns with surface water and those with brackish water is blurring. Often now, different parts in the same city need equipment for surface water versus ground water.

In response, EFL added the newer technologies of RO and resin in its product portfolio. This was in part precipitated by competitive pressures, both real and anticipated. These newer technologies, while opening up new market opportunities for EFL, also raised fresh challenges in branding, marketing channels, and marketing communications.

## Marketing Channels

Direct selling, traditionally the dominant go-to-market route for the company, was very well-suited for the focused, premium targeting of the Aqua-Guard brand platform. Its products sold at premium prices, typically 20 to 50 percent higher than the retail channel models; however, the cost of making or procuring products sold in this channel was also typically 20 to 40 percent higher than those sold in the retail channel. This was because very few vendors in the world were specialized and capable of making such high-quality products. It had always been the dominant earner for EFL, and even amid newer changes, continued to be its main breadwinner. To maintain the high margins, the direct sales channel needed to hire and retain hordes of talented salespeople capable of creating unique value for consumers through the "customized dialogue" and "magic of demonstration" mentioned earlier (see Exhibit 8).

The retail channel, formally called Consumer Division within the company, had an interesting role to play. Originally conceived as a "pre-emptive" move designed merely to capture the spillover sales potential from the direct channel rather than surrender such sales to competition, over time it began to gain the admiration of management: this was evident from the resources that were dedicated to exclusively retail brands, especially AquaSure. The market had changed as well: the water purifier product category was no longer the unknown entity it was in the 1980s. The children of the early customers had grown up in homes with water purifiers. This new generation knew these products well, and distinctly preferred to shop at retail sources. In recent years, the retail channel was seeing tremendous growth in revenues for EFL. Given the pattern of retail growth in India, the channel split its sales efforts across four different focus areas: retail existing (the traditional appliance dealer segment with long-standing presence and sizable customer base); retail new (newer, organized retailers and unique institutions with captive audiences such as military stores); rural (smaller retailers in towns and villages primarily engaged in agricultural output); franchise (a franchisee network developed to push low-end products through a mass-market approach).

The franchisee channel was the newest focus area, started only in 2004. By 2007, however, the network comprised 225 franchisees. Some of these franchisees were former employees of EFL, making it easier to recruit them for sales and service responsibilities as they already had product knowledge. Despite this success, the company's overall experience with franchisees had been mixed: many lacked good understanding of the water business and often seemed to pursue short-term, self-oriented goals at the expense of the long-term needs of the company.

## Marketing Communications

The demands of marketing communications for multiple brands represented a significant change in organizational culture for EFL. The principal mode

| Exhibit 8 | Channel Penetration |
| --- | --- |

|  | 2001–02 | 2002–03 | 2003–04 | 2004–05 | 2005–06 | 2006–07 |
| --- | --- | --- | --- | --- | --- | --- |
| Direct Channel: # of Customer Response Centers | 112 | 148 | 165 | 198 | 265 | 262 |
| Direct Channel: # of salespeople | 1,760 | 2,273 | 2,655 | 3,051 | 3,623 | 4,154 |
| Retail Channel: # of cities |  |  |  | 325 | 350 | 500 |
| Retail Channel: # of retailers |  |  |  | 4,150 | 5,500 | 6,900 |
| New Channel: # of salespeople |  |  |  | 40 | 40 | 81 |

*Source:* Company records.

of communication in direct selling was the in-depth and interactive contact between the customer and the EuroChamp, involving demonstration and question-answer sessions. Any advertising in direct sales was merely a supporting tactic. Palekar explained:

> A major principle of our communication for direct sales is not to focus overly on the product and its features but to urge the customer to phone our national call center number and invite a EuroChamp to visit.

Further, the AquaGuard name was already synonymous with pure water in urban Indian consumer minds. Marketing the newer AquaGuard Total as something that both retained the Aqua-Guard essence and was even more upmarket would thus be a significant challenge. The company entered into close collaboration with advertising agencies and released a slew of marketing communications to drive home this new, refined positioning.

EFL had to separately promote its AquaSure brand, which since its launch in 2004 had emerged a formidable brand entity of its own (aided by the growth of the retail channel). It presented a very different marketing communications challenge, as its target market was different from that of Aqua-Guard. While AquaGuard had always targeted urban middle-class households (about 18 million households), AquaSure—with average unit prices of about a quarter of AquaGuard—had a much wider mass target market (amounting to at least 30 million urban Indian households). Thus, AquaSure needed a distinctly "broadcasting" approach—something with mass appeal. Conveniently, there was a television soap opera that happened to be extremely popular in India at the time of the company's marketing communications conundrum. In this show called *Kyunki saas bhi kabhi bahu thi* (translated to "because the mother-in-law was at one time a daughter-in-law herself"), the lead actress Smriti Irani played the role of a wise and trusted family advisor to great viewer acclaim. Seeing a golden opportunity, EFL signed her on as its

brand ambassador, with a view to deeply connect with the audience of her show, which had the same demographics as AquaSure's target audience. Palekar remarked: "The advertising agency did a good job in the ad campaign by using a similar style and settings as the TV show to create a strong connect with the consumer."

In addition to the connection between television show and ad campaign, EFL found another marketing communications hook. Firstly, through long-term market observation, it came to the conclusion that the benchmark in Indian consumer minds for eliminating bacteria from water or milk was the humble, low-tech process of boiling. Palekar commented on this process:

> Simply put, boiling is the gold standard of water purification in India. Even after 30 years of marketing electrically powered water purifiers, the penetration of this category is only six to eight percent of urban households, whereas the traditional method of boiling still rules the roost at 12 percent."

Secondly, given the explosive growth of retail as a marketing channel, management had recently become convinced that UV technology, which was exclusively associated with the AquaGuard brand until then, needed to be deployed under the Aqua-Sure brand as well and sold at retail. These two developments provided a terrific branding opportunity, which EFL utilized by creating two new sub-brands within the AquaSure umbrella brand: Sureboil (for the resin-based, non-electrical models with which AquaSure was originally launched) and Powerboil (for the electrically-powered, UV-based models newly added to the AquaSure stable). The creation of these two sub-brands was a marketing communications breakthrough for EFL: as Aslam Karmali, chief executive officer (CEO), Consumer Division, put it:

> The tipping point came for us when we hit upon a way of leveraging both our technologies (UV and resin) with the same advertising rupee. By settling on the Indian reverence

to the boiling process, we came up with two labels (Powerboil and Sureboil) to denote our electricity-based and the non-electric purification processes respectively.

Advertising creativity was poised to create significant impact on the mass market. Market research indicated that as much as 45 percent of urban households did not do anything to purify their water, and a further 35 percent used drum filters or rudimentary methods such as cloth filtration: this meant that 80 percent of households drank unsafe water and could be exhorted through television-based marketing communications to "Powerboil" or "Sureboil" their water. Palekar described this marketing strategy:

In fact the best part of the AquaSure advertising campaign was cluing on to the typical Indian household practice of boiling! When the actress gently admonishes a mother in the advertisement who runs into the kitchen to retrieve milk that is about to boil over, saying "When you know you have to boil milk to make it safe, why do you not Sureboil (or Powerboil) your water using AquaSure?" The ad touches a chord in every Indian household. After us, almost every water purifier brand has been using some comparison with boiling to tell its own story because boiling is culturally deep-rooted in India.

## Marketing Water Purifiers—The Competition

When EFL first launched the AquaGuard in 1984, it was the only recognized player in the Indian water purifier business. Using its first-mover advantage, it was able to gradually build formidable barriers to competitive entry over the years: a large field sales force specialized in door-to-door selling, an extensive service network, an extensive support organization to assist both sales and service forces, a loyal customer base providing lifetime value, and

positive word of mouth. Nevertheless, competition inevitably emerged, and in recent years, fuelled by the promise of explosive growth in the economy and consumer demand, competition in the Indian water purifier market became intense.

**Hindustan Unilever Ltd. (HUL):** A leading multinational consumer goods company, HUL launched Pureit in 2004, based on resin technology. It positioned itself as a provider of water "as safe as boiled water" and "without needing gas, electricity or continuous tap water supply."[3] Priced at a low INR1,800 per unit, Pureit rapidly gained market share. Given its long-standing presence in the Indian consumer goods market in diverse product categories, HUL had an advantage that EFL did not have—an established distribution infrastructure with relationships nurtured over decades. In addition, in 2007 HUL had over 2,000 commissioned consultants delivering Pureit at consumer doorsteps in response to inquiries generated through print and television commercials, thus imitating the direct selling approach of EFL, albeit in a limited way. HUL was planning to double the number of direct selling consultants by 2008. The company had also outsourced its back end support services in each market to key service providers, which gave it a large third-party field sales force to make cold calls and consumer financing offers for appliance purchases. In short, HUL was riding on a massive strength in go-to-market infrastructure.

**Philips India Ltd. (Philips):** Another leading multinational company with an Indian heritage of several decades, Philips was planning to enter the UV market segment with its Intelligent Water Purifier brand. Scheduled for launch in May 2007, it had a price range of INR8,500 to INR12,500. In very clear competitive signaling, it announced its intention of becoming the long-run leader in the UV category of the water purifier market in India. The company was separately also planning to develop low-cost water purifiers aimed at the mass market. Given its similar profile to HUL in terms of having built a vast and loyal distribution network, Philips was in a good position to leverage this strength for the mass market. Aside from all its product development efforts, Philips was also experimenting with partnership initiatives, with some relationships established with real estate developers to pre-install its brand of water purifiers in their future residential home projects—a move that could potentially endow it with considerable competitive advantage.

**Kent RO:** Established in 1995, Kent RO had a mission of "producing innovative health care products that purify the water we drink, the food we eat and the air we breathe, thus helping people live healthier."[4] It had three water purifier brands, all based on RO technology: Kent Grand (which could be mounted on a kitchen wall), Kent Excell (which could be mounted on a kitchen sink) and Kent Elite (meant for industrial use). The prices ranged between INR10,000 and INR14,500 per unit. The company distributed its products using a franchise model, where individual franchisees sold water purifiers through direct marketing in their respective territories. The franchisees were responsible for demonstration, sales, revenue collection, product installation, and after-sales service.

**Ion Exchange (India) Ltd. (Ion Exchange):** Ion Exchange was positioned as a "total environment solutions company,"[5] offering water treatment and waste management services including generation of energy from waste. The company lobbied for end-to-end water management responsibility for industrial as well as residential communities; thus, unlike the other competitors, Ion Exchange was not merely a product-based player. It did, however, have consumer marketing pedigree: its consumer products division had successfully established Zero-B as a leading brand in home water purification as early as the 1980s. Over the years, the Zero-B platform developed numerous variants at different price points; for example, the Zero-B Pristine was priced at INR18,000. The company also set up a Zero-B Ultimate Watermart in all major cities, a one-stop shop for solutions to water purification problems.

**Bottled Water:** The bottled water industry could also be considered a source of competition for EFL. Generally speaking, it was a parallel industry catering to a very different consumer need (pure drinking water while traveling *outside* the

home) and operating at a completely separate and much higher price point (INR12/liter versus INR0.6/liter for water-purifiers). It was a much bigger industry (at INR20 billion versus the INR8 to 9 billion water purifier market), but was also much more fragmented and unorganized, with very few large, consolidated players. Hence it was believed to be less capable of launching a coherent marketing threat to water purifiers; however, the specific segment of large-capacity water bottles for home use (e.g., 18 liters), dubbed in the industry as "bubbles," could be interpreted as presenting some threat to the water purifier industry and hence to EFL. At approximately INR2 billion in revenues and being based on RO technology, it catered to the growing consumer demand for clean and good-tasting water at home.

## The Challenges Ahead

After 23 years of one dominant strategic template—"direct sell AquaGuard to relatively market-ready urban consumer households"—it seemed that the time had come to consider substantial changes in EFL's go-to-market strategy. Although the company had always been exploring alternative avenues as detailed earlier, these options were typically attempted on the sidelines, and with a risk-insurance mind-set rather than on their own strategic merit. As Goklaney looked ahead, several internal and external challenges presented themselves, fundamentally altering the market opportunity for water purifiers and EFL's competitive position within it.

## Internal

**Market coverage:** To date, AquaGuard had still only penetrated a tiny fraction of urban homes in India (seven percent of 56 million urban homes). In part, this had to do with geographic focus. In 2006, the EuroChamps sales force was present in 144 A-level cities (population greater than 100,000), a tiny fraction of the overall geographic distribution of the

Indian urban population (distributed across 4,000 towns and cities across the country); therefore, market penetration offered significant room for improvement.

**Relative value of business divisions:** Despite the coverage handicap, direct selling still represented more than 80 percent of AquaGuard revenues and almost all its profits. Clearly the two other divisions were not pulling their weight, despite having been in existence for a number of years and showing recent strong growth. Palekar reflected:

Although the two new divisions set up in 1988 were in theory supposed to help market penetration, in the management's mindset they were always viewed merely as "supplements" to the direct sales division, which was, by far, the company's primary income generator.

**Brand equity:** With the launch of AquaSure in 2004, the resulting two-brand platform in theory gave EFL an opportunity to pursue sharp market positioning: AquaGuard (now AquaGuard Total) targeted the upper end of about 18 million urban households, and AquaSure at the lower end with a potential target audience of about 30 million urban households. Despite this marketing position, with the distribution channels, technologies and customer groups in Indian cities seemingly blurred at their edges, it was not clear to Goklaney if this intended positioning would really work. As much as he really believed that AquaSure was another star in the making (initial results certainly suggested so), it was not clear how the two brands would play out their roles in the future.

For one thing, the AquaSure technology still had bugs that needed fixing; for example, it currently only worked in conditions of uniform temperature. With this handicap, the brand could hardly be expected to achieve wide geographical reach in the Indian mass market, where climatic conditions varied significantly from region to region; additionally, the company's initial assumptions regarding the ideal channel and ideal customer segment for the two brands now seemed a bit suspect. Palekar explained:

We originally believed that the customers for AquaSure were not as high profile as the customers for AquaGuard. That seems misplaced now, with sophisticated consumers responding to the brand's marketing communications and shopping at retail, especially in new formats such as high-end malls. We also traditionally believed that direct selling was ideally suited for upper-class consumers, but this was as much predicated on the social skills of the EuroChamps as on consumer profile. As newer employment options (e.g., call centers) take away much skilled talent in towns and cities, our EuroChamp recruits are now increasingly coming from somewhat lower strata of society, and thus short on the social skills necessary to connect with the core high-end audience of direct sales.

# External

## The Global Water Sustainability Concern

In recent years, another major issue hit home for EFL management: it became apparent that the global water scenario in the new millennium had placed considerable attention on the water purification industry (unlike when it started out in the 1980s). Water was increasingly scarce in the world due to a confluence of factors in supply and demand. On the supply side, climate change was causing significant drops in supply as well as variability in supply quality (see Exhibit 9). On the demand side, population growth, increasing demand for food and energy and growing industrialization (with concomitant rises in urbanization and consumer economies) were depleting global water resources. Over 2.8 billion people in 48 countries were expected to face water "stress" by 2025 (see Exhibit 10). Of these countries, 40 would be in West Asia, North Africa and sub-Saharan Africa.[6] A 2025 projection by the World Resources Institute on water availability in the world's major rivers (based on 1995 data) showed that much more than half the world would face major water stress.[7]

**Exhibit 9**    Vulnerabilities of Fresh Water Resources

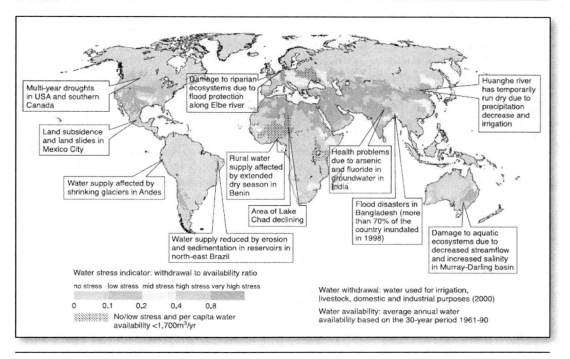

*Source:* "Watching Water: A Guide to Evaluating Corporate Risks in a Thirsty World," Global Equity Research, March 31, 2008, J.P. Morgan Securities, p. 6; available at www.wri.org/publication/watching-water, accessed on March 2, 2010.

**Exhibit 10**    Global Water Stress

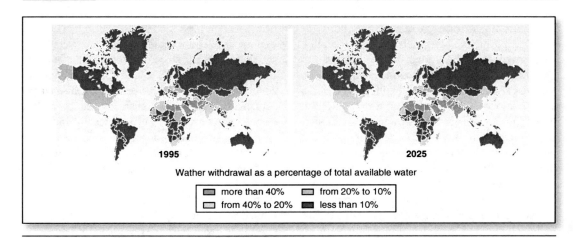

*Source:* "Increased global water stress," United Nations Environment Programme (UNEP), http://maps.grida.no/go/graphic/increased-global-water-stress, accessed on January 18, 2010.

In India, there were twin demand pressures; on the one hand, the country was rapidly industrializing as a result of policies favoring integration with the global economy being put in place almost two decades ago. This industrialization placed massive demands on water resources, as there were issues of availability as well as polluted fresh water at the output end. On the other hand, the industrialization also triggered urbanization and rises in income due to job opportunities, and these in turn induced significant changes in consumer lifestyles, all of which considerably raised per capita water usage.

It is clear that developing countries are most hurt by worsening water quality. In wealthier countries, industrial and household water pollution has been brought under control with the aid of technology. In developing countries, pollutants such as industrial waste and untreated sewage significantly reduce supplies of fresh surface water or at the very least increase the cost burden of water treatment. Excessive pumping of groundwater, common in India for example, can lead to salt water seeping into fresh water aquifers, permanently reducing fresh water availability.

## Market Growth, Competition, and Criticisms

As a result of the focus on water sustainability issues and their corresponding implications for global investment in clean water technologies, EFL anticipated that the Indian water purification industry was about to grow suddenly and rapidly. This was also entirely consistent with India's overall economic growth: the country was widely perceived to be on an irreversible, upward momentum, recording growth rates of seven to eight percent of gross domestic product (GDP) consistently throughout the 2000s, and was poised to grow at between six and nine percent up to 2025.[8]

The management felt that sizable competition was going to emerge not only for its traditional 18 million household market, but also for the much bigger 60 million household market of urban India. After easily being the market leader for two decades, this was a new challenge to face; thus, although lauded for its customer orientation, the new competitive scenario possibly meant that the company would have to acquire additional new skill sets adhering to a competitive orientation.

Significant new competencies in marketing channel orientation were called for: a key factor prompting this need was the explosive growth of Indian retail. Traditionally, retailing in India was extremely fragmented—millions of mom-and-pop *kirana* stores dotting the landscape of the country, catering to consumer needs at a very disaggregated neighborhood and community level. In just the past few years, however, there was a flood of market entry of numerous organized retail giants. The federal government had allowed, since January 2006, foreign direct investment (FDI) of up to 51 percent in single brand retailing, facilitating the entry of foreign retailers.[9] The move also spurred domestic corporations to diversify into retailing by collaborating with overseas retailers. Store formats grew rapidly—hypermarkets (greater than 55,000 sq. ft.), supermarkets (3,500–5,000 sq. ft), mini-supermarkets (1,000–2,000 sq. ft) and convenience stores (750–1,000 sq. ft)—and offered Indian consumers an unprecedented choice of shopping experiences. Mall space, approximately one million square feet in 2002, was expected to increase to 60 million square feet by 2008 in all of India.[10] Aided by professional and corporate technologies and management practices, retail business models also diversified quickly, leading to discount retailers, mass merchandisers, specialty stores and so on. The Indian retail industry was valued at INR13.5 trillion ($311.7 billion) in 2006[11] of which only three percent constituted the "organized retail" sector characterized by a clear demarcation of roles between ownership and management. The proportion of the organized sector was estimated to reach approximately 28 percent by 2017 (see Exhibit 11). This created significant implications for EFL concerning where and how it made its products available to consumers. Traditionally limited to apparel, organized retailers were rapidly expanding their category expertise to include everything from groceries to consumer durables.

| Exhibit 11 | Projected Growth of Indian Retail |

| | Market size (in INR billion) | | |
| | | Organized retail | |
| Year | Total retail | Size | % of Total |
|------|-------------|------|-----------|
| 2007 | 14,108 | 511 | 3.6 |
| 2008 | 15,792 | 714 | 4.5 |
| 2009 | 17,682 | 1,218 | 6.9 |
| 2010 | 19,782 | 2,142 | 10.8 |
| 2011 | 22,134 | 3,108 | 14.0 |
| 2012 | 24,780 | 4,074 | 16.4 |
| 2017 | 42,462 | 11,844 | 27.9 |

*Source:* www.indiaretailing.com/India_retail_report2007.

| Exhibit 12 | India—Socio-Economic Classes and Number of Urban Households 2006 |

| SEC Class | Est. no. of households (in millions) |
|-----------|--------------------------------------|
| A1 | 2.2 |
| A2 | 4.1 |
| B1 | 5.3 |
| B2 | 5.3 |
| C | 12.8 |
| D | 14.2 |
| E1 | 6.7 |
| E2 | 10.8 |
| R1 | 5.8 |
| R2 | 15.9 |
| R3 | 56.7 |
| R4 | 67.3 |
| Total | 207.1 |

*Source:* Market Research Society of India and Company records.

*Note:* The top band of purchasing power in India (urban A1 and A2) comprised a little over six million households. The next band, which would qualify, for the "middle class India" label, comprising B1, R1, B2, and C, harbored about 30 million households; The A, B, C, and R1 target group, which would form the broadest possible target group for most consumer goods was about 36 million households. The lower middle class comprised D, E1, and R2 at about 37 million households.

In the new climate of the water purification industry, there were plenty of criticisms forthcoming from non-governmental organizations (NGOs) and other consumer advocacy organizations. One was that water purifier companies made a lot of tall claims, not all of them factual. The NGOs argued that purifiers, however advanced, could not completely eliminate harmful pesticides, solvents, and other volatile organic compounds that were rampant in water polluted by the industrial sector. They also argued that in removing contaminants, many purifiers also removed some essential minerals vital to human health. Finally, giant corporations were generally seen as a part of the problem and not the solution, as they were believed to greatly contribute to the industrial polluting of the water in the first place.

## March 2007

Ahead of SMART 2007, one question held priority: If 25 years of "educating" the "elite" consumers of India on the merits of purified water has only helped penetrate four million of the top-bracket urban Indian households, how could EFL aspire to

break into the mass urban market? The company's brands, technologies and marketing channels were key levers that had to be somehow synchronized perfectly in the coming years if the company were to achieve its goal. In Goklaney's words:

AquaSure is an engine of growth in its own right now. But, although the resin category is growing at a rate faster than the UV category, AquaSure is growing at a rate lower than its principal competitor. Given the unfolding changes in the country's retailing landscape,

AquaSure has the potential to penetrate deeper into the market and change the fortunes of EFL. How do we realize that potential? This is the question for which we need to find answers at SMART 2007.

The board was not without concerns. It had already expressed worry on previous occasions that the company may be diversifying too much too fast with the advent of non-electric technology and retail channels.

---

### CASE QUESTIONS

1. Currently, AquaGuard had been sold through direct channels. Should Eureka Forbes alter this approach? Why or why not?

2. Should Eureka Forbes pursue a strategy of intensive, selective, or exclusive distribution?

3. If Eureka Forbes utilizes intermediaries, which types should be chosen and what tasks should they be given?

4. Should Eureka Forbes have a different distribution system for rural as opposed to urban customers, especially if the products are modified to meet differing specifications? Why or why not?

---

## Kraft Foods: The Coffee Pod Launch

*By Aleem Visram, under the supervision of Professor Robin Ritchie*

## Introduction

Geoff Herzog, product manager for coffee development at Kraft Foods Canada (Kraft), sat in his office after reviewing encouraging results for the single-serve coffee pod system in Europe. On a typical day, Herzog would have used the office coffee station for his morning cup of coffee, but today he had brewed his own cup using a single-serve coffee pod machine. It was July 6, 2004, and Herzog had just learned that Kraft Foods North America was planning an aggressive launch of coffee pods in the United States. He had less than a month to decide whether Kraft should proceed with a simultaneous launch in Canada, or await the U.S. results.

If Herzog went ahead with the launch, he would have to make several decisions. First, since Kraft owned two major coffee brands in Canada, Maxwell House and Nabob, a suitable branding strategy would be needed. Herzog would also have to set a wholesale and a suggested retail price for the coffee pods, choose which flavors to offer, and decide whether Kraft should use traditional distribution channels or direct-to-store delivery (DSD). In addition, he would have to develop an effective advertising and promotion strategy on a relatively limited budget. Herzog knew that whatever recommendations he made, he would need to make a convincing case that his plan would help Kraft expand its share of the Canadian coffee market, while generating a satisfactory return on the company's marketing investment.

## Kraft Foods Inc.

Founded as a cheese manufacturer in 1903, Kraft Foods Inc. (Kraft Foods) had evolved into North

Version: (A) 2009–09–11

America's largest food and beverage company and the number two player in the world. In 2004, Kraft Foods had operations in more than 155 countries. Although the company had previously been a division of Philip Morris Companies (since renamed Altria Group), it had become a public company in June 2001.

Kraft operations consisted of Kraft Foods North America and Kraft Foods International, and its business was divided into five product categories: beverages, convenience meals, cheese, grocery, and snacks. The Kraft brand portfolio was among the strongest of the global consumer packaged goods players, with more than 50 $100-million brands and five $1-billion brands. Along with its size and impressive brand portfolio, Kraft Foods boasted a strong distribution network and a well-earned reputation for developing innovative new products and food applications. The company's mission was to achieve leadership in the markets it served, which it pursued by fostering innovation, achieving high product quality and keeping a close eye on profit margins. Five operational objectives had been established to achieve these goals:

1. Build superior brand value for consumers by delivering greater product benefits at the right price, compared to the competition.

2. Enhance product demand among consumers by building relationships with trade partners.

3. Constantly adjust the product portfolio to align with consumer trends, especially in fast-growing channels and demographic groups.

4. Expand global scale by increasing business internationally, especially in the world's fastest-growing developing countries.

5. Build a leaner cost structure through better use of assets to generate savings for reinvestment in brand building.

Kraft Foods was the world leader in coffee sales with 15 percent of the global market. In Canada, Kraft's Maxwell House and Nabob brands enjoyed a combined 32 percent share, followed by Nestlé at 17 percent and Procter and Gamble with nine percent. Private labels accounted for nearly 23 percent of the market, with smaller companies making up the remaining 19 percent.

The company's Maxwell House line was Canada's top retail brand of roast and ground coffee, while Nabob was the leader in Western Canada and number two nationally. Both were available in a variety of flavors, sizes and formats (see Exhibit 1).

---

**Exhibit 1**   Maxwell House and Nabob Product Lines

|  | Brand Positioning | Current Products |
|---|---|---|
| MAXWELL HOUSE | *Maxwell House is "good to the last drop"* <br> Canada's number one brand and favorite mainstream coffee <br> Roasted to deliver peak flavor and aroma | 326g tin SKUs: <br> Original Roast <br> Mellow Roast <br> Rich Dark Roast <br> Decaffeinated <br> Half Caffeine |

---

*(Continued)*

| Exhibit I | (Continued) | |
|---|---|---|

| | Brand Positioning | Current Products |
|---|---|---|
| NABOB | *Nabob delivers a better cup of coffee, every time* <br><br> Canada's leading premium coffee <br><br> 100 percent Arabica Colombian beans, carefully chosen by Nabob for taste and quality <br><br> Custom roasted by Nabob to ensure perfect flavor and aroma | 350g "Nabob Tradition" SKUs: <br> Caffeinated — Regular Grind <br> Caffeinated — Fine Grind <br> 326g "Nabob Tradition" SKUs: <br> Decaffeinated — Regular Grind <br> Decaffeinated — Fine Grind <br> 326g "Nabob Blend" SKUs: <br> Full City Dark <br> Summit 100% Colombian <br> Summit Decaffeinated <br> Milano Espresso <br> Golden Java Sumatra <br> Carnival Brazil <br> 1kg "Nabob Tradition" SKU: <br> Caffeinated— Regular Grind |

*Source:* Company files.

All beans used by Kraft were custom-roasted to deliver peak aroma, and had a fine grind to ensure a fresh, rich flavor.

## Single-Serve Coffee Pods

The single-serve coffee pod (SSP) machine was the first major innovation to hit the coffee-brewing industry since the introduction of the drip coffee maker in the 1950s. First conceived of in 1978 by Italy's Illy Caffé, which targeted it to office users, the pod had been redesigned for consumer use by Kraft Foods, which introduced its home version in Switzerland in 1982. By 2003, Kraft Foods marketed consumer coffee pods in 10 European countries. Kraft Foods' most serious competitor in Europe was Senseo, a partnership between Dutch electronics and appliance maker Philips and the Douwe Egberts division of U.S.-based Sara Lee Corporation, the world's second-largest coffee roaster. Senseo had been launched in 2001, and some five million coffee makers and three billion pods were sold in the first three years.

By 2003, single-serve coffee pod units accounted for nearly 15 percent of all coffee makers sold in Europe, and 5.8 percent of coffee sales by value. By 2008, annual European sales were forecast to exceed both 82 million coffee pod machines and $150 million worth of coffee pods. By 2010, it was expected that SSP machines would account for 10 percent of the European home coffee brewer market. Significantly, as much as 30 percent of total coffee pod sales were expected to be incremental volume, drawn from individuals who would normally have bought their coffee out-of-home, or not consumed coffee at all.

## The Technology

Similar to machines used by coffee houses to make specialty coffee, SSP machines used pre-packaged single servings to make high-quality coffee in less than a minute. Instead of percolating water through the ground coffee via gravity like conventional coffee makers, SSP machines forced hot water through the coffee pod at high pressure. The pods were similar to teabags in that the ground coffee was encapsulated in perforated paper, but,

unlike tea, the coffee was packed tightly to ensure sufficient flavor. Each pod measured 59 to 62 millimeters in diameter, and contained between seven and 10 grams of ground coffee (see Exhibit 2).

Two types of SSP machines were available. So-called "open" systems used a standard-sized coffee pod that could be used interchangeably with pods from different manufacturers. Conversely, "closed" systems could only use a specific pod shape and size, and only accepted coffee pods compatible with these systems. In either case, the coffee produced was of similar quality to that available at cafés.

Although the cost per cup with SSP machines ($0.20 to $0.50 per cup) was higher than with

---

**Exhibit 2**    Operation of the Single-Serve Pod System

Single-serve pod systems use pre-heated water and high pressure to quickly extract the coffee from pre-ground coffee pods in less than a minute.

| Step 1 | Step 2 | Step 3 | Step 4 |
| --- | --- | --- | --- |
| First the water reservoir in the back is filled. The water is pre-heated so that it is dispensed hot without waiting. Most reservoirs hold between eight and 10 cups of water before needing to be refilled. | The coffee pod is then inserted into the machine and the desired size selected. Most brewers give consumers the choice of more than one size of cup. Two pods can be inserted for a stronger coffee. | The machine then brews the coffee directly into your cup in less than a minute. Coffee pods can be used only once per coffee serving to ensure optimal taste and freshness are maintained. | Once the brewing is finished, the pod is thrown out and another inserted. There is no flavor transfer between pods during usage. |

*Source:* Company files.

traditional drip coffee machines ($0.05 to $0.15 per cup), SSP systems provided several advantages. First, an SSP machine took less than a minute to make a cup of coffee, compared to nearly 10 minutes from a traditional brewing machine. As well, SSP machines were easier to use than the drip machines since there was no need to measure the ground coffee or use a filter. They were also easier to clean, with no messy ground coffee left over to toss, no leftover coffee to pour down the sink and no pot to clean—users simply disposed of the coffee pod in a garbage or compost bin.

The pod system was most advantageous when a person wanted to make coffee in small batches, or cater to several different tastes at the same time. For instance, if one person wanted a decaffeinated coffee after dinner, a single cup could be prepared without having to make an entire pot. Similarly, if family members each liked a different kind of coffee, separate coffees could be brewed simply by using a different flavor pod for each cup. Bill VandenBygaart, director of coffee development for Kraft Canada, was confident about the value of the system to consumers: "We believe Canadians will see real value in the convenience, choice and quality that single-serve pod machines provide."

## The Canadian Coffee Market

Because grocery stores carried a growing selection of coffee brands, flavors and formats, competition in the Canadian coffee market was intense. The past decade had also seen specialty retailers, such as Starbucks and Tim Hortons, enter the market in a serious way, selling their brands of ground coffee and coffee beans in grocery outlets as well as in their own stores. Brewed coffee from these restaurants and cafés was further cannibalizing grocery sales, with consumers willing to pay a substantial premium for the convenience, customization and variety they offered.

Retail sales of instant, ground and whole bean coffee in Canada topped $600 million in 2003, of which $425 million was sold by grocery, mass retail, and club stores. Sales of specialty coffees—a category

that included espresso and cappuccino, flavored coffees, and iced coffees—had dropped 12 percent in dollar terms and 11 percent by volume. Sales of instant coffee had increased two percent by volume, but declined by two percent in dollar terms, due to lower retail prices. This reflected the higher quality and availability of specialty coffee from coffee shops and cafes.

The home-prepared coffee category in Canada was also becoming increasingly polarized between premium and mainstream brands. The popularity of large-size containers of discount coffee had led to price wars between manufacturers of these brands in most mainstream retail channels, eroding margins and decreasing profitability. Conversely, at about 15 to 20 percent of total sales volume, higher priced premium coffee was a much smaller business that was enjoying double-digit sales growth. Herzog believed there was an opportunity for higher-end products to capture an even larger portion of the category over time, with higher price points and greater profitability.

## Coffee Consumption Behavior

Canadians were among the world's leading drinkers of coffee, consuming some 3.5 million cups of coffee daily in 2003—a number that had risen by an average of 4.5 percent over each of the previous five years. After water, coffee was easily the most popular daily beverage of Canadian adults (see Exhibit 3), with an average consumption of 2.6 cups per day among coffee drinkers. Roughly 63 percent of Canadians drank at least one cup daily, while 83 percent enjoyed coffee at least occasionally. Half of all Canadians drank at least some specialty coffee (espresso, cappuccino, or flavored coffee); these individuals tended to be younger than the average coffee drinker, with higher education and higher incomes. The percentage of regular coffee drinkers varied considerably across the country, from a high of 70 percent in Quebec, to 67 percent in the Prairies and the West, 60 percent in Ontario, and 53 percent in the Atlantic region.

By volume, more than two-thirds of the coffee consumed in Canada was prepared at home. Four

**Exhibit 3**    Canadian Coffee Consumption Data

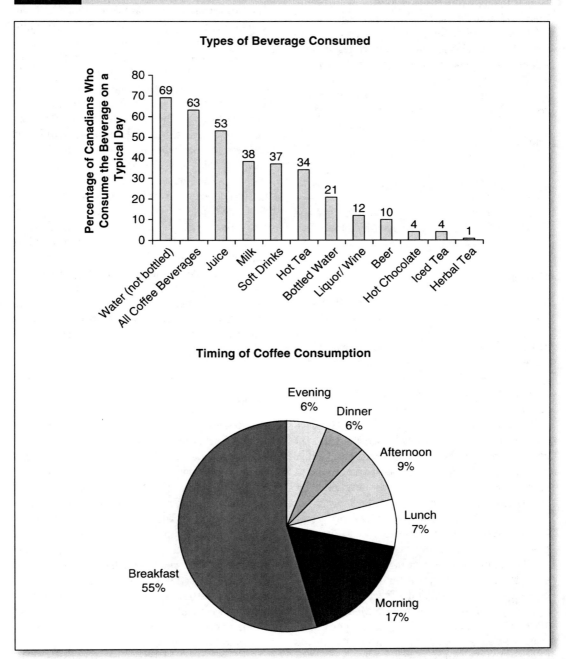

*Source:* Coffee Association of Canada.

out of five Canadian households made at least one store trip to buy coffee: These coffee-buying households averaged seven such trips per year, bought 0.7 kilograms of coffee on each trip, and spent $9 per kilogram. Coffee sales were greatest among middle- to upper-income Canadians, particularly 25 to 40 year-olds and middle-aged childless couples, who purchased more than 10 kilograms of coffee per year at an average price of $7 per kilogram. Nearly 38 percent of all coffee in Canada was purchased in bulk or on promotion.

## Competitive Landscape

Based on the major brands available in Europe and the United States, Herzog had identified four likely SSP competitors for Kraft in Canada:

### One-to-One

Germany's Melitta Group had joined with Salton, makers of the George Foreman Grill, to create the Melitta One-to-One SSP machine. The system was capable of brewing coffee in two sizes using a specially filtered system designed to deliver coffee-bar quality at home. The spout of the coffee machine could also be changed to make hot or iced tea. One-to-One machines were already available across Canada, and came with a six-flavor javapod sampler.

Melitta was the only SSP system to use 9.7 gram javapods, rather than the seven gram coffee pod sizes used by Home Café, Senseo and Bunn. As a result, while other coffee pods were all interchangeable across manufacturers, they could not be used in the Melitta One-to-One (and vice versa). Rumors were rampant, however, that Melitta was planning to switch to standard-sized coffee pods. Melitta javapods were sealed in oxygen-free foil packs to preserve flavor, and retailed for $4.99 for a package of 16 (see Exhibit 4). Three different varieties were available: 100% Arabica Medium Roast, 100% Colombian, and Light Roast. Pods were available from the same retailers where the Melitta One-to-One System was sold: Zellers, the Bay, Home Outfitters, and Canadian Tire.

### Home Café

The Home Café system was the result of a partnership between Procter and Gamble, and two leading makers of small appliances: Applica Inc. (owner of Black & Decker) and Jardine Corporation (owner of Mr. Coffee, Rival, and Sunbeam). Home Café used a specialized pressure-brewing technology to deliver single servings of fresh coffee in less than a minute while bringing out the full flavor of the coffee bean. The machine could brew three different cup sizes, and featured a removable cup platform to prevent spilling as well as an easy-clean removable drip tray. The water reservoir was also removable and could be rotated for fast and accurate filling. In the United States, Home Café machines came with a free bag of Folgers coffee pods. It was widely expected that the system would be introduced to Canada in September 2004 through Walmart.

Reliable sources had told Herzog that Home Café would launch with four different flavors of coffee pods under Procter and Gamble's Folgers brand: Classic Roast, Classic Decaf, 100% Colombian, and French Vanilla. The pods were expected to be available in packages of 16 and retail for $4.99 (see Exhibit 4).

### Senseo

Senseo was a partnership between Philips Electronics and Sara Lee Corporation, the world's second largest coffee roaster. The Senseo machine used balanced portions of coffee and water, mild pressure and a special spray head to produce an optimally balanced filtering process and a rich froth on top of each cup. The quick and easy one-touch system brewed a cup of coffee in 30 seconds, with auto shut-off after one hour. The machine was available in four colors and had dishwasher-safe removable parts for easy cleaning. As an added incentive, customers who registered their Senseo machine were sent a free bag of coffee pods and $2 off their next pod purchase. Senseo was expected to launch in Canada in early 2005.

Senseo coffee pods were marketed using Sara Lee's Douwe Egberts brand, using the slogan "one

| Exhibit 4 | Comparison of Coffee Pod Offerings | | | |
| --- | --- | --- | --- | --- |
| | Melitta One-to-One | Home Café | Bunn My Café | Senseo |
| Launch Date | In-Market | September 2004 | November 2004 | Early 2005 |
| Machine Manufacturer | Salton | Black & Decker | Bunn | Philips |
| Retail Selling Price for Machine | $60 – $75 | $75 – $89 (expected) | $150+ (expected) | $85 – $99 (expected) |
| System Type | Closed | Open | Open | Open |
| Primary Pod Supplier | Melitta | Folgers & Millstone (P&G) | Various | Douwe Egberts (Sara Lee) |
| Retail Selling Price for Pods | $4.99 for 16 | $4.99 for 16 (expected) | Varies | $4.99 for 18 (expected) |
| Beans Used | 100% Arabica, 100% Colombian | 60% Arabica, 40% Robusta | Varies | To be confirmed |

*Source:* Company files.

taste and you will know the extraordinary difference." They used premium-quality beans that had been carefully roasted and blended, and offered four flavors, including mild, medium, dark, and decaffeinated roast. Senseo pods came in packages of 18 for a retail price of $4.99 (see Exhibit 4).

## Bunn My Café

Bunn Home Brewers had announced plans to launch the My Café single-serve pod machine in Canada in November 2004. My Café claimed to offer great-tasting coffee quickly, simply and consistently. The system worked with a large array of pods and teabags, featured a removable easy-fill reservoir and patented spray head design for maximum flavor extraction, and could brew a cup of coffee in 30 seconds. The brew control had nine settings to alter coffee strength, and was made with dishwasher-safe parts. Bunn did not plan to manufacture its own coffee pods (see Exhibit 4).

## Marketing Strategy

With an annual budget of only $1 million for a potential launch, Herzog faced tight constraints on his ability to introduce Kraft coffee pods in Canada. If he proceeded with the launch, he would need to identify a cost-effective way to convince consumers that Kraft's pods delivered better value than competitors' pods. The goal was for 80 percent of SSP machine owners to try the product, and for 60 percent of those individuals to repeat purchase. Herzog was expected to at least break even by the end of 2006.

## Target Market

Although SSP machines had only recently been introduced to Canada, Herzog had access to market research on current Canadian coffee pod users. These individuals were typically coffee lovers between the ages of 25 and 54, tended to be well educated, and had an average household income of $91,000 (the Canadian average household income was $55,000). Nearly three-quarters were married, and 88 percent lived in single-detached homes in urban areas, primarily in the population-rich provinces of Ontario, Quebec, British Columbia, and Alberta. They were characterized by high levels of consumption, and their interests included exercising, entertaining at home, gourmet cooking, household decorating, gardening, and taking exotic vacations.

Maxwell House and Nabob buyers had similar profiles to SSP machine owners, except that they were typically over the age of 45. They also tended to be a mix of maturing, established families and single professionals.

## Buyer Behavior

Although most SSP machines used standard-sized coffee pods, experience in Europe had shown that consumers usually purchased pods of the same brand as the machine they bought (i.e., Folgers pods with Home Café machines, Senseo pods with Senseo machines, and Javapods with Melitta One-to-One machines). At the same time, focus group research suggested that SSP machine owners valued the flexibility of using different coffee brands in their brewers. Coffee quality was also critical, since it defined the entire coffee experience. Coffee drinkers were looking for a fresh, hot cup of coffee with peak flavor and aroma.

## Market Share

Kraft expected that, of the roughly 12.5 million households in Canada, SSP machines would be adopted by six percent by the end of 2004, and eight percent by the end of 2006. Average household consumption of coffee pods among SSP machine owners varied from seven to 14 pods per week. To maintain Maxwell House and Nabob's share of the Canadian coffee market, Herzog estimated that Kraft would need to capture at least 35 percent of the coffee pod segment. His actual goal

was to obtain a 45 percent market share by the end of 2006. Herzog knew this would require significant advertising and promotion to generate the necessary awareness and sales. He was uncertain whether he would be able to achieve his target and still break even.

## Product

If he went ahead with the launch, Herzog would also need to decide on a flavor selection for Maxwell House and/or Nabob coffee pods. He felt that a variety of pod offerings would be critical for building market share and category growth. Kraft's manufacturing facility also had the ability to offer the product in a re-sealable bag with zip closure, which would help keep the product fresh.

## Price

In the United States, Kraft planned to sell pods under the Maxwell House label at a lower price point than rival brands, retailing a pack of 18 pods for US$3.99. In contrast, Folgers charged US$3.99 for a pack of 16. This pricing would give retailers a 25 percent margin on Maxwell House and, at $0.22 per cup, revenue that was more than four times the $0.05 per cup from canned ground coffee.

Herzog was not sure whether to follow the U.S. lead on pricing. On one hand, a low price would serve to drive sales volume and establish Kraft as a market leader, but this strategy risked eroding brand image. Another consideration was the highly concentrated nature of the Canadian grocery sector and the relative power of retailers. Given the failure rate of new products, Herzog suspected that stores would only be willing to carry one or two brands of coffee pods. Canadian grocers typically enjoyed margins of 20 to 30 percent, but Herzog believed margins of 35 percent would be needed as an incentive to list Kraft's coffee pods. With an average production cost of $0.02 per pod, he was unsure of the best wholesale and retail selling price to recommend.

## Distribution

Most of Kraft's products were delivered to retailers via warehouse distribution. Under this system, Kraft was responsible for delivering all merchandise to the customers' warehouses. From these warehouses, retailers then distributed the goods to individual stores. Retailers were responsible for stocking products, refilling shelf space, maintaining inventories and maintaining displays—services for which Kraft paid in excess of $200,000 for national listing fees. Such a system eliminated the need for Kraft to constantly monitor and track inventories, distribution and stock.

The alternative was to use direct-to-store-delivery (DSD). Under this system, Kraft would be responsible for delivering merchandise to individual stores, holding inventories and restocking shelves. This method was currently used by Kraft for its Mr. Christie cookie products. A joint DSD program with Mr. Christie would enable Kraft to lower the overall cost for coffee pod distribution to approximately $150,000 by reducing supply chain expenses and minimizing inventory holding costs. DSD would also allow Kraft to control product displays, ensure superior product freshness, improve customer service, collect insights from retailers, and sidestep warehouse capacity restraints. Finally, since 40 percent of all coffee makers were sold in November and December, DSD would also provide Kraft with speed to market during this period.

Despite these advantages, Herzog was not convinced that DSD made sense. There was a reasonable probability that Kraft would not be able to maintain a DSD approach if the coffee pod sales increased significantly in the future, as the company had both limited space in its distribution center and a limited delivery truck fleet. Furthermore, with numerous retailers and thousands of stores spread across the country, he wondered whether Kraft had sufficient resources to adequately restock product shelves, update product displays and maintain inventory on a store-level basis. He also wondered how retailers would perceive the DSD system, instead of their preferred warehousing distribution system.

## Advertising and Promotion

Herzog expected the makers of rival SSP machines to engage in heavy advertising and promotion to generate consumer awareness of SSP technology and to educate them on the benefits. If Kraft entered the segment, it would need to be serious about building awareness and trial of Maxwell House and/or Nabob coffee pods. Herzog needed to select the promotional vehicles that would generate the greatest number of loyal customers. He had identified several possibilities:

### Print Advertising

Print offered a broad range of options. After meeting with his advertising agency, Herzog narrowed the choice to magazines in six categories: women's interest, decorating, gardening, food, travel, and regional and city magazines. Based on magazine features, readership, customer profiles and costs, Herzog would need to identify a specific set of publications for advertising inserts. He also had to determine the number of advertisement inserts for each magazine (see Exhibit 5).

### TV Sponsorship

Kraft's ad agency had also recommended a television sponsorship program in Toronto, Vancouver, and the province of Quebec to build awareness.

The Toronto and Vancouver initiatives would be conducted in partnership with CityTV, and would include coverage on popular local programs, such as Breakfast Television, CityLine, CityPulse News, and CityOnline. Kraft's coffee pod logo would also appear on all-news channel Cable-Pulse24 and the CityTV website.

The cornerstone of the Toronto/Vancouver TV sponsorship program was contests and giveaways. CityTV would air a 30-second promotional spot encouraging viewers to qualify for giveaways by watching CityPulse. During the telecast, viewers would be asked to e-mail the answer to a contest question, and CityTV would select one winner each night. To generate additional interest, CityTV

| Exhibit 5a | Print Ad Comparison—English Language |
|---|---|

| Category | Magazine | Features | Readership (000s) | Coverage (%) | Insertions | Total Cost ($) |
|---|---|---|---|---|---|---|
| Women's Interest | Chatelaine | Reader profile that fits (High household income, well educated) Appropriate environment with features on home and food | 2,950 | 24.9 | 2 | 55,900 |
| | Wish | New launch (September issue on sale in August) Targeting the busy, urban, upscale woman Home and food comprise half the editorial content | 1,100 | n/a | 1 | 14,900 |
| Decorating | Style at Home | Reader profile that fits (High household income, well educated) Appropriate environment featuring modern decorating | 1,600 | 14.0 | 1 | 9,300 |
| | Cottage Life | Appropriate environment featuring travel accessories, recipes and home design Reader profile that fits (High household income, well educated) Reach both males (53%) and females (47%) of the target market | 574 | n/a | 1 | 6,200 |
| | Canadian House & Home | Appropriate environment that includes features on home, garden, food, wine, travel, technology and lifestyle trends | 2,327 | 17.8 | 2 | 28,600 |
| Gardening | Gardening Life | Reader profile that fits (High household income, white collar professionals) Environment that is appropriate with the target including features such as food trends, entertaining, music and décor | 1,700 | 8.6 | 1 | 9,700 |

| Category | Magazine | Features | Readership (000s) | Coverage (%) | Insertions | Total Cost ($) |
|---|---|---|---|---|---|---|
| | Canadian Gardening | Appeals to both men (30+%) and women (60+%) Profile readership that matches (children in HH, high household income, educated) | 2,572 | 13.5 | 1 | 9,000 |
| Food | Food & Drink | Lifestyle magazine dedicated to the art of drink and entertainment Appropriate environment that features ideas and news of food trends Reaches both male (40%) and female (60%) of target market | 1,631 | 16.3 | 1 | 14,100 |
| Travel | enRoute | #1 ranked publication in terms of composition Targets frequent travelers with an above average disposable income Reaches both males (51%) and females (49%) of the target market | 863 | 17.2 | 2 | 42,000 |
| Regional / City | Vancouver Magazine | Reader profile that fits (High household income, well educated) Reaches both males (53%) and females (47%) of target market | 351 | 2.3 | 2 | 15,500 |
| | Toronto Life | Reader profile that fits (High household income, well educated) Reaches both males (53%) and females (47%) of target market Appropriate environment that reaches the affluent, sophisticated consumer who is engaged in the City of Toronto | 603 | 11.2 | 1 | 13,000 |

*(Continued)*

**Exhibit 5a**    (Continued)

| Category | Magazine | Features | Readership (000s) | Coverage (%) | Insertions | Total Cost ($) |
|---|---|---|---|---|---|---|
| | Western Living | Appropriate environment featuring travel tips, cuisine, home and garden<br>Reaches both the males (44%) and females (56%) of target market<br>Reader profile that fits (children >18 years, well educated) | 810 | 11.2 | 2 | 29,200 |
| | Ottawa City | Upscale, urban publication targeting Ottawa's affluent consumer<br>Covers art, entertainment, food and drink | 603 | n/a | 1 | 4,000 |

*Source:* Company files.

n/a = Data not available.

**Exhibit 5b**    Print Ad Comparison—French Language

| Category | Magazine | Features | Readership (000s) | Coverage (%) | Insertions | Total Cost ($) |
|---|---|---|---|---|---|---|
| Decorating | Décor Chez-Soi | Appropriate environment that features high-quality home décor tips<br><br>Reader profile matches target (affluent women, well educated, high household income) | n/a | 20.2 | 2 | $ 5,700 |
| Gardening | Les Idées de ma Maison | Appropriate environment that features trends and designs | n/a | 23.6 | 2 | 5,800 |
| | Fleurs, Plantes, Jardins | Reader profile that fits (High household income, well educated, children <18 years)<br><br>Appropriate environment that features gardening advice and new products for your home and garden | n/a | 12.4 | 2 | 5,700 |

| Category | Magazine | Features | Readership (000s) | Coverage (%) | Insertions | Total Cost ($) |
|---|---|---|---|---|---|---|
| Women's Interest | Châtelaine (French) | Reader profile that fits (live in urban areas, have children <18 years, well educated, high household income) | n/a | 21.3 | 2 | 9,300 |
| | Clin d'Oeil | Appropriate environment featuring money matters, fashion news and home<br><br>Reader profile that fits (live in urban areas, high household income, well educated) | 833 | 16.9 | 2 | 14,100 |
| | Plaisirs de Vivre | Reader profile that fits (High household income, well educated, professionals)<br><br>Reaches both males (40%) and females (60%) of target market | 191 | n/a | 2 | 6,000 |
| | Coup de Pouce | Ranked #1 in reach across the target market<br><br>Great publication to raise awareness of Maxwell House coffee pods | 1,213 | 32.6 | 2 | 9,200 |
| | Elle Québec | Reader profile that fits (live in urban areas, well educated, high household income)<br><br>Appropriate environment featuring home ideas, health advice, music and entertainment news | 830 | 13.5 | 2 | 16,900 |

*Source:* Company files.

n/a = data not available.

would also offer smaller draw prizes via its website, and offer random product giveaways during its other programming. Total cost of the Toronto and Vancouver sponsorship programs was $52,300, for a total reach of more than 364,000 viewers (see Exhibit 6).

The TV sponsorship plan for Quebec consisted of a low-key effort to generate awareness and educate viewers about the product. Coffee pods would be featured on two French-language programs on the TQS network: Caféine (a morning talk/variety show), and La Roue Chanceuse (a French-language version of *Wheel of Fortune*). In exchange, Kraft would agree to provide coffee pod gift baskets and coffee pod machines, which the hosts of these shows would give away to viewers.

| Exhibit 6 | Television Sponsorship Campaign |
|---|---|

### Audience Size

| Weekly Audience | Toronto | Vancouver | Total |
|---|---|---|---|
| *CityPulse at Six* (evening news) | 65,000 | | 65,000 |
| *Breakfast Television* (morning news show) | 105,000 | 3,000 | 108,000 |
| *CityLine* (mid-morning variety show) | 33,000 | 4,000 | 37,000 |
| *CityOnline* (interactive viewer-driven show) | 20,000 | | 20,000 |
| CityTV.com (website) | 109,000 | 25,100 | 134,100 |
| **Total** | **332,000** | **32,100** | **364,100** |

### Giveaways

| Program: | Week | # of Machines | Machine Costs | Misc. Basket Items | Total Cost |
|---|---|---|---|---|---|
| *Breakfast Television* (morning news show) | 1 | 10 | $1,000 | $500 | $1,500 |
| *CityLine* (mid-morning variety show) | 1 | 5 | $500 | $250 | $750 |
| *City Online* (interactive viewer-driven show) | 1 | 1 | $100 | $50 | $150 |
| *CityPulse News* | 2 | 5 | $500 | $250 | $750 |
| *Caféine Talk* (morning talk / variety show) | 1 | 5 | $500 | $250 | $750 |
| *La Roue Chanceuse* (Wheel of Fortune) | 2 3 | 10 | $1,000 | $500 | $1,500 |
| **Total Costs:** | | | | | **$5,400** |

### Total Promotional Costs

| Promotion | Cost |
|---|---|
| Production of a 30-second English-language contest spot | $10,000 |
| Airtime to run English-language spot for one week | $15,000 |
| Sponsorship of CityPulse Webtest news contest for one week | $16,900 |
| Giveaways | $5,400 |
| Promotional execution | $5,000 |
| **Total Cost:** | **$52,300** |

*Source:* Company files.

## Consumer Shows

A third option was to introduce the product at high-traffic home and garden shows across the country. This promotion would entail an elaborate exhibit, featuring hands-on, shopping channel-style demonstrations, taste tests and a projection screen TV (see Exhibit 7). The message would emphasize the café quality of Maxwell House and/or Nabob coffee pods, and the variety of flavor choices. Bunn My Café had contacted Kraft and suggested splitting the cost through a jointly operated booth. Regardless of whether he accepted this partnership, Herzog had the option of selecting a 10 × 30 foot booth for $485,200 or a 10 × 20 foot booth for $361,450. In addition, he would need to decide which trade shows would provide the most value and highest reach to the prospective target market. If Kraft attended all the fall and spring trade shows, they would be able to reach more than 1.4 million attendees for a total cost of $147,377 (see Exhibit 8).

## Direct Marketing

Herzog could also target existing Kraft customers through a direct mail campaign. Kraft had a database of more than one million subscribers, who voluntarily subscribed to receive its quarterly *What's Cooking* magazine. Herzog estimated that the cost of a direct mail insert, profiling the coffee pod product, would be $50,000.

An alternative was to target Kraft customers through an e-mail campaign. Customers that fit the profile of single-serve coffee machine purchasers

---

**Exhibit 7**    Coffee Pod Demo Program Booth

**FEATURES:**

- Choice of 30-foot or 20-foot wide booth
- 12-foot to 14-foot towers and back wall
- Counters kept to side to maximize traffic flow
- Potential for Nabob and Maxwell House co-branding (see above)
- Premium look and feel

*Source:* Company files.

| Exhibit 8 | Consumer Show Information |
|-----------|--------------------------|

| Show | City | Date | # of Days | Attendance | Cost | Cost per Thousand |
|------|------|------|-----------|-----------|------|-------------------|
| Barrie Fall Home Show | Barrie, ON | September | 2 | 12,000 | $3,002 | $0.25 |
| Ottawa Fall Home Show | Ottawa, ON | September | 3 | 25,000 | $3,436 | $0.14 |
| BC Fall Home Show | Vancouver, BC | October | 4 | 45,000 | $5,382 | $0.12 |
| Vancouver Home & Interior Design Show | Vancouver, BC | October | 4 | 25,000 | $5,054 | $0.20 |
| Edmonton Fall Home Show | Edmonton, AB | October | 3 | 20,000 | $4,968 | $0.25 |
| Autumn Home Show | London, ON | October | 2 | 50,000 | $3,415 | $0.07 |
| Fall Home Show | Toronto, ON | October | 4 | 75,000 | $6,365 | $0.08 |
| Markham Home Show | Markham, ON | October | 3 | 48,000 | $4,468 | $0.09 |
| International Home Show | Mississauga, ON | October | 4 | 60,000 | $7,418 | $0.12 |
| Guelph Fall and Leisure Expo | Guelph, ON | October | 3 | 25,000 | $3,278 | $0.13 |
| Fall Home Show | Montreal, QC | October | 5 | 45,000 | $4,347 | $0.10 |
| Fall Ideal Home Show | Halifax, NS | October | 3 | 20,000 | $2,898 | $0.14 |
| Royal Winter Fair | Toronto, ON | November | 8 | 100,000 | $9,315 | $0.09 |
| Homexpo | Calgary, AB | January | 4 | 24,000 | $4,312 | $0.18 |
| Toronto Home Show | Toronto, ON | January | 7 | 85,000 | $6,037 | $0.07 |
| Metro Home Show | Toronto, ON | January | 4 | 50,000 | $6,279 | $0.13 |
| BC Home and Garden Show | Vancouver, BC | February | 5 | 48,000 | $4,122 | $0.09 |
| Calgary Home & Garden Show | Calgary, AB | February | 5 | 55,000 | $4,312 | $0.08 |
| Edmonton Home & Garden Show | Edmonton, AB | March | 4 | 52,000 | $4,778 | $0.09 |
| Home Expressions | Winnipeg, MB | March | 5 | 12,000 | $3,657 | $0.30 |
| Barrie Spring Home Show | Barrie, ON | March | 2 | 20,000 | $3,277 | $0.16 |
| Guelph Home Show & Leisure Expo | Guelph, ON | March | 3 | 12,000 | $3,888 | $0.32 |
| Hamilton Home & Garden Show | Hamilton, ON | March | 3 | 20,000 | $4,123 | $0.21 |
| The Home Show Designs for Living | Hamilton, ON | March | 3 | 20,000 | $2,967 | $0.15 |

| Show | City | Date | # of Days | Attendance | Cost | Cost per Thousand |
|------|------|------|-----------|------------|------|-------------------|
| International Home & Garden Show | Mississauga, ON | March | 4 | 126,000 | $5,432 | $0.04 |
| Ottawa Home & Garden Show | Ottawa, ON | March | 4 | 15,500 | $6,210 | $0.40 |
| Montreal National Home Show | Montreal, QC | March | 10 | 183,500 | $7,762 | $0.04 |
| National Home Show | Toronto, ON | April | 10 | 100,000 | $6,727 | $0.07 |
| Hamilton Home Show | Hamilton, ON | April | 3 | 18,000 | $4,071 | $0.23 |
| London Spring Home & Garden Show | London, ON | April | 4 | 29,600 | $3,070 | $0.10 |
| Nova Scotia Ideal Home Show | Halifax, NS | April | 3 | 35,000 | $3,001 | $0.09 |

*Source:* Company files.

could be sent an e-mail inviting them to visit a website and register to win a free year's supply of coffee pods. When customers visited the website, they would be given information about the SSP machines and the benefits of Maxwell House and/or Nabob coffee pods. Total cost for the website, e-mail campaign, and giveaway was estimated at $30,000.

## Merchandising

Finally, Herzog was contemplating a variety of in-store merchandising. Kraft had previous experience with three different kinds of display systems. Off-shelf display bins could hold 24 packs of coffee pods and consisted of a stand, a colorful reader card to attract attention, and space for coupons. Herzog felt that a "buy one, get one free" coupon would provide sufficient incentive for SSP machine owners to try Kraft's coffee pods. Another possibility was on-shelf racks, which would ensure that the product would always be neatly and tidily presented. These racks were capable of holding specific point-of-sale merchandise to ensure customer visibility, and would be held down using magnets so that they could be easily moved. An additional option was to use metal shelf strips, which held a coupon attachment and up to 12 bags of coffee pods, and could attach easily to any retail shelf. The display bins, on-shelf racks and shelf-strips would cost a total of $70,000 and the coupons $13,800

(see Exhibit 9). Together, these in-store displays and coupon offerings were forecast to increase product trial by an additional 250 percent.

## Conclusion

With the high growth potential of the single-serve coffee machines in Canada, pressure to go ahead with the launch was high. By launching immediately, Kraft would also have a better opportunity to defend against Procter & Gamble, whose Folgers brand was linked to the Home Café SSP system. If Folgers gained a dominant position in the coffee pod market, there was a reasonable chance that its success could also spill over into the standard roast and ground coffee business.

Conversely, there was a chance that coffee pods would not be well received in North America; by waiting for the results of the U.S. launch, Herzog could minimize risk. Waiting would also enable Kraft to determine which customers were buying the SSP machines, enabling them to target marketing efforts more effectively.

In any case, if Herzog decided to launch the Maxwell House and Nabob Coffee Pods, he would need to create a marketing plan that could break even by the end of 2006. With that firmly in mind, Herzog took a final sip of his coffee and went to work.

| Exhibit 9 | Coffee Pod Merchandising Tools |
| --- | --- |

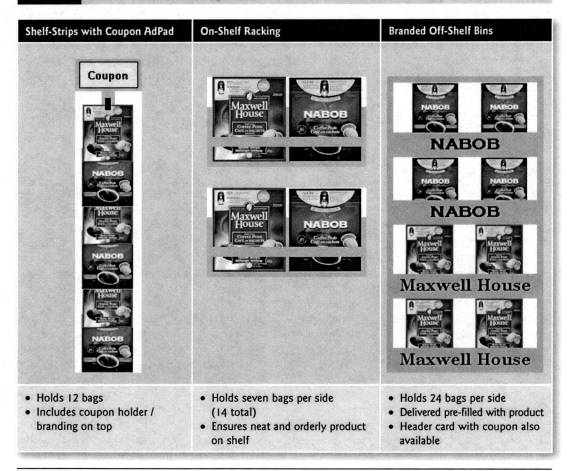

| Shelf-Strips with Coupon AdPad | On-Shelf Racking | Branded Off-Shelf Bins |
| --- | --- | --- |
| • Holds 12 bags<br>• Includes coupon holder / branding on top | • Holds seven bags per side (14 total)<br>• Ensures neat and orderly product on shelf | • Holds 24 bags per side<br>• Delivered pre-filled with product<br>• Header card with coupon also available |

*Source:* Company files.

## CASE QUESTIONS

1. Should Kraft use both the Maxwell House and Nabob brands for coffee pods? Why or why not?

2. Which channel of distribution would work best for single-serving coffee units: direct to consumers, the use of intermediaries, or both? Why?

3. Presuming the primary problem with the launch had been the coffeemakers rather than consumer acceptance of the single-serving size, what steps should Kraft take to correct the problem?

4. An alternative strategy to selling coffee pods to consumers first would have been to market them to other businesses, such as hotels, restaurants, and convenience stores. Discuss the implications of using a dual-channel marketing approach.

# Website and Internet Management

A website has become a necessity in today's marketing environment. Websites should complement all other marketing and management activities and contribute something more. On the marketing side, a site should facilitate customer acquisition, interactions, and retention. On the management side, a website should make the company more efficient and effective by providing a venue to streamline and customize operations. The essential ingredients that work in concert to create a high-quality web program are (1) developing the website functions, (2) designing an e-commerce program, and (3) promoting the website.

## ✉ Website Functions

Website designs vary widely. Each should be set up to serve a common set of functions. Customer support, the first function, includes any activity designed to assist customers who visit a website. The nature of the business or product often dictates the type of support offered.

Sales support will be provided to a company's sales staff and other employees. The site hosts quality information to be used by these workers. In business-to-business settings, websites support the sales staff by creating a separate portal for customers and company employees. Sales support for both consumers and other businesses should make sure the purchasing process works quickly and simply.

Brand support can be enhanced through a company's web program. All visitors routinely see the brand as part of each page, and links directing customers to the site are constructed. A consistently portrayed message comes across all communication channels.

Public relations support receives various degrees of emphasis by marketing managers. Some prominently display public relations releases, while others are less easy to locate. Cause-related marketing, green marketing, sponsorships, and event marketing programs are the most common types of public relations displays.

## ▨  The Value of a Website

A website helps create the opportunity to expand a company's market reach. A well-designed site promotes company visibility and enhances communications both within the company and as part of interactions with its publics. Improved communications builds even stronger relationships with customers. Websites offer convenience and often price advantages. Selling firms lower costs when fewer intermediaries are used. Direct communication can further benefit the bottom line. When companies engage in multichannel marketing, a website program helps integrate all the channels into a more coherent format.

## ▨  Designing an E-Commerce Program

The primary function of most websites is to facilitate e-commerce, because these activities are now commonplace, even among brick-and-mortar stores and retail chains. Marketing managers try to ensure websites are customer-friendly. Information technology experts make them easy to maintain and convenient to update. Some common activities that apply to all sites include (1) building the e-commerce foundation, (2) creating e-commerce components, and (3) finalizing methods of customer interaction.

## ▨  Building the E-Commerce Foundation

An e-commerce building program originates from the need to improve and revise ways to effectively serve customers. The foundation requires careful planning and analysis by the marketing department working in conjunction with information technology, human resources, and public relations. Several technical and operational problems will be resolved as the process unfolds.

E-commerce programs start with a study of the competition, including how competitor websites are organized, the approaches they take, and how competitors promote products. The type of cyber bait used by the competition is noted. Cyber bait includes marketing and financial incentives along with nonfinancial attractions. The marketing team seeks to meet or exceed the competition's online offers.

The second step in building an e-commerce foundation, defining the target market, should make it possible to more clearly define the company's customers and potential customers. Three groups are examined. First, the target market is defined. Then, any overlap between current customers and new prospects may be identified. The degree of overlap depends on how closely the firm's current customers fit the profile of the target market the company's marketing team intends to pursue. Also, the company's current customers may have additional needs that could be met to expand sales.

Choosing a positioning strategy, the third step, involves making sure the website aligns with the positioning that will be pursued. Positioning on a website consists of more than portraying price-quality relationships. Other forms such as product user, product class, or even a cultural symbol may be part of the positioning being presented.

Differentiating the website from the competition, the fourth step, involves finding ways to make the site unique. The unique feature should be appealing to customers and prospects. It should make the brand distinct.

The final part of the foundation, coordinating with other channel members, normally includes the establishment of a new distribution channel, such as a producer-to-end-user channel without the need for an intermediary. A balance should be created between fulfilling customer needs and satisfying the demands of other channel members. A manufacturer will take steps to make sure channel conflicts do not become major problems with retailers.

One of the primary benefits of e-commerce, reducing costs, will be realized only when the firm's management team carefully plans the logistics, warehousing, and inventory procedures for products to be sold online. For the program to succeed, the marketing team must create the best features to support the site through careful planning and coordination.

## ⬛ Creating E-Commerce Components

After the e-commerce foundation has been established, the marketing team works closely with information technology to create and finalize the various components of the e-commerce program. The terms *efficient* and *effective* apply to this process. The system should efficiently deliver information and products to customers. E-commerce becomes effective when the program entices new customers, maintains positive relationships with ongoing customers, and builds long-term relationships with them over time.

The first task in developing an e-commerce program, developing a product database, normally involves building something similar to a company catalog. The product database can carry a few items for a small operation or offer thousands of items for a large firm.

Building an internal search engine, another key e-commerce component, takes time. Each product will be tagged based on how customers search for it. Some customers do not always know the correct name of a product and may type in the generic category rather than more specific information. Every product should be tagged with all the names a person might use while shopping.

The shopping basket stores the items to be purchased in a single place. The customer can review what is about to be purchased, add or delete items, and send the signal that an order is ready. The basket provides a summary of the unit price, the total units ordered, any taxes or delivery charges, and the total charge. Some also include an expected delivery date.

Part of a complete e-commerce program will be the inclusion of various payment methods. The system should be flexible, acceptable to customers, easy to use, secure, reliable, and efficient. Typically, an increase in the number of payment methods made available increases sales.

Customer tracking offers the advantage of making it possible to customize and personalize content delivered to visitors. Systems used to track customers, such as basic authentication, cookies, a domain name, or an IP address, help the marketing team evaluate consumer behavior in terms of the products individuals examine and purchase.

A marketing database identifies various trends and types of consumers. The marketing database can make it possible to create better offers to entice shoppers to make online purchases.

The application interface connects the product database to the payment system, shopping basket, internal search engine, and other features of the site. Tags are placed on items to make it easier to search for products. When a customer finds the desired items, it should be easy to store the item in a shopping cart and then place the order.

Web design requires numerous features to be successful. Among them, the site should offer quality content, achieve consistency in the delivery of messages, be attractive, and allow for personalization and customization. A web design that is difficult to navigate costs the company customers. To achieve positive outcomes, the company's marketing team and information technology department ensure that a living website exists—one that is dynamic and interesting. The site should be closely monitored and maintained in order to facilitate quality customer usage.

## ✑ Finalizing Methods of Interaction With Customers

An e-commerce program achieves success when other matters are covered. Beyond the foundation—displaying items for sale, creating payment systems, and taking care of other e-commerce components—the system should allow the company to contact customers, customers to contact the company, and sometimes customers to contact one another. The website provides these methods of interaction through FAQs and web solutions, e-mail and live chat, social networks and blogs, customer reviews, customer-generated content, and newsgroups and newsletters.

FAQs and web solutions are one-way methods of communication with customers. Individuals access them and receive information without talking to or communicating with a specific company employee. Quality FAQs and web solutions are produced and edited based on two-way interactions with customers. Problems or concerns that have arisen should result in a new FAQ item or information placed on the web solution page.

E-mail and live chat are easy to use. Many customers enjoy them. The key is to ensure the company has sufficient personnel to handle the volume.

Social networks and blogs have grown in popularity. Companies can use them as means of communicating with customers. Facebook, Twitter, and MySpace are some of the main options. These networks reach customers based on key interests and other connections to friends.

Customer reviews are difficult to manage. Negative reviews may be taken down, receive a response from the company's viewpoint, or be left open to see how other customers react. When others agree, the company might wish to make changes to resolve the problem.

Customer-generated content includes discussion groups and methods to share experiences and upload videos. As customers share experiences and comments, others may be encouraged to purchase the brand. Effective customer content can increase sales and reduce marketing costs.

Newsgroups and newsletters often provide value-added methods of interaction. A newsgroup should receive something that is relevant to the products being sold. A newsletter is normally sent to a customer's e-mail account or is made available in a PDF file. Newsletters often contain information about the company, its products, and its activities.

## ✑ Promoting the Website

The final major ingredient in a website management program is promoting the site. Budgets for online advertising have steadily increased. Companies employ a variety of venues to promote a site, including banner ads, classified ads, media/video ads, search engine optimization, offline advertising, and consumer-generated advertising.

Banner ads account for a substantial percentage of advertising programs. Banners are placed on other sites and are exchanged with other organizations. Classified ads allow customers to shop for merchandise on major sites such as Craigslist. Media/video ads are place on mobile phones and other handheld devices.

Search engine optimization is the process of making certain a company's site appears prominently when a customer searches for a product or service. Three methods can be used. The first is a paid insertion. The second is the natural, organic emergence of the site. The third approach is to make use of paid search ads.

Offline advertising uses traditional methods of advertising to promote a site and attract customers to it. The process, also known as brand spiraling, helps more fully integrate any advertising or promotional campaign.

Consumer-generated advertising encourages individuals to make ads on behalf of a company. Several recent events have led to a great deal of publicity surrounding a contest that granted the winner air time at a major event, such as the Super Bowl.

## International Implications

Many of today's website management programs incorporate both domestic and international operations. The most basic problems to overcome, language and slang differences, can be addressed through careful translation and back-translation of content. Cultural assimilators make certain the use of colors, the portrayal of women and roles, religious symbols, and other matters of everyday life are presented in an appropriate fashion for each country. Often, methods of payment are adapted to the country or culture involved. Marketing managers take steps to protect intellectual property and address any legal restrictions on sites and content. As commerce becomes more global, the use of the Internet will continue to rise, and many companies have recognized the opportunities associated with more customers and target markets becoming available.

## The Cases

### The Entrepreneurs at Twitter: Building a Brand, a Social Tool, or a Tech Powerhouse?

Twitter is an easy-to-use, micro-blogging application, instant messenger, or social presence notifier. It relies on the simplicity of the 140-character tweet, or message, which does not need to be broken down to be transmitted. This, in turn, allows for nearly instant communication. Twitter reached a peak of 29 million users at one point but saw the number diminish to 24 million the next year. Investors had given the company nearly $150 million to start up, and the company was valued by some at more than $1 billion. The question remains as to whether Twitter is a great idea or potentially powerful new business.

### Anduro Marketing: Internet Services Vs. Software Sales

The essence of Anduro Marketing's key market offering had been a system to help companies make sure that a website would appear on the first two pages of any web search. Search engine optimization represents a key component of any Internet presence. The company experienced challenges in terms of cash flow from the time services were provided until payment was received; however, competitors were scarce and did not appear to compete directly with Anduro Marketing. The issue confronting the marketing managers at Anduro was the choice between remaining in the Internet services business (search engine optimization) and changing to a product-based business selling software packages that would allow companies to complete their own search engine optimization systems.

### Molson Canada: Social Media Marketing

Social media presents exciting new opportunities for various companies but also poses significant threats when improperly used. Molson Canada discovered this the hard way after creating a contest called "Cold Shot," which invited college students to post pictures of themselves enjoying beers and partying and then vote for the best party school in the country. Critics arose, suggesting the contest encouraged binge drinking and other irresponsible behaviors, including underage drinking.

The contest ended quickly, but the damage had been done. Molson executives wondered whether to continue to use social media in the future or take another route.

# The Entrepreneurs at Twitter: Building a Brand, a Social Tool, or a Tech Powerhouse?[1]

*By Ken Mark, under the supervision of Professor Simon Parker*

## Introduction

On February 9, 2010, a technology analyst working for a large Canadian bank was looking at Twitter as part of his analysis for an industry note on emerging technologies. Twitter is a micro blogging service that allows subscribers to send "tweets" of 140 characters or less to their "followers." It had been in the news as one of the hottest technology companies since Google and Facebook, and been cited as being an influential factor in socio-political events such as Senator Barack Obama's U.S. presidential campaign, as well as in political protests in Iran.

But Twitter's user numbers had fallen to 24 million by the end of 2009 after having peaked at 29 million in mid-2009. About half of Twitter's user base came from the United States.[2] The analyst wondered whether the drop in users was a blip or whether it signalled that Twitter needed to revisit its marketing strategy. After all, the service had attained its current level of popularity based on referrals, extensive (and free) media coverage, and the fact that it employed an open source platform, which encouraged the development of third-party applications by others.

While continuing to build a large user base was important, equally as interesting to many observers was how a company like Twitter planned to survive in the long run. Reminiscent of the dot-com start-ups in the late 1990s, Twitter had raised a total of $155 million from a consortium of investors in several rounds of funding—without having earned a single cent in profit.[3] The company was valued at US$1 billion following its latest round of funding.[4]

There continued to be much speculation over what the company would eventually adopt as a money-making business model, but Twitter was silent on specifics. Speaking about Twitter's business model, Ray Valdes, an analyst with Gartner Inc. commented:

> They have a dilemma. On the one hand, they need a robust revenue model. But they are also aware their perceived value is that they have a lot of potential. The moment they say one thing about their revenue model, whatever they choose will have a few limitations and risk associated with it. And that will diminish their perceived value.[5]

Twitter had an ambitious goal of reaching one billion users and earning over $1 billion in *net income* by 2013. The analyst wondered what steps the company needed to take to achieve those targets in three years.

## Company—History

Twitter founder's Evan Williams's early background hinted at the entrepreneurial path he would take. As a teenager growing up in Nebraska, he preferred the mental challenge of coming up with great business ideas to the physical demands of hunting or farming. Bored with university, he did not focus on a major and dropped out without completing his degree. He moved from job to job, pursuing entrepreneurial ideas on the side, but he struggled to follow through on any of his early projects, discarding them as soon

Version: (A) 2010–03–16

as a more alluring idea emerged. "It was turning into a constant pattern," recalled Williams.[6]

Looking to restart his career in 1996, Williams took a marketing job in Marin County before progressing to writing software code for large companies such as Intel and Hewlett-Packard. "For the first time, I learned what it was like to work in an office and have a normal career. To be in real meetings. I also learned that I did not want to do that," added Williams.[7]

In August 1999, several years before Twitter was founded, Williams and his friends were working as IT contractors on web projects during the day and thinking about their own Internet startup on the side. While in the midst of creating what they believed would be a much-sought after technology, they veered off-course on a whim, and ended up creating a landmark service that allowed Internet users to disseminate information to others, in real-time. With just a handful of employees, the company raised a small amount of venture capital and started releasing new versions of technology for free in order to build traction with users. As they reached a million users, competitors started to emerge. Less than four years after it started, the company had not yet generated any significant revenue and was not close to turning a profit. Even so, Google offered to buy it in exchange for stock, and Williams accepted the offer.

That company was Pyra Labs, the firm behind the blog creation tool Blogger.com, which was started in August 1999 and sold to Google in 2003. One of the business partners working on Blogger.com was Christopher Isaac "Biz" Stone, a fellow programmer whom Williams had met online. Stone had dropped out of college, lured by the prospect of designing book covers at Little, Brown Book Group. Soon after, he learned to write software code and design websites.[8]

Despite the fact that Pyra Labs had a willing buyer in Google, some observers were skeptical of the deal. Danny Sullivan of Search Engine Watch, for example, in an article titled "Google Buys Blogging Company—But Why?" speculated that "one chief reason Google has done this is for ad distribution reasons,"[9] which implied that Blogger.com, on its own, would not be profitable.

Williams stayed with Google until October 2004, and then launched a podcasting firm named Odeo, Inc. Podcasting—a play on the words "iPod" and "broadcasting"—i.e., the practice of recording and releasing digital media files via the web.

With just five people working from a walk-up apartment in San Francisco, Odeo's objective was to build a profitable company by building an "all-in-one system that makes it possible for someone with no more equipment than a telephone to produce podcasts," and "for users to assemble custom playlists of audio files and copy them directly onto MP3 audio players."[10] Williams commented: "Odeo aims to enable this new distribution channel and medium by creating the best one-source solution for finding, subscribing to, and publishing audio content."[11]

Once again, many observers were skeptical. A journalist commented in *The New York Times*:

> The question for Odeo, and for the many other entrepreneurial efforts almost certain to come, is whether there is any money to be made from podcasting. Recall that the dot-com boom was full of start-ups betting on one or another notion of the Web's potential. But for every felicitous pairing like Google and keyword searching, there were dozens of broken marriages like Pets.com and online dog food sales.[12]

Williams was undeterred as he saw huge potential in the podcasting industry. His excitement about the Odeo project and his belief that podcasting would become the next great technological medium convinced him to stay put on this particular path.[13]

Soon after Odeo shipped its major product, Odeo Studio, deep-pocketed competitors such as Apple, Inc. started to enter the market. In early 2006, faced with poor prospects for the company's future, Odeo's board of directors requested that Odeo revamp its strategy. It was during this period that one of Odeo's employees, an engineer called Jack Dorsey, presented an idea to the team that was based around a service that would enable users carrying standard cellular phones to update small groups of people on their current situation by pressing a few buttons and tapping out a message.

The key insight was that users would not need to enter the address of each recipient separately, every single time a message was to be sent. All the user had to do was enter a short numerical code before beginning the message. Odeo decided to adopt Dorsey's idea, initially for internal usage. At first, Odeo's team members kept the testing of the service close—no one affiliated with a large firm was allowed to participate in the test. By the spring of 2006, "Twttr Beta" was launched.

But Odeo's board was hard pressed to see the relevance of Twttr Beta and chose to conserve cash by trimming headcount. Six employees had their contracts terminated. Even so, in the midst of this turmoil, Twttr.com was made available to the public.

In an attempt to put more focus on this new project, Stone, Williams, Dorsey and their team set up Obvious Corp. in October 2006 to acquire the Twttr project. The URL www.twitter.com was acquired and the team rebranded the service.

## Twitter: How It Works

Twitter can be described as an easy-to-use, micro-blogging application, instant messenger or social presence notifier.[14] It is essentially a broadcasting system that allows users to transmit short bursts of information to lots of strangers as well as to friends. Twitter is built on open source software and allows users to send and receive messages to a mailing list of recipients ("followers") in real-time. Followers log on to Twitter and add themselves to an author's list of followers. To send a message to their list of followers, authors type in 140-character messages ("Tweets") via Twitter's website, by SMS (short message service) from cell phones, through an IM (instant messaging) client, through an RSS (really simple syndication) feed, or through third-party webtools. Authors can restrict their subscription lists to selected subscribers, or they can leave it open, which allows anyone to sign up to read their Tweets.

The original product name or codename for the service was "twttr," inspired by Flickr and the fact that American SMS short codes were five characters. From a technology perspective, Twitter is a web interface created using an "open source web application framework" called Ruby on Rails,[15] and using Starling as the primary message queue server.[16] Cell phone users can tweet using SMS, typing in one of five short telephone numbers—known as short codes—used to address SMS messages. There are short codes for the United States, Canada, India, and New Zealand and an Isle of Man-based number for international use.

The developers initially experimented with "10958" as a short code, but they later changed it to "40404"[17] for "ease of use and memorability."[18] Dorsey explained why the name "twitter" was chosen:

> The working name was just "Status" for a while. It actually didn't have a name. We were trying to name it, and mobile was a big aspect of the product early on. . . . We liked the SMS aspect, and how you could update from anywhere and receive from anywhere.
>
> We wanted to capture that in the name—we wanted to capture that feeling: the physical sensation that you're buzzing your friend's pocket. It's like buzzing all over the world. So we did a bunch of name-storming, and we came up with the word "twitch," because the phone kind of vibrates when it moves. But twitch is not a good product name because it doesn't bring up the right imagery. So we looked in the dictionary for words around it, and we came across the word "twitter" and it was just perfect. The definition was "a short burst of inconsequential information," and "chirps from birds." And that's exactly what the product was.[19]

Twitter is not a proprietary technology, as it offers the option of integrating other applications or web services with Twitter via an application programming interface (API).[20] APIs, which allow third-party software developers to build programs to interface with Twitter's data, were introduced by Twitter in September 2006.

An observer described how Twitter differed from online chat forums:

> We've all chatted online before—reserved our handle, entered a chatroom, and started

messaging away. Well, there are two problems with chat in that form. First, the chatroom is (usually) filled with strangers, and second, you must be logged into the chatroom to have access to messages. Twitter is essentially a net-based chatroom filled with your friends.[21]

Twitter also differs from Facebook, which has rapidly become the world's largest social networking site, counting over 350 million users worldwide. Facebook users can communicate with each other only by mutual consent, whereas anyone can log into Twitter and sign up to view any public tweets they like. Another difference between the two tools is that Facebook allows people to exchange videos and photos, whereas Twitter remains essentially text-based. For this reason, Stone has said that he sees a greater affinity between Twitter and Google than with Facebook, describing his business as an "information company."

## Promoting the Service

For the first six months of Twitter's existence, the company relied on its original users to become "personal evangelists" for the service.

By April 2007, Twitter.com was spun out of Obvious Corp. as its own company. A big break for the new Twitter came in March 2007, in Austin, at the South by Southwest festival. There, participants were able to see their tweets flash across television screens in real time. The number of tweets tripled to 60,000 per day, as participants talked about the service and the bloggers in attendance wrote about it.

Williams and his team were pleasantly surprised that their service was a hit. Referring to Twitter, he stated: "It took us a while to figure that it was a big deal."

Stone added: "I found myself watching groups of people twittering each other to coordinate their actions—which bar to go to, which speech to attend—and it was like seeing a flock of birds in motion."[22]

Building on the success at South by Southwest, Twitter added new features to its product such as RSS feeds and integration with IM. Each feature that was added boosted the number of users and usage per user.[23]

Over the next year and a half, Twitter's service was mentioned numerous times in the media. In addition, adoption of the service by new users came as a result of word-of-mouth promotion. As Twitter added employees, its founders marveled at the growing complexity of the organization. Stone stated: "We've never had a company that grew past 15 to 20 people. We're kind of excited about that."[24]

Organizations began to take note of Twitter's potential to reach out to a more technologically savvy audience. The service was especially valuable to small companies, with limited budgets, looking to gain recognition in the marketplace. With Twitter, these small firms could reach out and provide updates to a growing list of followers. Within larger organizations, there was the potential for managers to update and coordinate groups of employees. However, managers were aware of the downside as well—employees could be spending unnecessary amounts of time on the service.

Twitter gained in usage during the 2008 U.S. presidential campaign and was cited as a key tool during the 2008 attacks in Mumbai, India. During the Iranian presidential election, the popularity of Twitter as a tool used by protesters grew; participants relied on the service to coordinate their movements and to send message to the world outside Iran. Reliance on the service grew to such a point that Twitter delayed a 90-minute maintenance shutdown following a request from the U.S. State Department to keep the service available for the Iranian protesters.[25] In 2009, Twitter was constantly in the news. There were publicity stunts initiated by users, such as Ashton Kutcher's challenge to CNN in a "Twitter popularity contest"[26] and a Twitter name charity auction for "@drew," which attracted a US$1 million bid from comedian Drew Carey if he reached one million followers by the end of 2009.[27]

## Venture Capital Invests in Twitter

Seeking to capitalize on what seemed to be the next Google or Facebook, investors injected a total of $155 million into Twitter. Some investors in Twitter included Institutional Venture Partners, Benchmarks Capital, Union Square Ventures, Spark Capital, Digital Garage, Bezos Expeditions, and Insight

Venture Partners, among others. The latest round, completed at the end of September 2009, valued the company at US$1 billion.

Twitter's founders wanted to ensure that they had enough funds to continue building the company and supporting the millions of users who were using the service. Williams stated: "It was important to us that we find investment partners who share our vision for building a company of enduring value. Twitter's journey has just begun, and we are committed to building the best product, technology and company possible."[28]

David Garrity, principal of GVA Research LLC, stated: "It's interesting to see, almost 10 years since we had the first Internet bubble, that we've now got billion-dollar valuations on companies that haven't defined how they're going to monetize their traffic. It would be nice to see how the company is going to, one, generate revenues, and two, generate profits."[29]

Ellen Siminoff, a former Yahoo! Inc. executive who co-founded education the website Shmoop University Inc., disagreed, saying: "Where you have audiences, you will make money."[30]

Todd Chaffee, a Twitter board member and general partner at Institutional Venture Partners, one of Twitter's investors, suggested that e-commerce was an avenue the company could explore:

> Commerce-based search businesses monetize extremely well, and if someone says, "What treadmill should I buy?" then you, as the treadmill company, want to be there. As people use Twitter to get trusted recommendations from friends and followers on what to buy, e-commerce navigation and payments will certainly play a role in Twitter monetization. Over time, Twitter will develop filters to help users manage and classify their tweet streams into useful categories, such as tweets from friends, family, celebrities, news organizations, charities.[31]

Co-founder Stone suggested that Twitter would begin adding services for businesses to generate fees in the fourth quarter of 2009. At a Twitter management team meeting in April 2009, the team discussed licensing tweets to partners: "We can give people stuff for free, but not forever."[32]

Another potential route to realize value in the firm would be to somehow emulate Skype, an Internet telephone service that offers users "free and great value" calls. Skype has gained in popularity by offering users free Internet calls, and has now started to charge fees for certain connections while retaining free Skype-to-Skype calls. Skype has gained a critical mass of users and sold itself to eBay in 2005 for US$2.6 billion in up-front cash and eBay stock, and performance-based options.[33] By 2009, Skype was thought to be generating approximately US$600 million a year in revenues. That year, eBay changed its strategy, selling a controlling stake in Skype in a deal that valued the service at US$2.75 billion in 2009.

## Twitter's Business Model— Still in Question

Documents uncovered by hackers and posted on TechCrunch, with Twitter's (reluctant) approval, revealed, among other things, that Twitter was aiming to be more than just a micro-blogging service. One of the slides laid out in Twitter's strategy notes read as follows:

- Number of users?
- Be the first to one billion.
- Audience size: first to a billion = Awesome
- If we had a billion users, that will be the pulse of the planet.
- Are we building a new Internet?

Twitter described a "user" as being "a unique individual having a conscious twitter experience in a given week."[34] The types of revenue models being talked about were still very broad: business-to-business services; e-commerce, especially retailing recommended products; and advertising.

The technology analyst looked at Twitter's financial forecast and saw that, by 2013, Twitter expected to reach one billion users, employ 5,200 people, and earn net earnings of US$1.1 billion on revenues of US$1.54 billion. The estimate for 2009 and 2010 is shown here in Exhibit 1.[35]

**Exhibit 1** Twitter's Forecast Financials as Posted on TechCrunch

| | 2009 | | | | 2010 | | | |
|---|---|---|---|---|---|---|---|---|
| | Q1 | Q2 | Q3 | Q4 | Q1 | Q2 | Q3 | Q4 |
| Users in Millions | 8 | 12 | 16 | 25 | 35 | 48 | 72 | 100 |
| Revenue | $0 | $0 | $400,000 | $4,000,000 | $8,000,000 | $17,000,000 | $53,000,000 | $62,000,000 |
| Total Yearly | | | | $4,400,000 | | | | $140,000,000 |
| Number of Employees | 30 | 45 | 60 | 78 | 120 | 197 | 275 | 345 |
| | | | | Target: 65 | | | | Target: 500 |
| People Costs | $1,050,000 | $1,575,000 | $2,100,000 | $2,730,000 | $4,200,000 | $6,895,000 | $9,625,000 | $12,075,000 |
| Organization Costs | $2,030,000 | $3,045,000 | $4,060,000 | $6,343,750 | $8,881,250 | $12,180,000 | $18,270,000 | $25,375,000 |
| Gross Margin | $43,950,000 | $39,330,000 | $33,570,000 | $28,496,250 | $23,415,000 | $21,340,000 | $46,445,000 | $70,995,000 |
| Net Earnings | $28,567,500 | $25,564,500 | $21,820,500 | $18,522,563 | $15,219,750 | $13,871,000 | $30,189,250 | $46,146,750 |

The technology analyst wondered how the company planned to generate those numbers. For a better idea of which path the firm was likely to take, the analyst referred back to an internal Twitter document that talked about how the firm perceived and defined itself. In addition, the document described, in point form, how Twitter wanted to differentiate itself from its closest competitors, Facebook and Google (see Exhibit 2).

It was evident that Twitter had set very high targets for itself. Despite the firm's ambitions, the analyst suspected that Twitter would be eventually pressured by its investors to deliver a return on investment. In contrast, Twitter's founders did not seem to have an urgent need to develop a financial plan as they believed they had patient investors. Recognizing that the company had cash in the bank, Stone stated: "We are enamored with the idea of going all the way." Williams added: "We want to have as large an impact as possible."[36]

But even as the team was trying to find ways to generate revenues, Williams revealed to a

| Exhibit 2 | What's Twitter, the Company? |

- Facebook – social network
- Google – search engine
- Twitter is for discovering and sharing what is happening right now (Do other people describe Twitter in this way?)
- Twitter is the most varied communication network.
- Twitter introduced a new form of communication to the world.
- Twitter is an index to my friends' thoughts and I subscribe to that.
- The way to find out what's happening
- The way to share what's happening
- Google is old news.

*Source:* http://www.techcrunch.com/2009/07/16/twitters-internal-strategy-laid-bare-to-be-the-pulse-of-the-planet/, accessed March 2, 2010.

journalist that he was already thinking of his next "big" idea—how to revolutionize e-mail.[37]

## What Will Twitter's Future Look Like?

The technology analyst wondered how Twitter's growth could justify its current valuation. According to the internal documents, Twitter was looking to generate US$4 million in revenues by the end of 2009, and US$62 million by the end of 2010. Twitter, according to reports, had exceeded its 2009 revenue target by signing a non-exclusive deal with Google and Microsoft to provide these companies' search engines with access to real-time Twitter feeds. Based on an estimated value of $25 million in revenue from Microsoft and from other search deals, Twitter could have turned profitable in 2009.[38] But becoming barely profitable was not sufficient. Josh Bernoff, an analyst at Forrester Research, commented:

> By the end of 2010, Twitter will either have a business model capable of generating $100 million in revenue or it will get bought. This is not a company whose ambition is to be small and profitable. They are looking at a world where one billion people are Twittering. You have to be able to make money from that.[39]

But whether Twitter could achieve one billion users remained to be seen. According to Compete, a web analytics firm, Twitter's growth had peaked in July 2009 at just over 29 million global users per month, falling steadily over the next five months to under 24 million users per month by the end of 2009.[40] Another research firm, eMarketer, estimated Twitter's abandonment rate to be 60 percent after the first month.[41]

In addition, competitors had started to emerge, offering functionality that was unavailable from Twitter. Friendfeed allowed users to send text messages as well as import information from their blogs, Flickr photos, and YouTube videos. Identi.ca, another micro-blogging service, made its source code freely available, allowing users to create their own micro-blogging service. Present.ly, which was designed specifically for businesses, allowed companies to create their own micro-blogging network on its service and separate users into groups.[42]

In an attempt to win market share in this growing space, larger, more established companies have rolled out free services as well. In 2008, Facebook attempted to purchase Twitter for $500 million in Facebook stock, but Twitter's management team rejected the offer. After these takeover talks were abandoned, Facebook introduced several Twitter-like changes to its service, including updating users' home pages to allow them to provide real-time updates to friends. Facebook also gave more visibility to its pages for celebrities and other high-profile figures and lifted the ceiling on the maximum number of online fans they could have on the site.

Finally, in early February 2010, Google launched a Twitter competitor called "Google Buzz," which, among other things, allowed users to post updates in real time by using their mobile phones.[43] Google earned the bulk of its income from selling advertising and made no money from Google Buzz. Twitter aimed to enlist developers in creating applications for its service by highlighting its open source philosophy. In February 2010, Twitter launched a directory of all the open source projects on which Twitter employees were working or contributing.[44]

The technology analyst sat down at his desk and sifted through the rest of the news reports on Twitter. He switched on his computer and started to write down some conclusions about Twitter's potential impact and the challenges the firm could face as it tried to fend off other firms encroaching on its space. He wanted to make an educated guess at what the company's service represented to users, its likely business strategy, and how it planned to survive in the long-run.

---

## CASE QUESTIONS

1. Can Twitter be used to accentuate or replace some of the web functions for a company employing it to reach customers and potential customers? If so, how?

2. Should Twitter focus on advertising on the site or find some other method to generate revenues? If so, what methods should the company employ?

3. How should Twitter respond to other, new micro-blogging websites?

4. Does Twitter have a future as a business? Why or why not?

---

# Anduro Marketing: Internet Services Vs. Software Sales

### By Malcolm Munro and Sid Huff

"The revenue potential in developing this new software is huge—but the whole thing is risky. We could take the entire company down if we're wrong." Jeff Nelson, president of Anduro Marketing (Anduro), pondered a critical step in the future of the company. Anduro Marketing was a successful Internet marketing company located in Calgary, Canada. Amid the many web development companies in the

Copyright © 2007, Ivey Management Services                                           Version: (A) 2007–09–28

The Richard Ivey School of Business gratefully acknowledges Malcolm Munro at the Haskayne School of Business, University of Calgary, and Sid Huff at the School of Information Management, Victoria University of Wellington, in the development of this learning material.

market place, Anduro carved out a different niche, offering a variety of technical services to provide greater visibility for company websites. Nelson and his business partner Damon James started the company five years earlier and now had six employees and a growing list of increasingly high profile clients.

Anduro's future was bright. But Nelson and James had concluded that many of the technical services they offered—keyword tracking, link building, web statistics analysis, and a host of equally arcane functions—could be built into a pair of comprehensive website management and web marketing "software suites." Their vision was to develop the software and either sell the software suites directly to clients, or provide their clients access to the software via an application service provider subscription model—a decision to be made later.

Gradually expanding the company in its current form was a proven, safe, and profitable strategy—the market for Internet services expanded monthly. Still, bringing in outside investors and developing the software was an enticing option with the possibility of substantial additional profits. But some tough questions loomed. Was there really a market for such software products? Was Anduro better off in the long run selling Internet services than technology? Was the venture too risky—could Anduro survive if this project failed? Nelson realized this was a major fork in the road for the company and he needed to move very carefully.

## Background

Jeff Nelson was born in Uganda, the oldest of four siblings. His father was a surgeon, his mother a home economist. The family returned to Canada in 1972 as Jeff prepared to enter junior high school. Nelson later attended the University of Alberta where he earned a BA in recreation administration, thus acquiring the education he felt he would need to pursue his interest in outdoor recreation— running summer camps and the like. But during one class, a speaker referred to recreation as a thera-

peutic tool in hospitals. Nelson found the idea intriguing and developed his early career in this field for the next eight years. During this time he also started a recreational therapy company. While the company failed, Nelson discovered that he liked the idea of running a business. Along the way, while working at a hospital, he had access to a Mac computer and acquired a taste for technology.

He decided eventually to further his education and pondered law versus business. Concluding that he liked the creative opportunities that a business career presented, he enrolled in the evening MBA program at the University of Calgary. His MBA studies initially had a recreational focus but later he switched to marketing. On finishing his MBA, Nelson took a marketing job with Magellan Systems, a company involved in creating CD-ROM-based company catalogs, "leading edge stuff at the time," according to Nelson. The Magellan experience taught him about marketing, sales, and more about technology.

Jobs with several other technology companies followed. While working at one of these firms, Impact Blue, during the pre-Google era, Nelson listened to a presentation about search engines, and this was the first time he really became aware how companies could market their companies online. The idea that tinkering with the source code on a website could make a big difference to finding a webpage was "like a light bulb going on." He quickly saw that search engines were going to have a big impact on Internet marketing. When Impact Blue went out of business in 2001, Nelson teamed up with Damon James, another former Impact Blue employee. James' technical background nicely complemented Nelson's marketing expertise. Nelson and James decided to start their own web technology company—right at the start of the dotcom crash!

Damon James graduated from the multimedia program at Lethbridge Community College. Before becoming an Anduro partner, he worked for about three years for web design and technology companies such as Impact Blue and Big Picture. At Anduro he specialized in the technical aspects of website development but had a strong interest in search engine optimization. He also brought some entrepreneurial experience to the table, having previously started two companies of his own. One was Student Painters Canada that employed students during the summers. Damon sold off his share in that company but launched a second company called Ashen Films, a feature film production company that he continued to own and operate on the side.

Nelson and James initially called their company Anduro Technologies. The name Anduro was contrived. They wanted a name that was short and easy to type. Starting it with the letter "A" meant it would be listed higher on directories. They also thought the word conveyed a sense of authority, skill, and lasting value. They did an online search of names to ensure the name was not in use, eventually changing it to Anduro Marketing, which they felt better communicated their core activity. Financing for the business consisted of Nelson's bank account of $200 and an "advance on my inheritance from my parents," to get them through the lean startup months. Nelson served as Anduro's president and James as vice-president operations.

Finding and keeping good sales people was a challenge. Anduro employed several sales staff over the years and tried different compensation schemes but Nelson described it as "a constant issue and difficult to manage." Eventually Anduro appointed Matt Olah, a former supplier and competitor, as VP business development and another salesperson to do mostly cold calling on a part-time basis. Olah's experience in the field enabled him to close sales and perform well.

Early on, Nelson and James established business relationships with several companies and individuals as "referral sources" for their services. Referrers were on a commission-only basis, meaning that Nelson and James had no financial commitment beyond the commission for sales actually generated.

## Getting Established in the Internet Marketing World

Nelson and James saw that competition in the area of Internet marketing was fragmented and scattered. Oddly, most website development companies had yet to become involved in the Internet marketing segment of the industry. Instead such companies focused on building user friendly websites integrated with complicated databases; these websites also allowed content to be managed by users. At the same time, companies directly involved in search engine optimization usually relied on only one or two methods of generating traffic. Anduro found its niche by providing a broad range of offerings and services combining marketing and web design disciplines to create a full-service Internet marketing company. Nelson and James established the business in Calgary, a city with a highly educated workforce and a rapidly expanding high-tech community. In the first two years, Anduro signed contracts with more than 70 companies.

Nelson observed that there were three important drivers for the industry. First, he regarded Google as an important driver since it provided the world with lightning speed access to information. The search characteristics of Google and other search engines had given rise to the "keyword marketing" industry. Another important driver was high-speed Internet access: more and more people worldwide were subscribing to Internet access through either cable or ADSL. Anduro's local market, Calgary, was especially strong in this regard. Lastly, Nelson pointed to the significant change in the way consumers and buyers were using search engines to gather information before purchasing goods and services. Instead of relying on direct advertising, increasing numbers of customers were now actively seeking information about companies, products and services on their own, using Internet search engines such as Google, Yahoo!, and MSN. Nelson's plan was to grow the firm by leveraging the above industry drivers.

Initially operating out of a business incubator facility, Anduro focused on small to medium-sized businesses, including start-ups. Servicing a variety of clients with differing levels of sophistication and marketing budgets allowed Anduro to establish an excellent reputation and gain valuable experience (see Exhibit 1). Nelson then set about to expand the customer base by developing an aggressive targeted marketing campaign. Eventually Anduro signed up

| Exhibit 1 | A Diverse Partial Selection of Anduro Clients |
|---|---|
| Azusa Pacific University | www.apu.edu |
| Bernard Callebaut Chocolaterie | www.bernardcallebaut.com |
| Budco: The Dialogue Company | www.budco.com |
| Burger Boat Company | www.burgerboat.com |
| Bust Loose | www.bustloose.com |
| Canada Tourism Commission | www.canadatourism.com |
| Cash Advance.com | www.cashadvance.com |
| Enmax Corp. | www.enmax.com |
| Haskayne School of Business | www.haskayne.ucalgary.ca |
| Street Characters Inc. | www.mascots.com |
| NovAtel Inc. | www.novatel.com |
| Paisley | www.paisley.com |
| Syncrude Canada Limited | www.syncrude.ca |
| TeraGo Networks Inc. | www.terago.ca |
| Travel Alberta | www.travelalberta.com |

For a more complete list, see http://www.anduro.com/clients-industry.html.

such major high-profile clients as Syncrude Canada Ltd. (a giant oil sands mining company), Enmax Corporation (a Calgary city-owned energy distribution company), and Novatel Inc. (a leading provider of global navigation satellite systems components). Repeat business and referrals made up a significant portion of sales.

## The Anduro Business Model

Nelson explained their business model this way:

People refer to the Internet as the "information highway." There's a huge amount of traffic going back and forth. Just imagine that you started your little company a few blocks off the road. No one on that highway will ever see you or even know you are there. Our objective is to either draw the traffic directly to your company or pull your company right up onto the highway!

Anduro used a free "10 Point Inspection" as a unique and effective marketing vehicle and "attention grabber." The inspection could be done quickly, and enabled clients to easily grasp the value of Anduro's services.

Another key to generating sales was a specially designed spreadsheet referred to as a calculation sheet. "With only the client's URL, we can do an examination of their entire website in a few minutes." With a wry smile Nelson admitted that he sometimes delayed providing the work estimate to the client for at least a day to avoid giving the mistaken impression that business was so slow they had nothing to do but provide quick estimates! But the reality was "we can prepare a complete estimate in approximately half an hour."

The calculation sheet was the core document in generating the sale, organizing the work, managing the project, tracking the billable hours, and securing payment from the client. The spreadsheet specified the various Internet services Anduro provided, and from past experience Anduro had developed flat rates for each activity. In effect, this was akin to having one's car serviced with the mechanic charging a flat rate for each piece of work regardless of the amount of time taken. In preparing the quote for each individual client, spreadsheet lines for which no work was required were deleted from the spreadsheet, and the remaining spreadsheet was pasted directly into a form letter, which was then further edited for the individual client (see Exhibits 2a and 2b). As the actual work was completed, time was billed to each project according to the categories on the spreadsheet. Substantial changes were subject to additional charges but minor changes were provided free of charge. Anduro's accounting system enabled them to track the profit generated, accuracy of estimates, accounts receivables, and so on for each

**Exhibit 2a** Portion of Typical Anduro Calculation Sheet

| H Deliverable | I Quantity | J Units | K Estimated Hours | L Estimated Fee | M 3rd Party Fees |
|---|---|---|---|---|---|
| **Strategy & Baseline** | | | | | |
| Discovery Phase | 0 | Hours | 0.0 | $0 | |
| Website Analytics Report | I | Hours | 7.0 | $495 | |
| Strategy Planning Session | I | Hours | 1.0 | $150 | |
| **Natural Traffic** | | | | | |
| High Performance Keywords | 15 | Keywords | 5.0 | $750 | |
| Baseline Positioning Report | I | Reports | 0.5 | $75 | |
| Source Code Recommendations | 5 | Pages | 5.0 | $750 | |
| Website Optimization | 0 | | 0.0 | By Client | |
| eSignpost Content Pages | 5 | Pages | 20.0 | $3,000 | |
| Set-up Google Analytics | 0 | Hours | 0.0 | $0 | |
| Yahoo! Search Submit | 5 | Pages | 0.5 | $75 | $59 |
| Verify Website with Google SiteMaps | 0 | Submission | 0.0 | $0 | |
| Create a Glossary Page | 0 | Definitions | 0.0 | $0 | |
| Add 404 Re-direct to Server | 0 | Re-directs | 0.0 | $0 | |
| **Link Quality** | | | | | |
| Registration with Major Directories | II | Directories | 2.8 | $413 | $550 |
| Article Syndication | 0 | Sites | 0.0 | $0 | $0 |
| Initial Research for Link Purchasing | 0 | Hours | 0.0 | $0 | $0 |
| Peer-to-Peer Chat on Forums | 0 | Campaign | 0.0 | $0 | $0 |
| Froogle Set-up | 0 | Hours | 0.0 | $0 | |
| Links Page for Out-bound Links | 0 | Hours | 0.0 | $0 | |
| **Banner Advertising** | | | | | |
| Researching Sites | 0 | Hours | 0.0 | $0 | $0 |
| Creative for Banner Ads | Depends | Ads | 0.0 | $0 | $0 |
| Media Buys/Placement | 0 | Hours | 0.0 | $0 | $0 |
| Meetings | 0 | Hours | 0.0 | $0 | $0 |
| Reporting | 0 | Hours | 0.0 | $0 | $0 |
| **eMedia Communications** | | | | | |
| Optimized Press Release | 0 | Submission | 0.0 | $0 | $0 |
| Writing the Press Release | 0 | Releases | 0.0 | $0 | |

*(Continued)*

**Exhibit 2a**    (Continued)

| H Deliverable | I Quantity | J Units | K Estimated Hours | L Estimated Fee | M 3rd Party Fees |
|---|---|---|---|---|---|
| Develop HTML Template | 0 | Template | 0.0 | $0 | |
| Set-up eNewsletter System | 0 | System | – | $0 | |
| **Project Management** | | | | | |
| Search Engine Positioning Report | I | Reports | 0.5 | $75 | |
| Review Meeting | I | Hours | 1.0 | $150 | |
| Project Management (10%) | | Hours | 3.6 | $544 | |
| **Totals for Initial Work** | | | **39.9** | **$6,476** | **$609** |

**Exhibit 2b**    Excerpt From Client Letter Including Data From Calculation Sheet

## Estimate for Online Marketing Program

We know that you want visitor traffic to your website as soon as possible. The best way to start an online marketing campaign is to develop a solid strategy. In the strategy we will select the action steps that will generate the most traffic from various online sources to your website.

*Initial project*

The initial project would include the following deliverables:

| Deliverable | Quantity | Units | Estimated Hours | Estimated Fee | 3rd Party Fees |
|---|---|---|---|---|---|
| **Strategy & Baseline** | | | | | |
| Website Analytics Report | I | Hours | 7.0 | $495 | |
| Strategy Planning Session | I | Hours | 1.0 | $150 | |
| **Natural Traffic** | | | | | |
| High Performance Keywords | 15 | Keywords | 5.0 | $750 | |
| Baseline Positioning Report | I | Reports | 0.5 | $75 | |
| Source Code Recommendations | 5 | Pages | 5.0 | $750 | |
| Website Optimization | 0 | | 0.0 | By Client | |
| eSignpost Content Pages | 5 | Pages | 20.0 | $3,000 | |
| Yahoo! Search Submit | 5 | Pages | 0.5 | $75 | $59 |

| Deliverable | Quantity | Units | Estimated Hours | Estimated Fee | 3rd Party Fees |
|---|---|---|---|---|---|
| **Link Quality** | | | | | |
| Registration With Major Directories | 11 | Directories | 2.8 | $413 | $550 |
| **Project Management** | | | | | |
| Search Engine Positioning Report | 1 | Reports | 0.5 | $75 | |
| Review Meeting | 1 | Hours | 1.0 | $150 | |
| Project Management (10%) | | Hours | 3.6 | $544 | |
| **Totals for Initial Work** | | | **39.9** | **$6,476** | **$609** |

*Monthly Ongoing Improvements*

If required, a program to maintain improvements on an ongoing basis will be determined at a later date. Typically, this would include a stronger link-buying campaign and other measures to improve the power of the website and its capability to rank higher for more competitive keyword phrases.

individual project. Companies appreciated Anduro's fixed price approach for professional services, as it enabled them to budget for the expenditure and avoid surprises when they received their invoices.

## Marketing Anduro's Services

Anduro believed that establishing credibility and rapport with clients was critical. Consequently, their most effective means of making a sale was through relationship selling. Since identifying promising clients could be a time-consuming process, Anduro relied on a local call center to create quality leads. Anduro managers also invested considerable time in personal networking by attending various functions each month to create exposure, increase awareness, and generate leads. To establish a referral network, Anduro created formal partnerships with several complementary technology services companies. If a referred business became a client, Anduro paid the referring company a referral fee. Anduro eventually established strategic alliances with 16 other technology companies.

Public relations efforts took the form of presentations to service clubs, writing newspaper and magazine articles, and competing for awards to create a positive company image and establish credibility. Anduro developed a media kit that was sent to local media outlets explaining the Internet marketing business. This was done in part to counter some of the negative image that stuck to the industry in the wake of the dot-com crash that occurred in 2000–2002. This tactic proved successful in gaining access to radio talk shows and small business publications. Finally, Nelson produced a monthly online newsletter that was distributed to their customers and served as a reminder of their presence.

## Anduro's Competition

In Nelson's view, Anduro's only direct competition in Calgary, perhaps even in western Canada, was another local company known as Found-Pages. Perhaps due to the referral nature of the business however, Nelson said that Anduro and FoundPages had never "gone head-to-head" over a contract. Nelson said that some web development companies had claimed they could do the same work as Anduro but he doubted if any, even in the whole of Western Canada, could justify this claim. There were some aspects of the business that were easy to do but when things got complicated, it required a high level of expertise that Nelson asserted most web developers simply didn't have in-house. There were many companies in the United States offering such services but Anduro was still able to draw business from there. As a result of Anduro's focused "relationship selling" approach, Anduro got a lot of business from repeat customers, and secured all of the business of its technology partners.

In short, Nelson was not losing any sleep worrying about the competition. But managing cash flow was a constant concern. Anduro's normal contracts required a 50 percent payment up front and the balance when the work was completed. Collecting receivables was often a slow matter, however, since many companies took 60 days or longer to make payment. In addition many companies took a long time to complete their action items, which delayed some projects. For a small company with a payroll to meet, and the business being somewhat seasonal anyway, cash flow was a matter for continuous attention.

## The Anduro Product Line

Imagine that a retailer set up a website to sell electronic amusements for children. Typing the words "electronic amusements for children" into Google provided a listing of 1,160,000 web pages in 0.12 seconds. However, unless the retailer's website appeared in the first 20 or so sites on the list, the merchant would receive almost no traffic from the search engine because few people read past the first page or two of listings. This is where Anduro came in.

The goal of Anduro was to boost a company's website onto the first page or two of the various search engine listings for specific keyword phrases. In business community presentations Nelson selected five items to illustrate a quick preliminary website diagnosis. In less than five minutes, using any URL provided by the audience, Nelson could show: (1) the number of pages archived by Google for that website; (2) the number of back links, which are links from other sites to the site; (3) the volume of daily traffic to the site and its traffic ranking; (4) the Google PageRank that represented a website's importance; and (5) the names of the search engines that listed the website. Like a mechanic checking the oil level, tire pressure, and compression test, Nelson was able to quickly develop a preliminary picture of the "performance" of the website using these website "vital signs" (see Exhibit 3).

A key competitive advantage Anduro brought to the marketplace was its intimate knowledge of how the various search engines' algorithms worked to determine the order in which pages were listed. Search engines based their listing order on dozens of factors, but keywords, number of links to a website and the "quality" or relevance of such links, were particularly important. To

---

**Exhibit 3** | 5 Point Inspection

✖ anduro marketing                          **5 Point Inspection**

- **Pages on Google:**
  - site: www.mysite.com
- **Backlinks on Yahoo!:**
  - siteexplorer.search.yahoo.com
- **Alexa Traffic Rank:**
  - www.alexa.com
- **Google PageRank:**
  - www.seochat.com/seo-tools/pagerank-lookup/
- **# of Search Engines Listed:**
  - www.marketleap.com/verify/default.htm

complicate matters, individual search engines employed differing ranking criteria, and such criteria changed frequently as processes and technology evolved. The goal of a search engine was to return a set of results as relevant as possible to the user's interests. The goal of Anduro was to ensure that its clients' web pages appeared at or near the top of the listing in a search engine's results whenever a search relevant to the client's product line occurred.

Anduro provided the following services:

1. Strategy and Baseline Services: this included the 10 Point Inspection Service, competitor analysis from an Internet marketing perspective, and an Ongoing Maintenance Plan that provided monthly reports tracking Key Performance Indicators.

2. Pay-per-Click Advertising Services: Anduro would set up an account on selected pay-per-click search engines to drive traffic to a client site whenever particular keywords were searched for.

3. Search Engine Keyword Marketing: High-performance keyword research, source code optimization, and special eSignpost (an Anduro term) content pages to deal with a variety of web development techniques that were not search engine-friendly, to improve the success of search engine acceptance.

4. Link Quality: this consisted of an evaluation of all inbound links to help improve the "relevance" or "authority" of the site on major search engines, and to increase exposure of the website in niche areas.

5. Other services including an optimized Internet press release, and electronic newsletter management in which Anduro enabled a client to set up and create an informative company electronic newsletter, including the means to automate all new subscriptions and deal with un-subscribers.

See Exhibit 4 for links to websites that provide glossaries of website terminology; see Exhibit 5 and the Anduro website at www.anduro.com for greater detail on the above services.

Nelson used the term "productizing" to describe Anduro's practice of charging flat rates for individual services and packages of services, essentially creating a set of discrete products. Examples were the Deluxe Instant Traffic Package, Home Page Optimization Package, and Internet Marketing Analysis Package, typical services that included the 10 Point Internet Marketing Inspection, pay-per-click keywords, and competitor analyses.

Anduro's business thrived and the company moved to attractive offices in a busy, trendy area close to downtown. The building into which they relocated was a hotbed of high technology companies, and several of Anduro's own business partners shared the generous upscale reception area and related office facilities with Anduro.

| **Exhibit 4** | Search Engine Terminology Glossaries |
|---|---|

http://www.sempo.org/learning_center/sem_glossary/

http://www.zeromillion.com/webmarketing/search-engine-glossary.html

http://www.mcanerin.com/EN/search-engine/glossary.asp

http://www.searchengineguide.com/whalen/2002/1205_jw1.html

For a listing of all Search Engine Glossaries:

http://searchenginewatch.com/showPage.html?page=2161401

| **Exhibit 5** | Anduro Marketing Home Page |
|---|---|

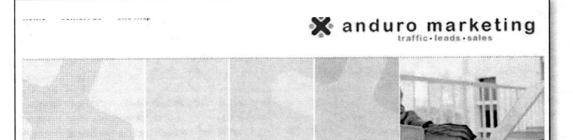

## anduro marketing
traffic·leads·sales

> Services
> Products
> Resources

> Our Company
> Our Clients
> Our Partners

Sign up for Our
Monthly Newletter

See our
Proof of Results

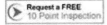
Request a FREE
10 Point Inspection

2006 MEMBER
sma
NORTH AMERICA
BOARD MEMBER

ADWORDS
QUALIFIED
PROFESSIONAL
Google

YAHOO! SEARCH MARKETING
AMBASSADOR

### welcome to anduro marketing

**Anduro Marketing** provides effective Internet Marketing strategies designed to increase the visibility of a company, its website, and the products and services it offers. We work with our clients to do more than increase traffic to their sites. We build strategic partnerships that deliver targeted leads and increased sales.

There are many reasons to begin an online marketing campaign, and Anduro Marketing can help you understand how to not only increase your rankings on the search engines, but how to improve your conversions so you realize the ultimate benefit: increased sales.

When choosing an Internet marketing company it is important to find a company that has the experience and the flexibility to customize its services to your unique situation. Anduro Marketing tailors its offerings to our clients' needs so each client achieves its online marketing goals. Our capabilities include optimized content creation, natural search engine optimization, paid search campaigns, e-newsletters, link building, and more. One size indeed does not fit all, and Anduro Marketing is your trusted partner who can guide your company to online success.

*seo-browser.com*™

### Anduro News

- **January, 2007**
  Anduro Marketing Signs Enmax Corporation (Enmax).

- **January, 2007**
  Anduro Marketing Signs the Canada Tourism Commission.

- **December, 2006**
  Invitation: Anduro Marketing Chistmas Party, Five Year Anniversary.

### Services

- **Strategy & Baseline**
  Critical planning procedures to assess website strategies and metrics

- **Pay-Per-Click Traffic**
  Generate instant & valuable traffic through Pay-per-Click campaigns

- **Natural Traffic**
  Allow potential customers to find your website naturally

- **Link Quality**
  Build authority & relevance through link building campaigns

- **Other Services**
  From press releases to eNewsletters, Anduro offers many additional services

## A New Strategic Opportunity

Nelson and James recognized that many of Anduro's technical services were highly structured and hence amenable to automation. They foresaw the possibility that a better-financed company might exploit this potential vulnerability. They also noted that Anduro relied heavily on third-party companies to deliver several of its core consulting services. Consequently, some of the company's principal offerings were subject to the business and pricing whims of these other firms. Furthermore, as a small company Anduro experienced periodic cash flow problems from longer than anticipated sales cycles, low margins on loss-leader offerings, delays in accounts receivables, and occasional downturns in the business cycle.

Nelson and James considered whether they could reduce these risks and business problems by making a pre-emptive strategic move. They reasoned that if their broad range of services could be appropriately packaged into "software suites," Anduro would not only be somewhat more cost effective in providing such services to their own clients, but the software could also either be sold or leased to clients who preferred to do their own Internet marketing. Overall, such software would create a significant barrier to entry for new competitors, reduce Anduro's reliance on third-party

suppliers, and ameliorate Anduro's cash flow problems by generating additional revenue year-round. Though there were numerous competitors for each of Anduro's individual services, Nelson and James felt that an integrated comprehensive software package would firmly establish Anduro as the industry leader.

Nelson and James prepared a formal business plan to attract outside investors to finance the development of two major software suites to automate the full range of Anduro's services. The two new products were called the Website Management Suite and the e-Marketing Suite. Website Management would enable a customer to manage the content on their website, send out eNewsletters, design and offer surveys, and sell products. eMarketing would provide tools enabling subscribers to increase qualified traffic to their websites and measure the results, i.e., search engine marketing. With the eMarketing suite, Anduro would target a variety of web design professionals including webmasters in-house staff of web design companies, and e-commerce companies that might consider offering Anduro's software to their own clients. Each suite would provide a scalable solution, in that clients could either select different packages of services or pick and choose their own tools according to their needs (see Exhibits 6a and 6b). For larger clients or perhaps those desiring a custom solution, Anduro would continue to offer consulting services

---

**Exhibit 6a**  Website Management Suite

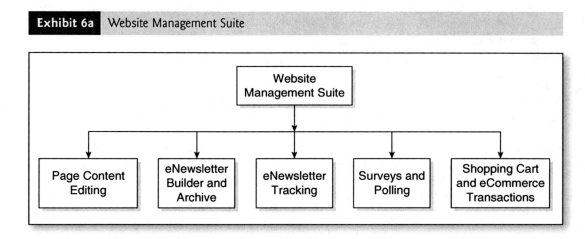

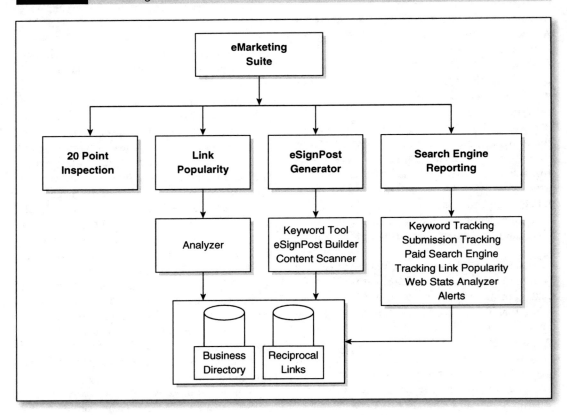

in conjunction with selling the software suite. For getting the software into their customers' hands, Nelson and James favored an application service provider (ASP) subscription model as opposed to selling a software product using a physical sales and distribution channel. A final decision would be made during the research and development (R&D) phase.

From their detailed projections Nelson and James determined that to research, develop, market and improve the Website Management and eMarketing Suites, $400,000[1] of investment capital was required. They forecasted the revenue from the Website Management and eMarketing Suites to grow to more than $6 million per year within five years with growth at roughly 100 percent

per year and breaking even in two years from the start of software development. The software development itself would be outsourced to a local company.

## Software or Services?

The potential revenue flow from sales of the new software suites could be huge. The newness and complexity of the web environment, and its expansion worldwide, generated seemingly endless opportunities. But Nelson also realized that getting into software development and sales would fundamentally change Anduro Marketing. Anduro would have to evolve from a company oriented around providing services into one in which the focus would be on developing and selling technology solutions. Furthermore, if his projections were accurate, Anduro would become heavily financially reliant on these activities. Rapid shifts in technology also presented inherent risks to any company working in the software industry. In order to reduce the risk of obsolescence, Anduro would have to aggressively research and develop new technologies and products. The ever-changing Internet would guarantee that continuing investments in R&D to maintain and upgrade the software would be necessary for survival. Ongoing reviews of competitors, suppliers, and technology shifts within the industry would be imperative for maintaining an advantage over the competition. In short, if Anduro were to be successful, it would have to adopt a very different business model. Nelson and James would have to acquire a whole new set of management skills.

Both Nelson and James had reservations. They reflected on the countless number of now-forgotten companies that had cast their fate in this direction; but they also thought about the few mind-boggling exceptions. In the short term, what if the software took longer to develop than planned? In a company in which meeting the payroll depended on monthly cash flow, additional capital and resources would likely be required to complete the project. Anduro could attempt to meet these additional costs through the maintenance and continued nurturing of its current business but it would be imperative

to attain full efficiency and maximum profitability before undertaking the software project. Otherwise, Anduro might have to face the daunting task of pursuing other outside investors to raise additional funding for a software project already in trouble.

For the longer term they pondered the ongoing interest in the market place for this very special kind of software. Internet marketing directors, a prime target for this software, might prefer to outsource activities such as search engine optimization and focus instead on the creative side, i.e., content development, aesthetic appeal, and so on. Also, Anduro could not simply assume that the new software suites would be entirely user-friendly, at least not in the early versions. Therefore, a marketing director deciding to adopt such a product might also need to hire or develop an in-house expert on the use of the software—something many companies might not be willing to do. Such matters could have severe implications for acceptance of the products in the marketplace.

For Jeff Nelson and Damon James the options boiled down to staying the course and focusing on services—a proven, safe, profitable but gradual growth strategy—versus embarking on software development and sales, a much riskier path but with much greater upside potential. Nelson and James knew they had to evaluate their alternatives with great care and caution. Anduro was their "baby," and a misstep at this point could be fatal.

## CASE QUESTIONS

1. Explain the value-added component of search engine optimization that Anduro was able to provide for a flat-rate fee.

2. A new term has emerged in the area of search engine optimization, *bull-dozing*, which means the company not only has its website located on the first page of a web search, but sufficient numbers of additional postings push other sites to the third or fourth page of the search. Would this type of service be more valuable for Anduro to provide than moving into software sales? Why or why not?

3. Should Anduro move into the software business, stay in the Internet service business, or attempt to do both? Defend your answer.

# Molson Canada: Social Media Marketing[1]

### By Israr Qureshi, under the supervision of Professor Deborah Compeau

On November 23, 2007, the Molson brewing company pulled its promotion on Facebook, after numerous complaints that it promoted binge drinking. The promotion in question involved a photo contest targeting 19- to 24-year-old college and university students. The failure of this promotion on a social networking site forced Molson to think hard about its strategy vis-à-vis social media. What should be Molson's next move? How should it handle one of the fast emerging marketing channels? Should Molson use the social media for any commercial activities?

## Molson Company

The Molson Company was founded by John Molson in 1786, in Montreal. It was the second-oldest company in Canada, preceded only by the Hudson's Bay Company. Molson Canada was part of the Molson Coors Brewing Company. At 41 percent market share by volume in 2006, Molson was Canada's most preferred brand, slightly ahead of Labatt beer. Worldwide, Molson had 3.8 percent market share, placing it fourth behind InBev NV, Anheuser-Busch, and SABMiller. Molson offered a range of brands in Canada, including Molson Canadian, Coors Light, Rickard's Red and Pilsner. Molson Canada also partnered with other leading brewers to offer such brands as Heineken and Miller Genuine Draft. Molson employed 3,000 Canadians and operated six breweries, including the boutique brewery in Creemore, Ontario.

Molson Canada invested in communities from coast to coast through its various charitable initiatives and through sports and entertainment sponsorships. It was proud to be a socially responsible company, which was reflected in its code of conduct:

> As a manufacturer of alcohol beverages, Molson Coors is committed to promoting

legal and responsible decisions about drinking our products. In our sales and marketing practices, Molson Coors promotes the responsible use of our products by adults of legal drinking age. The Company makes every effort to avoid even the appearance of condoning underage drinking, drunk driving or other irresponsible activity involving consumption. When pursuing your work responsibilities or representing the Company, you should be aware that any inappropriate behavior reflects negatively upon the Company's reputation and the equity of its brands. If you choose to consume alcohol beverages, you are expected to set a positive example of responsible alcohol consumption.[2]

Following what it espoused in its code of conduct, Molson organized annual awareness programs to encourage responsible drinking. In December 2007, Molson spent more than $100,000 to raise awareness and support communities across Canada in their efforts to encourage responsible drinking during the holiday season. Molson's sponsorship included complimentary New Year's Eve transit service in Ottawa and supporting Operation Red Nose in western and eastern Canada.

Elaborating on the company's efforts, Ferg Devins, vice-president Government and Public Affairs, Molson, explained:

> Community involvement is a major part of Molson heritage. Molson has long promoted responsible choices and this year's local initiatives across the country are consistent with how Molson has built its business in communities from coast to coast. This is our way of celebrating those who choose to make sure all their holiday memories are good ones.[3]

Version: (A) 2008–10–02

Over the years, the company had focused its efforts on brewing quality beers and taking social and community obligations seriously. The responsible drinking program was an example of Molson's commitment to consumers making responsible choices (see Exhibit 1). Because it was producer of alcohol, Molson directed its community investment donations to programs that encouraged adult audiences to make responsible decisions regarding drinking. Historically, Molson had focused most of its efforts on traditional marketing channels. However, since the beginning of 2007, Molson had started experimenting with social media and social marketing tools as means of targeting its potential young customers.

## Social Media

Molson had already experimented with blogs and had tried having a static web presence at social networking sites. However, both these attempts had been at very early stages. Molson did not fully engage the social media (i.e., online technologies and practices used by people to share their experiences, opinions, and perspectives others).

Like many other companies, Molson was still trying to make sense of how best to integrate its marketing efforts with various online activities that used technology for social interaction by integrating words, pictures, and videos. Some examples were web content, such as blogs and wikis, created by individuals or a collaboration of individuals. Molson's executives found it intuitive that social media was a way of using the Internet to instantly collaborate, share information or have a conversation on anything—or everything. However, how to use these features to promote Molson products was a bit of intellectual exercise.

To make the matter more complex, in social media, anyone can be an expert, a poet, a musician, a photographer, a publisher, or a reporter. Thus, how a potential community member would respond to content created by Molson and how much credence Molson should give to that response was very difficult to ascertain. This quandary was one of the primary reasons why many organizations had hesitated to enter the social media realm. In addition, in social media, the contents of one service could be mashed up with data from other services:

> Mashup is a web application that combines data from more than one source into a single integrated tool. An example is the use of cartographic data from Google Maps to add location information to real-estate data from Craigslist, thereby creating a new and distinct web service that was not originally provided by either source.[4]

Mashups led to issues of control and ownership. Content in social media could not be controlled by the individual who created it, especially in terms of how content could be used by others and the sorts of evolutionary trajectories they could take. Thus, nobody had complete control over social media content, which had great implications on how businesses could to use social media for promotion of their image and products.

| Exhibit I | A Diverse Partial Selection of Anduro Clients Responsible Choices Campaign |
| --- | --- |

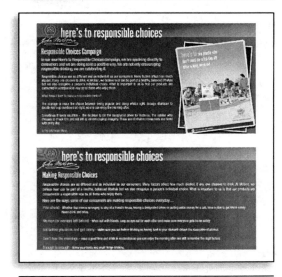

*Source:* Molson Canada, "Here's to Responsible Choices," http://www.responsiblechoices.ca/, accessed January 29, 2008.

Social media was characterized by such features as connectivity, community and inclusiveness that made it fundamentally different from traditional media, such as newspapers, television, books and radio. Exhibit 2 provides a partial list of social media characteristics. Primarily, these characteristics were related to interactions between people that were facilitated by the technology and design aspects of the social media websites. Companies tried to leverage one or more of these features of social media for building awareness and creating communities around their products.

For creating awareness about its product, Molson could choose from a variety of social media, such as blogs, forums, microblogging, and news aggregation. To create communities, Molson could resort to sites that offered photo sharing, video sharing, social bookmarking, and social networking. Some of the common categories of social media are described in the Exhibit 3. Based on the primary objectives of the social media sites, they could be classified into various communities that organized and shared particular kinds of content. Some of the most popular content communities tended to form around friendship (Facebook), photos (Flickr), bookmarked links (del.icio.us) and videos (YouTube). Similar to other media, the type of social media and the features that were leveraged were determined by the target customers, the type of product and the marketing strategy.

## Social Media Marketing

Social networking sites like MySpace.com and Facebook attract large numbers of mostly young users who are eager to engage with their favorite brands. But most marketers use traditional marketing tactics like run-of-site advertising[5] and static microsites[6] to push messages into these networks. Instead, to realize the full value of marketing on social networking sites, marketers should be

| Exhibit 2 | Characteristics of Social Media |
| --- | --- |
| Archival and retrieval | In social media, all the events are automatically archived and normally available for retrieval to anyone who may have interest in looking them at later date. Retrieval of information in traditional media is not that easy. |
| Community | Social media facilitates community building. It allows communities to form around a common interest, such as a favorite celebrity, a political issue, a sport, a hobby, etc. |
| Connectedness | Social media is also characterized by the endless possibility of connectedness, which may manifest itself in the form of links to other individuals, groups, forums, or web resources. |
| Democratic | Most social media services are open to feedback and participation, which are actively encouraged. They also encourage discussion, voting, comments and at times some sort of ranking about shared information. |
| Dialogue | Traditional media, such as newspaper, radio and television, work on the principles of broadcast where readers, listeners and viewers are passive receivers. Social media is seen as a two-way conversation in which roles of "broadcasters" and "receivers" are continuously changed back and forth. |
| Dynamic | Traditional print media cannot be changed once it is off the press. Similarly, radio and TV programs once delivered are in the public domain without any possibility of revision. However, social media can be modified or corrected instantaneously. Moreover social media continuously evolves due to regular feedback and comments. |

| Inclusive | Contributions and feedback are encouraged from anyone who may be interested. No entry barriers exist. Digital divide issues may limit some people, but otherwise it is absolutely open. |
|---|---|
| Lack of control | In social media, the content of one service can be mashed up with data from other services. Thus, nobody has complete control over any content. |
| Real-time evaluation | It is very easy to evaluate the popularity of a social media service in real time, based on a site visit, comments left, growth of membership and number of links that the service solicits. Sites such as Wordpress (http://wordpress.org/) can identify how much traffic each blog receives. Visitors to Digg (http://digg.com/) can see voting on someone's blog items. In addition, sites such as TechMeme (http://www.techmeme.com/), provide statistics on which blog items received the most links in the past few hours. Traditional media provide some statistics on popularity but they are very coarse and available at the best in annual intervals and generally with the lag of one or two years. |

*Source:* Compiled from various sources and authors' own experiences. Sources include: *What Is Social Media?* An e-book from iCrossing – available at www.icrossing.co.uk/ebooks, accessed January 15, 2008. *What Is Social Media?* available at http://scobleizer.com/2007/02/16/what -is-social-media/, accessed on January 16, 2008.Social Media Sociology, available at http://social-media-sociology.com/, accessed on January 15, 2008.

| **Exhibit 3** | Some Examples of Social Media |
|---|---|
| Blogs | Blogs are the most common form of social media. Blogs are online journals, with the most recent entries appearing first. These journal entries are available for other to read and comment on. |
| Forums | Forums are websites for online discussion, often around specific topics and interests. These online spaces provide an outlet for debates, arguments and counter-arguments. |
| Microblogging (Presence apps) | Microblogging is combination of social networking with bite-sized blogging, where micro blog-like posts, such as an announcement of what you are currently doing, are distributed online and through the mobile phone network. Twitter (http://twitter.com/) is a well-known example of microblogging website. |
| News aggregation | News aggregator websites provide a list of the latest news stories published by users from a range of different websites. Digg (http://digg.com) is one of the web's largest news aggregators. |
| Online gaming | Online gaming is often based around communities. World of Warcraft (http://www .worldofwarcraft.com/index.xml) is one of the popular examples of online gaming. Some aspects of Second Life (http://secondlife.com/) may also be included in online gaming. |
| Photo sharing | Photo-sharing sites facilitate uploading of pictures and images to a personal account, which can then be shared or viewed by web users the world over. A well-known example of a photo-sharing website is Flickr (http://www.flickr.com). |

*(Continued)*

| Exhibit 3 | (Continued) |
|---|---|
| Social bookmarking | Social bookmarking sites allow users to publicly bookmark web pages they find valuable in order to share them with other Internet users. One famous example is del.icio.us (http://del.icio.us). |
| Social Networking sites | Social networking websites provide opportunities for individuals who either want to build online social networks to share their interests and activities or are interested in exploring the interests and activities of others. These sites allow people to build personal web pages and then connect with friends to communicate or share content. Some of the common social networking sites are Linkedin, MySpace, Facebook, and Orkut. |
| Video sharing | Video-sharing sites facilitate the uploading and sharing of personal videos with the rest of the web community. A common example of a video-sharing website is YouTube (www.youtube.com). |
| Wikis | These websites allow people to add, edit, challenge or debate their content. The contents are collectively owned and act as a communal document or database. The best-known wiki is Wikipedia, the online encyclopedia, which has more than 2.3 million English language articles and more than 6.5 million articles in all the available languages (information as of March 29, 2008 on http://www.wikipedia.org). |

*Source:* Compiled from various sources and authors own experiences. Sources include: *What Is Social Media?* An e-book from iCrossing – available at www.icrossing.co.uk/ebooks, accessed January 15, 2008. *What Is Social Media?* available at http://scobleizer.com/2007/02/16/what-is-social-media/, accessed on January 16, 2008. Social Media Sociology, available at http://social-media-sociology.com/, accessed January 15, 2008.

prepared to engage in a personal relationship with users by providing something of value. Promotions are good in this context, but even better are information or brand elements that users can pass on to their friends.[7]

Social Media Marketing (SMM) is a form of Internet marketing that utilizes social media to achieve branding and marketing communication goals. Social media sites, such as MySpace, Facebook, Bebo, YouTube, Digg, Flickr, and Twitter, are used to communicate information about a company and its brand and products. Which social medium is most effective and how it can best be targeted depends in part on the goals of SMM campaign and the product offered by the company. In general, most campaigns involved propagating an idea, creating brand awareness, increasing visibility, encouraging brand feedback and dialogue and, in some cases, selling a product or service.

Social media marketers took advantage of the fact that average users of social networking sites were young. In a Forrester survey conducted in 2006, only 20 percent of adults reported using social networking sites. In contrast, almost 47 percent of teenagers, and 69 percent of young adults (ages 18 to 21) had a profile and had interacted with other users on social networking sites, such as MySpace and Facebook. Among the users of social networking sites, young adults' (18- to 21–year-olds) usage rate was higher compared with other groups, using social networking sites much more frequently (68 percent reported making a daily visit) than 12- to 17-year-olds (60 percent reported daily visits) or adult users (42 percent reported daily visits).[8]

Another interesting aspect, from a social media marketer's perspective, was that social networking site users wanted to engage with their favorite brands. A Forrester survey found that the most common approach to marketing on social networking sites was to set up a profile for the brand, which members could then join, or "friend," as some social networking sites preferred to call it. For example, Molson's Facebook profile, Molson Canadian Nation, had more than 19,000 members (other Facebook users) as friends.[9] The Forrester survey also found that many social networking site users welcomed interactions with the brands that they loved: more than one-third of 18- to 26-year-old social networking users admitted that they would be interested in seeing a marketer's profile (see Exhibit 4).

## Cold Shots Campus Challenge

In mid-October, on behalf of Molson Canada, Toronto-based ad agency Henderson Bas announced the launch of a campaign targeted at the 19- to 24-year-old demographic. The goal of this campaign was to use Facebook, a social networking site, to increase brand awareness of Molson products in Canada to reach Molson's "target demographics in most efficient manner."[10] The plan was to use the Molson Canadian Nation group profile on Facebook, which then had more than 17,500 members, to spread the word about Molson's products.

| **Exhibit 4** | Age and Frequency of Usage (indicators of willingness to engage with favorite brands) |

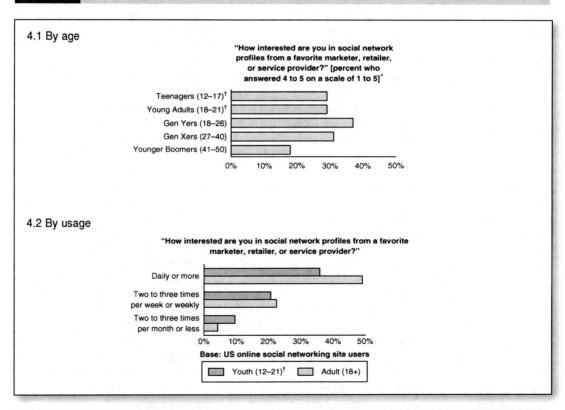

*Source*: Charlene Li, "Marketing on Social Networking Sites," Forrester Research Inc., Cambridge, MA, 2007.

*Source*: Forrester's NACTAS Q3 2006 Media & Marketing Online Survey.

[†]*Source*: Forrester's NACTAS Q4 2006 Youth Media & Marketing and Finance Online Survey.

[*]*Note*: Bases for Older Boomers (51–61) and Seniors (62+) were too small to report values.

"Utilizing Facebook for this program made strategic sense," stated Heather Clark, creative strategy director at Henderson Bas, at the launch of the campaign.[11] The demographics present on most social network websites, including Facebook, were "ideal" for marketers such as Molson. Facebook, primarily created for college and university students, had a very young membership base. Moreover, these websites provided an environment where friends interacted in a trusted and open setting. Thus, social network websites presented opportunities to marketers to build their brands and promote their products through viral marketing as word of "mouse" spread among friends. These websites were a virtual space "where they hang out and it's a great opportunity to engage them in a dialogue. If you do it right, you can find yourself with a whole nation of brand ambassadors," claimed Heather Clark.[12] The campaign was planned to run from the end of October to the end of November, 2007.[13]

The *modus operandi* of the campaign was to have a virtual "dorm room" in the name of each university or college, where students from those institutions could post photos of themselves and their friends in full party mode. The school with the most photos would be awarded the title of number-one party school in Canada. The best photo, as determined by a panel of Molson judges, would win the Spring Break Trip Give Away Contest—a trip for the winner and three friends to Cancun, Mexico, for Spring Break 2008, sponsored by Breakaway Tours.[14] In addition, the Molson Canadian Nation group on Facebook would provide some features to attract members, including the Cold Shots Amped Up game, screen savers, wallpaper and MSN icons, the "Party Finder" section and customized searches for pictures and polls.

The students who were the target of this campaign grew up in the age of Internet and felt comfortable sharing their personal details in an online environment. They routinely upload their personal photos, shared their videos and spent more time on the social networking website than in a physical social space. Social networking sites such as Facebook were a common "hanging around place" for them. For these reasons, the contest became popular among students, particularly those from Memorial University of Newfoundland (MUN). By November 23, students from MUN had uploaded 67 photos, much ahead of University of Victoria, which was in second place with 26 photos. However, not all the students were proud of having their university "leading" this competition. Some argued that students in skimpy costumes who had consumed excess quantities of alcohol hardly matched their image of a wonderful time at university.

## Criticism of the Contest

Many students and administrators across the Canadian universities felt that Molson's "Cold Shot" was giving their school's image a bad reputation. They felt that the contest encouraged irresponsible behavior by inciting students to post their photos in outrageous situations. To get noticed, students who were posing for photos may have felt the need to present themselves in an extraordinary condition, which typically meant wearing skimpy costumes, behaving unusually and drinking more than what could be considered safe and responsible amounts of alcohol.

The non-participating students at the front-runner MUN felt this contest was giving their university image a "hangover." *The Muse,* a student-run newspaper at MUN, published an editorial bashing the competition. Editor Kerri Breen labeled the contest "really kind of lame." She criticized Molson's approach as inappropriate and stated "beer bongs and letterman's jackets, it's really not something MUN should strive to be associated with."[15] Another student at MUN found the contest frustrating because it gave an impression of the school that wasn't fair to students who attended MUN to study and achieved good grades. In her view, it was unfair "to have other people coming in, looking at the school as a whole and saying that we're a group of people who don't care about the academics, that we're just here to party."[16] Many students at MUN agreed that Molson's contest presented the wrong view about having a good experience at the university.

The University of Western Ontario (Western), which prided itself in providing best student experience wasn't amused with its eighth overall ranking (only 10 entries had been received by November 22) of "best party" school, which, according to Cynthea

Galbraith, a Molson spokesperson, meant "the context of celebrating good times with friends after the academics are over for the day."[17] Students and officials at Western argued that if this was what "best party" school meant, then Western should be at the top of the list and not at the eighth place:

> Party school is a very narrow definition of what we believe to be the best student experience in the country. When we talk to students, alumni and the public we emphasize [Western] has both an in-class component but also a great social experience . . . social experience means many different things. It means having great student government and opportunities to involve yourself in that, along with clubs, organizations, and the opportunity to involve yourself in varsity sport. It's the opportunity to build great networks because so many of our students live on campus. There are more important things to the student experience than just partying and drinking[18]

Responses from other universities also followed the same lines. Jason Laker, associate vice-principal and dean of Student Affairs at Queen's University, felt disgusted:

> Such an apparent and dangerous disregard . . . promotes an abusive use of alcohol. . . . In order for the photos to be eligible, to be notable, would require outrageous behavior or profoundly dangerous levels of drinking, and of course the kind of decision making and behavior that follow that. [Molson] are either unaware of it or simply placing profits above ethics.[19]

Similar sentiments were expressed by Joe MacDonald, dean of Students Affairs at St. Francis Xavier University:

> These kinds of programs put added stress on our ability to ensure that students have a very positive, successful academic and non-academic development. . . . This is not something that is welcome within our campus community.

It's cheap marketing, I'm concerned about Molson's lack of contrition.[20]

Phil Wood, associate vice-president of student affairs at McMaster University agreed, "It is hard to believe that a leading corporation like Molson would stoop to such a . . . way of doing business."[21] He expressed his dismay especially because Molson Coors Brewing Co. was targeting students in residence even though many of them were too young to legally consume alcohol. Zach Churchill, national director of the Canadian Alliance of Student Associations, termed the Molson campaign as unfortunate because it stereotyped university students as being interested only in partying.[22]

However, the best articulation of universities' opposition to Molson contest came in the letter sent by Brenda Whiteside, chair of Ontario Committee on Student Affairs, the University of Guelph. In her letter to Molson she wrote:

> As professionals dealing with the transition of young students to university, we are continuously combating the stereotype of universities being places to party. . . . One of the risks of a "party university" culture is the increased potential for over consumption of alcohol by students with no previous experience. Each year we send a small but concerning number of students to hospital with alcohol poisoning. Some of us have had to deal with a student death due to over consumption. In addition, we continually struggle with the by-products of over consumption—vandalism, assault, sexual assault, and academic failure . . . we devote endless energy, resources and programming towards responsible drinking campaigns. . . . Imagine our dismay when we learned of this campaign—a competition for a party environment in residence. This campaign not only dismantles university efforts to create a culture of academics in residences, it also helps to establish an environment that could encourage irresponsible drinking. Our second concern with this campaign is the use of Facebook. . . . Facebook has the potential to be dangerous for students. . . . Of particular concern is students posting pictures of themselves in behavior that

could impact negatively on future careers or opportunities. There are numerous examples of students who have regretted the posting of such pictures. Thus, please understand again our dismay with a program that encourages students to potentially place such damaging photos on the internet. . . . This present campaign runs counter to Molson's commitment to responsible drinking. We hope that your company will be more thoughtful about possible risks of advertising campaigns prior to future launches[23]

Her letter raised two critical aspects: (1) this contest was run against the often cited Molson virtue that it encourages responsible drinking and (2) this contest overlooked the privacy risk of sharing objectionable photos on a public website such as Facebook. Most of the objections from students and university administrators were around the first issue; however, some objections were raised about the second issue as well.

Administrators were of the view that Molson's Facebook initiative could jeopardize students' future career, especially those seeking jobs in near future, if potential employers stumble upon their not-so-graceful photos on Facebook. Phil Wood was concerned that some students' pictures may have been viewed by prospective employers or graduate schools, and these students could face biased treatment that could compromise their chances of landing a job or gaining admission to graduate school. He felt that encouraging students to post pictures of themselves engaging in excessive drinking or dangerous behavior was not a good idea in itself because students "don't understand the danger of the publicness of Facebook. You're not anonymous."[24]

Because Facebook was a public virtual space, these photos were accessible to potential future employers, administrators, and society at large. This exposure created a potential risk of students not being hired, being pre-judged if hired and being monitored in prejudiced way. Moreover, some students had become unconsenting participants. Not everyone who was partying and happened to be in photo wanted to be part of the contest, which had privacy implications. It was not clear whether Molson

had any guidelines in place to ensure the consent of all those who appeared in the photographs was obtained before photo was uploaded for the contest. Many similar issues were raised regarding privacy and future implications of compromising this privacy.

One blogger's comment about Molson contest summed it up humorously:

Capturing these young heavy drinkers in Facebook is a great idea. We will have a vibrant montage of "before" pictures to mix with the "after" pictures of:

- people killed by drunk drivers
- students choking on their vomit
- students sexually assaulted or robbed while incapacitated (by heavy drinking)
- students later running for public office or other positions of trust etc.

Then as the years go by, and Molson tracks their "best customers," we can see whether they reach their potential from a university degree, or struggle with alcoholism and its social and physical effects. Without using Facebook, we would never have such a well-organized audit trail, with poignant photographs, on which to base lawsuits for those who drink to tragic ends.[25]

The final proverbial straw in the coffin of Molson's photo contest came when administrators from four universities wrote letters to Molson and also expressed their opinions in the *Globe and Mail*, squarely criticizing the contest. They slammed Molson's contest saying it promoted irresponsible drinking and demanded immediate withdrawal of the contest. They argued that Molson should pull the campaign because it was inconsistent with the company's own promotion of safe and responsible drinking.

## Molson's Response

Sensing the probable outrage from the academic community, Molson pulled its contest on November 23, almost a week before its scheduled end. Molson, however, argued that the contest was simply an effort to engage its target market with socially oriented advertising and should not be interpreted as any attempt to encourage irresponsible drinking. The company also initiated damage control by issuing public statements through various officials. Molson issued a public note on its Facebook page explaining why it withdrew the contest: "we promote responsible choices and wanted to be pro-active in responding to concerns expressed from a number of different audiences."

However, Molson executives felt that the company's initiative had been misunderstood and misinterpreted as promoting irresponsible drinking. Ferg Devins, Molson's vice president, Government and Public Affairs, agreed that Molson had learned a lot from the contest:

> The whole realm of social media—there's lots to learn. It's really a new area. We're probably groundbreaking and leading in a lot of things we've been doing.[26]

Similar sentiments were expressed by Cynthea Galbraith, a spokeswoman for Molson: "Our take is that this whole social media realm is new. There's going to be some experimentation, there's going to be some learning." In spite of this failure, Galbraith was very positive about the future possibility of social media. She expressed cautious optimism:

> I don't know if surprised is the word, but we learn from these things. Our intention is to become a leader in that area and we'll go back and develop some new innovations in communications for next time.[27]

Like many others at Molson, Galbraith identified social media as one of the most important channels to communicate with the 19- to 24-year-old demographic. She observed "Social interaction is key with that [demographic], it seems to be all the rage right now." Ferg Devins was in total agreement: "We need to be communicating with our consumers because that's where our consumers are communicating among themselves. . . . We need to make sure we're in that relevant channel." Despite the setback to its contest, Molson planned to expand its social media marketing, and Devins highlighted the efforts Molson had initiated in terms of blogs and other social technologies.

With its marketing vision firmly rooted in the exploitation of social media, some Molson executives wondered whether they had really done the right thing by calling off the photo contest a week ahead of its scheduled conclusion. Had they given into unreasonable pressure or had they acted responsibly? Did they forgo the opportunity of using social media in its true sense by not taking the view of the participants of the contest into account? Should they continue to try to use social media as part of their marketing, and if so how? How would they combat the challenges they had encountered with the Facebook promotion, and what other challenges should they foresee?

Whether future attempts of Molson with social media would bear fruit would depend on how the company applied the lessons learned from the failure of the photo contest. How should Molson address the privacy issues? Should Molson include all the relevant stakeholders in the loop? And how could Molson best put the potential of social media to use?

## CASE QUESTIONS

1. How is social media, such as Facebook, different from creating a company website?

2. Do you think the "Cold Shot" promotion was effectively targeted at the right market or represented a major miscalculation by the Molson marketing team?

3. Should Molson respond to critics using social media or more traditional forums such as press releases? What would be the advantages and disadvantages of each approach?

4. Should Molson's marketing managers continue to pursue social media events? If so, what kinds? If not, why not?

# 14

# Customer Retention and Recovery

A great deal of marketing management involves spending money, time, and energy acquiring customers. The next crucial moment occurs following the initial purchase. Will the customer come back? The ones that return do not require the investment of additional funds, making them the most profitable type of customer. Customer retention rests on three pillars: (1) customer loyalty, (2) quality customer relationships, and (3) customer recovery.

## ▧ Developing Customer Loyalty

Customer retention begins with the application of the AIDA (Awareness, Interest, Desire, Action) process. Following the action of buying an item, the goal quickly becomes to motivate the customer to make additional purchases. Building a pathway from awareness to loyalty includes encouraging the customer to bypass the brand-switching option.

## ▧ Types of Customer Loyalty

Customers are not all the same. Types and levels of loyalty vary. Brand loyalty consists of two components: (1) emotional attachment, where the customer becomes connected with and attached to the brand, and (2) behavior, where the customer takes action—most often making a purchase. Four forms of brand loyalty may be derived from these two dimensions.

No loyalty occurs in individuals without emotional attachment to the brand who also infrequently purchase the item. Brand names carry little meaning. The costs of retaining these customers tend to be higher than revenues gained.

Latent loyalty may be found when individuals have high levels of attachment but the purchase volume remains low. Some other factor may prevent more frequent purchases. When that factor can be overcome, the customer becomes more valuable.

Inertia loyalty means the individual makes frequent purchases but maintains a low level of emotional attachment. Convenience explains repeat purchases without loyalty. Only when a relationship can be built with this type of customer will loyalty grow.

Brand loyalty expresses high levels of emotional attachment and high purchase levels. Those holding this point of view do not make substitute purchases and may make extra effort to buy the favored brand. A totally brand-loyal consumer may not be feasible; however, those with strong levels are a company's most valuable customers.

## ⬚ Factors That Generate Loyalty

Marketing managers emphasize customer retention and brand loyalty as highly desirable outcomes. Often, the factors that would on the surface appear to generate loyalty, such as quality products, quality service, and comparable prices, may actually lead to perceptions of brand parity. To overcome this outcome, the marketing team can tip the scale by developing quality relationships with customers and consistently exceeding their expectations. Doing so can lead to brand-loyal customers who become the advocates who are willing to pass along positive word of mouth to others.

Exceeding expectations results from taking the factors of product quality and service quality and moving them beyond what is offered by the competition. Only then will comparable prices result in loyalty rather than perceptions of brand parity. In essence, exceeding expectations leads to the conclusion that the customer receives "more bang for the buck."

## ⬚ Maintaining Customer Relationships

The second pillar of customer retention is maintaining quality relationships. It results from the creation of meaningful interpersonal attention, the delivery quality of products and services, responding to problems and complaints, and effectively using marketing tools such as advertising and promotional programs. Customer relationships are maintained through programs such as (1) cross-selling, (2) frequency or loyalty programs, (3) direct marketing and permission marketing programs, and (4) customer relationship management systems.

Cross-selling is the attempt to sell a second or additional product to a customer who has already purchased at least one product. It can lead to increases in customer retention, earnings and profits, and opportunities to sell additional products. Cross-selling increases switching costs for customers while maintaining a relationship that already exists. Cross-selling is easier and cheaper than acquiring new customers.

Frequency or loyalty programs retain customers by giving rewards to those who make additional purchases. The goal should be to obtain 100% of the share of the customers in a product category. Marketing managers carefully consider the costs of a frequency program before implementing it. The costs include recruiting members, making initial offers, administration expenses, making secondary offers to return customers, managing the database, and continuing lines of communication. Successful frequency programs feature high levels of service and reward the best and most loyal customers.

Direct marketing programs attempt to sell goods or services without an intermediary. They can entice new sales and create repeat business. Direct marketing programs succeed when they are used in conjunction with the firm's database or with a commercial database, thereby reaching the customers most likely to make additional purchases. Permission marketing involves the individual or business agreeing to receive marketing materials and offers. When true permission has been granted, the opportunity to build and sustain relationships appears.

Customer relationship management programs are designed to increase customer retention. Effective programs identify the company's customers, differentiate those customers in terms of needs and overall value to the company, efficiently interact with them, and customize interactions. Unfortunately, many programs have failed to follow these steps and instead violate the company's culture, rely too heavily on technology, and make customers feel as though they are being stalked rather than "wooed."

## Customer Recovery

The third pillar of customer retention, customer recovery, goes into action when a customer has been frustrated by a company, is dissatisfied with an experience, and has become angry as a result. These individuals are most likely to look for new options.

To overcome customer dissatisfaction, the first step will be to diffuse the customer's anger. Although the customer may not have a valid complaint, the company representative can still acknowledge that the person has the right to be upset. Second, an apology should be offered. The apology can be for some type of service failure or merely to say the company is sorry the person has been inconvenienced. Third, the process should move toward restoring loyalty through reconciliation. The goal of finding a solution that will be agreeable to the customer may be difficult to achieve, but simply making the effort may restore some faith in the company's good intentions.

Customer defections take place when some patrons move on to other companies or brands. Customer defections, which are also known as churn, can be lessened through brand loyalty programs, which address the problems of dissatisfaction with the product, employees' attitudes of indifference, and competitive offers. High-quality customer service alleviates the most likely cause of churn, employee indifference.

## The Benefits of Customer Retention

Many marketing experts believe it costs five to six times more to acquire a new customer than to retain a current customer. Beyond that statistic, other benefits of customer retention include increases in purchase frequency, purchase volume, and cross-purchases. Loyal customers who have been retained offer positive word-of-mouth endorsements. These positive comments circulate to a much wider audience due to the presence of social media and the Internet. Service costs for repeat purchase accounts become lower over time, and greater profitability results.

## Implications for Marketing Managers

Customer retention and recovery largely rests with entry-level employees and their supervisors. It is the individual salesperson, telephone operator, complaint department employee, delivery person, and service technicians who will meet face-to-face with customers. These interactions largely determine the relationship with the company that follows. Consequently, the marketing manager should use every tool possible to make sure each contact point creates a positive experience.

Selection programs, training programs, and reward systems should all be geared to finding and motivating the highest-quality team that can deliver quality customer service.

##  The Cases

### Ten Thousand Villages of Cincinnati: The First Year and Beyond

Ten Thousand Villages is an organization consisting of more than 200 stores in the United States. The North American Mennonite Church and the Brethren in Christ Churches support its operations. The company purchases items from individuals in less-developed countries. This allows them the opportunity to support themselves and their families through the production and sale of local, high-quality crafts in the United States. Ten Thousand Village's key customers are female, educated, and have strong incomes—known as cultural creatives—who enjoy making purchases that support less-advantaged individuals. Although sales in the Cincinnati store had been satisfactory over the initial period, the marketing manager was looking for ways to increase sales and maintain a solid customer base over time.

### Personal Shoppers at Sears: The Elf Initiative

Sears in Canada launched a new marketing initiative in 2006. The Elf program created a set of personal shoppers (Elves) to serve each retail location. The Elf program's purpose was to improve and personalize customer service, assist in selecting merchandise, suggest additional merchandise, and generate larger sales per purchase. Services ranged from pre-selecting merchandise so the shopper could simply pick it up at the store to full assistance throughout an extended visit to Sears. The program began during the Christmas shopping season and would feature larger numbers of Elves during other holidays, with at least one Elf in the store at other times. The program was a response to flat sales in the highly competitive retail market.

# Ten Thousand Villages of Cincinnati: The First Year and Beyond

### By Professor Mary Conway Dato-on

Spring always brings renewal: that was Karen's focus as she reminisced about how she became involved with the fair trade organization, Ten Thousand Villages (TTV), in her hometown of Cincinnati, and contemplated the next steps to build on the local store's first year. Karen, a full-time mom most of her adult life with little to no business experience, had been a Mennonite church member for as long as she could remember. As church members, both she and her husband were involved in various volunteer/service endeavors throughout their lives; therefore, it seemed natural for Karen to become involved in an internationally focused mission when the opportunity presented itself through her church. She never imagined that such humble beginnings would lead her to the chairperson position of the board of directors for the first and only TTV retail store in Cincinnati. Karen seemed overwhelmed as she recalled the brief history of Ten Thousand Villages Cincinnati

Version: (A) 2010–05–31

(TTVC) and thought about its future. The memory seemed surreal; through Karen's leadership, TTVC opened in November 2002. Karen maintained a "pinch me, it can't be true" attitude, while also feeling a sense of pride about her accomplishments.

While there was much excitement about the store's first year of operation, Karen was eager to discover new strategies for increasing sales in year two and beyond. She believed that the TTVC store could repeat and even improve upon the first year's successes; at the same time, she was quick to note that staying true to the TTV mission was crucial. Because soliciting advice was part of the TTVC store's recipe for success, Karen willingly sought recommendations to help more impoverished artisans across the world by generating more fair trade sales in Cincinnati.

## History of Ten Thousand Villages

Ten Thousand Villages started in 1946 when Joe Byler, a volunteer with the Mennonite church, visited a Puerto Rican community the church was sponsoring. Byler's wife, Edna Ruth, accompanied him on this trip. During the trip, Ruth observed the intricate embroidery work of the local Puerto Rican women. Realizing that there were few places to sell the embroidery in Puerto Rico, Ruth purchased samples to sell in her hometown of Lancaster County, Pennsylvania. Having sold the initial pieces in Lancaster County, Ruth purchased more products from the women in Puerto Rico—she even expanded her product selection to include other handcrafted Puerto Rican items. Soon, Ruth began traveling to Mennonite churches throughout Pennsylvania displaying samples of handmade products from Puerto Rico, told stories of the artisans who made the various products and took orders. Ruth contacted Mennonite-sponsored communities in other developing countries to see if they too would be interested in supplying handmade products to sell in the United States. As word spread about the high-quality, handcrafted products produced by artisans from around the world, U.S. consumers inside and outside the Mennonite church clamored for more. Before too long, demand

for these unique, international handmade products exceeded Ruth's capacity to supply and manage.

In the early 1970s, the successful project moved out of Ruth's home and became an official Mennonite Central Committee (MCC) undertaking. MCC is the service, relief and development agency of the North American Mennonite and Brethren in Christ churches. For more than 50 years (1946–1996), the Ten Thousand Villages program of the MCC was known as SELFHELP Crafts of the World. This name and logo was familiar to the thousands of loyal customers and volunteers who helped build the program into the strong alternative trading organization that became Ten Thousand Villages in 1996.[1] Ten Thousand Villages launched as a nonprofit organization specifically to foster the sale of indigenous handicrafts in the United States; as part of this endeavor, the church opened stores throughout North America to sell the handcrafted items.

At the beginning of 2004, there were nearly 200 stores in the United States and Canada that sold TTV products. TTV always operated as a nonprofit program affiliated with the MCC, and the stores were mainly managed by volunteers. Based on the MCC's belief in fair trade, TTV became a member of the International Fair Trade Association (IFAT)[2] and the U.S.-based Fair Trade Federation (FTF)[3]. The following mission statement and operating principles adopted by TTV clearly articulate the organization's role in a global economy:

> Ten Thousand Villages provides vital, fair income to Third World people by marketing their handicrafts and telling their stories in North America. Ten Thousand Villages works with artisans who would otherwise be unemployed or underemployed. This income helps pay for food, education, health care and housing.
>
> - We work with disadvantaged artisans.
> - We purchase from craft groups that are concerned for their members and that promote member participation.
> - We pay fair prices for handicrafts. We pay promptly.

- We pay up to half the value of a handicraft order when it is placed; the balance when the items are shipped to North America. This provides operating capital for artisans to purchase raw materials and for craft groups to pay workers.
- We offer handicrafts that reflect and reinforce rich cultural traditions.
- We promote fair trade.
- We use marketing strategies and messages consistent with our mission and ideals.
- Our ideals include responsible lifestyle choices, efficiency and Christian ethics. We seek integrity in all our actions and relationships.
- Whenever possible, we work with volunteers in North American operations.[4]

## Fair Trade

IFAT defined fair trade as

[A] "trading partnership, based on dialogue, transparency [being open to public accountability] and respect that seeks greater equity in international trade. The fair trade organization contributes to sustainable development by offering better trading conditions to, and securing the rights of, marginalized producers and workers. Backed by consumers, fair trade organizations engage actively in supporting producers, raising awareness, and campaigning for positive change in conventional international trade practices. Fair trade organizations have a clear commitment to fair trade as the principal core of their mission."[5]

According to IFAT, fair trade was better than aid because fair trade was built on the premise of a sustainable future for artisans based on their own abilities. The following 10 standards of fair trade,

coincide with TTV's operating principles, demonstrate the values upon which fair trade organizations based their decisions:

1. "Create Opportunities for Economically Disadvantaged Producers—poverty reduction through trade

2. Transparency and Accountability—transparent in its management and commercial relations and accountable to all its stakeholders

3. Trading Practices—trades with concern for the social, economic and environmental well-being of marginalized small producers

4. Payment of a Fair Price—one that has been mutually agreed by all through dialogue

5. Child Labor and Forced Labor—adheres to the UN Convention on the Rights of the Child, and national/local law on the employment of children

6. Non Discrimination, Gender Equity and Freedom of Association

7. Working Conditions—provides a safe and healthy working environment for employees

8. Capacity Building—seeks to increase positive developmental impacts for small, marginalized producers

9. Promotion of Fair Trade—raises awareness of the aim of Fair Trade and of the need for greater justice in world trade through Fair Trade

10. Environment—maximize the use of raw materials from sustainably managed sources in products, buying locally when possible".[6]

TTV became a member of FTF—a coalition of more than 200 craft producers, wholesalers, and retailers. Among other things, the FTF developed "a workable agenda for handicrafts and agricultural products within the context of fair trade."[7]

Operations such as TTV came to be known as alternative trade organizations (ATOs):

> ATOs were non-governmental organizations designed to benefit artisans and not maximize profits. They marketed products from handicraft and agricultural organizations or cooperatives established in low-income countries. They provided consumers around the world with products that have been fairly purchased from sustainable sources. ATO's put fair trade into practice and campaigned for more equitable terms of trade for artisans from low-income countries.[8]

Other retail ATO operations that offered products from developing countries included Oxfam (United Kingdom), Twin Trading (United Kingdom), SERRV (United States), Bridgehead (Canada), Trading Partners (Australia), and Nepali Bazaro (Japan). Product selection at these retail outlets generally included handicrafts (e.g., clothing, household decor and giftware) and agricultural-based commodities such as tea, coffee, chocolate, and cocoa.[9] In 2002, total sales for the fair trade industry in North America were $180 million[10], an increase of 44 percent from 2001. The sales for the Pacific Rim (Australia, Japan and New Zealand) were $70.6 million in 2002: this represented a 23 percent increase from 2001.[11] The popularity of fair trade products was on the rise: "Fair trade products also became increasingly conspicuous on supermarket shelves, and if choice was what consumers wanted then the future looked prosperous."[12] Consumers who purchased ATO products shared demographic and psychographic profiles, regardless of their geographic location.

## Ten Thousand Villages' Customers

ATO consumers comprised the primary target market for TTV stores. These socially conscious consumers became known as "cultural creatives."

The estimated 50 million U.S. cultural creatives were motivated to purchase high-quality products with social value. In other words, these well-educated consumers, most with college and post-baccalaureate degrees, sought to make a difference in their world. Demographically, cultural creatives were predominantly women in their early 40s with an above average annual income of $52,200.[13]

Cultural creatives wanted to know everything they could about the products they might purchase. They became knowledgeable consumers based on extensive research about global current events and production sources.[14] Their research drove them to ask question about who made products, under what conditions, and using what processes. Cultural creatives consistently read package labels and product reviews; they did not purchase on impulse.

Products offered by TTV and other ATOs were perfect offerings for cultural creatives. The practice of fair trade and the operating principles of TTV mirrored the values of cultural creative consumers. This segment actively sought stores, products and services from fair trade organizations via the Internet and other media. The identification and pursuit of this segment was logical for TTV Cincinnati.

According to the 2000 U.S. Census Bureau, the Cincinnati market (the geographic market segment), which constituted approximately 7.4 percent of Ohio's population, comprised approximately 331,280 people. Within that population, 38.5 percent were between the ages of 35 and 64, and 51.4 percent were female. Twenty-nine percent of Cincinnatians held a bachelor's degree or higher and earned a median annual income of $40,964. This demographic data suggested the possible existence of a cultural creatives segment in Cincinnati. More specific, in-depth primary data would be necessary to understand if a group of cultural creatives existed within the demographic segment.

## Ten Thousand Villages' Competitors

Research by local MBA students discovered four main competitors (three national and one local) in the Cincinnati area that sold home decor and handcrafted items similar to the TTVC store.[15] A brief description of the competitors follows.

## Pier 1 Imports

Pier 1 Imports was North America's largest importer of decorative home products. According to Pier 1 Imports' 2003 annual report, its stores carried a variety of 4,000 products from more than 40 countries. Pier 1 Imports divided its products into five categories: furniture, decorative accessories, housewares, bed and bath, and seasonal. The annual report showed sales for the previous three fiscal years were driven by the furniture category (38 percent of sales in 2003, 39 percent in 2002 and 40 percent in 2001).

Pier 1 Imports targeted women aged 25 to 34 and advertised aggressively to reach its target audience. Nationwide advertising in 2001 totaled $55 million, and was nearly $30 million in 2002. Advertising campaigns were designed to position Pier 1 Imports as "relaxing, stimulating and a sanctuary at the same time. It's a place that is fun, warm and inviting. It is not hectic like a mall environment."[16] More than 2,000 items were available for sale on Pier 1's website,[17] including furniture and decorative items. The site also included a bridal gift registry and a furniture guide. Pier 1 Imports targeted children through its subsidiary CargoKids. The company defined its competitive advantages as price, merchandise variety and visual presentation. Based on its volume, visibility online and multiple store locations, Pier 1 Imports enjoyed a competitive advantage of vast name recognition.

## Cost Plus World Market

The 2003 Cost Plus World Market (World Market) annual report noted products imported from more than 60 countries; the company's marketing strategy targeted women aged 22 to 55. World Market differentiated itself from Pier 1 Imports and others in two ways: it carried food items and relied heavily on creating a unique atmosphere in the store.

World Market operated under the assumption that consumers wanted the same international flair in food items as they had in home furnishings; to accommodate these needs, World Market offered consumables including wines, beers and olive oils among others. Consumables made up 33 percent of World Market's product mix.[18]

World Market stores were designed to evoke a feeling of being in a world market: items were displayed in open barrels as if displayed in a bazaar. World Market made use of in-store activities such as cooking demonstrations and food and drink samples to generate excitement and increase impulse purchases. The stores' atmosphere was designed to capture the customers' imagination and encourage exploration of new items. World Market identified its competitive advantages as low prices, a variety of products and a unique shopping experience.

## Z Gallerie

Twenty-four years ago, Z Gallerie started in California as a store offering dormitory-room posters. In 2003, Z Gallerie maintained 47 stores in 13 states (including Ohio) and offered a comprehensive product selection of 3,000 items.[19] Z Gallerie merchandise displays encouraged exploratory shopping by constantly changing its products. Unlike Pier 1 Imports and Cost Plus World Market that strove for a pleasant and relaxing atmosphere, Z Gallerie designed stores to be dynamic, to energize the customer with a bohemian flair.[20]

## From the Ridiculous to the Sublime

A small boutique store, From the Ridiculous to the Sublime was located down the street from TTVC. It was a local establishment with small monthly sales that fit the odd mix of O'Bryonville (the section of town where both stores were located) store offerings. The store's products included unique handicraft items, jewelry, and giftware. From the Ridiculous to the Sublime followed Z Gallerie's dynamic layout and bohemian atmosphere.

## Unique Selling Point for Cincinnati Ten Thousand Villages

The competitive review showed competitors that carried similar product offerings but held limited appeal to the values of the cultural creatives target segment. TTV was the only store in Cincinnati to tender fair trade merchandise; no other store could match the mission of TTV, in which "shopping makes a difference." In addition to this distinctive character, comparison shopping showed that TTV's products were competitively priced and at times offered better quality. TTV had a competitive advantage in its mission: the key to success might be promoting that mission to the "right" customers. This was particularly difficult given the monetary constraints of TTVC as a non-profit endeavor.

Fair trade products were not without any competition in the Cincinnati area, however. As fair trade coffee and teas gained more acceptance in mainstream grocery stores, TTVC found itself competing with supermarket giant and local corporate power house, Kroger. Due to its nation-wide buying volume, Kroger sold the same brand of fair trade coffee for less than TTVC's wholesale purchase price. Interestingly, TTVC also found itself competing against the Cincinnati Catholic Church. The Cincinnati archdiocese took a strong position on promoting and selling fair trade coffee. Once again, the diocese's prices for the same coffee were below cost for TTVC.

## Ten Thousand Villages Cincinnati: Setting Up Shop

The TTVC store was started by the Cincinnati Mennonite Fellowship (one of several Mennonite churches in Cincinnati). In 2001, after having orchestrated twelve years of successful Christmas season weekend sales events, members from the Cincinnati church decided to begin raising funds to open a permanent, year-round retail outlet where Cincinnatians could purchase unique, international handmade products. Karen served as the chairperson of the board of directors for the newly proposed TTV store. With the assistance of her husband, who was an attorney, Karen developed the bylaws and filed for the store's nonprofit status in January 2002. The goal was to open the store in time for the 2002 Christmas shopping season. With the help of the board, the following mission statement was developed:

> Ten Thousand Villages of Cincinnati will promote global understanding and connectedness by
>
> - providing innovative markets for artisans in developing countries,
> - telling the artisans' stories and celebrating their artistic spirit,
> - empowering the artisans to provide basic needs for themselves and their families by purchasing their handcrafted products at fair prices, and
> - creating local awareness of, and involvement with, global economic issues through an ecumenical community.

To open the store, Karen needed to raise $52,000 (the amount set by TTV headquarters in Akron, Pennsylvania). Although many people told Karen that she would never raise the needed capital, she remained committed and believed in the mission of TTV. She was confident that others would support her as they heard the TTV story. To generate the necessary funds, Karen pursued two main avenues. Firstly, she organized a large-scale church craft sale. When assisting with the Christmas season weekend sales events, Karen received inventory on consignment from TTV's headquarters. For this fundraising event—as well as for a permanent store—the goods would be the responsibility of the TTVC group, whether or not they sold. Thus, Karen selected the items for the craft sale carefully: the items that did not sell might become inventory for the planned store. She relied on both her past experience and recommendations from others to judiciously select a wide range of items from TTV's headquarters' list of imported products from 36 different countries. Secondly, Karen embarked on a fundraising campaign; specifically, she wrote letters soliciting donations from loyal customers of the past Christmas sales events and members of both her own and other local church communities.

The church craft sale generated $12,000; the remainder of funds came from donations. Karen recalled the fundraising period with awe and pleasure:

> I was so scared. I had no idea how the store's fair trade mission would be received outside the Mennonite community. I mean within the community we're so familiar with the project it seemed natural, but how would I convince those not so intimately involved in the process? I decided to start with people who had purchased products before. I figured this would be a good indication of a belief in the mission and an appreciation for the quality of the handicrafts themselves. In the end [she laughs nervously], it wasn't as difficult as I thought it would be. The artisans tell their own stories so well; I simply served as a mouthpiece in the local community.

## Finding a Store Location

With funds in hand and a board of directors (mostly Mennonite Church members) in place, Karen began to search for the "ideal" store location. Everyone told her this would be the most critical element pertaining to the success of the TTVC store. She was nervous and felt somewhat overwhelmed by the task, but she again relied on her community of supporters and friends. Karen found a realtor who was an acquaintance of a church member: she and the realtor spent much of the spring and early summer of 2002 looking at and rejecting numerous store locations. Karen was becoming frustrated; she decided to take the matter into her own hands.

It was August 2002, and time was running out if Karen was going to open the store in time for the 2002 holiday shopping season. She began looking on the Internet for available and affordable commercial real estate in the areas of Cincinnati that she felt would be receptive to the ideals of fair trade. Cincinnati, traditionally a conservative city, had few shopping districts with significant foot traffic—a criteria that other TTV store managers told Karen was critical to success. There were no "bohemian" sections of town populated by liberal thinkers who actively supported fair trade, like there were in other cities, such as Seattle, Washington, and Saint Paul, Minnesota. One potential location for the TTVC store was the area surrounding the University of Cincinnati (the largest university in the city). There were, however, no available commercial locations in the area, and some perceived the neighborhoods around the school to be unsafe.

Ideally, Karen wanted the store to be in Hyde Park—an upscale neighborhood with a popular shopping square that integrated restaurants, ice cream shops, and boutiques in an area where people walked morning, noon and night. When available, real estate in Hyde Park was expensive and beyond Karen's projected budget of $2,000 per month for rent. Feeling a bit dejected, Karen was driving to her church one day through an area just west of Hyde Park called O'Bryonville. She could not believe her eyes: there was a "for lease" sign in a store front on the main street in O'Bryonville. She quickly jotted down the number and vowed to call as soon as she reached her church.

Karen was elated to learn that the store in O'Bryonville, with 1,017 square feet of retail space, was available immediately, needed only minimal work before the store could open and rented for $1,900 per month. She consulted with the board members; some members were not as excited as Karen. They said, for example, that O'Bryonville had more drive-by traffic than foot traffic. Others pointed out that the consignment, antique and furniture shops in the area did not attract "fair trade-type" customers (i.e., cultural creatives). Aware of these risks, Karen pondered the situation: she believed strongly that if she did not have a store location secured by September 2002, TTVC would not open by November. Karen signed the lease.

### Hiring a Store Manager

While looking for the commercial retail site, Karen and the board members were also trying to find a store manager. They did not have any contacts in the retail business, so they simply placed a want ad in a local newspaper. By August, the advertisement had appeared twice and there were no suitable candidates. Just as Karen was about to pursue other means of finding a store manager, she opened a letter and resume from a woman named Cheryl. Cheryl had retail management experience in a small home decor store, expressed a desire to stay in Cincinnati long-term and was available immediately—Karen eagerly contacted the board to schedule an interview with Cheryl.

When Karen met Cheryl, she knew it was a perfect match. Cheryl was well prepared for the interview: she researched TTV, had visited the store location, asked specific questions about sales objectives, and queried specifically about the relationship between the store manager and board. Cheryl had applicable experience, was extremely energetic, boldly honest and showed a sincere interest in the TTV mission. She provided an excellent balance to Karen's more reserved approach to the project. The board unanimously agreed to hire Cheryl as the first manager of the TTVC store. It was now the end of September 2002, and the race was on to get the store up and running by the beginning of November.

Cheryl started her tenure at TTVC by logging almost 80 hours per week, seven days a week for all of October and November and most of December. She recalled the start-up time as both exciting and exhausting: "I definitely wouldn't want to do it again! As a matter of fact, if the Ten Thousand Villages headquarters asked me, I'd tell them to never let anyone open this close to the holidays no matter how much they begged." She recalled walking into the store and seeing "boxes . . . floor to ceiling, front to back; really, there was nothing but boxes."

Cheryl was certainly impressed by the volume of goods Karen had purchased with the $50,000 loan from TTV's headquarters.[21] Cheryl managed three shifts of volunteers for almost two days to unpack the merchandise. Although TTV stores were largely run by volunteers, Cheryl was—like managers in most other TTV outlets—a full-time, paid employee.

After unpacking, Cheryl and the volunteers began to attach price tags to the products. Cheryl initially priced the products according to recommendations from TTV headquarters: although the price recommendations were not mandated by TTV, Cheryl felt comfortable adhering to them until she gained a clearer understanding of her customers. The volunteers also made store fixtures to display the merchandise. As was customary, TTV headquarters sent a small group of volunteers to assist with both merchandising displays and the setting up of computers. Although work on the displays progressed, the computers arrived late; thankfully, the computers were set up in time for the official store opening on November 1, 2002.

## The First Year of Operations

### Overview

As Karen stated time and time again, "The story included so much more than just the numbers." TTV's headquarters estimated that for every $1,200 in sales at a TTV store, one impoverished artisan could be employed for an entire year. Based on this estimate, the Cincinnati store employed approximately 294 artisans in 2003 (see Exhibits 1 and 2).

TTVC turned its first profit of $546 in April 2003: this was likely the result of traffic generated by TTVC's booth at the Cincinnati Flower Show. Cheryl remembered the excitement and hard work on the part of the volunteers during this profitable period. November was the next significantly profitable month, when TTVC netted $1,902, with sales of $45,767. November sales coincided with the beginning of the store's first major advertising campaign and the rush of the holiday shopping season. Sales in December were the highest for the year at $109,990, resulting in $28,262 profit.

As expected, store traffic mirrored sales. Cheryl noted, "Visits to the store were definitely

**Exhibit 1** Store Income Statement—2003 (in US$)

| | Jan | Feb | Mar | Apr | May | Jun | Jul | Aug | Sep | Oct | Nov | Dec | 2003 |
|---|---|---|---|---|---|---|---|---|---|---|---|---|---|
| **Sales** | 15,968 | 13,748 | 19,898 | 25,676 | 23,243 | 21,293 | 21,125 | 19,022 | 19,440 | 18,068 | 45,767 | 109,990 | 353,238 |
| **Expenses** | | | | | | | | | | | | | |
| Personnel | 4,806 | 8,309 | 6,820 | 6,128 | 6,128 | 6,440 | 6,128 | 6,128 | 6,440 | 6,128 | 6,128 | 10,380 | 79,963 |
| Bank services | 285 | 260 | 328 | 391 | 365 | 343 | 341 | 318 | 323 | 308 | 612 | 1,319 | 5,193 |
| Gen. operating | 559 | 459 | 1,193 | 759 | 609 | 459 | 459 | 459 | 1,193 | 459 | 459 | 459 | 7,526 |
| Equipment & building | 3,756 | 2,940 | 2,940 | 2,940 | 2,940 | 2,940 | 2,940 | 2,940 | 2,940 | 2,940 | 2,940 | 2,940 | 36,096 |
| Marketing/ promotion | | | | | | | | | | | 9,498 | 9,498 | 18,996 |
| Finance fee & loan payment | 650 | 650 | 650 | 650 | 650 | 650 | 650 | 650 | 650 | 720 | 720 | 720 | 8,010 |
| Other | 517 | 167 | 317 | 1,167 | 167 | 317 | 167 | 167 | 317 | 167 | 167 | 317 | 3,954 |
| **Total Exp.** | 10,573 | 12,785 | 12,248 | 12,035 | 10,859 | 11,149 | 10,685 | 10,662 | 11,863 | 10,722 | 20,524 | 25,633 | 159,738 |
| **Total COGS** | 8,144 | 7,011 | 10,148 | 13,095 | 11,854 | 10,859 | 10,774 | 9,701 | 9,914 | 9,214 | 23,341 | 56,095 | 180,150 |
| **Net income** | −2,749 | −6,048 | −2,498 | 546 | 530 | −715 | −334 | −1,341 | −2,337 | −1,868 | 1,902 | 28,262 | 13,350 |

*Source:* Company records.
*Note:* COGS = cost of goods sold.

| Exhibit 2 | Statement of Financial Position, December 31/2003 (in US$) |
|---|---|

| ASSETS | |
|---|---|
| Current assets | |
| Checking/savings | 89,469.98 |
| Merchandise inv. | 21,039.34 |
| TOTAL current assets | 110,509.32 |
| Fixed assets | |
| Total computer system | 12,247.73 |
| Total furniture & fixtures | 2,198.17 |
| Total leasehold improvements | 9,376.24 |
| TOTAL fixed assets | 23,822.14 |
| TOTAL ASSETS | 134,331.46 |
| LIABILITIES & EQUITY | |
| Total current liabilities | 3,348.68 |
| Total long-term liabilities | 40,197.55 |
| Total liabilities | 43,546.23 |
| Equity | |
| Retained earnings | 77,435.23 |
| Net income | 13,350.00 |
| Total equity | 90,785.23 |
| TOTAL LIABILITIES & EQUITY | 134,331.46 |

*Source:* Company files.

not consistent over the course of the year. We increased store hours for the holidays, adding Sunday hours, and one additional hour Monday through Saturday. We were swamped in the last two months of the year." Cheryl kept track of the number of customers served by having the volunteers keep count. The volunteers were also trained to ask shoppers how they heard about the store and if this

was their first visit. The store served approximately 10,880 customers throughout the year.

## Getting the Word Out

Promotions played a vital role during the first year of operations; for example, the store received a local advertising agency grant for $25,000. The grant stipulated that the ad agency would work to develop TTVC print ads at no cost to the store. Cheryl negotiated several advertising placement contracts so the ads would be seen on city buses, strategically placed billboards and in one newspaper, *CityBeat*—the weekly alternative press paper. All ads were placed in November and December 2002 (see Exhibit 3). As with most retailers, these two months were critical sales periods and ads were placed to drive customers to the store. TTVC also received some good publicity through an article in *Catholic Telegraph,* a national Catholic magazine emphasizing social services. Cheryl was particularly proud of being named as a "2002 top retail choice" in *Cincinnati Magazine.* The other main promotional strategy was the "shopping days" campaign. With this promotion, local nonprofit organizations (e.g., Red Cross, YWCA, Salvation Army, and local churches) scheduled days when they would encourage members and friends to shop at the store. In exchange for promoting the store, the designated nonprofit organization would receive a percentage of the store's sales. To augment in-store sales, Cheryl and volunteers staffed booths at local craft shows, such as the Cincinnati Flower Show and the Northern Kentucky Holiday Market. TTVC did not engage in Internet (online) marketing during its first year of operations.

## Year Two

According to Cheryl and Karen, the most important objective for 2004 (year two) was to increase sales. Given that increasing sales was often achieved by considering one's marketing strategy, Cheryl and Karen considered the "four Ps of marketing" (product, price, place, and promotion) as they pertained to TTVC and its target market.

| Exhibit 3 | TTVC Advertisements From Grant Money |
|---|---|

*Source:* Company files.

## Target Market

In the eyes of Cheryl and Karen, TTVC had done a fairly good job of targeting the local cultural creative consumer segment. Toward the end of 2003, for example, MBA students from a local university conducted marketing research as part of their class project. The data indicated that customers were similar to cultural creatives in several ways. The majority of customers were female (88 percent), between the ages of 41 and 60 and earned more than $50,000 per year. An overwhelming majority had at least a bachelor's degree (82 percent). Survey responses also indicated that, like cultural creatives, TTVC shoppers bought fair trade items to help the less fortunate but also found the products to be of high-quality and unique variety. Although there were clearly more cultural creatives in Cincinnati that TTV needed to reach, Cheryl and Karen felt comfortable that their current promotion strategy could be successfully implemented again in the second year to further penetrate this important market segment; in fact, Cheryl and Karen planned to increase the promotional budget in year two.

## Place

Karen felt comfortable with the location of the store, despite the fact that, during the first year, Cheryl had suggested other possible locations and a store expansion. Although they both believed that the O'Bryonville neighborhood was ideal, Cheryl felt that the store was quickly outgrowing the current space (1,000 square feet of retail space) and therefore needed more room. For the time being, however, Karen and the board of directors decided to stay at the current O'Bryonville location.

## Product

The products sold by TTVC were somewhat dictated by TTV's headquarters. Given that the TTV organization guaranteed its artisans 90 percent of last year's purchase volume, TTVC—like other TTV outlets—was obligated to purchase the items that

TTV's headquarters sent to the store. During 2003, TTV's headquarters sent 700 (unordered) products to Cincinnati. Merchandise was received monthly, and although Cheryl was able to select approximately 90 percent of these products from what TTV headquarters had available, 10 percent of the items came "sight unseen." Product availability at TTV headquarters varied throughout the year. Assuming that Cheryl could sell the products that headquarters supplied, she could purchase goods from non-TTV sources as long as they were FTF-approved. In 2003, TTVC sold most of the products supplied by TTV, and had even purchased some supplementary items from SERRV and other FTF-certified suppliers. Cheryl was not overly concerned about products for the upcoming year: goods from Ten Thousand Villages sold well thus far, and although the procurement process was partially out of her control, she felt comfortable in being able to secure additional product if and when necessary. Cheryl repeatedly emphasized that focusing on the mission—employing artisans for sustainable living—was more important than terrific inventory turn.

## Price

TTV's headquarters provided suggested retail prices for products sent to the store: Cheryl could charge these suggested prices, or change them. Over the course of the first year, Cheryl made several adjustments—both increases and decreases—to the prices of various items as she learned the preferences of her customers; for example, due to strong demand, Cheryl raised the price of flower pots from Vietnam by almost 25 percent. She would likely continue to adjust prices as she saw fit throughout the upcoming year.

## A Strategy for Year Two

At this point in their assessment, and in keeping with the primary objective for the second year (i.e., increasing sales), Cheryl and Karen decided to focus on existing customers. While interested in acquiring new customers, Cheryl and Karen were committed to reaching the entire cultural creative segment in Cincinnati, as well as other (non-cultural creative) segments in the area who might be interested in the TTV mission or products. The women seemed convinced they could achieve their goal of increasing sales by focusing on existing customers. Data from the above-mentioned survey suggested to Cheryl and Karen that the store attracted many repeat buyers (almost 60 percent) who were satisfied with their in-store experience and were likely to shop the store again (almost 70 percent). The task at hand was to ensure that those who intended to return acted on their intentions—multiple times throughout the year.

Based on her many interactions with the customers, Cheryl was also convinced that most shoppers could and would—with the right incentives—purchase more items, as well as more expensive items. Cheryl and Karen envisioned having actual *relationships* with their customers, wherein the needs of these customers were more fully satisfied, ultimately making the store more profitable.[22] By setting up procedures and implementing strategies to assure customer longevity and profitability, Cheryl and Karen hoped to insure the long-term success of TTVC. Although they planned to focus on existing customers for the time being, they knew that whatever new policies and procedures they set into motion should be readily applicable to future customers.

## Conclusion

Karen anxiously contemplated what the next year at Ten Thousand Villages Cincinnati would bring: How would she and Cheryl effectively focus on existing customers? They needed sound, workable ideas complete with details. What exactly should they do, and how and when should they do it? What problems might they encounter and/or what actions should they avoid? What aspects of such a strategy were most important? Clearly, they needed a plan.

## CASE QUESTIONS

1. How could Ten Thousand Villages of Cincinnati build customer loyalty that would endure over time? What factors might lead to customers exhibiting latent loyalty rather than brand loyalty?

2. Two features that might help Ten Thousand Villages of Cincinnati succeed would be exceeding expectations and developing quality relationships. How could the marketing team build these two factors into daily operations?

3. Should Ten Thousand Villages of Cincinnati offer a frequency program? Why or why not?

4. How could Ten Thousand Villages of Cincinnati establish and maintain a strong customer relationship management program, especially with cultural creatives?

# Personal Shoppers at Sears: The Elf Initiative

*By Ramasastry Chandrasekhar, under the supervision of Professor Kyle Murray*

In October 2006, Ethel Taylor, senior vice-president (Corporate Store Sales), Sears Canada (Sears), was reviewing a new retailing initiative scheduled for launch in early November in all 123 Sears full-line department stores across Canada. For the 2006 holiday shopping season, Sears was to offer the services of an Elf—the equivalent of a personal shopper—to customers in its full-line department stores. The time for execution was nearing, and Taylor wondered, as she examined the new service offering, how customers would respond to this novel concept in Canadian retailing.

The idea had surfaced at Sears headquarters, in Toronto, only three months earlier. It was motivated by internal market research that indicated 60 to 70 percent of Christmas shoppers at Sears shopped at its stores only during the Christmas season, not during the rest of the year. In addition, a national survey conducted for Sears in 2006 found that 70 percent of women in Canada shopped for gifts up to a year before the holidays as compared to 13 percent of men. Thirty-four percent of Canadians began their holiday shopping one month before Christmas. An estimated 40 percent of men started purchasing gifts in the 14 days before Christmas. About 10 percent of Canadians avoided shopping during the holiday season. At a general level, market research allowed Sears to segment its holiday shoppers into four distinct categories (see Exhibit 1).

Said Taylor:

A department store is widely perceived as the best place to shop, particularly for gifts. Its main attraction is the convenience of a one-stop shop. But, often, customers feel intimidated in a department store. The size of the store, the variety of merchandise on offer and the volume of traffic are daunting for them. Invariably, they postpone shopping until the last moment. They are, as a result, stressed while shopping and could, therefore, do with some help. We see a customer need here and a business opportunity for Sears in building repeat customers.

Version: (A) 2008–01–10

| Exhibit 1 | Holiday Shoppers—Canadian National Survey | | | |
|---|---|---|---|---|
| | **"Keener"** | **"Gambler"** | **"Slacker"** | **"Avoider"** |
| *Personality traits* | Loves the holiday season<br><br>Can't wait to start shopping each year for friends, family, extended relatives, neighbors, the postman, the sales clerk...<br><br>Provides some yuletide cheer to everyone around | May or may not have a list for each member of the family<br><br>Waits until a few weeks before Christmas to start shopping in hopes of scoring great holiday deals | Waits until the last few days before the holidays start to head out to the stores<br><br>Puts off shopping until it is absolutely necessary | Would rather not shop during the holidays and might try to pass off shopping duties to friends and family<br><br>Likely a serial "Can-I-add-my-name-to-that-card?" giver<br><br>Prone to re-gift |
| *Shopping traits* | Starts holiday shopping several months before most others<br><br>Prepares a detailed list in advance—and checks it twice<br><br>Looks through flyers for special promotions and sales | Shops later in the holiday season than the keener<br><br>Likely to rush from store to store in search of the best gifts<br><br>Looks for last-minute deals when shopping | Shops very late in the season<br><br>Wants a one-stop shop to find all gifts<br><br>Might resort to shopping on-line for last-minute gifts, especially if all the "good gifts" aren't available in stores so close to the big day | Shops very little—if at all—for the holiday season<br><br>Does not think out gifts in advance<br><br>Looks for easy one-fits-all purchases |
| *Percentage* | 70 percent of women in Canada are keeners who will shop for gifts up to a year before the holidays as compared to 13 percent of men | 34 percent of Canadians begin their holiday shopping one month before Christmas | An estimated 40 percent of men are slackers, waiting until the 14 days before Christmas before starting to purchase gifts | Approximately 10 percent of Canadians are avoiders who don't shop at all during the holiday season |

*Source:* Sears Canada holiday shopping survey conducted by Maritz Omnitel for Sears Canada among 1,002 interviewees in 2006. http://www.newswire.ca/en/releases/archive/December2006/14/c7266.html.

# Personal Shoppers

Personal shoppers had been operating in Canada for some time, but on a limited basis at higher-end stores, such as Holt Renfrew. The practice was more widespread in the United States, at stores such as Bloomingdales and Saks Fifth Avenue. The basic idea was that by providing customers with a level of individual attention and service beyond what retail associates would normally offer, personal shoppers could add to the ambience of the retailer. In doing so, personal shoppers could have a positive effect on the brand and help to draw traffic to the store. They could re-energize the shopping routine, making it more enjoyable, while saving time for customers. Personal shoppers offered a new level of service and interactivity designed to enhance the shopping experience. Their involvement was wide ranging and could include presenting an array of items for review in a private setting at the store, identifying consumers' preferences and suggesting items tailored to specific personal tastes. Some personal shoppers specialized and became experts in a particular area, such as shopping for busy families or wealthy individuals, buying groceries for senior citizens, and purchasing gifts for corporate clients or holiday gift giving.

Sears Canada had designated its personal shoppers as Elves, building on the word's use in folklore to describe magical or mystical beings who do good and help others. Elves at Sears were chosen from among the 9,000 associates, currently employed at the full-line department stores (i.e., those stores that were "primarily engaged in retailing a wide range of products, with each merchandise line constituting a separate department within the store").[1] After a rigorous process of selection and training, the company had identified approximately 1,000 associates as Elves.

Customers looking for an Elf in a Sears store could find one at a "wish station" that would be easy to locate within the store. From there, the Elf would help customers with whatever they were shopping for, keeping an eye out for complementary merchandise and matching the customers' needs to products across departments throughout the store. In addition, Elves were trained to move consumers through the entire sales process, including finalizing the sale and accepting payment. Elves were compensated by the hour, similar to other sales associates; however, being an Elf meant more hours and, in many cases, the opportunity for more interesting work. Before entering the store, customers could call ahead and have Elves set aside recommended products or even complete a purchase and have the merchandise ready for pick-up. Although the Elf program would only be in full swing during key holiday shopping seasons—e.g., Christmas, Valentine's Day,

Mother's Day and Back-to-School—at least one Elf would be available in each store throughout the year. Although the role of the Elf was still evolving, Sears was committed to ensuring that the program provided customers with a superior level of service and a more enjoyable shopping experience.

Taylor commented:

> The Elves represent the best among Sears' associates, with a track record of excellence in identifying customers' needs and wants, and achieving sales goals. One of their mandates is to convert a gift-purchasing visit to a Sears department store from a chore to a pleasurable experience. The launch of the Elf program during the 2006 holiday season will be followed by a phased introduction, during 2007, at specific times, including Valentine's Day, Easter, Mother's Day, Father's Day, and Back-to-School. At each department store, a dedicated Elf leader and designated associates will execute the program on an on-going basis. In all of Sears' full-line department stores in Canada, 350 Elves will be deployed throughout the year, while an additional 700 will be drafted to cope with the demands of the holiday season.

Sears saw the selection of Elves and their ongoing education as the two factors that would be critical for a successful program. To date, the company had made a significant investment in human capital for the Elf program: in addition to paying elves for training (a total of 9,225 hours: 123 stores × 10 Elves × 7.5 hours), 114,000 incremental hours had been budgeted to staff the program during the fourth quarter of 2006.

## Building Customer Loyalty in a Competitive Retail Market

The Elf program represented the beginning of a new service at Sears Canada, at no charge to the customer. The new strategy was motivated by a number of factors.

In the month of December, the number of transactions at Sears department stores was approximately double the average of the other 11 months of the year (see Exhibit 2). During the holiday season, the stores were attracting both new and existing customers who were visiting Sears with a clear intent to make a purchase. However, the average transaction value was not as strong as the company would like it to be. Sears believed that an opportunity existed to increase the average transaction value and, ultimately, the overall sales volume, during the holiday season.

Sears had redefined merchandising as its core business in 2005. The company had divested its Credit and Financial Services operations to JPMorgan Chase Bank in November 2005. Subsequently, it had consolidated its buying offices at one location, reduced staff by 2,200 (including 1,000 associates relocated to Chase) and pared down non-customer-serving activities.[2] Sears aimed to be a more focused, efficient, and profitable retailer.

The benefits of higher consumer spending in the United States in 2005 had been enjoyed primarily by firms situated at either the high end or the low end of the pricing spectrum. The mid-market U.S. department stores had, on average, underperformed their high-end and low-end competitors. A similar trend was affecting Sears in Canada, which, as a mid-level player, was competing with discounters such as Walmart at one end and specialty retailers at the other end. Sears was also competing with local department stores, such as Canadian Tire.

Sears had embarked on a long-term productivity drive aimed at attaining a cost structure that could compete with the best of Canadian retailers. This drive, to be completed in 2008, was expected to generate pre-tax annualized savings in the order of $100 million.[3] Improving the productivity of store associates, a major company resource, was thus an integral part of the drive. The average sales per hour of non-commissioned associates were $231 at Sears Canada stores. The sales per hour of Elves were expected to be considerably higher.

Sears Canada was committed to "recharge" (as the company called it) various product categories with continuous investments. It was particularly targeting categories such as women's wear, men's wear, home furnishings, major appliances, home décor and cosmetics and accessories. These areas were considered "destination" categories in which the company had established an authority position with customers. Aimed at building on and growing in these areas of strength, investments were made to launch new products, increase selling space, expand in-store departments, increase catalogue pages, improve the product knowledge of salespeople and generally enhance the in-store customer experience. The introduction of Elves fit well with this strategy.

Sears had four types of full-line department stores, classified on the basis of sales volume, store size, location and market demographics (see Exhibit 3). It was also experimenting with new store formats in response to research indicating that "customers wanted an easy-to-shop environment with exceptional customer service." In 2003, the company had unveiled a new department store prototype, as part of a multi-year strategic plan. The prototype consisted of an easy-to-shop interior with wider aisles, clear and bright sightlines and color-coded departments allowing customers to navigate through the store more quickly and easily. Customer service centers had also been set up next to fitting rooms to allow associates to better serve customers. As of February 2006, Sears had 14 full-line department stores utilizing this design.

Said Yvette Corriveau-McGee, manager of Workforce Development, Corporate Store Support:

> There is also recognition at Sears that it is not enough to have satisfied customers. We believe that satisfaction and loyalty do not, at a deeper level, move in tandem. A loyal customer is necessarily satisfied, but a satisfied customer would not necessarily be loyal. It is not enough to satisfy customers. To win, we have to astound them with products and services that exceed their expectations. The introduction of Elves is consistent with the objective of providing a high-quality customer service at the stores, resulting in very satisfied customers that are likely to shop at Sears again and more likely to recommend Sears to others.

**Exhibit 2**  Sears Canada Full-Line Traffic and Sales History

| | Year | JAN | FEB | MAR | APR | MAY | JUN | JUL | AUG | SEPT | OCT | NOV | DEC |
|---|---|---|---|---|---|---|---|---|---|---|---|---|---|
| Transaction Count (billlions) | 2004 | 4,006.3 | 3,922.5 | 5,222.3 | 4,633.4 | 4,648.1 | 5,819.3 | 4,502.5 | 4,344.9 | 5,996.3 | 4,524.7 | 5,990.0 | 10,892.9 |
| | 2005 | 4,116.6 | 3,745.6 | 5,070.4 | 4,628.4 | 4,425.7 | 5,866.9 | 4,482.6 | 4,144.3 | 5,379.2 | 4,640.4 | 5,589.6 | 10,755.1 |
| | 2006 | 3,942.6 | 3,557.4 | 4,692.7 | 4,505.7 | 4,355.7 | 5,422.2 | 4,198.9 | 3,977.3 | 5,562.6 | – | – | – |
| Average Transaction Value ($) | 2004 | 43.49 | 49.00 | 49.99 | 54.00 | 51.60 | 50.89 | 51.39 | 53.02 | 54.54 | 53.56 | 50.24 | 45.69 |
| | 2005 | 43.68 | 48.46 | 48.36 | 53.57 | 50.17 | 49.90 | 49.50 | 51.37 | 54.42 | 55.58 | 53.29 | 46.91 |
| | 2006 | 44.77 | 49.04 | 51.85 | 54.40 | 52.00 | 51.83 | 52.85 | 53.47 | 55.33 | – | – | – |

*Source:* Company files.

| Exhibit 3 | Sears Canada Store Formats |
| --- | --- |

| Type | Number of Stores | Attributes |
| --- | --- | --- |
| Core Plus | 2 | Larger, urban markets that tend to offer more upscale merchandise, usually two or more floors with store size in excess of 300,000 square feet |
| Core | 74 | Urban markets, usually one or two floors with store size ranging from 80,000 to 150,000 square feet |
| Satellite | 33 | Markets with store size ranging from 40,000 to 80,000 square feet |
| Small | 14 | Smaller markets with store size ranging from 25,000 to 40,000 square feet |

*Source:* Company files.

For Sears, Customer Experience is a key retail value proposition. The dimension of Customer Experience is inclusive, as opposed to other retail value propositions like, for example, Price, Convenience, or Selection. It encompasses all of the many ways in which a retailer can not only satisfy but delight customers. Delighting customers is central to customer loyalty as we see it at Sears. The launch of Elves is a step in that direction.

## The Canadian Retailing Industry

According to the Retail Council of Canada, in 2004, more than 227,200 retail locations in Canada provided more than 11 percent of all jobs in every community across the country and representing Canada's second-largest labor force. Valued at about $366 billion in 2006, the Canadian retail market had grown by an average of 5.1 percent since 2002 (see Exhibit 4). Sales from general

| Exhibit 4 | Canadian Retail Trade by Industry (Unadjusted, $Millions) |
| --- | --- |

| | 2002 | 2003 | 2004 | 2005 | 2006 |
| --- | --- | --- | --- | --- | --- |
| All retail trade groups | 319,525.40 | 331,143.40 | 346,721.50 | 366,170.70 | 389,567.40 |
| Total excluding new, used and recreational motor vehicle and parts dealers | 236,061.40 | 248,565.90 | 264,021.20 | 279,353.70 | 297,523.70 |
| New car dealers | 69,161.00 | 68,183.60 | 68,141.10 | 71,515.60 | 74,663.20 |
| Used and recreational motor vehicle and parts dealers | 14,303.00 | 14,393.90 | 14,559.20 | 15,301.40 | 17,380.50 |
| Gasoline stations | 28,138.40 | 29,951.30 | 33,363.80 | 38,356.80 | 41,606.90 |
| Furniture stores | 7,467.30 | 7,923.80 | 8,506.50 | 8,914.40 | 9,585.50 |
| Home furnishings stores | 3,701.20 | 3,971.60 | 4,438.90 | 4,686.30 | 5,339.90 |
| Computer and software stores | 1,967.70 | 1,883.90 | 1,581.80 | 1,557.50 | 1,517.60 |

| | 2002 | 2003 | 2004 | 2005 | 2006 |
|---|---|---|---|---|---|
| Home electronics and appliance stores | 8,361.10 | 9,089.70 | 9,443.10 | 10,164.80 | 11,157.00 |
| Home centers and hardware stores | 12,517.40 | 14,595.20 | 16,597.80 | 18,220.70 | 20,126.50 |
| Specialized building materials and garden stores | 4,234.10 | 4,316.00 | 4,372.80 | 4,340.40 | 4,627.90 |
| Supermarkets | 54,343.60 | 56,874.10 | 59,760.90 | 62,196.30 | 63,512.50 |
| Convenience and specialty food stores | 7,694.40 | 8,371.40 | 8,806.90 | 9,128.60 | 9,356.40 |
| Beer, wine, and liquor stores | 12,696.70 | 13,293.70 | 13,789.80 | 14,343.90 | 15,160.30 |
| Pharmacies and personal care stores | 20,410.40 | 21,266.60 | 22,769.30 | 23,642.70 | 26,070.30 |
| Clothing stores | 14,220.00 | 14,567.10 | 15,311.60 | 16,069.30 | 17,248.50 |
| Shoe, clothing accessories, and jewellery stores | 4,925.60 | 4,903.80 | 4,876.80 | 4,981.30 | 5,400.30 |
| General merchandise stores[1] | 38,419.50 | 40,011.00 | 42,123.70 | 43,758.40 | 46,518.30 |
| Department stores[1] | 20,112.50 | 20,800.80 | 21,849.90 | — | — |
| Other general merchandise stores[1] | 18,307.00 | 19,210.20 | 20,273.80 | — | — |
| Sporting goods, hobby, music, and book stores | 8,501.20 | 8,676.10 | 8,831.40 | 9,379.30 | 10,003.10 |
| Miscellaneous store retailers | 8,462.80 | 8,870.70 | 9,446.10 | 9,613.10 | 10,292.80 |

*Source:* Statistics Canada, "Retail and wholesale: Retail sales by type of store" – accessed at: http://www40.statcan.ca/l01/cst01/trad15a.htm, December 17, 2007.

1. Suppressed to meet the confidentiality requirements of the Statistics Act, as of December 2005 Statistics Canada is no longer publishing separate figures for these categories. Instead, "Department store sales" are combined with "Other general merchandise stores" sales and published under "General merchandise stores."

merchandise stores, which included both department stores and other general merchandisers, were about $46.5 billion.

The Canadian retail market was competitive. Existing players and new entrants were both fighting aggressively for market share. Global retailers were continuing to target and expand into Canada. Sears was facing competition from not only the traditional full-line department stores but also from ever-expanding big-box stores, specialty retailers, and online merchants. The company's competitors ranged from general purpose Walmart stores to niche outlets, such as Reitmans (for women's wear), Best Buy (for electronics), The Home Depot Canada (for hardware), and Shopper's Drug Mart (for cosmetics).

## Sears Canada

Established in 1953 as an equal partnership between Sears Roebuck, Co. of Chicago and Robert Simpson, a mail-order company in Toronto, Sears Canada (as it became known in 1984 on acquisition of majority holdings by Sears Roebuck) had been a major player in the evolution of Canadian retail. Sears Canada reached $1 billion in sales for the first time in 1973, and it became the largest general retailer in Canada by 1976. In 2006, Sears had a presence in all Canadian provinces and territories, with a Sears location within a 10-minute drive of 93 percent of Canadians. In 2005, the company sourced goods from more than 3,000 suppliers, resulting in 2006 sales of nearly $6 billion (see Exhibit 5).

| Exhibit 5 | Sears Canada—Statement of Earnings |
| --- | --- |

| (in million $) | 2006 | 2005 | 2004 | 2003 | 2002 |
| --- | --- | --- | --- | --- | --- |
| Total Revenue | 5,932.8 | 6,237.6 | 6,230.5 | 6,222.7 | 6,535.9 |
| Cost of goods sold | 5,468.3 | 5,814.6 | 5,816.9 | 5,775.9 | 6,107.9 |
| Depreciation and amortization | 152.1 | 164.2 | 166.0 | 146.6 | 148.7 |
| Interest expense net | 48.0 | 48.9 | 55.0 | 59.5 | 59.8 |
| Unusual items – (gain) expense | 25.2 | (747.7) | 3.2 | 5.0 | 189.1 |
| Earnings before income taxes | 239.2 | 957.6 | 189.4 | 235.7 | 30.4 |
| Income tax | 86.6 | 186.8 | 60.7 | 101.0 | (21.8) |
| Net earning | 152.6 | 770.8 | 128.7 | 134.7 | 52.2 |

*Source:* Sears Canada annual reports.

As per its vision statement, "Sears is committed to improving the lives of our customers by providing quality services, products and solutions that earn their trust and build lifetime relationships."

## Merchandising

The company's merchandising strategy was fourfold: recharging destination businesses, improving category productivity and profitability, securing strategic sourcing, and delivering "Sears Value."

The full-line department stores, featuring national brands, were located primarily in suburban enclosed shopping centers. Their merchandise consisted of two broad categories in nearly equal proportions: home and hardlines (comprising appliances, home furnishings, home décor, lawn and garden, hardware, electronics, leisure and seasonal products) and apparel and accessories (comprising women's, men's and children's apparel, cosmetics, jewelry, footwear, and accessories). Some Sears department stores offered home installation products and services, and served as pick-up locations for catalogue merchandise. Many of the stores leased space to other businesses, such as optical centers and photo studios.

## Retail Channels

The company had a multi-channel distribution model—known as "Click, Call or Come In"—consisting of the Net, Catalogue and Retail stores respectively (see Exhibit 6). The Elf program was limited to the retail channel and, specifically, to the full-line department stores within it.

The day-to-day objective at the store level was to maximize the stores' productivity and profitability. Sears Canada was therefore tracking two key metrics: sales per square foot and return on net assets. It had opened its first off-mall, free-standing department store (of 108,000 square feet) in Charlottetown in 2005. The company's Product Repair Services business, which serviced Sears' products and products sold by other retailers, was designed to enhance customer relationships and contribute to a "helpful" brand image.

**Exhibit 6** Sears Canada—"Click, Call or Come In" Multichannel Strategy

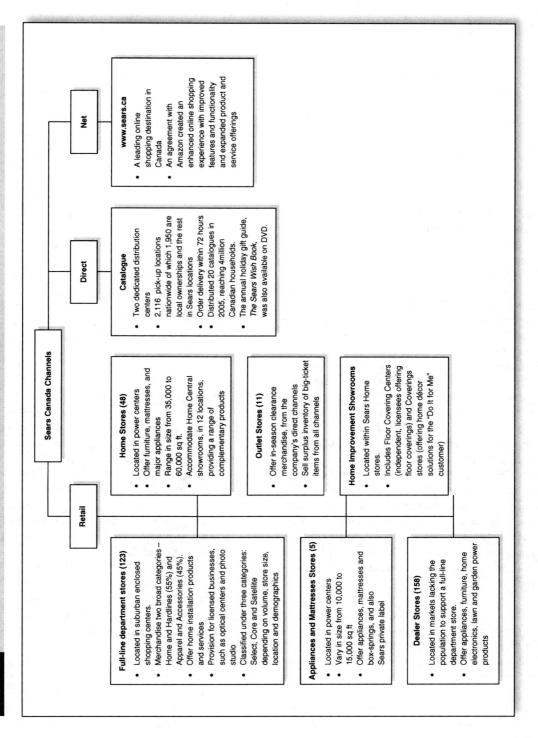

**Sears Canada Channels**

**Retail**

**Full-line department stores (123)**
- Located in suburban enclosed shopping centers.
- Merchandise two broad categories – Home and Hardlines (55%) and Apparel and Accessories (45%).
- Offer home installation products and services
- Provision for licensed businesses, such as optical centers and photo studio
- Classified under three categories: Select, Core and Satellite depending on volume, store size, location and demographics

**Home Stores (48)**
- Located in power centers
- Offer furniture, mattresses, and major appliances
- Range in size from 35,000 to 60,000 sq ft.
- Accommodate Home Central showrooms, in 12 locations, providing a range of complementary products

**Outlet Stores (11)**
- Offer in-season clearance merchandise, from the company's direct channels
- Sell surplus inventory of big-ticket items from all channels

**Home Improvement Showrooms**
- Located within Sears Home stores.
- Includes Floor Covering Centers (independent, licensees offering floor coverings) and Coverings stores (offering home décor solutions for the "Do It for Me" customer)

**Appliances and Mattresses Stores (5)**
- Located in power centers
- Vary in size from 10,000 to 15,000 sq ft
- Offer appliances, mattresses and box-springs, and also Sears private label

**Dealer Stores (158)**
- Located in markets lacking the population to support a full-line department store.
- Offer appliances, furniture, home electronics, lawn and garden power products

**Direct**

**Catalogue**
- Two dedicated distribution centers
- 2,116 pick-up locations nationwide of which 1,950 are local ownerships and the rest in Sears locations
- Order delivery within 72 hours
- Distributed 20 catalogues in 2005, reaching 4million Canadian households.
- The annual holiday gift guide, *The Sears Wish Book,* was also available on DVD.

**Net**

**www.sears.ca**
- A leading online shopping destination in Canada
- An agreement with Amazon created an enhanced online shopping experience with improved features and functionality and expanded product and service offerings

## Support Initiatives

Prior to the Elf program, Sears Canada had taken several steps to increase both the attractiveness of its stores and demand for its products; now these individual initiatives were being included under the umbrella of the Elf program and aimed at enhancing the overall in-store experience. In June 2006, the company had relaunched its website, in partnership with Amazon, to offer a more user-friendly interface. It introduced a broader assortment in women's apparel and created specialized merchandise shops in men's wear. The advertising was modified to be simpler, easy to understand and focused on compelling offers. The company was also working towards a reduction in the frequency of out-of-stock situations and the number of product returns. In addition, the retailer had expanded its electronics assortment to appeal to younger customers. Sears had launched five "specialogues"—smaller and more seasonally relevant catalogues.

Sears Canada had also launched "Operation Wish," a partnership between Sears Canada and the Canadian Armed Forces, to offer its catalogue (with a special discount) to Canadian soldiers serving overseas. This initiative had not only increased sales but generated a great deal of satisfaction among associates.

Pricing at Sears was built around what the company called its Value Strategy, offering everyday value for a major portion of its product offerings. The focus was on solutions for the customer—from coordinating a particular look to providing easy-to-understand product benefits and features. This strategy also helped to increase the size of the average transaction.

To be faithful to the overall objective of enhancing the customer experience, Sears had refrained from adopting some of the current trends in retailing. For example, it would not offer self-checkouts—cost-cutting tools popular with some big-box retailers—because they shifted the burden of tallying prices and packing merchandise onto the customer. Similarly, no price detectors were available on the shelves; instead, each Elf carried a mobile point-of-sale device that would scan the material, print out the bill, and even accept payment. In addition, when the Elves were away from their desks, they would be available to customers through an "on-call" pager system.

Said Donna-Lee Waymann, events promotion coordinator, Corporate Store Support:

> The success of the Elf program depends to a large extent on individual associates. Elves are not new hires. Selected from among the best associates within the company, they are trained to get to know the clients, understand their needs, budgets and time constraints, and generally develop a knack for matching people with products. Their selection and training is an ongoing process at Sears. Elves have opportunities to earn extra hours. This is a financial incentive. They are perceived as having strong leadership potential within the company. That is an incentive in its own right.

## The Big Issues

As Taylor reviewed the Elf strategy on the eve of its execution, she realized that some important issues still needed to be resolved.

The company planned to track the following metrics to monitor the progress of the Elf program: sales per square foot, sales per hour per associate, traffic count, number of transactions and average transaction size. What else should be measured and monitored as a part of the Elf program?

Employees were very excited about the program, particularly the new Elves. Could the momentum be maintained over time? Would Elves lose focus as the novelty wore off? How could the freshness of the program be retained in the months and years to come?

Sales varied by store size, merchandize and location. Stores experiencing the greatest sales were classified as being in the Core category. These 76 stores were located in key market areas with high traffic. Satellite and Small category stores (numbering

33 and 14, respectively) were seeking sales through community involvement by interacting with local retirement centers, schools and businesses. Could the Elves play a role in these stores?

The company's customers were largely the middle-income group who were attracted to the value offered at Sears stores. Whether these customers would seek the help of personal shoppers who were associated with promoting fashions at high-end stores was uncertain. How could the Elf program ensure customer buy-in?

Historically, associates at each Sears department store enjoyed a great deal of specialization. Each associate was focused on a particular category; the Elves, however, were generalists. Chosen from among existing associates, they were taken out of their product categories to serve the general needs of a particular set of customers. The new deployment would likely be seen by store managers as the loss of a valuable resource at the store. Would this reassignment lead to any significant problems?

Finally, after associates became Elves, they would experience a shift in roles. Traditionally, an associate provided a service to the customer in terms of finding the right product suited to a particular requirement. Elves would be "closing the sale," which required a different mind-set.

Sears was launching an innovative retailing initiative to ensure it remained competitive in a dynamic marketplace. The Elf program was an aggressive strategic decision that had been developed very quickly and was being introduced during the critical Christmas season. Taylor wondered what, if anything, they might have overlooked.

## CASE QUESTIONS

1. Sears identified the key metric as sales per hour. How might the Elf program improve this statistic?

2. Which shoppers are the best targets for the Elf program—those with no loyalty, latent loyalty, inertia loyalty, or brand-loyal customers? How might the program also benefit sales to other groups?

3. Do you believe the Elf program will help Sears exceed expectations and build relationships? What about customers who want an Elf but none is available when they are at the store? What might the impact be on them?

4. Is the Elf program a cross-selling program or more of an attempt to create a better customer relationship management system?

5. What role should Elves play when customers are dissatisfied? Should they become immediately involved or leave the task to other store employees?

6. The Elves are being paid an hourly rate. Should they receive some type of commission or bonus? Defend your answer.

# Marketing Control

The five functions of management include planning, organizing, staffing, directing, and control. Of these, planning and control have one very strong linkage: the use of standards. Setting standards will be a key ingredient in the planning process. These targets then become the basis of control.

## Planning Systems: The Basis of Control

Planning consists of five major activities, including scanning the external environment, forecasting future events, making decisions about which plans to undertake, carefully crafting or writing the plans, and setting goals and standards. When company managers set standards, two areas deserve particular attention. The first involves making sure quality standards are set. This will be accomplished by gathering quality forecasting information. The second area is eliminating politics from the planning and goal-setting process, including over-asking for budgets, horse-trading for favors, and hedging one's bet when setting standards. Effective control will not be possible when the planning process is tainted.

## Control Systems

Control may be defined as comparing performance with standards, making corrections when needed, and rewarding success. The control process consists of four steps: (1) restate the standard, (2) measure performance, (3) compare performance to the standard, and (4) make a decision (i.e., make corrections or reward success).

In current terminology, standards are also known as metrics, which is another term for performance measures. Metrics tie the planning and control systems together. They become the basis for making quality corrections to company operations.

## Strategic Controls

Strategic controls are those that apply to the CEO and any other manager involved in directing the portfolios of businesses or activities conducted by a single company or corporation. Typically, these standards are somewhat beyond the reach of the marketing department. They include corporate profitability figures, the value of a share of common stock, overall company growth in assets, and similar measures.

Various units of analysis are used to assess the strategic well-being of an organization. Strategic business units are clusters of activities linked together by a common thread. A profit center is a business unit or department that is treated as a distinct entity enabling revenues and expenses to be determined so that profitability can be measured. Strategic marketing controls revolve around decisions made by the top-level management team and CEO regarding these company portfolios. These efforts go beyond the scope of marketing to encompass a variety of company activities and functions.

## Strategic Marketing Controls

The highest-ranking member of the marketing department is likely to hold the title of vice-president of marketing and sales or director of marketing. This individual has the ultimate responsibility of directing the marketing department and establishing strategic marketing standards. The size of the company and marketing department dictates the types of controls to be put in place. The typical objectives and goals established for the marketing department's planning and control systems are found in the areas of (1) market share, (2) sales, (3) profitability, (4) customer satisfaction, and (5) corporate and brand image.

Market share can be assessed in a number of ways. Company market share reflects the percentage of total industry sales held by the firm. Brand market share is the share of any line of products carrying the same brand, such as when the Pepsi brand is considered separately from the Mountain Dew line even though both are made by the same company. Product market share is the share of sales held by an individual product.

Sales figures are evaluated using roughly the same levels of analysis as market share. Total sales constitute a general measure of the well-being of the sales department and overall organization. Sales are also tallied by brand or product line. A third level consists of figures for individual products. Sales will be considered in relation to past sales and competitor sales, including company versus company, brand versus brand, and product versus product.

Profitability figures apply to the overall organization and specific areas. Among them, assessments of profitability are made for products, territories, customers, segments, trade channels, and order sizes. Profits are never the solitary goal for a marketing program. Those early in a life cycle may lose money, as might a product being introduced into a new territory, country, or to a different market segment.

Customer satisfaction can be assessed in a variety of ways. Among them, measures may be taken for customer reactions to the company or purchase experience, for negative customer reactions, and for positive customer responses. Each provides insight into the overall degree of satisfaction that in turn affects customer loyalty and customer retention.

Customer reactions to the company or purchase experience may be studied in several ways. Evaluation cards can be given during or after a purchase. Post-purchase follow-up calls or e-mails provide additional information. Survey data provides a richer context for customer responses. Blogs and customer-generated reviews provide other insights.

Negative customer responses take the forms of product returns, warranty work that is required, and complaints. Complaints may be made in person, by mail, online, or through blogs and reviews. A full assessment includes how the company responded to the complaint and the customer's reaction to the company's efforts.

Positive customer responses include repeat purchases and complimentary remarks. Compliments are made in person, by mail, online, through blogs and reviews, and in other ways. Positive responses can lead to high levels of brand loyalty as well as word-of-mouth endorsements.

Corporate and brand image may be evaluated using the criteria of share of mind and share of heart. Share of mind indicates consumer awareness of the company and its products. Share of heart indicates fondness or loyalty. To understand brand and image, primary sources such as surveys, interviews, and focus groups are helpful. Secondary sources include information collected from various media. In summary, the strategic level of control in the marketing department contains the evaluation of the most general features of the marketing program.

## Brands and Product Lines

Three primary objectives with regard to brands are to build brand awareness, brand loyalty, and perceptions of brand equity. Also, evaluations of new products and brand extensions will be undertaken. When a company carries only a single brand, the goal for the brand will also be the companywide goal. Large firms assess portfolios of brands.

Measuring brand awareness begins with finding out how many consumers or businesses are aware of the company's products. One method, studying media figures, includes ratings of programs, circulation figures of newspapers and periodicals, traffic counts of billboards, and other rough measures. Trade show traffic indicates exposure to other businesses. More direct measures of awareness can be made using mall intercepts, surveys, and Internet questionnaires.

Brand loyalty can be examined through the repeat-business indicator. Also, lifetime values of customers and RFM (recency, frequency, and monetary value) figures may be evaluated. Brand loyalty occurs when customers have moved beyond awareness and liking to prefer a brand. It bodes well for the company's future.

Brand equity, the perception that a firm's products are different and better, is examined through market research, such as surveys, questionnaires, and focus groups. Brand equity takes time to build and can easily be damaged by negative publicity. The marketing team works hard to defend and build brand equity perceptions.

New products and brand extensions are evaluated using metrics such as rate of trial, repeat purchases, and cannibalization rates. Rate of trial indicate the success level of a product launch. Repeat purchase rates measure consumer acceptance of the product. The cannibalization rate shows whether sales of a new product came at the expense of existing products or added new customers.

## Marketing Function or Departmental Controls

The five primary functions carried out under the leadership of a director or vice-president of marketing are (1) marketing activities, (2) sales activities, (3) advertising and promotional activities, (4) distribution activities, and (5) the public relations function. Each is assessed for current success and contributions to the firm's long-term well-being, with an eye focused on the best types of corrections to be made going forward.

Sales activities are assessed using input measures, output measures, and financial measures. Input measures include presales activities, selling activities, post-selling activities, and nonselling activities. Metrics are selected based on the firm's goals, the type of selling position, and other specific company circumstances.

Advertising and promotional activities will be evaluated in three areas (1) advertising and promotional cost measures, (2) psychological responses, and (3) behavioral responses. Advertising and promotional costs are studied using the percentage-of-sales metric or the revenue-per-ad-dollar ratio. Psychological responses include recognition, recall, persuasion, emotional responses, and liking. Behavior responses consist of observable reactions to promotions and advertisements.

Distribution activity assessments normally include average delivery time, the percentage of stores carrying a product, the months of inventory in the dealer's possession, and the distribution cost per unit. The goals of efficient delivery (low cost) and effective distribution (serving the marketing program) remain key areas of concern.

Public relations activities affect the firm's image and positioning. Any hit, or mention in a news story or public service announcement, should be reviewed. Other metrics are the number of clippings generated, calculating impressions (the number of hits multiplied by the medium's audience), and the advertising equivalence of the hit or story. Public relations evaluations also examine the number of positive versus negative stories.

## Individual Controls

Performance appraisal metrics seek to achieve three outcomes (1) perceptions of relevance, (2) perceptions of fairness, and (3) perceptions that rewards are tied to performance. Individual performance objectives succeed when they are difficult, attainable, clearly stated, measurable, and flexible. It is crucial to link individual performance goals with overall company goals.

## Strategic Corrections

Several perspectives exist regarding strategic standing. One approach focuses on the company's core competence, with the goal of creating a distinctive competence. Any time an organization enjoys competitive superiority, the long-term strategic plan is working. When a company faces a plateau of brand parity, corrections may be made to achieve brand equity through various marketing actions.

A second perspective examines strategic direction in terms of becoming the low-cost provider, creating broad differentiation, remaining the best-cost provider, or any focused marketing strategy. Company activities should align with the desired approach. Corrections are made when they do not.

Standard responses or corrections to a company's strategic course of action include (1) rapid-growth strategies, (2) slow-growth strategies, (3) stability strategies, or (4) decline strategies. Rapid-growth strategies consist of mergers, acquisitions, or takeovers of other companies, vertical integration, horizontal integration, a joint venture, or a globalization strategy. Two slow-growth strategies are possible: incremental growth by adding customers or markets and efficiency strategies that concentrate on achieving greater profits by eliminating waste or unnecessary costs.

Decline strategies may be implemented through divestment, liquidation, or retrenchment. Divestment means the company sells off part of the operation intact. Liquidation strategies are those that reduce the size of a company by selling component parts rather than a full operation. Retrenchment strategies consist of reducing outlets, reducing products and services, eliminating entire markets, or eliminating employees. The goal of any retrenchment or decline strategy should be to allow the company to become smaller but stronger.

## ⊠ Tactical Corrections

Tactical corrections made within the marketing department provide additional guidance to company activities. Three areas given attention are (1) product-line tactics, (2) product-based tactics, and (3) functional tactics. Product-line tactics are made by cutting or adding depth to a product line or by cutting or adding breadth to product lines. Product-based tactics involve finding new users, finding new uses for a product, and encouraging more frequent use. Functional tactics are in the areas of advertising, promotions, personal selling, distribution, and channel arrangements.

## ⊠ Individual Rewards and Corrections

The fourth step of control results in either corrections or rewards. Rewards for successful performance are granted to top managers, middle managers, and entry-level employees. The rewards are adjusted to the individual's rank. The same holds true for corrections. Quality individual performance appraisal systems consistently focus on the future.

## ⊠ Implications for Marketing Managers

To effectively manage the marketing control system, marketing managers avoid overemphasizing short-term results and single indicators. This will be accomplished by seeing the big picture, encouraging participation, using the system for diagnosis rather than blame, remaining flexible in changing circumstances, and staying future-oriented. Successful control programs lead the organization into the future, where new plans and activities can be devised and implemented.

## ⊠ The Cases

### Microsoft and the Xbox 360 Ring of Death

The Microsoft Xbox 360 was to be a console that went far beyond gaming. Instead, it was an entertainment hub featuring high-definition games plus digital movies and music. Both the Premium and Core models were supposed to become the next generation in this type of entertainment. The products quickly captured a substantial market share. Unfortunately, technical problems emerged, and the product was at times unreliable. Nintendo's Wii overtook the Xbox as the dominant market product, followed by the Sony Blu-ray Disc player. Microsoft's inability to resolve quality problems caused a loss of goodwill among core customers. Extending the product's warranty to 3 years helped, but the Xbox never recaptured its initial momentum in the gaming marketplace.

### Kenexa

Kenexa consults in the area of human resources. Led by Jack W. Wiley and Scott Brooks, the company developed a High-Performance Model that could be applied to various clients. The National Choice Bank (NCB) was interested in understanding perceptions of both employees and customers. The linkage between employees, customers, and the business serves as a measure of current success and a predictor of future outcomes. The underlying concepts are that customer loyalty will be a potent predictor of business performance and that specific leadership practices can enhance or inhibit employees seeking to develop quality bonds with those customers. Leader behaviors include a customer orientation, an emphasis on quality, methods of employee training, and the focus on employee involvement.

# Microsoft and the Xbox 360 Ring of Death[1]

*By David Wesley, under the supervision of Professor Gloria Barczak*

On the eve of the Xbox 360's North American launch, Microsoft was poised to become the world leader in video game entertainment. By launching its console in 2005, one year ahead of rivals Sony and Nintendo, Microsoft was able to establish a customer base of more than five million users before the first Nintendo Wii or Playstation 3 (PS3) hit store shelves. "In 2001, [the original] Xbox launched many months after Sony, and the all-conquering PS2 by then had cemented its position in the local games market," observed one journalist. "This time the boot is on the other foot."[2] Most industry observers agreed: analysts at Piper Jaffrey, an investment bank, predicted that the Xbox 360 would lead the market through 2011. By the end of 2008, Piper Jaffrey predicted sales of nearly 20 million Xbox 360s, compared to 15 million PS3s and only five million Nintendo Wiis.[3]

Despite this positive projection, somewhere along the line the Xbox 360 took a wrong turn. The Nintendo Wii, which many had written off as an underpowered toy, quickly captured the lead in monthly sales in every major market, although Sony had a slow start, its PS3 was gaining ground. Major design flaws in the Xbox 360 resulted in more than US$1 billion[4] in warranty repair costs, and contributed to a nearly $2 billion loss for the 2006–07 fiscal year (see Exhibit 1).[5]

Although some outside observers were doubtful that the Xbox division would ever be profitable, Robbie Bach, president of Microsoft Entertainment and Devices, assured them that the Xbox 360 would be profitable in 2008. It "will be profitable next year," he said. "We'll make money next year and that will be the first time, which is pretty exciting. And then the next two or three years are the place where you need to make tracks, and the next two or three years are where you have to make money."[6]

Not everyone agreed that the focus should be on profitability; instead, they argued that Microsoft's immediate concern should be to restore consumer confidence in the Xbox 360 by addressing the console's serious technical shortcomings.[7]

## Background

### The Entertainment and Devices Division

Microsoft Windows had long been the most popular operating system for playing computer games; however, the rise of inexpensive gaming consoles in the 1990s caused Microsoft some concern, as sales

| Exhibit 1 | Entertainment and Devices Division Financial Results ($ millions) | | | | | |
|---|---|---|---|---|---|---|
| | **2002** | **2003** | **2004** | **2005** | **2006** | **2007** |
| Revenues | 2,453 | 2,748 | 2,876 | 3,242 | 4,256 | 6,080 |
| Expenses | (3,588) | (3,939) | (4,213) | (3,727) | (5,518) | (7,970) |
| Operating loss | (1,135) | (1,191) | (1,337) | (485) | (1,262) | (1,890) |

*Source:* Cesar A. Berardini, "Robbie Bach: Xbox Will Be Profitable Next Year," Team Xbox, May 4, 2007: http://news.teamxbox.com/xbox/13401/Robbie-Bach-Xbox-Will-Be-Profitable-Next-Year/, accessed February 17, 2010 and Microsoft (2007 figures).

Version: (A) 2010–03–09

began to shift away from home computers. Microsoft saw gaming as a way to assure its dominance in computer-based home entertainment. According to Seamus Blackley, the Microsoft executive who co-wrote the Xbox business plan, "If the Xbox successfully landed Microsoft in the world's living rooms, it could count not only on the substantial profits from big-time game publishing, but also on one day controlling an empire of movies and TV-on-demand, Internet, and . . . as-yet-undreamed services."[8]

Microsoft launched the original Xbox in 2001, after nearly two years of development.[9] Microsoft sold the Xbox for approximately $40 less than it cost the company to manufacture and distribute, leading to some speculation that Microsoft could lose as much as $3.3 billion over the life of the console. On the other hand, the software giant hoped that by getting its console in the hands of as many consumers as possible, it could earn enough revenue through software sales and third-party licenses to offset those losses.

In 2003, Microsoft hired Peter Moore to head the Xbox division. At the time, Moore had been managing Sega's video game console business. In 1991, Sega launched a popular console known as the Sega Genesis, along with several highly successful game franchises, such as "Sonic the Hedgehog." In 1999, while Moore headed the console business, Sega introduced the Dreamcast, a console that was well ahead of its time with built-in support for online gaming and advanced graphics. However, when Sony and Nintendo responded by dropping the price of their consoles and Microsoft entered the market with the Xbox, Sega felt it could no longer compete. Less than two years later, Sega decided to pull the console from the market.[10]

Moore was livid. He blamed the failure of the Dreamcast on a "pre-emptive guerrilla PR" campaign by Sony, "where they promised the consumer something they probably believed they were going to deliver, but they never did." What that did in consumers' minds was create "fear uncertainty and doubt" (FUD):

It was a massive FUD campaign. The consumer thought twice and they started to read, "can the Dreamcast make it?" It had a

tough time in Europe; it had a really disastrous time in Japan. . . . It was like, "well, what do you do?" You just do it yourself. You start talking, you don't wait for the Japanese to give you messaging—because PR is something they don't do very well . . . the only thing we could do was be passionate. But it was too little too late unfortunately.[11]

In January 2003, Steve Ballmer, chief executive officer (CEO) of Microsoft, asked Moore to head up the Xbox division. For Moore, it was a chance to get even with Sony, "to put on my suit of armor, get on my horse and take on Sony again—but with a little bit more money this time!" A month later, Moore installed himself at Microsoft, once again ready to take on his archrival. One idea was to acquire Nintendo, but ultimately Microsoft determined that Nintendo was becoming too marginalized to be an important player in the video games market: "We were just completely fixated on Sony," recalled Moore. "Nintendo didn't even come into the conversation."[12]

Moore's primary task would be to oversee the development and launch of Microsoft's next generation console, the Xbox 360. Sega had spent enormous sums of money publicizing the launch of the Dreamcast, only to see it fail. This time, Moore wanted to do things differently: "I'm sick of consoles being launched with massively expensive ad campaigns," he told his colleagues at Microsoft. "I'm going to do this differently."[13]

## The Launch of the Xbox 360

In the months leading up to the unveiling of the Xbox 360, Microsoft created an online video game known as OurColony. Information about the game was sent to Xbox fans around the world with cryptic messages and instructions on how to participate in the new game. The final step in the game was revealed on May 12, 2005. Users who successfully completed all the steps were shown a video demonstration of the Xbox 360.[14] That day, a global MTV special presentation hosted by actor Elijah Wood, star of the Lord of the Rings trilogy, revealed the

Xbox 360 for the first time. The show provided fans with a first look at the console's specifications, capabilities and online gameplay through a new version of the Xbox Live service. After the show, viewers were invited to get more information about the console from MTV.com, including product details and previews of upcoming game titles.[15]

"Tonight's unveiling is a signal to the world that the next generation of gaming is here," Microsoft announced in a news release.

> Every Xbox 360 game is designed for high-definition, wide-screen televisions. Regardless of the television Xbox 360 connects to, gamers will experience smooth, cinematic experiences that far exceed anything they've seen or felt in games before. And these experiences are never more than a click away. The Xbox Guide Button is the launch pad that connects gamers to their games, friends and music from the wireless controller.[16]

The benefits of the console went far beyond gaming. The Xbox 360 was designed to be a high-definition entertainment hub that included games, movies and music.

> As high-definition entertainment becomes more pervasive, Microsoft will offer more ways to experience HDTV and movies in any room in the house, any way people want it. Whether it's by the dropping of an optical disc in a drive, streaming to Xbox 360, or through broadband distribution, Xbox 360 will let players choose how to light up their high-definition content.[17]

Two models of the Xbox 360 were to be offered. The "Premium" package included a hard drive and headphones for $399. A stripped-down "Core" version with no hard drive would be priced at $299. High-definition movie playback would eventually be supported through the Xbox Live store for downloadable content and through an HD-DVD add-on drive capable of playing high-definition video discs.

The official unveiling came four days later at the Electronics Entertainment Expo (E3), in Los Angeles, California. E3 was the gaming industry's most important trade event, providing a venue for new product announcements and demonstrations. Sony and Nintendo also used E3 to announce their own next-generation consoles. However, unlike Microsoft's console, the Sony and Nintendo consoles would not become available to consumers until the following year. Both companies hoped that by announcing the inevitable availability of their consoles, potential Xbox 360 customers would wait to make their purchase until all three consoles became available. At that point they could evaluate all the consoles side by side and choose the best one for their needs.

On launch day, November 22, 2005, Microsoft held an official launch party at a 200,000 square-foot aircraft hangar in the Los Angeles suburb of Palmdale, California. Attendees were chosen by random drawing after filling out entry forms on one of several popular gaming websites. The 2,000 winners of the draw were given an opportunity to play 18 launch titles on the 500 Xbox 360 consoles arranged throughout the hanger.[18]

## Early Problems

Microsoft only had 69 days from the Xbox 360's initial production date until launch day; this short window caused significant supply shortages during the console's first few months on the market.[19] Within days of the console's launch, thousands of units began to appear on grey market sites, such as eBay, where they commanded prices that were two to three times the retail price.[20] Moore blamed the supply shortages on problems with the production line:

> Nothing's perfect. . . . You've got a complex piece of hardware that's got 1,700 different parts in it, every now and again the line will slow down because something's happened and there'll be a component that didn't make it that morning . . . That's just the way of the beast, particularly when you are ramping up factories from ground zero all the way up to full capacity.[21]

Although Microsoft claimed that the launch of the Xbox 360 was a great success, some analysts were doubtful. The day after the launch, one analyst wrote that the results were "not pretty":

> From unconfirmed rumors of near-riots as employees apparently hoarded Xbox 360 systems in front of waiting customers, to numbers of pre-orders that went unfulfilled, some are saying Microsoft mishandled the launch. But those who actually got the systems in hand are breathing easy and living it up, right? *Some* of them are. But others are posting a plethora of problems with their brand-new 360s, from game crashes to hard drives that simply don't work. . . . Just how widespread is the scope of 360 problems, though? It's a little too early to call whether these problems are systemic or isolated bugs. [22]

In fact, the technical problems reported on launch day were early signs of design and production defects that would plague Microsoft's entire Xbox 360 line.

Despite the initial supply shortages and reports of console malfunctions, Microsoft's one-year advantage allowed it to win significant market share. By the time the Nintendo Wii and Sony Playstation 3 were launched in November 2006, Microsoft had a huge lead with sales of nearly five million consoles and a library of approximately 160 games. [23]

# The Xbox Live Experience

Microsoft's strategy had always been to dominate the sphere of online gaming through its Xbox Live online gaming service. Online gaming increased the challenge and playability by allowing gamers to face off against similarly skilled opponents or form teams with other online players. Online gaming also had the advantage of downloadable add-on content, such as new levels, landscapes or characters. Finally, developers could test new games online and marketers could use the data gathered through online services to better understand customers.

The launch of the Xbox 360 coincided with rapid growth in broadband Internet subscriptions in the United States. [24] More than 60 percent of Xbox 360 owners subscribed to Xbox Live at an annual cost of $50, [25] and the number surpassed 10 million members at the end of 2007. [26] Even though Microsoft was the only console maker to charge a fee for its online service, it had a strong lead over Sony and Nintendo. [27]

Xbox Live also gave Microsoft unprecedented information about its customers. "[W]e've got this consumer demographic nailed," observed Moore. "[W]e know exactly who they are, what they're doing, what they're playing, what they like, what they don't like every second of every day." [28]

Although Sony sought to unseat Microsoft by enhancing its own online service, Microsoft's lead proved to be a significant barrier to entry. "Is it possible that Sony could create a network the size and scale of Xbox Live in such a short time?" asked one analyst when Sony announced its decision to challenge Microsoft. "It has cost Microsoft, the world's largest software company, billions [of dollars] and taken years just to lay the framework for the current Xbox Live service."

> [I]t seems unlikely they could take the crown from Microsoft on their first try, but any attempt is a huge relief. It was beginning to look like Sony didn't think the Xbox Live service was a valuable addition to console gaming, or a serious competitor to their hegemony. [29]

For many users, the PlayStation Network was already good enough to meet their needs. Online play was almost identical for non-exclusive games. The fact that Sony offered its service for free was enough to sway some gamers toward the PlayStation Network. Sony made no secret of the fact that it was competing on price: "I think what we're doing is pretty cool," offered Peter Dille, senior vice president for marketing and PlayStation Network. "I also think it comes back to great value. There's an awful lot of content you can get on the PlayStation Network.

We're not charging consumers a subscription fee to get online and play games head to head."[30]

Nintendo, on the other hand, still had a lot of catching up to do. "The current gold standard of online gaming services is Microsoft's Xbox Live," observed one video games journalist. "The Wii, by comparison, doesn't have a consistent online network, forcing each developer to devise its own solutions. . . . What the Wii's online games all have in common is that they're shamefully primitive."[31]

## The Red Ring of Death

Rob Cassingham was the ideal Xbox fan. On launch day, he and his spouse attended the launch event with large "XBOX" signs hanging from their necks. Cassingham loved games and he loved the Xbox. He even had a personalized license plate that read "Xbox 360." That was in 2005; in 2006, his first unit stopped working after displaying a red ring of light around the power button. That ring would later become infamously known among gamers as the "Red Ring of Death."

In early 2007, after returning his seventh failed unit to Microsoft, Cassingham surrendered: "Xbox Live is great," he noted, but the general hardware failures were too much.

> When [the repaired unit] comes, I'm going to sell it. . . . That's a hard thing to give up. I gave up cigarette smoking so I've been through worse. I've had game systems since the Coleco machine. Intellivision. The first machine I had was the Magnavox Odyssey in 1972. I have never had to send any of them back.[32]

Cassingham's experience was far from unique. An online survey conducted by a popular gaming website found that 59 percent of registered members (2,111 people) experienced at least one Xbox 360 failure. Survey administrator David Abrams acknowledged that the failure rate represented in the survey was almost certainly higher than normal: "It's probably safe to assume that members of an online video game community use their systems more than

others. I'd imagine that increased use could lead to increased console failures," he wrote.[33]

Surveys of retailers and repair centers showed average failure rates of between 16 and 33 percent.[34] However, such reports did not include console owners who returned defective units directly to Microsoft. By comparison, the failure rates for the Nintendo Wii and the Sony PlayStation 3 were estimated to be 2.7 percent and 10 percent respectively, according to a study conducted by Square Trade, the largest independent warranty provider.[35]

In February 2007, a British Broadcasting Corporation (BBC) television news program highlighted the problems faced by Xbox 360 owners. Initially, Microsoft denied that it had a problem.[36] In its official response, Microsoft stated the following:

> The return rate is significantly lower than the consumer electronics industry average of 3 to 5 percent. Customer satisfaction is our highest priority, and we do everything we can to take care of gamers who may be having problems with their consoles.[37]

In the United Kingdom, Micromart Ltd., which handled video game console repairs for major retailers, was inundated with defective systems. Finally, it refused to accept Xbox 360 units. "The problem with three red lights was there fairly regularly, but over two or three months it became a real issue," explained a Micromart representative.[38] "These days, it's harder to find someone with an original 360 than it is to find one who has had problems," observed one journalist.

> Everyone online is complaining about overheating, red lights of death, and being on their third systems (if not more). I've had two die. . . . [o]ther game journalists and reviewers have complained about having to replace the office system often.[39]

On July 5, 2007, Microsoft finally admitted that it had a serious problem; that day, Moore published an open letter on the company's website (see Exhibit 2). "You've spoken, and we've heard

| Exhibit 2 | Open Letter From Peter Moore, Corporate Vice-President, Microsoft Interactive Entertainment[1] |
|---|---|

To our Xbox Community:

You've spoken, and we've heard you. Good service and a good customer experience are areas of the business that we care deeply about. And frankly, we've not been doing a good enough job.

Some of you have expressed frustration with the customer experiences you have had with Xbox 360; frustration with having to return your console for service after receiving the general hardware error message on the console.

The majority of customers who own Xbox 360 consoles have had a terrific experience from their first day, and continue to, day in and day out. But when anyone questions the reliability of our product, or our commitment to our customers, it's something I take very seriously.

We have been following this issue closely, and with on-going testing have identified several factors that can cause a general hardware failure indicated by three flashing red lights on the console. To address this issue, and as part of our ongoing work, we have already made certain improvements to the console.

We are also implementing some important policy changes intended to keep you in the game, worry-free.

As of today, all Xbox 360 consoles are covered by an enhanced warranty program to address specifically the general hardware failures indicated by the three flashing red lights on the console. This applies to new and previously-sold consoles. While we will still have a general one year console warranty (two years in some countries), we are announcing today a three-year warranty that covers any console that displays a three flashing red lights error message. If a customer has an issue indicated by the three flashing red lights, Microsoft will repair the console free of charge — including shipping — for three years from the console's purchase date. We will also retroactively reimburse any of you who paid for repairs related to problems indicated by this error message in the past. In doing so, Microsoft stands behind its products and takes responsibility to ensure that every Xbox 360 console owner continues to have a fantastic gaming experience.

If we have let any of you down in the experience you have had with your Xbox 360, we sincerely apologize. We are taking responsibility and are making these changes to ensure that every Xbox 360 owner continues to have a great experience.

This will take a few days to roll out globally, and I appreciate your continued patience as we launch this program. I've posted an FAQ that should address some additional questions, and we'll update it over the next few days.

I want to thank you, on behalf of all us at Microsoft, for your loyalty.

---

1. "Open Letter From Peter Moore," Xbox.com, July 5, 2007, xbox.com/en-GB/support/petermooreletter.htm, accessed on April 16, 2008, http://web.archive.org/web/20080705194728/http://www.xbox.com/en-GB/support/petermooreletter.htm.

---

you," he wrote. "Good service and a good customer experience are areas of the business that we care deeply about. And frankly, we've not been doing a good enough job." [40] Microsoft agreed to take "responsibility to repair or replace any Xbox 360 console that experiences the 'three flashing red lights' error message within three years from time of purchase free of charge, including shipping costs." Microsoft estimated the cost of repairs to be between $1.05 billion and $1.15 billion.[41]

Less than two weeks later, Moore resigned from Microsoft for "personal reasons."[42]

## Scratched Discs

A commonly reported problem that was not covered under Microsoft's warranty extension program was scratched game discs. As early as launch day, some owners reported circular scratches to their game discs, often rendering them unusable.[43] An investigation by a Dutch television news program found that between one and two million consoles had a missing component in the drive mechanism that is used to stabilize discs while they are spinning. Again, Microsoft's initial response was to deny the problem.[44] At the same time, Microsoft launched a disc-replacement program that allowed console owners to send in scratched discs for replacement.[45] Microsoft also encouraged owners to seek warranty repairs if they believed the scratches were caused by a hardware defect.

Many believed that Microsoft had not done enough to address the problem; for example, not all game titles were covered under the replacement program, nor did Microsoft offer to extend the warranty on consoles affected by disc scratches as it had done for the Red Ring of Death. As a result, the European Commission launched an official investigation of the problem,[46] and in the United States, some Xbox 360 owners launched a class action suit against Microsoft.[47]

## Design Flaws

Microsoft outsourced production of the Xbox 360 to three Chinese electronics manufacturers: Celestica, Flextronics, and Wistron. All three had been contract manufacturers for a wide range of automotive, industrial, medical, and technology companies. Flextronics and Wistron also produced the original Xbox, while Celestica was a new partner for Microsoft. In early 2007, Wistron announced that it would phase out production of the Xbox 360, which accounted for 10 percent of the firm's total revenues, due to declining margins.[48]

One former Microsoft engineer, who was interviewed by Jacob Metcalf, editor of *Digital*

*Joystick,* under condition of anonymity believed that the problems encountered by Xbox 360 owners were the result of design flaws and poor quality control at the company's Chinese manufacturing sites. In an effort to beat Sony to market, Microsoft decided to overlook apparent problems. However, the company never anticipated the full extent of the impact the flaws would have on the console.

> Whenever something failed and there was a question about whether the test result was false, they would remove that test, retest and ship, or see if the unit would boot a game and run briefly and then ship. The 360 is too complex of a machine to get away with that.
> I'm sure [the management team] thought that somehow they would figure it out and everything would end up ok. Plus, they tend to make big decisions like that in terms of dollars. They would rationalize that if the first few million boxes had a high failure rate, a few 10's of millions of dollars would cover it. And contrasting that cost with a big lead on Sony, they would pay it in a heartbeat.[49]

Microsoft was quick to defend its partners: "You should think of this as an issue that is Microsoft's responsibility," replied Bach.

> The partners who have done assembly and component work for us have done good work; we're very proud of working with them; we're going to continue to work with them. So you should think of it as a Microsoft design issue. Again, since it's multiple things [that are causing the Xbox 360 failures], I hate to even point at design. To get at the heart of your question, it's really our responsibility, not anybody else's.[50]

Wistron's decision to phase out production of Xbox 360 seemed to support Bach's assertion.

After six years as a Microsoft subcontractor, Wistron decided to end its relationship with Microsoft.[51] Shortly thereafter, Nintendo contracted with Wistron to produce the Wii,[52] a console with a defect rate of less than three percent.

Bryan Lewis, research vice president and chief analyst at Gartner, Inc., agreed that Microsoft alone was to blame for the Xbox 360's high failure rate. He blamed the problems on Microsoft's decision to cut costs by not using a traditional microchip designer; instead, Microsoft took its own processor design directly to a Taiwanese chip manufacturer. This helped reduce design costs by "tens of millions of dollars." Although a specialist firm would have cost more, it "could have been able to design a graphics processor that dissipates much less power."[53]

Although the former Microsoft engineer interviewed by Metcalf agreed that the Red Ring of Death was most frequently caused by poor thermal design, he contended that other flaws could produce the same result. Although these types of problems were more likely to affect avid gamers than casual gamers, less frequent use only delayed the inevitable. He believed that eventually every console "will probably fail."[54]

## Declining Market Share

The launch of the Nintendo Wii and Sony PlayStation 3 in November 2006 had a major impact on Xbox 360 sales. During the first half of 2007, sales were less than half of 2006 sales over the same time period. In its fiscal fourth quarter, Microsoft's gaming division lost $1.2 billion on sales of 700,000 consoles, compared to a loss of $423 million on sales of 1.8 million consoles in the fourth quarter of 2006.[55]

### The Halo Effect

Microsoft pinned its hopes for a turnaround on the release of Halo 3 in September 2007. Halo was a highly successful video game series developed by Microsoft subsidiary Bungie Studios. It was first released in 2001 exclusively for the Xbox. It went on to sell more than six million copies. Halo 2 was released in 2004 and sold more than two million copies on the day of its launch, making it the best-selling media product in history.[56]

Although Halo 3 was one of the most expensive games ever produced by Microsoft, with an estimated production cost of $30 million (about twice the average production cost of an Xbox 360 or PlayStation 3 game),[57] it proved to be money well spent. Launch day sales exceeded three million copies. During the first week, Halo 3 contributed gross revenues in excess of $300 million.[58] The game also propelled the Xbox 360 to first place in console sales for the month of September, with 528,000 units sold in the United States (approximately double the previous month's sales).[59] Shortly after Halo 3's launch, Microsoft announced that it was spinning off Bungie into an independent privately held company.[60]

The boost Halo 3 gave to Xbox 360 sales was short-lived, however, as the console resumed its downward trend in October. By early 2008, the Xbox 360 had fallen to last place among next-generation consoles sold in the United States (see Exhibits 3 and 4).[61]

In the future, Microsoft would be forced to rely less on exclusive games to succeed. Due to skyrocketing development costs, fewer game developers were willing to commit to exclusivity. Grand Theft Auto (GTA), for example, had been a PlayStation-exclusive up until the release of the fourth installment in the franchise. Developer Rockstar Games decided to abandon exclusivity for GTA IV after its costs spiraled to an estimated $100 million, according to the game's producer. Undoubtedly, Rockstar's decision helped GTA IV post record revenues of more than $500 million during its first week,[62] easily surpassing the previous record set by Halo 3.

| Exhibit 3 | United States Monthly Console Sales[1] |
|---|---|

| | PS2 | Xbox | Gamecube | Xbox 360 | PS3 | Wii |
|---|---|---|---|---|---|---|
| November-05 | 530,000 | 200,000 | 270,000 | 326,000 | | |
| **December-05** | **1,500,000** | **420,000** | **600,000** | **281,000** | | |
| January-06 | 270,000 | 90,000 | 70,000 | 250,000 | | |
| February-06 | 300,000 | 90,000 | 70,000 | 161,000 | | |
| March-06 | 270,000 | 80,000 | 60,000 | 192,000 | | |
| April-06 | 210,000 | 40,000 | 40,000 | 295,000 | | |
| May-06 | 230,000 | 25,000 | 30,000 | 221,000 | | |
| June-06 | 310,000 | 25,000 | 50,000 | 277,000 | | |
| July-06 | 240,000 | 10,000 | 40,000 | 206,000 | | |
| August-06 | 260,000 | 10,000 | 40,000 | 205,000 | | |
| September-06 | 310,000 | 5,000 | 40,000 | 259,000 | | |
| October-06 | 240,000 | 5,000 | 30,000 | 218,000 | | |
| November-06 | 660,000 | 5,000 | 70,000 | 511,000 | 197,000 | 476,000 |
| **December-06** | **1,400,000** | **5,000** | **200,000** | **1,130,000** | **491,000** | **604,000** |
| January-07 | 299,000 | | 34,000 | 294,000 | 244,000 | 436,000 |
| February-07 | 295,000 | | 24,000 | 228,000 | 127,000 | 335,000 |
| March-07 | 280,000 | | 22,000 | 199,000 | 130,000 | 259,000 |
| April-07 | 194,000 | | 13,000 | 174,000 | 82,000 | 360,000 |
| May-07 | 188,000 | | 11,000 | 155,000 | 82,000 | 338,000 |
| June-07 | 270,000 | | | 198,000 | 99,000 | 382,000 |
| July-07 | 222,000 | | | 170,000 | 159,000 | 425,000 |
| August-07 | 202,000 | | | 277,000 | 131,000 | 404,000 |
| September-07 | 215,000 | | | 528,000 | 119,000 | 501,000 |
| October-07 | 184,000 | | | 366,000 | 121,000 | 519,000 |
| November-07 | 496,000 | | | 770,000 | 466,000 | 981,000 |
| **December-07** | **1,100,000** | | | **1,260,000** | **798,000** | **1,350,000** |
| January-08 | 264,000 | | | 230,000 | 269,000 | 274,000 |
| February-08 | 352,000 | | | 255,000 | 281,000 | 587,000 |
| March-08 | 216,000 | | | 296,000 | 301,000 | 593,000 |
| **TOTAL** | **11,507,000** | **1,010,000** | **1,714,000** | **9,932,000** | **4,097,000** | **8,824,000** |

1. *Source:* Compiled from various news sources using data from NPD Group Market Research (npd.com).

| **Exhibit 4** | Monthly Console Sales |

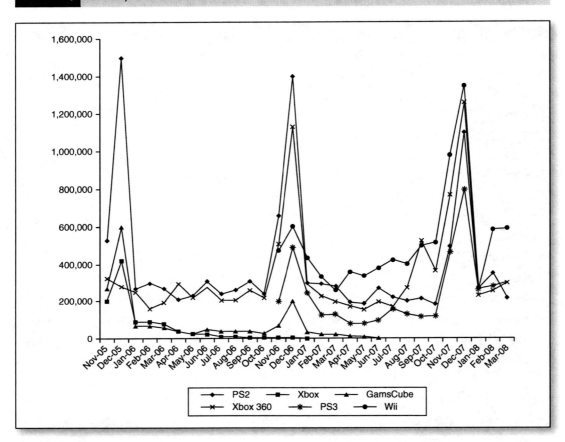

## International Markets

In Europe, production problems prevented Sony from releasing a European version of the PlayStation 3 until early 2007. This gave the Xbox 360 a 16-month lead over the PS3. Nevertheless, by early 2008, Microsoft had fallen to last place in overall sales in Europe, despite having a retail price that was almost half the price of a PS3. [63]

Japan was the third most important market for video games after North America and Europe. When Microsoft launched the Japanese version of the Xbox 360 in December 2005, the company hoped to win a significant share of a market traditionally dominated by Nintendo and Sony. However, the dominance of Microsoft's Japanese rivals proved impenetrable. Even though Microsoft

priced the Japanese console lower than the U.S. version, initial sales were sluggish. [64] In 2007, Microsoft sold 250,000 Xbox 360 consoles in Japan, compared to 3.6 million Nintendo Wiis and 1.2 million Sony PS3s. [65]

Factors other than the Xbox 360's high failure rate also played a role in the console's declining market share. Sony, which had few popular gaming titles available for the launch of the PS3, introduced a number of popular titles in 2007 and 2008. More importantly, it dropped the price of its base console to $400 and offered other buying incentives such as free high-definition movies by mail-in rebate and free accessories. Finally, the demise of HD-DVD in February 2008 made the PS3, with its Blu-ray drive, the only console capable of playing high-definition movies.

Unlike the original Xbox, which lost money over its lifespan, Microsoft expected the Xbox 360 to show a profit. For Robbie Bach, profitability was "what it's all about . . . you [must] have the right metrics in place to know which [investments] are paying off."[66] Therefore it was with some consolation that despite the console's problems, the Entertainment and Devices division turned a profit for the first time in the fiscal quarter ending March 31, 2008, with earnings of $89 million.[67] Analysts, however, were less impressed: "Microsoft reported $4.4 billion in net income for the quarter, which means the contributions of the Entertainment and Devices division was barely a rounding error," noted one. "[I]nvestors aren't playing the game."[68] "Microsoft is far from being on the ropes," noted another, "but Sony has every indication of being on a roll, and Microsoft needs to come up with a plan to fend off the growing threat."[69]

## Restoring Confidence

Some believed that the first thing Microsoft needed to do was restore its reputation by improving product quality. One way to do this was to partner with another manufacturer with more experience in designing complex computer hardware. A *Newsweek* editorial urged Microsoft to take more immediate action: "Microsoft must either be thoroughly forthcoming about the Xbox 360's flaws, or initiate a recall."[70]

Others wondered if a software company such as Microsoft should even be in the hardware business:

> Microsoft has lost unthinkable amounts of money on its Xbox business. In the six short years it's been in the industry, the company

hasn't made a dime. When adding the recently announced $1.9 billion losses incurred in fiscal 2007, total life-to-date Xbox losses are conservatively estimated at somewhere around $6 billion dollars. . . . Every man has a breaking point, and anyone can pull a Sega and quit the hardware business—even a rich kid with deep pockets.[71]

"Pulling a Sega" referred to the 2002 decision by Sega Corporation to pull out of the video game hardware business. Although software development had significant up-front costs, it benefited greatly from economies of scale; as a result, within one year, Sega Corporation began to show strong earnings on its software sales.[72]

## Leveraging the Xbox Empire

When Microsoft posted its first quarterly profit ever for the Xbox business, it did little to allay the fears of investors. There was no denying the fact that the video game business was a drain on overall company earnings. At the same time, video games as a whole were winning a larger share of the overall entertainment market, and Microsoft owned some of the most valuable brands within that market. The question was how to leverage those assets in ways that contributed to the financial performance of Microsoft Corporation, while maintaining the company's long-term strategic vision of "one day controlling an empire of movies and TV-on-demand, Internet, and . . . as-yet-undreamed services."[73]

---

**CASE QUESTIONS**

1. Explain the problems encountered by Microsoft across the goals of (1) market share, (2) sales, (3) profitability, (4) customer satisfaction, and (5) corporate and brand image.

2. The issue of quality control in design and production created a major problem for the marketing department. Explain how the CEO and top management team should respond to this situation.

3. What strategies should Microsoft undertake with regard to gaming in the coming years?

4. Can the problems in this case be resolved at the functional and individual levels? If so, how? If not, why not?

# Kenexa

*By Chetan Joshi, under the supervision of Professor Joerg Dietz*

On September 14, 2006, Jack W. Wiley and Scott Brooks, executives at Kenexa, an human resources (HR) consulting firm, sat in the meeting room of Kenexa's Minneapolis office discussing the survey data they had received on the National Choice Bank (NCB). About 15 months previously, Katharine Graham, senior vice-president of Organization and Leadership Development at NCB, had first contacted Wiley and Brooks in order to conduct an employee opinion survey and a customer satisfaction survey. Once both the employee and customer survey data had been collected, the challenge for Wiley and Brooks was to identify issues in the data that they needed to address in their presentation to NCB's leadership in Chicago on October 9, 2006.

## Kenexa[1]

Kenexa, a Wayne, Pennsylvania-based HR consulting firm, was founded in 1987. During the initial eight years, Kenexa focused on providing talent management solutions to its clients. Later on, it broadened its products and services offerings to include employee and customer satisfaction research, performance management technology and consultation, and employee process outsourcing. On June 24, 2005, Kenexa announced its initial public offering and began trading on the NASDAQ National Market. As a full-service consulting firm, Kenexa provided solutions (see Exhibit 1) aimed at helping corporate clients to maximize their performance by improving their human capital management. Its list of approximately 2,400 clients, including approximately 130 companies on the *Fortune* 500 list published in April 2005, spanned many key industries—financial services, life sciences, retail, health care, call centers, education, and hospitality. For the year ending December 31, 2005, Kenexa reported total revenues of $65.6 million,[2] an increase of 42 percent compared to the prior year. As of September 2006, Kenexa employed approximately 1,000 people and had offices throughout the United States in Wayne, Lincoln, Philadelphia, Lexington, Englewoods, Minneapolis, San Francisco and New York, as well as in London (United Kingdom), Hyderabad (India), Taipei (Taiwan), and Toronto (Canada).

In the last 19 years, Kenexa had garnered extensive experience and expertise in providing clients tools for human capital management. The team-oriented workforce at Kenexa played a vital role in this regard. The personnel comprising these teams had strong analytical, cross-functional and multi-industry expertise. Numerous Kenexa employees had PhDs in Industrial/Organizational Psychology and were well-recognized experts in both the practitioner and academic communities.

## Jack W. Wiley

Jack Wiley, executive director of the Research Institute at Kenexa, had 30 years of experience with research on linking employee opinion survey results to organizational performance measures of customer satisfaction and business performance. Based on his research, Wiley had developed WorkTrends™, a unique database of employee opinions. Previously, Wiley had been president and CEO of Gantz Wiley Research—a consulting firm he co-founded in 1986—that was acquired by Kenexa in August 2006. Prior to that, he was director of organizational research at Control Data Corporation (now Ceridian) and held personnel research positions at National Bank of Detroit and Ford Motor Company. With a PhD in Organizational Psychology from the University of Tennessee, Wiley was also a licensed psychologist and an accredited senior professional in

Version: (A) 2008–03–25

| **Exhibit 1** | Solutions Offered by Kenexa |

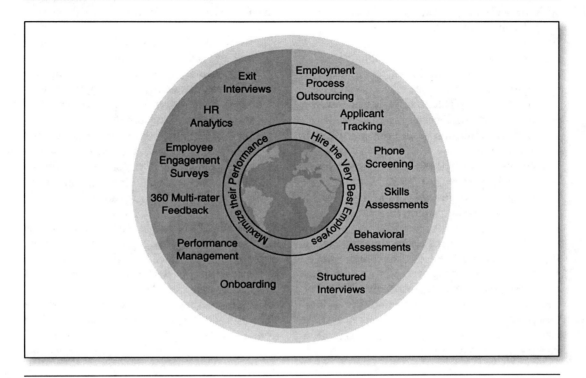

*Source:* Company files.

human resources. He had written numerous articles and book chapters on conducting organizational surveys and had made many presentations to professional associations around the globe. His professional affiliations included memberships in the Society for Industrial and Organizational Psychology (SIOP), the Human Resources Planning Society (HRPS), and the Academy of Management (AoM).

## Scott M. Brooks

Brooks, who had a BA from Cornell University and a PhD in Industrial and Organizational Psychology from the Ohio State University, shouldered responsibility for managing WorkTrends™ and developed customized employee and survey research products

for Kenexa's projects. Additionally, he worked closely with Wiley to prepare feedback for Kenexa's clients based on the analysis of employee/customer survey data. Previously, Brooks worked for the retailer Mervyn's, a division of Dayton Hudson Corporation. He had 15 years of survey research experience and had authored many presentations and publications on employee measurement topics. He was a member of SIOP, AoM, the Society for Human Resource Management and the American Psychological Association.

## Rationale Underlying Wiley's and Brooks' Approach to Projects

Wiley firmly believed in the notion that effective workforce management was the key to better performance. This belief was grounded in research by others, but also in his own research and work with many clients. Stanford Professor Jeffrey Pfeffer had summarized relevant research:

Achieving competitive success through people involves fundamentally altering how we think about the workforce and the employment relationship. It means achieving success by working with people, not by replacing them or limiting the scope of their activities. It entails seeing the workforce as a source of competitive advantage, not just as a cost to be minimized or avoided. Firms that take this perspective are often able to successfully outmaneuver and outperform their rivals.[3]

Wiley's own research aimed at diagnosing the organizational practices that were indicative of better workforce management and, at the same time, were predictors of organizational success. For that purpose, he used data from employee surveys, customer surveys, and business performance measures. The findings from his consulting projects consistently showed

- Customer loyalty was a potent predictor of business performance. Moreover, customer loyalty could be forecasted from employee perceptions of an organization's customer orientation and the extent of emphasis on service quality.
- Specific leadership practices—customer orientation, quality emphasis, employee training and employee involvement—created an environment of service excellence and separated leading organizations from lagging ones. Organizations focusing on these four practices had employees who knew their tasks, worked well in teams, were more satisfied, and were better able to deliver quality service to customers. That capability translated into the delivery of products and services of better value, thereby contributing to customer loyalty, higher market share, and better bottom-line organizational performance.

According to Wiley, these findings suggested a chain of activities (see Exhibits 2a and 2b) that built a high-performance organization (see Exhibit 3):

The more visible and present certain organizational values and leadership practices (e.g., customer orientation, quality emphasis, employee training, and employee involvement) are in a given work environment, the more energized and productive the workforce. In turn, the more energized and productive the workforce, the greater the satisfaction and loyalty of customers, and with a time lag, the stronger the long-term business performance of the organization.[4]

The High Performance Model illuminated the interrelationships among organizational practices, employee perceptions of their work environment, customer satisfaction and business performance. It provided a well-grounded argument to clients. Organizational success was contingent on the ability to build "long-term and mutually beneficial relationships among the company, employees and customers."[5] For that reason, organizations needed to embrace the leadership practices outlined in the High Performance Model and create a work environment where employees felt capable of, and were able to deliver top-quality service to customers. The ability to deliver exceptional service translated into improved customer satisfaction and retention, ultimately improving the company's growth and bottom-line. Employees, too, felt more satisfied with their jobs as a result of their ability to provide excellent service and their continued positive interactions with satisfied customers.

Wiley noted that the interrelationships articulated in the High Performance Model were affected by elements of the work characteristics and contextual factors. In a retail bank setting, for example, certain bank-branch characteristics (e.g., frequency of customer contact at a branch) might differentially influence the relationship between employee opinions about elements of their work environment and customer satisfaction. Furthermore, he suggested that the interrelationships among employee perceptions of their work environment,

| Exhibit 2a | The High Performance Model: Conceptual Model |
|---|---|

The High Performance Model

Leadership Practices

Business Performance

Employee Results

Customer Results

Custome orientation
Quality emphasis
Training
Involvement

Communication
Teamwork
Engagement
Retention

Sales growth
Market share
Productivity
Profitability

Elapsed time

Work characteristics

Responsiveness
Product quality
Overall satisfaction
Loyaty

© 1996, 2004 Cantz Wiley Research

| Exhibit 2b | The High Performance Model: Analytical Model |
|---|---|

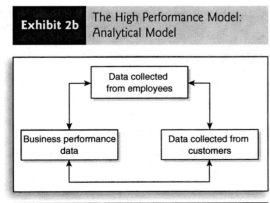

*Source:* Company files.

customer satisfaction and business performance grew stronger with a time lag. For example, positive customer perceptions translated into potential repeat purchases and word-of-mouth recommendations of a bank's products and services to friends and relatives, resulting in improved performance over the long term rather than over the short term.

When applied for organizational diagnoses, the High Performance Model involved integration and correlation of data from employees, customers, and business performance metrics. Both employees and customers were considered as subject matter experts of the service environment. Kenexa gathered customer and employee reports using surveys.

| **Exhibit 3** | Characteristics of High Performance Organizations |

What does it take to be a leading organization? Focusing on the Leadership Practices and Employee Results themes, the characteristics of a high-performance organization arc defined below.

| **Leadership Practices** | **Employee Results** |
| --- | --- |
| *Customer orientation* <br><br> • Employees see a strong emphasis on customer service. They use customer-friendly processes and procedures. designed with customer input. <br> • Customer needs are attended to quickly, whether in initial delivery of products and services, or in the resolution of problems. | *Communication* <br><br> • Management creates and communicates a compelling vision and direction for the company. <br> • Work group goals are clear, and employees know how well they are being met. They are recognized for achieving these goals, in particular for providing outstanding service. <br> • Employees report having enough information to do their jobs, including company information, advance warning of changes, and information from other departments. |
| *Quality emphasis* <br><br> • Senior management is committed to quality, and demonstrates this priority in day-to-day decisions. These values are effectively translated and implemented by lower level managers. <br> • Clear standards exist to help employees know what to do and whether they are doing it well. <br> • Employees believe their work groups do quality work, as judged by clear quality standards, and are able to continuously improve. | *Teamwork* <br><br> • Employees cooperate to get the work done. Different work groups are aligned toward the same goals, and mutually support each other to serve customers. <br> • This teamwork is actively supported by management. Problems and conflicts are addressed quickly. <br> • Workload is managed effectively within a given work group—the load is divided fairly, and short staffing is not a significant barrier. |
| *Involvement* <br><br> • Employees have the authority and support they need to serve their customers. <br> • They are encouraged to participate in decisions affecting their work, and perhaps more importantly, to innovate. <br> • Management solicits and uses opinions of employees in such a way that employees can see the connection. | *Engagement* <br><br> • Employees derive intrinsic satisfaction from their work, see a good match between their job, their interests, and their skills and abilities. <br> • Employees are satisfied with and proud of their organization. <br> • There is confidence in the company's ability to succeed, leading to long-term stability for the employee. |

| Leadership Practices | Employee Results |
|---|---|
| *Training* | *Retention* |
| • Employees are well trained and otherwise prepared to meet the demands customers present; needed tools, equipment and other systems are also available to help get the job done. <br> • Whether on-the-job or formal, employees have the training to perform their current jobs well. This can include specific training on products and services, or explicitly on customer service. <br> • New employees are oriented and able to come up to speed quickly, without undue burden on existing staff. | • Employees value their relationship with the organization, and have no short-term interest in leaving. <br> • Longer-tenured employees are both more efficient and create more value for the organization and customers. |

*Source:* Company files.

A typical employee survey focused on employee descriptions of the aspects of their business-unit's work environment (e.g., the extent to which top management emphasized the importance of top-quality service) that were relevant for building service capability. Similarly, the customer survey collected data on customer perceptions of service quality, customer satisfaction, and customer loyalty. Finally, the data from employee and customer surveys were integrated with organizational performance data.

The integrated data were analyzed for the interrelationships among employee perceptions, customer reports, and business-unit performance. These interrelationships pointed out the key drivers of customer satisfaction and performance that separated better-performing business units from the lower-performing ones. This was critical to understanding where an organization stood in terms of managing the core drivers and what managers could change in their organizations to better realize the full potential of these drivers. Kenexa's consultants focused on providing tangible action-planning recommendations to clients so that the reformulated organizational practices reflected an increased emphasis on the crucial drivers.

# How Kenexa Executed Projects

Kenexa followed a five-phase model to design and execute a research project for its clients. During the initial planning phase, members of the Kenexa research team developed a customized project plan for serving the needs of the client. This was followed by the survey development phase during which Kenexa's consultants tailored their standard survey instruments and incorporated the key indicators that determined employee/customer opinions for the clients. Once adapted, the survey instrument was administered using a variety of formats, including interactive voice recognition (IVR) and the Internet, as well as with paper and pencil. Kenexa also provided help desk support for the survey respondents during the administration phase. Once the data had been collected, Kenexa's consultants, using a Web-enabled technology platform, organized and analyzed the data and prepared it for reporting back to the client. Finally, Kenexa's executives provided action-planning feedback to the client, translating the linkage research results into actions for improving workplace performance.

# The NCB Project

On April 16, 2005, Wiley and Brooks gave a presentation on the High Performance Model at the annual conference of the Society for Industrial and Organizational Psychology in Los Angeles, California. Katharine Graham, senior vice-president of Organization and Leadership Development at NCB, was in the audience and was intrigued by the possibility of how insights from the High Performance Model approach could help make NCB more effective. Graham's informal discussions with Wiley and Brooks at SIOP materialized into NCB's decision, in June 2005, to conduct employee and customer opinion surveys that would (1) provide an understanding of employee/customer opinions and their relation to performance of NCB's branches in order to differentiate better-performing branches from the poorer ones, (2) identify priorities for organizational development activities, and (3) serve as a benchmark to track the progress of organizational development activities.

# NCB

NCB, headquartered in Chicago, was a large retail branch banking organization that provided the full range of retail banking services (e.g., accepting deposits, consumer lending, wealth management services and safe deposit box operations) to its clients through 128 branches located in six mid-western states. It also had a network of 264 ATMs and an on-line full-service electronic banking center. Based on 2005 financial data, NCB had approximately $7.5 billion in assets, $5.1 billion in deposits and a net income of $104 million. As of year-end 2005, NCB served about 70,000 customers and employed a workforce of 2,884, including 84 at its Chicago headquarters.

At NCB, headquarters was responsible for setting the overall strategic direction. The headquarters' role included new product design, branch layout design, public and media relations, and marketing strategy conceptualization. Branches, on the other hand, were responsible for execution of the products. Branches acted independently, catered to their geographic region and reported to the

headquarters. A typical branch was comprised of about 20 employees, including a branch manager, assistant branch managers, personal bankers, banking assistants, and tellers.

The branch manager was responsible for coordinating with the headquarters and managing the day-to-day functioning of the branch. With ultimate responsibility for branch performance, the branch manager needed to motivate the team, drive sales, and lead the way in how the branch delivered excellent customer service. The manager also served as the bank's liaison with local community groups and institutions. The assistant branch managers were responsible for working closely with the manager to create a high-energy, high-performance culture within the branch. As "champions" of customer service and sales practices, they were expected to focus on meeting and exceeding branch targets. They were specifically required to identify opportunities for training of the branch personnel if branch performance was falling behind.

The personal banker(s) were responsible for the portfolio of personal services offered to existing and new consumers: personal loans, credit card applications, and day-to-day banking—savings and checking account plans, safety deposit offerings, travel and medical insurance products, and wealth management products. Banking assistants worked in the banking hall of the branch and were usually one of the first employees who came in contact with the customers. As such, they were responsible for talking to the customers about the bank's products and services and guiding them to the appropriate banking personnel.

The tellers were responsible for cashing checks, accepting deposits and loan payments, processing withdrawals, accepting payments for customers' utility bills and charge cards, processing necessary paperwork for certificates of deposit, and selling travelers' checks and foreign currencies. As the quintessential face of NCB, tellers were expected to be courteous, attentive and patient in dealing with the customers. They needed to work as a team, and, together with banking assistants, they were expected to be resourceful in spotting potential sales opportunities.

The personnel at NCB were focused on providing value-enhancing and need-satisfying services to its clientele. In that vein, NCB was dedicated to meeting and exceeding the banking needs of current and new customers. That was an ongoing challenge given that the competition for banking customers continued to be intense. NCB management firmly believed in the bank's ability to offer a broad array of services and products at competitive prices and counted on its committed and knowledgeable employee base to deliver its products and services.

## The NCB Project Gets Underway

Wiley and Brooks led the team that designed and administered the surveys for the NCB project. Their project plan included (1) the administration of two surveys for all the 128 branches of NCB— an employee opinion survey in the fourth quarter of 2005 and a branch-level customer satisfaction survey shortly thereafter, (2) organization of the data collected from the two surveys at the branch level, (3) collection of performance data available from NCB headquarters for the 128 branches, and (4) integration of the resulting data for the purposes of conducting the analyses.

## The Employee Opinion Survey

Wiley and Brooks began the NCB project during July and August of 2005 with the design of the employee opinion survey. For that purpose, they adapted a standard employee survey instrument to NCB's requirements. The resulting survey contained 54 questions and assessed employee opinions on specific elements of their work environment. These elements were organized along nine themes in the survey: customer orientation, quality emphasis, employee training, involvement/empowerment, communication, teamwork, engagement, intention to leave, and satisfaction with compensation and benefits (Exhibit 4 provides examples on questions[6] intended to measure different themes). While answering the survey, employees indicated their agreement with the survey questions on five-point scales ranging from 1 (*Strongly Disagree*) to 5 (*Strongly Agree*). The survey package identified employees on the basis of their branch affiliation and not their names. This confidential survey was administered, during October to November 2005, on company time to the employees in 128 branches; 2,230 employees returned usable surveys.

| Exhibit 4 | Illustrative Questions From the Employee and Customer Surveys |
|---|---|

### Illustrative Questions From the Employee Opinion Survey

| Theme | Illustrative Questions/Items |
|---|---|
| Customer Orientation | 1. Where I work, customer problems are corrected quickly |
| | 2. Senior management shows by its actions that customer service is a top priority |
| Emphasis on quality | 1. Where I work, day-to-day decisions demonstrate that quality is a top priority |
| | 2. Where I work, we set clear performance standards for service quality |
| Involvement | 1. Sufficient effort is made to get the opinions and thinking of people who work here |
| | 2. Where I work, employees are encouraged to participate in making decisions which affect their work |
| Training | 1. I receive enough training to help me continually improve my job performance |
| | 2. I receive adequate training on National Choice Bank's products and services |

*(Continued)*

| Exhibit 4 | (Continued) |

| Theme | Illustrative Questions/Items |
|---|---|
| Communication | 1. Senior management gives employees a clear picture of the direction in which the company is headed |
| | 2. I get enough warning about changes that are going to take place at National Choice Bank |
| Teamwork | 1. Where I work, management encourages a teamwork approach to getting things done |
| | 2. The people I work with cooperate to get the work done |
| Engagement | 1. I like the kind of work I do |
| | 2. My work gives me a feeling of accomplishment |
| Compensation and Benefits | 1. The amount of pay I get at National Choice Bank |
| | 2. The total benefits program at National Choice Bank |

## Illustrative Questions From the Customer Satisfaction Survey

| Theme | Illustrative Questions/Items |
|---|---|
| Satisfaction with Service Quality | 1. National Choice Bank is innovative in finding new and better ways to meet my needs |
| | 2. Compared to other banks I know of, National Choice Bank offers more convenient ways for me to do my banking |
| Satisfaction with Branch Teller | 1. How satisfied are you with the service you receive from tellers at the National Choice Bank's branch you use most often in terms of the tellers' courtesy and friendliness? |
| | 2. How satisfied are you with the service you receive from tellers at the National Choice Bank's branch you use most often in terms of the tellers' ability to resolve your problems quickly? |
| Satisfaction with Bank Branch in General and Facilities | 1. How satisfied are you with the convenience of lobby hours at the National Choice Bank Branch you use most often? |
| | 2. Thinking about the National Choice Bank branch you use most often, how satisfied are you with the overall service you receive |
| Satisfaction with Personal Bankers | 1. How satisfied are you with the service you receive from personal bankers at the National Choice Bank's branch you use most often in terms of giving you individualized, personal attention? |
| | 2. How satisfied are you with the service you receive from personal bankers at the National Choice Bank's branch you use most often in terms of following up on what they say they will do for you? |
| Customer Loyalty | 1. I would recommend National Choice Bank to friends and family |
| | 2. The next time I need additional financial services, National Choice Bank would be my first choice |

*Source:* Company files.

## The Customer Satisfaction Survey

In September 2005, the NCB project's team developed a customized retail branch customer opinion survey for the NCB project. The resulting survey had 40 questions aimed at measuring customer opinions on specific service issues (these issues were organized along four themes: satisfaction with service quality, satisfaction with teller, satisfaction with branch in general and facilities at the branch, and satisfaction with personal banker) and opinions on customer loyalty. Exhibit 4 provides examples of questions[7] intended to measure different themes. Similar to the employee opinion survey, customers indicated their extent of satisfaction with the survey questions on five-point scales ranging from 1 (*Very Dissatisfied*) to 5 (*Very Satisfied*). In addition, the survey assessed the frequency of contact these customers had with the branch's service personnel. The questions, intended for this purpose, asked the customers to indicate the number of times they had used the services of bank tellers or personal bankers during the last six months. The response categories were: 1, *not at all*; 2, *1–3 times*; 3, *4–6 times*; 4, *7–10 times*; and 5, *11 or more times.*

The survey was mailed to customers' homes (with around 300 randomly selected customer households per branch) during December 2005. The survey did not ask for customer names but identified customers on the basis of branch affiliation; 14,114 customers returned usable surveys.

## Business Performance and Branch Location Data

In May 2006, Graham sent data on two key indicators of bank-branch performance for all 128 branches: (1) teller productivity, computed as the volume of transactions handled by tellers in relation to the number of full-time equivalent teller staff, and (2) overall productivity ratio, a measure of the amount of revenue generated by the branch for every dollar of personnel expense. The business performance measures were based on 2005 year-end data. In her email, Graham mentioned that the NCB management speculated about the possibility of different business dynamics in branches located in metropolitan areas versus those in non-metropolitan areas. She provided data on branch location (i.e., whether a branch was located in a metropolitan or non-metropolitan area).

## Data Aggregation Team for the NCB Project Gets to Work

Once the data from the two surveys had been collected and business performance data from NCB were available, research assistants at Kenexa's Minneapolis office entered the employee and customer survey data as two separate data files, with responses from 2,230 employees and 14,114 customers, respectively, and cross-checked for data entry errors.

Once the initial screening was complete, the research assistants calculated scores for the employee/customer opinion themes by computing the averages for the set of questions intended to measure a particular theme. The resulting files were sent to the project consultants who conducted initial statistical tests on each of the two surveys to assess whether or not respondents of the same branch responded similarly to the survey questions and if these responses differed across branches. These tests involved testing for within-bank branch versus between-bank branch variance. The project consultants found support for within-branch similarity in responses and between-branch variance in responses and therefore aggregated each of the data files such that they represented employee and customer[8] data for the 128 branches.

Finally, these two data files were merged and combined with the business performance and branch location data and sent to Wiley and Brooks for analysis (see Exhibit 5 for a list of variables included in the final data file; Exhibit 6 provides a sample from the NCB data file).

| Exhibit 5 | Names and Definitions of Variables for the NCB Datafile |

| Variable Name | Definition |
| --- | --- |
| bnum | Branch number; numerical variable ranging from 1 to 128 |
| badd | Branch address |
| bloc | Branch location; categorical variable:<br> 0 = non-metropolitan branch, 1 = metropolitan branch |
| bsize | Branch size (the number of employees at the branch who responded to the employee survey) |
| ecuso | Employee opinion on the extent of customer orientation |
| equal | Employee opinion on the emphasis of quality |
| einvol | Employee opinion on the extent of their involvement |
| etra | Employee opinion on the training they receive |
| ecomm | Employee opinion on communication levels |
| eteam | Employee opinion on teamwork |
| eeng | Employee opinion on engagement |
| eitl | Employee intention to leave |
| eben | Employee opinion on the compensation and benefits received |
| cserq | Customer satisfaction with service quality |
| cbrtel | Customer satisfaction with branch teller |
| cbr | Customer satisfaction with branch in general and facilities at the branch |
| cbrpb | Customer satisfaction with personal bankers |
| cloy | Customer loyalty for the bank |
| ccon | Customer's frequency of contact with branch's service personnel; categorical variable:<br> 0 = branch with customers who interact less frequently with branch's service personnel, 1 = branch with customers who interact more frequently with branch's service personnel |
| teltr | Teller productivity for the branch |
| prod | Overall productivity ratio for the branch |

**Exhibit 6** NCB Data File

| bnum | badd | bloc | bsize | ecuso | equal | einvol | etra | ecomm | eteam | eeng | eitl | eben | cserq | cbrtel | cbr | cbrpb | cloy | ccon | teltr | prod |
|---|---|---|---|---|---|---|---|---|---|---|---|---|---|---|---|---|---|---|---|---|
| 1 | Anoka (E) | 1 | 38 | 3.52 | 3.47 | 3.21 | 3.24 | 3.18 | 3.37 | 3.12 | 2.57 | 3.58 | 3.26 | 4.29 | 4.15 | 4.13 | 3.76 | 1 | 3946 | 412 |
| 2 | Anoka (W) | 1 | 15 | 3.75 | 3.58 | 3.39 | 3.02 | 3.11 | 3.44 | 3.36 | 2.93 | 3.79 | 3.43 | 4.48 | 4.54 | 4.34 | 3.84 | 1 | 4041 | 317 |
| 3 | Apple Valley | 1 | 19 | 3.63 | 3.63 | 3.44 | 3.28 | 3.23 | 3.49 | 3.29 | 2.42 | 3.42 | 3.45 | 3.91 | 4.18 | 3.93 | 3.81 | 1 | 3510 | 232 |
| 4 | Blaine | 1 | 12 | 3.83 | 3.58 | 3.32 | 3.26 | 3.61 | 3.25 | 3.48 | 2.58 | 3.92 | 3.29 | 4.13 | 3.96 | 4.06 | 3.73 | 0 | 4184 | 323 |
| 5 | Bloomington | 1 | 27 | 3.22 | 3.16 | 3.19 | 3.08 | 2.85 | 2.91 | 2.68 | 3.3 | 3.52 | 3.67 | 4.13 | 4.15 | 4.09 | 3.98 | 1 | 3484 | 242 |
| 6 | Brooklyn | 1 | 28 | 3.7 | 3.6 | 3.36 | 3.09 | 3.24 | 3.68 | 3.03 | 2.07 | 4.04 | 3.59 | 4.06 | 4 | 3.92 | 4.05 | 0 | 4406 | 351 |
| 7 | Burnsville | 1 | 31 | 3.88 | 3.72 | 3.42 | 3.42 | 3.39 | 3.66 | 3.39 | 2.32 | 3.77 | 3.15 | 4.14 | 4.33 | 4.11 | 3.61 | 0 | 4642 | 324 |
| 8 | Columbia hts. | 1 | 36 | 3.47 | 3.45 | 3.28 | 3.26 | 3.29 | 3.31 | 3.13 | 2.61 | 3.86 | 3.28 | 4.21 | 4.2 | 4.06 | 3.72 | 0 | 4344 | 391 |
| 9 | Cottage groove | 1 | 51 | 3.8 | 3.54 | 3.39 | 3.13 | 3.08 | 3.46 | 3.16 | 2.51 | 3.8 | 3.4 | 4.1 | 3.98 | 3.96 | 3.76 | 0 | 4060 | 342 |
| 10 | Hopkins | 1 | 23 | 3.95 | 3.7 | 3.38 | 3.22 | 3.14 | 3.59 | 3.27 | 2.17 | 4 | 3.18 | 4.18 | 4.24 | 4.09 | 3.61 | 0 | 4399 | 314 |
| 11 | Minneapolis | 1 | 34 | 4.29 | 4.04 | 3.94 | 3.48 | 3.66 | 3.87 | 3.89 | 2.15 | 3.61 | 3.46 | 4.3 | 4.33 | 4.09 | 3.77 | 1 | 4056 | 309 |

*(Continued)*

**Exhibit 6** (Continued)

| bnum | badd | bloc | bsize | ecuso | equal | einvol | etra | ecomm | eteam | eeng | eitl | eben | cserq | cbrtel | cbr | cbrpb | cloy | ccon | teltr | prod |
|---|---|---|---|---|---|---|---|---|---|---|---|---|---|---|---|---|---|---|---|---|
| 12 | Minneapolis (NE) | 1 | 12 | 3.39 | 3.42 | 3.53 | 3.17 | 3.36 | 3.72 | 3.21 | 1.75 | 3.67 | 3.29 | 4.3 | 4.08 | 4.05 | 3.84 | 0 | 4186 | 305 |
| 13 | Minnetonka | 1 | 24 | 3.84 | 3.81 | 3.8 | 3.35 | 3.47 | 3.51 | 3.45 | 2.13 | 4.08 | 3.26 | 4.11 | 3.87 | 3.87 | 3.63 | 0 | 4051 | 311 |
| 14 | Little Canada | 1 | 19 | 3.43 | 3.38 | 2.98 | 3.01 | 3.16 | 3.39 | 2.78 | 2.58 | 3.68 | 3.19 | 4.05 | 4.23 | 4.06 | 3.6 | 0 | 4413 | 287 |
| 15 | Oakdale | 1 | 16 | 3.75 | 3.63 | 3.68 | 3.22 | 3.73 | 3.82 | 3.37 | 2.25 | 3.88 | 3.36 | 4.38 | 4.22 | 4.27 | 3.78 | 0 | 4502 | 294 |
| 16 | Plymouth | 1 | 9 | 4.19 | 3.56 | 3.65 | 3.34 | 3.26 | 3.63 | 3.58 | 1.44 | 3.56 | 3.18 | 4.2 | 4.24 | 4.15 | 3.78 | 0 | 3839 | 346 |
| 17 | Robbinsdale | 1 | 10 | 3.33 | 3.55 | 3.41 | 3.53 | 3.9 | 3.93 | 2.95 | 1.9 | 3 | 3.07 | 4.06 | 3.9 | 4.01 | 3.54 | 0 | 4588 | 363 |
| 18 | St. Louis Park | 1 | 12 | 3.31 | 3.38 | 3.25 | 3.17 | 3.33 | 3.4 | 3.33 | 2.08 | 3.83 | 3.26 | 4.07 | 4.16 | 4.03 | 3.7 | 0 | 4506 | 296 |
| 19 | St. Paul (E) | 1 | 16 | 4.28 | 3.84 | 3.76 | 3.19 | 3.19 | 3.77 | 3.59 | 2.31 | 3.73 | 3.37 | 4.47 | 4.17 | 4.24 | 3.85 | 0 | 3611 | 313 |
| 20 | St. Cloud | 1 | 13 | 3.4 | 3.33 | 3.1 | 3.03 | 3.31 | 3.18 | 3 | 2.23 | 3.46 | 3.24 | 4.12 | 3.8 | 3.95 | 3.63 | 0 | 4286 | 372 |
| 21 | Willmar | 1 | 10 | 4.25 | 4.15 | 3.93 | 3.65 | 3.47 | 3.97 | 4 | 1.9 | 3.8 | 3.63 | 4.27 | 4.21 | 4.18 | 3.92 | 1 | 4288 | 346 |
| 22 | Eagan | 0 | 29 | 3.41 | 3.34 | 3.2 | 2.88 | 2.62 | 3.16 | 3.16 | 2.97 | 3.97 | 3.42 | 4.3 | 3.99 | 4.11 | 3.72 | 0 | 3150 | 247 |

*Source:* Company files.

## CASE QUESTIONS

1. Is the High-Performance Model a strategic, tactical, or individual performance metric, or does it measure all three aspects?

2. Should the analysis of NCB lead to the conclusion that employees are somewhat dissatisfied and that relations with customers are strained, what strategic corrections should be made?

3. Should the analysis of NCB lead to the conclusion that employees are somewhat dissatisfied and that relations with customers are strained, what tactical corrections should be made?

4. Should the analysis of NCB lead to the conclusion that employees are somewhat dissatisfied and that relations with customers are strained, what individual corrections should be made?

5. Should the analysis of NCB lead to the conclusion that employees are highly satisfied and customers are strongly loyal, what types of rewards should be given to employees at all ranks in the company?

# Notes

## Chapter 1

### Case 1.1 Chantale and Clinton Call for Service

1. Christopher A. Ross is a professor in the Department of Marketing at the Molson School of Business, Concordia University.

2. In Quebec, a student makes the following progression through the educational system: kindergarten, primary, secondary, CEGEP and university. CEGEP is an acronym for Collège d'enseignement général et professionnel and students normally attend for two years.

3. Nitrogen is a colourless, tasteless and odorless inert gas.

## Chapter 2

### Case 2.1 GENICON: A Surgical Strike Into Emerging Markets

1. All prices are in U.S. dollars.

2. Millennium Research Group, U.S. Markets—Medical Technology Laparoscopic Devices 2008.

3. Business Monitor International: India Pharmaceuticals & Healthcare Report Q4 2009, p. 11.

4. Ibid.

5. Ibid.

6. Ibid.

7. Business Monitor International: Brazil Pharmaceuticals & Healthcare Report Q4 2009, p. 39.

8. Ibid., p. 32.

9. Ibid., p. 57.

10. Ibid.

11. Business Monitor International: Russia Pharmaceuticals & Healthcare Report Q4 2009, p. 54.

12. Ibid.

13. Ibid., p. 56.

### Case 2.2 HyundaiCard's Marketing Strategy

1. www.koreanclick.com, 2007, accessed May 22, 2008.

2. White paper of Korean Ministry of Information and Communication, 2007.

3. Korean Credit Finance Association, 2005.

4. Number of cards distributed = [(total login number / customer period) × 100].

5. Rankey Monthly Report (MediaChannel Inc., 2002, 2005), www.rankey.com, accessed December 15, 2007.

### Case 2.3 TerraCycle Inc.

1. The mixture of organic waste as it is being fed to the worms prior to it being separated and liquefied. The resulting worm excretions were a solid, granular plant fertilizer which was then liquefied to create the liquid plant fertilizer.

2. Affluent individuals who provide capital for business start-ups, usually in exchange for an equity stake.

3. Twenty fluid ounces are approximately equal to 591 milliliters.

4. A garden that uses water for growing in place of soil, sometimes referred to as hydroponics.

5. Subsequent to the time of the case, sales of these products were discontinued.

6. Economies of scale refers to the expected cost savings that result from higher levels of production.

7. Spectrum also had other brands outside the gardening industry, such as Rayovac, a line of batteries.

8. Mixture of partially decomposed organic waste, bedding, and worm castings (excretions).

9. All prices and costs are in U.S. dollars.

10. Calculated using cost of goods sold.

11. There are 128 fluid ounces in one gallon.

## Chapter 3

*Case 3.1 AIR MILES Canada: Rebranding the Air Miles Reward Program*

1. Page 7 of the company's Form 10-K filing, dated March 3, 2006.

2. Page 8 of the company's Form 10-K filing, dated March 3, 2006.

3. Page 31 of the company's Form 10-K filing, dated March 3, 2006.

4. Ibid.

5. All funds in Canadian dollars unless specified otherwise.

6. Caroline Papadatos, "The Art of Storytelling," *Journal of Consumer Marketing*, vol. 23, no. 7, 2006, pp. 382–384.

7. "Loyalty Program Participation Rate on the Rise According to New ACNielsen Study," PanelTrack Loyalty Card Study 2005, ACNeilsen Canada, September 16, 2005, available at http://www.acnielsen.ca/news/20050916.shtml, accessed August 30, 2006.

8. Caroline Papadatos, "The Art of Storytelling," *Journal of Consumer Marketing*, vol. 23, no. 7, 2006, pp. 382–384.

## Chapter 4

*Case 4.2 Boman Communications*

1. This acronym refers to the *Bo*man *Co*mmunications *S*ystem, the firm's business concept.

2. In the case of its largest client, HIAB, for example, Boman Communications selected the HIAB representatives, who would have access to the BOCS database, on the basis of their demonstrated thorough understanding of the BOCS concept and how it works, rather than on the basis of rank.

3. HIAB was a global market leader in on-road load handling solutions. Its product range featured loader cranes, truck-mounted forklifts, forestry cranes, etc. The firm was a subsidiary of Cargotec Inc. Both were headquartered in Finland. HIAB maintained a number of offices in Sweden, including one in Hudiksvall. In 2005, HIAB had 3,400 employees, sales of €844 million and profits of €67 million. Cargotec's sales were €2,358 million and profits €179.4 million. For more information, see the companies' websites: http://www.cargotec.com and www.hiab.com.

4. Boman Communications usually worked in Swedish krona, which is relatively stable with respect to the euro. Figures have been converted to euros at a rate of 9.125 krona per euro.

5. This metaphor illustrates the effect of BOCS. Ketchup is notoriously hard to get out of glass bottles. You bang the bottle repeatedly, but nothing happens, until suddenly ketchup is everywhere!

6. Client proposal drafts were usually pictures and computerized images illustrating general ideas and information flows.

## Chapter 5

*Case 5.1 Ruth's Chris: The High Stakes of International Expansion*

1. Ruth's Chris Steak House 2005 Annual Report, pg. 7.

2. Due to damage caused by Hurricane Katrina, Ruth's Chris was forced to temporarily close its restaurant in New Orleans, Louisiana.

3. Ruth's Chris Steak House 2005 Annual Report, pg. 10.

4. This diagram is based on Ansoff's Product/Market Matrix, first published in "Strategies for Diversification," *Harvard Business Review*, 1957.

5. World Resources Institute, "Meat Consumption: Per Capita (1984–2002)," retrieved on June 7, 2006, from http://earthtrends.wri.org/text/agriculture-food/variable-193.html

*Case 5.2 The Ultimate Fighting Championships (UFC): The Evolution of a Sport*

1. Jon Show, "UFC Finalizes Team with CMO Hire," *Sports Business Journal,* June 1, 2009, p. 25; available at http://www.sportsbusinessjournal.com/index.cfm?fuseaction=article.preview&articleid=62699, accessed August 8, 2009.

2. Sean Gregory and James Osborne, "White vs. Fedor: Ultimate Fighting's Cold War Gets Hotter," *Time Magazine,* July 10, 2009; available at http://www.time.com/time/arts/article/0,8599,1909703,00.html, accessed September 3, 2009.

3. Ipsos-Reid Canadian Sports Monitor, "UFC (Ultimate Fighting Championship) Tops List of Sports Gaining Momentum in Canada," Toronto, ON, June 22, 2009.

4. Ibid.

5. Arnold M. Knightly, "UFC Sells 10 Percent to Mideast Company," *Las Vegas Review-Journal,* January 11, 2010; available at http://www.lvrj.com/news/breaking_news/UFC-sells-10-percent-to-Mideast-company-81192552.html, accessed January 22, 2010.

6. Steve Cofield, Interview, Yahoo! Sports cage writer, *ESPN Radio 1100,* January 21, 2010; available at http://mmablips.dailyradar.com/video/ufc-112-marshall-zelaznik-talks-about-abu-dhabi-s/, accessed February 1, 2010.

7. Clyde Gentry III, *No Holds Barred: Evolution,* Archon Publishing, Richardson, TX, 2001, pp. 38–39.

8. Ibid., p. 41.

9. Ibid., p. 29.

10. John Paul Newport, "Blood Sport," *Details,* March 1995, pp. 70–72.

11. Clyde Gentry III, *No Holds Barred: Evolution,* Archon Publishing, Richardson, TX, 2001, pp. 106, 123.

12. David Plotz, "Fight Clubbed," Slate.com, November 7, 2009; available at http://www.slate.com/id/46344, retrieved October 3, 2009.

13. Staff, "John McCain—Enter the Opportunist & Sports Biggest Enemy," *MMAMemories.com,* December 14, 2007; available at http://www.mmamemories.com/2007/12/14/john-mccain-enter-the-opportunist-sports-biggest-enemy.html, accessed October 3, 2009.

14. Ivan Trembow, "New Jersey Commission Corrects Mainstream UFC Stories," *Ivansblog.com* (originally published by MMAweekly.com), July 21, 2006; available at http://www.ivansblog.com/2006/07/mixed-martial-arts-new-jersey.html, accessed October 3, 2009.

15. *Zuffa* is Italian for "brawl," "scuffle." or "fight with no rules."

16. Daniel Schorn, "Mixed Martial Arts: A New Kind Of Fight," *60 Minutes* (website) (CBS News), December 12, 2006, p. 2; available at http://www.cbsnews.com/stories/2006/12/08/60minutes/main2241525_page2.shtml, accessed November 3, 2009.

17. Todd Martin, "UFC Retrospective Series Part 3: The New Ownership, Todd Martin," *CBSSports.com,* June 1, 2009; available at http://www.cbssports.com/mma/story/11809856, accessed October 13, 2009.

18. UFC Press Release, "Robbie Lawler vs. Melvin Manhoef, Joe Riggs vs. Jay Hieron set for Strikeforce: Miami Jan.30," prommanow.com, January 6, 2010; available at http://prommanow.com/index.php/2010/01/06/robbie-lawler-vs-melvin-manhoef-joe-riggs-vs-jay-hieron-set-for-strikeforce-miami-jan-30/, accessed January 11, 2010.

19. Ivan Trembow, "UFC's Pay-Per-View Buys Explode in 2006," *Ivansblog.com* (originally published by MMAWeekly.com), July 13, 2006; available at http://www.ivansblog.com/2006/07/mixed-martial-arts-ufcs-pay-per-view.html, accessed November 12, 2009.

20. Joel Stein, "The Ultimate Fighting Machines," *CNNMoney.com* (originally published by *Business 2.0* magazine), November 8, 2006; available at http://money.cnn.com/2006/11/07/magazines/business2/stationcasinos.biz2/index.htm, accessed December 3, 2009.

21. Ibid.

22. Kevin Lole, "Trigg gears up for one more run," *Yahoo! Sports,* September 10, 2009; http://sports.yahoo.com/mma/news?slug=ki-trigg091009&prov=yhoo&type=lgns, accessed December 4, 2009.

23. Kevin "Kimbo Slice" Ferguson is a streetfighter with no formal training in any form of martial arts who became hugely popular through his impressive displays of bare-knuckle fighting in backyards and other illegal fighting circles. Videos of Kimbo featured on YouTube drew millions of views and earned him a spot on the 10th season of the *Ultimate Fighter.* He signed an endorsement contract with Tapout, an MMA retail clothing company, before he had ever won a single fight.

24. Kelsey Philpott, "TUF 10 Breaks Another Ratings Record," *MMAPayout.com,* October 1, 2009; available at http://mmapayout.com/2009/10/page/8/, accessed October 5, 2009.

25. Dave Meltzer, "UFC 52: Chuck Strikes Back," *Yahoo! Sports,* May 24, 2009; available at http://sports.yahoo.com/mma/news?slug=dm-ufcfiftytw0052409&prov=yhoo&type=lgns, retrieved December 4, 2009.

26. A "rubber match" is the third fight between two fighters after the first two matches have been split. This third fight is meant to

determine which fighter will have the winning record. The UFC has often used this term to create anticipation for upcoming fights and to increase the number of PPV buys.

27. Kelsey Philpott, "UFC Establishes New Mark for PPV Buys in 2009," *MMAPayout.com*, December 28, 2009; available at http://mmapay-out.com/2009/12/ufc-establishes-new-mark-for-ppv-buys-in-2009/, accessed January 3, 2010.

28. Ivan Trembow, "UFC 66 Breaks Records; UFC Business Year-In-Review," *MMAWeekly.com*, January 6, 2007, available http://www.mmaweekly .com/absolutenm/templates/dailynews.asp? articleid=3235&zoneid=1, accessed November 27, 2009.

29. Ivan Trembow, "UFC PPV Revenue Tops $200 Million in 2006," *MMAWeekly.com*, March 1, 2007; available at http://www.mma weekly.com/absolutenm/templates/dailynews.asp? articleid=3520&zoneid=3, accessed November 24, 2009.

30. John Hartness, Bodog says UFC will overtake Boxing," gambling-weblog.com, July 11, 2007; available at http://www.gambling-weblog .com/50226711/bodog_says_ufc_will_overtake_ boxing.php, accessed December 5, 2009.

31. Associated Press, "UFC Buys Pride for Less than $70M," *ESPN.com*, March 27, 2007; available at http://sports.espn.go.com/sports/news/ story?id=2814235, accessed October 3, 2009.

32. Ibid.

33. Taro Kotani (translated by Korey Howard), "Pride Worldwide Japan Office Officially Closed," *MMAWeekly.com*, October 5, 2007; available at http://www.mmapower.com/ news.asp?dismode=article&apage=2&artid=231, accessed October 4, 2009.

34. Kris Karkoski, "Dana White: "PRIDE Is a Mess," *MMAFrenzy.com*, June 26, 2007; available at http://mmafrenzy.com/623/dana-white-pride-is-a-mess/, accessed October 23, 2009.

35. UFC 75: Champion vs. Champion featured UFC light heavyweight champion Quinton Jackson and PRIDE champion Dan Henderson; UFC 82: The Pride of a Champion featured UFC middleweight champion Anderson Silva and PRIDE welterweight champion Dan Henderson (at the time he held both PRIDE belts).

36. Matthew Miller, "Ultimate Cash Machine," *Forbes Magazine*, May 5, 2008; available at http://www.forbes.com/forbes/2008/0505/080 .html, accessed January 12, 2010.

37. Interview, UFC fighter (name withheld), October 14, 2009.

38. Sean Gregory and James Osborne, "White vs. Fedor: Ultimate Fighting's Cold War Gets Hotter," *Time Magazine*, July 10, 2009; available at http:// www.time.com/time/arts/article/0,8599,1909703,00 .html, accessed September 3, 2009.

39. Ibid.

40. Dan Arritt, "Showdown," *Los Angeles Times*, July 18, 2008; available at http://articles .latimes.com/2008/jul/18/sports/sp-mma18, accessed December 17, 2009.

41. Ibid.

42. John Morgan and Dan Stupp, "'Affliction: Trilogy' Event Canceled," *MMAJunkie .com*, July 24, 2009; available at http://mmajunkie .com/news/15621/aug-1-affliction-trilogy-event-canceled.mma, accessed January 4, 2010.

43. Loretta Hunt, "Carano Shuns Freak Show One-Woman Act," Sherdog.com, June 18, 2009; available at http://sherdog.com/news/ articles/carano-shuns-freak-show-one-woman-act-18045, accessed November 22, 2009.

44. Dave Meltzer, "Ortiz vs. White Is UFC's Hottest Feud," May 16, 2008; available at http:// sports.yahoo.com/mma/news?slug=dm-tito dana051608&prov=yhoo&type=lgns, accessed November 22, 2009.

45. Staff, "Mark Cuban's HDNET to air Japan's Dream," *MMAWeekly.com*, April 26, 2008; available at http://mmaweekly.com/absolutenm/ templates/dailynews.asp?articleid=6167& zoneid=13, accessed October 11, 2009.

46. Damon Martin, "Pro Elite & Dream Announce Partnership," *MMAWeekly.com*, May 10, 2008; available at http://www.mmaweekly .com/absolutenm/templates/dailynews.asp? articleid=6248&zoneid=13, accessed October 12, 2009.

47. Steven Marrocco, "Strikeforce and Dream Formalizing 'Alliance,'" *MMAWeekly .com*, August 2, 2009; available at http://www .mmaweekly.com/absolutenm/templates/dailynews .asp?articleid=9288&zoneid=4, accessed October 15, 2009.

48. Interview, UFC Fighter (name withheld), October 14, 2009.

49. Ibid.

50. Ibid.

51. Ibid.

52. Dave Meltzer, "Ortiz vs. White Is UFC's Hottest Feud," *Yahoo! Sports,* May 16, 2008; available at http://sports.yahoo.com/mma/news?slug=dm-titodana051608&prov=yhoo&type=lgns, accessed November 22, 2009.

53. Dana White, Twitter.com, July 17, 2009; available at http://twitter.com/danawhiteufc.

54. Interview, UFC fighter (name withheld), October 14, 2009.

55. An undercard fighter is featured on a UFC card before the main advertised events are shown live on television. Often, the undercard fights were televised only at the end of the show, if at all, to fill empty air time when the main-event fights ended sooner than was expected. For example, all main-event fights featured first-round knockouts that ended the fight.

56. Jacob Camargo, "Fedor, Kimbo Slice and Silva vs. Belfort and More," Interview, *fiveknuckles.com,* October 4, 2009; available at http://www.fiveknuckles.com/mma-news/Video-Dana-White-talks-Fedor,-Kimbo-Slice,-Silva-vs-Belfort-and-more.html, accessed November 13, 2009.

57. Ibid.

58. Steve Cofield, Yahoo! Sports Cagewriter, Interview, *ESPN Radio 1100,* January 21, 2010; available at http://mmablips.dailyradar.com/video/ufc-112-marshall-zelaznik-talks-about-abu-dhabi-s/, accessed February 1, 2010.

59. Ibid.

60. Ibid.

61. Andy Samuelson, "UFC Inks TV Deal in Mexico," *LasVegasSun.com,* July 9, 2009; available at http://www.lasvegassun.com/blogs/sports/2009/jul/09/ufc-inks-tv-deal-mexico/, accessed February 1, 2010.

62. Ibid.

63. Josh Stein, "UFC Expands to Portugal," *MMAOpinion.com,* May 30, 2009; available at http://mmaopinion.com/2009/05/30/ufc-expands-to-portugal/, accessed September 30, 2009.

64. Jon Show, "UFC Expands TV Reach to China and Mexico," *Sportsbusinessjournal.com,* June 29, 2009. http://www.sportsbusinessjournal.com/article/62917, accessed September 30, 2009.

65. Ibid.

66. GLAAD is an acronym for Gay & Lesbian Alliance Against Defamation.

67. Joel Stein, "The Ultimate Fighting Machines," *CNNMoney.com* (originally published by *Business 2.0* magazine), November 8, 2006; available at http://money.cnn.com/2006/11/07/magazines/business2/stationcasinos.biz2/index.htm, accessed December 3, 2009.

68. Staff, "Lorenzo Fertitta to Work Full-Time as UFC Chair and CEO," *Sportsbusinessjournal.com,* June 19, 2008; available at http://www.sportsbusinessdaily.com/article/121737, accessed February 4, 2010.

69. Standard and Poor's, "Zuffa's $100M Incremental Term Loan Rated 'BB-' (Recover Rating: 4); 'BB-' Corporate Credit Rating Affirmed," S&P Credit Research (Abstract), October 1, 2009; available at http://www.alacrastore.com/research/s-and-p-credit-research-Zuffa_s_100M_Incremental_Term_Loan_Rated_BB_Recover_Rating_4_BB_Corporate_Credit_Rating_Affirmed-749666, accessed November 2, 2009.

70. Ibid.

### Case 5.3 Best Buy Inc.—Dual Branding in China

1. "Best Buy Snaps up Future Shop for $580 Million," *CBCNews.*ca, August 14, 2001, http://www.cbc.ca/money/story/2001/08/14/futureshop140801.html, accessed September 12, 2008.

2. Best Buy 10-K filings 2001 p 5.

3. Ibid.

4. www.ce.org/research/US.CE industry growth 2004–2009(e), referenced March 31, 2009.

5. Consumer Electronics Association, "Global Consumer Electronics Industry Will Grow to $700 Million by 2009, CEA/GfK Study Finds," press release, July 9, 2008, http://www.ce.org/Press/CurrentNews/press_release_detail.asp?id=11535, accessed March 31, 2009.

6. Diana Farrell et al., From "Made in China" to "Sold in China": The Rise of the Chinese Urban Consumer,' McKinsey Global Institute, November 2006.

7. Instat, "China's Consumer Electronics Manufacturing Will More Than Double by 2010," press release, October 11, 2006, http://www.instat.com/press.asp?ID=1768&sku=IN0602785CSM, accessed November 28, 2008.

8. In May 2008, Best Buy and Carphone Warehouse announced the creation a new joint venture company, in which Best Buy acquired 50% of The Carphone Warehouse's European and U.S. retail interests for a cash consideration of £1.1 billion, or US$2.1 billion.

9. Jean Zhou, Deutsche Bank equity research report on Suning Appliances, dated April 7, 2006.

10. Andrew Grant, "The New Chinese Consumer," *The McKinsey Quarterly*, Special Edition, June 2006 p 1.

11. Claudia Suessmeth-Dykerhoff et al., "Marketing to China's New Traditionalists," *Far Eastern Economic Review*, April 2008. p 29.

12. Kevin P. Lane et al., "Building Brands in China," *The McKinsey Quarterly*, Special Edition, June 2006. p 39.

13. Normandy Madden, "Tier Tale: How Marketers Classify Cities in China," *Advertising Age*, March 19, 2007 p 21.

14. Sandy Chen, Citigroup equity research report on Gome, dated October 12, 2005.

15. Russell Flannery, "Best Buy's Art of War," Forbes.com. http://www.forbes.com/services/forbes/2007/1015/066.html, accessed November 27, 2008.

16. Sandy Chen, Citigroup equity research report on Gome, dated October 12, 2005.

17. Jean Zhou, "Suning Appliance," Deutsche Bank Equity Research Report dated April 7, 2006.

18. Russell Flannery, "Best Buy's Art of War," Forbes.com, http://www.forbes.com/services/forbes/2007/1015/066.html, accessed November 28, 2008.

## Chapter 6

*Case 6.1 Hanson Production*

1. www.broadwayworld.com/shows/tickets/ (calculated average), accessed December 18, 2008.

*Case 6.2 Sy.Med
Development. Inc.*

1. www.symed.com/about.htm, accessed December 4, 2001.

2. According to Robert B. Taylor, physicians do not like to be called "providers," because, although the term may be "politically correct," it "lumps my physician colleagues and me with individuals who are frankly less qualified and yet aspire to do the same work we do." Taylor says that the term "diminishes" physicians as professionals. The term is beneficial, however, in this case to differentiate between physicians who provide care (providers) and health-care organizations that pay for the care (payors). Robert B. Taylor, "Please Don't Call Me Provider," *American Family Physician*, June 15, 2001, p. 2340.

3. www.aafp.org/online/en/home/publications/news/news-now/practice-management/20070420credentialingform.html, accessed April 19, 2009.

4. Personal interview with the author, November 3, 2001.

5. Ibid.

6. www.cactussoftware.com, accessed August 2001.

7. Personal communication with the author, December 18, 2001.

8. Personal communication with the author, December 20, 2001.

*Case 6.3 Arvind Mills:
Re-Evaluating Profitability*

1. www.idt.org/issues/india4.

2. All amounts in U.S. dollars unless otherwise specified.

## Chapter 7

*Case 7.1 La Hacienda Del Sol*

1. The months when travel activity was at its lowest.

2. One mile is equivalent to 1.609 kilometers.

3. State Government of Baja California: www.bajacalifornia.gob.mx/english/home.htm, July 19, 2004.

4. All-terrain vehicles.

5. Rooms represented 60 percent of revenue with remaining revenues derived from restaurant and spa sales.

6. All prices in the case are in U.S. dollars.

7. The weekend prior to the first Monday in September of each year.

8. Maquiladoras are assembly plants in Mexico that import raw materials from a foreign country, namely the United States, and export the finished goods to the same foreign country.

9. All costs converted to U.S. dollars as at January 7, 2004.

### Case 7.2 Shoppers Stop—Targeting the Young

1. US$1 was equivalent to INR44.95 in June 2006, http://www.economywatch.com/exchange-rate/rupee.html, accessed April 28, 2009.

2. An interview by *Business Barons* magazine with Sundara Rajan, CEO, Market Search, http://www.market-search.com/news01.html, accessed April 28, 2009

3. The figures pertained to 2004/05. See "Retail—Market and Opportunities," Ernst & Young and India Brand Equity Foundation. www.ibef.org/download/Retail_220708.pdf.

4. Kaushik Basu, "India's Demographic Divide," *BBC News*, July 25, 2007, http://news.bbc.co.uk/1/hi/world/south_asia/6911544.stm, accessed January 12, 2009.

5. "YouSumerism: Youth in India—Opportunity Knocks," Ernst & Young India Retail Advisory Group, 2007, www.ey.com/Global/Assets.nsf/India/Youth_Final/$file/Youth_Final.pdf, accessed March 9, 2009.

6. Shoppers Stop draft Red Herring prospectus, p.46.

7. *Shoppers Stop Equity Research Report*, B&K Securities, February 2007, p.5.

8. Don Tapscott, *Grown up Digital: How the Net Generation Is Changing Your World*, McGraw-Hill, Columbus, OH, 2009.

9. Ibid

10. Mark Bauerlein, *The Dumbest Generation: How the Digital Age Stupefies Young Americans and Jeopardizes Our Future (or Don't Trust Anyone Under 30)*, Penguin Books, New York, 2008.

### Case 7.3 Eat2Eat.com

1. While the example of hotel restaurants gave birth to the concept in Aggarwal's mind, he believed there were also innumerable restaurants not affiliated with hotels that could also benefit from online reservations.

2. First-time users of the service were required to register as customers and provide some personal details. Registration was free.

3. Coordination with the restaurants could be automated and conducted online. For restaurants that were not connected to the Internet, the process was conducted using facsimile (fax) machines. Thus, restaurants did not require Internet access to participate, although Internet access made the process more efficient for both the restaurants and for Eat2Eat.com.

4. WAP, or wireless application protocol, was an open international standard for applications on wireless communication devices. A common example was Internet access on mobile phones.

5. Alibaba.com operated the world's largest online marketplace for international and domestic China trade, as well as China's most widely used online payment system, AliPay. It had a community of more than 15 million businesses and consumers in more than 200 countries and territories. In 2004, Alibaba.com facilitated more than US$4 billion in trade. In August 2005, Yahoo! Inc. and Alibaba.com announced a long-term strategic partnership in China. The arrangement would promote the Yahoo! brand in China. Also, Yahoo! purchased US$1 billion of Alibaba.com shares, giving Yahoo! approximately 40 percent economic interest in the company.

## Chapter 8

### Case 8.1 SC Johnson: Planning Coupon Promotions

1. A line extension is often a new fragrance or application for an existing product line

2. Integrated promotional campaigns combine more than one type of promotion

### Case 8.2 Phillips Foods, Inc.— Introducing King Crab to the Trade

1. Hoover's Profile, 2008.

2. *Baltimore Business Journal*, January 11, 2008.

3. *Seafood Business*, June 15, 2007.

4. *Seafood Business*, January 28, 2008.

5. *Seafood Business*, June 15, 2007.

6. Mintel, U.S. Fish and Seafood Industry Report, January 2008.

7. Mintel, U.S. Fish and Seafood Industry Report, January 2008.

8. MRI+, Spring 2006 Product Survey.

9. Mintel, U.S. Fish and Seafood Industry Report, January 2008.

10. *Refrigerated & Frozen Foods,* June 2007.

11. Food Marketing Institute, Key Facts & Figures, 2006.

12. *Encyclopedia of American Industries,* Vol. 2, pp. 710–711, 2005.

13. Mintel, U.S. Fish and Seafood Industry Report, January 2008.

14. Mintel, U.S. Fish and Seafood Industry Report, January 2008.

15. Center for Exhibition Industry Research, 2006 Census.

16. The Global Association of the Exhibition Industry, Exhibitions Work, 2006.

17. B2B Media Trends and Forecast, Expo, 2006.

18. Center for Exhibition Industry Research, ACRR 1120, 2000.

19. Center for Exhibition Industry Research, ACRR 1130, 2007.

20. Center for Exhibition Industry Research, AC32, 1999.

21. Center for Exhibition Industry Research, PE II, 2000.

22. Center for Exhibition Industry Research, AC31, 1999.

23. Center for Exhibition Industry Research, SM36, 2000.

24. Center for Exhibition Industry Research, SM17.01, 2001.

25. Exhibit Survey Inc., ROI Toolkit, 2008.

26. Exhibit Survey Inc., ROI Toolkit, 2008.

27. B2B Media, Expo, November/December 2006.

28. Forrester Research Inc., "The Power of Industry-Specific Business Magazines," 2007.

29. Direct Marketing Association, Response Rate Report, 2004.

### Case 8.3 Boots: Hair-Care Sales Promotion

1. £1 = 100 pence (p). £1 = Cdn$2.35, December 2004.

2. http://www.alberto.com, accessed May 2005.

## Chapter 9

### Case 9.1 Global Source Healthcare: Allocating Sales Resources

1. As reported by the American Hospital Association (AHA) in 2003. Registered hospitals are those hospitals that meet AHA's criteria for registration as a hospital facility.

### Case 9.2 Spectrum Brands, Inc.— The Sales Force Dilemma

1. All funds are in Canadian dollars unless otherwise indicated.

### Case 9.3 Biomed Co., Ltd.: Designing a New Sales Compensation Plan

1. The exchange rate was $1 US = 38.25 Thai Baht (THB) in mid-2006.

2. GMP is a set of regulations, codes and guidelines for the manufacture of drugs, medical devices, etc.

## Chapter 10

### Case 10.1 Retail Execution: Linens 'n Things

1. Data from preceding paragraphs taken from International Directory of Company Histories, Vol. 24, St. James Press, 1999,www.funding universe.com/company-histories/Linens-n-Things-Inc-Company-History.html, accessed June 2009; and G. Lemieux and K. Peippo, "Linens 'n Things, Inc.," www.answers.com/topic/linens-n-things-inc, accessed June 2009.

## Chapter 11

### Case 11.1 Walmart Puerto Rico: Promoting Development Through a Public–Private Partnership

1. http://idbdocs.iadb.org/wsdocs/get-Document.aspx?DOCNUM=1828461, accessed February 5, 2010.

2. www.walmartpr.com/Pages/Conoce Walmart/culturaWalmart.aspx, accessed February 5, 2010.

3. All funds in U.S. dollars unless otherwise stated.

4. http://walmartstores.com/AboutUs, accessed February 5, 2010.

5. PBS Frontline, "Is Wal-Mart Good For America?" November 16, 2004, www.pbs.org/wgbh/pages/frontline/shows/walmart, accessed February 5, 2010.

6. www.walmartwatch.com.

7. http://economia.uprrp.edu/ensayo%20121.pdf, accessed April 5, 2010.

8. http://walmartstores.com/sites/sustainabilityreport/2009/s_d_majorDiversity Programs.html, accessed April 5, 2010.

9. www.aec.msu.edu/thefoodscene/seminars/wal-mart.htm, accessed April 5, 2010.

10. www.walmartstores.com, accessed April 5, 2010.

11. The United States Department of Agriculture defines sustainable agriculture development as an integrated system of plant and animal production practices that could help satisfy, in the long term, the need for food and fiber; help increase the efficiency of the environment and natural resources; allow the use of more efficient non-renewable resources and utilize natural biological controls and cycles; help maintain the economic viability of farms; and improve the quality of life of farmers and the whole society alike. www.nal.usda.gov/afsic/pubs/terms/srb9902.shtml.

12. http://walmartstores.com/Sustainability, accessed April 5, 2010, and http://walmartstores.com/Diversity, accessed April 5, 2010.

13. Puerto Rico Enterprises, or Puerto Rico Emprende, was the name eventually given to the EDB's banner CSR program. It was an umbrella project that involved the social responsibility programs of four companies that had come to the EDC for company financing and which had sought López's advice. They were Walmart's Siembra el Desarrollo Del País; Cemex's Arte en Concreto vocational training for prisoners program; Bacardí's waterfront development project, Desarrollo Frente Portuario de Cataño; and W Hotels Martineau-Vieques's local value chain micro-enterprise project.

14. The agreement was signed by Walmart PR president Renzo Casillo, EDB President Annette Montoto, Esq., Secretary of Agriculture Hon. Gabriel Figueroa and the leader of Caborrojeños Pro Health and Environment, Luis Valderrama.

15. Financing program coordinated between the DA and the EDB to promote the development and creation of small and medium agribusinesses.

16. Besides the EDB, the only financial institutions in Puerto Rico that granted agricultural loans were the PR Production Credit and the Farm Service Agency.

17. The BBVA Foundation was established in 2007 in Spain with 200 million euros in capital and was governed by Spanish law. www.fundacionmicrofinanzasbbva.org/castellano, accessed April 5, 2010.

18. www.bdepr.org/bdepr/download/AnualReport2008.pdf.

19. K. Weiermair, M. Perters and J. Frehse, "Success factors for public private partnership: cases in alpine tourism development," *Journal of Services Research*, February 2008, pp. 7–21.

20. The government created the Puerto Rico Authority for Public-Private Partnerships with a mission to guide and facilitate the establishment of partnerships between the government and private companies to further the development and innovation of Puerto Rico's infrastructure and service. www.app.gobierno.pr/SobreAutoridad/Autoridad.html, accessed April 5, 2010.

### Case 11.2 "Hips Feel Good"—Dove's Campaign for Real Beauty

1. "Vitality," *Unilever Magazine*, 132, 2004, p. 19.

2. A situational influence is a temporary force that influences behavior usually associated with the immediate purchasing environment. Dimensions of situational influence include the time when purchases are made, the physical surroundings, and the emotional state or mood of the purchaser. Where consumers buy are the physical surroundings. How consumers buy refers to the terms of the purchase. Conditions under which consumers buy relates to states and moods.

3. Nancy Etcoff et al., "The Real Truth about Beauty: A Global Report: Findings of the Global Study on Women, Beauty and Well-Being," September 2004, available at www.campaign forrealbeauty.com/uploadedfiles/dove_white_paper_final.pdf.

4. "Vitality," *Unilever Magazine,* 132, 2004, p. 9.

5. "Dove's Flight of Fancy," Marketing Magazine (Ireland), April 2006, www.marketing. ie, accessed April 16, 2007.

6. "Medaillenflut für deutsche Agenturen, *Horizon*", October 6, 2005, p. 34.

7. "Dove's 'The Campaign for Real Beauty,' Created by Ogilvy & Mather Wins the 2006 Grand Effie Award," Company Press Release, June 8, 2006.

8. "Vitality," *Unilever Magazine,* Issue 132, 2004, p. 11.

9. "Super Bowl Spot Launches Multi-Tiered Effort Encouraging Girls to Feel More Confident, Recognize Their Unique Beauty," Campaignforrealbeauty.com, January 27, 2006, available at http://sev.prnewswire.com/advertising/20060127/NYF01927012006-1.html, accessed August 28, 2006.

10. "How Real Curves Can Grow Your Brand," Viewpoint Online Magazine, Ogilvy.com, April 2005, available at http://www.ogilvy.com/uploads/koviewpoint/dove.pdf, accessed August 28, 2006.

## Case 11.3 New Balance: Developing an Integrated CSR Strategy

1. In this case, the term corporate social responsibility is used interchangeably with corporate citizenship, responsible leadership and sustainability.

2. The Boston College Center for Corporate Citizenship (BCCCC) is a membership-based research organization associated with the Carroll School of Management. New Balance had been a member of the Center since 1999.

3. Kim B. Clark, "New Balance Athletic Shoes," *Harvard Business School Publishing,* 1980, p. 680–710.

4. All funds are in US$ unless otherwise stated.

5. The acquired brands included men's traditional and everyday shoes, apparel, footwear, and equipment for lacrosse, hockey, and volleyball, among other sports.

6. Lean production was pioneered by Toyota and represents flexible manufacturing technologies to deliver goods on demand, minimize inventory, maximize the use of multi-skilled employees, flatten management structure, and focus resources when and where they were needed.

7. Source: Hoovers, "Industry Overview: Footwear Manufacture, Wholesale and Retail," www.hoovers.com/footwear-manufacture,-wholesale,-and-retail-/—ID__130—/free-ind-fr-profile-basic.xhtml.2009, accessed December 4, 2009.

8. The Play Fair campaign was an alliance of Oxfam, Global Unions, the Clean Clothes Campaign, and their constituent organizations worldwide, which aimed to push sportswear and athletic footwear companies, the International Olympics Committee (IOC) and national governments toward eliminating the exploitation and abuse of workers in the global sporting goods industry. For more information, see www.playfair2008.0rg. While Oxfam did not participate in the 2008 campaign, it remained a member of the Play Fair Alliance.

9. The list of Timberland supplier factories in 2008 is available at www.justmeans.com/usercontent/companydocs/docs/company_docs_1213368647.pdf; Nike's list of suppliers in 2009 is available at www.nikebiz.com/responsibility/documents/Dec09_Collegiate_Disclosure.pd, both accessed January 13, 2010.

10. See Massachusetts Department of Environmental Protection, Global Warming Solutions Act Implementation, www.mass.gov/dep/air/climate/index.htm, accessed on December 7, 2009.

11. See EUROPA Environment, "What is REACH?" http://ec.europa.eu/environment/chemicals/reach/reach_intro.htm, accessed on December 7, 2009.

12. 2007 Corporate Social Responsibility Report (published in 2008 and available only internally).

13. Michael Blowfield, "New Balance Case Study," unpublished paper prepared for the Business Network on Integration at the Boston

College Center for Corporate Citizenship, November 2006.

14. Reputation Institute and Boston College Center for Corporate Citizenship, "Building Reputation Here, There and Everywhere: Worldwide Views on Local Impact of Corporate Responsibility," March 2009, www.bcccc.net/index.cfm?fuseaction=document.showDocumentByID&nodeID=1&DocumentID=1270, accessed January 13, 2010.

15. For more information see Boston Consulting Group (BCG) 2008 Survey, "Capturing the Green Advantage for Consumer Companies," www.bcg.com/publications/files/Capturing_Green_Advantage_Consumer_Companies_Jan_2009.pdf, accessed January 13, 2010, Remi Trudel and June Cotte, "Does Being Ethical Pay?," MIT *Sloan Management Review,* Winter 2009, 50.2.

16. Harada, C., Hawthorn, A., Kilbride, J., and Redding, C., "New Balance Athletic Shoe, Inc.: Brand Audit," Jones Graduate School of Management, Rice University, December 2004. Unpublished report.

17. A separate but related initiative included an assessment of the New Balance Foundation's charitable contributions and provided recommendations for improving the focus and alignment with the company's business strategy.

18. This case focuses only on the first initiative. There was, however, communication between the research team and CREA to ensure that key findings and recommendations from the assessment were taken into consideration when developing the CSR report.

19. For more information on the framework see Christopher Pinney, "Framework for the Future: Understanding and Managing Corporate Citizenship from a Business Perspective," Boston College Center for Corporate Citizenship, briefing paper, February 2009, www.bcccc.net/index.cfm?fuseaction=document.showDocumentByID&DocumentID=1259, accessed January 13, 2010.

20. For more information on the framework see Vesela Veleva, "Managing Corporate Citizenship: A New Tool for Companies," *Corporate Social Responsibility and Environmental Management,* 17, 2010, pp. 40–51, published online in Wiley InterScience, www.interscience.wiley.com, June 15, 2009, DOI: 10.1002/csr.206, accessed January 26, 2010.

21. Established in 1994, the Maquila Solidarity Network (MSN) is a group of labor and women's rights organization committed to supporting the efforts of workers in global supply chains to win improved wages, working conditions, and a better quality of life. For more information see http://en.maquilasolidarity.org, accessed January 13, 2010.

22. Interview with Anne Davis, February 12, 2009.

23. For example, in the footwear division, New Balance was the only company that its overseas factories manufactured for. In the apparel and accessories division, however, New Balance was one of many customers, and therefore, it had limited leverage in enacting changes.

24. With the lack of corporate-wide policy on PVC it was not clear whether all acquired brands were also PVC-free.

25. The 070 shoe was made with recycled materials, reduced waste, and water-based adhesives. For more information see www.nbwebexpress.com/newbalanceME070SN.htm, accessed on January 13, 2010.

26. For more information on product stewardship see www.productstewardship.us and Vesela Veleva, "Product Stewardship in the U.S.: The Changing Policy Landscape and the Role of Business," *Sustainability: Science, Practice and Policy,* Fall/Winter 2008, 4.2, http://ejournal.nbii.org/archives/vol4iss2/communityessay.veleva.html, accessed on January 13, 2010.

27. See Boston Consulting Group 2008 Survey "Capturing the Green Advantage for Consumer Companies," http://209.83.147.85/impact_expertise/publications/files/Capturing_Green_Advantage_Consumer_Companies_Jan_2009.pdf accessed January 13, 2010.

28. For more information see Bea Boccalandro, "Mapping Success in Employee Volunteering: The Drivers for Effectiveness in Employee Volunteering and Giving Programs and Fortune 500," Boston College Center for Corporate Citizenship, April 2009, www.bcccc.net/index.cfm?fuseaction=document.showDocumentByID&DocumentID=1308, accessed January 13, 2010.

29. Some of the questions came from an earlier assessment of New Balance conducted by the Boston College Center for Corporate

Citizenship: Blowfield, Michael, "New Balance Case Study," October 2006.

## Chapter 12

### Case 12.1 YesCreations LLC: Alex Goes to Hollywood

1. Swiss cinematographer Ueli Steiger was best known for his work in big-budget blockbusters, such as *Austin Powers, The Day After Tomorrow,* and *10,000 BC.*

2. Caduff's credits included *The Visual Language of Herbert Matter, Charlie Haden,* and *A Crude Awakening: The Oil Crash.*

3. Burke, Leslie, "IndieVest Seeks Investors for Independent Feature Films," *South Florida Business Journal,* April 6, 2009, southflorida.bizjournals.com/southflorida/stories/2009/04/06/smallb1.html, accessed June 8, 2009.

4. Romano's screen credits included starring roles in *Kim Possible, Campus Confidential, Cadet Kelly* and *Even Stevens.*

5. Harris had appeared in more than 70 films since the late 1960s. Harris's recent screen credits included *Toy Story 2, Seinfeld* and *The Suite Life of Zack and Cody.*

6. Brauen's screen credits included *Æon Flux, The Big One, Salomaybe?* and *Asudem.*

7. Gill, Mark, "Yes, the Sky Really Is Falling," *IndieWire,* June 22, 2008, indiewire.com/article/first_person_film_departments_mark_gill_yes_the_sky_really_is_falling, accessed June 8, 2009.

8. Festivus Mission Statement, festivusfilmfestival.com/filmmakers.html, accessed June 8, 2009.

9. The Sundance Festival was the largest independent film festival in the United States. Lynn Tryba, "Adventures in Self Distribution: Three Case Studies," *Independent Magazine,* April 8, 2008, independent-magazine.org/08/04/adventures-self-distribution, accessed April 7, 2009.

### Case 12.2 Eureka Forbes Ltd: Growing the Water Purifier Business

1. Method of water purification using ultraviolet (UV) light.

2. The Tatas eventually divested their stake in EFL in 2001. Thus 60 percent ownership of the company came to SP Group (Shapoorji Pallonji Group) who themselves had a significant stake in Tata Sons Limited. SP Group later bought out 40 percent from Electrolux also and thus by 2004 EFL came to be owned entirely by SP Group.

3. http://www.pureitwater.com/index1.htm Referenced March 03, 2010

4. http://www.kent.co.in/introduction.html Referenced March 03, 2010

5. http://www.ionindia.com/about_us Referenced March 03, 2010

6. "Increased global water stress," *United Nations Environment Programme (UNEP),* http://maps.grida.no/go/graphic/increased-global-water-stress, accessed on January 18, 2010.

7. Watching Water: A Guide to Evaluating Corporate Risks in a Thirsty World," *Global Equity Research,* March 31, 2008, J.P. Morgan Securities, p. 6; available at www.wri.org/publication/watching-water, accessed on March 2, 2010.

8. "The 'Bird of Gold': The Rise of India's Consumer Market," *McKinsey Global Institute,* McKinsey & Company, May 2007, p. 10; available at www.mckinsey.com/mgi/publications/India_consumer_market/index.asp, accessed on March 2, 2010.

9. "Wholesale FDI in retail," http://www.thehindubusinessline.com/2009/06/04/Referenced March 03, 2010.

10. "Retail: wholesale growth" http://www.indiaretailshow.com/Industry.htm Referenced March 03, 2010.

11. "The Indian retail revolution," page 4 of 30 Indian Retail 2005–06 www.ibef.com Referenced March 03, 2010.

## Chapter 13

### Case 13.1 The Entrepreneurs at Twitter: Building a Brand, a Social Tool, or a Tech Powerhouse?

1. This case has been written on the basis of published sources only. Consequently, the interpretation and perspectives presented in this case are not necessarily those of Twitter or any of its employees.

2. http://www.cnn.com/2010/TECH/01/26/has.twitter.peaked/index.html?hpt=C1, accessed March 5, 2010.

3. http://blog.pff.org/archives/2009/09/will_our_twitter_free_ride_end_or_will_targeted_ad.html, accessed March 5, 2010.

4. http://techcrunch.com/2009/09/16/twitter-closing-new-venture-round-with-1-billion-valuation/, accessed March 5, 2010.

5. http://www.marketwatch.com/story/teens-arent-into-twitter-but-they-love-facebook-2010–02–09?reflink=MW_news_stmp, accessed February 9, 2010.

6. http://online.wsj.com/article/SB124000817787330413.html, accessed March 2, 2010.

7. Ibid.

8. Ibid.

9. http://searchenginewatch.com/2165221, accessed October 15, 2009 and http://www.blogger.com/about, accessed October 15, 2009.

10. http://www.nytimes.com/2005/02/25/technology/25podcast.html?_r=1, accessed July 15, 2009.

11. http://evhead.com/2005/02/how-odeo-happened.asp, accessed July 15, 2009.

12. http://www.nytimes.com/2005/02/25/technology/25podcast.html?_r=1, accessed July15, 2009.

13. http://evhead.com/2005/02/how-odeo-happened.asp, accessed July 15, 2009.

14. http://dev.aol.com/article/2007/04/definitive-guide-to-twitter, accessed November 15, 2009.

15. http://www.techcrunch.com/2008/05/01/twitter-said-to-be-abandoning-ruby-on-rails/, accessed November 15, 2009.

16. http://www.artima.com/scalazine/articles/twitter_on_scala.html, accessed November 23, 2009.

17. "40404" is the U.S. short code.

18. Dom Sagolla, (2009–01–30). "How Twitter Was Born," 140 Characters, http://www.140characters.com/2009/01/30/how-twitter-was-born/, accessed June 25, 2009.

19. David Sano, (2009–02–18), "Twitter creator Jack Dorsey illuminates the site's founding document," *Los Angeles Times*, http://latimesblogs.latimes.com/technology/2009/02/twitter-creator.html, accessed September 15, 2009.

20. http://apiwiki.twitter.com/Things-Every-Developer-Should-Know, accessed November 15, 2009.

21. http://dev.aol.com/article/2007/04/definitive-guide-to-twitter, accessed November 15, 2009.

22. http://online.wsj.com/article/SB124000817787330413.html, accessed March 2, 2010.

23. http://www.140characters.com/2009/01/30/how-twitter-was-born/, accessed Mary 2, 2010.

24. http://online.wsj.com/article/SB124000817787330413.html, accessed March 2, 2010.

25. Andrew LaVallee, (2009–06–15). "Web Users in Iran Reach Overseas for Proxies," *The Wall Street Journal*, http://blogs.wsj.com/digits/2009/06/15/web-users-in-iran-reach-overseas-for-proxies/, accessed June 16, 2009; and Mike Musgrove, (2009–06–17), "Twitter Is a Player In Iran's Drama," *The Washington Post*, http://www.washingtonpost.com/wp-dyn/content/article/2009/06/16/AR2009061603391.html?hpid=topnews, accessed July 09, 2009.

26. http://www.cnn.com/2009/TECH/04/15/ashton.cnn.twitter.battle/index.html

27. http://mashable.com/2009/10/07/drew-carey-twitter-bid/, accessed October 15, 2009.

28. http://blog.twitter.com/2009/09/new-twitter-funding.html

29. http://www.bloomberg.com/apps/news?pid=20601087&sid=aPAHFu.jBrhM

30. http://www.bloomberg.com/apps/news?pid=20601087&sid=aPAHFu.jBrhM

31. http://bits.blogs.nytimes.com/2009/06/19/twitter-plans-to-offer-shopping-advice-and-easy-purchasing/

32. http://www.techcrunch.com/2009/07/16/twitters-internal-strategy-laid-bare-to-be-the-pulse-of-the-planet/

33. http://about.skype.com/2005/09/ebay_to_acquire_skype.html, accessed March 2, 2010.

34. http://www.techcrunch.com/2009/07/16/twitters-internal-strategy-laid-bare-to-be-the-pulse-of-the-planet/, March 2, 2010.

35. Adapted from http://www.techcrunch.com/2009/07/15/twitters-financial-forecast-shows-first-revenue-in-q3–1-billion-users-in-2013/.

36. http://online.wsj.com/article/SB124000817787330413.html, accessed March 2, 2010.

37. Ibid.

38. http://www.marketwatch.com/story/teens-arent-into-twitter-but-they-love-facebook-2010–02–09?reflink=MW_news_stmp, accessed February 9, 2010.

39. Ibid.

40. http://mashable.com/2010/01/11/twitter-growth-stats/, accessed February 9, 2010.

41. http://mashable.com/2009/09/14/twitter-2009-stats/, accessed February 9, 2010.

42. http://news.cnet.com/8301–17939_109–10120401–2.html, accessed February 9, 2010.

43. http://news.cnet.com/8301–30684_3–10449662–265.html, accessed February 9, 2010.

44. http://techcrunch.com/2010/02/16/twitter-open-source/, accessed March 2, 2010.

### Case 13.2 Anduro Marketing: Internet Services Vs. Software Sales

1. All funds in Canadian dollars unless specified otherwise.

### Case 13.3 Molson Canada: Social Media Marketing

1. This case has been written on the basis of published sources only. Consequently, the interpretation and perspectives presented in this case are not necessarily those of Molson Canada or any of its employees.

2. Molson Coors Brewing Company, *Living Our Values,* p. 4, available online at http://www.molsoncoors.com/templates/molson_coors/pdf/Code_of_Business_Conduct.pdf, accessed May 10, 2008.

3. Molson Coors Brewing Company, "Molson Celebrates Responsible Choices across Canada This Holiday Season," press release, December 19, 2007, available online at http://www.molsoncoors.com/newsroom/press-releases/2007, accessed February 17, 2008.

4. Wikipedia, available online at http://en.wikipedia.org/wiki/Mashup_(web_application_hybrid), accessed September 16, 2008.

5. Run-of-site advertising is an advertisement buying option, in which advertisements can be placed on any pages of the target site. This option is usually inexpensive and hence advertisers generally give up their say over placement. Advertisements may be placed in the unsold, less valuable portions of the target site randomly.

6. Static microsites are related pages on a website that have their own URL, which is not a derivative of home page. These websites are used for contextual advertisements or pay-per-click advertisements and are created with topic-specific, keyword-rich contents to attract web traffic; however, they are not dynamic and have very low customizability.

7. Charlene Li, "Marketing on Social Networking Sites," Forrester Research Inc., Cambridge, MA, 2007.

8. For more details on consumer usage of social networking sites, refer to Charlene Li, "How Consumers User Social Networks," Forrester Research Inc., Cambridge, MA, 2007.

9. Molson Canadian Nation Facebook group had 19,063 members as of March 29, 2008.

10. Marina Strauss, "Molson Photo Contest Brews up Anger," *Globe and Mail,* available at http://www.theglobeandmail.com/servlet/story/RTGAM.20071122.wmolsonface1122/BNStory/Technology, accessed January 6, 2008

11. Kara Nicholson, "Molson Using Facebook to Engage Canadian Students," available at http://www.mediaincanada.com/articles/mic/20071122/molson.html, accessed January 6, 2008.

12. Ibid.

13. Karen Rouse, "Molson Ends Facebook 'Party School' Contest," *Denver Post,* November 26, 2007, available at http://www.denverpost.com/business/ci_7562948, accessed January 12, 2008.

14. Kara Nicholson, "Molson Using Facebook to Engage Canadian Students," available at http://www.mediaincanada.com/articles/mic/20071122/molson.html, accessed January 12, 2008.

15. "Molson's Facebook Contest Leaves Some MUN Students Frothing," CBC News, November 20, 2007.

16. Ibid.

17. Ken Meaney, "Anger Brews over Molson Contest," *Calgary Herald,* November 21, 2007, p. 5.

18. Ted Garrard, vice-president external at Western, quoted in Mike Hayes, "Memorial Is the

Number One Party School? Really?" *The Gazette,* November 15, 2007, pp. 1–2.

19.   Sarah Miller, "Molson Promo Challenged by Universities," *The Gazette,* November 28, 2007, p. 3.

20.   Marina Strauss, "Molson Photo Contest Brews up Anger," *Globe and Mail,* available at http://www.theglobeandmail.com/servlet/story/RTGAM.20071122.wmolsonface1122/BNStory/Technology, accessed January 6, 2008.

21.   Ibid.

22.   Ibid.

23.   Brenda Whiteside "A Cold Shot to Responsible Drinking," available at www.macdrphil.wordpress.com/2007/11/27/a-cold-shot, accessed on January 27, 2008.

24.   Mary Jane Credeur, "Molson Coors Ends Facebook Contest after Complaints," available at http://www.bloomberg.com/apps/news?pid=newsarchive&sid=aFC760lDqrJQ, accessed January 9, 2008.

25.   Ziad Fazel, comments on the article "Molson Photo Contest Brews up Anger," available at http://www.theglobeandmail.com/servlet/story/RTGAM.20071122.wmolsonface1122/CommentStory/Technology, accessed January 11, 2008.

26.   "A Cold Shot to Responsible Drinking," available at www.macdrphil.wordpress.com/2007/11/27/a-cold-shot, accessed January 27, 2008.

27.   Sarah Miller, "Molson Promo Challenged by Universities," The Gazette, November 28, 2007, p. 3.

## Chapter 14

*Case 14.1 Ten Thousand Villages of Cincinnati: The First Year and Beyond*

1.   www.tenthousandvillages.org, accessed July 13, 2004.

2.   At the time of the case, the organization was known as IFAT. It has since changed to World Fair Trade Organization (WFTO).

3.   www.fairtradefederation.org/ accessed July 13, 2004.

4.   www.tenthousandvillages.com/php/about.us/about.vision.php, accessed July 13, 2004.

5.   www.ifat.org accessed July 13, 2004.

6.   www.wfto.com/index.php?option=com_content&task=view&id=2&Itemid=14, accessed April 11, 2010.

7.   www.fairtradefederation.com/index.html, accessed December 2004.

8.   www.ifat.org, accessed December 2004

9.   Mark S. Leclair, "Fighting the Tide: Alternative Trade Organizations in the Era of Global Free Trade," *World Development, 30* (6), 2002, p. 949–58.

10.   All funds are in US$ unless otherwise noted.

11.   "2003 Report on Fair Trade Trends in US, Canada & the Pacific Rim," Fair Trade Federation, Washington, DC, 2003.

12.   Higher Education & Research Opportunities 2003, "Ethics the Easy Way." www.hero.ac.uk/business/archive/ethics_the_easy_way5043.cfm?archive=yes accessed December 4, 2003.

13.   Paul H. Ray, "The Emerging Culture," *American Demographics,* 19 (2), 1997, p. 29–34.

14.   Paul H. Ray and Sherry Ruth Anderson, *The Cultural Creatives: How 50 Million People Are Changing the World,* Harmony Books, New York, 2000.

15.   Donald Hicks, Shigeaki Wakana and John Dine, "Marketing Plan for Ten Thousand Villages," Unpublished paper by students at Xavier University, Cincinnati, Ohio, 2003.

16.   Rebecca Flass, "Pier 1 Gets in the Holiday Spirit," *Adweek Southeast Edition,* 23 (45), November 11, 2002, p. 4.

17.   www.pier1.com, accessed July 13, 2004.

18.   Cost Plus World Market, 2003 Annual Report.

19.   http:///www.zgallerie.com/t-about.aspx, accessed June 10, 2004.

20.   "Furnishing the Cocoon," *Chain Store Age,* 79 (3), March 1, 2003.

21.   The loan was to be paid back in five years at a "very reasonable" rate.

22.   Mary Conway Dato-on, Mary Joyce and Chris Manolis, "Creating Effective Customer Relationships in Non-profit Retailing: A Case Study," 2006, Special Issue of *International Journal of Nonprofit and Voluntary Sector Marketing* on "Nonprofit and Voluntary Sector Marketing: An International Perspective," 11 (4), pp. 319–333.

*Case 14.2 Personal Shoppers
at Sears: The Elf Initiative*

1. Statistics Canada, "Special Aggregation: Retail Trade and Wholesale Trade Based on the North American Industry Classification System (NAICS) 2002," http://stds.statcan.ca/english/spec-aggreg/trade-2002/retailnaics02-class-search.asp?criteria=45211, accessed December 17, 2007.

2. Sears Canada Inc. Annual Report 2005, p. 14.

3. Ibid.

## Chapter 15

*Case 15.1 Microsoft and
the Xbox 360 Ring of Death*

1. This case has been written on the basis of published sources only. Consequently, the interpretation and perspectives presented in this case are not necessarily those of Microsoft or any of its employees.

2. Greg Thom, "Xmas Joy for Xbox," *Herald Sun*, October 11, 2006, p. C03.

3. Aaron McKenna, "Analysts Predict Xbox 360 Will Beat PlayStation 3," *The Inquirer*, September 30, 2005, www.theinquirer.net/inquirer/news/1047560/analysts-predict-xbox-360-will-beat-playstation, accessed on May 7, 2008.

4. All funds in U.S. dollars unless specified otherwise.

5. Nick Wingfield, "Microsoft's Videogame Efforts Take a Costly Hit," *The Wall Street Journal*, July 6, 2007, p. A3.

6. César A. Berardini, "Robbie Bach: Xbox Will Be Profitable Next Year, *Team Xbox*, May 4, 2007, news.teamxbox.com/xbox/13401/Robbie-Bach-Xbox-Will-Be-Profitable-Next-Year/, accessed on May 7, 2008.

7. N'Gai Croal, "Confession is Good for the Soul: Why Microsoft Must Be More Forthcoming About the Xbox 360's Flaws—Or Initiate a Recall," *Newsweek*, July 10, 2007, http://blog.newsweek.com/blogs/levelup/archive/2007/07/10/why-microsoft-must-be-more-forthcoming-about-xbox-360-flaws-or-initiate-a-recall.aspx, accessed on May 16, 2008.

8. Heather Chaplin and Aaron Ruby, *Smartbomb: The Quest for Art, Entertainment, and Big Bucks in the Videogame Revolution*, Algonquin Books, Chapel Hill, NC, 2005, p. 236.

9. John C. Dvorak, "Intel's Albatross," *PC Magazine*, March 22, 2005, p. 53.

10. Kelly Zito, "Newest, Fastest Video Consoles / Dreamcast is Season's Hot Hardware," *The San Francisco Chronicle*, December 2, 1999, http://articles.sfgate.com/1999–12–02/business/17708357_1_128-bit-processor-gaming-capabilities-sega-s-dreamcast, accessed March 1, 2010.

11. "Peter Moore Interview: Part Two," *The Guardian*, September 11, 2008, www.guardian.co.uk/technology/gamesblog/2008/sep/11/playstation.microsoft, accessed on September 18, 2008.

12. Ibid.

13. Ibid.

14. Tor Thorsen, "Ad Campaign Offering Glimpse of Next-Gen Xbox?," *Gamespot*, April 6, 2005, www.gamespot.com/news/2005/04/06/news_6121811.html, accessed on October 24, 2007.

15. "Microsoft Teams With MTV to Provide Exclusive Sneak Peek at the Debut of the Next-Generation Xbox," *Microsoft News Center*, April 11, 2005, www.microsoft.com/presspass/press/2005/apr05/04–11MTVXboxPR.mspx, accessed on October 24, 2007.

16. "Xbox 360 Officially Announced," *Team Xbox*, May 12, 2005, http://news.teamxbox.com/xbox/8233/Xbox-360-Officially-Announced/, accessed on March 1, 2010, news.teamxbox.com/xbox/8233/Xbox-360-Officially-Announced/, accessed May 6, 2008.

17. Ibid.

18. Daniel Terdiman, "Xbox 360 Makes Desert Debut," *CNET News*, November 20, 2005, http://news.cnet.com/Xbox-360-makes-desert-debut/2100–1043_3–5963915.html, accessed on April 28, 2008.

19. Chris Morris, "Nintendo's Wii May Get Early Launch," *CNN Money*, July 5, 2006, money.cnn.com/2006/07/05/commentary/column_gaming/index.htm, accessed on April 28, 2008.

20. "Xbox 360 Sells Out Within Hours, *BBC News*, December 2, 2005, news.bbc.co.uk/2/hi/technology/4491804.stm, accessed on April 28, 2008.

21. Brendan Sinclair, "Moore On 360 Launch: 'Nothing's perfect,'" *Gamespot*, January 9, 2006, gamespot.com/news/6142087.html, accessed on April 28, 2008.

22. Jane Pinckard, "Xbox 360 Crashes, Defects Reported," *1up.com,* November 23, 2005, www.1up.com/do/newsStory?cId=3145847, accessed on April 28, 2008.

23. "Living Room New Internet Battlefield: Apple vs. Microsoft," *The National Post,* December 28, 2006, p. FP1.

24. "Over Half of U.S. Households Subscribe to Broadband Internet," *Leichtman Research Group,* June 7, 2007, http://leichtman research.com/press/060707release.html, accessed on July 24, 2007.

25. John Markoff and Matt Richtel, "Battleground For Consoles Moves Online," *The New York Times,* October 18, 2006, www.nytimes.com/2006/10/18/technology/18game.html?fta=y, accessed on March 1, 2010.

26. Luke Plunkett, "Xbox Live: 10 Million Gold Subscribers," *Kotaku,* January 6, 2008, http://kotaku.com/341399/xbox-live-10-million-gold-subscribers, accessed on April 25, 2008.

27. Tim Surette, "Xbox Live: 6 Million Sstrong and Counting," *Gamespot,* March 6, 2007, www.gamespot.com/news/6166851.html, accessed on March 12, 2007.

28. Interview with Peter Moore, *E3 Financial Analyst Briefing,* May 9, 2006, www.microsoft.com/msft/download/Transcripts/FY06/PeterMoore050906.doc, accessed on October 24, 2007.

29. Christopher Grant, "Sony Declares "Full-On Assault" on Xbox Live," *Joystiq,* January 31, 2006, http://joystiq.com/2006/01/31/sony-declares-full-on-assault-on-xbox-live/, accessed on April 25, 2008.

30. "Sony Explains How PSN Can Trump Xbox Live," MTV Multiplayer, July 24, 2008, http://multiplayerblog.mtv.com/2008/07/24/sony-explains-how-psn-can-trump-xbox-live/, accessed on August 27, 2008.

31. Jack Patrick Rodgers, "Smashing Failure," *Slate,* March 27, 2008, http://slate.com/id/2187562/, accessed on August 27, 2008.

32. Takahashi, Dean "Xbox 360 Failures: A Loyal Fan Returns Seven Machines," *The Mercury News,* February 22, 2007, http://blogs.mercury news.com/aei/2007/02/xbox_360_failures_a_loyal_fan_returns_seven_machines.html/, accessed on April 15, 2008.

33. CAG Community Xbox 360 Failure Survey Results, conducted March 2008, http://cheapassgamer.com/forums/showthread.php?t=175137, accessed on April 15, 2008.

34. Ben Kuchera, "Xbox 360 Failure Rates Worse Than Most Consumer Electronics, *Ars Technica,* February 14, 2008, http://arstechnica.com/gaming/news/2008/02/xbox-360-failure-rates-worse-than-most-consumer-electornics.ars, accessed on April 16, 2008. Steve Watts, "Report Claims Xbox 360 Failure Rates at 16%," *1up.com,* February 13, 2008, www.1up.com/do/newsStory?cId=3166259, accessed on April 16, 2008.

35. Thorsen, Tor, Xbox 360 failure rate 23.7%, PS3 10%, Wii 2.7%—Study, Gamespot, September 2, 2009, http://www.gamespot.com/news/6216691.html, accessed March 1, 2010.

36. "Xbox 360," *BBC Watchdog,* February 13, 2007, http://bbc.co.uk/consumer/tv_and_radio/watchdog/reports, accessed on April 16, 2008.

37. Emma Boyes, "Xbox 360s Investigated by Watchdog," *Gamespot,* February 14, 2007, www.gamespot.com/news/6165896.html?page=3, accessed on April 16, 2008.

38. Martin, Matt "Repair Specialists Refuse To Take 360s," *gamesindustry.biz,* June 28, 2007, accessed on April 15, 2008.

39. Ben Kuchera, "Microsoft to Extend Warranty Against Red Rings of Death to 3 Years," *Ars Technica,* July 5, 2007, http://arstechnica.com/gaming/news/2007/07/microsoft-to-extend-warranty-against-red-rings-of-death-for-3-years.ars, accessed on April 16, 2008.

40. "Open Letter From Peter Moore," *Xbox .com,* July 5, 2007, xbox.com/en-GB/support/peter mooreletter.htm, accessed on April 16, 2008.

41. "Xbox 360 Warranty Coverage Expanded," *Xbox.com,* July 5, 2007, xbox.com/en-GB/support/systemsetup/xbox360/resources/warrantyupdate.htm, accessed on April 16, 2008; http://www.xbox.com/NR/exeres/5CC2A2B9–5434–43BC-BCAD-24544E885660.htm, accessed March 1, 2010.

42. "Peter Moore Resigns From Microsoft to Return to Northern California," *Microsoft News Center,* July 17, 2007, www.microsoft.com/Presspass/press/2007/ju107/07–17MooreMattrick PR.mspx, accessed on April 16, 2008.

43. Jane Pinckard, "Xbox 360 Crashes, Defects Reported," *1up.com,* November 23, 2005, www.1up.com/do/newsStory?cId=3145847, accessed on April 28, 2008.

44. Alexander Sliwinski, "Scratch That: The Xbox 360 Might Damage Discs After All, *Joystiq,* April 16, 2007, www.joystiq.com/2007/04/16/scratch-that-the-xbox-360-might-damage-discs-after-all/, accessed on April 28, 2008.

45. César A. Berardini, "Xbox Disc Replacement Program Kicks Off," *TeamXbox,* April 3, 2007, http://news.teamxbox.com/xbox/13175/Xbox-Disc-Replacement-Program-Kicks-Off/, accessed on April 28, 2008.

46. "EC buigt zich over problemen X-box," *NOS.nl,* June 1, 2007, http://nos.nl/nos/artikelen/2007/06/, accessed April 28, 2008.

47. Eric Bangeman, "Lawsuit Claims Xbox 360 System Scratches Discs," *The International Herald Tribune,* July 10, 2007, http://arstechnica.com/gaming/news/2007/07/scratched-xbox-360-discs-lead-to-lawsuit-against-microsoft.ars, accessed March 1, 2010.

48. Cesar Berardini, "Wistron to Discontinue Production of Xbox 360," *Team Xbox,* March 26, 2007, accessed on October 23, 2007, http://news.teamxbox.com/xbox/13096/Wistron-to-Discontinue-Production-of-Xbox-360/.

49. Jason Metcalf, Inside Source Reveal the Truth About Xbox 360 "Red Ring of Death" Failures, Digital Joystick, January 17, 2008 http://blog.seattlepi.com/digitaljoystick/archives/129866.asp Accessed March 1, 2010.

50. N'Gai Croal, "Confession is Good for the Soul: Why Microsoft Must Be More Forthcoming About the Xbox 360's Flaws—Or Initiate a Recall," *Newsweek.com,* July 10, 2007, http://blog.newsweek.com/blogs/levelup/archive/2007/07/10/why-microsoft-must-be-more-forthcoming-about-xbox-360-flaws-or-initiate-a-recall.aspx, accessed on May 16, 2008.

51. Chen, Y and Tsai, J. "Wistron quits on Xbox 360," *Digitimes,* November 14, 2007, http://digitimes.com/systems/a20071113PD219.html, accessed on August 27, 2008.

52. "Asia's Fab 50 Companies," Forbes, September 6, 2007, http://www.forbes.com/lists/2007/37/biz_07fab50_Wistron_SDWV.html, accessed March 1, 2010.

53. Junko Yoshida, "The Truth About Last Year's Xbox 360 Recall," *EE Times,* June 9, 2008, http://eetimes.com/showArticle.jhtml?articleID=208403010, accessed on June 12, 2008.

54. Metcalf, Jacob, Inside Source Reveal the Truth About Xbox 360 "Red Ring of Death" Failures, Digital Joystick, January 17, 2008 http://blog.seattlepi.com/digitaljoystick/archives/129866.asp Accessed March 1, 2010

55. Paul McDougall, "Microsoft Xbox 360 Sales Plunge 60% As Problems Mount," *Information Week,* July 20, 2007, www.informationweek.com/news/personal_tech/showArticle.jhtml?articleID=201200157, accessed on March 1, 2010.

56. Tor Thorsen, "Microsoft Raises Estimated First-Day Halo 2 Sales to $125 Million-Plus," *Gamespot,* November 10, 2004, www.gamespot.com/news/2004/11/10/news_6112915.html, accessed on April 28, 2008.

57. David Gibbon, "'Halo 3' Cost £15 Million to Develop," *Digital Spy,* December 28, 2007, www.digitalspy.co.uk/gaming/a82352/halo-3-cost-gbp15-million-to-develop.html, accessed on August 28, 2008.

58. Scott Hillis, "Microsoft Says 'Halo' 1st-Week Sales Were $300 Mln," *Reuters,* October 4, 2007, http://uk.reuters.com/article/technologyNews/idUKN0438777720071005, accessed on August 28, 2008.

59. Christopher Grant, "September NPD: Xbox 360 Takes the Lead, Halo 3 to Thank," *Joystiq,* October 18, 2007, www.joystiq.com/2007/10/18/september-npd-xbox-360-takes-the-lead-halo-3-to-thank/, accessed on April 28, 2008.

60. "Bungie Studios Becomes Privately Held Independent Company," Company Press Release, October 5, 2007, bungie.net/News/content.aspx?type=news&cid=12835, accessed on August 28, 2008.

61. Brandon Boyer, "Pachter: 'Smash Bros,' Wii To Drive $850m In March U.S. Sales," *Gamasutra,* April 14, 2008, www.gamasutra.com/php-bin/news_index.php?story=18233, accessed on April 16, 2008.

62. Barbara Ortutay, "Take-Two's 'Grand Theft Auto IV' Tops $500M in Week 1 Sales," USA Today, May 7, 2008, www.usatoday.com/money/topstories/2008-05-07-1908764460_x.htm, accessed on August 28, 2008.

63. Waters, Darren, Europe PS3 sales 'overtake 360,' BBC News, May 6, 2008, http://news.bbc.co.uk/2/hi/technology/7386879.stm, accessed March 1, 2010.

64. "Muted Hello for Xbox 360 in Japan," *BBC News,* December 10, 2005, http://news.bbc .co.uk/1/hi/technology/4517362.stm, accessed on May 7, 2008.

65. Alexander Sliwinski, "Wii Outsold PS3 3-to-1 in Japan During '07; Xbox Pens Memoir On Neglect," *Joystiq,* January 7, 2008, http:// joystiq.com/2008/01/07/wii-outsold-ps3–3-to-1-in-japan-during-07-xbox-pens-memoir-on/, accessed on May 7, 2008.

66. "Thinking Inside the Xbox," *The Edmonton Journal,* January 9, 2008.

67. Dustin Burg, Microsoft's Xbox division turns a profit (again!), Joystiq, April 25, 2008, http://xbox.joystiq.com/2008/04/25/microsofts-xbox-division-turns-a-profit-again/, accessed March 1, 2010.

68. Brian Caulfield, "The Xbox Trap," *Forbes,* April 24, 2008, www.forbes.com/ 2008/04/24/microsoft-xbox-earnings-tech-ebiz-cx_bc_0424xbox.html, accessed on March 1, 2010.

69. Ben Kuchera, "Why Microsoft Should be Worried About New NPD Sales Figures," *Ars Technica,* March 14, 2008, http://arstechnica .com/gaming/news/2008/03/why-microsoft-should-be-worried-about-new-npd-sales-figures .ars, accessed May 16, 2008.

70. N. Croal, "Confession Is Good For the Soul: Why Microsoft Must Be More Forthcoming About the Xbox 360's Flaws—Or Initiate a Recall," *Newsweek,* July 10, 2007, http://blog.newsweek .com/blogs/levelup/archive/2007/07/10/why-microsoft-must-be-more-forthcoming-about-xb ox-360-flaws-or-initiate-a-recall.aspx Accessed March 1, 2010 .

71. Blake Snow, "Six Reasons the Xbox 360 Is In Trouble," *Gamepro,* July 20, 2007, www .gamepro.com/microsoft/xbox360/games/ features/124008.shtml, accessed on May 16, 2008.

72. "Sega's Earnings Exceed Estimates On Software Sales," *Asian Wall Street Journal,* August 11, 2003.

73. Heather Chaplin and Aaron Ruby, *Smartbomb: The Quest for Art, Entertainment, and Big Bucks in the Videogame Revolution,* Algonquin Books, Chapel Hill, 2005, p. 236.

## Case 15.2 Kenexa

1. Source: http://www.kenexa.com/abou_ hist.html; http://www.kenexa.com/abou_over .html, accessed December 1, 2006.

2. All funds are in U.S. dollars unless noted otherwise.

3. J. Pfeffer, "Producing Sustainable Competitive Advantage Through the Effective Management of People," Academy of Management Executive, 19(4), 2005, pp. 95–106.

4. J. W. Wiley and B. Campbell, "Using linkage research to drive high performance: A case study in Organizational Development," in *Getting Action from Organizational Surveys: New Concepts, Techniques, and Applications,* San Francisco: Jossey-Bass Inc. Publishers, 2006, pp. 150–180.

5. S. D. Pugh et al., "Driving service effectiveness through employee-customer linkages," *Academy of Management Executive, 16*(4), 2002, pp. 73–84.

6. The employee opinion survey contained at least two questions intended to measure each theme of employee opinions. While each employee responded to individual questions, an average of the responses on the set of questions intended to measure each theme served as corresponding employee opinion score for that theme.

7. The customer satisfaction survey contained at least two questions intended to measure each theme of customer opinions. While each customer responded to individual questions, an average of the responses on the set of questions intended to measure each theme served as corresponding customer opinion score for that theme.

8. For the purposes of making the branch level customer data on the frequency of usage of the services of bank tellers or personal bankers amenable for analyses, project consultants for the NCB project team did a median split and transformed the frequency of contact variable into a categorical variable (see Exhibit 5 for the two categories represented by the transformed variable "ccon").

# About the Editors

**Kenneth E. Clow** is a Professor of Marketing and holds the Biedenharn Endowed Chair of Business in the College of Business Administration at the University of Louisiana at Monroe. Previously, he served as Dean at both the University of Louisiana at Monroe and the University of North Carolina at Pembroke. He teaching career began at Pittsburg State University where he also served as the MBA Director. He obtained his PhD from the University of Arkansas in 1992.

Dr. Clow has published a total of 190 articles in academic journals and proceedings and has written 13 textbooks. He has published articles in journals such as *Journal of Services Marketing, Services Marketing Quarterly, Journal of Business Research, Marketing Management Journal, Journal of Economics and Finance Education, International Journal of Business, Marketing, and Decision Sciences, Journal of Internet Commerce, Health Marketing Quarterly,* and *Journal of Restaurant and Foodservices Marketing.*

Books co-authored by Professor Clow include *Integrated Advertising, Promotion, and Marketing Communications, 4th edition* (Prentice Hall), *Concise Encyclopedia of Advertising* (Haworth), *Essentials of Marketing, 3rd edition* (Cengage), *Services Marketing, 2nd edition* (Atomic Dog), *Concise Encyclopedia of Professional Services Marketing* (Routledge, Taylor and Francis Group), *The IMC PlanPro Handbook,* and *Marketing Management* (SAGE).

Prior to earning his doctorate, Clow owned and operated a commercial cleaning service in Joplin, Missouri, and Fayetteville, Arkansas. He started as a sole employee and the company grew to become one of the largest cleaning services in Northwest Arkansas with 40 employees. He is married to Susan and has four sons, Dallas, Wes, Tim, and Roy.

**Donald Baack** holds the rank of University Professor of management at Pittsburg (Kansas) State University, where he has taught since 1988. He previously held positions at Southwest Missouri State University, Missouri Southern State College, and Dana College. Baack received his PhD from the University of Nebraska in 1987. His primary area of study was Organization and Management Theory.

Professor Baack is a Consulting Editor for the *Journal of Managerial Issues* and has published in the journal. He has also published in *Human Relations, Journal of High Technology Management Research, Journal of Ministry Marketing and Management, Journal of Management Inquiry, Journal of Customer Service in Marketing, Journal of Professional Services Marketing, Journal of Global Awareness, Journal of Business Ethics, Journal of Euromarketing, Journal of Nonprofit and Public Sector Marketing,* and the *Journal of Advertising Research.*

Dr. Baack has authored *Organizational Behavior* (Dame), *International Business* (Glencoe/McGraw-Hill), and *Integrated Advertising, Promotion, and Marketing Communications* (Prentice Hall, co-author to Kenneth E. Clow). Clow and Baack also wrote the *Concise Encyclopedia of Advertising* (Haworth) and *Marketing Management* (SAGE). Baack and his son Daniel W. Baack recently prepared a series of 10 modules titled "Ethics Across the Curriculum" for Pearson Custom Publishing. He also published three popular press books in the area of romance/self-help.

Baack has been active in the Southwest Academy of Management (SWAM) for many years, serving as its President in 1996. He has been nominated for SWAM's Distinguished Educator award four times. He is married (Pamela) with three children.

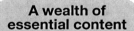

CPSIA information can be obtained
at www.ICGtesting.com
Printed in the USA
FSOW02n1902141216
28567FS